D1435956

# The Illustrated Encyclopaedia of
# SHELLS

The Illustrated Encyclopaedia of

# SHELLS

Kenneth R. Wye

HEADLINE

A QUARTO BOOK



First published in Great Britain in 1991
by HEADLINE BOOK PUBLISHING PLC



British Cataloguing in Publication Data
Wye, Kenneth R.
The illustrated encyclopaedia of shells.
1. Molluscs. Shells.
I. Title
594.0471

ISBN 0-7472-0468-3

This book was designed and produced by
Quarto Publishing plc
The Old Brewery, 6 Blundell Street,
London N7 9BH

Senior Editor: Sally MacEachern
Editor: Diana Brinton
Indexer: Dorothy Frame
Creative Director: Terry Jeavons
Art Editor: Anne Fisher
Designer: Stuart Walden
Illustrators: David Kemp, Jenny Millington
Photographer: Paul Forrester
Art Director: Moira Clinch
Publishing Director: Janet Slingsby

Typeset by ABC Typesetting, Bournemouth
Manufactured in Singapore by
Chroma Graphics (Overseas) Pte. Ltd
Printed in Hong Kong by Leefung Asco

HEADLINE BOOK PUBLISHING PLC
79 Great Titchfield Street, London W1P 7PN

This book is dedicated to, and is in memory of, a dear family friend,
Leonardo P. Igot, who died 4 April, 1991, aged 31 years, Cebu, Philippines. REVELATION 21 V.4.

# Contents

# Introduction

*I can always remember the thrill of owning my first few seashells. I recall exchanging several, and I went on to develop the interest, along with a close friend, purchasing still more in what must have been London's only specialist shop for shell collectors. Some 25 years on, I am still just as enthralled by them.*

*These exquisite wonders of creation have demanded a response from mankind, and indeed have been inextricably linked with the human story since the dawn of civilization. The appreciation, study, enjoyment and collecting of seashells is probably as widespread now as at any time in history. Appreciation, because few have failed to be intrigued and amazed at their diversity and complexity of colour, shape and form; shells have stimulated the artistic, promoted ideas in design and architecture, inspired musicians and poets, and have led to the publication of some of the most beautiful books ever produced for natural historians.*

*Scientifically known as marine molluscs, seashells are the hard outer covering of highly adaptable snails that inhabit the world's oceans in a wide range of environments and at varying depths. These shells can be found washed ashore, emptied of the soft bodies that once inhabited them, in rock pools, beneath mud and sand at low tide and beneath the seas in shallow waters and down to dark abyssal depths. As objects of scientific study, shells have much to offer. They are of interest to medical research, in general education, and in relation to environmental and ecological issues. Most importantly, they are also an important food source and are linked to the relatively new science known as mariculture.*

*The "golden age" of shell collecting was during the 200 years of discovery and exploration that drew to a close at the turn of this century, but conchology – as the study and collecting of shells is correctly termed – has entered a new era. Thanks to modern fishing methods, rare shells that were once known only from a handful of old and faded specimens in museum vaults are now available to all. Modern colour photography captures the intricate beauty of shells in all their wonder, and there are many excellent books on the subject.*

*Conchologists and amateur collectors have an infectious enthusiasm, and along with the increasing awareness of the need for environmental protection is a growing need to discover more about the natural world. I believe that conchology will continue to enhance mankind in both work and leisure for generations to come.*

ABOVE *Penchinat's Murex* (Chicoreus penchinatti) *found from Japan to the Philippines.*

RIGHT *Scallop* (Pecten maximus) *showing marginal tentacle and eyes.*

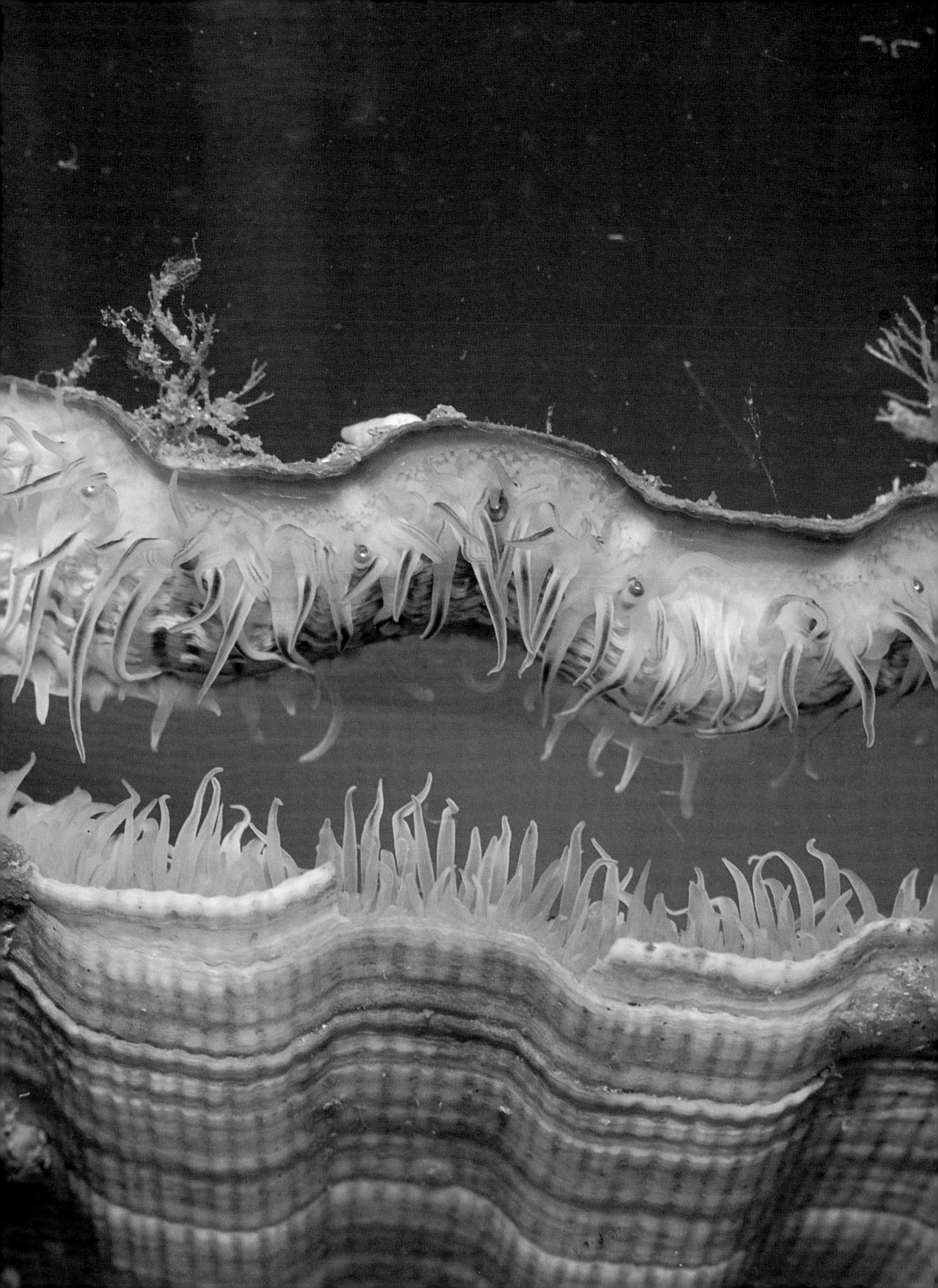

# *The influence of shells*

A stroll through the ethnological gallery of almost any reputable museum will reveal examples of man's widespread use of shells, for both decorative and practical purposes. It would be easy to write a book on the subject, and only a handful of examples can be given here.

## *Food*

Discarded shells have been found in the waste-heaps of prehistoric settlements, but the Romans may have been one of the earliest peoples to farm molluscs, particularly oysters, as a food source. Today, virtually every nation with a seashore has its own seafood speciality. A Japanese delicacy is *Cypraea tigris*, roasted alive on hot coals. In the Philippines, the people in some areas consume virtually every mollusc fished, including even the toxic cone shells; most shells are boiled and eaten with rice. The USA is famous for her abalone steaks and clam chowder, while French cuisine boasts the culinary delights of *coquilles St. Jacques* and *moules marinieres*.

## *Currency and trade*

In times past, the use of cowrie shells, primarily *Cypraea annulus* and *C. moneta*, as a form of currency was widespread in Asia, Central Africa, the Indian Ocean and the Malaysian islands. Easy to collect and handle, they were strung into lengths and used for bartering. Early traders made fortunes by carrying cowries from the Indian and Pacific oceans to West Africa, where they were exchanged for ivory, palm-oil, and semi-precious stones. These shells have been discovered in aboriginal sites in parts of the United States, which suggests that they may have been imported at the time of Columbus, or even before that.

The North American Indians used to grind down pieces of bivalves, which they called *wampum*, and use them for trading. Certain clams were pierced and strung on sinew, the most prized shells being those with a purple interior. American Indian traders journeying from the coast to the hinterland bore abalones, olives for beads, tusk shells for currency, *Glycymeris* for bracelets, and also varieties of helmet, whelk and venus shells.

Other shells were traded and used for their dye secretions. *Murex trunculus* and *M. brandaris* produce the deep purple dye which in ancient times was known as Tyrian purple, because Phoenician traders had made Tyre and Sidon the main distribution centres.

## *Religion*

The emblem of St. James is the scallop, and in times past pilgrims who visited his shrine at Santiago de Compostela would bring back a shell as proof of their pilgrimage. A papal ruling allegedly declared that anyone selling scallops outside the town would be excommunicated.

The chank shell, *Turbinella pyrum,* is sacred to the Hindu god Vishnu. Left-handed, or sinistral, specimens are extremely rare and much coveted. In ancient times they were sometimes covered with gold and encrusted with precious jewels; these days, Hindus will accept the more common and naturally left-handed *Busycon contrarium* as a substitute.

## *Fashion and jewellery*

Shells have been used for adornment from the earliest times. Cowries, which were consecrated to Venus, were worn by Roman women and were often given as bridal gifts. The Golden Cowrie, *Cypraea aurantium*, was (and possibly still is) worn pendant-style as an emblem of rank by main chieftains on the islands of Fiji and Vanuatu.

The development of collecting and conchological interests in the 18th and 19th centuries was accompanied by a fashion for shell jewellery and ornamental objects. Hairslides, earrings, brooches and necklaces were exquisitely fashioned out of mother-of-pearl, from various nacreous oysters; while articles such as shell-backed mirrors, calling card cases and perfume bottles were highly popular in Victorian times. Cameos were primarily

made from *Cypraecassis rufa*, craftsmen carving into the thick walls of the shell through layers of rich orange, red and off-white.

Most modern shell jewellery comes from Taiwan and the Philippines. Mother-of-pearl is still popular, but there is also an increasing demand for the paua shell, *Haliotis iris*, the native abalone of New Zealand.

## Art and architecture

Shells are, and always have been, a great source of inspiration for artists. Of all shells, the scallop has perhaps been most frequently used – ornamenting Roman lead coffins, decorating niches and porticoes, carved above church doorways, chosen by Botticelli as a vehicle for Venus rising from the waves, and in modern times picked as the logo for the Shell Oil Company.

Leonardo da Vinci made drawings of spiral shells, and one of these is thought to have provided the inspiration for the famous spiral staircase at the Château de Blois, in France.

Nautilus shells were much used for goblets and chalices in the 16th and 17th centuries, and the Dutch in particular were great collectors of exotic shells during this period, a passion reflected in Rembrandt's etching *The Shell* or in Vander Ast's *Still Life with Shells*.

In the 19th century, sailors returning from a long voyage would make shell collages as Valentines for their sweethearts. Today, this art form is enjoying something of a revival, and even relatively small "floral arrangements" of shells can command hundreds of pounds.

At the other end of the scale is the pagoda-like Guggenheim Museum in New York, designed by Frank Lloyd Wright, who was allegedly inspired by that wonderful species, *Thatcheria mirabilis*.

ABOVE LEFT *Botticelli:* The Birth of Venus.

ABOVE RIGHT *Carved nautilus shell mounted in silver-gilt and coral, c. 1630.*

LEFT *The Shell emblem.*

BOTTOM *The Guggenheim Museum, New York.*

# The phylum Mollusca

All living things are grouped by zoological classification into major sections known as phyla. The phylum Mollusca is second in numerical size only to the insects (Arthropoda), and some experts suggest there may be in excess of 100,000 species. In order to understand such a large and varied group better, they have been divided up into six sections, referred to as classes.

## *Class Gastropoda*

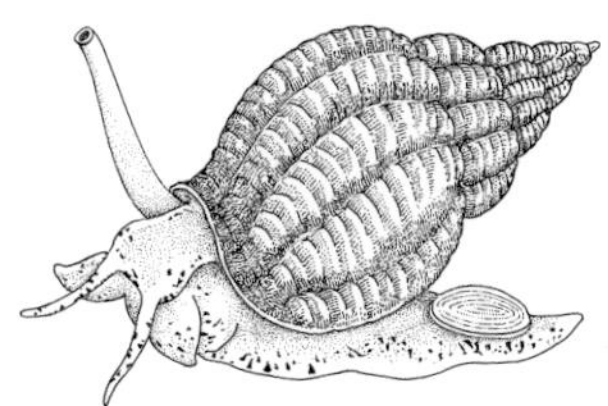

At least three-quarters of the world's molluscs are included in this, the largest class, and approximately half the species are marine. The snails are soft bodied, with tentacles, eyes, a mantle and a broad, flat foot. The visceral mass where most internal organs are situated is contained in a one-piece, usually coiled, hard shell. The majority of gastropods are mobile, highly active creatures. There are perhaps between 20,000 and 30,000 described species and these include such well-known families as limpets, cowries, murex, cones and olives.

## *Class Bivalvia*

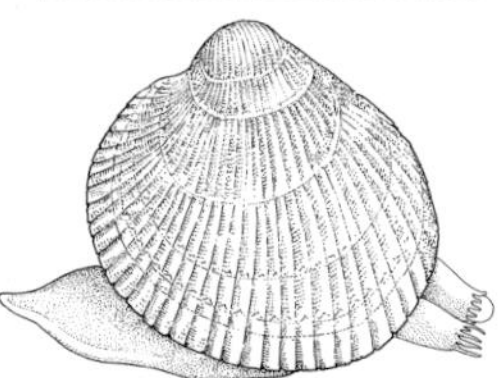

The outer shell of a bivalve comprises two pieces, or valves, which are hinged and are joined by means of a supple ligament. The valves are opened and closed by means of strong muscles located in the interior. The majority of species, of which there are around 10,000, possess a large foot, a pair of siphons and a mantle. Most are sessile creatures, but a few – such as the scallops – are very active. Oysters, mussels, cockles and clams are all included in this class.

## *Class Cephalopoda*

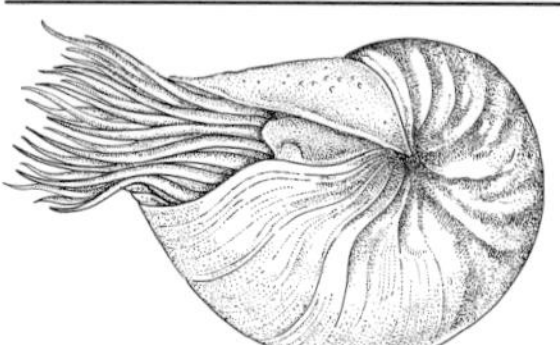

This is a relatively small group of highly mobile molluscs that possess large eyes, tentacles with suckers, and powerful beak-like mouths. All species are carnivorous. These creatures are most unlike other molluscs – especially as far as the soft parts are concerned. Some do possess an external shell, such as the Nautilus, while others, such as Spirula, have internal shells. Other species such as the octopus and squids, have no shell at all.

## *Class Scaphopoda*

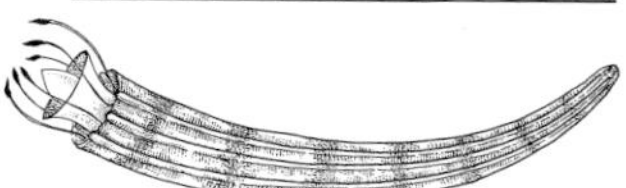

A small class of 200-400 species, these are known as tusk or tooth shells and are the most primitive of all molluscs. They have a long, narrow, tubular shell which is open at both ends. The narrower posterior end usually protrudes above the sand in which most species live. They have no head, eyes or gills, but possess a large foot and a radula.

## *Class Polyplacophora*

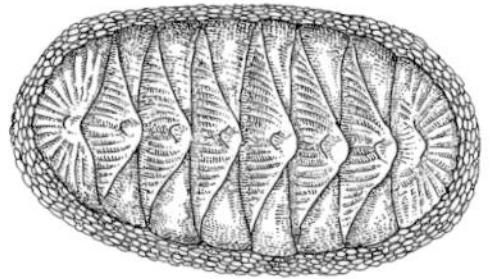

Known as chitons or "coat of mail" shells and much resembling woodlice, these possess eight segmented plates which are held together by a leathery and tough band known as a "girdle". They have either a broad or narrow foot and microsensory organs that are situated on the shell and girdle surfaces. They lack tentacles. There may be 600 or so species.

## *Class Monoplacophora*

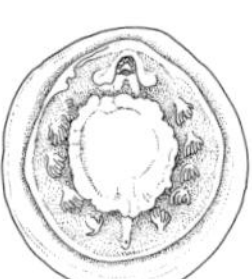

The earliest-known gastropods, these were long thought to be extinct. However, some of these very primitive limpet-like shells, with paired muscles and segmented body parts, were discovered this century in very deep water. They are exceptionally rare and are seldom if ever found in amateur collections.

# Fossil shells – the link with the past

Creationists, among whom I would certainly be counted, believe these words, found in Genesis 1:20, "God said, let the waters bring forth swarms of living creatures". When one considers the wealth and complexity of natural forms, and especially of molluscan design, it is hard to believe that they all "just happened". Science argues that molluscs derive from a unifying original life form, but the evolution of molluscs cannot easily be traced or explained. Some genera clearly developed and changed under environmental influences, while others ceased to exist, but there is no scientifically proven common ancestor of all the mollusc species known today. Several "recent" (present day) species, such as chambered nautilus and species of slit-shells, have unsevered links with the very earliest geological times. These incredible shells have withstood the passage of time without noticeable change, while other far less sophisticated and adaptable species have disappeared and are known only from fossils.

Some species, such as the tusk shells, have changed little in shape since they first appeared; others have evolved considerably, and there is a vast range of molluscs, often with bizarre shapes, which can only be found in fossil form. These include *Caprine, Spinigera* and early long-spined forms of the family Aporrhaidae, all of which provide a fascinating subject for study.

Gastropods, bivalves, scaphopods and cephalopods are all well represented in fossil records, but species of the order Polyplacophora, although first appearing in the late Cambrian period, are scarce and rare. Monoplacophora, another very ancient group, also date back to early Cambrian.

With the onset of the Mesozoic era, there took place a great increase in family and generic variation, especially among shells of the Volutidae, Muricidae and Cerithiidae families. During the Tertiary era, especially the Eocene period, the Gastropods were the most numerous of all molluscs, and many species have changed little from that time to the present day. Significant numbers of bivalves did not appear until the late Devonian and early Carboniferous periods, when swampy conditions appear to have suited them.

**GEOLOGICAL KEY**

| ERA | PERIOD | MILL. OF YRS. |
|---|---|---|
| **TERTIARY** | Pliocene | 5-10 |
| | Eocene | 40-70 |
| **MESOZOIC** | Jurassic | 200 |
| **PALAEOZOIC** | Carboniferous | 350 |
| | Devonian | 400 |
| | Cambrian | 500-600 |

Geological periods referred to in text.
Dating is according to scientific estimate and is open to argument.

LEFT *A selection of what are known as "recent" fossil gastropods, dating from the Pliocene period.*

ABOVE *A halved and polished section of a Jurassic ammonite. Note its similarity to the Nautilus shells on p277.*

# The nomenclature and classification of molluscs

Most living things are referred to by their common or colloquial names. Shells, for example, are often just called "whelks", "cockles" or "conch" and the like. However, this can be very misleading and confusing when you realize that these names can vary greatly from place to place and country to country. All natural creatures and plants, including shells, have therefore been given a two-part Latin name which has been universally adopted. But this has not always been so.

It was only in comparatively recent times that order came from the chaotic mess of names for seashells. Various species often possessed several different names and it was only a matter of time before someone developed an orderly and carefully arranged system of classification and identification.

The naming of a particular species of seashell is structured as follows. Let us take, for example, a popular and large species, commonly known as the triton's trumpet, but correctly named thus: *Charonia tritonis*. Linné 1758.

The first of the two Latin names refers to the genus, the group to which this species and its close relatives belong, and is correctly started with a capital letter. The second name, not capitalized, is the species or specific name. Generic names cannot be used for more than one group of animals and the specific name cannot be used for any other species in that particular genus. It is therefore simple to deduce that there can only ever be one species called *Charonia tritonis* – making life a lot easier for everyone concerned!

For every species so described there is an authority, known as the author – the biologist, scientist or even layman who first published a valid description of this species and named it. This is usually and most correctly via a scientific publication or journal. The date of this publication of the name is often given in more formal literature.

Our example, as it so happens, was described by Carl Linnaeus in 1758. He is referred to in some descriptions as Linné (a name attributed to himself after receiving a knighthood). Linnaeus is the only author whose name can be abbreviated to "L" (L.1758), and this prefix is used in this book when species described by Linnaeus are included.

Within the phylum Mollusca, *Charonia tritonis* is classified as follows;

| **PHYLUM** | **MOLLUSCA** |
|---|---|
| Class | Gastropoda |
| Subclass | Prosobranchia |
| Order | Mesogastropoda |
| Super family | Tonnoidea |
| Family | Ranellidae |
| Subfamily | Cymatiinae |
| Genus | Charonia |
| Species | tritonis |

Related genera are placed within a family, although some families contain only one genus, e.g. Haliotidae, genus *Haliotis*. Large families such as Muricidae contain numerous genera. Similar or related families are, in turn, placed within super

## CARL LINNAEUS

A Swedish naturalist, Carl Linnaeus, took up the challenge of tackling classification. In the 10th edition of his momentous work, *Systema Naturae*, published in 1758, he carefully listed and described every animal and plant, including seashells, known to him, using two Latin names for each species. For the first time in history, a uniform and concise system of nomenclature for natural things had been formulated but the binomial system, as it was named, was not widely accepted until the late 18th and early 19th centuries. The common names were slow to disappear from scientific publications, and it is perhaps surprising and interesting to note that shell dealers and collectors were among the slowest to adopt the system, which they considered too "revolutionary" and "unnecessary".

*LEFT A living specimen of a European Painted Top* (Calliostoma zizyphinum). *This is a common shallow water dweller found throughout western European waters.*

*BELOW This fine example of a handpainted lithograph is taken from a plate in* Reeve's Conchologia Iconica, *1848. The shell depicted is* Phalium strigatum.

families; then comes the order, occasionally the subclass, and finally the largest category is the class. (see also the section on systematic arrangement on p.28).

Sometimes there are three Latin names. In this case, the last name refers to a sub-specific name – a variety close to the specific form. I refer, where necessary, to forms or varieties in the main text by using "f." (form) or "var." (variety). In these cases the third name is not capitalized, and the author of the subspecies form or variety automatically replaces the author of the species.

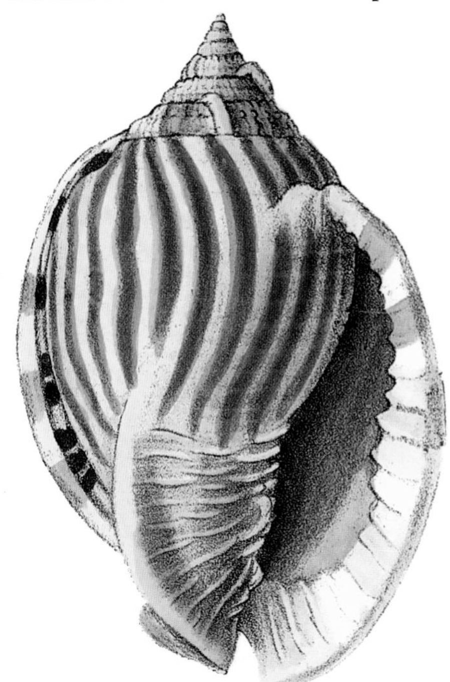

In some publications, the author's name and date appear in parentheses. This is because the species has been recognized, accepted and re-classified into another genus (a usage not employed in this book).

Both the serious student and amateur collector will at once be aware that there has been much splitting of families into sub-families, genera into numerous sub-genera and so on. I believe that the current trend, which I hope will long continue, is to reduce the confusing number of classifications, eliminating those that are superfluous. There has been much controversy and confusion on the subject of shell classification over the years, and I doubt if the situation will ever be completely settled; as one collector once said to me: "There are as many opinions as there are books on the subject!".

# The biology of molluscs

The gastropods are a large and diverse class that live in almost every conceivable environment, from high tide levels to the dark depths of the ocean floor. But the majority, and certainly the most colourful and attractive, inhabit varying substrates in shallow waters relatively close to the shore, where all manner of marine life is to be found in great variety and abundance. Purple Sea Snails (Janthinidae) live pelagic lives floating on the surface of the ocean far from land.

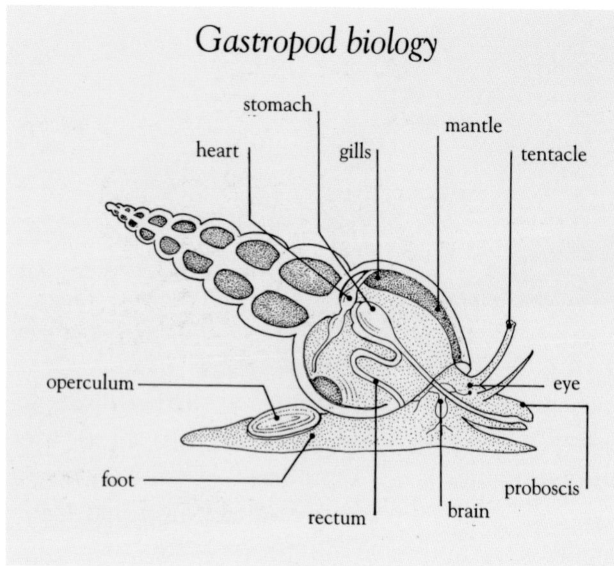


## FEEDING

All gastropods possess an intestinal tube and stomach. The "new" gastropods (order Neogastropoda) – such as murex, cone and turrid shells – are carnivorous and will often eat other shells. Those within the order Archaegastropoda (ancient gastropods), the most primitive families, are all herbivores, feeding on algae and minute suspended vegetable matter. Shells within the order Mesogastropoda ("middle" gastropods) comprise shells that are generally either herbivorous or carnivorous, and some groups feed on almost anything. Most gastropod snails carry a retractable organ – a ribbon of chitin – called a radula, which bears rows of rasping "teeth" (often examined under a microscope as a means of close species identification). The snail gathers its food by rasping against vegetable or plant matter, or flesh. As radula teeth wear out they are constantly replaced by others.

Predatory species, such as moon snails, are able to bore a neat circular hole in the shell of their prey by means of an adapted radula. The radula of a cone shell is further adapted into miniature harpoons or darts, and is connected to a venom gland by a duct. The teeth of the radula are barbed and hollow and, when the animal encounters its prey, a single highly toxic poison-filled tooth is injected into the unfortunate creature, which becomes paralyzed. The sting of cones has been known, primarily due to careless handling of live specimens, to have caused paralysis and even death in humans.

## RESPIRATION

Gastropods have gills. Respiration can also take place in and through the mantle, but only in a small number of species. The majority possess a trunk-like siphon through which water is conducted to the gills. This extrudes from the anterior end of the snail.

## REPRODUCTION

Although some snails possess both male and female organs, most species are a separate sex. Some, such as slipper shells, start life as male and develop female characteristics as they mature.

After fertilization, most female snails place their eggs in capsules or cases, which are released to float freely or are attached to solid material, such as rocks or coral. Each species has its own characteristic egg-containers.

Once gastropod eggs hatch they attain the so-called free-swimming veliger stage. Many at once sink to the substrate to commence miniature shell growth, others swim or are borne far and wide by ocean currents.

## GROWTH

The hard, outer covering of the snail, its shell, is produced by a special secretion from the animal's outer skin or mantle, and is called conchiolin. This hardened material is formed basically of calcium carbonate. Both colour and pattern, and sculpturing, are laid down in layers as the shell building proceeds via the mantle edges. On the surface of many species is a skin-like covering of fine or very coarse, often brown, material called periostracum, which can totally obscure any colouring or pattern beneath. It can be smooth, rough, scaly or flaky, or covered in short, coarse hairs.

Growth is usually intermittent with resting stages, clearly seen as varices, as in murex shells, and these can often bear long and elaborate ornamentation. If damage occurs to the shell's surface for whatever reason the mantle can "repair" holes or cracks including repeats of both pattern and colour. Resultant repairs are known as "growth scars" or "healed breaks".

In the larval or veliger stage, the snail's body undergoes a twisting process, known as torsion, which re-orientates several organs and brings some to the front, while the anus and reproductive apparatus and other organs end up in the coiled part of the shell, away from the aperture.

All gastropods, in growth, are spirally orientated and seemingly all variations on this theme have been exploited by them.

### GENERAL ANATOMY

The heads are usually well-developed, and comprise one or two pairs of tentacles, often carrying highly developed eyes, which can perceive light, darkness and shape. The foot is strong and muscular and is used primarily as an organ of locomotion. In numerous species a structure known as the operculum is grown on the rear portion of the foot. The operculum can be calcareous, corneus or horny, and can often be ornamented and colourful. It serves to close the aperture like a kind of door after the animal has withdrawn into its shell. In the Strombidae and Xenophoridae it is an aid to movement or can also be used as a weapon. In the Conidae, the operculum is very small and virtually useless – known as degenerate.

Gastropods have a heart, arteries and blood sinuses. The nervous system is restricted to simple "touch organs" situated on the mantle surface, foot and tentacles.

## *Bivalves*

The bivalve shell consists of two halves, which are constructed in layers laid down by the mantle. They are joined together by a rubbery connection known as the ligament, and there is also a hinge structure with interlocking teeth, some simple, others rather complex. Classification and grouping of bivalves is often arranged by this hinge and teeth structuring.

The shapes of the valves vary considerably. When both valves are identical both in shape and size, they are referred to as being equal. Some species have gaping valves; others overlap, and yet others have convex upper valves and virtually flat lower ones.

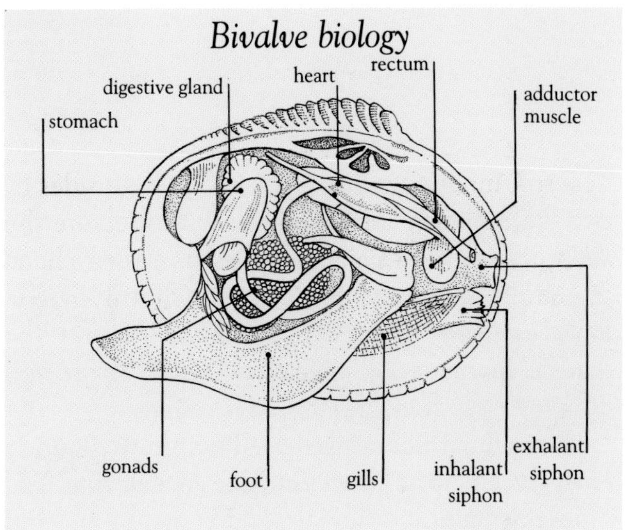


### REPRODUCTION AND GROWTH

Most bivalve sexes are separate and their system is relatively simple. Generally, both eggs and sperm are shed into the water where they meet, and here fertilization takes place. After the eggs hatch, the veligers eventually settle on the sea bed and commence to grow their shells.

Growth of the shell starts more or less at the dorsal side, at the umbo. In proximity to this the dorsal edges develop internal teeth to fit similar structures on the opposite valve; when fully developed, these can vary considerably in both size and shape. The inner faces of bivalves are often white and porcellaneous, or they may be nacreous. Many species have highly patterned or coloured exteriors, whilst others are rather drab looking. Many species also possess a periostracum.

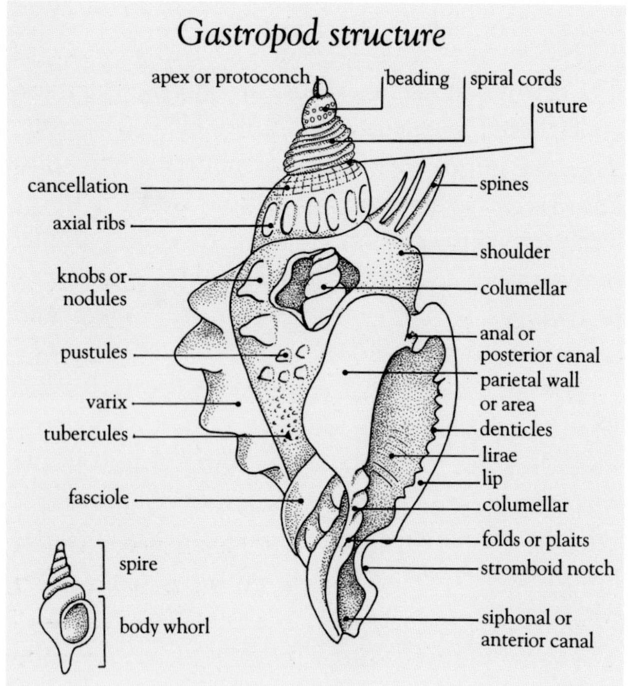


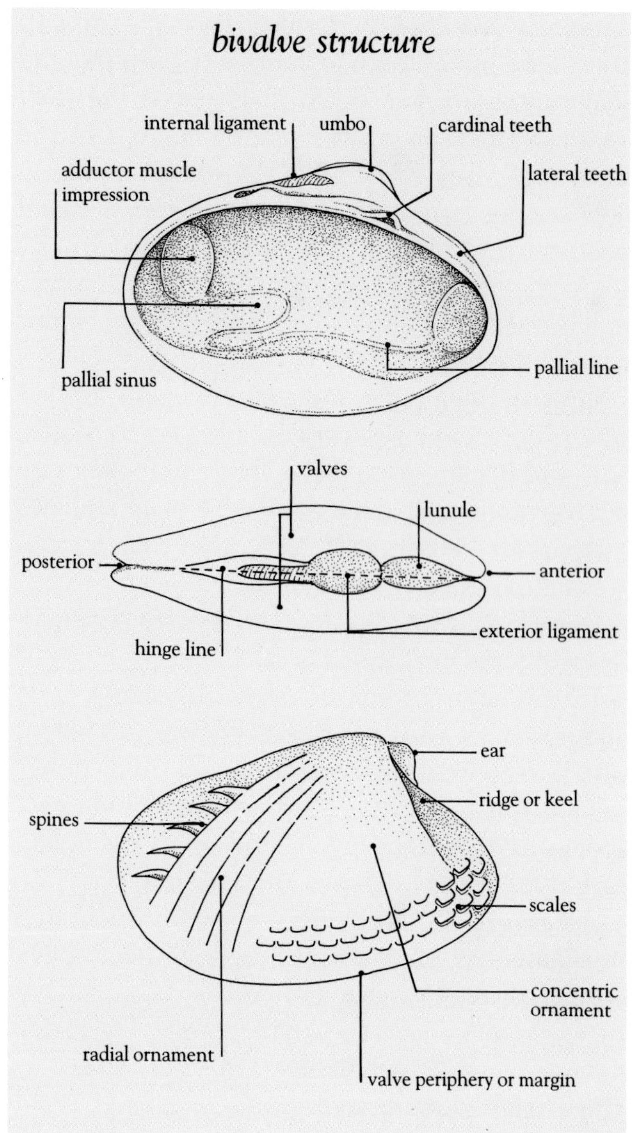


## THE BIVALVE BODY

The soft inner parts are enclosed on both sides by two large mantle lobes and these also secrete the shell-making material. No species possesses a head or radula, but some scallops and thorny oysters have light-sensitive "eyes" situated around the mantle margins. All species possess a heart and circulatory system, and digestive organs.

The gills, which are situated within the mantle cavity, act as food filters for those species that feed on plankton and other suspended organisms, and are drawn in on the respiratory current by beating hair-like cilia in the cavity. A portion of the mantle of most bivalves is drawn out at the posterior into two siphons, one of which inhales water, while the other exhales. These can be retracted in order to close the shell. Generally the longer the siphons the deeper the shell lives in the substrate; in some cases, the siphons may be up to twice as long as the actual shell.

Oxygen is taken up by means of the mantle, the gills having little to do with respiration. The exhalent siphon is responsible for carrying away waste products.

Bivalves close their shells by means of strong adductor muscles, many species having two of these. Scars or impressions of the muscles can be observed on the valve's inner walls and are used as an aid in identification. The rubbery ligament situated close to the umbones (where the young shell commenced growth) has the opposite effect to the muscles, tending to push the valves apart. It is these opposing forces that enable the shell to open and close at will.

The shape of the foot varies according to whether it is used for creeping, burrowing or for attachment by byssus threads. It can be described as axe, tongue or worm like. In free-swimming and sessile species, the size of the foot is much reduced.

## MOVEMENT

Immature shells, or those of primitive families, such as ark shells, move by slowly creeping over substrate, but most burrow in sand or mud with the help of the foot. Some species, such as mussel and pen shells, remain sessile and fix themselves in one place. Other species are capable of boring into timber or even soft rock. Some swim by forcing water held within the shell through a jet at the rear edge or by clapping their valves like bellows. The pedal gland secretes filament-like threads which are used to attach shells to coral, rock or other stable or firm material.

## Cephalopods

Although this is an order which contains groups such as the octopus and squid, we are primarily concerned with the families Nautilidae and Argonautidae.

With few exceptions, the sexes are separate. There is no free-swimming larval or veliger stage; the embryo emerges fully developed from its egg.

The head and foot are united and there are gills and highly developed sensory organs. All members of this order are carnivorous and have long suckered tentacles with which the animal seizes its prey, tearing at it with a powerful parrot-like beak.

The chambered nautilus has a large coiled shell with sealed internal chambers in a perfect spiral, each being larger than the preceding one. A central tube, the siphuncle, connects these chambers. A kind of nitrogenous gas passes through this tube and, together with an amount of fluid, creates buoyancy for mobility. By varying the amounts of these two substances, the shell can rise or submerge at will; shells however, rarely ever come to the surface of the water. Recent study has shown that these incredible molluscs are not the sole survivors of their primitive fossil ancestors (ammonites), but highly advanced and sophisticated shells, well-adapted to their peculiar life-style.

The "shells" of the family Argonautidae are not shells in the real sense, but are actually protective egg cases produced by the female of an octopus-like creature.

## Scaphopods

These uniquely shaped molluscs, with their hollow, tube-like and tapering shells, live buried in sand with the narrow, posterior end of the shell projecting just above the surface. The foot is situated at the opposite end and can be used to draw the animal deeper into the substrate. They possess no eyes but have a large radula.

Because they have no true gills, they breathe by inhaling water; this passes over the folds of the mantle lining, which is modified to form a tube. The animal utilizes a form of adhesive at the ends of its long tentacles to grab microscopic organisms from the substrate.

There are separate sexes. The embryonic form consists of two minute valves; these fuse together to form the tube-like shape and the mantle produces the shell as it grows in size.

## Polyplacophora

These are fairly primitive molluscs, possessing a unique flexible shell comprised of eight plates or pieces which can be tightly coiled when attacked or when removed from rocks. The foot is powerful and is extremely difficult to remove once attached to a rock.

Within its mantle cavity are the gills and sexual and excretory organs. Some species have tactile organs and primitive "eyes" which are situated in cavities on the exposed parts of the shell. The chitons breathe by lifting part of the encircling girdle to take in water, which then passes over the gills.

All have a well-developed radula, which is used to tear at algae and other vegetable matter. The sexes are separate, and although a few species have a veliger stage, most young shells remain under the mother until they are able to fend for themselves.

## Monoplacophora

This is an ancient order long considered extinct since the Devonian period. However, in May 1952, a Dutch research vessel *Galathea* off Costa Rica, fished up a "living fossil". A shell resembling a circular flat limpet was taken from a muddy substrate at 11,850ft (3,590m) and this long-lost mollusc, a truly amazing and sensational find, was named *Neopilina galatheae*. Since that time, several other species have been discovered and named. The soft parts are segmented and there are gills, mouth and excretory, but no visual, organs. Research continues on these primitive and extremely rare shells. I doubt any are yet owned by private amateur collectors.

# Habitat and world distribution

Seashells are able to inhabit almost any environment where water can offer an adequate supply of food, but the majority of species, and certainly the most highly coloured and patterned shells, exist in shallow waters. The sea and seashore can, and for the purposes of this book, be divided up into the following zones or areas:

*Intertidal* The area between the highest and lowest tides, also often referred to as the littoral zone. Some species also occupy the area above the high-tide line, known as the splash zone.

*Sub-tidal* Also known as the shallow-water zone, this includes waters below the low-tide line, coral reefs and continental shelves.

*Abyssal* Also called the deep-water zone, this describes the lightless regions, down to the ocean floor.

*ABOVE Numerous marine plants and animals thrive in shallow-water rock pools. Limpets, sea urchins, anemones and starfish are among the inhabitants of this cold-water pool in South Africa.*

Many species thrive in sand or in muddy habitats, and burrowing shells such as olives, mitres and numerous bivalves, find sandy substrates ideal. Mangrove swamps also provide a food-rich habitat for numerous species, such as horn shells and mud creepers.

On rocky coasts, where rougher conditions prevail, you will find species with strongly constructed shells (limpets, top shells and chitons) that are adapted to cling to rock faces and boulders without being washed away. Other, less sturdy, species tend to live under rocks and slabs, or in rocky crevices.

Coral reefs are an ideal habitat for numerous species of mollusc, and here the majority of the highly coloured and attractive shells are found, mostly in tropical areas.

So-called pelagic species live on or near the surface of the sea, away from shores and land attached to a "raft" of bubbles. In deep water or the abyssal zones, other well-adapted species exist; these are often thin-walled whitish or mostly colourless shells. (For further detail on depths, see depth guide, p.31.)

## Distribution

Numerous factors are to be considered when determining how and why seashells are distributed in the world's seas. These include climatic conditions, water currents and depths, and food supply.

In the mid 19th century, S. P. Woodward showed that the oceans could be divided into zoogeographical provinces reflecting molluscan distribution, basing his analysis on the grounds that at least half of all marine molluscs do not occur in any other area.

The 16 areas designated by Woodward are still generally accepted. Although I have not strictly adhered to his provinces, they still provide a reasonable basis on which to work and are shown on the map (right). The localities in parentheses also fall into these broad categories, and are often used in the text as an aid to more precise location.

## MARINE ZOOGEOGRAPHICAL PROVINCES

ARCTIC ALEUTIAN AUSTRALIAN BOREAL CALIFORNIAN CARIBBEAN INDO-PACIFIC JAPONIC

MAGELLANIC MEDITERRANEAN PANAMIC PATAGONIAN PERUVIAN SOUTH AFRICAN TRANSATLANTIC WEST AFRICAN

ARCTIC
(North polar seas, Northern Alaska and Canada; Greenland and Northern Siberia)

ALEUTIAN
(North Pacific from Siberia and Southern Alaska to the Bering Sea and south to British Columbia)

AUSTRALIAN
(Western, Southern and Eastern Australia; New Zealand)

BOREAL
(Eastern Canada, Northern and North-eastern Atlantic; North Sea)

CALIFORNIAN
(Western USA, California to Baja California)

CARIBBEAN
(Gulf of Mexico, Florida, West Indies, Caribbean Sea, Venezuela, North-eastern Brazil)

INDO-PACIFIC
(East Africa, Mauritius, Madagascar, Red Sea, Gulf of Oman, Indian Ocean, India and Sri Lanka, Thailand, China Sea, Taiwan, Malaysia, Indonesia, Philippines, Papua New Guinea, Solomon Islands, Vannatu, New Caledonia, Northern Australia, Western and South-West Pacific, Tahiti, Easter Islands, Marquesas Islands, Andaman Sea, Hawaiian Islands, Sulu Sea, Bay of Bengal)

JAPONIC
(Japan, Okinawa, Korea)

MAGELLANIC
(Southern Chile, Southern Argentina)

MEDITERRANEAN
(Mediterranean Sea, North-West Africa, Canary Islands)

PANAMIC
(Gulf of California, West Mexico, Western Central America, Panama)

PATAGONIAN
(Eastern South America, Brazil and Argentina)

PERUVIAN
(Western South America, Peru, Northern Chile)

SOUTH AFRICAN
(South and South-East Africa)

TRANSATLANTIC
(Eastern and South-eastern USA)

WEST AFRICAN
(Western Africa, Senegal, Angola, Cape Verde Islands)

# *Conservation*

All natural objects, including molluscs, as well as the environment in which they live, are under threat, primarily due to the selfishness, carelessness and irresponsibility of man.

The single most important threat to molluscs is the destruction of their habitat. Pollution is the prime killer – our oceans having become vast dumping grounds for rubbish, sewage and industrial waste products. News of oil spillage and slicks from commercial tankers is commonplace, resulting in the death of much marine life. In addition, natural disasters, such as typhoons, are capable of irreparable damage to shallow water reefs in a matter of hours. Large, shallow water areas and reefs have been destroyed to provide material for building harbours, runways, land reclamation and other projects.

Indiscriminate overfishing of shells is a major problem. This is partly to supply large commercial concerns in the U.S.A., Europe and the Far East.

TOP *A dead specimen of European Prickly Cockle* (Acanthocardia echinata) *on sand flats at low tide.*

ABOVE *European Jingle Shell* (Anomia ephippium) *revealed by a receding tide.*

*LEFT The numerous varieties of dead shells, particularly limpets, are typical of cold or temperate waters.*

Countries like India, the Philippines and Malaysia export many tons of seashells annually; the mother-of-pearl, jewellery, shell curio and fertilizer industries all depend on regular supplies. Here, there is a good argument for tough controls.

Several countries such as Kenya, Australia and the Seychelles have established marine nature reserves where fishing and collecting is totally banned. In some South African locations you may only collect specimens over a certain size and in limited number. A sign on a beach on Sanibel Island, Florida clearly states: "only two mature specimens of any one species may be taken".

In recent years, an international body known as the Convention on International Trade in Endangered Species (CITES) has been formed to control the movement and thus the overfishing and collecting not only of endangered species of any kind, but also those that if not carefully monitored and controlled could also become endangered. There are as yet no seashells that are endangered, but all species of the giant clam family are on the controlled list due to overfishing for food and ornament. There is an increasing need, however, for more species of shells to be added to this list.

In many underdeveloped countries the poor depend on shells for both their food and livelihoods. A great need exists to educate and promote sensible harvesting of the seas' produce and to conserve and nurture stocks for future generations. Commercial farming on a large scale and the relatively new science of mariculture could be key issues in the future.

Collectors are often accused of depleting numerous species of molluscs, but there is little evidence to support this claim; it is of course essential that serious collectors, students and conchologists take a lead in promoting a responsible attitude as far as collecting in the wild is concerned. Indeed some collectors prefer to specialize in beached or dead-collected material.

## A SHELLER'S CREED

The following rules, published by the Hawaiian Malacological Society, provide a useful code of conduct for shell collectors everywhere.

1 Leave the coral heads alone! Shells do not live there; look amongst the rubble, under slabs, in the sand and amongst loose chunks of coral.
2 Replace coral and rocks exactly as found, even in deeper water, something lives under them and continued exposure will kill it.
3 Look out for and protect shell egg masses. The survival rate is slim at best. Do not take a shell that is guarding eggs and avoid disturbing breeding groups.
4 Collect only what you need. Take time to examine your finds. Imperfect or immature shells are of no use to you. Leave them to grow and breed.

# Making a collection

Conchology is a broad enough subject to encompass people of all ages and all levels of commitment from amateurs to scientists. Some people collect shells simply because they appreciate natural objects; others because they derive an artistic pleasure in their varied shapes and colours, while for others collecting becomes almost an obsession.

It is fashionable nowadays to specialize in one group or family, or in certain types of shell, perhaps because a more comprehensive collection would consume too much space or cover too broad a field for detailed study. Cowries are the most popular group, closely followed by cones, volutes and murex species. Little display space is required for cowries, and they offer a wide variety of pattern and colour. They are relatively easy to collect in the wild, and the majority can be bought for affordable prices.

Some collectors take an active interest in very tiny adult shells, known as "micro-shells", which are perhaps no more than ⅜in (1cm) long at maturity. Another fascination to collectors is the collecting of abnormalities, or freaks. The natural world has been marvellously arranged but, as we all know, deviations from the normal do occur and shells can suffer from pollution, predatory attack or some unexplicable upheaval in lifestyle, the result being a shell with growth scars, an abnormally curved spire, excessively long – or stunted – spines, or general deformities. The cowries of New Caledonia can develop unusually lengthened and recurved extremities and are known as "rostrate" specimens; also, possibly due to chemical presence in the water, many are an unnatural dark brown or, rarely, totally black (known as melanistic). These variations from the normal are most sought after by collectors and can command high prices.

## Collecting shells

The beach or shoreline is the most accessible area in which to commence your collecting exploits. Without undue difficulty, you will find beach-worn specimens on the sand or pebbles, or, after rough storms, good "fresh dead" shells. Washed up devoid of the snail inhabitant, these can be most acceptable.

Many species that exist below the sand or mud are within reach of a spade or shovel at low tide. When beachcombing, be aware of the tide movements and, especially in the tropics, of the sun, which can be fierce and harmful without suitable head and body protection.

Rocky terrain is also a good hunting ground – many well-adapted molluscs are to be found in shallow pools, under rocks and stones and in crevices. Stout footwear is required, waterproof plastic shoes being ideal. This also applies when searching on coral reefs, which can be extremely sharp. You should also watch out for those spinose shells that lurk on the surface or just below, and are able to scratch or sting. The minimum requirements are a bucket or strong plastic bag for your finds, gloves, a knife, and perhaps forceps.

Those wishing to collect below the low-tide zones will initially require a face mask and snorkel and, if available, a small vessel to reach areas that cannot be reached by wading. Free diving can be useful, but requires stamina and strength. Scuba diving has enabled those of us with the correct training to enter a hitherto undiscovered world, and as diving has gained in popularity, so uncommon and rare shells have become available.

If you have no wish to enter the water, a simple dredge can be made which, providing you have a boat, can prove very useful in bringing up all kinds of specimens from the substrate. This method should not be used over coral as you could damage coral heads.

Commercial lobster and crayfish vessels often take deep-water species at depths down to about 660ft (200m). Deep-sea dredgers and trawlers, along with fishing vessels, are the best source for rare deep-water shells. Fishermen have discovered that these shells – which they would once have thrown away – are worth money. With modern methods of fishing, most of the world's known rare species are available, occasionally, at a price.

ABOVE *A beachcomber's paradise – mounds of beached, or dead molluscs on Shell Beach, Herm, Channel Islands.*

In the central Philippines, where seashells are an important seafood as well as being required by collectors and by the commercial shell market, fishermen often use what are known as tangle nets. These are suspended in the water overnight to retrieve whatever molluscs fall foul of the netting.

Many species are regularly caught "ex-pisce" – retrieved from stomachs of fish who pick up food, including molluscs, from the substrate. In general, these specimens are in excellent condition, having been totally cleaned by gastric juices. Probably the world's rarest cowrie, *Cypraea fultoni*, has in past years only been collected in this way, in fish caught off the coast of south-east Africa, but the price has been halved since 1990 due to the discovery of new habitats off Mozambique.

## *Cleaning shells*

Shells purchased from dealers normally require no cleaning other than a periodic dusting or a wash in warm soapy water. Grubby specimens have even been known to benefit from a cycle in the dishwasher. Beached, faded or dull shells respond to a light rub with baby oil. This can be applied with a finger or, in the case of spinose shells, with a soft brush, and the excess wiped away with a tissue.

Live-collected shells must be cleaned of their inhabitants. Sometimes, of course, these will be edible, but in other cases a period in the deep freeze will cause the contents to fall away from the inner surface, facilitating their removal with forceps or wire.

Once the soft parts have been dealt with, it may be desirable to remove the periostracum. Place the specimen in a solution of household bleach and water for a few hours; the skin will either dissolve completely or can be gently brushed away.

Stubborn areas may require a longer period of soaking and stronger bleach solution.

Exterior encrustations can cause problems, and I have encountered numerous methods of removing hard lime encrustations and other marine debris. A wire brush can be used with care on solidly built shells that have a non-glossy surface; other methods entail careful "picking" with pins or forceps, or gently tapping with a small blunt instrument.

*ABOVE Glass-fronted wooden showcases display a naturalist's collection, c. 1900.*

Shells that have coarse ornamentation and are dull or have a chalky appearance respond very well to a second or two's dip in a weak solution of hydrochloric acid. Although this method is frowned upon by some experts, I have found that when it is used with due care excellent results can be obtained with some species, like those of *Murex*, *Pecten* and *Spondylus*. Often the full potential of colour and pattern can be realized only with this apparently extreme treatment.

I am often asked how to renovate shells that have been kept outdoors and have totally lost their colour. Alas, once a shell has deteriorated to this condition, little or nothing can be done to retrieve its former glory. Seashells, like other cherished collectable items, have to be safeguarded against external elements, especially sunlight, which can seriously fade the colour of a shell in a relatively short period of time. Specimens are best housed indoors away from direct sunlight.

## *Display*

However you have collected your shells, they deserve to be displayed to their best advantage. A growing collection will eventually need to be moved away from shelves or coffee tables, where they are open to damage from bright natural light, and into cases or specially designed drawers.

I am fortunate in being able to house my collection in a shellroom-study, where many specimens are on permanent display in purpose-built, glass-fronted cases. The curtains are, however, drawn in daylight hours, especially during summer.

It has been said that a shell collection without correct data relating to each specimen is worthless. Arguably, each shell should bear at least a note of its name, location and other relative data, such as depth and habitat, but not every collector is interested in such scientific details. If your collection has been compiled with interest and love – and this will certainly be evident to the onlooker – it will be as valid as those housed in the world's foremost museums and scientific collections.

# Purchasing shells

Shells can be purchased in numerous places nowadays, ranging from seaside gift shops, florists and fishmongers, to specialist dealers. The new collector will soon be able to differentiate between what are known as commercial shells – those available primarily from gift or seaside shops, and those termed specimen quality, which are generally obtained from shell dealers.

Commercial quality material consists, for the most part, of common or abundant varieties. These are often attractive and collectable, but you would expect to find faults, chips or breakages. It is doubtful that the rarer species would be found among such material, although good "finds" have been known and it pays to look out for the odd rarity. Once you are on the way to becoming a collector, you will tend to look for specialist shell dealers from whom you might expect a greater selection, quality specimen shells and useful advice. You can also expect to pay more for your shells.

Some dealers travel and visit shell shows and club meetings while others have retail (and sometimes wholesale) shops. Get to know your dealer – hopefully he will advise you of new or interesting specimens that have just arrived – he may even be coaxed into showing you his own ultra-rare or special items. If you have doubts about a dealer – ask other collectors.

Many dealers offer a mail order service – indeed many overseas traders exist solely in this way – producing and mailing periodic lists of specimen shells from worldwide locations. New customers are usually required to pay at least some cash in advance and this can be somewhat daunting to the uninitiated. The sale is often backed by a clause promising "full return if not satisfied", but this is little comfort if your dealer is thousands of miles away! Again, check by asking other collectors.

Dealers are often happy to exchange specimens. If you have self-collected material that is surplus to requirements, offer it to your dealer – he or she may well be able to use what you have.

Prices of specimen shells vary, and there are several factors to consider. All shells are individual and unique and one specimen may be infinitely more desirable than another of the same species; the actual cost to the dealer must vary – he may have had the shell sent by airmail, which is far more expensive than surface mail, and if his premises are in the centre of a town, his overheads will be high. The only customer guideline is satisfaction in what you have purchased for the price paid. Tom Rice, in his catalogue (see bibliography), lists thousands of species at current American dealers' prices, and this can be a useful general guide.

Do not be afraid of always having to pay high prices for shells. Hundreds of common and popular shells are available at very low and reasonable prices.

On many dealers' lists you will see "w/o" beside a description; this means that the shell possesses its original operculum (preferred by some collectors). "Full data" means that a shell is supplied with details of its country and place of origin, depth, habitat, date of collecting and possibly the name of the diver. Some collectors insist on these full data, but in many cases shells are supplied with basic data, often detailing only the country or location of origin.

Can a collection of shells be considered an investment? I would suggest not, for the following reasons. Over the years, so-called rare species have become less rare and more readily available; inevitably, prices drop. A sudden craze for a particular species or a newly named species will force the price up, but it will fall when more shells come on the market or the fashion ceases.

## SHELL PRICES

| | |
|---|---|
| **Abundant or Common** | Can cost from a few pence to perhaps £5 each. |
| **Uncommon** | Prices between £5 and possibly £50 each. |
| **Rare** | In excess of £50; some species fetch perhaps £500 or £1,000 each. |

Although shells remain, if cared for, in pristine condition for many years, they do age and very old shells from Victorian collections look their age. Generally shells cannot be revived, and antique value is seldom a consideration unless a collection is from a famous conchologist. My advice would be to exercise caution in the subject of expensive shells – collect, exchange or purchase for study or enjoyment, this should be your ultimate aim.

## SHELL GRADES

In order that collectors can, with some degree of trust and reliability, purchase from dealers without prior sight of a given specimen, many have adopted the following internationally-accepted shell grading standard.

**GEM** A virtually flawless shell, without visible breaks or flaws. The spire should be perfect; the lip unchipped and not filed; spines, if evident, unbroken. Well cleaned, without excessive oiling. Adult.

**FINE** An adult specimen with minor flaws and no more than one shallow growth scar. It must bear the original colour and gloss (if any). The outer lip or edge may have one small crack or chip, and the shell – a *Murex* or *Spondylus*, for example – may have a slightly broken spine. There will be no human 'repairs', and it should be well cleaned.

**FAIR OR GOOD** A shell which is considered reasonable, but perhaps has a few flaws. It will have growth scars or breaks, broken spines or worn lip or spire. It can be immature, but display the main species characteristics.

**POOR** This can be assumed to be a commercial grade, and will be worn, broken, chipped or holed. It will naturally have very obvious flaws.

## *Shells – common or rare?*

Why are shells common, uncommon or rare? A great deal can influence the status of a given species and the situation has changed much over the last two or three centuries. Deep-water shells that at one time were virtually unobtainable were said to be "rare", whereas nowadays, with modern fishing methods, these once-elusive species are available in reasonable numbers, and tend to appear on the market as "uncommon". There are of course numerous species that live in very restricted ranges or in difficult habitats, and these factors render the shell at least scarce and usually very expensive.

Nature reserves and conservation areas are subject to severe collecting or fishing restrictions, rendering all endemic species difficult, if not impossible, to come by. Species solely occurring in the Galapagos Islands are most difficult to obtain, and, when they are, usually originate from old collections formed before the days when these islands became a total nature reserve.

The golden cowrie (*Cypraea aurantium*) is reasonably plentiful in places such as Samar Island, Philippines, but due to its beauty and popularity, the demand has for many years exceeded the supply.

Offshore fishing habits change. Several species mentioned in this book were commonly fished off the coasts of south-west Taiwan during the 1970s. More recently it was less expensive for the Taiwanese to purchase their fish direct from mainland China, many of these shells (by-products of the industry) were no longer available; the situation however is changeable.

## Counterfeits and shell "doctoring"

*Sooner or later most collectors will encounter "doctored" shells. These may be imperfect specimens with holes and scars which have been filled in, and chipped lips which have been filed smooth. Alternatively, they may be the amazing and cleverly constructed over-spinose or expertly hand-painted "rarities" offered by unscrupulous central Philippine dealers.*

*Although never really substantiated, probably the best known story of shell counterfeiting is that of the precious wentletrap* (Epitonium scalare)*. In the 19th century this was extremely rare, and enterprising Oriental craftsmen were supposed to have made counterfeits from rice-flour paste. The fraud was only detected when shells fell apart after washing. The specimen shown was long considered a fake and, although now proved genuine, is valued by its present owner because of its history as an imitation. Note the broken areas about the aperture where curious owners have removed pieces to investigate its construction.*

*RIGHT A full plate of Cassidas from Reeve's* Conchologia Iconica, *1848.*

Cassis. Pl. VIII.
18. a.
19 a.
19. b.
20 a
20. b.
20. c.
18. b.
Sowerby del et lith.
Reeve, Benham & Reeve, imp.

# *Systematic Arrangement of Taxonomic Classification down to Subfamily Level used within the text of this book*

*Phylum Mollusca*
**CLASS GASTROPODA**
*Subclass Prosobranchia*
Order Archaegastropoda

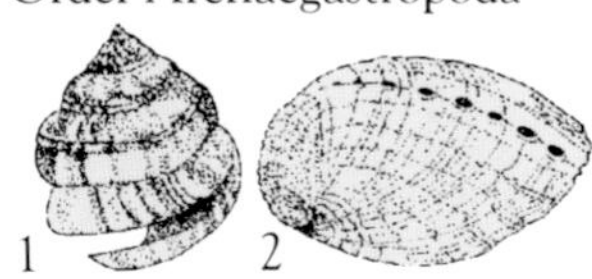


PLEUROTOMARIOIDEA
Pleurotomariidae (1)
Haliotidae (2)

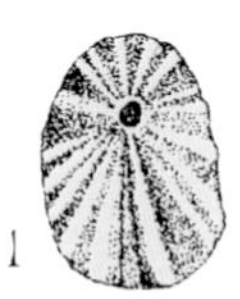


FISSURELLOIDEA
Fissurellidae (1)
s/f Emarginulinae
s/f Diodoriinae
s/f Fissurellinae

PATELLOIDEA
Acmaeidae (1)
s/f Acmaeinae
Lottiidae (1)
s/f Lottiinae
s/f Patelloidinae
Patellidae (1)
s/f Patellinae

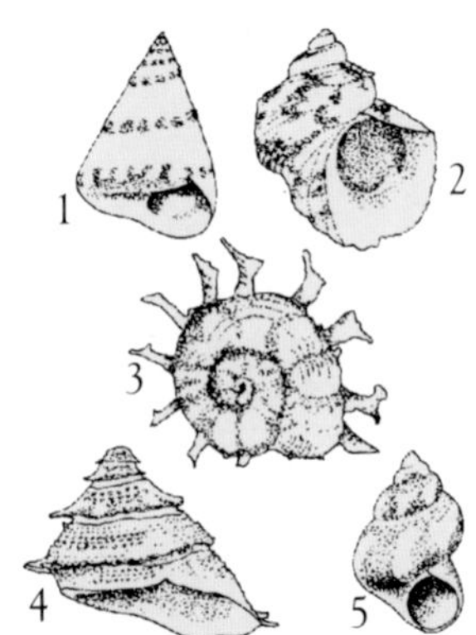


TROCHOIDEA
Trochidae (1)
s/f Margaritinae
s/f Monodontinae
s/f Gibbulinae
s/f Calliostomatinae
s/f Trochinae
s/f Umboniinae
Turbinidae (2) (3)
s/f Angariinae
s/f Turbininae
s/f Astraeinae (4)
Phasiandlidae (5)
Tricolicdae

1

NERITOIDEA
Neritidae (1)
s/f Neritinae
s/f Smaragdiinae
Order Mesogastropoda

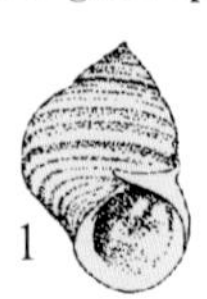


LITTORINOIDEA
Littorinidae (1)
s/f Littorininae
s/f Tectariinae

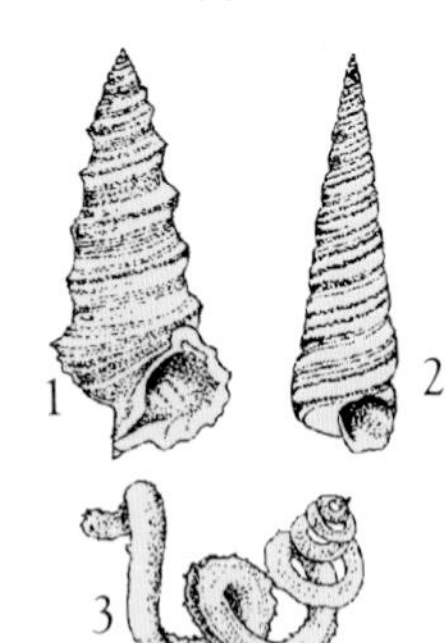


CERITHIOIDEA
Cerithiidae (1)
s/f Cerithiinae
Campanilidae
Potamididae
s/f Potamidinae
Turitellidae (2)
s/f Turitellinae
s/f Vermiculariinae
Siliquariidae (3)

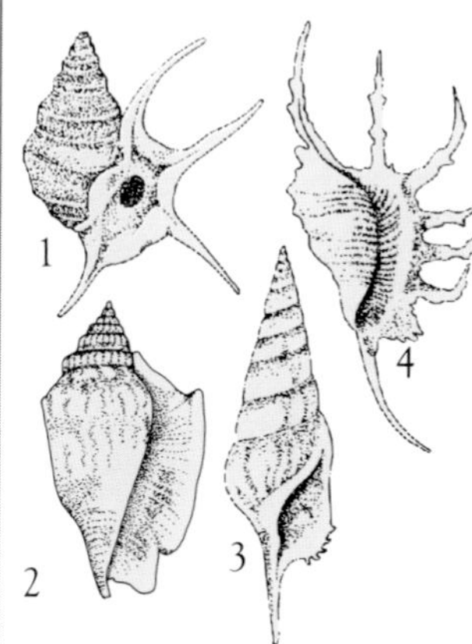


STROMBOIDEA
Aporrhaidae (1)
Strombidae (2, 3, 4)

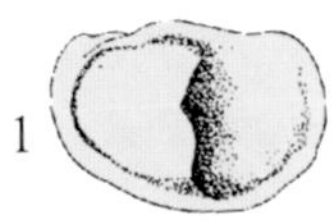


CREPIDULOIDEA
Crepidulidae (1)

XENOPHOROIDEA
Xenophoridae (1)

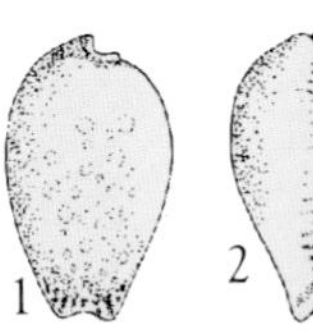


3

CYPRAEOIDEA
Cypraeidae (1, 2)
Ovulidae (3)
s/f Ovulinae
Triviidae
s/f Triviinae

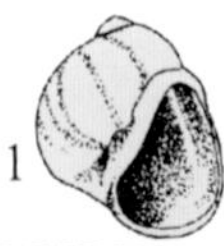


NATICOIDEA
Naticidae (1)
s/f Ampullospirinae
s/f Polinicinae
s/f Naticinae

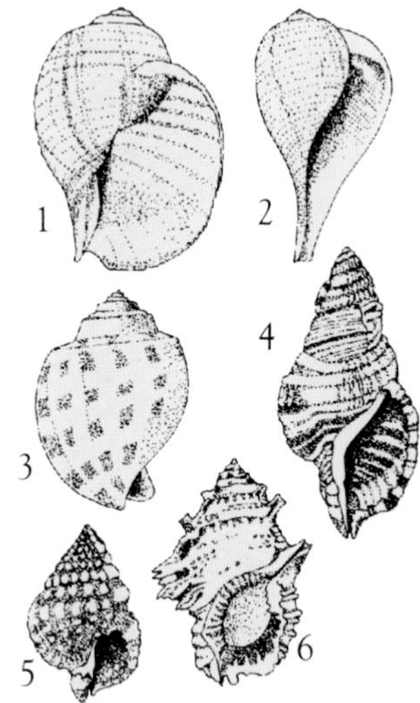


TONNOIDEA
Tonnidae (1)
Ficidae (2)
Cassidae (3)
s/f Cassinae
s/f Phaliinae
Ranellidae (4, 5)
s/f Ranellinae
s/f Cymatiinae
s/f Personinae
Bursidae (6)
*Suborder Heteroglossa*

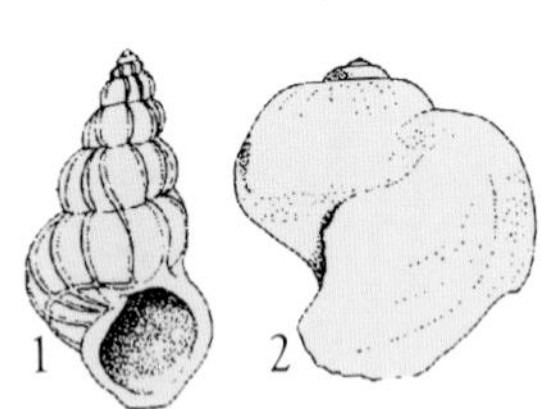


EPITONIOIDEA
Epitoniidae (1)
s/f Epitoniinae
Janthinidae (2)
Order Neogastropoda
MURICOIDEA

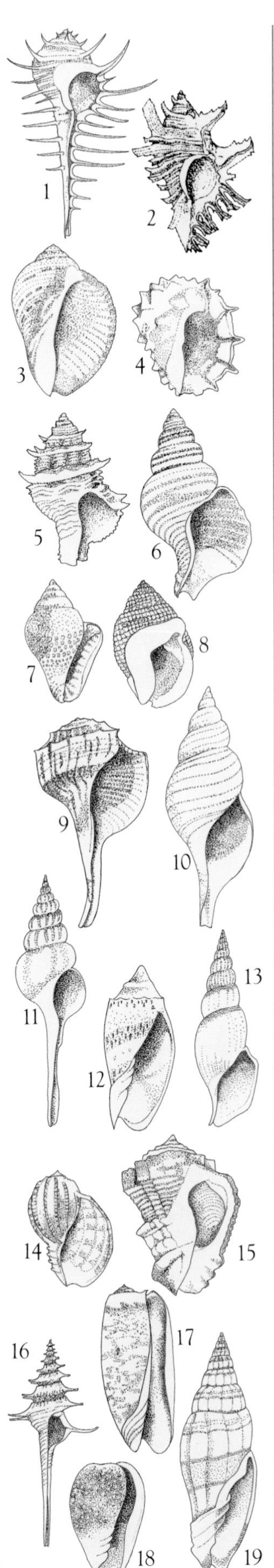

Muricidae (1, 2)
s/f Muricinae
s/f Muricopsinae
s/f Ocenebrinae
s/f Trophoninae
s/f Thaidinae (3, 4)
s/f Rapaninae
Coralliophilidae (5)
Buccinidae (6)
s/f Bucininae
s/f Volutopsinae
s/f Photinae
s/f Pisaniinae
Columbellidae (7)
s/f Columbellinae
s/f Pyreninae
Nasariidae (8)
s/f Nasariinae
s/f Dorsaniinae
Melongenidae (9)
Fasciolariidae (10)
s/f Fasciolariinae
s/f Fusininae (11)
s/f Peristerniinae
s/f Colubrariinae
Volutidae (12, 13)
s/f Volutinae
s/f Athletinae
s/f Lyrinae
s/f Fulgorariinae
s/f Cymbiinae
s/f Zidoninae
s/f Odontocymbiolinae
s/f Scaphellinae
s/f Calliotectinae
Harpidae (14)
s/f Harpinae
s/f Moruminae
Vasidae (15)
s/f Vasinae
s/f Turbinellinae
s/f Columbariinae (16)
Olividae (17)
s/f Olivinae
s/f Ancillinae
s/f Olivellinae
s/f Agaroniinae
Marginellidae (18)
s/f Marginellinae
Mitridae (19)
s/f Mitrinae
s/f Cylindromitrinae

s/f Imbricariinae
Costellariidae

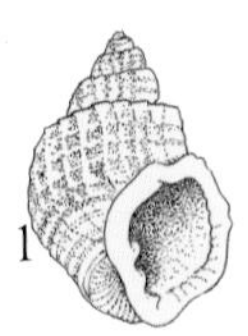

CANCELLARIOIDEA
Cancellariidae (1)
s/f Cancellariinae

CONOIDEA
Conidae (1)
Turridae (2)
s/f Pseudomelatominae
s/f Drillinae
s/f Turrinae
s/f Turriculinae
s/f Crassispirinae
s/f Clavatulinae
s/f Borsoninae
s/f Daphnellinae
s/f Thatcheriinae
Terebridae (3)
*Subclass Heterobranchia*
*Suborder Allogastropoda*

ARCHITECTONICOIDEA
Architectonicidae (1)
*Subclass Opisthobranchia*
Order Cephalaspida

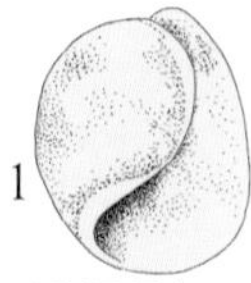

PHILINOIDEA
Acteonidae (1)
Hydatinidae (1)
Bullidae (1)
Hamineidae

**CLASS BIVALVIA**
*Subclass Pteriomorphia*
Order Arcoida

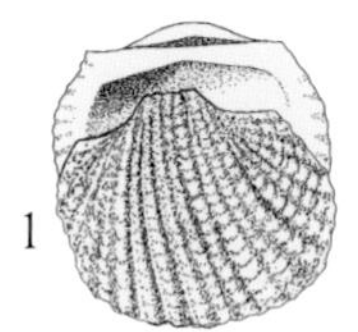

ARCOIDEA
Arcidae (1)
s/f Arcinae
s/f Anadarinae
Cuculaeidae

LIMOPSOIDEA
Glycymerididae (1)
Order Mytiloida

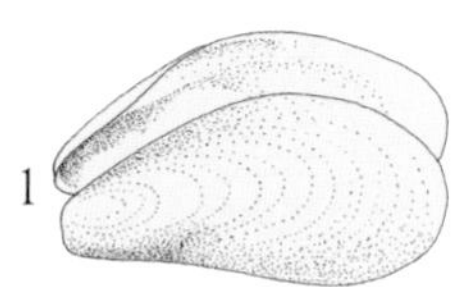

MYTILOIDEA
Mytilidae (1)
s/f Mytilinae
Order Pterioida
*Suborder Pteriina*

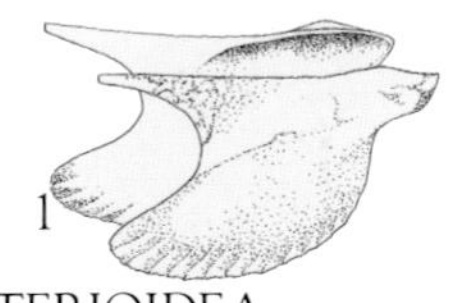

PTERIOIDEA
Pteriidae (1)
Malleidae
*Suborder Pinnina*

PINNOIDEA
Pinnidae (1)
Order Limoida

LIMOIDEA
Limidae (1)
Order Ostreoida
*Suborder Ostreina*

OSTREOIDEA
Ostreidae (1)
s/f Ostreinae
s/f Crassostreinae
s/f Lophinae (2)
*Suborder Pectinina*

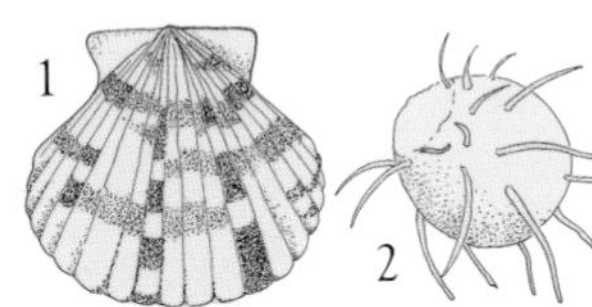


PECTINOIDEA
Pectinidae (1)
s/f Chlamydinae
s/f Pectininae
s/f Patinopectininae
Propeamussiidae
Spondylidae (2)

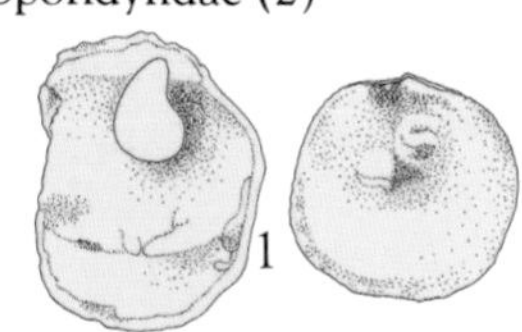


ANOMIOIDEA
Anomiidae (1)
Placunidae
*Subclass Paleoheterodonta*
Order Trigonoida

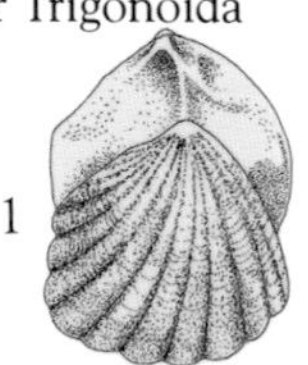


TRIGONIOIDEA
Trigoniidae (1)
*Subclass Heterodonta*
Order Veneroida

LUCINOIDEA
Lucinidae (1)
s/f Lucininae
Fimbriidae

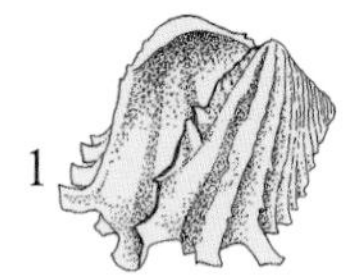


CARDITOIDEA
Carditidae (1)
s/f Carditinae

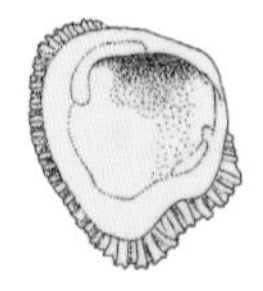

CHAMOIDEA
Chamidae (1)

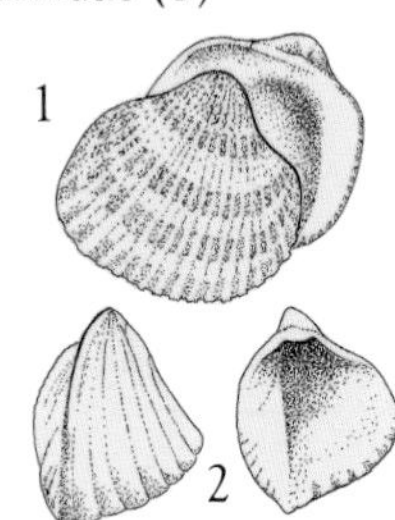


CARDIOIDEA
Cardiidae (1, 2)
s/f Cardiinae
s/f Trachycardiinae
s/f Fraginae
s/f Laevicardiinae

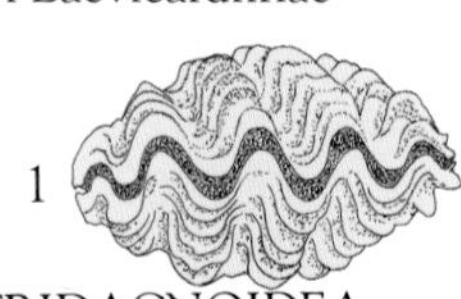


TRIDACNOIDEA
Tridacnidae (1)

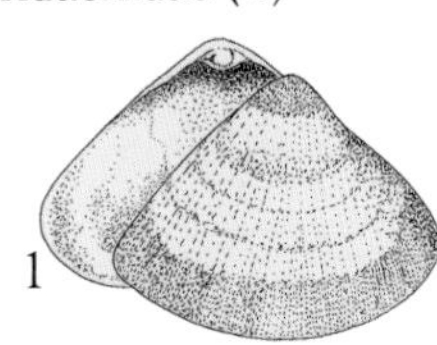


MACTROIDEA
Mactridae (1)
s/f Mactrinae

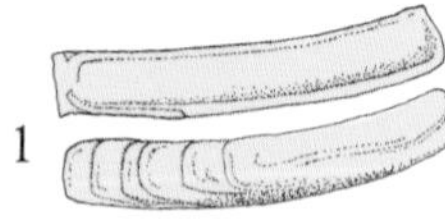


SOLENOIDEA
Solenidae (1)
Cultellidae

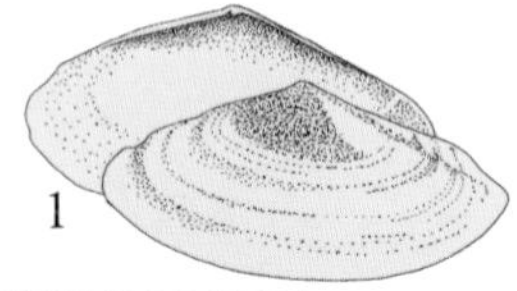


TELLINOIDEA
Tellinidae (1)
s/f Tellininae
Donacidae

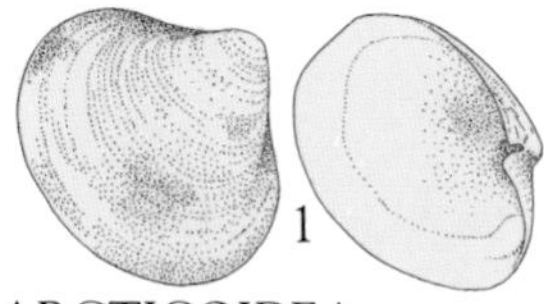


ARCTICOIDEA
Arcticidae (1)

GLOSSOIDEA
Glossidae (1)

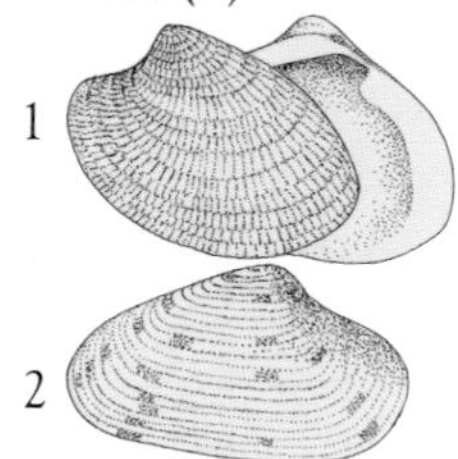


VENEROIDEA
Veneridae (1, 2)
s/f Venerinae
s/f Circinae
s/f Chioninae
s/f Meretricinae
s/f Pitarinae
s/f Tapetinae
s/f Dosiniinae
Order Myoida
*Suborder Pholadina*

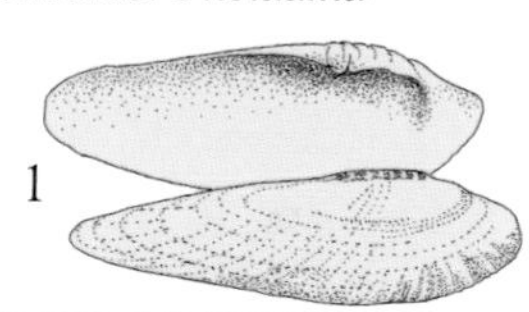


PHOLADOIDEA
Pholadidae (1)
s/f Pholadinae

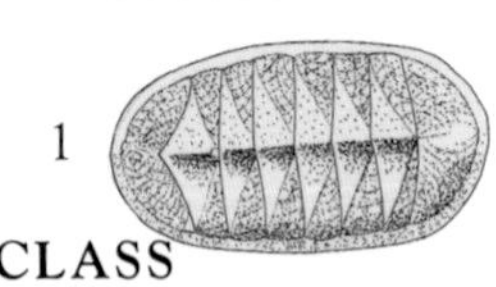


**CLASS POLYPLACOPHORA**
Order Neoloricata
*Suborder Ischnochitonina*
Ischnochitonidae (1)
s/f Ischnochitoninae
s/f Chaetopleurinae
s/f Lepidochitoninae
Chitonidae (1)
s/f Chitoninae

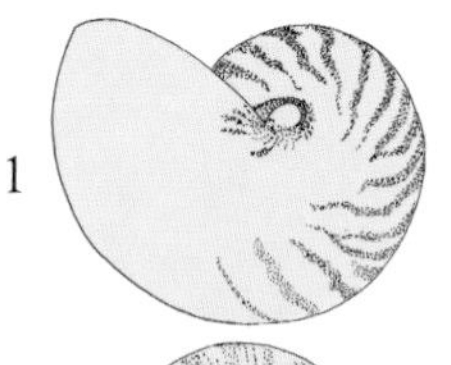

**CLASS CEPHALOPODA**
*Subclass Nautiloidea*
Order Nautiloida
Nautilidae (1)
*Subclass Coleoidae*
Order Sepiida
*Suborder Spirulina*
Spirulidae (2)
Order Octopoda
*Suborder Incirrata*

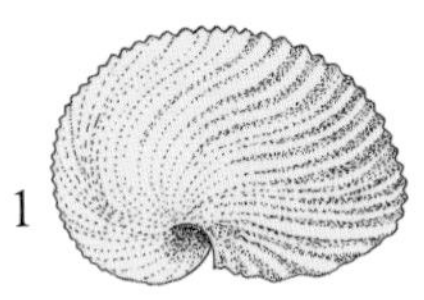


ARGONAUTOIDEA
Argonautidae (1)

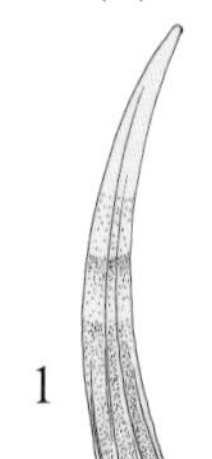


**CLASS SCAPHOPODA**
Order Dentaliida
Dentaliidae (1)

# How to use this book

The systematic arrangement of shells in the directory section of this book has, for the most part, followed that established in *A Classification of the Living Mollusca* by Kay Cunningham Vaught. This book is the result of a ten-year study of all available literature worldwide on molluscan systematics. I have deviated from the listings only in the placing of genera in alphabetical order, except when subfamily groupings dictate otherwise.

The full systematic arrangement of the directory is listed on pages 28–30: each Class is split into Subclass, Order (ending in -a), Suborders (occasionally), Super families (-oidea), and Families (-idae). The final division – Subfamilies (-inae) – is not shown in the directory but can be found in the index (in brackets after the species).

The small line drawings of the more common shapes of shells within each family are designed to aid identification of species.

The information in the directory is arranged to supply the reader with as much information as possible about each species. The example will help to clarify the system used and explain the symbols which appear in each entry. The generic title and species name are given in capital letters in the headings and italic in the text. (See pages 12–13 and 19 for full explanations of name, author, date and locality.)

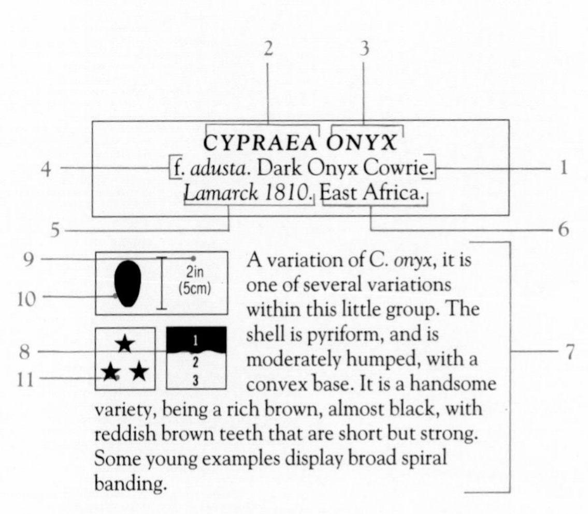


**1** Common or colloquial name

**2** The generic title (*Cypraea*)

**3** The species name (*onyx*)

**4** Form or variation (*adusta*), sometimes known as the subspecies

**5** The author of the species, form or variety and the date of publication

**6** Locality

**7** General description of the shell and any other relevant or interesting facts

**8** Habitat depth

All figures are approximate and peculiar only to this book. Some species may be found at more than one depth.

1 2 3 — extends to about 83ft (25m)

1 2 3 — between 83 and 495ft (25–150m)

1 2 3 — between 495 and 1,650ft (150–500m)

**9** Average size of mature shell

**10** Stylized shape for size reference

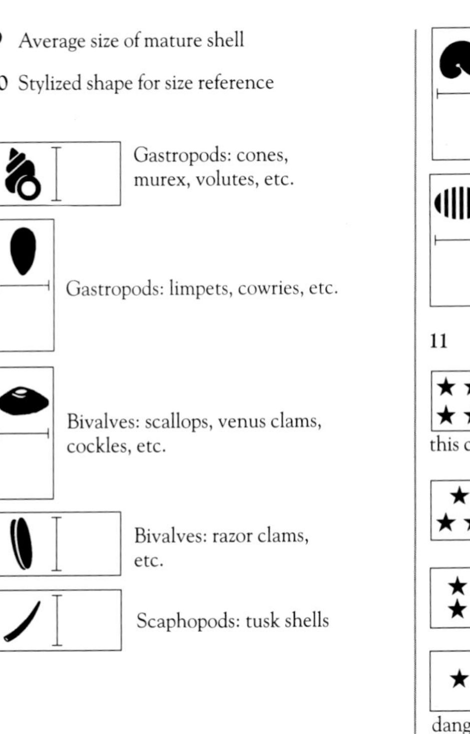

Gastropods: cones, murex, volutes, etc.

Gastropods: limpets, cowries, etc.

Bivalves: scallops, venus clams, cockles, etc.

Bivalves: razor clams, etc.

Scaphopods: tusk shells

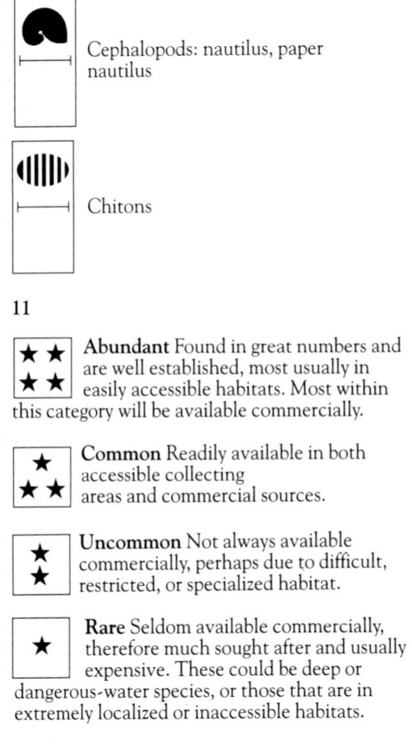

Cephalopods: nautilus, paper nautilus

Chitons

**11**

**Abundant** Found in great numbers and are well established, most usually in easily accessible habitats. Most within this category will be available commercially.

**Common** Readily available in both accessible collecting areas and commercial sources.

**Uncommon** Not always available commercially, perhaps due to difficult, restricted, or specialized habitat.

**Rare** Seldom available commercially, therefore much sought after and usually expensive. These could be deep or dangerous-water species, or those that are in extremely localized or inaccessible habitats.

# CLASS: GASTROPODA

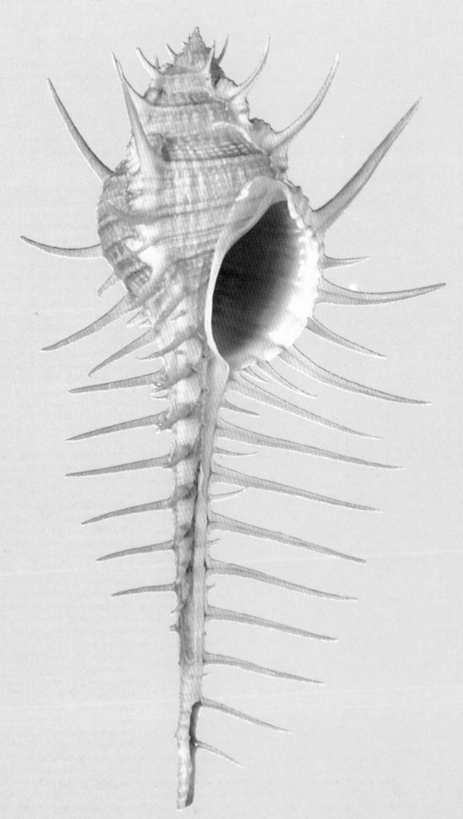

SUPER FAMILY
PLEUROTOMARIOIDEA

FAMILY

## PLEUROTOMARIIDAE

(Slit Shells)

This is an ancient group of molluscs, its ancestors dating back to early Cambrian times. The 16 or so surviving species – all vegetarians – occur in very deep waters, some down to 1,980ft (600m), in areas as widespread as the China and Caribbean Seas and off the coast of Southern Africa. They are therefore considered rare shells (indeed, apart from fossil evidence, the first recent species was only discovered in the mid-19th century in the Caribbean), and are seldom seen in amateur collections. The shells are generally rounded and conical, relatively large – *Pleurotomania rumplii* can reach over 8in (20cm) – and all have the characteristic anal slit through which waste water escapes, and a horny rounded operculum. There are three genera: *Entemnotrochus, Perotrochus* and *Mikadotrochus*.

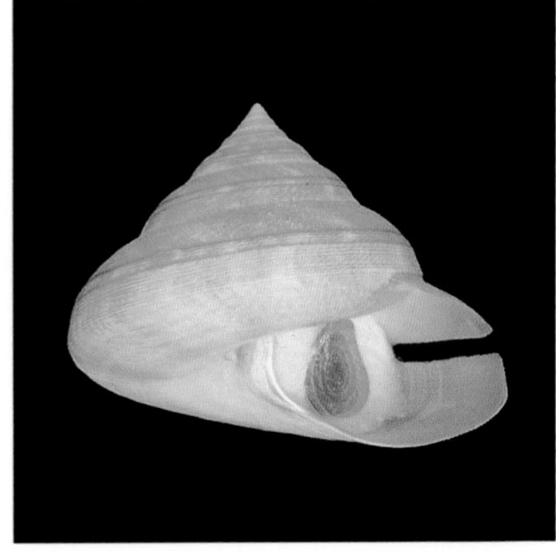

### PEROTROCHUS AFRICANA

African Slit Shell. *Tomlin 1948.*
South Africa.

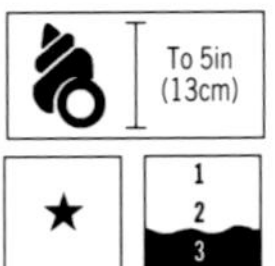


Compared to *P. hirasei*, this is a very light, thin shell, less conical and more angular. It is pale beige or orange in colour and has minute spiral cording. Two thin spiral bands of a deeper orange wind back and upwards on the shoulders of each whorl, running from the rear of the slit to the apex of the shell.

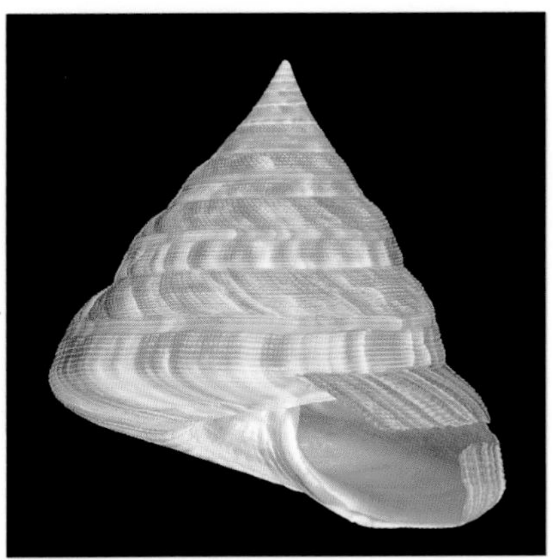

### PEROTROCHUS HIRASEI

The Emperor's Slit Shell. *Pilsbry 1903.*
Taiwan and Japan.

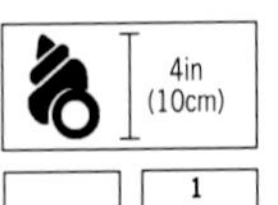


One of the more common species from this family, this is probably also the most attractive, having a thick heavy shell with rounded rather flat shoulders. Spiral cording and beading ornamentation give a latticed effect. The umbilicus area is highly nacreous and the coloration generally ranges from pale to deep orange red in the form of haphazard diagonal streaking on a cream background. This species, along with others fished in similar waters, was once known to fishermen as the "millionaire shell".

### PEROTROCHUS TANGAROANA

West Australian Slit Shell. *Bouchet and Metivier 1982.* Western Australia.

Only described relatively recently, this species closely resembles both *P. africana* and *P. teramachii* and could be a local variation of either. It was previously known as *P. westralis* and has since been re-named. In shape, it is similar to *P. africana*, perhaps with a slightly higher spire; it is virtually devoid of colour save for faint thin orange streaks on a dirty white or beige background. It is often trawled at depths down to 1,500ft (450m).

SUPER FAMILY
PLEUROTOMARIOIDEA

FAMILY

## HALIOTIDAE

(Abalones)

A large family, numbering perhaps 100 recognized named species, abalones are also commonly known as ormers or sea ears in various localities. They are a valuable seafood and several species – notably the larger abalones of California – have been farmed for lucrative commercial markets. The shape is fairly constant, being flat, with little evidence of a spire, and either rounded or oval. All possess a series of holes on the body whorl through which water and waste are passed. All interiors are highly nacreous and iridescent and can be very colourful. Most show evidence of a central muscle scar in the interior. Their habitat ranges from low tide zones – in shallow water attached firmly to rocks – down to, on occasions, some hundreds of feet. There is one genus: *Haliotis*.

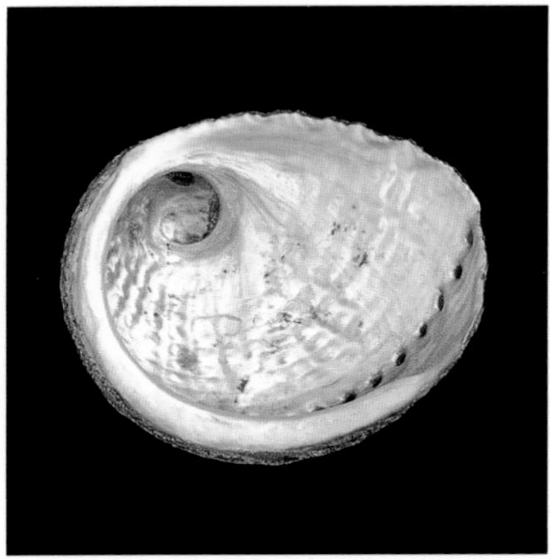

### HALIOTIS ROEI

Roe's Abalone. *Gray 1847.*
Southern and South-western Australia.

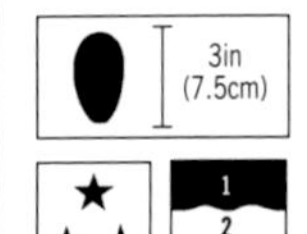


This has a rounded stout shell with coarse spiral ridges, usually encrusted with marine algae and lime deposits. Any faint tinge of colour that may be evident will be a greenish brown. The spire is often worn, revealing some nacre. The interior is predominantly green, a small muscle scar being evident. The initial whorl is slightly depressed.

**HALIOTIS MARIAE**
Marie's Abalone. *Gray 1831.*
Oman.

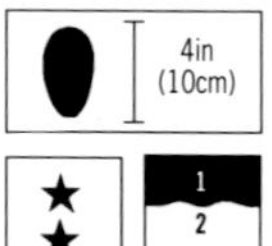

4in (10cm)

Strong thickened rounded ridges are the major characteristic on the exterior or dorsum of this shell. The coloration ranges from beige to pale red, with a delicate pinkish green pearly interior. Specimens are often encrusted with marine deposits and small barnacles.

**HALIOTIS CORRUGATA**
Corrugated Abalone. *Wood 1828.*
California.

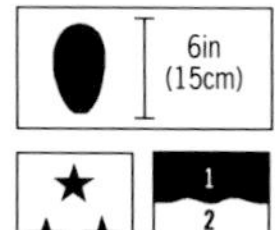

6in (15cm)

One of the larger abalones, this is an attractively sculptured species, the dorsum of which is covered with low but prominent haphazard ridges, giving a "corrugated" effect. There is a large muscle scar on the highly colourful and iridescent interior. Usually only the largest of the dorsal holes remain open.

**HALIOTIS CRACHERODI**
Black Abalone. *Leach 1814.*
North-western USA to Mexico.

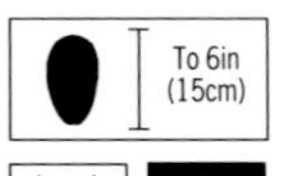

To 6in (15cm)

In this ovate species, which is thick and heavy, with a smooth dorsum, the larger adult shells are usually encrusted with lime. The exterior coloration is a slate grey to black with hints of blue green shining through. The interior nacre is predominantly green, the prominent muscle scar being somewhat raised and irregular.

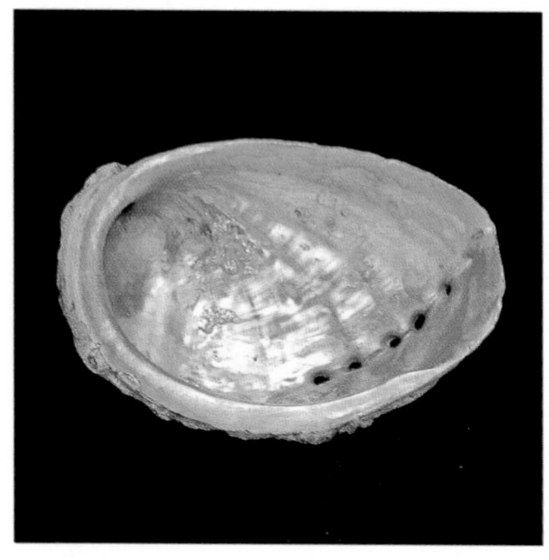

**HALIOTIS TUBERCULATA**
European Edible Abalone. *L. 1758.*
Mediterranean and North-East Atlantic.

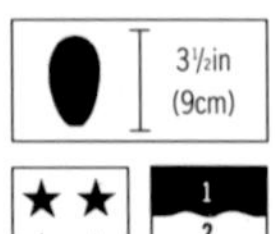

3½in (9cm)

Known as the sea ear by Channel Islanders and the French, this species is a popular food. It is thick and heavy for its small size, though the weight can possibly be attributed to the abundance of marine debris supported on its dorsum. *H. tuberculata* is found in great numbers in shallow water on rocks in tidal pools.

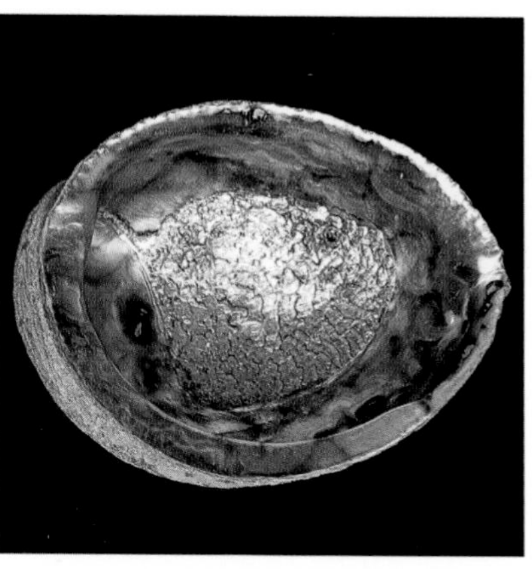

**HALIOTIS FULGENS**
Green Abalone. *Philippi 1845.*
Southern California to Mexico.

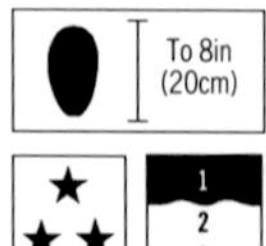

To 8in (20cm)

*H. fulgens* is one of the most beautiful and attractive of the family, the interior being a highly iridescent bluish green. The large muscle scar is patterned with irregular black lines and waves, often with peacock-blue colouring. The species is also one of the largest abalones. The exterior usually reveals little or no sculpturing due to heavy encrustation and erosion. The mother-of-pearl is used extensively for inlay work, especially in antique restoration.

**HALIOTIS SORENSONI**
Sorenson's Abalone. *Bartsch 1940.*
California.

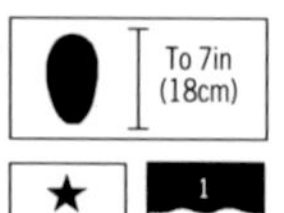

To 7in (18cm)

This is sometimes known as the white abalone, due to its white pearly interior, although the dorsal coloration is a dull reddish grey. There are raised dorsal holes, and the exterior ornamentation consists of fine spiral undulating ridges. This is one of the larger species, but it is not particularly thick or heavy.

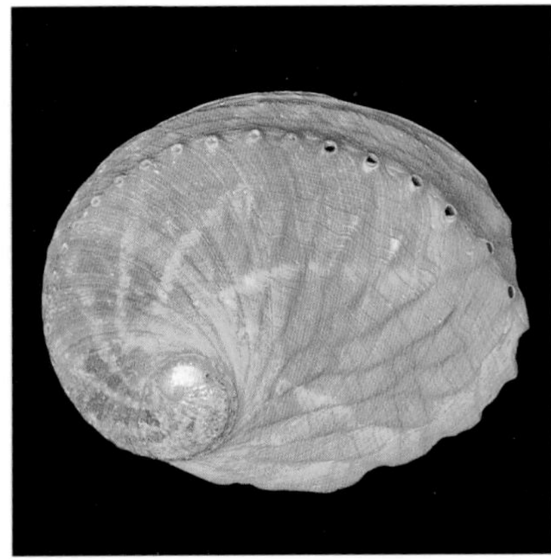

### HALIOTIS RUBER

Ruber Abalone. *Leach 1814.*
Southern Australia.

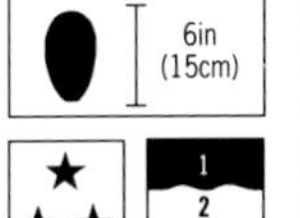

*H. ruber* is a very beautiful large abalone with a pale red dorsum. The interior nacre is primarily white, and features wide radiating flattened ridges. The spire is often eroded to show the lower layers of nacre. A shallow-water dweller.

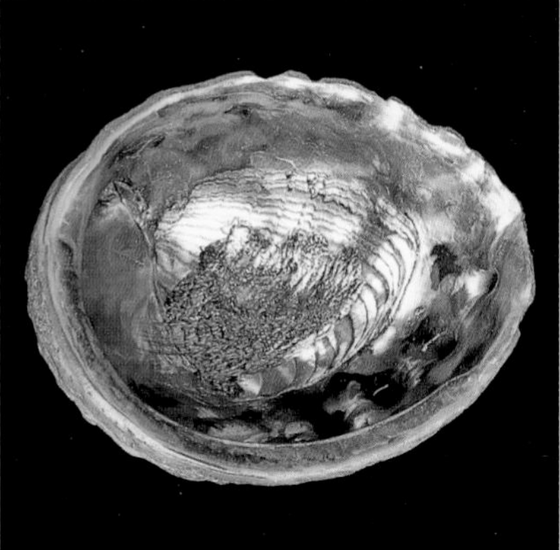

### HALIOTIS RUFESCENS

Red Abalone. *Swainson 1822.*
Southern California to Mexico.

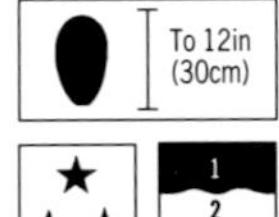

The largest species of the family, this has a thick and very heavy shell. The exterior, when unencrusted, is pale red, with large low rounded nodules and fine growth lines. The huge muscle scar dominates the interior, and the iridescence varies from blue greens, to reds and pinks, and even golds. The dorsal red extends over the margins of the shell.

### HALIOTIS GIGANTEA

Giant Abalone. *Gmelin 1791.*
Japan.

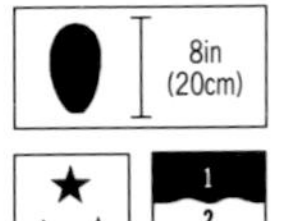

Although called the giant abalone, this commercially fished seafood species is not as large as some of the family. The interior of the shell is nacreous white, while the exterior is a pale green tinged with red. There are uneven rounded ridges, with irregular undulating bumps at right angles to them. The holes are raised, and the largest four are normally open.

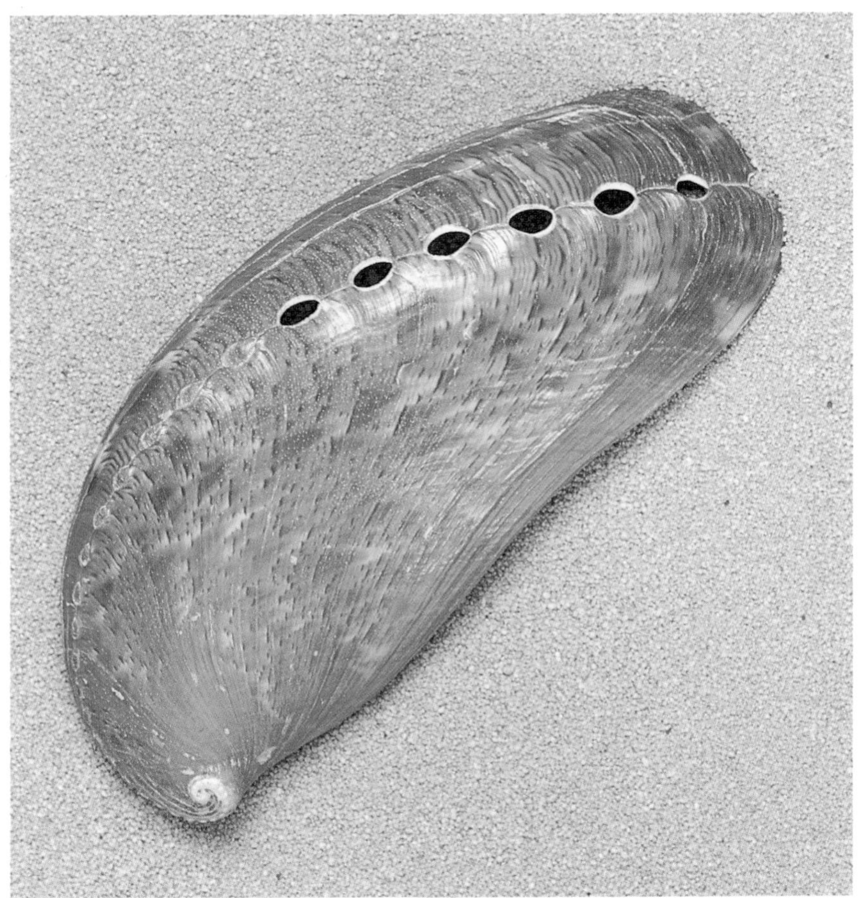

### HALIOTIS ASININA

Ass's Ear Abalone. *L. 1758.*
Central Indo-Pacific.

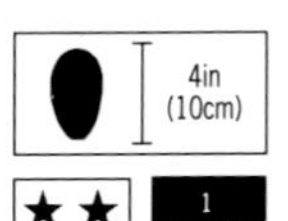

This curved smooth shell is elongated in shape and is aptly named. The exterior is a pale olive green, enlivened with odd splashes of brown. The interior is white with hints of green. For the size of the shell, the holes are large. The dorsum is sometimes commercially polished to show the fine nacreous layers below.

**HALIOTIS SCALARIS**
Staircase Abalone. *Leach 1814.*
Southern and Western Australia.

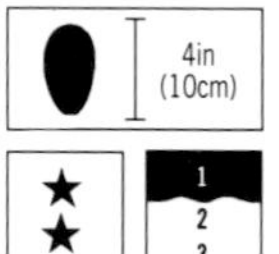


A beautiful shell, with delicate sculpturing, this features raised holes, a thick rounded spiral ridge and thin radial "blades", all of which are basically dull red on a cream background. The interior is no less attractive, having a bright pearly nacre. A choice collectors' item.

**HALIOTIS EMMAE**
Emma's Abalone. *Gray 1846.*
Southern Australia.

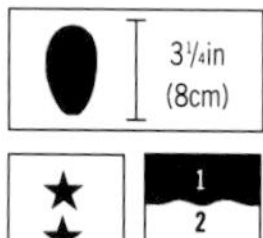


A pretty little shell, this is similar to *H. scalaris*, but the dorsum is less sculptured. The holes are raised and rounded, and there are spiral ridges. It is a pale pink, with large dull reddish brown radial patches. This specimen was found off Port Lincoln.

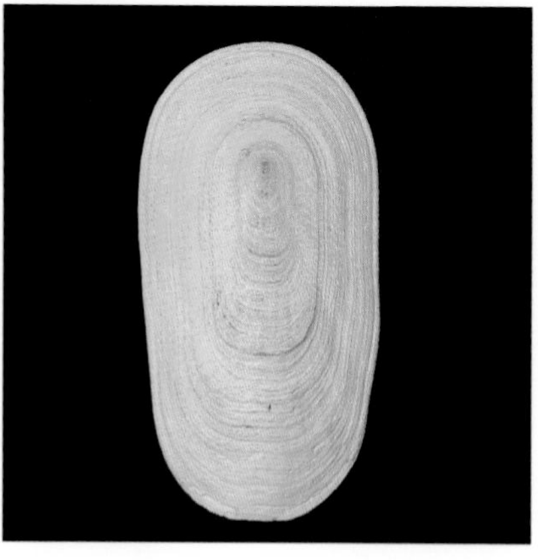

**SCUTUS ANTIPODES**
Roman Shield Limpet. *Montfort 1810.*
South Australia and north New Zealand.

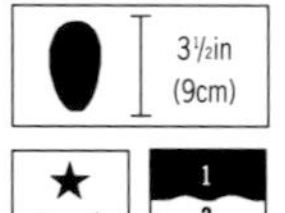


None of the *Scutus* species has holes and all are generally flat and elongated – the common name of this species being an apt reference to its shape. The exterior is a yellowish beige, and the growth stages of the shell are clearly evident. The interior is porcellaneous white – and odd callouses and blemishes occasionally occur, possibly because sand and grit have been trapped beneath the glaze.

**HALIOTIS AUSTRALIS**
Austral Abalone. *Gmelin 1791.*
New Zealand.

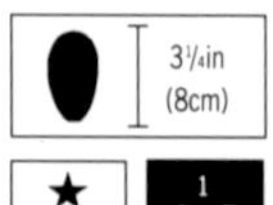


Known locally as the Silver Paua, this smallish species is pale beige to green and bears evenly spaced radial ridges. Fine growth lines are evident. The nacreous interior is primarily white, with hints of pink and green. About seven or eight holes are usually open.

SUPER FAMILY
## FISSURELLOIDEA

FAMILY
## FISSURELLIDAE
(Keyhole Limpets)

This is a large family of primitive snails with shells that are generally rounded to ovate in shape. They have a worldwide distribution, including the coldest seas, inhabiting rocky coastlines and coral below the low tide areas. None possesses an operculum. All are egg-laying vegetarians. Most have the natural hole at the top of the shell, though a few have a marginal slit or indentation at the front. The interior of most species is porcellaneous. An interesting group, this promotes little interest amongst amateur collectors, perhaps because the shells are comparatively dull and ordinary in appearance.

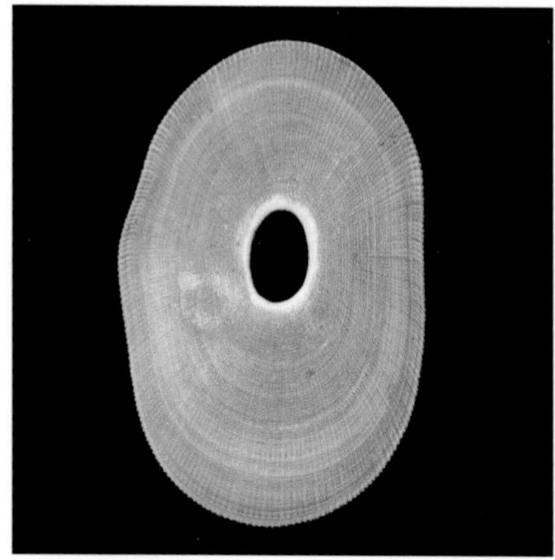

**MEGATHURA CRENULATA**
Great Keyhole Limpet. *Sowerby 1825.*
California to Mexico.

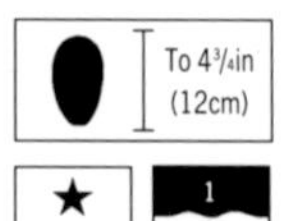


One of the larger of the keyhole limpets, this species has a large oval hole edged in white and a finely radiating ridged dorsum, grey beige in colour. When viewed from below, the surface is porcellaneous white and the margin bears many fine indentations, or teeth. A subtidal rock dweller.

### *FISSURELLA MAXIMA*

Giant Keyhole Limpet. *Sowerby 1835.*
Western South America.

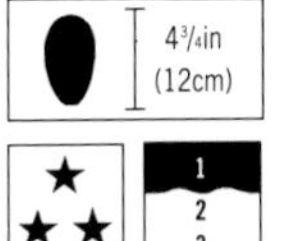

The large heavy shell is mainly cream, with wide red-to-brown rays, radiating from the slightly ovate hole. The surface is ridged with growth lines. The interior is white, with a cream margin edged with reddish brown. There is a finely ridged horseshoe-shaped muscle scar. *F. maxima* inhabits rock reefs.

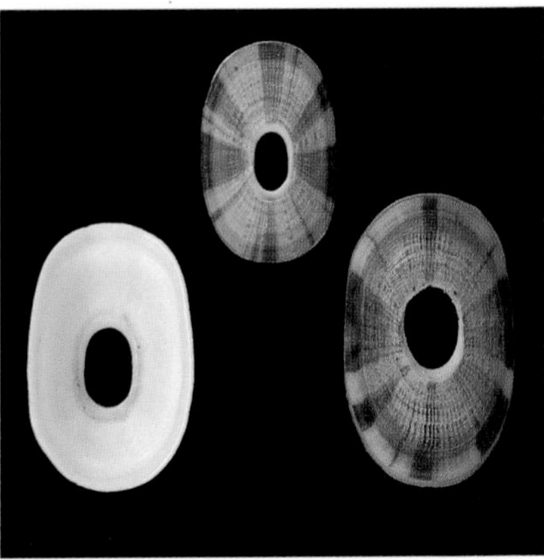

### *FISSURELLA APERTA*

Double-edged Keyhole Limpet.
*Sowerby 1825.* South Africa.

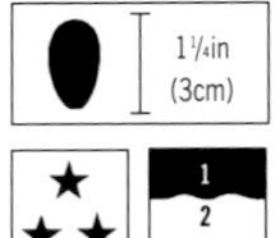

This endemic shell lives on and under rocks in intertidal waters. The small but solid shell is elongated and features a large hole in relation to its overall size. The coloration is beige to pink, overlaid with fine radial lines and rays. The margin is white, giving the appearance of two edges. The interior is pure white.

### *FISSURELLA NODOSA*

Knobbed Keyhole Limpet. *Born 1778.*
Florida and West Indies.

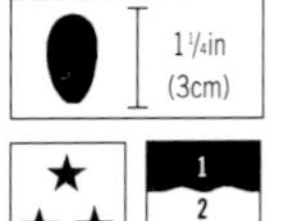

Heavily nodulose radiating ridges and a figure-of-eight hole are the main characteristics of this species. The shell is ovate, with a relatively high spire. The interior is white, with fine incised grooves radiating from the hole to the margins. Found on rocks in the intertidal zone.

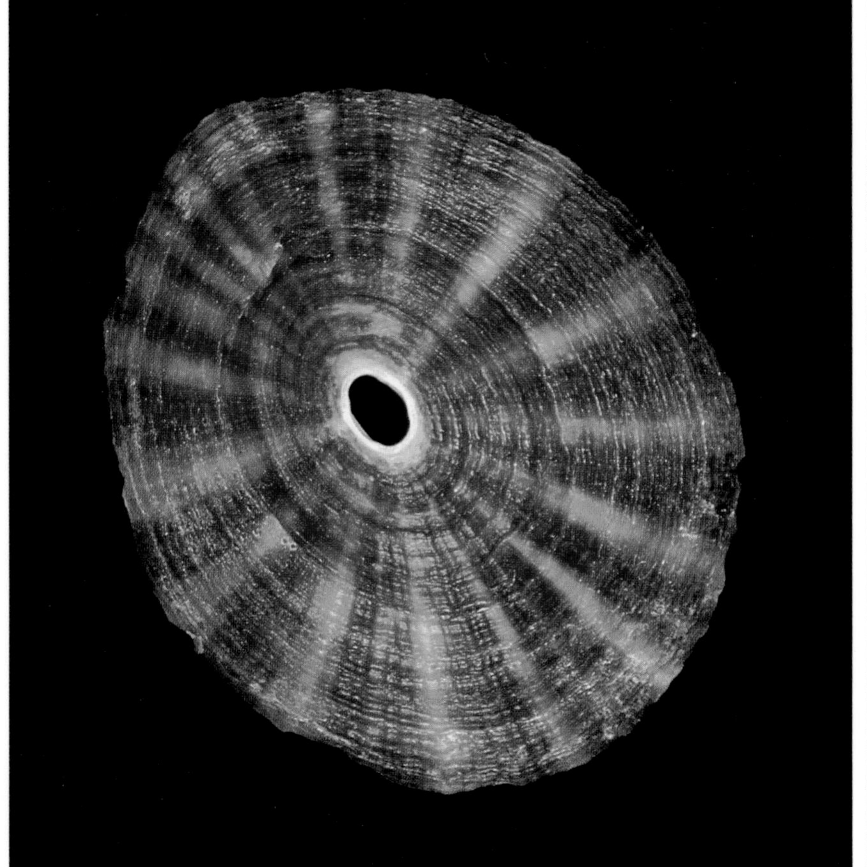

### *FISSURELLA PERUVIANA*

Peruvian Keyhole Limpet. *Lamarck 1822.*
Western South America.

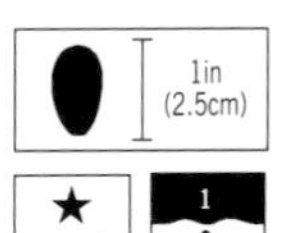

A small rounded shell with a pointed conical spire, it has relatively straight sides and is pale crimson in colour, with wide dark greyish brown rays. The small hole is edged in cream. The interior is white with a crimson margin.

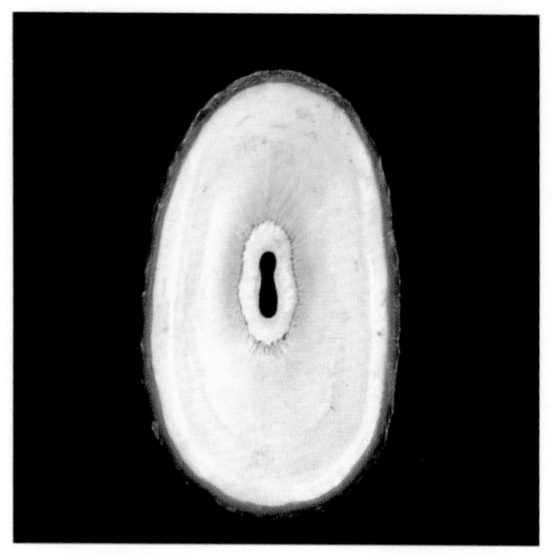

**FISSURELLA CRASSA**
Thick Keyhole Limpet. *Lamarck 1822.*
Western Central to South America.

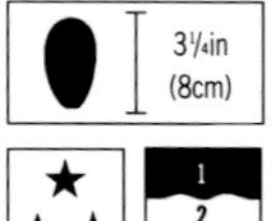


This has a stout ovate shell with a long narrow slit edged in white. Apart from this, the colouring is beige brown, and there are fine growth lines. The interior is off-white with a thick brown margin. In some cases, the slit is surrounded by a pinkish tinge.

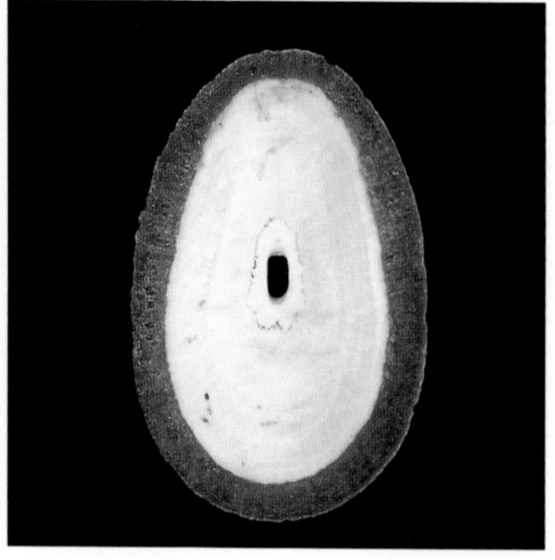

**FISSURELLA NIGRA**
Black Keyhole Limpet. *Lesson 1830.*
Western South America.

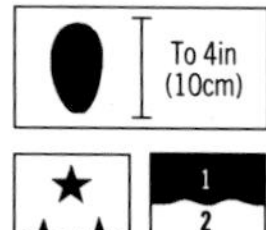


Ovate in shape, the shell is slightly convex when viewed from the side. Although termed "black", the colouring is generally a dark red or grey. Fine radial ridges are apparent. The interior is white with a thick greyish brown margin. *F. nigra* is an intertidal rock dweller.

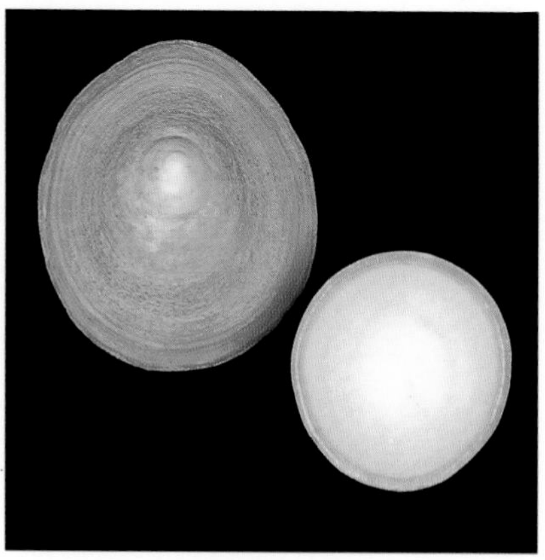

**ACMAEA MITRA**
White Cap Limpet. *Rathke 1833.*
Alaska to Mexico.

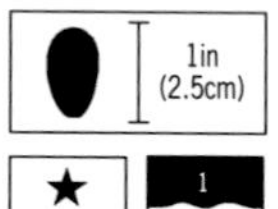


A high domed spire, dirty beige in colour and with little or no ornamentation, is characteristic of this species. The interior is a porcellaneous white with a thin beige marginal band.

**FISSURELLA BARBADENSIS**
Barbados Keyhole Limpet. *Gmelin 1791.*
West Indies to Brazil.

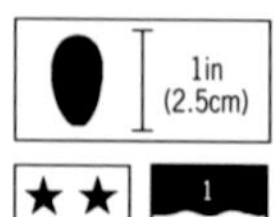


A well-known species, this has a characteristic green interior. Although the dorsum is radially ridged in many specimens, this ridging is entirely covered with lime deposits and marine debris. The hole is a figure-of-eight shape. This limpet is found on intertidal rocks throughout the region.

SUPER FAMILY
## PATELLOIDEA

FAMILIES
## ACMAEIDAE and LOTTIIDAE
(True Limpets)

There are small biological differences between these two families and the Patellidae, but the collector need only consider the appearance of the shells. The shapes are all somewhat similar, being rounded, oval, or regular. However, the interiors of these two families are porcellaneous and often colourful, whereas the Patellidae tend to have nacreous and iridescent interiors. The main genus of Acmaeidae is Acmaea, while Lottia and Scurria belong to Lottiidae.

**LOTTIA GIGANTEA**
Giant Owl Limpet. *Sowerby 1834.*
California to Mexico.

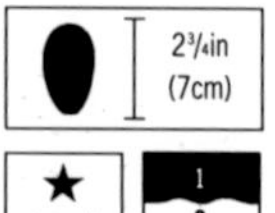


A flat, ovate and rather light species, the giant owl limpet inhabits on-shore rocks near the high-tide line. Beneath the dorsum, which is usually encrusted, there is a maculated patterning which can often be noticed at the margin. The interior bears a white or pale blue oval scar and the surround is a uniform dark to mid-toned brown. The margin edge has a thick black band.

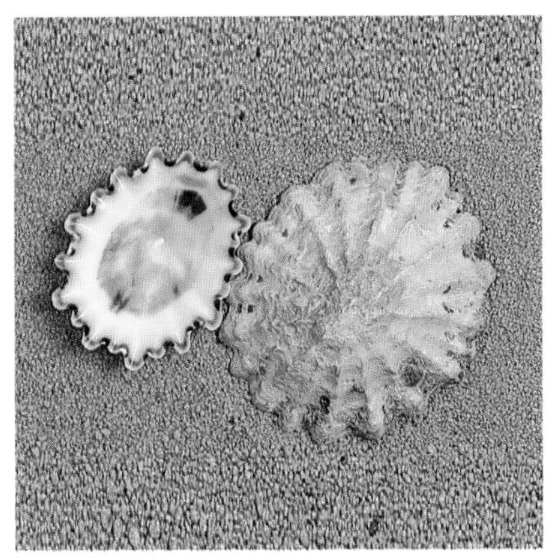

**PATELLOIDA ALTICOSTATA**
High Ribbed Limpet. *Angas 1865.*
Southern Australia.

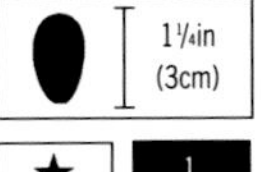


Widespread on intertidal rocks, its main food source is the marine plant, ulva. The dorsum of this small but solid limpet bears about 18-20 rounded moderate radial ribs between which, on younger less-encrusted specimens, are fine grey spiral lines. Interiors vary slightly between white and off-white, and have a grey or pale brown central scar. The more colourful shells are edged with black between the interior marginal crenulation.

**SCURRIA VARIABILIS**
Variable Scurria.
Chile.

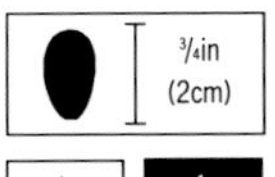


The author is unknown to me, but the shell had to be included due to its sheer prettiness! This tiny species has a dirty greyish brown dorsum that is usually encrusted. The central scar area inside is highly attractive and variable in patterning – several are shown here. Brown, beige or white and even pale blue rims occur, with short radial lines and dashes on the margin.

SUPER FAMILY
PATELLOIDEA

FAMILY
## PATELLIDAE
(True Limpets)

A large group, with limpet-like, flat-to-conical shells possessing no hole at the apex, they tend to move about at night time and return to their sites at dawn, when they become firmly attached to rocky surfaces. All are vegetarian and none possesses an operculum. Patellidae are divided into two subfamilies, Patellinae and Nacellinae, of which there are several genera and subgenera, notably *Patella, Nacella* and *Cellana*. The shapes of limpets show clearly how well they are adapted to their harsh environment, their more or less flat shape and their ability to cling tightly to rocks enabling them to withstand fierce wave action and strong currents.

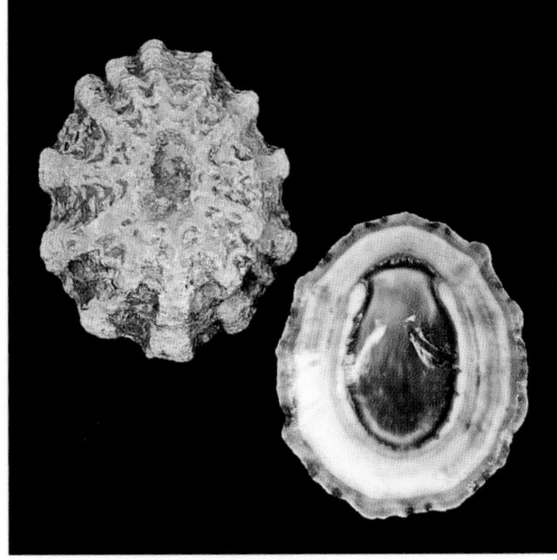

**SCURRIA ZEBRINA**
Zebrina Limpet. *Lesson 1831.*
Western South America.

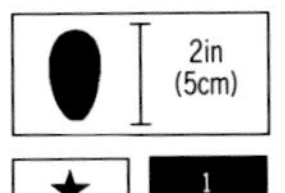


Not unlike *P. alticostata*, this has only approximately 12 coarse low rounded ribs, normally concealed beneath marine encrustation. The shell is slightly ovate and the interior decoration varies from a plain off-white to specimens with dominant oval scars in a greyish brown, with marginal rims of brown or duck-egg blue. It lives on intertidal rocks.

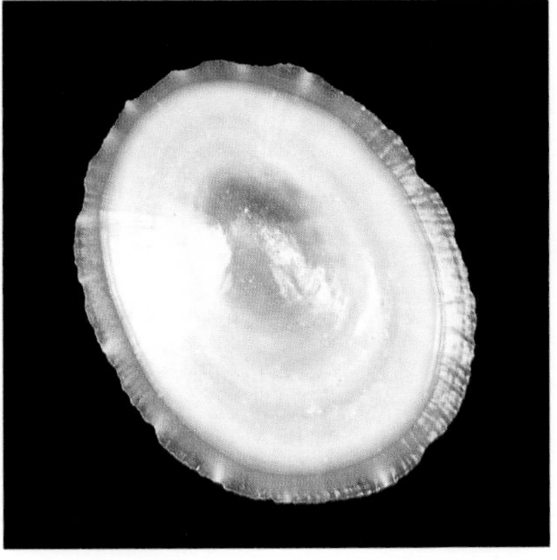

**SCURRIA MESOLEUCA**
Half-white Limpet. *Menke 1851.*
Western Central America.

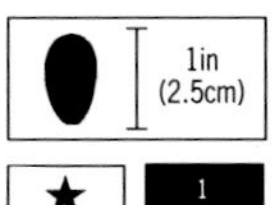


A thin, rather fragile, flat limpet with fine radial dorsal ridges and white dashes on a mud-brown background. The interior colour is pale duck-egg blue with a grey central scar flecked with orange. The margin is edged with blue, and brown at the extremities. An intertidal rock dweller.

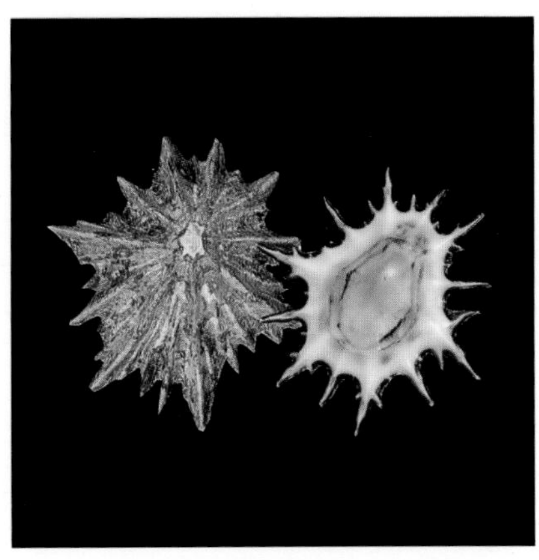

**PATELLA LONGICOSTA**
Star Limpet. *Lamarck 1819.*
South Africa.

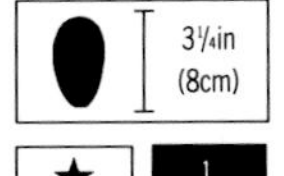


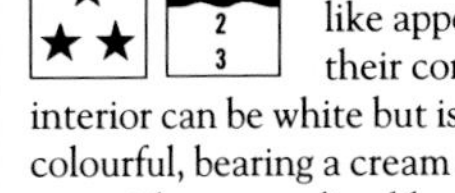

This attractive species features long exterior ribs that radiate from the apex to the margins, creating the "star"-like appearance indicated by their common name. The interior can be white but is generally very colourful, bearing a cream and orange central scar with surrounding blue and yellow undertones towards the margin. Found on all rocky shorelines, this is a collectors' favourite.

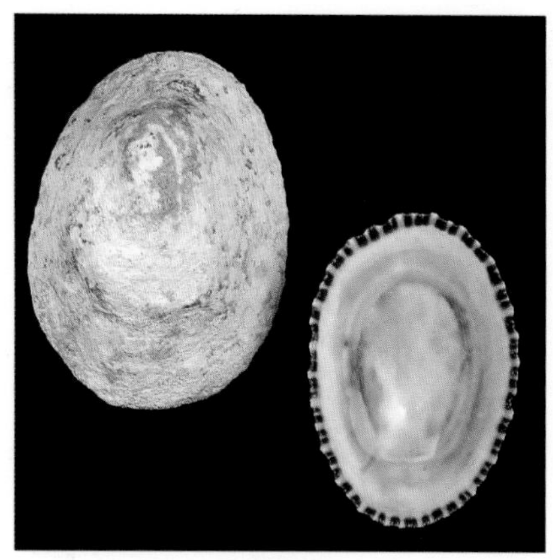

## PATELLA LATICOSTATA

Giant Australian Limpet. *Blainville 1825.*
Southern and Western Australia.

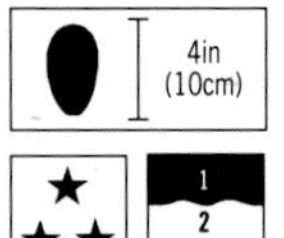

The large heavy shell is ovate, with a large conical spire. The exterior is usually heavily encrusted with marine debris, including other limpets. There is a large central scar, off-white in colour, surrounded by a deep reddish brown horseshoe mark. Towards the margin, the colour tends to a beige yellow, and there are fine brown indentations at the very edge. When prepared correctly, the foot can make a pleasant meal.

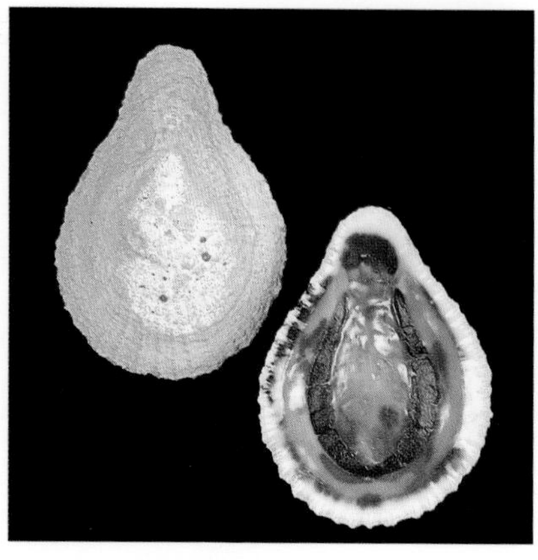

## PATELLA COCHLEAR

Spoon Limpet. *Born 1778.*
South Africa.

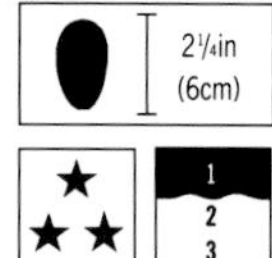

A smaller species, this has a distinctive spoon-like shape. It is extremely variable in internal coloration, although the slate-grey horseshoe mark is constant. The background colour is usually a pale blue grey, darker towards the margins. The margin is neatly indented with fine grooves. The central scar is tinged with yellow and grey. The exterior is often heavily encrusted, but moderate radial grooves are sometimes evident. This is one of the few shells to show much blue coloration.

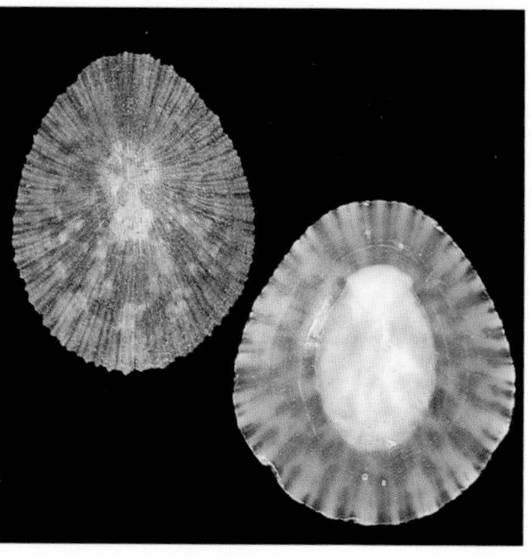

## PATELLA CONCOLOR

Variable Limpet. *Krauss 1848.*
South Africa.

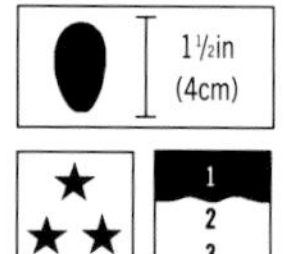

As the common name suggests, this is an extremely variable species – not in shape, but in colour and patterning. The dorsum generally bears fine radial ridges, sometimes obscured by deposits of marine debris. The interior is nacreous and prettily patterned with pale and dark radial dots and dashes. The overall colour ranges from off-white to deep yellow or orange. There is a faint central scar mark. There are several named varieties, with differing patterns and colours. This species is found on intertidal rocks.

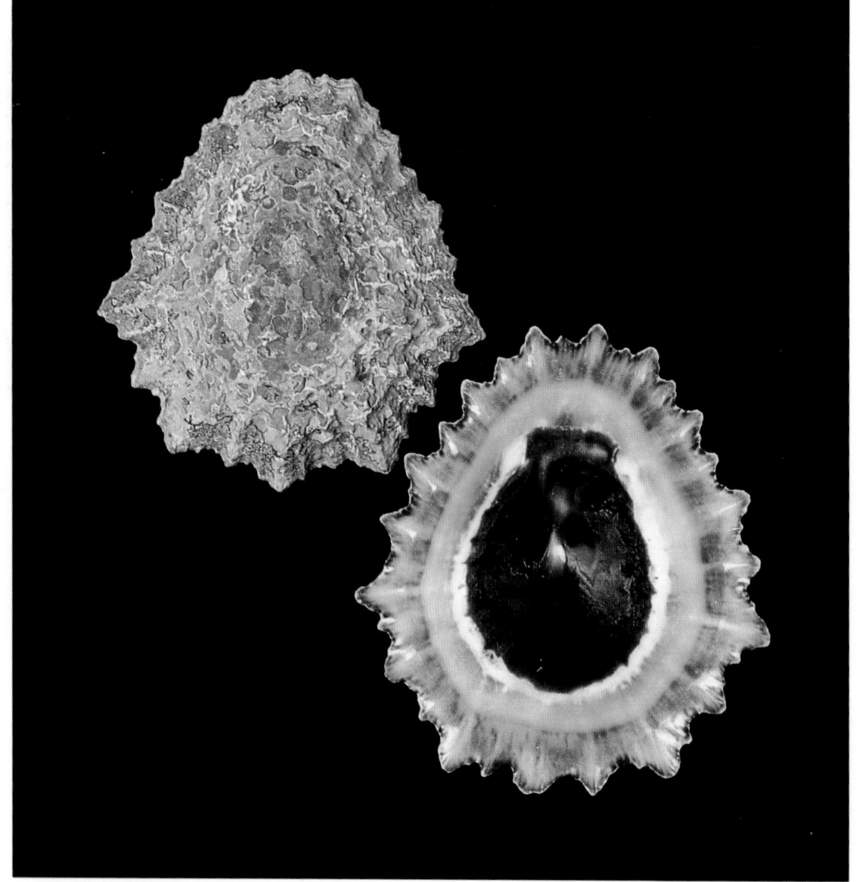

## PATELLA GRANATINA

Sandpaper Limpet. *L. 1758.*
South Africa.

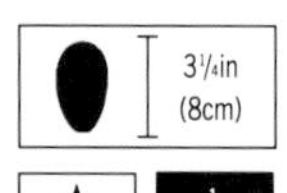

This has a rather stout shell, with sharply angular radial ridges. On mature specimens the dorsum is usually partly eroded away due to the conditions of its habitat. The colour ranges from grey to beige. Interior colours vary, although there is always a large dark brown central scar. Some are a pale yellowish green with flecks and flashes of grey at the margins, while others show a white horseshoe mark and are edged with deep yellow or blue. All in all, a very attractive species.

## PATELLA GRANULARIS

Granular Limpet. *L. 1758.*
South Africa.

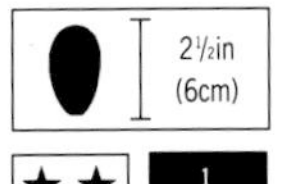


This limpet occurs on all rocky South African shorelines. As with many molluscs in this area, collecting may be limited to only 15 specimens per day. The shell is smallish but stout, with radiating ribs, sometimes with sharp nodules. Large shells can be eroded on the spire. The interior bears a large brown central scar on a background that is usually a pale blue grey. There is a thick dark grey or black marginal rim, indented with shallow grooves.

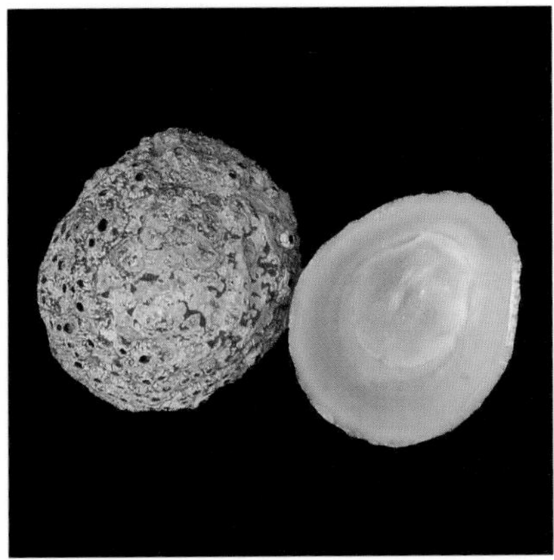

## PATELLA VULGATA

Common European Limpet. *L. 1758.*
North Atlantic coastlines.

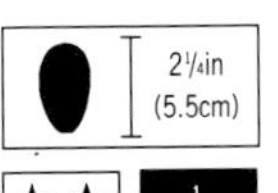


A well-known species, this is found on rocky coastlines throughout Britain and North-West Europe. The solid shell may have either a high or low spire, with fine or coarse radiating ribs, and is often heavily encrusted with marine deposits and small barnacles. The porcellaneous interior ranges from off-white to a dirty grey colour. The central scar is usually paler.

## PATELLA FERRUGINEA

Ribbed Limpet. *Gmelin 1791.*
Mediterranean.

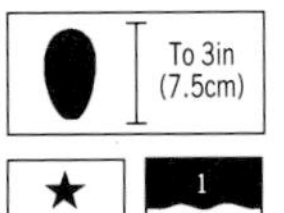


An elongated or ovate species, its dorsum bears coarse sometimes nodulose, ribs that extend to the margin, giving a crenulated effect. Somewhat convex when viewed from the side, the shell has a pale grey porcellaneous interior, bearing a prominent oval scar; the edges of the crenulated margin are brown. Found on intertidal rocks.

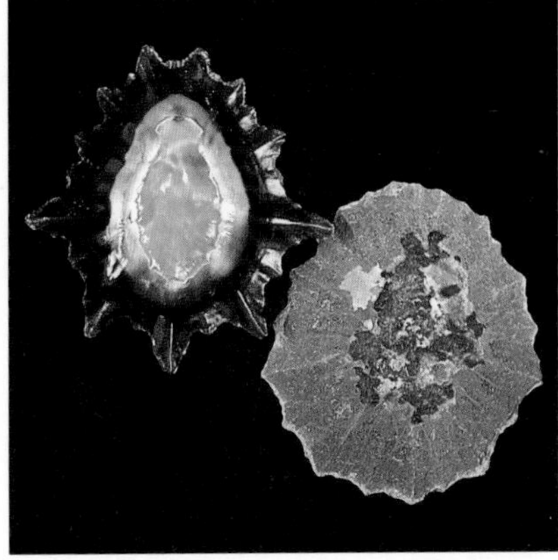

## PATELLA OCULUS

Eye Limpet. *Born 1778.*
South Africa.

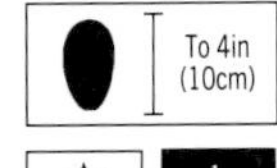


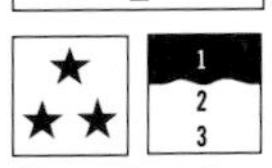


This is variable only in shape, ranging from more or less rounded to slightly ovate. The moderate dorsal ridges extend to the margins, sometimes reaching outwards in a "finger"- or "star"-like fashion. The interior is dominated by a wide marginal band of dark brown. There is usually a pale blue edge to the large light brown oval scar. A generally flat shell.

**PATELLA BARBARA**
Barbara Limpet. *L. 1758.*
South Africa.

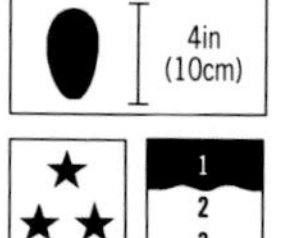

4in (10cm)

The solid heavy shell has a white porcellaneous interior. The large central scar is often tinged pale orange. The dorsum bears coarse radiating ribs, which are deeply angled and project outwards from the margin edge, and is usually a chalky white.

**PATELLA MEXICANA**
Giant Mexican Limpet. *Broderip and Sowerby 1829.* Western Central America.

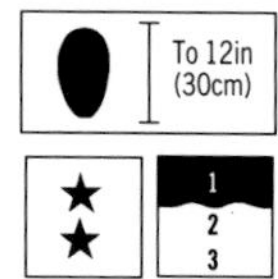

To 12in (30cm)

A shallow water rock-dweller, this is the largest species in the family. The chalky white dorsum, which is often encrusted, bears approximately ten low radial ribs, and distinct growth stages can be seen on large specimens. The interior is a creamy white, with a darker marginal rim. Because of its size, this collectors' item is understandably thick and heavy.

**PATELLA MINIATA**
Cinnabar Limpet. *Born 1778.*
South Africa.

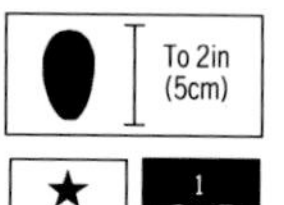

To 2in (5cm)

The light, delicate shell, with its beautiful coloration, seems to avoid excessive dorsal encrustation, and collected specimens nearly always portray the lovely ridged exterior, which can be brown, pink or grey. The interior bears a large white oval scar surrounded by brown, red or pink rays that extend to the slightly crenulated margin.

**PATELLA TABULARIS**
Tabular Limpet. *Krauss 1848.*
South Africa.

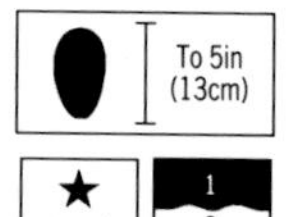

To 5in (13cm)

This is the largest of all African limpets. It is ovate, and the dorsum has many moderate-to-coarse angled ribs extending radially to form a crenulated margin. The shell, when not encrusted, ranges in colour from a dull pale to bright red. Large specimens bear sponge or worm holes on or near the apex. The interior is porcellaneous white. Younger small shells have a pale red rim around the margin.

**PATELLA LUGUBRIS**
Grey Rayed Limpet. *Gmelin 1791.*
Cape Verde Islands.

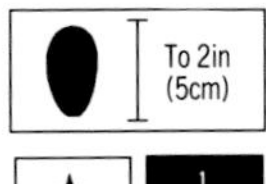


A pretty limpet, with low radiating ribs and a usually eroded apex. The semi-nacreous interior bears attractive grey rays towards the crenulated margin. The central scar area is a pale greyish white.

**BATHYBEMBIX ARGENTEONITENS**
Silvery Magarite. *Lischke 1872.*
Japan.

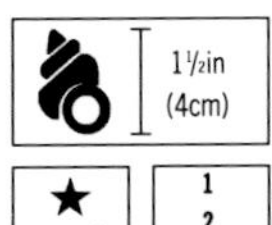


A light, fragile shell, it has a moderately high spire. Each whorl bears a row of blunt nodules at the shoulder and there are several raised spiral ridges below the nodules on the body whorl. The off-white shell is thin, allowing the pearly interior to show through. It inhabits deep water, between 165 and 1,320 feet (50-400m).

**LISCHKEIA UNDOSA**
*Kuroda and Kawamura 1956.*
Philippines.

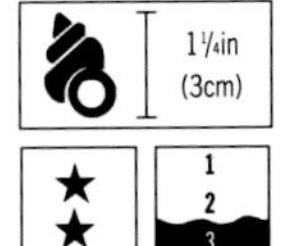


A lightweight elegant shell, it has a moderately high spire and off-white coloration. There are fine spiral cords and two rows of sharp nodules on each whorl. These shells are found in deep waters in the Sulu Sea, southern Philippines.

SUPER FAMILY
## TROCHOIDEA

FAMILY
## TROCHIDAE
(Top Shells)

The hundreds of species that make up the Trochidae are divided biologically into subfamilies, including Monodontinae, Gibbulinae Calliostomatinae and Trochinae. These are further divided into many genera, some of which are named here. The Trochidae enjoy worldwide distribution and habitats vary from shallow rock pools down to the abyssal zones. Most species are herbivores, some feeding on sponges. The shapes often determine habitat – the high-spired species usually dwell in calmer sheltered waters, whereas the flatter, low-spired shells live in areas where rough seas are prevalent. Virtually all are conical or top-shaped, however. All possess horny operculae.

**LISCHKEIA IMPERIALIS**
Imperial Top. *Dall 1881.*
Off Florida and Caribbean.

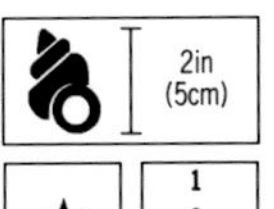


An extremely rare species, this is occasionally dredged or caught in fish or crab traps down to depths of about 1,000 feet (330m). Usually these shells are dead collected and badly worn. The depicted specimen was hauled up in a trap from a depth of 1,000 feet (330m) off Carlisle Bay, Barbados. There are about six whorls, decorated with four or five rows or spiral nodules which are sharp to the touch. The shell is a dirty off-white, and the aperture is highly nacreous.

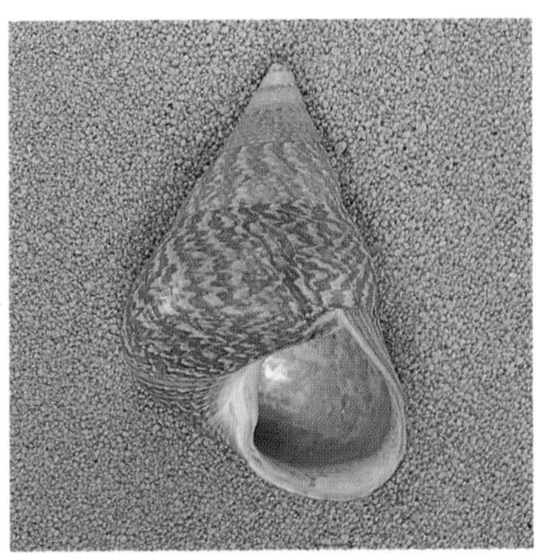

**CANTHARIDUS OPALUS**
Opal Top Shell. *Martyn 1784.*
New Zealand.

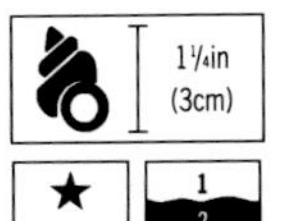


A tall shell with a large aperture, this has slightly rounded whorls and is pale grey overlaid with dull reddish brown axial zigzag lines. The nacre below the outer shell covering – and within the aperture – is of a wonderful greenish blue. Lives on seaweeds in fairly deep water.

**MONODONTA LABIO**
Toothed Monodont. *L. 1758.*
Indo-Pacific.

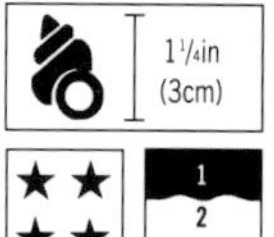


Thick and heavy, this species has a low spire and a large rounded body whorl. There are several rows of incised ridges on each whorl and the pale greenish brown is overlaid with squares and patches of dark brown and grey. The columella supports two large white "teeth". The interior of the aperture is chalky white, has strong lirae and a thin nacreous edge.

**PHASIANOTROCHUS EXIMIUS**
Green Jewel Top. *Perry 1811.*
Southern Australia.

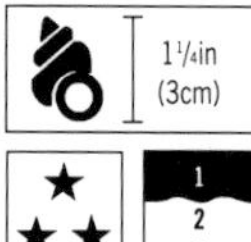


A small delicate shell, with rounded whorls extending to a tall narrow spire, its overall colour is a greenish brown with fine spiral striae. Within the yellowy green aperture is vivid peacock-blue nacre. These shells live among seaweeds in shallow waters.

**CITTARIUM PICA**
Magpie Shell. *L 1758.*
Caribbean.

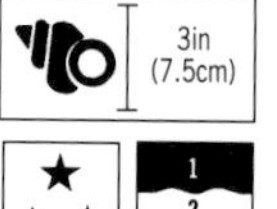


A well-known and popular edible species, it inhabits subtidal rocky areas and is thick and heavy, with rounded whorls and a large gaping aperture. The umbilicus is open. The background colouring is white and the entire shell is covered with thick black wavy axial lines. The operculum is horny and circular.

**OXYSTELE SINENSIS**
Rose-based Top. *Gmelin 1791.*
South Africa.

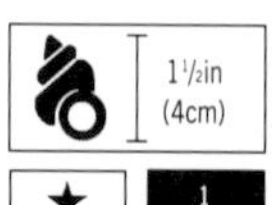


This thick squat rounded shell is rather unattractive, with dirty greyish black exterior colouring. The apex is often worn or worm infested. The base is smoother than the sides and the umbilical area is of porcellaneous white with a rose-red edging. The interior is nacreous. These shells inhabit intertidal rock pools. This specimen was collected from East London.

**TEGULA REGINA**
Regal Top. *Stearns 1892.*
California to Mexico.

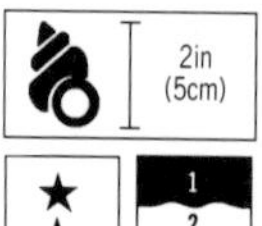


This has a large dark grey shell with four to six overlapping whorls bearing wavy axial ribs. The aperture is nacreous and stained with deep yellow and there is a vivid orange spiral band around the umbilicus. The operculum is circular and horny. It is generally a difficult shell to rid of marine deposits. The apex is often worn and can show worm holes and other signs of damage.

**GIBBULA MAGUS**
Great Top. *L. 1758.*
North-East Atlantic and Mediterranean.

This small squat depressed shell has a low spire and a large body whorl. The angled shoulders can either be smooth or bear low blunt nodules. Several fine spiral grooves are evident. Shells are extremely variable in patterning and colour, as the photograph shows. The interior is highly nacreous. A shallow-water dweller.

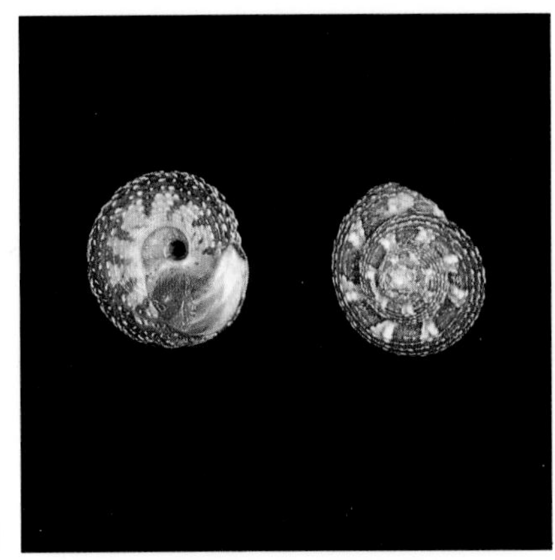

**GIBBULA ARDENS**
Ardens Top. *Von Salis 1793.*
Mediterranean.

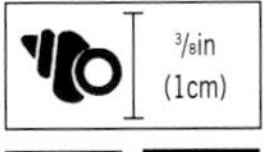


This tiny species has a low spire and a large rounded body whorl. The background colouring is beige grey with mottled patches and spiral dots of pale brown to deep grey. The suture is incised. The umbilicus is open and relatively large and the internal nacre is a deep blue green. These specimens were collected in marine grass in shallow water, Malta.

**CALLIOSTOMA MONILE**
Monile Top. *Reeve 1863.*
Western Australia.

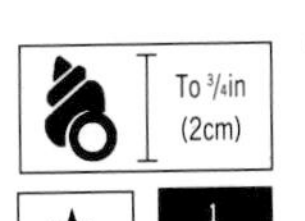


This is a pretty and delicate little shell with straight sides and a tall spire. There are minute spiral striae on the whorls. The colour is pale beige with a dominant band running above the sutures of pale purple squares and "flames" on white. It lives on sponges in shallow water.

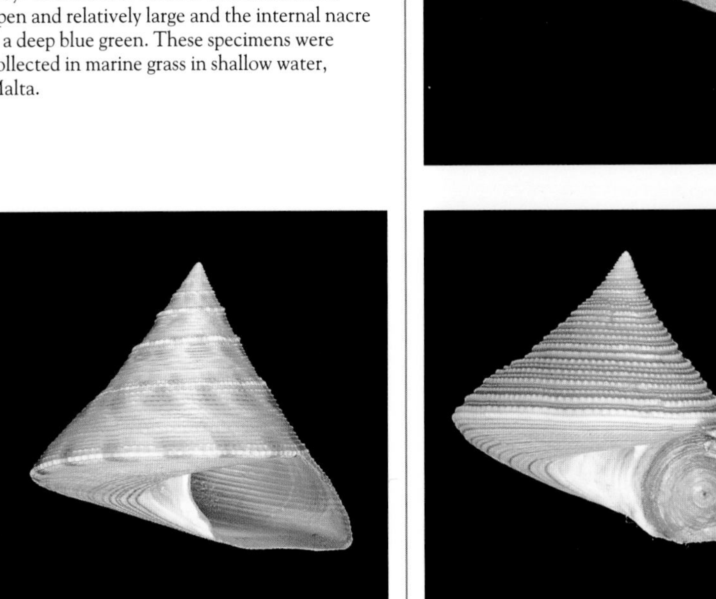

**CALLIOSTOMA FORMOSENSE**
Formosan Top. *E. A. Smith 1907.*
Taiwan.

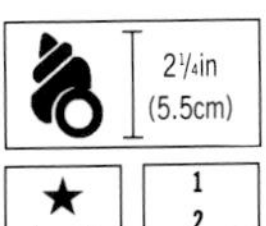


A large, but rather thin shelled, species, it has a moderate-to-high spire, with slightly concave sides. Fine rows of spiral beading are coloured a mid-toned reddish brown in places. The overall base colour is a nacreous beige. The rows of spiral beading at the suture are slightly raised. Fished in deep water off South and West Taiwan.

**CALLIOSTOMA SPRINGERI**
Springer's Top. *Clench and Turner 1960.*
Northern Gulf of Mexico.

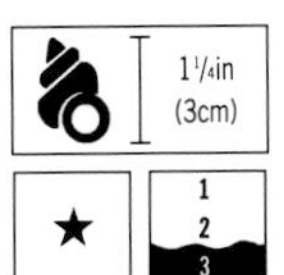


A delicate species, the shell of *C. springeri* is rather depressed and has a moderate spire and slightly concave sides. Against the pretty base colour of pale nacreous bronze run five or six spiral rows of off-white beading. This specimen was fished at a depth of 825 feet (250m) off southern Pensacola, Florida.

**CALLIOSTOMA ANNULATUM**
Ringed Top. *Lightfoot 1786.*
California.

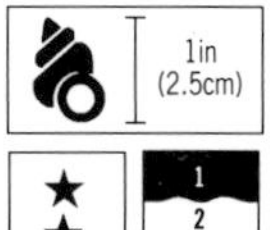

A popular collectors' shell, perhaps because of its attractive sculpturing and colour, it has straight sides with a moderate spire. Each whorl bears rows of fine spiral beading which appear as red and white dots, and a broad spiral band of lavender runs above the suture. The background colour is pale brown or beige, and lavender also occurs around the sealed umbilicus.

**MAUREA TIGRIS**
Tiger Top. *Martyn 1784.*
New Zealand.

The genus *Maurea* are a small group, mainly composed of lightweight shells with fine and delicate ornamentation. This species is the largest, and has a high spire and rounded shoulders. There are many rows of fine spiral beading. Their colour is beige, overlaid with axial or diagonal brown "flames". The aperture is large and the operculum circular and horny.

**MAUREA BLACKI**
Black's Maurea. *Powell 1950.*
New Zealand.

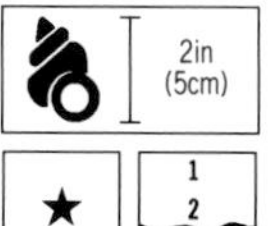

A pale pink shell, this is one of the rarest in the genus, and is thicker and heavier than most related species. The seven or so whorls are straight-sided and bear rows of slightly nodulose cording. The narrow suture is at right angles to the whorls. This specimen was dead collected in deep water off Canterbury, South Island.

**MAUREA PUNCTULATA**
Punctate Maurea. *Martyn 1784.*
New Zealand.

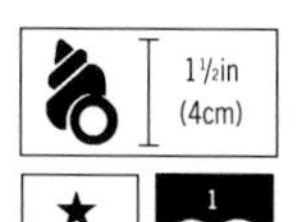

A short rather squat species, with a large rounded body whorl, it bears many rows of fine spiral cording. The background colour is beige or mid-brown and the cords bear alternate white and brown dots and dashes. These specimens were found on rocks at low tide, Mahanga Beach, New Zealand.

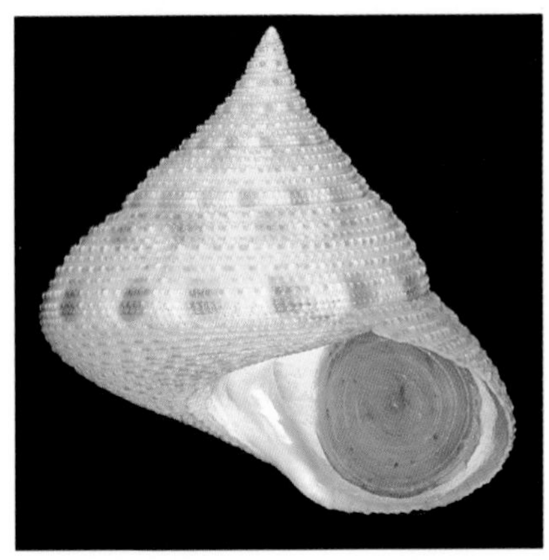

### MAUREA PELLUCIDA

Pellucid Maurea. *Valenciennes 1846.*
New Zealand.

2in (5cm)

This maurea has eight or more whorls, each bearing rows of spiral cording, and the sides of the high spire are either straight or slightly concave. The body whorl is large and has a rounded shoulder. The overall colour is pale beige, decorated with spiral dots and dashes with larger pale orange or brown blotches around the lower part of each whorl.

### CLANCULUS PHARAONIUS

Mantle Clanculus. *L. 1758.*
Red Sea and Indian Ocean.

3/4in (2cm)

Although it closely resembles *C. puniceus*, this species appears to be more squat and the spiral beads or ridges more coarse. It is a darker red, with at least three rows of black or black and white dots per whorl. There are several variations of this intertidal rock or coral rubble dweller.

### TECTUS TRISERIALIS

Tall Top. *Lamarck 1822.*
Philippines.

2 1/4in (5.5cm)

A very elegant, tall and narrow species, *T. triserialis* has slightly rounded shoulders. The 13 or so whorls bear several broken rows of blunt white nodules set against a background that is generally pale green or brown. The base is white with fine spiral grooves.

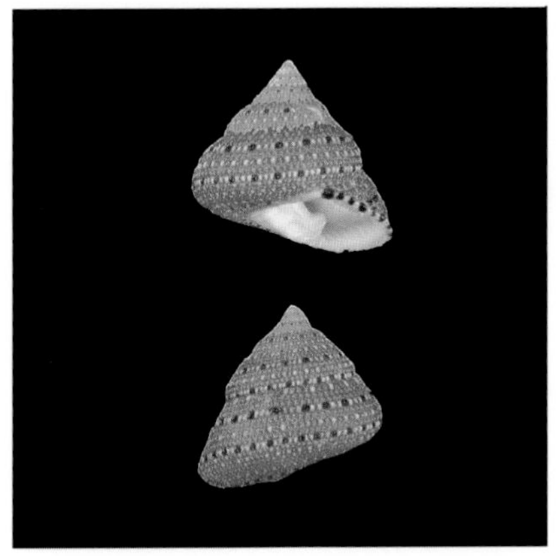

### CLANCULUS PUNICEUS

Strawberry Top. *Philippi 1846.*
East Africa.

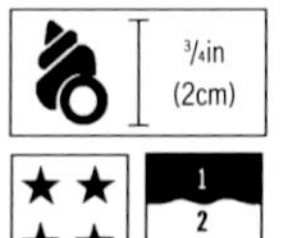

3/4in (2cm)

A pretty species and collectors' favourite, this small but solid shell has slightly rounded whorls, bearing rows of spiral beading with two bands of alternating black and white dots on each whorl. The background colour is deep red. There are white extended "teeth" on the columella and small white spiral ridges on the upper wall of the aperture. Found under rocks in the intertidal zone.

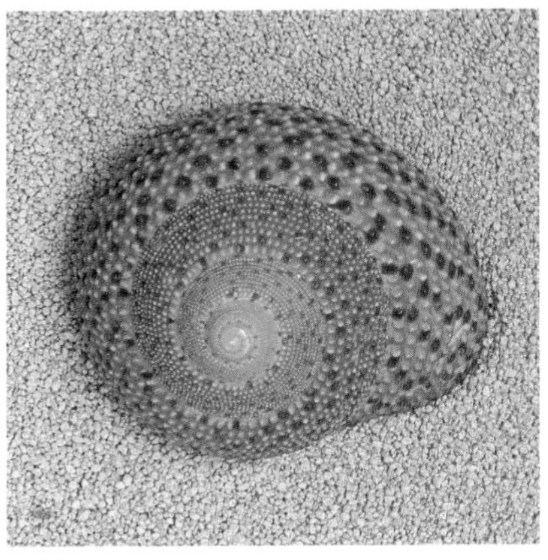

### CLANCULUS UNDATUS

Wavy Australian Clanculus. *Lamarck 1816.*
Southern Australia.

To 1 1/4in (3cm)

One of the largest of the genus, its squat shell has rounded flattened whorls and is mid-brown, with rows of black dots running diagonally from the apex. Many small-to-moderate spiral ridges or beading are evident. It has a nacreous aperture with fine "teeth" on the columella and fine lirae on the inside of the outer aperture wall. Found on intertidal rocks.

### TROCHUS MACULATUS

Maculated Top. *L. 1758.*
Indo-Pacific.

To 2in (5cm)

*T. maculatus* is a very variable species only in colour and pattern. The shape is fairly constant – a solid thick shell, with straight or slightly convex sides, the whorls bearing rows of spiral pustules and raised nodules. The base has fine spiral grooves which are white with radial or random lines and dashes. The exterior colours range from beige through reds, greens and browns, some being one colour, others a mixture. The three included here show a typical range.

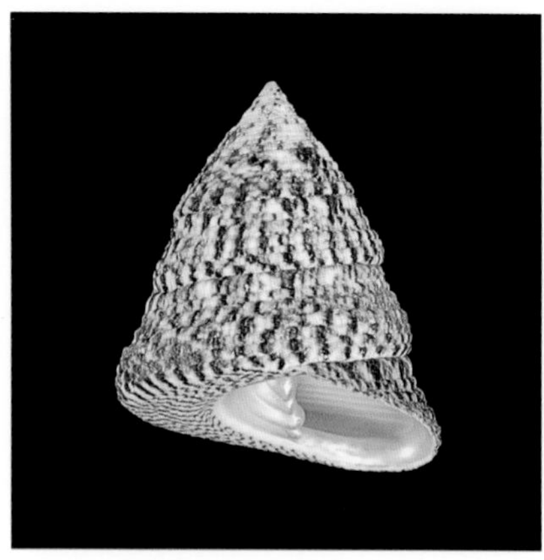

**TROCHUS VIRGATUS**
Striped Top. *Gmelin 1791.*
Indo-Pacific.

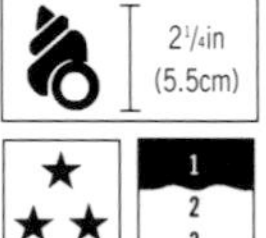

Rather similar to *T. maculatus*, this species has a somewhat higher spire and slightly rounded whorls. There is much coarse spiral beading and the pattern consists of axial "flames" and patches of green, grey or red on a white background. It inhabits coral reefs and is often heavily encrusted with lime when collected.

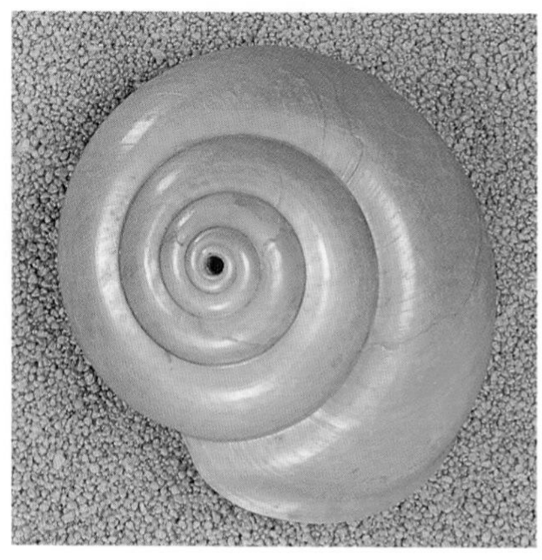

**GAZA SUPERBA**
Superb Gaza. *Dall 1881.*
Gulf of Mexico and West Indies.

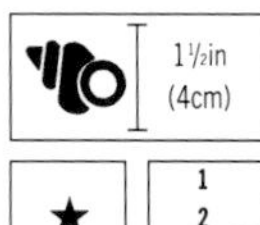

A very light fragile species, rounded and depressed, its shell is much desired by collectors. The gazas are a small rare genus and all appear to be thin shelled with the pearly interior showing through. *G. superba* is pale lime green with gold and pink undertones. A nacreous parietal wall partly covers the otherwise wide umbilicus. This specimen was dredged at a depth of 1,650 feet (500m) off Pensacola, Florida.

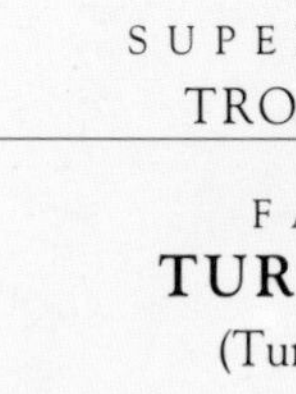

SUPER FAMILY
## TROCHOIDEA

FAMILY
## TURBINIDAE
(Turban Shells)

The turban shells are a large family comprising several hundred species which are divided into three subfamilies, Angariinae (Dolphin Shells), Turbininae (True Turbans) and Astraeinae (Star Shells). The Angariinae are a small group of relatively large shells with spiral ornamentation. Some have long curved spines. *Angaria* is the only genus and all are collectors' items. The turbans tend to have solid top-shaped shells with large body whorls and apertures. Genera include *Turbo*, *Ninella* and *Lunella*. The Astraeinae are popular and varied collectors' shells which are generally conical to top-shaped with flat bases, often highly ornamented with long spines. The main genera are *Astraea*, *Bolina* and *Guildfordia*. Most species of the family are vegetarian and usually prefer warm shallow water.

**TROCHUS DENTATUS**
Toothed Top. *Forskal 1775.*
Red Sea and Indian Ocean.

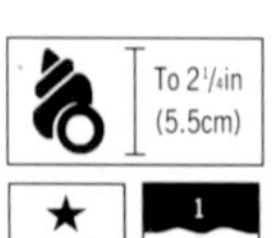

Solid and fairly heavy, this has about 10 whorls, the sides of which are slightly concave. Prominent extended nodules occur on the lower part of each whorl, overlapping the suture. The pale beige or pink shell is often heavily encrusted. The base is mainly chalky white. It feeds on algae on reef flats in shallow water.

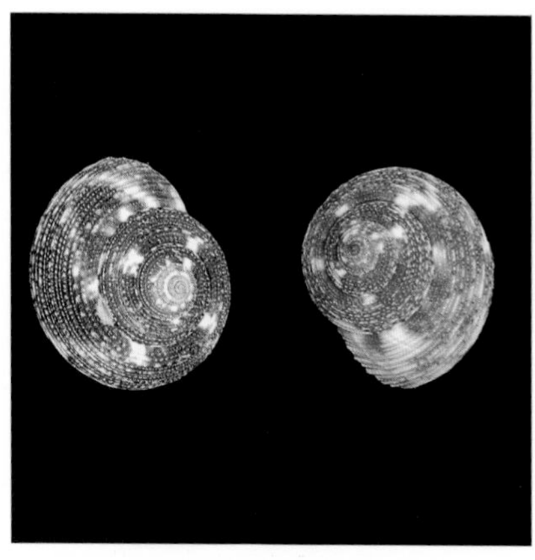

**MONILEA BELCHERI**
Belcher's Top. *Philippi 1850.*
Western Pacific.

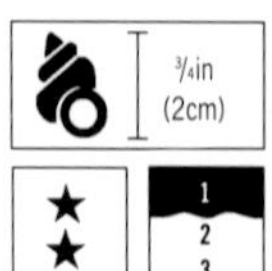

Button-like in shape, this has a low spire and a large body whorl. Fine spiral striae are evident and the umbilicus is open on the base. The ground colour is white with irregular markings of red, grey or pale brown. The specimens depicted were supposedly collected off Queensland, Australia.

**ANGARIA DELPHINULUS MELANACANTHA**
Imperial Delphinula. *Reeve 1842.* Philippines.

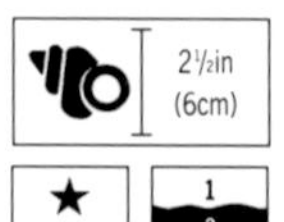

A thick highly spinose species, it has a flat spire with virtually only an enlarged body whorl which swings out and drops downward revealing an open and spinose umbilicus. The sides and top of the whorl bear black spines of varying length, while those on the shoulder project outward and upward, occasionally touching each other. The background colour is a pale greyish purple. The aperture is highly nacreous.

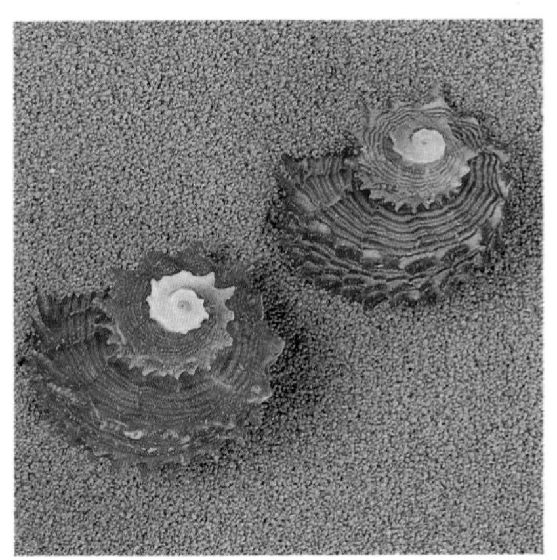

## ANGARIA DELPHINULUS

Common Delphinula. *L. 1758.*
Indo-Pacific.

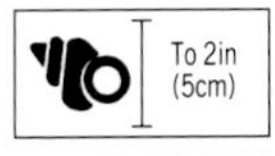


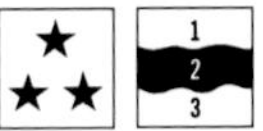


This is the best-known form of the *Delphinulus* group. It has a flat spire, only about two whorls, and a large umbilicus. Each whorl supports many spinose spiral ridges, the spines being longer and sharper at the shoulders. Colours vary from pale pink to almost black. These specimens are from southern India.

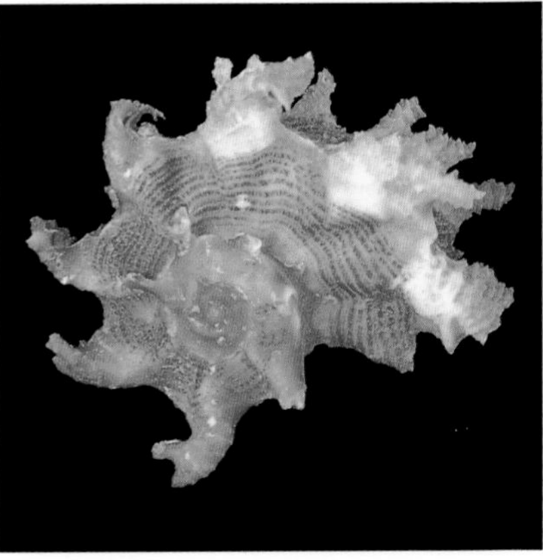

## ANGARIA DELPHINULUS ACULEATA

Aculeate Delphinula. *Reeve 1842.*
Japan and Philippines.

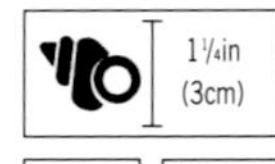


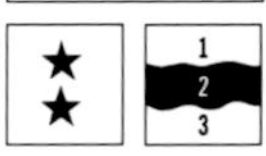


Another very variable but attractive form of *A. delphinulus*. The depicted specimen was fished in 33 feet (10m) at Sinabe, Okinawa and shows typical characteristics of a flat spire, and an enlarged and very spinose body whorl. The colour is exquisite, consisting of pale red and pink, with golden tipped spines.

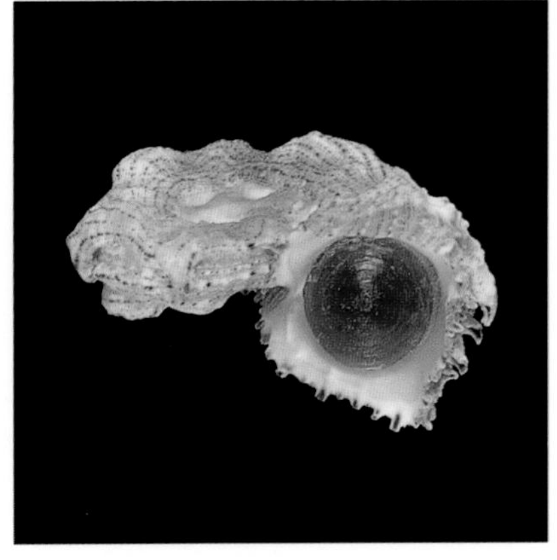

## ANGARIA NODULOSA

Knobbed Delphinula. *Reeve 1846.*
Japan.

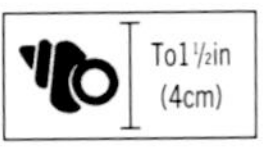


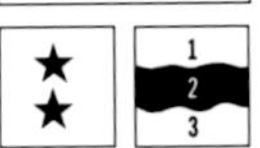


Some people consider this a variety of *A. delphinulus*, but I will treat it as a species in its own right. A large, virtually continuous body whorl radiates from a flat or depressed spire (when viewed from above). There are several large rounded or scaled nodules, both on the shoulder and below the whorl, and a delicate spiral beading of fine dark red dots on a pale pink background. This shell was collected at a depth of 66 feet (20m) off Sinabe, Okinawa.

## ANGARIA TYRIA

Tyria Delphinula. *Reeve 1842.*
South-West Pacific and Australia.

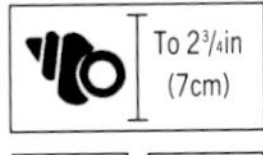

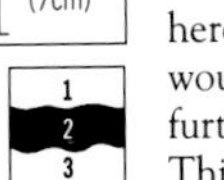


Two forms of this extremely variable species are depicted here. Again, some experts would put *A. tyria* as yet a further form of *A. delphinulus*. This may well be, but I am treating it as a species in its own right. The smaller of the two is probably a Philippine shell, whereas the larger was fished off North-West Australia. Extremely variable.

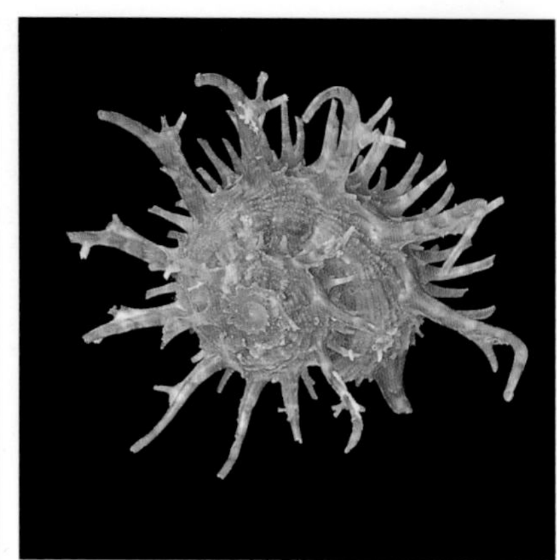

## ANGARIA VICDANI

Victor Dan's Angaria. *Kosuge 1980.*
Philippines.

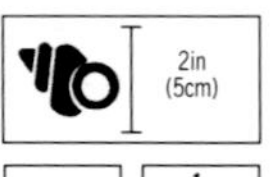

Perfect specimens of this sought-after collectors' favourite are a rarity. A flat spire and large body whorl characterize the species. There are many spines, those on the shoulders being the longest. Generally pink over a golden bronze nacreous background. The shell is fished in deep water in tangle nets, the spines often bearing small corals and marine debris. Cleaning must be a nightmare!

## ANGARIA SPHAERULA

Kiener's Delphinula. *Kiener 1839.*
Philippines.

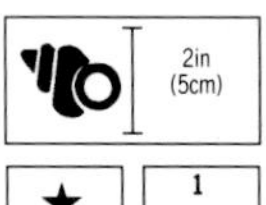

This beautiful species can be pink, bronze or yellow, with a nacreous base colour showing through. Spines are numerous, many spatulate, the specimens with the longest spines being fished from calm deep waters.

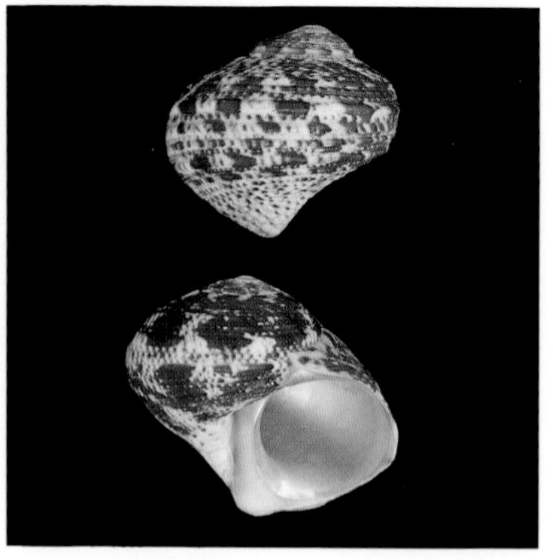

## LUNELLA CINEREA

Smooth Moon Turban. *Born 1778.*
Indo-Pacific.

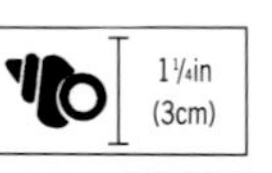

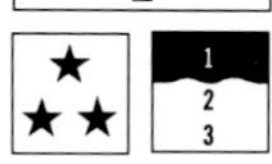

This is a globose shell with a flat spire and large rounded body whorl. Below the open umbilicus the columella extends down to the aperture base with a lobe-like structure. There are fine spiral grooves and rounded ridges on some specimens. *L. cinerea* is variable in colour but generally white, overlaid with green or brown axial streaks and patches. It inhabits rocky shorelines.

## NINELLA WHITLEYI

Whitley's Turban. *Iredale 1949.*
Australia.

When well cleaned, *N. whitleyi* is an attractive shell with a strongly ridged shoulder bearing bumps and low nodules. There is also a row of nodules on the upper part of the body whorl, below the suture. The shell is overlaid with a closely spaced pattern of sharp diagonal ridges and is a beige grey, some specimens bearing pale green axial streaks. The spire is flat and often eroded. The umbilicus is open and the operculum is heavily ornamented.

## *SUBNINELLA UNDULATA*

Lightning Moon Turban. *Lightfoot 1786.*
Southern and South-western Australia.

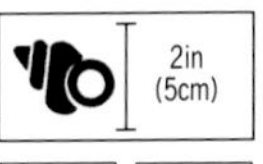


*S. undulata* has a large rounded body whorl and its spire is virtually flat. The shell is similar in shape to *L. cinerea*, but the former has an open umbilicus. The colour varies from a beige brown to green, with many dark axial zigzag lines. These shells live on reefs down to about 100 feet (30m).

## *TURBO PETHOLATUS*

Tapestry Turban. *L. 1758.*
Indo-Pacific.

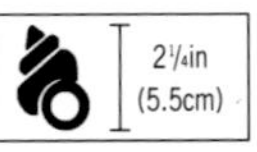


This beautifully patterned species is found in a wide range of colour variations. Very popular, it has proved an inspiration to artists and designers as well as lovers of natural objects. The shell is rather bulbous and stout, smooth and glossy, and is covered with bands and axial streaks and "flames" of various colours, including browns, greens and beiges. The operculum – known as a "cat's eye" – is thick and is predominantly dark green.

## *TURBO PULCHER*

Beautiful Turban. *Reeve 1842.*
Western Australia.

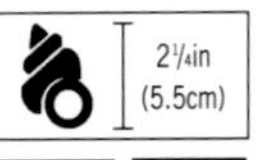


Another solid shell, this is somewhat coarsely sculptured, with both strong and weak axial ridges, the whole surface feeling rather like a file. The pale grey green shell is waved or zigzagged with darker grey green axial lines. The operculum bears stunted nodules similar to those of *T. sarmaticus*. A shallow-water reef dweller.

## *TURBO SPECIOSUS*

Green Ridged Turban. *Reeve 1848.*
South-eastern Australia.

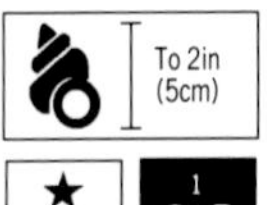


This shallow-water dweller has a moderate spire and an enlarged body whorl. There are many coarse spiral ridges, some of which bear short spines. The background colour is beige, with brown axial stripes and patches. There are at least four distinctive green ridges on the larger whorls. The operculum is granulose, being white with some brown staining.

## *TURBO CRASSUS*

Heavy Turban. *Wood 1829.*
Central and South-West Pacific.

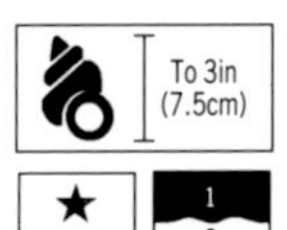


As the name implies, this is a thick robust shell. It has many rounded axial ridges, and while some colour variations occur, most appear to be a beige-toned green. The depicted specimen is vividly patterned in two shades of green. The operculum is granulose white, with a brown centre.

## *TURBO CANALICULATUS*

Channelled Turban. *Hermann 1781.*
Caribbean Sea.

An attractively sculptured species, it has a moderately tall spire and rounded whorls. There are strong low rounded spiral ridges and the upper part of each whorl is angled or "channelled" below the suture. The beige ground colour is offset by axial patches of deeper brown, with dashes and dots on the ridges. An offshore reef dweller in shallow water.

### TURBO CORNUTUS

Horned Turban. *Lightfoot 1786.*
Japan.

A large solid shell, *T. cornutus* combines a moderate spire with a large body whorl and aperture. Although some shells are relatively smooth, many bear strong rows of spines on the body whorl, and specimens can be either brick red or greenish in colour. The operculum has a low rounded radial ridge and is finely granulose. It is an important seafood in Japan.

### TURBO SARMATICUS

South African Turban. *L 1758.*
South Africa.

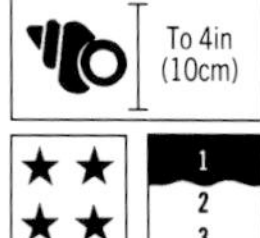

A large globose shell, this has a very low spire and giant body whorl. The distinctive operculum bears many rounded nodules. Locally known as the alikreukel, its meat is often used in fish patties. In recent years it has become a popular commercial shell as it looks quite stunning when polished and the pearly structure of the shell is revealed. (Both natural and pearlized versions are shown here.)

### TURBO REEVEI

Reeve's Turban. *Philippi 1847.*
Philippines.

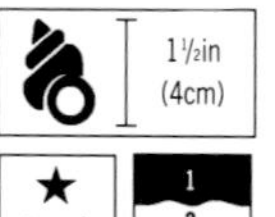

This species varies from *T. petholatus* by being rather smaller and having less dramatic patterning. The colour variations are no less vivid, however, ranging from pale to deep orange, green and reddish brown through to near black, many having mottling or axial zigzag lines. The depicted specimens were collected from the Sulu Sea.

### TURBO ARGYROSTOMA

Silver Mouthed Turban. *L. 1758.*
Indo-Pacific.

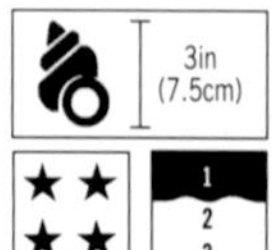

A large and heavy turban, its name comes from the silver nacre around the aperture. A low spire and very large body whorl and aperture characterize this species. Some shells are finely ridged and spinose; others develop longer blunt nodules on the shoulder of the body whorl. The background may be either beige or pale green and is overlaid with dark brown axial streaks and patches. Apart from its food value, it is widely used commercially for its nacre.

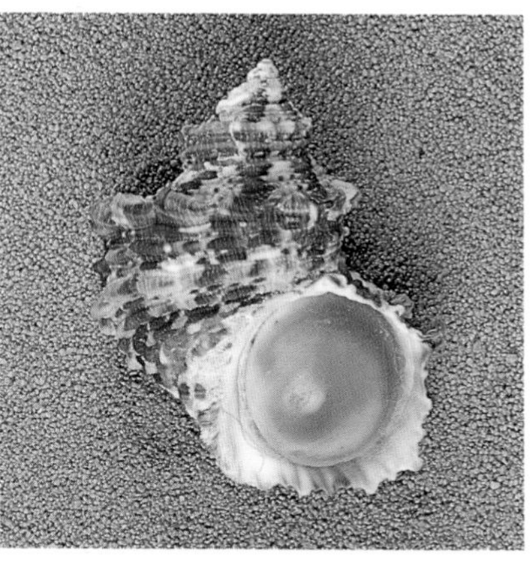

### TURBO RADIATUS

Radial Turban. *Gmelin 1791.*
Red Sea and Gulf of Oman.

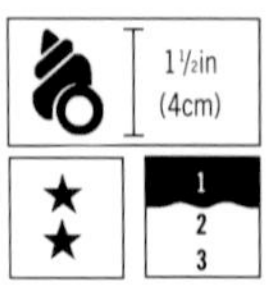

*T. radiatus* has a moderate spire and an enlarged body whorl and aperture, coarsely sculptured with rows of out-turned blunt nodules – three rows per whorl. The colour range extends from mottled beige through to dark brown. The thick operculum is smooth. An intertidal reef dweller.

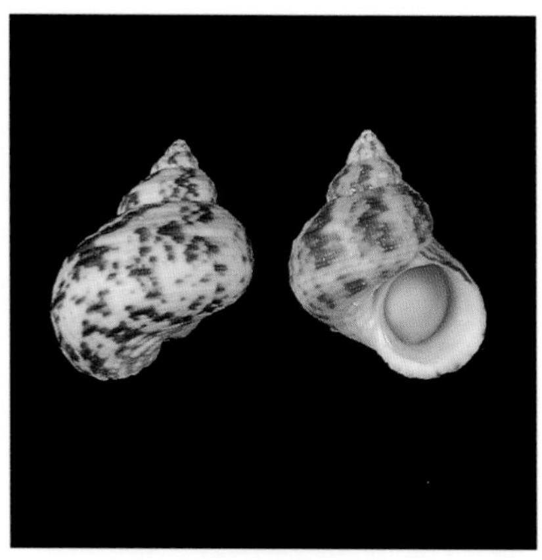

### TURBO BRUNEUS

*Röding 1798.*
Western Pacific.

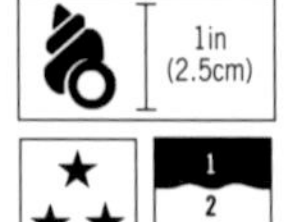

This relatively small species possesses a moderate spire and rounded whorls, decorated with very fine spirally beaded ribs. The colouring is extremely variable, ranging from off-white to yellow, with axial bands and patches of brown, green and grey. The two specimens shown here are from Tryon Island, Queensland.

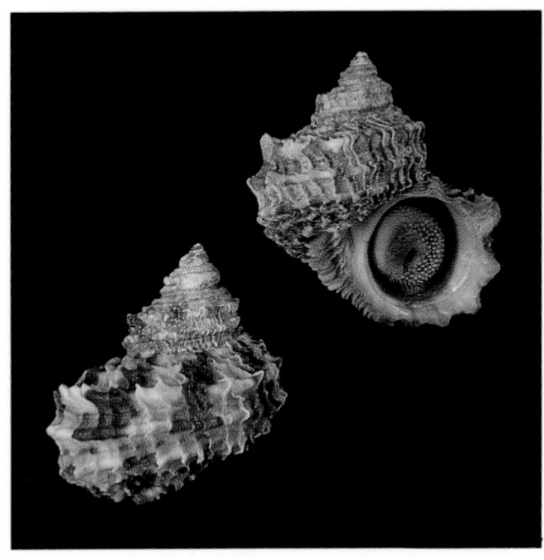

**TURBO LAMINIFEROUS**
Crinkly Turban. *Reeve 1848.*
Northern Australia to Papua New Guinea.

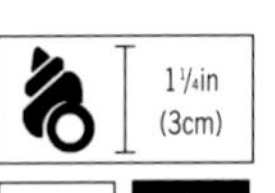

1¼in (3cm)

Coarsely ornamented, the shell has many fine axial growth ridges, giving a "crinkled" effect. There are three raised spiral cords, from which the growth ridges protrude slightly. The dirty beige brown base colour is decorated with splashes or mottling of a darker shade. The operculum is pustulose.

**TURBO GRUNERI**
Gruner's Turban. *Philippi 1846.*
Southern and Western Australia.

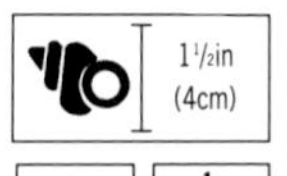

1½in (4cm)

This species has a low spire and an enlarged body whorl. The whorls bear prominent spiral rounded ridges and alternating rows of fine beading. The operculum is thick and features spiral decoration. The colour varies from cream to pink or beige, overlaid with fine axial zigzag lines and patches. *T. gruneri* inhabits deeper water, down to about 495 feet (150m).

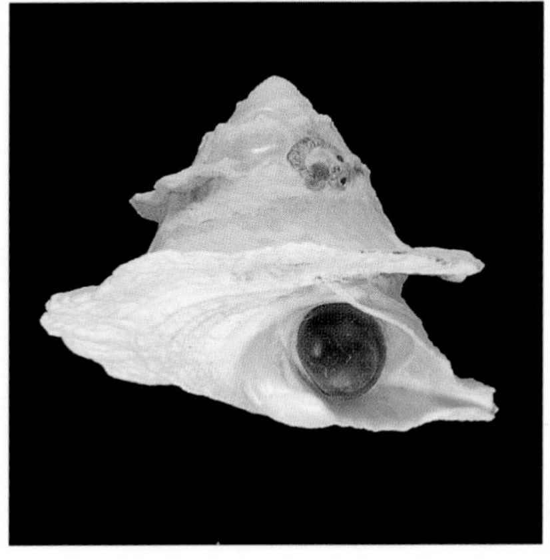

**ASTRAEA PILEOLA**
*Reeve 1842.*
Western Australia.

To 2in (5cm)

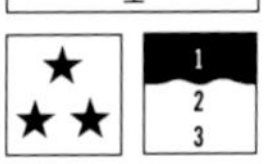

The chalky white shell has a moderate spire and slightly convex sides. The shoulders on larger whorls extend outward in flat, keel-like wavy projections, rather like the brim of a soft hat. The aperture is nacreous and the ovate operculum is a dark blue grey. The apex is often worn, revealing mother-of-pearl. Found on intertidal rocks.

**TURBO SPARVERIUS**
Corded Turban. *Gmelin 1791.*
South-West Pacific.

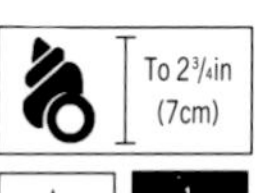

To 2¾in (7cm)

*T. sparverius* has a moderate spire and enlarged rounded body whorl, on which many rounded spiral cords are evident. The background colour varies from beige to green, and is patterned with axial mottling and patches of brown or black. The operculum is smooth and stained brown. This specimen was collected on Honiara Reef, Solomon Islands, in shallow water.

**ASTRAEA HELIOTROPIUM**
Sunburst Star Shell. *Martyn 1784.*
New Zealand.

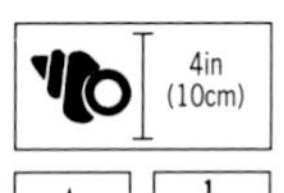

4in (10cm)

This deep-water shell is seldom obtained in pristine condition – it is usually entirely covered with lime and marine encrustations and is difficult to clean. The species was reputedly discovered on the cable of a vessel belonging to Captain Cook's fleet in the waters later to be named Cook Strait. (Martyn, its author, was one of several gentlemen interested in obtaining the material that was brought back by such voyages.)

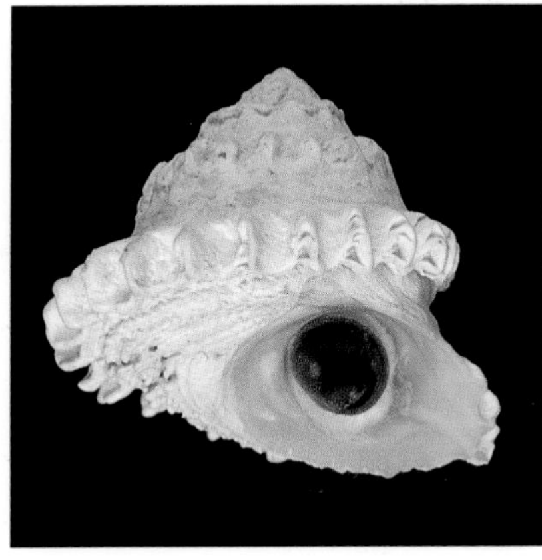

**ASTRAEA ROTULARIA**
Rotary Star. *Lamarck 1822.*
Western Australia.

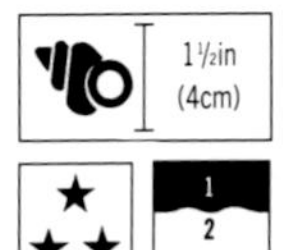

1½in (4cm)

In shape this is similar to *A. pileola*, as is its chalky appearance. The shoulders of this species, however, bear a row of strong outward-turning nodules, which can be up to ¼in (6mm) long. Many shells of this type are so encrusted that they are hardly recognizable. The operculum is a dark blue grey.

## ASTRAEA PHOEBIA

Circular Saw Shell. *Röding 1798.*
Caribbean to Brazil.

Well-cleaned adult shells can be spectacular. The spire is relatively low and the whorls are covered with rows of coarse spatulate triangular spines, which are extended at the periphery of the whorls. The umbilicus can be open or closed. The aperture is nacreous white and the overall shell colour ranges from dirty beige to pale orange. They live on sand flats in intertidal areas.

## ASTRAEA CAELATA

Carved Star Shell. *Gmelin 1791.*
Off Florida and West Indies.

The shell, which has a moderate spire and large body whorl, is coarsely sculptured with sharp oblique spines, many part-open. The ground colouring is off-white and there is much emerald-green mottling. The aperture is nacreous and there is no umbilicus. Usually heavily encrusted, it is found on or under rocks in shallow water.

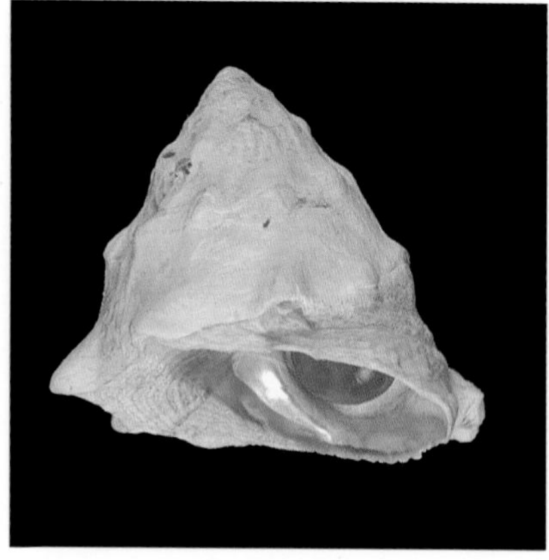

## ASTRAEA STELLARE

Blue-mouthed Star Shell. *Gmelin 1791.*
Western Australia.

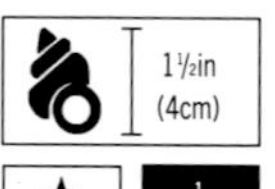

This is another white species, usually heavily encrusted. It is notable for its vivid turquoise-blue ovate operculum and the pale blue tinge around the umbilical area, making it to my knowledge the only true blue to be found in the Phylum Mollusca! The shell is rounded and conical with odd blunt nodulose projections along the lower edges or shoulders of the whorls.

## ASTRAEA OLIVACEA

Blood-spotted Turban. *Wood 1828.*
West Mexico.

Round and conical with rounded whorls, this shell is a mixture of olive green and pale reddish brown. It has saw-like flat projections at the whorl periphery and small diagonal raised ridges. The umbilical area is encircled with a deep orange red. *A. olivacea* inhabits rock ledges in subtidal waters.

## ASTRAEA TECTA

Caribbean Star Shell. *Solander 1786.*
Florida and Caribbean.

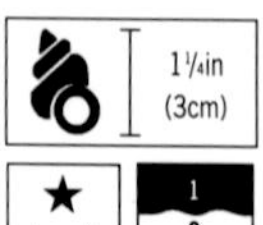

A small solid shell, it has straight sides. There are several local variations, two of which are depicted here. Some possess rows of rounded protruding nodules; others are relatively smooth. Colours vary, but in general a beige background is overlaid with green or beige to brown mottling. The columella is white. This shell is found on rocks and grass flats.

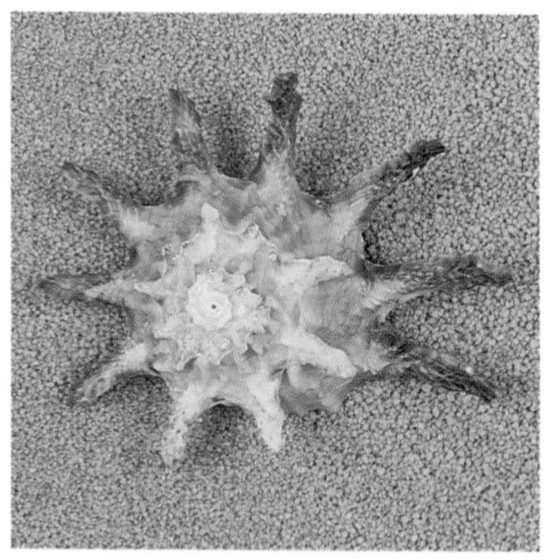

## ASTRALIUM CALCAR

Philippine Star Shell. *L. 1758.*
Philippines.

Long spines sometimes protrude from the whorl periphery of this almost flat shell. The base colour is a green beige, and the slightly ovate operculum is dark green. There is fine spiral beading on the base of the shell. The aperture is nacreous. Many specimens are heavily encrusted and eroded at the apex.

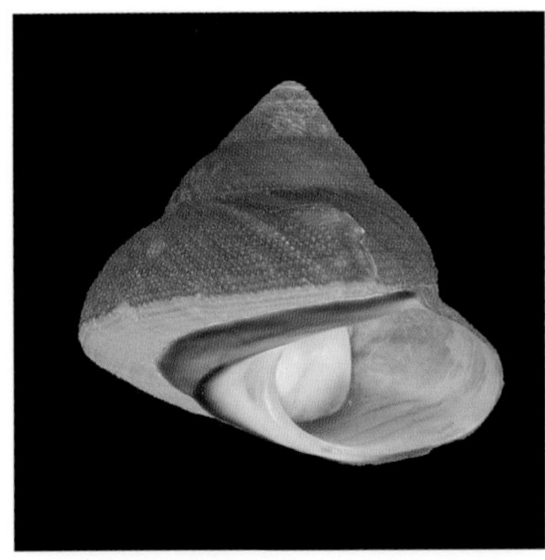

**BOLMA TAYLORIANA**
Taylor's Star Shell. *E. A. Smith 1880.*
South Africa.

A round conical shell with rounded whorls, its entire surface is covered with fine spiral beading, making it rough to the touch, like a file. The overall colour is dirty pink, the columella being white and encircled with an orange brown calloused area. The operculum is pure white. *B. tayloriana* inhabits deep water, in excess of 330 feet (100m), and when freshly caught it is often covered with brown marine algae.

**BOLMA MODESTA**
Modest Bolma. *Reeve 1843.*
Taiwan to Japan.

A species of small-to-medium size, it has a moderate spire and rounded nodulose whorls. The shell is a pretty shade of pale lavender, and the operculum is pure white. The columella is tinged with pale orange. *B. modesta* inhabits water down to 330 feet (100m), and is often heavily encrusted with marine debris.

**BOLMA RUGOSA**
Orange-mouthed Star. *L. 1767.*
Mediterranean and North-East Atlantic coasts.

*B. rugosa* has a moderate spire, with angular whorls bearing rows of irregular spiral cords. Below the suture are a row of low rounded nodules. The shells, which are often heavily encrusted, are a grey green or brown, with orange around the nacreous columella and covering the umbilical area. The spirally grooved operculum is bright orange.

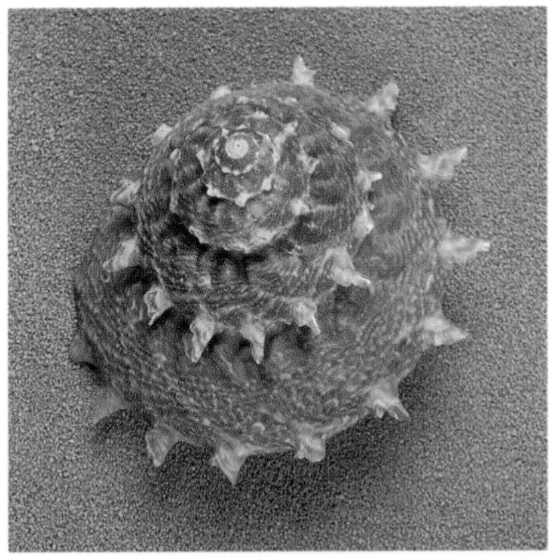

**BOLMA AUREOLA**
Bridled Bolma. *Hedley 1907.*
Queensland, Australia.

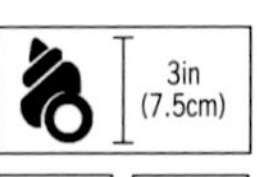

Found only off Queensland in depths to 130 feet (40m), this shell is large, with straight sides. The whorls are slightly angled at the suture. The shoulders bear a single row of short sharp spines which project outward and elsewhere there are haphazard rows of low nodular ridges. The shell is orange brown with a pale orange and white operculum. The aperture and columella are edged in bright orange.

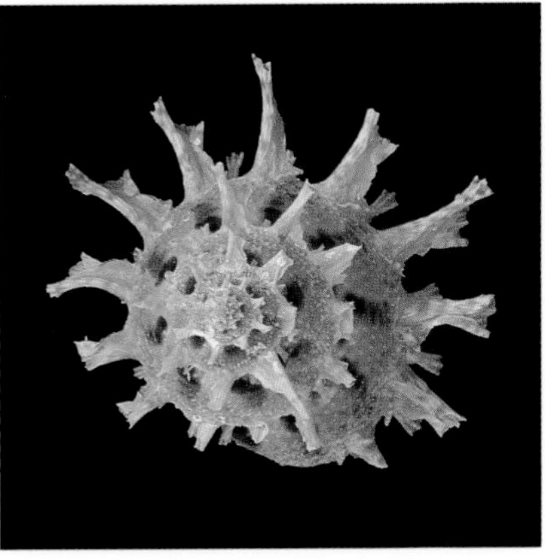

**BOLMA GIRGYLLUS**
Girgyllus Star. *Reeve 1861.*
Philippines.

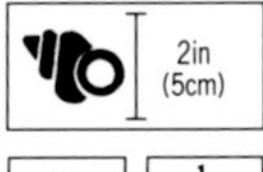

Probably the most spectacular of the genus; it has a fairly tall spire with rounded whorls. The shoulders of these bear a double row of outward-projecting foliated spines, the upper row being the largest. Elsewhere, there are neat spiral rows of small rounded nodules. The shell colour is extremely variable, ranging from pale lemon to deep orange; some have diagonal "flames" and patches of brown, grey or purple. Perfect specimens are rare, for a slight touch will damage a spine.

**COOKIA SULCATA**
Captain Cook's Turban. *Gmelin 1791.*
New Zealand.

One of several species possibly first discovered on the voyages of Captain James Cook of South Sea Island fame, this is a robust squat shell with a low spire. There are rows of nodulose diagonal ridges and the overall colouring is a dull beige. Many collected specimens are highly encrusted. The operculum is off-white and has the appearance of an "ear". An intertidal rock dweller.

## GUILDFORDIA TRIUMPHANS
Triumphant Star. *Philippi 1841.*
Taiwan and Japan.

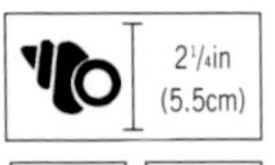


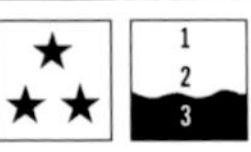


Another almost flat shell with a low spire, this has long projecting spines at right angles to the body whorl and much fine spiral beading overall. The colour is a pink-toned bronze and the base is off-white to cream. The operculum is white and ovate. A collectors' favourite. It is a deep-water species.

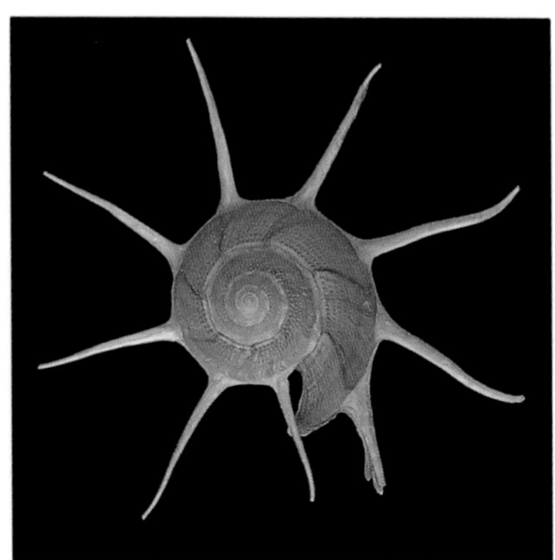

## GUILDFORDIA YOKA
Yoka Star Shell. *Jousseaume 1888.*
Japan to Philippines.

It is amazing that perfect, or near perfect, specimens survive after being fished from their habitat in depths possibly as low as 1,650 feet (500m). This flat shell is a true wonder of creation! It is very similar to G. *triumphans*, but its body whorls bear only seven to nine extremely long spines. It is also a pale bronze pink colour, the base being cream. Unlike G. *triumphans*, it has no spiral beading. This specimen comes from Bohol Island, Philippines.

## MEGASTRAEA TURBANICA
Turban Star Shell. *Dall 1910.*
Southern California to Mexico.

The bigger of the two species in this genus, large live specimens – over 3in (7.5cm) – have only been fished from deep-water kelp beds since the 1950s, prior to which the only evidence had come from dead shells and fossils. The shell has straight sides to the apex and each whorl bears rows of stunted and pronounced nodules. The colour is generally off-white, but the early whorls are often dull brick-red or pinkish. This deep-water species is popular with collectors.

## MEGASTRAEA UNDOSA
Wavy Turban. *Wood 1828.*
California to Mexico.

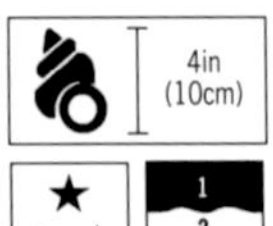


Similar in appearance to M. *turbanica*, it is generally smaller and the nodules are smaller and neater. From my specimens it would appear that M. *undosa* bears only one nodulose ridge, while the former has two. The operculum is also different, being minutely granulose, whereas that of M. *turbanica* is smooth. The colour of M. *undosa* is pale pink-tinged brown throughout, with little white showing.

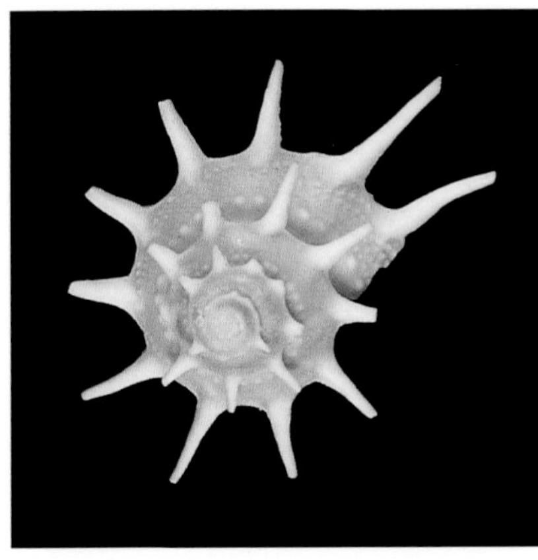

**PSEUDASTRALIUM HENICUS GLORIOSUM**
Glorious Star. *Kira 1959*. Japan.

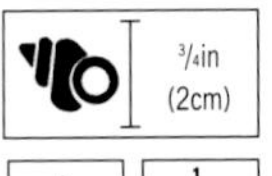


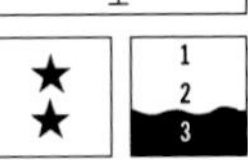


A dainty low conical shell, it is encircled by long rounded spines, protruding from the periphery of each whorl. There are several rows of minute spiral beading, the more prominent one being that below the suture. The base is semi-nacreous and the columella white. The overall colour is pale cream or white. It inhabits deep water, down to 465 feet (140m).

SUPER FAMILY
## TROCHOIDEA

FAMILY
## PHASIANELLIDAE and TRICOLIIDAE
(Pheasant Shells)

These two families contain the genera *Phasianella* and *Tricolia*, but have relatively few species. The shells possess smooth exteriors that are usually colourful and patterned, the apertures being non-nacreous but porcellaneous. The operculae are chalky white, smooth and glossy. Most species are vegetarian.

**PHASIANELLA AUSTRALIS**
Australian Pheasant. *Gmelin 1791*.
Southern Australia.

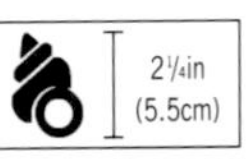


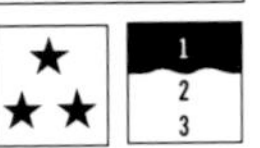


A tall fairly narrow shell, with rounded whorls, its surface is smooth and glossy and is highly patterned. There are many variations, and I have selected several here to show a range. The thick white operculum is almond-shaped.

**PHASIANELLA VENTRICOSA**
Swollen Pheasant. *Swainson 1822*.
Southern Australia.

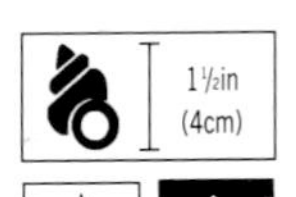


Although in texture it is identical to *P. australis*, the shape of *P. ventricosa* differs in that the spire is relatively low and the body whorl large and bulbous. Once again, patterns and colours can be extremely variable. The operculum is white and calcareous.

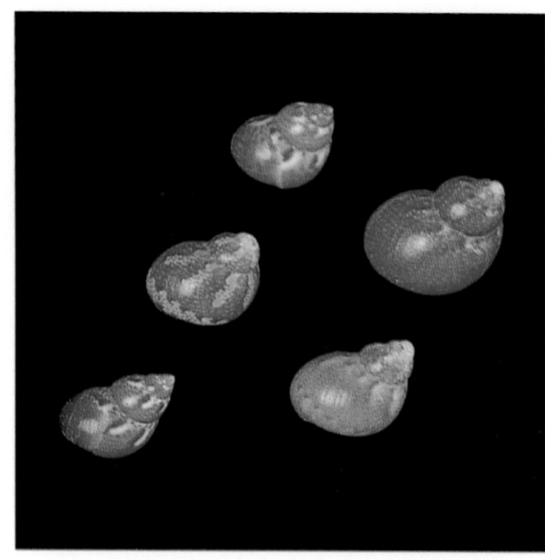

### TRICOLIA PULLA

Red Pheasant. *L. 1758.* Mediterranean and North-East Atlantic coasts.

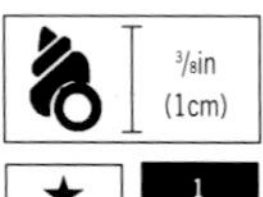


The *Tricolia* genus consists of very small shells, and you will have to inspect this particular species with an eye-glass to appreciate its beauty. It is globose, with rounded whorls and a moderate spire. The colour of this tiny gem is a rich reddish pink overlaid with tiny deeper red spots and zigzag lines. There are larger patches of cream and brown just below the suture. The neat tiny operculum is calcareous, and off-white in colour. These two examples are from Sines, Portugal.

SUPER FAMILY

## NERITOIDEA

FAMILY

## NERITIDAE

(Nerites)

The nerites are arguably one of the less popular families. This group of smallish shells comprises only about 50 species. There are several genera and subgenera, including *Nerita, Neritina, Smaragdia* and *Theodoxus.* Nerites are able to store water within the shell – the operculum is close fitting – and can therefore withstand periods without moisture, for example at low tide or in the splash zone. They are all vegetarian. Although there is little interest in the group as a whole, one or two species are nonetheless collectors' favourites.

### NERITA POLITA

Polished Nerite. *L. 1758.*
Indo-Pacific.

This occurs in an almost endless array of colours and patterns. Indeed, many experts have split the species into a range of subspecies and variations. The polished nerite has a flat spire and one large body whorl. The aperture is semi-circular and the columella bears two or more blunt "teeth", which can either be tinged with colour or off-white. I have selected a range of colours and patterns from several localities to portray the variety. They are to be found among rocks in the intertidal zone.

### NERITA EXUVIA

Snake-skin Nerite. *L. 1758.*
South-West Pacific.

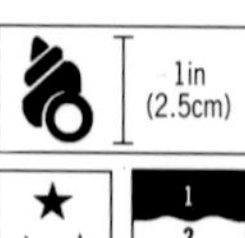


The body whorl has stout rounded spiral ribs of dark grey, and between these it is a cream or pale beige, dotted with grey. The aperture wall is incised with grooves and is white, while the columella and parietal wall are granulose. This species lives in or near mangroves.

### NERITA PELORONTA

Bleeding-tooth Nerite. *L. 1758.*
Caribbean.

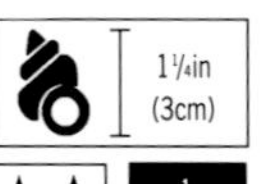


Although very common, it is a popular species, with its characteristic blood-stained-tooth pattern on the columella and parietal area. The exterior can be either smooth or ridged and the colours vary. Most have a cream background, overlaid with spiral broken bands and dashes of red, lavender, grey and black. This nerite inhabits rocky shorelines.

### NERITA BALTEATA

Lined Nerite. *Reeve 1855.*
South-West Pacific.

A plain little shell, it is covered with fine black spiral ribs on a grey background. The aperture and parietal area are a smooth white, but there is often a slight lemon staining on the columella. The operculum is grey and is finely pustulose.

**NERITA TEXTILIS**
Rough Nerite. *Gmelin 1791.*
Indo-Pacific.

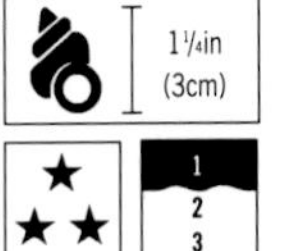


Solid and chunky, this species has coarse round spiral ribs, broken everywhere with fine axial growth lines. The colour is off-white, with broken grey patches on virtually every rib. The aperture is dentate and the parietal wall is pustulose. The operculum is a mid-grey and is also covered with tiny pustules. Found on shore rocks.

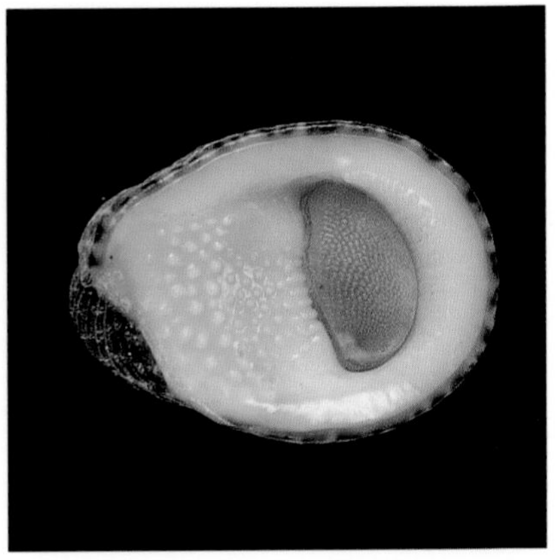

**NERITA ALBICILLA**
Ox-palate Nerite. *L. 1758.*
Indo-Pacific.

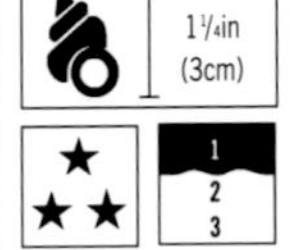


The depicted specimen has coarse but low flat ribs and is generally dark grey, but I believe this could be another variably patterned species. The shape is rather flatter than many nerites. The aperture and whole parietal area is pale lemon white and there are pustules both on the operculum and the parietal wall, the former being very fine.

**NERITINA COMMUNIS**
Candy Nerite. *Quoy and Gaimard 1832.*
Philippines.

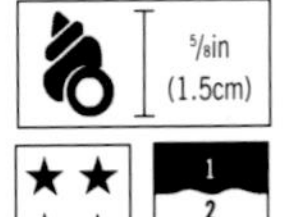


Probably the most variably patterned of all Gastropod species, its colours and patterns are virtually limitless! Most popular with collectors and shell lovers everywhere, this small shell is found among mangroves. It is smooth and glossy: the aperture being white or cream, tinged with pale orange, pink or red.

**CLYPEOLUM LATISSIMUM**
Wide Nerite. *Broderip 1833.*
Western Central America.

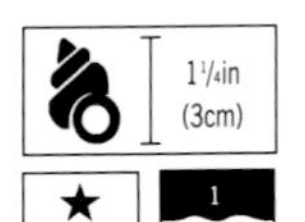


A species with a most unusual shape, this is one of several in the subgenus *Clypeolum.* It has a wide flaring mouth and a broad parietal shield. The exterior colouring is brown, grey or pale mauve, decorated with a fine black netted pattern. The aperture is grey and the columella and parietal area is a creamy yellow. The dark grey operculum is half-moon shaped. The species lives in estuaries and river mouths.

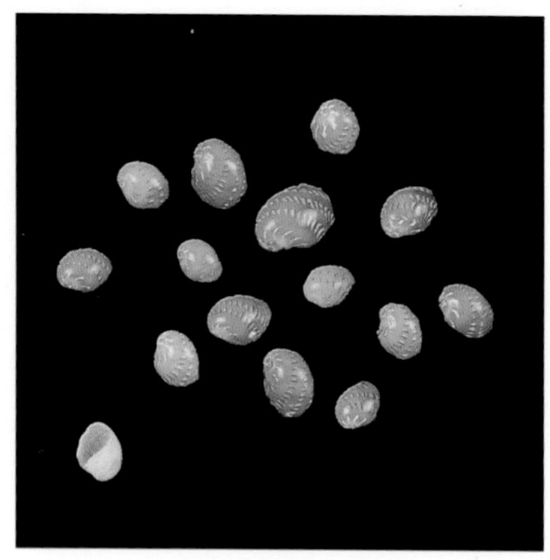

**SMARAGDIA VIRIDIS**
Emerald Nerite. *L. 1758.*
Caribbean.

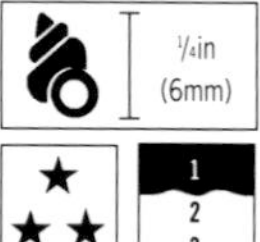


A minute species, this is probably the most popular of the very small nerites, due to its vivid green colouring. It has a very low spire and a greatly enlarged body whorl. Two or three rows of white axial lines spiral against the green background. The dentate columella extends to a large callous parietal shield in off-white. Emerald nerites live in shallow water.

**LITTORINA LITTOREA**
Common Periwinkle. *L. 1758.*
North Atlantic coastlines.

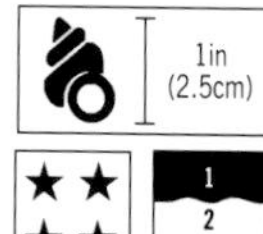


A rounded shell, it has a low spire and enlarged body whorl. It is generally a dark grey brown, marked with fine spiral striae. The aperture and columella are white and the operculum is dark brown and horny. A popular seafood, it is extremely common on both sides of the Atlantic.

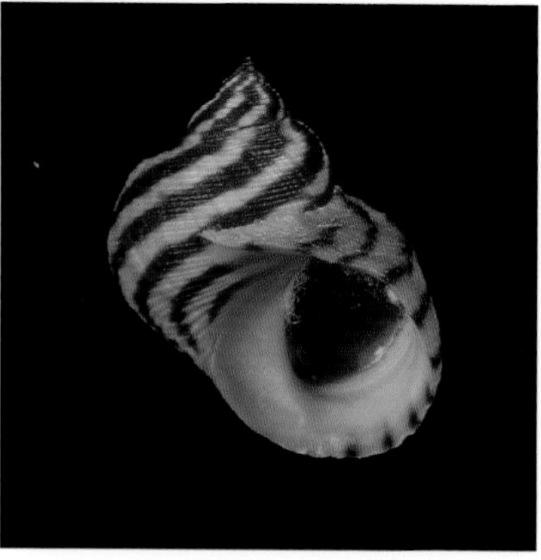

**LITTORINA ZEBRA**
Striped Periwinkle. *Donovan 1825.*
Costa Rica to Colombia.

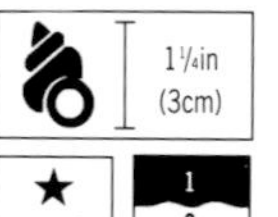


A solid and low-spired shell, it is one of the most attractive in the genus, having a terracotta background with oblique brown stripes and tiny spiral grooves. The horny ovate operculum is dark brown in colour. This shell is found on intertidal rocks.

SUPER FAMILY
## LITTORINOIDEA

FAMILY
## LITTORINIDAE
(Periwinkles)

The periwinkles are a group of smallish shells numbering some 100 species – certain authorities suggest fewer – some of which inhabit rocky shores, while some are to be found in mangroves. They are vegetarian and feed on seaweed and algae. The group is divided into several subfamilies, such as *Littorininae* and *Tectariinae* (in both of which we have an interest here) and is further divided into many genera. The family as a whole is not of great interest to amateur collectors.

**LITTORINA LITTORALIS**
Dwarf Periwinkle. *L. 1758.*
North Atlantic.

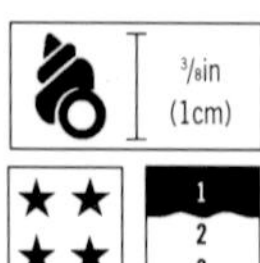


Another species found on both sides of the Atlantic on rocky coastlines, the dwarf periwinkle is a very rounded small shell with a flat spire and a greatly enlarged body whorl. It is generally smooth in texture, but very fine growth striae are to be seen on close examination. Shells are very variable in colour, only some of the range being depicted here.

**LITTORINA SCABRA ANGULIFERA**
Angulate Periwinkle. *Lamarck 1822.*
Caribbean and Queensland, Australia.

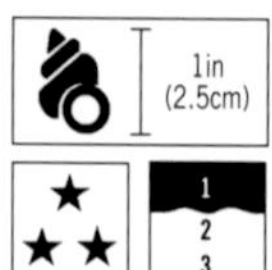


Possibly two local variations exist: the Caribbean forms appear to be generally mottled, whereas the two depicted here, which are from Yeppoon, Queensland, bear no patterning and are very lightweight, with sharp spiral ribbing. Although angular by name, they tend to have generally rounded whorls.

**_LITTORINA COCCINEA_**
Scarlet Periwinkle. *Gmelin 1791.*
Central and South-West Pacific.

A relatively high spire and large angulate body whorl distinguish this species, which is mostly smooth and has no patterning. The colour can be white, beige or lilac, and the aperture is presumably scarlet when alive, the colour later fading to a pale orange.

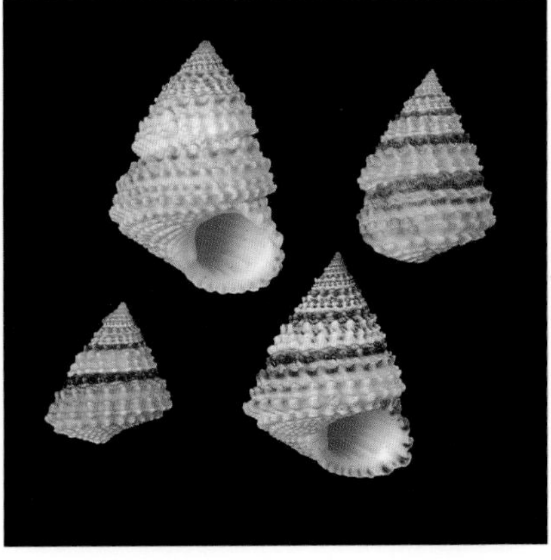

**_TECTARIUS CORONATUS_**
Beaded Prickly Winkle. *Valenciennes 1832.*
Philippines.

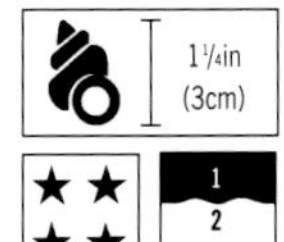


A solid conical shell, it has spiral bands of coarse rounded nodules. The colours vary from overall cream or apricot to forms with strongly contrasting bands of orange and purple or pale and dark grey. They live on intertidal rocks.

SUPER FAMILY
CERITHIOIDEA

FAMILY
## CERITHIIDAE
(Cerith Shells)

Most species of this major family are small. They are widely distributed in shallow, tropical seas, very few being found in European seas. All are vegetarian, living on diatoms and plant detritus, and they inhabit sandy substrates, often in large colonies. They are generally long, tapering shells with many whorls, some with distinct sculpturing and patterns. In most species, the lower edge of the aperture develops an angled siphonal canal. The numerous genera include *Cerithium*, *Aluco* and *Rhinoclavis*.

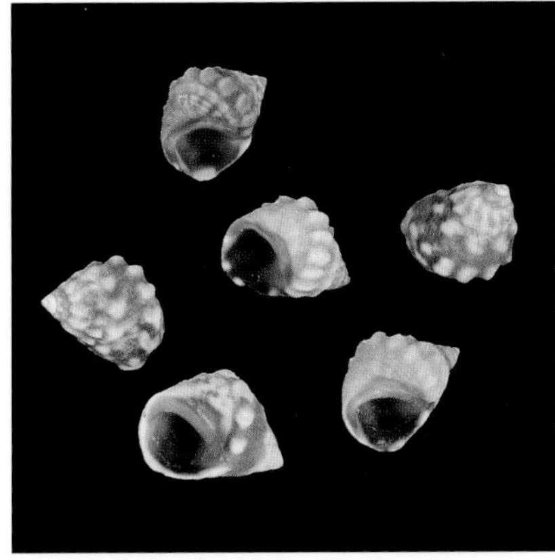

**_NODILITTORINA PYRAMIDALIS_**
Knobbly Periwinkle. *Quoy and Gaimard 1833.* Western Australia.

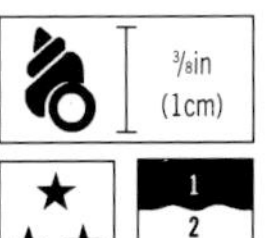


This tiny conical shell has an enlarged body whorl and two spiral rows of rounded nodules, which give rise to its common name. The colour is a pale beige or brown, the nodules being cream. The aperture is a light orange brown.

**_TECTARIUS PAGODUS_**
Pagoda Prickly Winkle. *L. 1758.*
South-West Pacific.

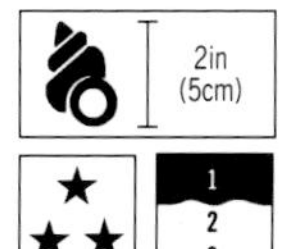


A large heavy species, with a moderate spire, it has rows of coarse uneven spiral cords, some oblique and axial, ending in blunt spines. The base is convex, with a smooth white columella. There are spiral ridges inside the lip. The overall colour is a pale brownish grey. This shell inhabits rocks above the high-tide line.

**_CERITHIUM NODULOSUM_**
Giant Knobbed Cerith. *Bruguière 1792*
Indo-Pacific.

Possibly the largest species in the family, it has coarse spiral cords with blunt heavy nodules. The white shell is decorated with spiral dashes and a mottling of brownish black. There are grey or black spiral lirae on the aperture wall. The depicted shell is slightly juvenile – in adults, the lip is usually thickened and white.

## CERITHIUM MUSCARUM

Fly-specked Cerith. *Say 1832.*
Southern Florida and West Indies.

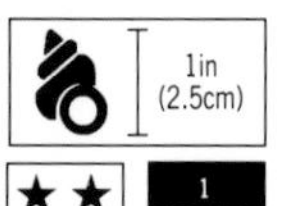

A small slender species, with coarse spiral nodules, it is middle-to-dark brown. The nodules, which in some shells are joined axially into ridges, are off-white. This is a shallow-water species – the two depicted were collected from Tarpoon Beach, Florida.

## CERITHIUM ERYTHRAEONENSE

Red Sea Cerith. *Lamarck 1822.*
Red Sea.

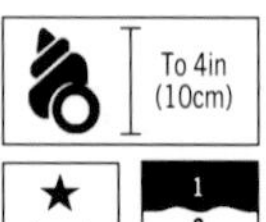

Rather similar in shape and texture to C. *nodulosum*, the Red Sea cerith varies in having an off-white background with light brown axial stripes. The aperture is pure white and the crenulate lip curves and crosses over the canal at an angle of about 90 degrees. A shallow-water dweller; this specimen is from Jeddah.

## CERITHIUM NOVAEHOLLANDIAE

New Holland Cerith. *Sowerby 1855.*
Northern Australia.

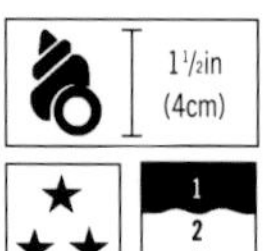

A medium-sized cerith, this species has stepped whorls, each bearing rows of axial rounded ridges. There is a neat little ovate operculum. The aperture is white, and the overall colour of the shell is cream, with a broad light brown spiral band around the lower half of each whorl. It is found in shallow water.

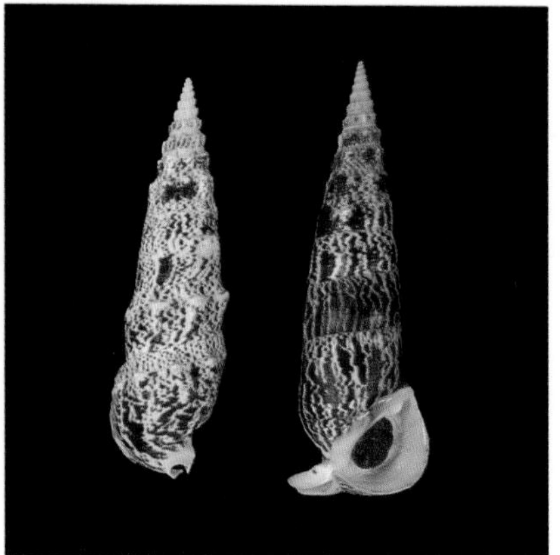

## CERITHIUM CUMINGI

Cumming's Cerith. *A. Adams 1855.*
Western Australia.

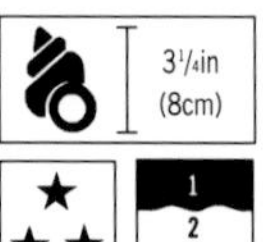

In markings and size this species is not unlike *P. aluco*, but is smoother with less prominent nodules on the whorls. The two depicted shells are both from Port Hedland, Western Australia. The shell is off-white, with mainly axial zigzag stripes and lines of dark grey or brown.

**PSEUDOVERTAGUS ALUCO**
Aluco Cerith. *L. 1758.*
South-West Pacific.

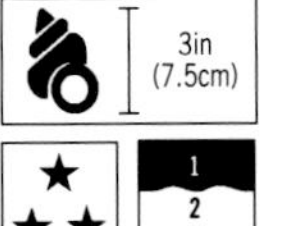

A heavy robust shell, it can have either smooth or nodulose whorls. The beige background is overlaid with many small flecks and patches that are dark brown to black. The aperture is off-white with yellowish margins. It is found in intertidal waters, in sand.

**RHINOCLAVIS FASCIATA**
Striped Cerith. *Bruguière 1792.*
Indo-Pacific and Australia.

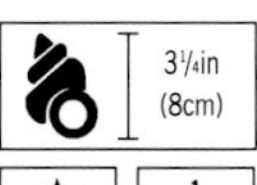

The striped cerith has a tall slightly convex spire, with about 13 or 14 whorls, mainly flat-sided, and a distinct outward-curving siphonal canal. It is white, with variable spiral bands of cream, brown and black, and inhabits subtidal waters down to about 50 feet (15m). The specimens shown here are from Queensland, Australia.

**RHINOCLAVIS BITUBERCULATA**
Bituberculate Cerith. *Sowerby 1855.*
Northern Australia.

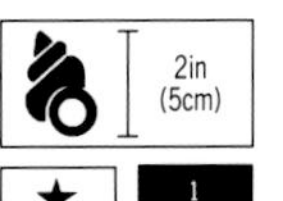

A coarse chalky shell in appearance, it has a moderate spire and slightly convex sides. There is a row of rounded nodules, arranged spirally below the suture, and one or two narrow flat spiral ridges. A pale beige colour is evident between the sculpturing. It inhabits intertidal waters.

**PSEUDOVERTAGUS CLAVA**
Club Vertagus. *Gmelin 1791.*
Polynesia.

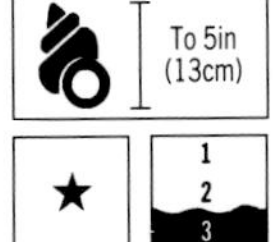

One of the larger species in the family, its impressive shell is tall, with straight-sided whorls, the body whorl being rather flat at the anterior end. There are axial rows of low rounded nodules and incised spiral grooves. The colour is cream, with haphazard lines and patches of mid-brown. It lives in sand at depths to 132 feet (40m).

**RHINOCLAVIS SINENSIS**
Obelisk Cerith. *Gmelin 1791.*
Indo-Pacific.

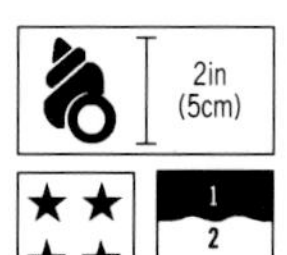

This dainty shell has a high sheen, and very fine spiral grooves, interspersed with three or more rows of cords. Below the suture are prominent fairly sharp nodules. It is beige in colour, with spiral flecks and dashes of middle-to-dark brown. There are also odd pale grey or brown patches, irregularly placed. It is a shallow-water dweller. This specimen was taken from Rarotonga Atoll, Cook Islands.

**RHINOCLAVIS GEMMATUM**
Gem Cerith. *Hinds 1844.*
Western Central America.

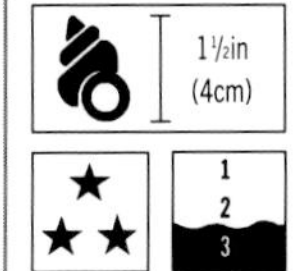

A small lightweight species, with a tall slender spire, the gem cerith is ornamented with beaded spiral ribs, and the columella has a fold near the base. The shell is white, marbled and spotted with mid-brown. It lives in depths of as much as 330 feet (100m). This particular specimen was collected from Gubernadora Island, Panama.

SUPER FAMILY
CERITHIOIDEA

FAMILY
## CAMPANILIDAE
(Bell Clappers)

This was once a very large family of at least 700 species, all but one of which are known only from fossil remains. Many of these were found in the Paris Basin, France. One particular species grew to a length of at least 20in (51cm) – *Campanile giganteum*. The sole survivor, *C. symbolicum* is vegetarian and lives in a very restricted area in South-western Australia.

SUPER FAMILY
CERITHIOIDEA

FAMILY
## POTAMIDIDAE
(Horn Shells or Mud Creepers)

A group of shells of varying size, primarily brown in colour and more or less pointed and conical, they differ from the ceriths in that the outer lip of the aperture tends to be larger and expanded and the siphonal canal is short. They inhabit warm, muddy brackish waters in large groups and feed on marine detrital matter and algae. There are several genera, including *Cerithidea*, *Telescopium* and *Terebralia*.

**TELESCOPIUM TELESCOPIUM**
Telescope Shell. *L. 1758.*
Indo-Pacific.

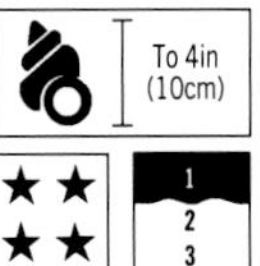


A curious and popular shell, its sharply tapering sides define a perfect spiral, with numerous pronounced grooves and flat ridges which are alternately cream and dark brown in colour. The columella is strongly twisted and the lip is extended at the anterior. It inhabits mangrove mud flats.

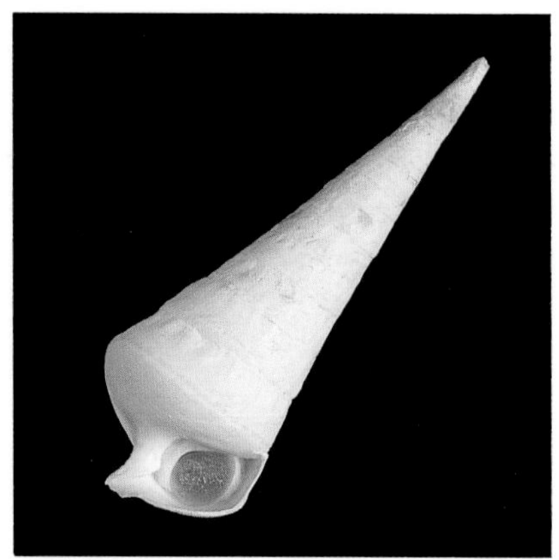

**CAMPANILE SYMBOLICUM**
Bell Clapper. *Iredale 1917.*
South-western Australia.

There is only one genus in the Campanilidae family, and this, the only surviving species, is endemic to South-western Australia. The odd chalky white appearance gives it a fossil-like look. The spire is tall and has somewhat concave sides, the whorls bearing faint spiral grooves. There is no patterning. The glossy white columella is rather twisted.

**PYRAZUS EBENINUS**
Ebony Mud Creeper. *Bruguière 1792.*
Eastern Australia.

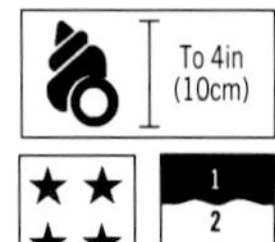


Dark brown to black, with fine spiral ridges, it has pronounced axially arranged nodules on a tall spire. The aperture is white on the columella but dark brown on the outer edge, and there is an upward fold at the posterior. Shells live in colonies on mud flats.

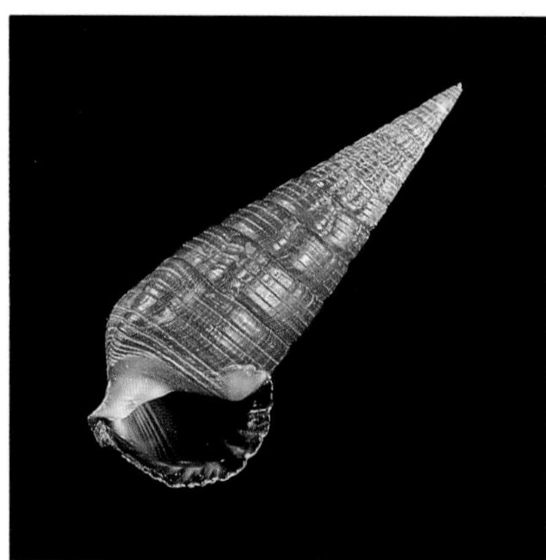

**TEREBRALIA PALUSTRIS**
Mud Creeper. *L. 1767.*
Indo-Pacific.

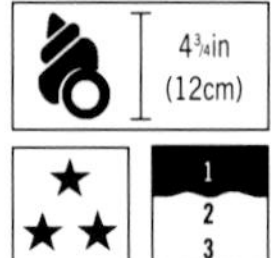


A large species, with flat axial ribs and rows of spiral grooves, the mud creeper has a flaring aperture which is shiny inside, with black spiral striae. The columella is creamy white. The outer colour is a mid-brown. This is another mangrove mud-flat dweller.

**TYMPANOTONUS FUSCATUS**
West African Mud Creeper. *L. 1758.*
Central West Africa.

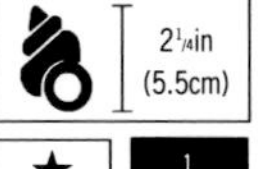

2¼in (5.5cm)

This beautifully ornamented shell has a tall slender spire. Rows of small rounded spiral tubercules and most prominent sharp and slightly upturned nodules characterize this species. The variety *T. fuscatus radula* lacks the sharp nodules, but is covered with spiral tuberculose beading. The spires are usually partly eroded. Both forms are shown here, and both samples come from Sazaire, Angola.

**MESSALIA OPALINA**
Opal Screw Shell. *Adams and Reeve 1850.*
West Africa.

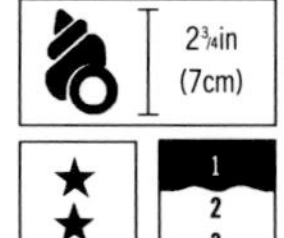

2¾in (7cm)

This is a solid shell, with well rounded whorls and one spiral groove below the suture. It is off-white, with tan-coloured axial streaks. The aperture and columella are white. This particular specimen is from Senegal.

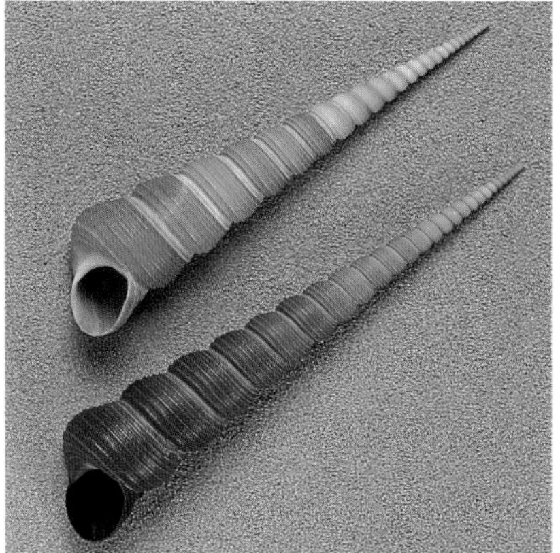

**TURRITELLA TEREBRA**
Common Screw Shell. *L. 1758.*
Indo-Pacific.

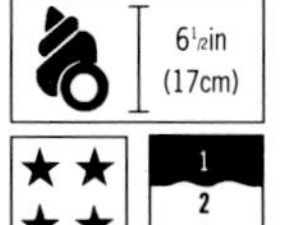

6½in (17cm)

Mature specimens of this beautiful tall shell, which has a perfect spiral, can have up to 30 whorls. There are fine rounded spiral ribs and the colour is generally middle-to-dark brown. The operculum is circular and horny. This screw shell is a shallow-water dweller, found in sandy mud.

SUPER FAMILY

## CERITHIOIDEA

FAMILY

## TURRITELLIDAE

(Screw Shells)

Two main genera within this family concern us here – *Turritella* and *Vermicularia.* The former genus are the true screw shells and have very tall spires and regular tightly coiled whorls, whereas the latter begin with several regular whorls and then suddenly grow in a haphazard and quite unruly direction. Neither type possesses a siphonal canal. There are over 100 species, all of which are vegetarian, and inhabit offshore waters in coarse sand or mud. This is not a particularly popular family with collectors.

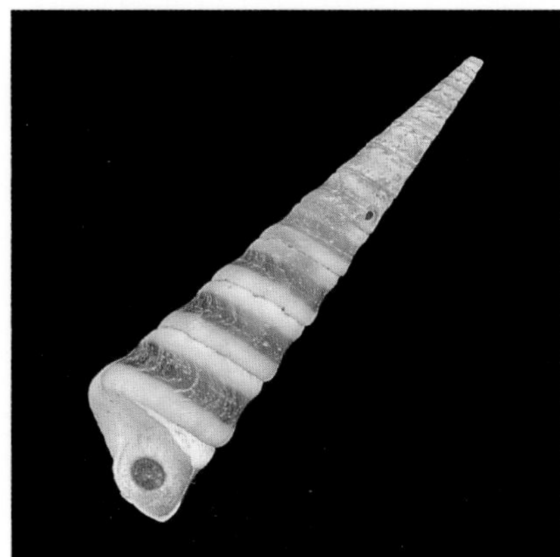

**TURRITELLA DECLIVIS**
Girdled Screw Shell. *Adams and Reeve 1850.*
South Africa.

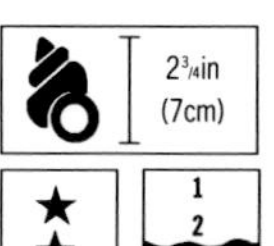

2¾in (7cm)

A relatively small and lightweight species with about 12 whorls, each slightly concave, it is off-white, with a broad brown spiral band running around the centre of each whorl. The operculum is very small – perhaps ⅛in (3mm) – and round. This species lives in deep water, as far down as 575 feet (175m).

**TURRITELLA DUPLICATA**
Duplicate Screw Shell. *L. 1758.*
Indian Ocean.

4¾in (12cm)

Not unlike *T. terebra*, this aptly named shell is, however, shorter and much more solid and heavy. The rounded whorls bear two distinct parallel rows of spiral ribbing, and this shell is also paler in colour. It lives in subtidal sand. This specimen comes from Sri Lanka.

### *TURRITELLA CINGULATA*

Banded Screw Shell. *Sowerby 1825.*
Chile.

A short solid species, it is cream in colour, with several rows of broad dark brown spiral bands. The whorls are generally straight sided and number between eight and ten. It lives in subtidal waters. The shell depicted here was fished at Tongoy, Chile.

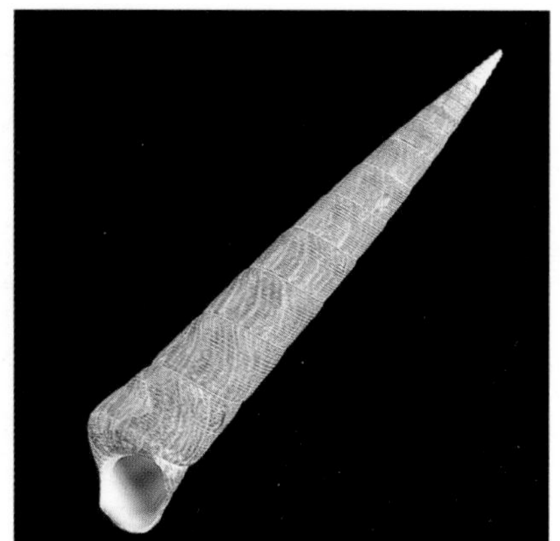

### *TURRITELLA BRODERIPIANA*

Broderip's Screw Shell. *Orbigny 1847.*
Western Central America.

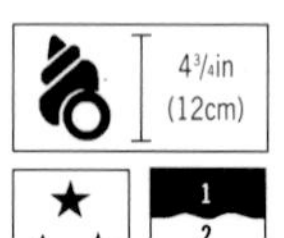


A fairly tall solid shell, with almost straight-sided whorls, it has many very fine spiral grooves and several axial growth lines. The colour is pale brown or cream, with dark brown axial streaks and "flames". The aperture and columella are white.

### *TURRITELLA LIGAR*

Ligar Screw Shell. *Deshayes 1843.*
West Africa.

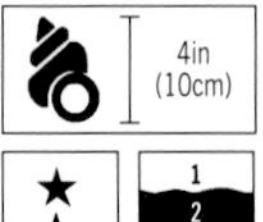


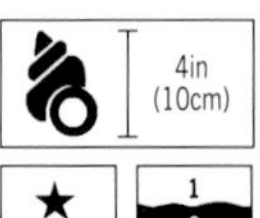

This species has a moderately tall spire comprising about 17 rounded whorls with strong rounded spiral ridges. It can be beige, off-white or pinkish, with pale grey axial patches. This particular shell was fished at 50 feet (15m), and comes from Casamance, Senegal.

### *TURRITELLA TORULOSA*

Projecting Screw Shell. *Kiener 1843.*
West Africa.

3in
(7.5cm)

Delicate and lightweight, it has about 14 whorls bearing coarse rounded spiral ribs, and is cream to beige with brown axial bands and zigzag lines. The operculum is rounded, with fine concentric lines. The shell shown here was found at a depth of 17 feet (5m), in Baie de Hann, Senegal.

**TURRITELLA CONSPERSA**
Angled Screw Shell. *Adams and Reeve* 1850. West Africa.

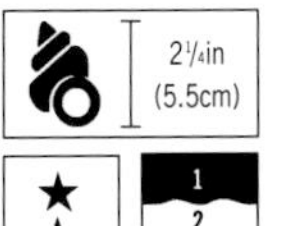

A medium-sized turritella, it has about 14 angled whorls bearing two spiral rounded ribs. The top third of each whorl is patterned with axial lines or "flames" of russet brown on an overall cream background. There are very fine axial growth striae throughout. A shallow-water dweller, often found in Senegal.

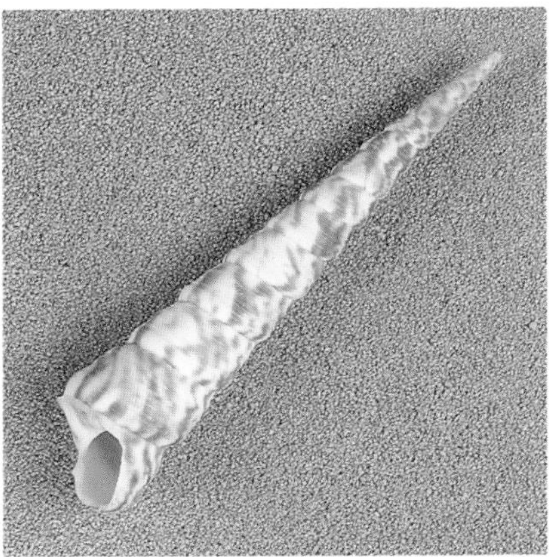

**TURRITELLA RADULA**
Dart Turritella. *Kiener 1843.* Gulf of California to Mexico.

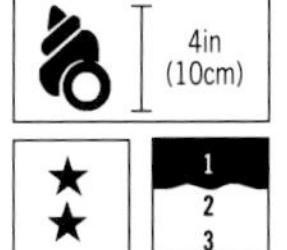

The dart turritella is a fairly tall species, with at least 18 spirally ribbed whorls. The suture is slightly impressed. The colour is cream with conspicuous tan wavy axial lines and blotches. A subtidal sand dweller.

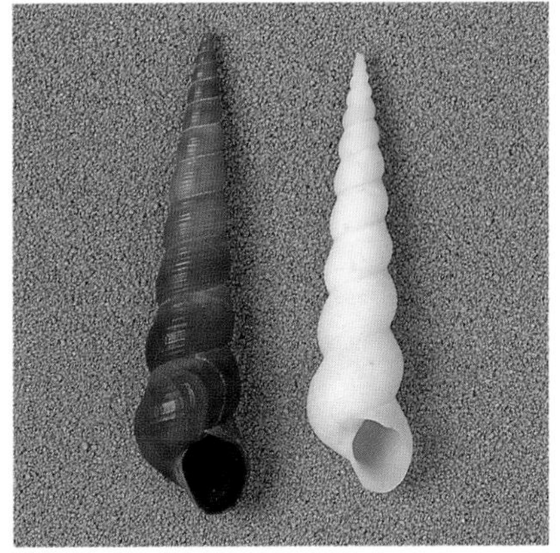

**TURRITELLA UNGULINA**
Rounded Screw Shell. *L. 1758.* West Africa.

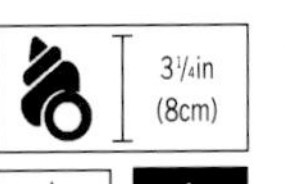

A robust species, its well rounded whorls – about 14 on mature specimens – bear fine spiral ribs. The colour varies from pure white through to a near black, most being middle-to-dark brown. This shell is often used in local native jewellery.

**TURRITELLA GONOSTOMA**
Angle-mouthed Screw Shell. *Valenciennes 1832.* Western Central America.

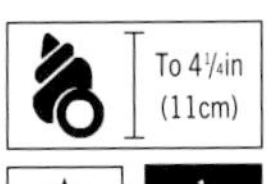

Similar in shape to *T. broderipiana*, it is slightly smaller, and perhaps the suture is more impressed and the pattern – a cream background with large axial patches and streaks of dark grey or black – is more evident. There are very fine spiral striae. The aperture is somewhat angular, following the shoulder line of the body whorl.

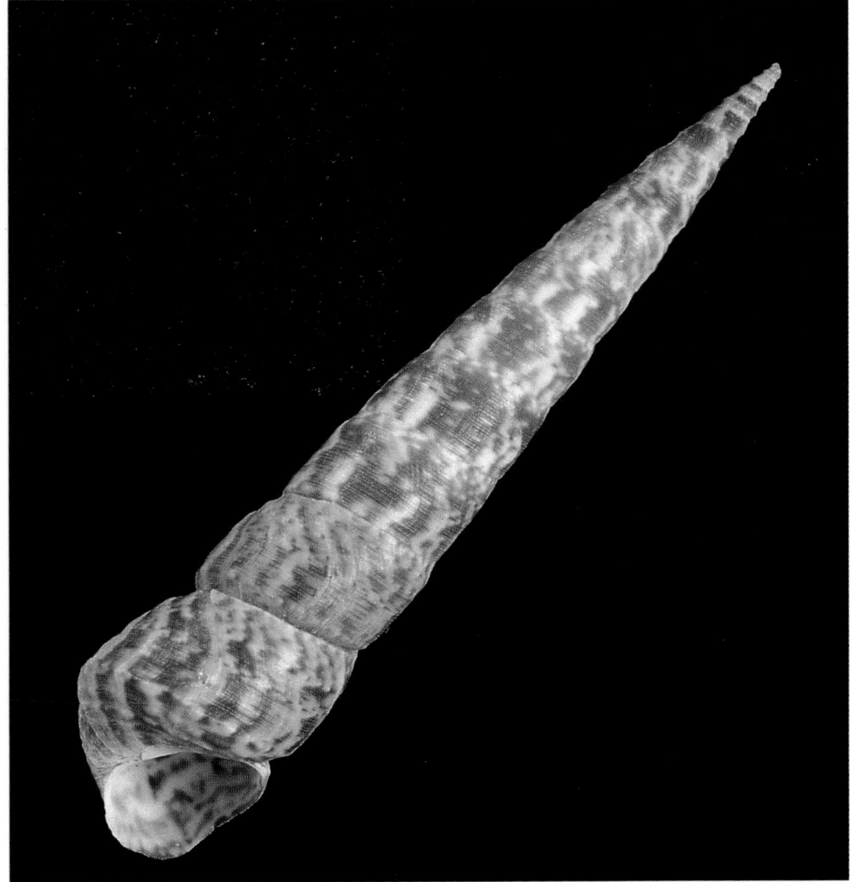

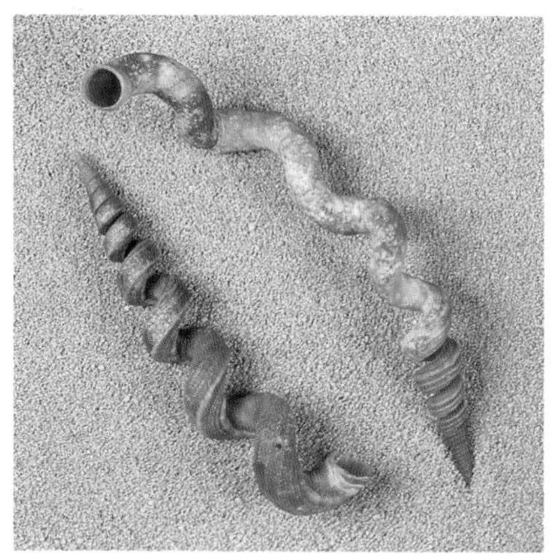

**VERMICULARIA SPIRATA**
Caribbean Worm Shell. *Philippi 1836.*
Southern Florida and Caribbean Sea.

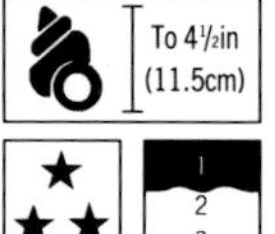

For obvious reasons, the common name is very apt. The shell in its early growth period starts very much like other turritellas, but after about six whorls the growth becomes open and haphazard. There are two or three spiral ribs which are not evident nearer the aperture. The shells live among sponges in shallow water.

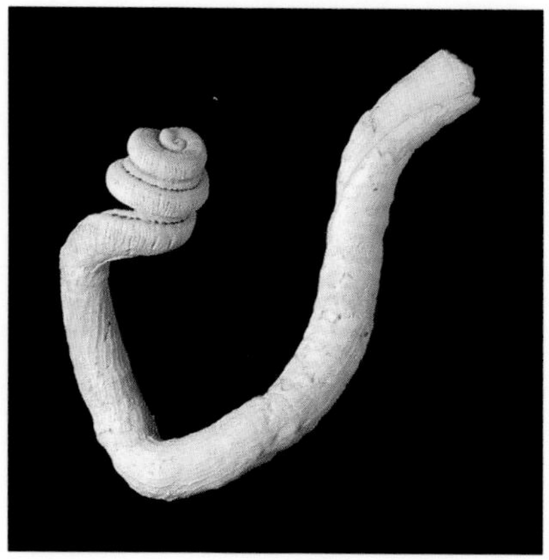

**SILIQUARIA PONDEROSA**
Giant Worm Shell. *Mörch 1860.*
Taiwan, Indo-Pacific.

This bizarre species is a popular collectors' item. Large flatly-coiled early whorls grow out into strange haphazard forms, taking no set shape. The sculpturing is scaly and off-white, with many growth lines and scars. The open slit is more evident on the earlier growth, becoming somewhat covered with age. This specimen was fished off Taiwan.

SUPER FAMILY

STROMBOIDEA

FAMILY

## APORRHAIDAE

(Pelican's Foot Shells)

A small family of about six species, the pelican's foot shells occur in the cooler waters of the North Atlantic and Mediterranean. The outer lip bears characteristic finger-like processes from which the common name derives. Many strangely shaped fossil species are known. The living species are fairly mobile and are mainly sand dwellers.

SUPER FAMILY

CERITHIOIDEA

FAMILY

## SILIQUARIIDAE

(Worm Shells)

Although previously placed with the genus *Vermicularia*, these worm shells are now within a family of their own. They differ from the former group in that they produce virtually no spire, but a kind of tubular chamber. The early whorls are often flat or depressed and, where these two grow in a haphazard manner, there is a distinct slit or opening running along the entire length of the shell, except at the apex. They often live in colonies on substrate.

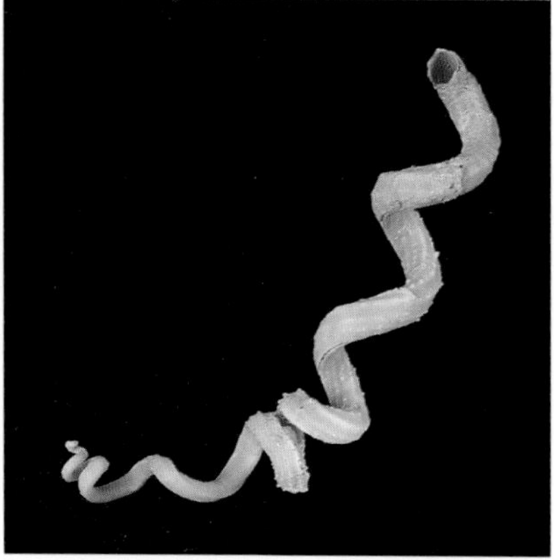

**SILIQUARIA CUMINGI**
Scaled Worm Shell. *Mörch 1860.*
Taiwan to Philippines.

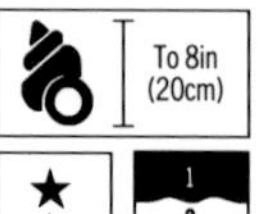

Another greatly distorted species, it is finer than *S. ponderosa*, and has several spiral ribs on which are small scaly projections. The slit is evident through the entire length of the shell. The dirty pink or beige surface is often lime-encrusted.

**APORRHAIS PESPELICANI**
Common Pelican's Foot. *L. 1758.*
Mediterranean to Norway.

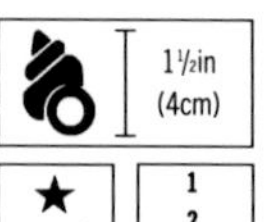

Coarsely sculptured, with angled and nodulose whorls, its extended and thickened lip bears four projections – one growing alongside the spire, two growing outward and the fourth forming the siphonal canal. The colour is generally cream or off-white. The aperture, columella and interior of the processes are often calloused and glazed. It inhabits relatively deep water, to about 575 feet (175m).

**APORRHAIS SENEGALENSIS**
Senegalese Pelican's Foot. *Gray 1838.*
West Africa.

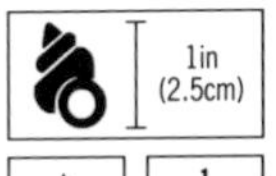


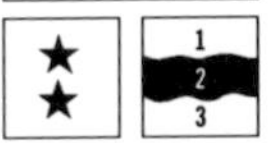


This is the smallest member of the family. It has a medium-sized spire and each whorl bears spiral rounded nodules. It has three projections and a narrow siphonal canal. The shell is a beige brown. The specimen seen here came from Gabon.

**APORRHAIS OCCIDENTALIS**
American Pelican's Foot. *Beck 1836.*
Eastern Canada to North Carolina.

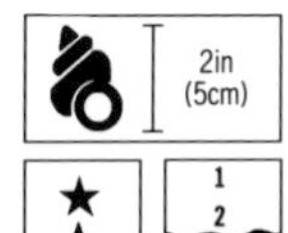


The thickest and heaviest of the group, this shell inhabits deep water to about 1,980 feet (600m). It is usually heavily encrusted or eroded but some ornamentation – coarse axial ribs and fine spiral lirae – can be seen. The thickened outer lip does not bear projections as in the other aporrhais. This specimen was dredged off Maine, USA.

**APORRHAIS PESGALINAE**
African Pelican's Foot. *Barnard 1963.*
South-West Africa to Angola.

A delicate and lightweight shell, it has long narrow projections and angular whorls. There are very fine spiral lirae and the colour is beige or light brown. On the whorl shoulders is a row of fine cording. The columella, parietal wall and lip margins are calloused and shiny white.

**APORRHAIS SERRESIANUS**
Mediterranean Pelican's Foot.
*Michaud 1828.* Mediterranean.

Although similar to *A. pesgalinae*, this is smaller, usually white or off-white and has four projections, two of which are partly joined, and a siphonal canal. There are three spiral rows of nodulose ribbing on the body whorl and one row thereafter to the apex. This specimen was collected at 120 feet (36m), off Elba.

SUPER FAMILY
STROMBOIDEA

FAMILY
## STROMBIDAE
(Conch Shells)

This is a large, well-known and diverse family. *Strombus* possess what is known as the stromboid notch – an indentation at the anterior end of the aperture through which the animal can protrude its stalked eye. The operculum is seldom large enough to close the aperture but is often used as an aid to mobility or as a defensive weapon against predatory crustaceans and fish. The *Lambis* all have flaring lips with long digit-like projections, siphonal canal and a pronounced stromboid notch. The *Tibia* species, however, are generally fusiform, with extended canals, curved anal canals and tall multi-whorled spires. The two species of *Varicospira* discussed are not unlike *Tibia* species, but with short canals, while *Terebellum* bear little resemblance to the true conches. All species are vegetarian.

### LAMBIS TRUNCATA
Giant Spider Conch. *Humphrey 1786.*
Indo-Pacific.

This is the largest species in the genus. The spire is depressed and appears truncated; the body whorl is long and ovate, and the wide flaring lip bears six long finger-like digits, all of which are grooved on the interior. The siphonal canal is long and the stromboid notch is prominent. The overall colour is off-white to beige, with irregular patches of a pinkish brown on the underside of the body whorl. The aperture is creamy brown and smooth, and the columella and parietal area are calloused. It inhabits shallow waters.

### LAMBIS WHEELWRIGHTI
Wheelwright's Spider Conch. *Greene 1978.*
Philippines.

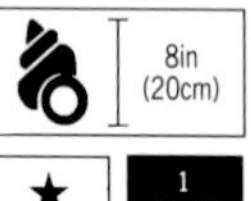


Many experts believe this to be a hybrid between *L. millepeda* and *L. truncata*, and it certainly bears characteristics from each! The digits are short, and there are rounded nodules on the whorls. The aperture is a pale pinkish orange, with darker streaked lirae inside. The columella and spire are calloused.

### LAMBIS LAMBIS
Common Spider Conch. *L. 1758.*
Indo-Pacific.

One of the most well known of shells, this differs from *L. truncata* in that it is much smaller and has large rounded nodules on the body whorl. Of the two depicted specimens, the deep orange form is a rarer, larger variation from Western Australia. The female is generally larger and has longer projections.

**LAMBIS CHIRAGRA CHIRAGRA**
Chiragra Spider Conch. *L. 1758.*
Indo-Pacific.

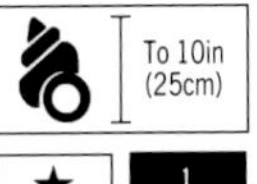


This is a large shell, with five large closed hollow digitations, all of which are curved, except the one nearest the spire. The siphonal canal projects at right angles to the axis of the shell. There is a large stromboidal notch. The outer colour is white, with mottled or zigzag axial lines, the aperture being a pale pink or yellow.

**LAMBIS VIOLACEA**
Violet Spider Conch. *Swainson 1821.*
West Indian Ocean.

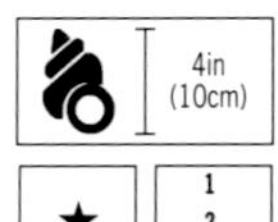


This sought-after collectors' item is one of the rarest in the genus and is usually fished off Mauritius in fairly deep water. There are about 12 short open digits; these are slightly longer at the posterior, the last two being "joined" (bifurcated). The body whorl bears quite coarse rounded spiral ribs and several blunt nodules; the aperture is white and spirally lirate and inside is a beautiful violet stain. The columella bears a low raised hump at the anterior.

**LAMBIS CROCATA CROCATA**
Orange Spider Conch. *Link 1807.*
Indo-Pacific.

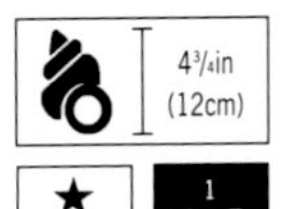


The aperture of this vividly coloured species is a rich orange. There are six long thin closed digits, some touching each other, and the siphonal canal is long, slender and curved. The body whorl is bulbous and supports both fine and coarse spiral ribs, some of which bear blunt nodules. It is a coral reef dweller.

**LAMBIS CHIRAGRA ARTHRITICA**
Arthritic Spider Conch. *Röding 1798.*
East Africa.

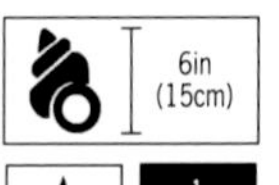


Resembling *L. chiragra chiragra*, but much smaller, the body whorl of this shell is rather bulbous and bears very strong rounded ribs. The hollow digits are relatively short and curved and the columella and parietal area is strongly lirate. There is dark brown or purple staining around the aperture of the mottled brown shell. It inhabits coral reefs.

**LAMBIS MILLEPEDA**
Millipede Spider Conch. *L. 1758.*
South-West Pacific.

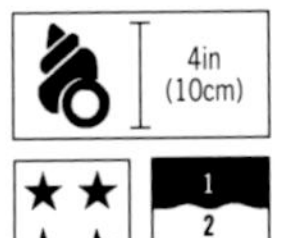


The millipede spider conch has a short spire and a large spirally-ribbed body whorl, on which occur odd blunt nodules. There are nine closed hollow digits extending toward the posterior, and both sides of the aperture are strongly lirate. The exterior colour is beige brown, with a pale greyish pink in the aperture. The shell is deep orange inside.

**LAMBIS SCORPIUS SCORPIUS**
Scorpion Spider Conch. *L. 1758.*
Western Pacific.

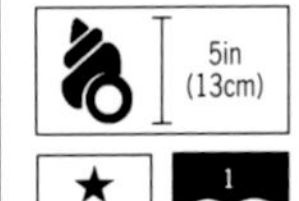


A dramatic shape and deep colouring make this a popular shell among collectors. The slender crimped digits are closed and rather flat, and are most striking; the exterior is coarsely ribbed, and there are many rounded nodules. The inner lip bears strong spiral striations, tinged between with deep purple; the columella is also striated, but has a dark brown background colouring. This conch lives on coral reefs.

**LAMBIS DIGITATA**
Finger Spider Conch. *Perry 1811*.
South-East Africa.

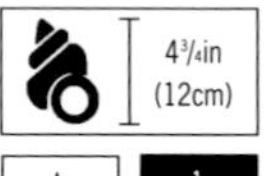

An unusual species, with very coarse spiral ribs and nodules, it displays an overall mottling of brown on a cream background. The eight or so closed digits are short, with the exception of the last two at the posterior end; the one nearest the spire is bifurcated. There are distinctive white raised lirae set against a dark purple black on both the columella and the inner lip. The interior of the shell is a beautiful deep yellow.

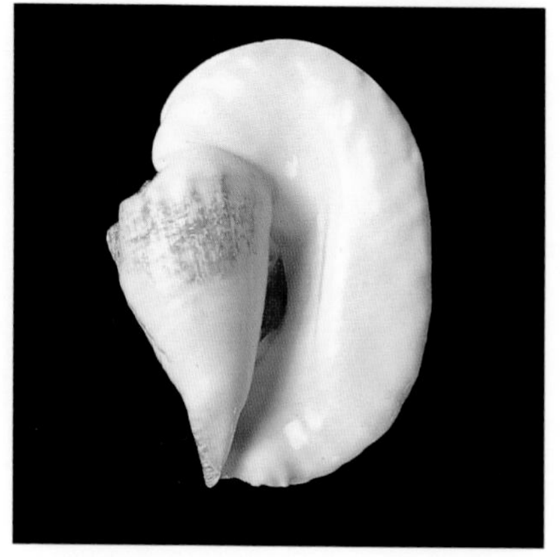

**STROMBUS GOLIATH**
Goliath Conch. *Schröter 1805*.
Brazil.

A collectors' favourite, this endemic is the largest species of the genus. The outside of the spire is low, sharply pointed and has slightly concave sides. There is a row of low blunt spiral nodules on the shoulder of the body whorl. The lip is huge and flaring and inside, along with the columella and parietal area, it is calloused. The exterior is a beige brown and the inside is a creamy peach.

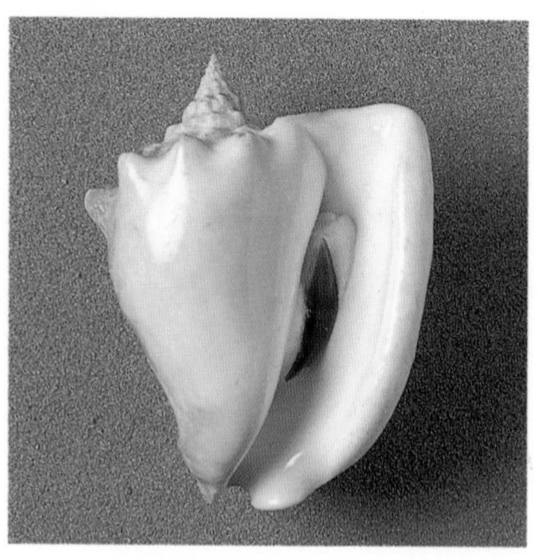

**STROMBUS COSTATUS**
Milk Conch. *Gmelin 1791*.
Southern Florida, Caribbean, to Brazil.

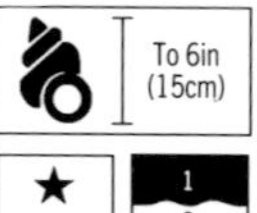

A short but robust shell, it has a low spire and small rounded nodules on the shoulders which extend outward in longer projections on the body whorl. There is a fine brown periostracum, under which the shell is beige. The whole of the off-white interior is calloused. A shallow-water dweller.

**STROMBUS GIGAS**
Queen Conch. *L. 1758*.
Southern Florida and Caribbean.

This shell is prized for its size and colour and as a major seafood. It is one of the largest in the group, with a wide flaring lip. The spire is low and the shoulders of the whorls bear blunt protruding nodules, which are particularly large on the body whorl. The species occasionally produces pink pearls, and the shell can be used, after the apex has been removed, as a type of trumpet (the conch trumpet in Golding's *Lord of the Flies*). It is found in shallow water, on sandy substrates.

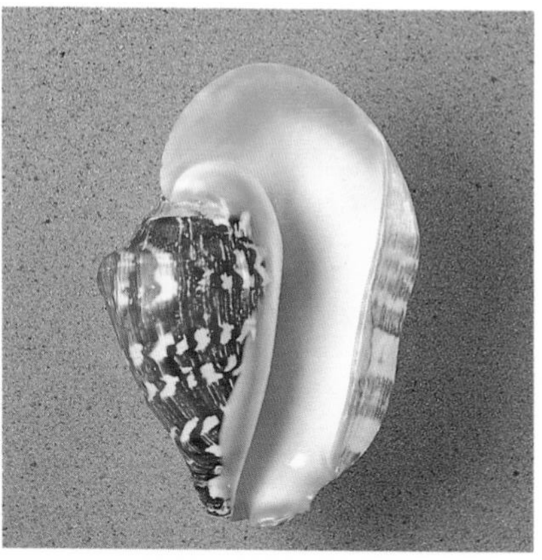

**STROMBUS LATISSIMUS**
Wide-mouthed Conch. *L. 1758*.
West Pacific.

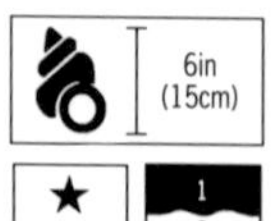

The solid and very heavy shell has a wide flaring lip, which is much thickened at the margins, opposite the columella. The spire is low and partly obscured by the posterior part of the lip. Shells are generally encrusted with marine deposits, but when clean they are a pale or middle shade of brown, with axial lines and blotches which become darker and more vivid on the underside of the body whorl. The aperture interior is white. The shell seen here is from the Central Philippines.

**STROMBUS PERUVIANUS**
Peruvian Conch. *Swainson 1823*.
Western Central America.

Another heavy species, this has a short concave spire, a bluntly nodulose body whorl and a large thickened lip, which extends at the posterior into a longish curved projection. The canal is relatively short and the stromboid notch is pronounced. The exterior is brown, whereas the highly glossy and calloused interior is a pale orange pink. There are spiral grooves at the top of the columella and slight bumps and ridges on the lip margin. This particular shell is from Panama, and was collected in a low-tide pool.

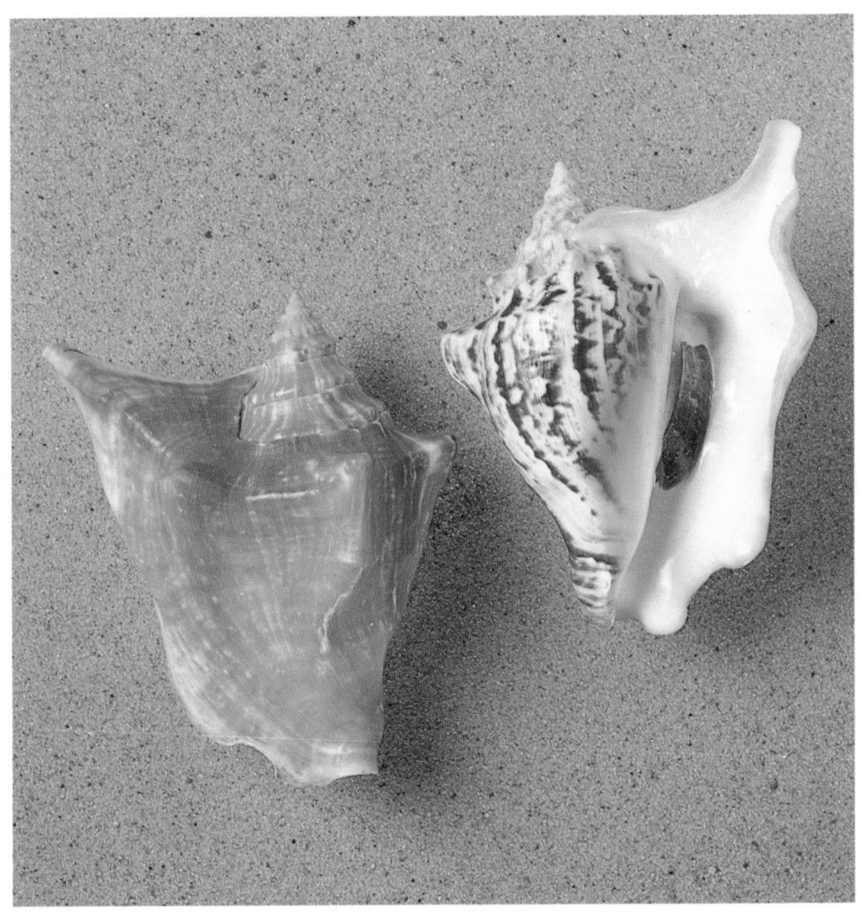

## STROMBUS TRICORNIS

Three-knobbed Conch. *Lightfoot 1786.*
Red Sea and Gulf of Aden.

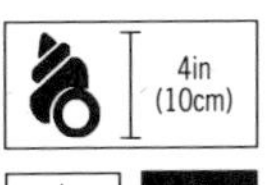

Although there are many rounded nodules on the shoulders, there are usually two or three that are larger, and it is from these that the common name is derived. A smaller conch, it has a wide lip that extends into a finger-like projection at the posterior. Colours and patterns vary greatly. It is found in shallow water on sand and is endemic.

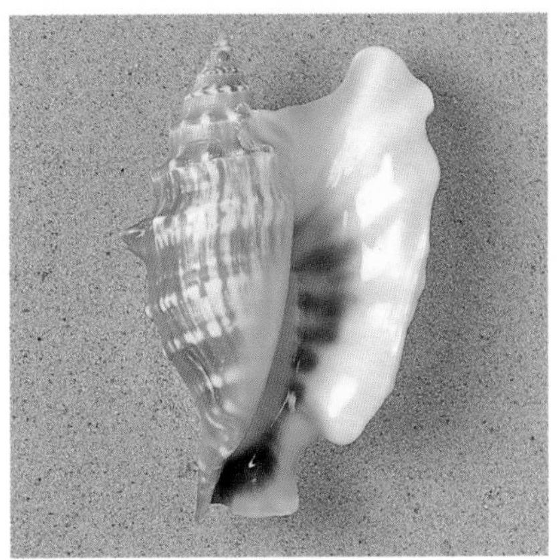

## STROMBUS OLDI

Old's Conch. *Emerson 1965.*
Somalia, East Africa.

1
2
3

This rare species has only become available in appreciable numbers in the last few years and is much sought-after by strombus enthusiasts. The spire is moderate and the body whorl long and rather convex. The lip is fairly thin and the margin extends at the posterior into a sort of projection rather like a tab; the notch is pronounced. There are strong rounded nodules on the body whorl and spiral ridges on the exterior of the lip. There are generally brown axial patches, and the aperture is a pink orange with dark brown stains.

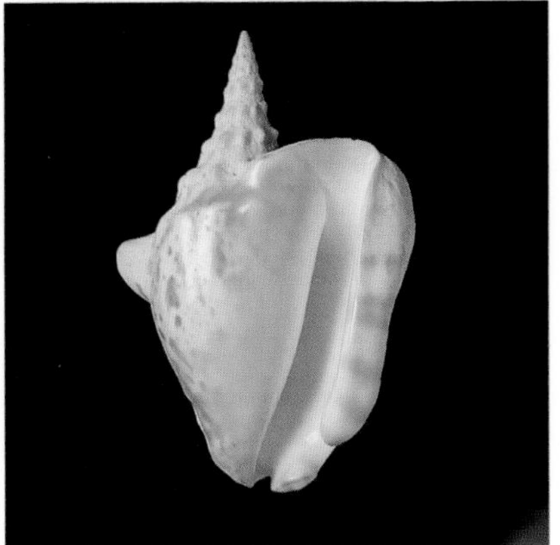

## STROMBUS THERSITES

Thersite Stromb. *Swainson 1823.*
South-West Pacific.

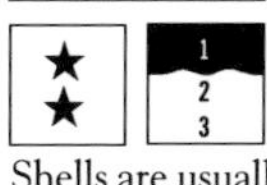


The thersite stromb is distinguished by a tall slender nodulose spire and a thick heavy rather flattened body whorl. The lip is much thickened at the margin. Shells are usually heavily encrusted, but cleaned specimens are off-white, with occasional russet axial "flames". The aperture and parietal wall are calloused and white. This species lives in shallow waters.

## STROMBUS LENTIGINOSUS

Silver Conch. *L. 1758.*
Indo-Pacific.

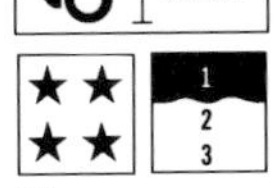


A shallow-water dweller, found in sand, it has a coarsely sculptured exterior with heavy blunt nodules on the body whorl. The spire is low, and there are strong spiral ribs. The aperture and underside is prettily patterned with irregular grey and brown patches on a yellow cream background. On the rather crenulated lip edge are about eight broad grey broken bands.

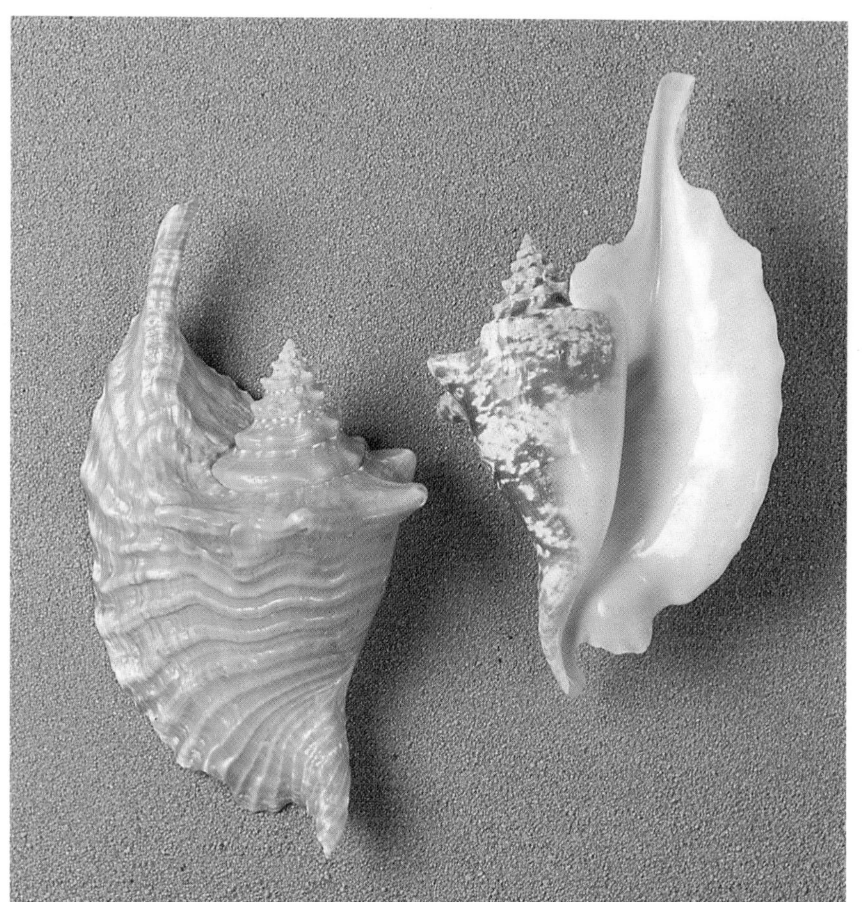

## STROMBUS GALLUS
Rooster Tail Conch. *L. 1758.*
Caribbean to Brazil.

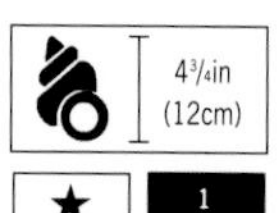

A distinctive shell, it has a very pronounced process which extends upward from the posterior lip margin, suggesting a rooster's tail. The relatively low spire is nodulose and the shoulder of the body whorl bears four or five strong high rounded nodules. The lip margin is slightly undulating. Two of many colour forms are shown here, both coming from Haiti.

## STROMBUS LISTERI
Lister's Conch. *T. Gray 1852.*
Eastern India to Thailand.

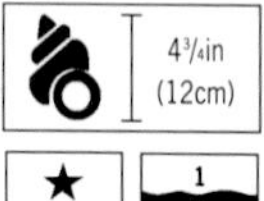

Since the early 17th century and up until possibly the 1970s, this species was said to be one of the most rare and desirable of the genus. Now, shells have fallen to a mere fraction of their former value and are to be found in virtually every conchologist's cabinet. This tall rather thin elegant shell lives in moderately deep water.

## STROMBUS SINUATUS
Laciniate Conch. *Lightfoot 1786.*
South-West Pacific.

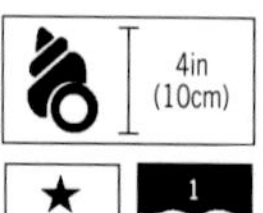

This is a lovely shell, with attractive colouring, a moderate spire, and a long convex body whorl. The outer lip, thickened opposite the columella, extends at the posterior with four or so short rounded tab-like projections. The shell is off-white, with russet axial striations and blotches. The aperture is pale pink, with deep purple staining. The specimen shown here was collected on coarse coral sand in shallow water, Central Philippines.

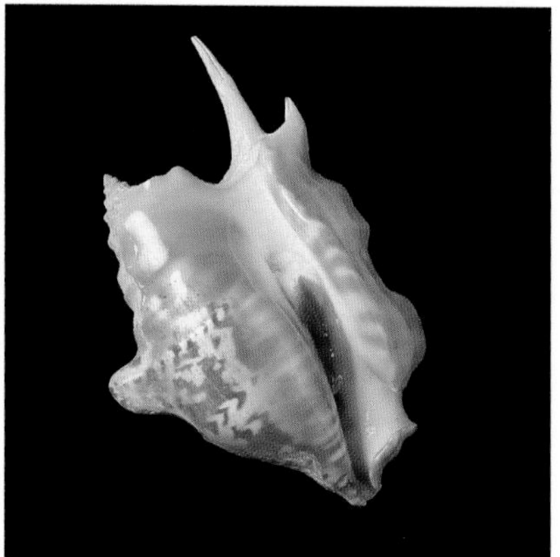

## STROMBUS TAURUS
Bull Conch. *Reeve 1857.*
Marshall Islands.

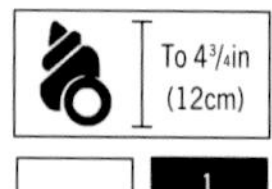

A rare collectors' item, the bull conch is a solid thick shell, rather flattened. The exterior is often encrusted and there are several coarse rounded nodules. The underside is heavily calloused and "lumpy". The lip margin is much thickened, with a tall sharp spine at the posterior. The shell has an orange brown staining and wavy axial lines. There is a vivid magenta tinge inside the aperture. It inhabits fairly shallow water and is endemic.

**STROMBUS CANARIUM**
Dog Conch. *L. 1758.*
South-West Pacific.

A solid chunky shell, it has a wide size range, most adult specimens growing to about 2in (5cm). Only exceptionally do they reach the size quoted here. The spire is low and concave; the body whorl enlarged and bulbous. The lip is thickened marginally and can be slightly upturned at the posterior. Shells are generally beige brown, with fine axial streaks, lines and zigzag marking. The larger of the two shown is from the Philippines, the smaller coming from the New Hebrides.

**STROMBUS GRANULATUS**
Granulated Conch. *Swainson 1822.*
Western Central America.

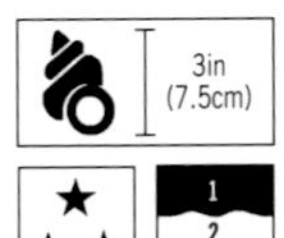


The granulated conch is rather tall and slender, with strong tubercules and rough spiral ribs. It features broad bands of brown on white. The aperture is white, and fine granulations occur on the inside of the lip in mature specimens. The margins are tinged with creamy yellow, as is the parietal wall. This specimen is from Gubernadora Island, Panama.

**STROMBUS EPIDROMIS**
Swan Conch. *L. 1758.*
South-West Pacific.

A bulbous rounded shell, its moderate spire is formed of angular whorls that are smooth in texture, although early whorls bear minute spiral striae and axial ribs. The shell is off-white, overlaid with a fine pale brown "netting" pattern. The aperture is pure white and highly glossy. A shallow-water dweller, it is found in mud or sand.

**STROMBUS PUGILIS**
West Indian Fighting Conch. *L. 1758.*
Florida and Caribbean.

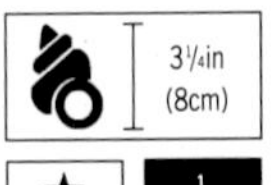


This is a short but rather wide and angular shell, with pronounced sharp nodules on the shoulders. The variation *S. pugilis alatus* is to my mind a rather dubious species, although this name is usually applied to those shells with a purple interior. The orange form is the typical *S. pugilis*. Both are shown here.

**STROMBUS AURISDIANAE ARATRUM**
Brown-lipped Diana Conch. *Röding 1798.*
North-eastern Queensland and East Malaya.

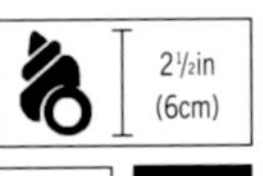


This is the lesser known subspecies of *S. aurisdianae*, varying in its interior colour, which is pale orange, with a darkly blotched calloused area above the parietal wall that extends two-thirds up the spire. The lip margins are edged in dark brown. The ornamentation is coarse, with spiral ribs and nodulated shoulders.

**STROMBUS VOMER VOMER**
Vomer Conch. *Röding 1798.*
South-West Pacific.

This is an attractive species, its tall spire and angular whorls bearing a row of spiral nodules that are virtually coronated. The shell is slender, with a wide lip extending at the posterior into a long finger-like projection, and is off-white, with pale orange mottled markings. There are distinct spiral striae in the aperture, between which is orange tinting. A prominent dark brown blotch lies above the white calloused parietal wall. The canal extends upward at right angles to the shell body.

**STROMBUS URCEUS**
Little Bear Conch. *L. 1758.*
Western Pacific.

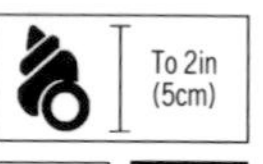


Some of this variable species have rounded whorls, while others have angular ones. There are fine striae at the anterior end of the body whorl and the inner lip bears fine spiral striae. Certain authors have been encouraged by the wide range of colour variations, a selection of which are shown here, to re-name some forms.

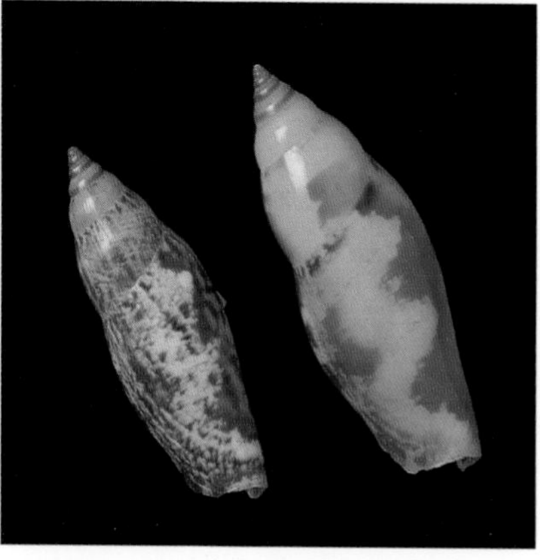

**STROMBUS TEREBELLATUS**
Little Auger Conch. *Sowerby 1842.*
South-West Pacific.

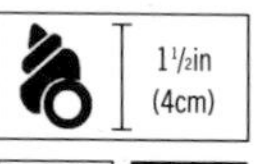


Not unlike *S. dentatus* in shape, it is generally taller and less rounded. The smooth shell is cream or beige, with irregular patches of darker red brown axial markings. There is little or no evidence of a stromboid notch.

**STROMBUS MINIMUS**
Minute Conch. *L. 1771.*
Western Pacific.

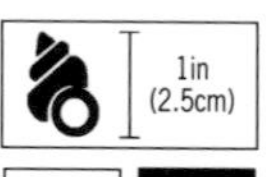


A small but solid shell, it has angulate shoulders and a thickened lip that extends at the posterior to the side of the spire, where it is met by an upward extension of a calloused columella, forming the anal canal. The exterior colour is basically brown; the aperture margins are white and the interior is yellow. It dwells in sand or mud, in shallow water.

**STROMBUS DENTATUS**
Toothed Conch. *L. 1758.*
Indo-Pacific.

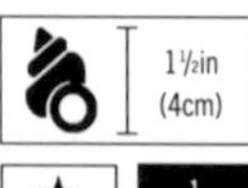


The toothed conch has whorls which bear rounded axial ridges. The lower margin of the lip is dentate and the columella is thickly calloused and white. The inner lip wall has strong spiral striae, stained black. Overall, the colour is a mottled orange brown and the texture is smooth. An inhabitant of coral reefs in shallow waters.

**STROMBUS MUTABILIS**
Mutable Conch. *Swainson 1821.*
Indo-Pacific.

A very variable little shell, it has a large angular body whorl and short spire. Patterns and colours vary enormously, two forms being shown here. Generally, the aperture is orange or pink with fine spiral striae extending in from a thickened lip. It inhabits shallow water in coral sand.

**TEREBELLUM TEREBELLUM**
Little Auger Shell. *L. 1758.*
Indo-Pacific.

These slim highly glossy and smooth shells bear little resemblance to true conchs. They are bullet-shaped and slightly convex, with short spires and an enlarged body whorl that is truncated at the anterior end. The patterns are highly variable – several forms are shown here. They inhabit subtidal sandy areas.

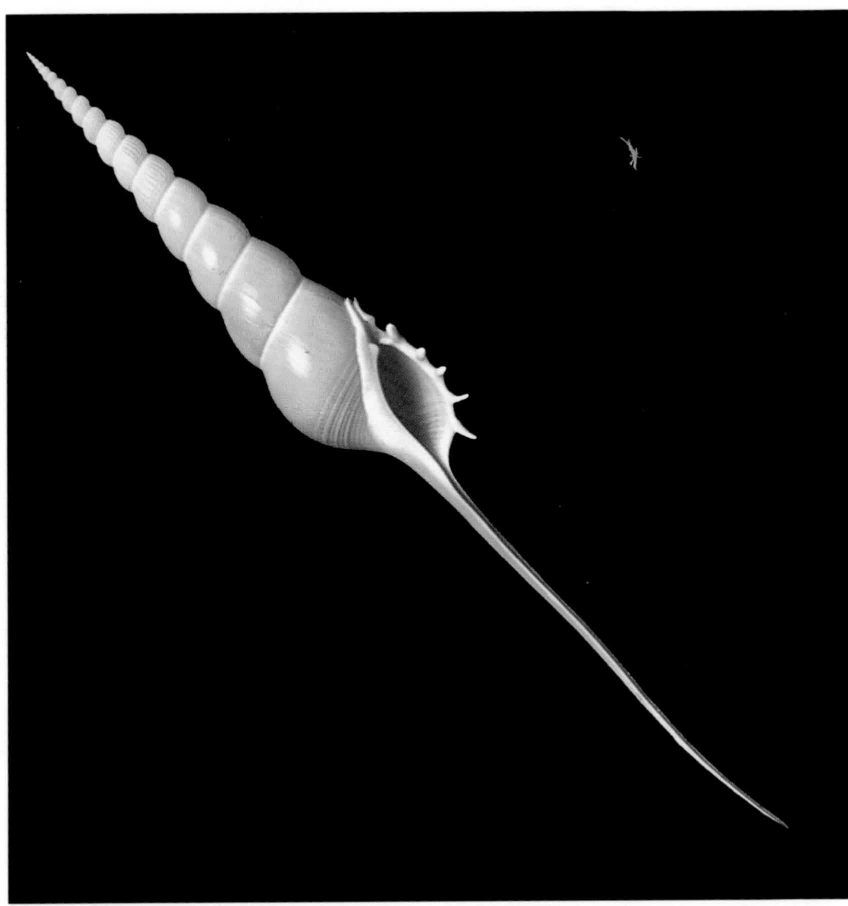

### *TIBIA FUSUS*
Spindle Tibia. *L. 1758.*
Philippines.

An incredible species and firm collectors' favourite, it has a very tall slender spire of about 19 whorls and a long narrow canal that may be either straight or gently curved. There are five finger-like projections on the lip margin and the anal canal is curved against the side of the body whorl in a semi-circle. There are fine axial ridges on the early whorls; otherwise the shell is smooth and pale golden brown. The aperture and columella are white. It is an inhabitant of moderately deep water.

### *TIBIA INSULAECHORAB*
Arabian Tibia. *Röding 1798.*
Indian Ocean.

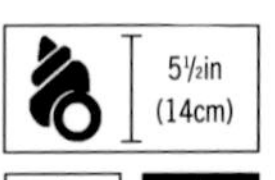


A solid thick and heavy shell, with a high spire, the Arabian tibia has gently rounded whorls and its body whorl is wide and bulbous. It has minute axial ribs near the apex and faint growth striae throughout. The siphonal canal is very short and slightly curved; the posterior canal of the sample shown here has grown against the spire for about 1in (2.5cm) and is heavily calloused. The overall colour is mid-brown and glossy, and there is a white aperture and columella. The lip margin bears six or seven stunted denticles.

### *TIBIA CURTA*
Indian Tibia. *Sowerby 1842.*
Indian Ocean.

Similar in appearance to *T. insulaechorab*, it is less bulbous and the siphonal canal is straighter and longer. The outer shell has a very smooth highly glossy texture with distinctive growth striae. It is a rich tan-brown, and some specimens have a broad dark brown spiral band below the suture. The aperture and columella are white. The lip margin bears about five short rounded projections. This specimen was collected off the South-East Indian coast.

### *TIBIA DELICATULA*
Delicate Tibia. *Nevill 1881.*
Indian Ocean.

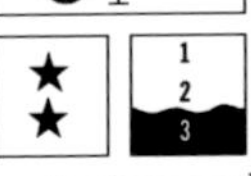


The delicate tibia is rather like a miniature *T. insulaechorab*, but with a quite different aperture. The canal is very short and slightly curved and there are about four short projections on the lip margin. The posterior canal is virtually non-existent. It is pale beige overall, with four cream thin spiral bands on the body whorl. The aperture is pale creamy white. This is a deep-water species.

### TIBIA MARTINI
Martin's Tibia. *Marratt 1877.*
Philippines.

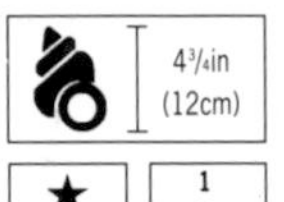


This generally thin and lightweight shell has rounded whorls and a fairly short straight siphonal canal. There are four or five very stunted denticles on the lip margin. A one-time rarity, it has now become readily available, due to deep-sea commercial fishing in the late 1960s.

### TIBIA POWISI
Powis's Tibia. *Petit 1842.*
Japan to Northern Australia.

A short narrow species, with a high spire, it has numerous spiral cords. The lip is thickened, white and prominently striate, and the margin bears four or so short sharp projections. The anal canal is curved but short; the siphonal canal is moderate. This deep-water shell is a pale beige colour.

### VARICOSPIRA CANCELLATA
Cancellate Tibia. *Lamarck 1822.*
Indo-Pacific.

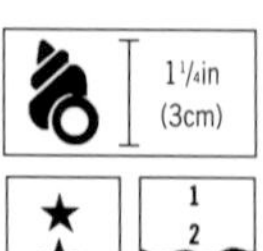


A small ovate shell, it has a moderate spire and rounded whorls. Fine spiral lirae are evident, as well as strong rounded axial ribs, these two features giving the shell its cancellate texture. The aperture is white; the siphonal canal short; and the anterior canal extends at least half-way up the side of the spire. This shell is found in offshore waters.

### VARICOSPIRA CRISPATA
Netted Tibia. *Sowerby 1842.*
Philippines.

A tiny delicate-looking species, its fine ornamentation of small rounded axial ribs and spiral bands give it a netted effect. The lip margin is thickened and serrated; the canal is short. The main colour is dull beige, with broad grey spiral bands that show through to the interior wall of the body whorl. This shell lives in deep water.

SUPER FAMILY
## CREPIDULOIDEA

FAMILY
## CREPIDULIDAE
(Slipper, Cup and Saucer Shells)

A relatively small group of gastropods, these are either rock dwellers or live on the backs of other shelled creatures. All possess either a shelf-like or a cup-shaped structure in order to protect the soft organs. They are generally flat, rounded or slipper-shaped and can be smooth, ridged or spiny. They are distributed globally, filter-feeding on vegetable matter. There are several genera and subgenera, notably *Crepidula, Calyptraea, Trochita* and *Crucibulum.*

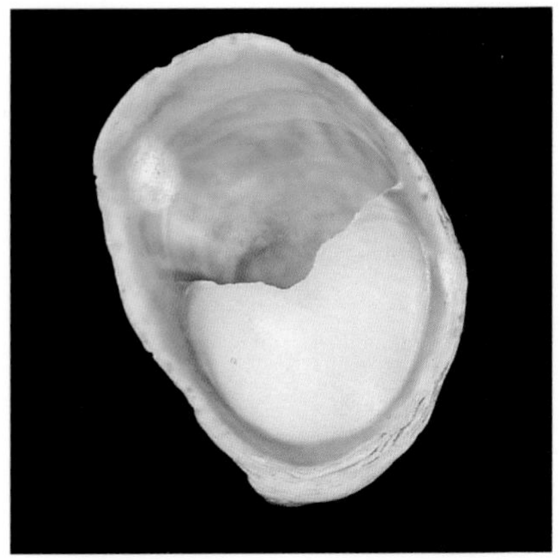

### CREPIDULA FORNICATA
Common Atlantic Slipper. *L. 1758.*
Eastern USA, North-East Atlantic coasts.

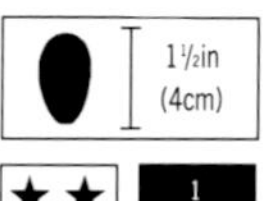

This is a subtidal, rock-dwelling species, which lives in colonies, many specimens crowded on top of each other. A flattish shell, it has little or no sculpturing save for growth lines and scars. The interior "shelf hair" is white; the exterior is beige or pale pink, with fine haphazard lines and zigzags.

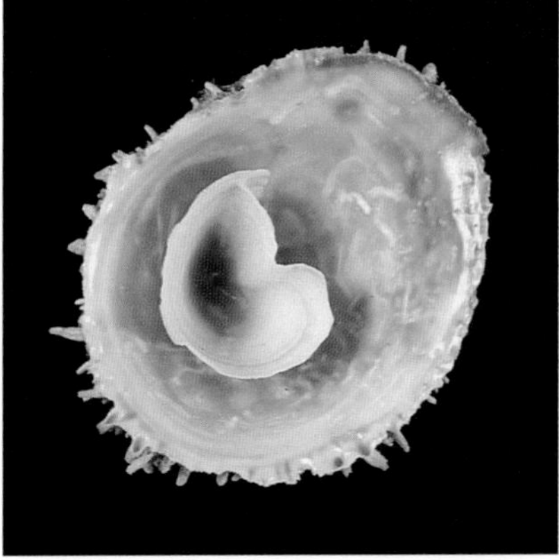

### CRUCIBULUM SPINOSUM
Spiny Cup and Saucer. *Sowerby 1824.*
Western Central America.

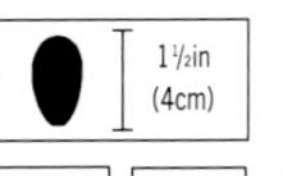

This is another irregularly shaped species that takes on the shape of its habitat. The rough dorsum is covered with coarse upturned sharp spines and is often encrusted. The apex is usually free of spines. It lives in depths down to 165 feet (50m).

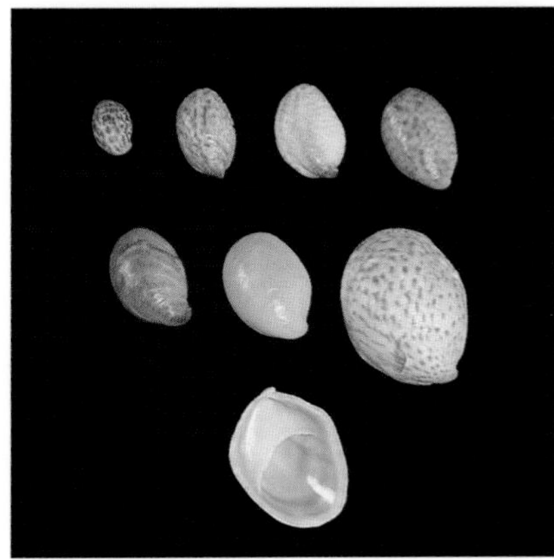

### CREPIDULA MACULOSA
Spotted Slipper Limpet. *Conrad 1846.*
Gulf of Mexico and Bahamas.

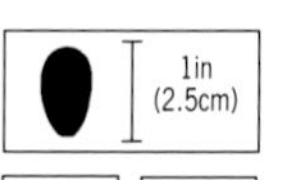

A small flat ovate species, it invariably lives on the backs of other shells. Colours and patterns vary, a selection being shown here. The small shelf-like structure occupies a third to half of the interior cavity. It is an inhabitant of subtidal waters, these examples coming from Yucatán, Mexico.

### CRUCIBULUM SCUTELLATUM
Shield Cup and Saucer. *Wood 1828.*
Western Central America.

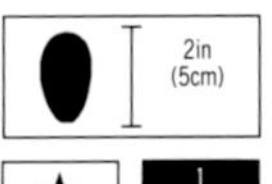

An irregularly shaped species, it tends to grow into the shape of the base – such as a rock crevice – in which it lives. The unencrusted dorsum has radial ridges, and the margin is usually crenulated. The interior "cup", which is often white against a darker background, is prominent. It is found in subtidal waters.

### TROCHITA TROCHIFORMIS
Peruvian Hat. *Born 1778.*
Western South America.

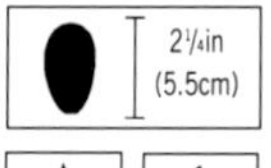

A rounded flattish shell, it is often heavily encrusted with marine debris. The dorsum, where obvious, is ridged. The underside is similar to trochus shells; the "shelf hair" area occupies at least half of the shell. An inhabitant of offshore rocks, this specimen is from Iquique, Chile.

SUPER FAMILY
XENOPHOROIDEA

FAMILY
## XENOPHORIDAE
(Carrier Shells)

One of the most fascinating families in the phylum Mollusca, these are truly the "original shell collectors"! The group is fairly small, with a single genus – *Xenophora* – which contains several subgenera, including *Stellaria*, *Tugurium* and *Onustus*. They are all basically trochoidal in shape, with flattish bases. The animal uses its foot to gather dead shells, pebbles, coral and marine debris and uses a secretion to cement these objects to its own shell. A few species of *Xenophora* do not collect material; nor do *Stellaria* species. There are several theories as to why this group covers itself with marine objects: camouflage against predators; to add strength and rigidity to a fragile shell; and to stop the carrier shell from sinking into muddy substrate. Measurements given are for mature shells without attachments.

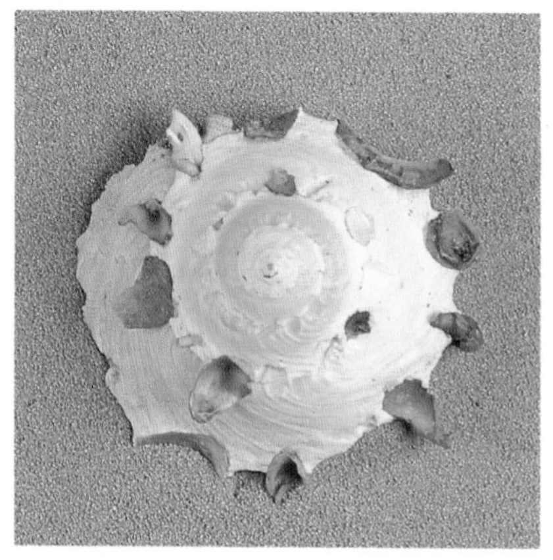

**TUGURIUM GIGANTEUM**
Great Carrier Shell. *Schepman 1909.*
South Africa and Japan.

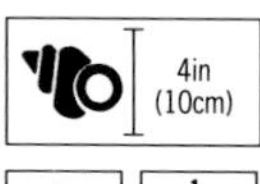


This large thin shell has flat sides and a broad base. Small shell fragments are attached along the suture and at the periphery of the body whorl. There are very fine axial growth striae and very fine radial striae on the underside. It is a pale beige or white colour. This specimen was dredged at 990 feet (300m) off Natal, South Africa.

**XENOPHORA PALLIDULA**
Pale Carrier Shell. *Reeve 1842.* Indo-West Pacific, Indian Ocean and South Africa.

A white conical shell, it has strong growth lines and indentations and fine wavy spiral lirae. The underside is slightly concave, with a wide half-circular aperture. It is one of the most spectacular of the genus, with many and various gastropod attachments and odd bivalves; in addition, it often bears large growths of sponge or soft coral. This specimen was collected in the central Philippines.

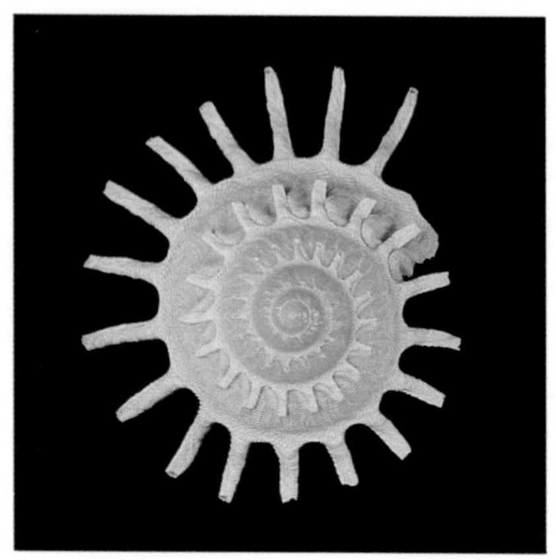

**STELLARIA SOLARIS**
Sunburst Carrier Shell. *L. 1767.*
Indo-Pacific.

The superbly attractive sunburst carrier bears no shells or attachments at all. It is conical, with a low spire and broad base. At the suture and body whorl periphery grow long flat thin projections – these are seldom all perfect. Its overall measurement includes the spines. The shell is covered with fine growth striae. The umbilicus is open and there is pronounced flat radial beading. This specimen was fished in deep water off south-western Taiwan.

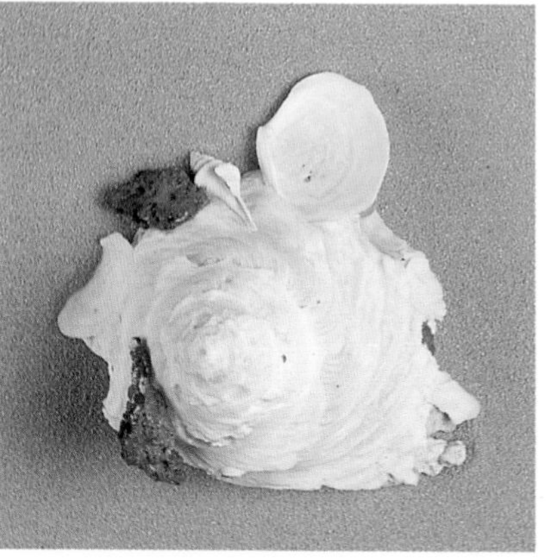

**TUGURIUM LONGLEYI**
Longley's Carrier Shell.
South-eastern USA and Caribbean.

One of the largest shells in the family, it has a fairly tall rounded spire and a wide gaping base, the periphery of which – usually with only a few attachments – far extends below and outward from the base proper; there is a deep open umbilicus. This carrier dwells in very deep water, as far down as 2,475 feet (750m).

**XENOPHORA CONCHYLIOPHORA**
Atlantic Carrier Shell. *Born 1780.*
South-eastern USA, Caribbean to Brazil.

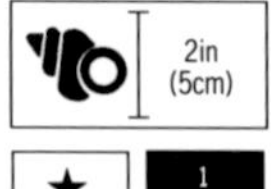


The underside of this rough conical shell is usually beige brown, with radial growth striae. Of the specimens I have seen the spire is, in all cases, completely covered. Usually the covering contains both rough and rounded stones and various attractive corals – occasionally the odd bivalve is attached. The depicted shells were collected in shallow water off Florida Keys.

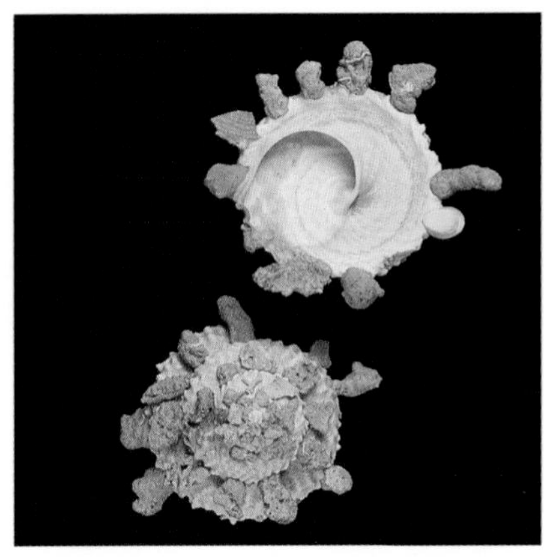

**XENOPHORA CORRUGATA**
Rough Carrier Shell. *Reeve 1843.*
Indo-West Pacific and Indian Ocean.

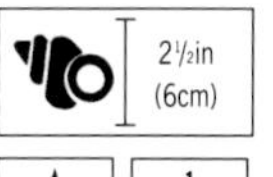

A conical white species, this is characterized by rounded heavily corrugated whorls. The underside is smoother, but still granular in texture. It appears to prefer rough stones and coral, with very few shell attachments. These two specimens are from Central Philippines.

**XENOPHORA JAPONICA**
Japanese Carrier Shell. *Kuroda and Habe 1971.* Japan to Philippines.

Rather delicate and lightweight, the Japanese carrier covers itself with broken bivalves, coral rubble and odd stones. The underside has very fine radial lirae and there is a horny ovate operculum. It is found in depths to about 990 feet (300m).

**XENOPHORA DIGITATA**
Finger Carrier Shell. *Von Marten 1878.*
West Africa.

This shell has very few, if any, attachments. It has a rounded conical spire and the periphery of each whorl bears short downward-pointing flat projections, the lowest ones holding the base above the muddy substrate on which it lives. The small umbilicus is open and there is a thin ovate horny operculum.

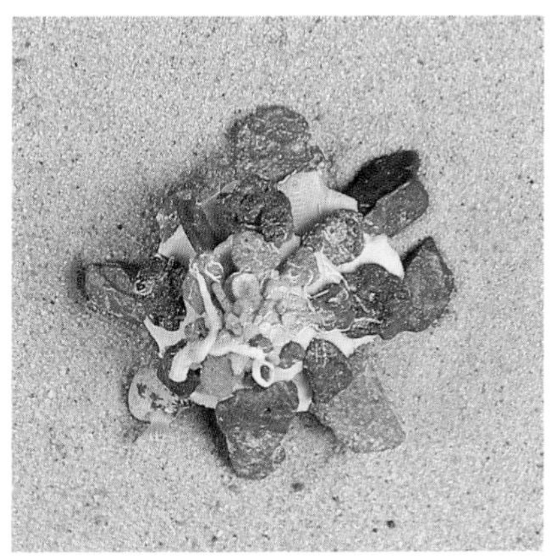

**XENOPHORA CRISPA**
Mediterranean Carrier Shell. *Koenig 1831.*
Mediterranean and North-East Atlantic.

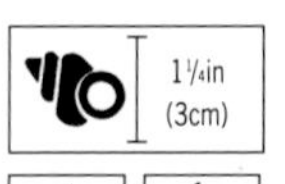

This small but solid conical shell has fine spiral lirae. These also occur on the underside, radiating from a part-open umbilicus. The creature collects smooth and rough pebbles. This shell was trawled at 215 feet (65m) off Malaga, Spain.

**XENOPHORA NEOZELANICA PERONIANA** Australian Carrier Shell. *Iredale 1929.* Southern and Eastern Australia.

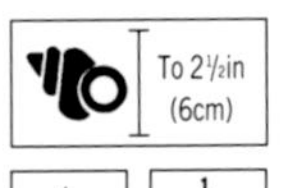

A smallish species with a rough beige conical shell, it has a slightly concave underside and the beige base has strong brown radial growth lines. The cover consists of stones, pebbles and corals. This specimen is from 360 feet (110m), Cape Moreton, Queensland.

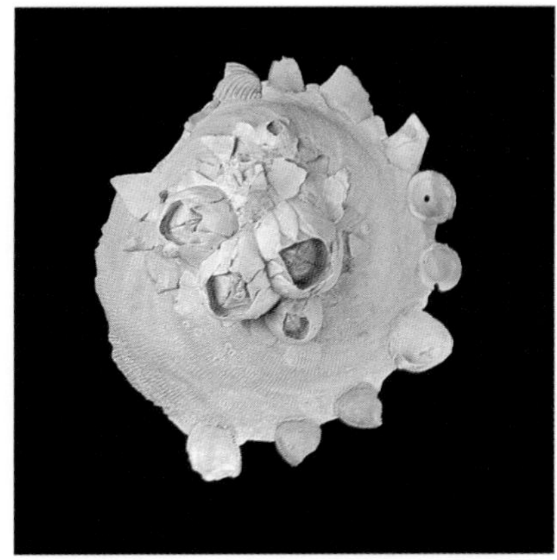

**XENOPHORA CALCULIFERA**
Fragment Carrier Shell. *Reeve 1843.*
Indo-West Pacific.

A rounded conical shell, with convex sides and broad concave base, it has fine diagonal lirae on the whorls and fine, spiral and radial grooves on the underside. The umbilicus is large and open. Small attachments – shells and barnacles in this case – are found around the apex and body whorl periphery.

SUPER FAMILY

CYPRAEOIDEA

FAMILY

## CYPRAEIDAE

(Cowrie Shells)

Among collectors, this is probably the most popular family of molluscs, possibly due to their very smooth, glossy porcelain-like texture and vivid patterning and coloration. It is a large group, in excess of 200 named species, with many varieties and local variations, and the number is constantly being augmented. There is one main genus, *Cypraea*, which over the years has been divided into many and various subgenera, taking into account differences of anatomy as well as shell structure. Kay Vaught lists 55 subgenera. However, for simplicity's sake this book will adhere to *Cypraea* throughout, although mention will be made of subgeneric names where necessary. The listed specimens are arranged approximately according to their global distribution.

### CYPRAEA CERVUS

Atlantic Deer Cowrie. *L. 1771.*
Florida and Caribbean.

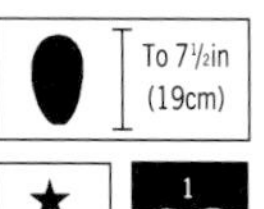


Although the largest species of the genus, it is rare nowadays to find specimens over about 6in (15cm). The shell is large, ovate and rather inflated but lightweight. It is mid-brown in colour, with pale grey dots which cease at the margins. There is a wide dorsal line. The prominent teeth are dark brown and more numerous on the columella lip. The interior is pale lavender.

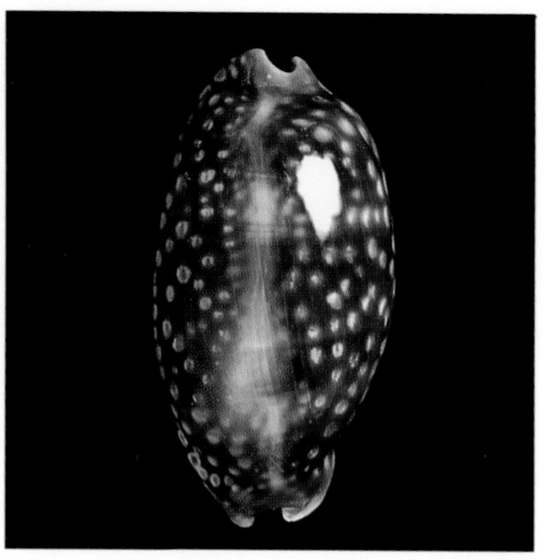

### CYPRAEA ZEBRA

Measled Cowrie. *L. 1758.*
South-eastern USA to Brazil.

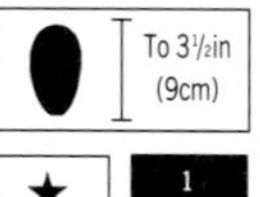


Sometimes confused with small *C. cervus*, this can be distinguished by its more slender, less inflated shape and more importantly by the occurrence of ocellated spots on the lateral margins. It is dark brown with grey spots and fairly coarse, almost black, teeth, especially on the outer lip. It dwells in shallow water.

### CYPRAEA CINEREA

Atlantic Grey Cowrie. *Gmelin 1791.*
South-eastern USA to Brazil.

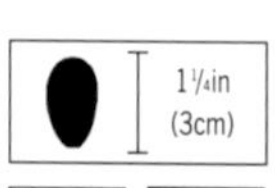


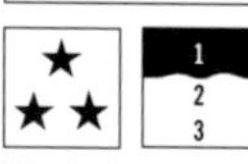


A sturdy little shell, with a rather humped dorsum and convex base, it has fine grooved teeth at either side of a curved aperture. The colour is a pinky grey, overlaid with black dots and blotches, more so at the margins, which are slightly inflated on mature specimens. This shell inhabits rocky reefs in shallow water.

**CYPRAEA ANNETTAE**
Annette's Cowrie. *Dall 1909.*
Western Central America.

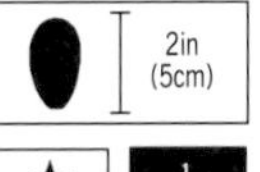

A distinctly marked shell, Annette's cowrie has a mottled brown-on-beige dorsum and pale brown base with white teeth. It is a slender ovate shape, with a convex base and relatively wide aperture, particularly at the anterior. It is found in shallow water, under rocks.

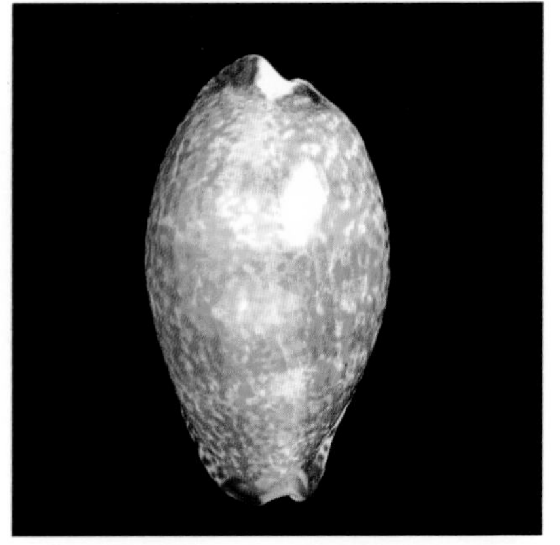

**CYPRAEA NIGROPUNCTATA**
Black-spotted Cowrie. *Gray 1828.* North-west South America and Galapagos Islands.

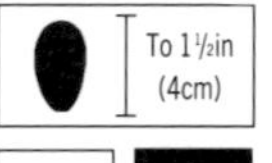

Although rather similar in shape to C. *annettae*, it has more pronounced extremities, posterior and anterior terminal spots, and dark brown or black spotting on and above the margins. The dorsum is pale grey overlaid with pale green reticulation at either side of a dorsal line that is usually wide. This has become rare, due to a ban on collecting that was imposed in 1983 in the Galapagos Islands, where it is fairly common.

**CYPRAEA LURIDA**
Lurid Cowrie. *L. 1758.*
Mediterranean to North and West Africa.

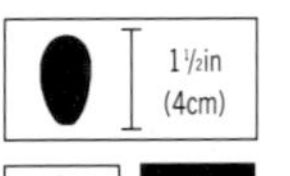

A well-known shell, the lurid cowrie is distinctly marked with prominent black posterior and anterior terminal spots. The dorsum is pale grey brown with two lighter spiral bands. The thickened margins are a pale creamy orange. The convex base is white, as are the short teeth. The dwarf variety, C. *lurida minima*, from West Africa, is also shown here.

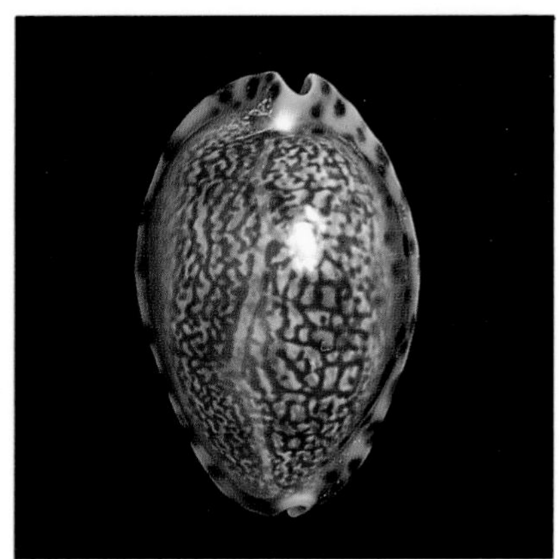

**CYPRAEA ARABICULA**
Little Arabian Cowrie. *Lamarck 1810.*
Western Central America.

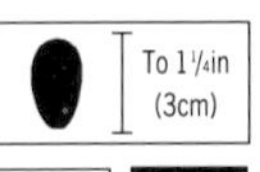

The humped dorsum, ovate shape and sharply defined margins provide the identification points of this little shell. The dorsal colour is pale green, overlaid with brown reticulation; the margins are pale grey with strong black spots. The flattish base is a pinkish beige, and the teeth are fine. It lives under rocks and slabs at low tide levels.

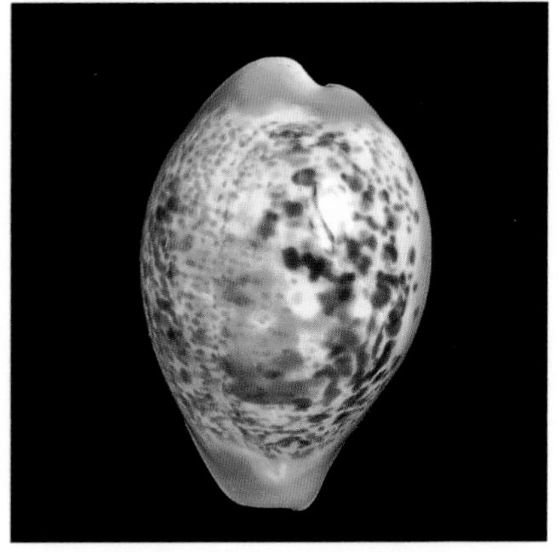

**CYPRAEA ACHATIDEA**
Agate Cowrie. *Sowerby 1837.*
North-West Africa to West Mediterranean.

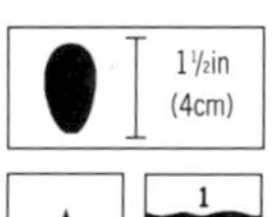

The rarest cowrie in this location, it is fairly lightweight, and is inflated and pyriform. It has pretty colouring – an off-white dorsum with irregular spots and blotches of tan-brown. The margins and extremities are a lovely pinkish orange, and the convex base is white. The teeth are very short and difficult to discern. An inhabitant of relatively deep water.

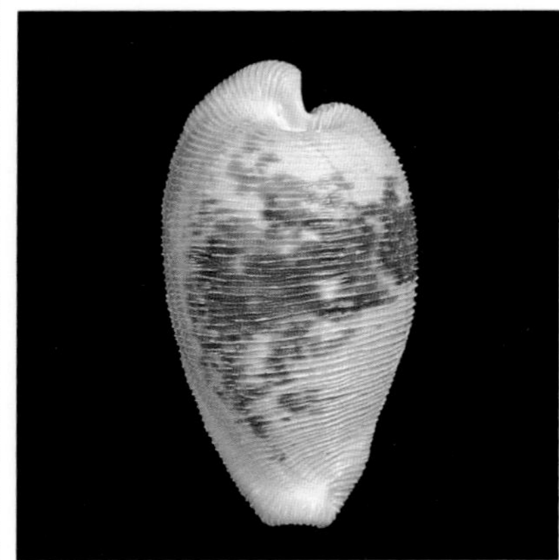

**CYPRAEA CAPENSIS**
Cape Cowrie. *Grey 1828.*
South Africa.

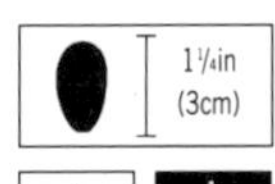

Until recent scuba diving activity, South African cowries were rarely found alive. In this species, coarse ribs spiral around the entire shell, thinning at the columella lip and thickening at the labial lip. There is a distinct, dark brown blotch on the dorsum. Its range extends from shallow to moderately deep water.

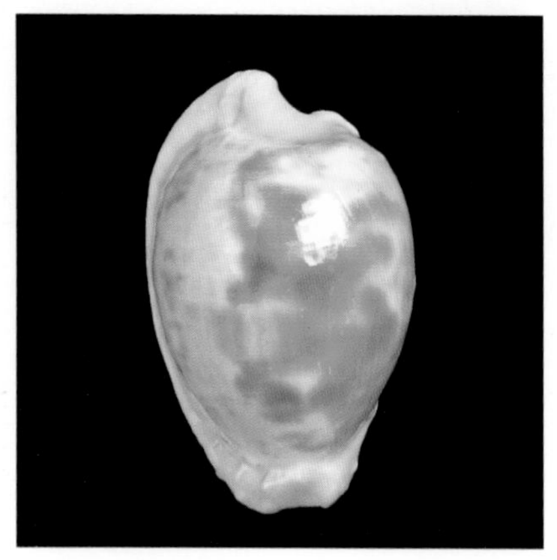

**CYPRAEA CORONATA**
Coronated Cowrie. *Schilder 1930.*
South Africa.

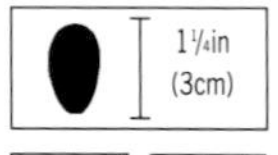

Apart from a few specimens, this species has only become available in any appreciable numbers since the 1980s, and is still rare and sought-after. It is almost deltoid in shape, with a humped dorsum and a solidly ridged labial margin, and is creamy pink in colour, some with a mottled brown dorsum. Its habitat extends from shallow to moderately deep water, to 132 feet (40m).

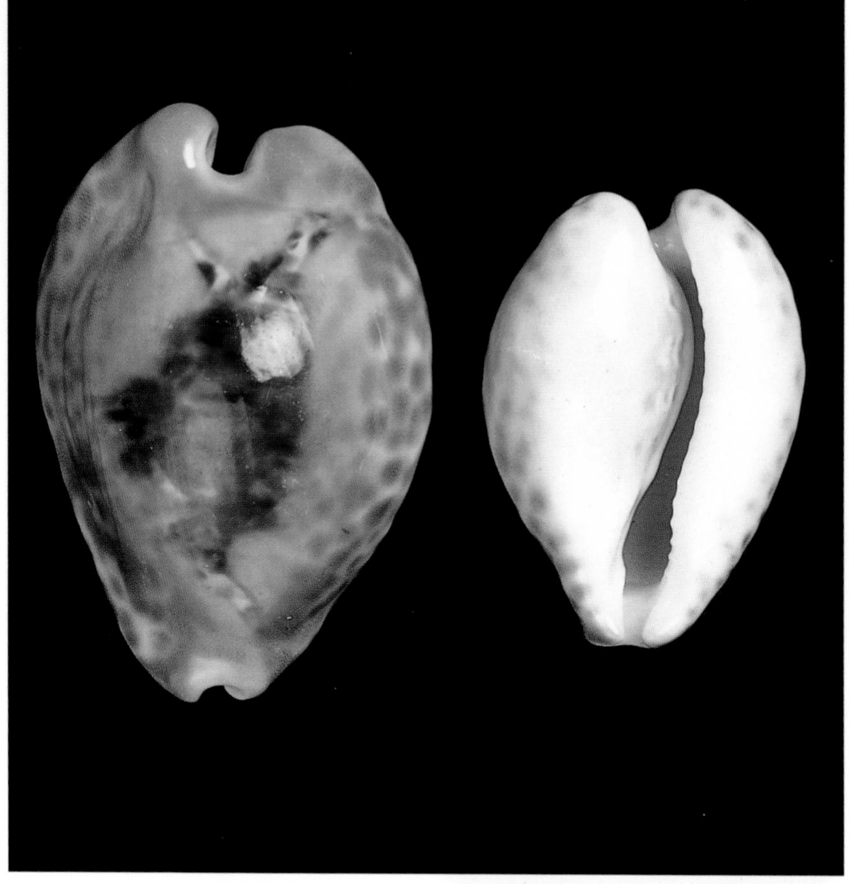

**CYPRAEA TEULÈREI**
Teulère's Cowrie. *Cazevanette 1845.*
Gulf of Oman (Masirah Island).

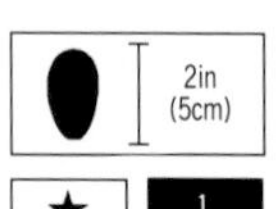

Once a great rarity, this endemic shell eventually came to be collected in great numbers in the late 1960s, after its habitat had been discovered. A thick and heavy, irregularly-shaped species, it has distinctive markings and no teeth. There is no veliger stage in this species, so its restricted habitat may be due to lack of dispersion.

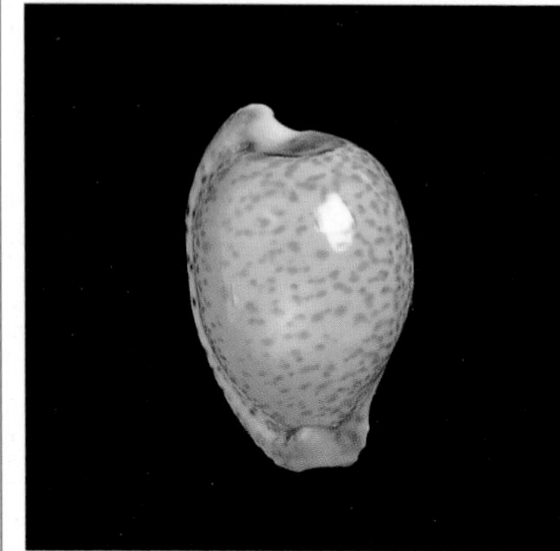

**CYPRAEA ALGOENSIS**
*Gray 1825.*
South Africa.

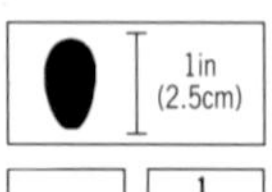

Another rare and sought-after species, it is small and lightweight. The dorsum is beige, pale grey or orange, with minute dots of darker brown, while the extremities and labial margin are thickened and are grey or brown with darker, larger spots. A callus covers the flat spire. The teeth are coarse, especially labially. This specimen was found by divers at a depth of 122 feet (37m) off the West Cape coast.

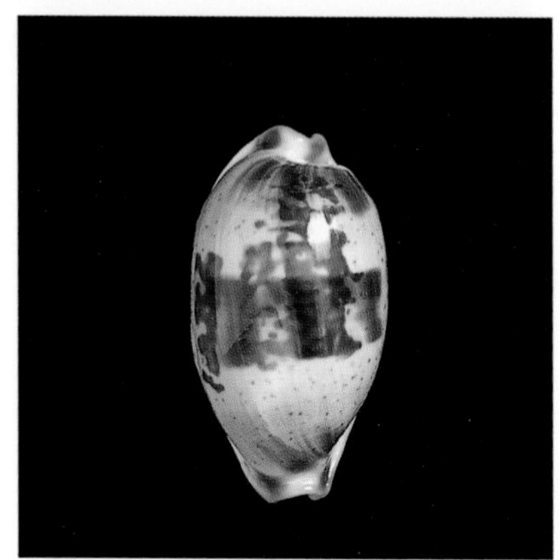

**CYPRAEA ERYTHRAENSIS**
Red Sea Cowrie. *Sowerby 1837.*
Red Sea.

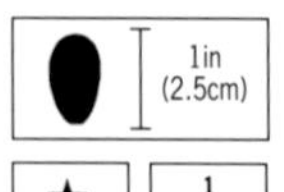

A small cylindrical endemic shell, with produced extremities, its finely ridged teeth cross the entire base. It is a pale blue grey, overlaid at the centre and posterior with a spiral band of dark reddish brown, on which there is mottling. There are minute pale reddish spots on the white margins. It lives subtidally under rocks.

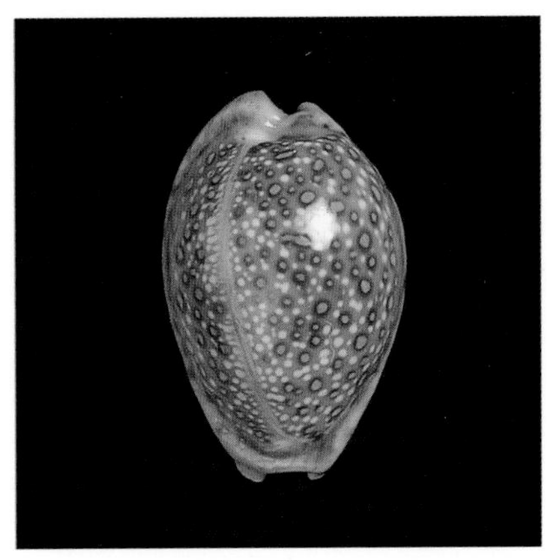

## CYPRAEA MARGINALIS

Margin Cowrie. *Dillwyn 1827.*
East Africa.

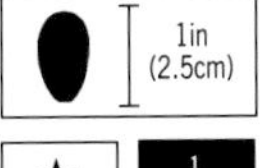

This is a pretty cowrie, with lavender margins and base. The dorsum is pale brown, covered with blue-ringed spots and small white dots, and has a distinct line. This small shell is ovate and slightly humped, and has thickened margins, a convex base and short, moderately strong teeth. This specimen was collected on the southern Somalian coast.

## CYPRAEA ONYX

f. *adusta.* Dark Onyx Cowrie.
*Lamarck 1810.* East Africa.

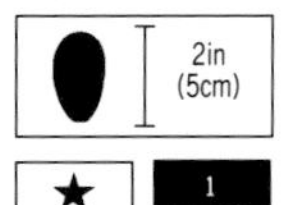

A variation of C. *onyx*, it is one of several variations within this little group. The shell is pyriform, and is moderately humped, with a convex base. It is a handsome variety, being a rich brown, almost black, with reddish brown teeth that are short but strong. Some young examples display broad spiral banding.

## CYPRAEA ARABICA

f. *immanis.* Giant Arabian Cowrie. *Schilder & Schilder 1939.* South and East Africa.

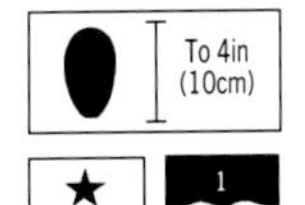

A large handsome variant of the quite complex C. *arabica* group, this shell is ovate and humped, with calloused margins and a broad flat base. It is a pale grey beige, overlaid with rich brown reticulation. The margins are a grey blue with hazy large grey spots; the base is a pinkish beige, and there are short red brown teeth. Alongside is a mature dwarf of C. *arabica* from Zula Bay, Ethiopia.

## CYPRAEA AURANTIUM

Golden Cowrie. *Gmelin 1791.*
Philippines, Solomon Islands and Fiji.

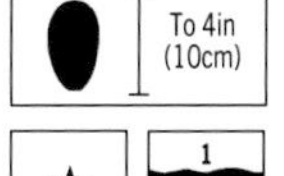

Highly prized among collectors, the purchase price is usually totally out of proportion to its rarity; indeed they are relatively common shells in Samar Island, Philippines, where they inhabit rocky ledges and holes at depths of about 65 feet (20m). However, demand exceeds supply. The large, ovate and inflated shell is not "golden" in fact, but a deep magenta when fresh, fading to a deep orange. The base is pinkish beige and the teeth are tinged with orange.

**CYPRAEA EGLANTINA**
Eglantine Cowrie. *Duclos 1833.*
Western Pacific.

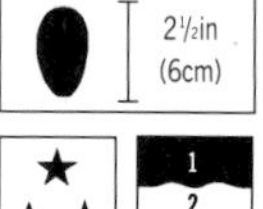

The base of this cylindrical and elongated shell is fairly flat, with a virtually straight aperture. The overall colour is a pale grey or pinkish beige, with a fine reticulated "netting" of light brown. The dorsal line is distinct, and there are terminal spots. The teeth are short, fine and red brown. It lives in shallow water.

**CYPRAEA MONETA**
Money Cowrie. *L. 1758.*
Indo-Pacific.

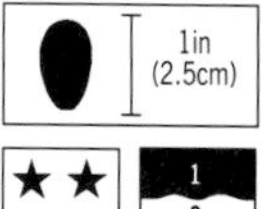

A variable species, shells can be ovate, angular, humped or flat, with or without inflated margins or low blunt nodules. The colours range from white to deep orange. These shells have been – and perhaps still are – used as a form of currency or barter by the natives of tropical areas.

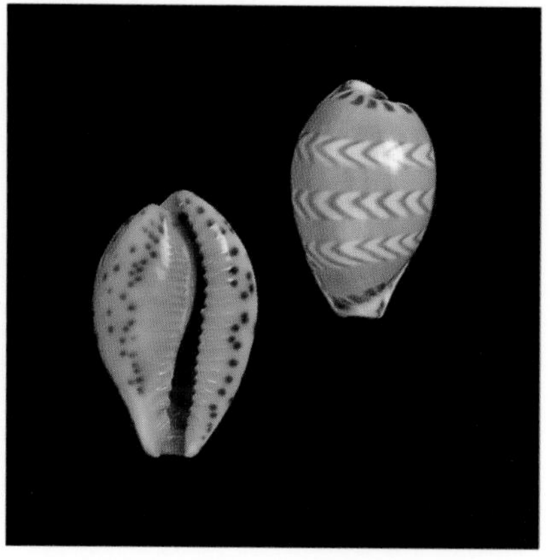

**CYPRAEA ZICZAC**
Zigzag Cowrie. *L. 1758.*
Indo-Pacific.

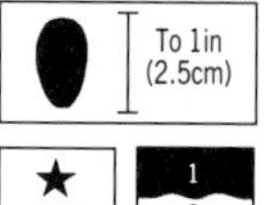

This attractive shell varies little in shape and pattern. The distinct spiral banding of brown zigzag lines on white is unique among *Cypraea*. The base and teeth are pale orange, and there are dark brown spots on the margins. The spire is depressed. The two shells shown here come from Mombasa, Kenya.

**CYPRAEA EGLANTINA**
f. *niger. Roberts 1855.*
New Caledonia.

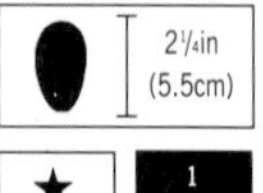

Cowries from New Caledonia often appear "black" and can also develop into strange abnormal shapes, some known as "rostrate". It can easily be seen how these collectable "freaks" differ from the normal *C. eglantina*. The theory is that the waters off New Caledonia contain cobalt, which could affect the shell's growth and colour.

**CYPRAEA CRIBRARIA**
Sieve Cowrie. *L. 1758.*
Indo-Pacific.

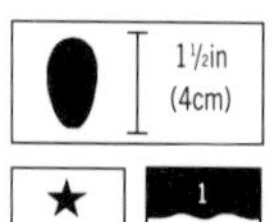

A very strikingly marked shell, it occurs in many forms and locality variations. This species is pure white, both above and below, and the dorsum is overlaid with a rich ochre and brown network, producing stark large white circular spots. It is probably the most common of all the *cribraria* varieties.

**CYPRAEA ONYX**
Onyx Cowrie. *L. 1758.*
Indo-Pacific.

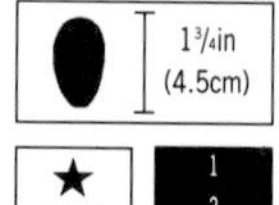

This must be one of the most beautiful cowries. The base, teeth, margins and extremities are a rich dark brown, the dorsum is pale orange brown transversed with two or three broad spiral bands of darker brown. Over this, on either side of a wide dorsal line, is a lovely pale smoky blue. The habitat varies from shallow to moderately deep water.

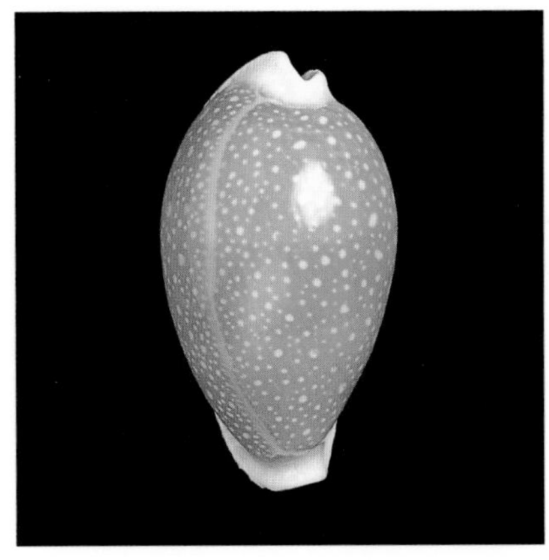

**CYPRAEA MILIARIS**
Millet Cowrie. *Gmelin 1791.*
Western Pacific and Northern Australia.

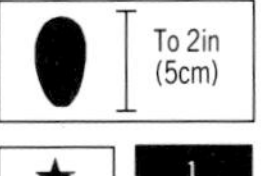

The slightly humped and pyriform dorsum narrows at the anterior. The shell is a pale mustard yellow, occasionally with a green tinge, and is covered with irregular small spots. The dorsal line is distinctive. The base and margins are white and there are short coarse teeth. This is an inhabitant of shallow water.

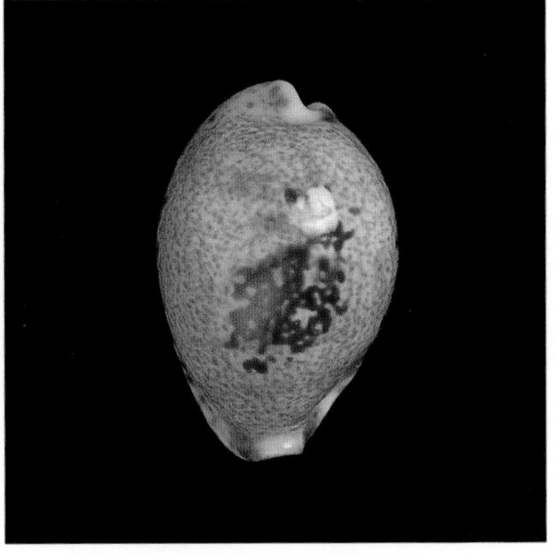

**CYPRAEA PALLIDA**
Pale Cowrie. *Gray 1824.*
Persian Gulf, South Indian Ocean to Borneo.

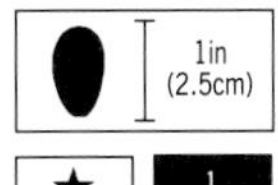

A somewhat rounded and humped little cowrie, it has a slightly convex base, and is pale green, with tiny pale brown dots. There is often a distinctive, irregular dorsal blotch, although some shells do not have this. The base is creamy white. The teeth are short and moderately coarse.

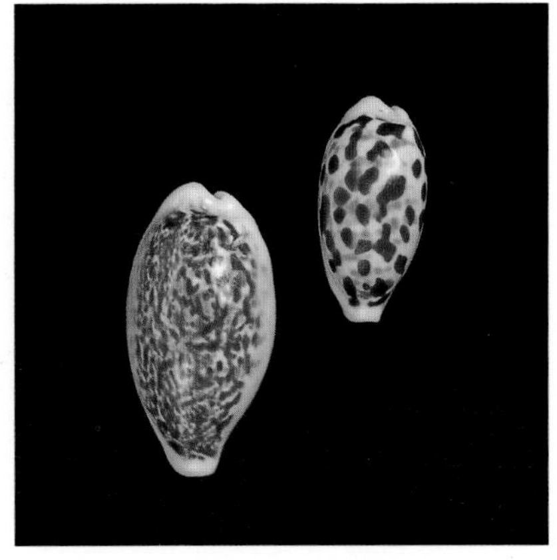

**CYPRAEA COXENI**
Cox's Cowrie. *Cox 1873.*
New Guinea to Solomon Islands.

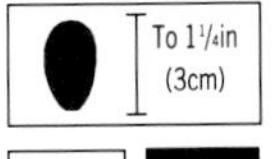

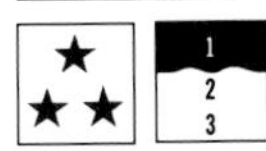

This is an easily recognizable species, being ovate, with a flat dorsum and base, and long strong teeth. It is cream coloured, with irregular rich brown mottling on the dorsum. The variant *hesperina* is slimmer, smaller and has fewer, but larger and usually darker, dorsal spots or blotches. Both types are depicted here and come from Honiara Reef, Solomon Islands.

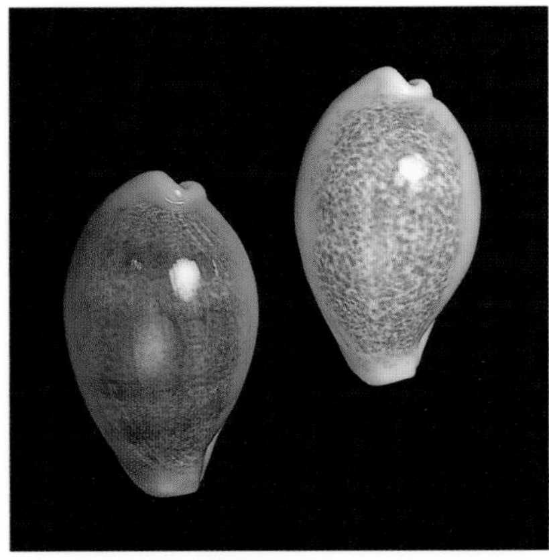

**CYPRAEA OVUM**
Orange-toothed Cowrie. *Gmelin 1791.*
South-West Pacific.

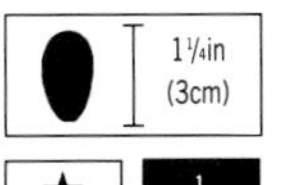

The base of this small solid pyriform species is somewhat convex. The overall colour is a creamy yellow, and there is a mass of concentrated small green and light brown dots and blotches on the dorsum. The teeth are very short and have distinctive orange staining. The much darker form is also shown here – it was collected in Marau Sound, Guadalcanal.

**CYPRAEA QUADRIMACULATA**
Four-spotted Cowrie. *Gray 1824.*
South-West Pacific.

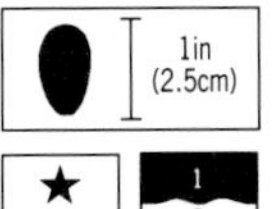

A narrow elongated ovate species, the four-spotted cowrie has a low dorsum and flat base. The shell is cream, with a pale blue grey dorsum covered with tiny pale green flecks. There are very distinctive posterior and anterior terminal spots, after which the shell is named. The teeth are fairly coarse and long.

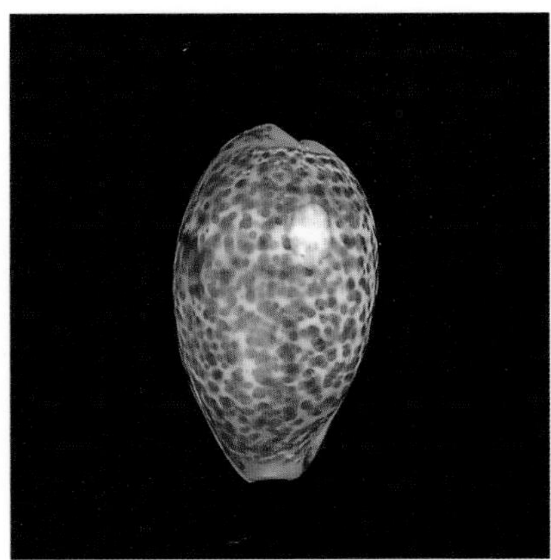

**CYPRAEA HUMPHREYSI**
Humphrey's Cowrie. *Gray 1825.*
Western Pacific.

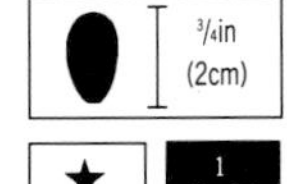

Dr C. M. Burgess, the eminent *Cypraea* expert, suggests that this shell is merely a heavily spotted *C. lutea*; more scientific study may be required in order to ascertain its proper status. I am inclined to consider it a true species in its own right. The colour and patterning of this little shell is virtually always constant. The specimen shown here is from the Solomon Islands.

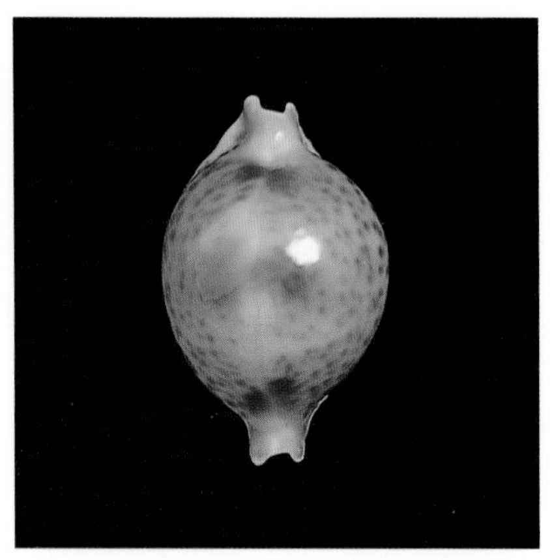

**CYPRAEA BISTRINOTATA**
Treble-spotted Cowrie. *Schilder and Schilder 1937.* Western and Central Pacific.

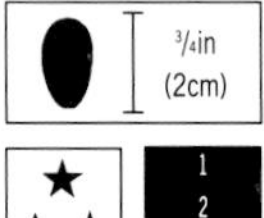

A rounded humped little species, with characteristic protruding posterior and anterior canals, it is a beige orange with mid-brown dorsal blotches. There are also small spots, particularly at the margins, where they are slightly raised and granulose. The teeth are short, very fine and a pale red brown. This particular shell came from the Central Philippines.

**CYPRAEA ISABELLA**
Isabelle's Cowrie. *L. 1758.* Indo-Pacific.

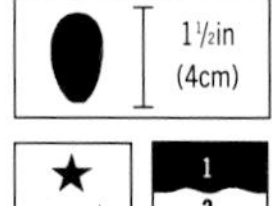

A cylindrical shell, with a flat dorsum and base, it has distinctive orange terminal markings and fine axial black streaks, lines or dots on a beige grey background. The variation *atriceps*, which is endemic to Hawaii and is much smaller and narrower, is shown alongside a true C. *isabella* from the Philippines.

**CYPRAEA CAPUTDRACONIS**
Dragon Head Cowrie. *Melvill 1888.* Easter Island.

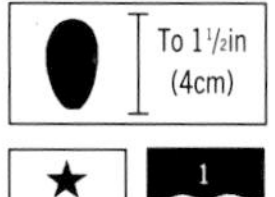

This endemic ovate-to-rounded shell has a moderately humped dorsum. The teeth are short and coarse, and the base is flat. It is dark brown overall, with small dorsal spots and blotches of white. The posterior and anterior canal areas are coloured a pale blue grey, and the base is a paler grey brown, with off-white teeth. It inhabits shallow rough water, living under rocks and coral.

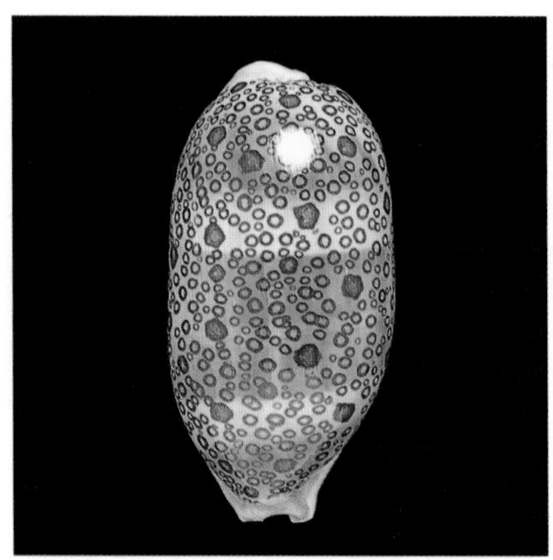

**CYPRAEA ARGUS**
Eyed Cowrie. *L. 1758.* Indo-Pacific.

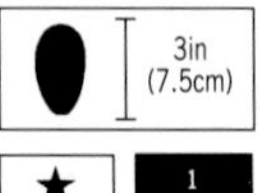

A well-known and widespread species, it is characteristically cylindrical and elongated. There are brown stained, moderately coarse teeth; three dark brown basal blotches and one that is less dark; and the dorsum is covered with irregular rings or "eyes" and odd blotches of dark brown over a beige ground colour. Another unmistakable shell.

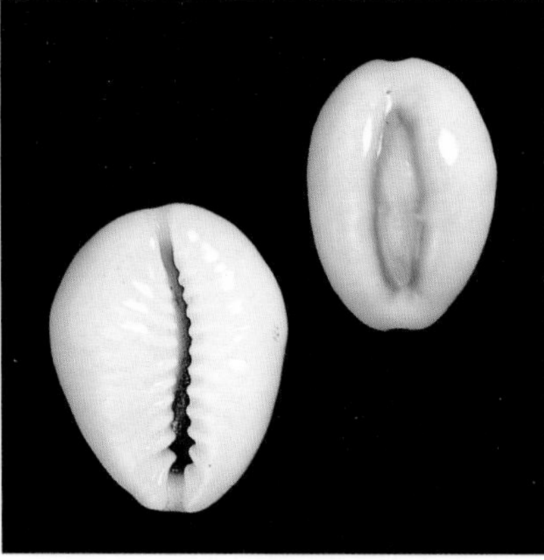

**CYPRAEA OBVELATA**
Tahitian Gold Ringed Cowrie. *Lamarck 1810.* Tahiti and Marquesas Islands.

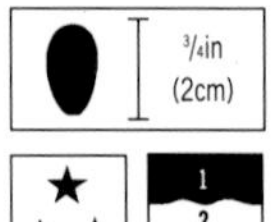

A small species, with wide inflated margins and a narrow depressed dorsum, its long coarse teeth cover the rather concave base. The aperture is straight. The colouring is off-white to pale grey, the dorsal area being a grey blue and encircled with a thin orange band.

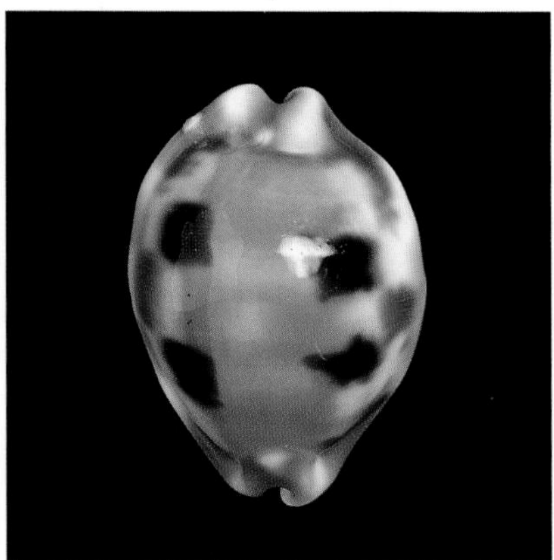

**CYPRAEA TESSELLATA**
Checkerboard Cowrie. *Swainson 1822.* Hawaiian Islands.

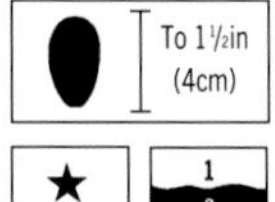

This endemic shell cannot be confused with any other cowrie. A popular, but on occasions difficult to obtain, collectors' shell, four distinctive dark brown dorsal squares or blotches are the distinguishing characteristic of this species. It is probable that the inaccessible habitat of this shell, which lives in depths to 43 feet (13m) inside coral heads and crevices, makes it difficult to collect with ease.

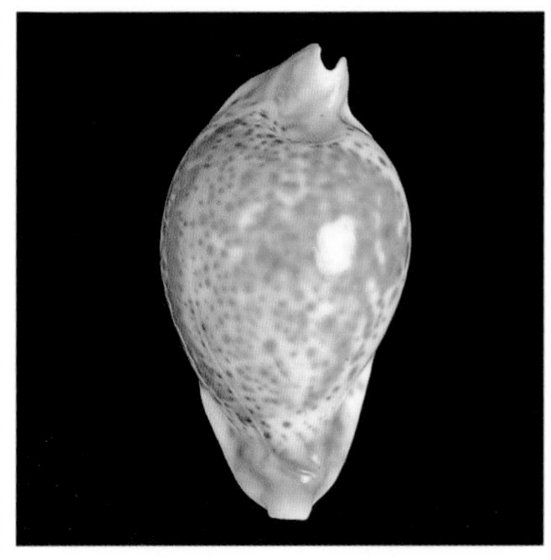

**CYPRAEA HESITATA**
Umbilicate Cowrie. *Iredale 1916.*
South-eastern Australia.

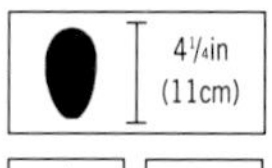


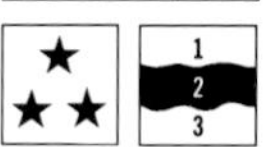


This strikingly shaped shell is ovate and slightly curved, with extended posterior and anterior canals, a humped dorsum and a flat base with short fairly fine teeth. The spire is depressed. Once rare, specimens are now trawled in reasonable numbers. The coloration is off-white and the entire dorsum is spotted or blotched with a fawn brown.

**CYPRAEA FRIENDII**
Friend's Cowrie. *Gray 1831.*
Western and South-western Australia.

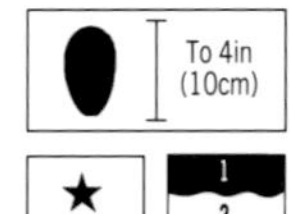


A sponge dweller found in both fairly shallow and deep water, it is a very attractive distinctly shaped and marked collectors' favourite. The shell is elongated and ovate, with a slightly humped dorsum, with angled margins and a pronounced, raised and flanged posterior canal. Specimens are often chipped at one or other extremity – the result of attacks by hostile predatory fish. The shell shown here was collected at Ocean Reef, Western Australia.

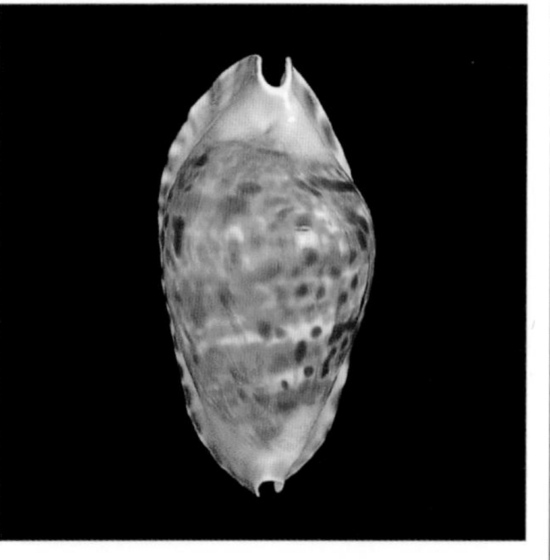

**CYPRAEA MARGINARTA**
Margined Cowrie. *Gaskoin 1849.*
Western and Southern Australia.

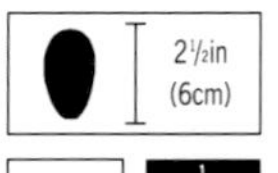

Another beautiful and popular Australian species, the shell may be ovate or almost rounded, or angled toward the extremities. The name refers to the sharply edged and protruding margins, which are irregular or pitted. The base is flat, with short moderately fine teeth. Colour and pattern can vary from pure white throughout to a dorsum bearing distinct spots or uneven, hazy blotches of mid-to-dark rich brown. It can be found in shallow or deep water.

**CYPRAEA ROSSELLI**
Rossell's Cowrie. *Cotton 1948.*
South-western Australia.

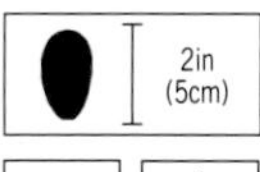


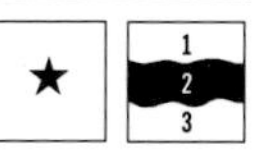


Probably the rarest of the sub-genus *Zoila*, to which *C. friendii* and *C. marginarta* also belong. It is almost deltoid in shape, with a steeply humped dorsum, and is a very rich dark brown to black, usually with a creamy white and irregularly patched dorsum. A moderately deep-water species, it is collected in crayfish pots or by scuba divers.

SUPER FAMILY
## CYPRAEOIDEA

FAMILY
# OVULIDAE
(Egg Shells)

Closely related to and not dissimilar from true cowries, Cypraeidae, the egg shells or false cowries are a family of species that are generally pyriform or spindle shaped, with few or no teeth. There are some anatomical differences between these and true cowries, and egg shells lack patterning or markings. Most inhabit tropical seas, mainly in the Indo-Pacific areas, where they live in close proximity to sponges, sea fans and soft corals and gorgonians. There are several well-known genera, such as *Jennaria, Ovula, Calpurnus, Cyphoma, Phenacovolva, Primovula* and *Volva*, each differing in characteristic shape or form. They are therefore varied enough to promote more than a cursory interest among collectors.

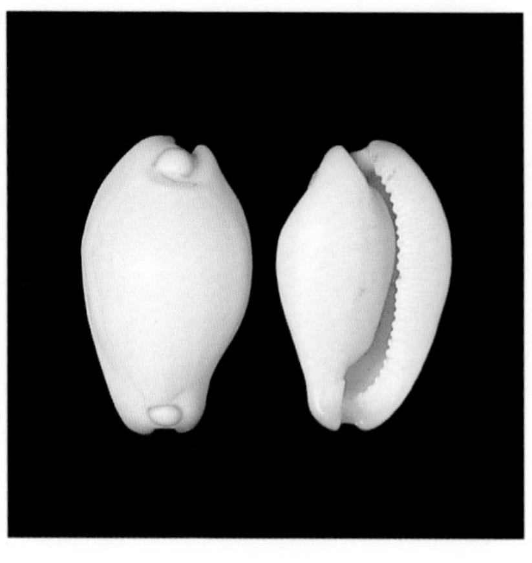

### CALPURNUS VERRUCOSUS
Warted Egg Shell. *L. 1758.*
Indo-Pacific.

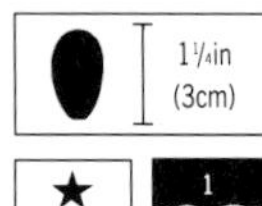

A strange species, the warted egg shell has a raised rounded tubercule just above the posterior and anterior canals. It is ovate, with a raised spiral ridge on the dorsum. The lip bears coarse teeth. The extremities are tinged with pink. This shell inhabits shallow-water reef areas.

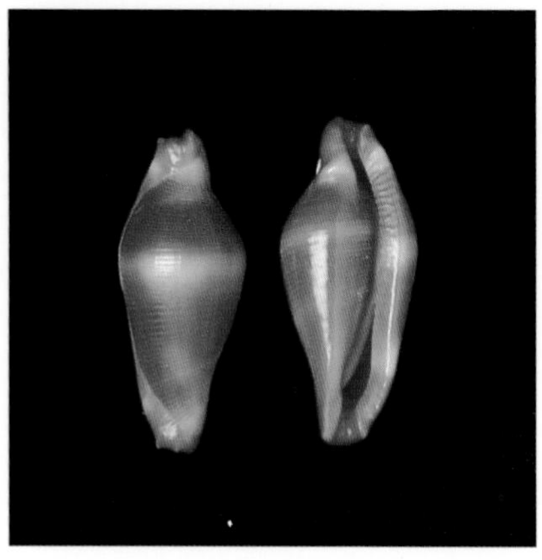

### CRENAVOLVA ROSEWATERI
Rosewater's Volva. *Cate 1973.*
Philippines.

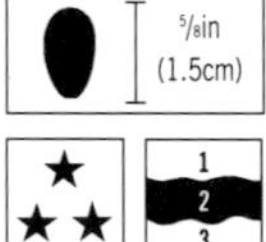

A tiny beautifully coloured shell of deep rose red and crimson, its shape is a long oval, with a central hump. The canals are extended, and there are extremely fine spiral lirae on both the dorsum and the lip. The specimen shown here came from Mactan Island.

### CYPHOMA GIBBOSUM
Flamingo Tongue. *L. 1758.*
South-eastern USA to Brazil.

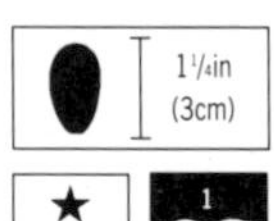

A thick solid calloused shell, with a strong rounded spiral ridge, it has no teeth on its lip. In colour, it is a creamy apricot, with a slender area of white along the dorsum. The base and aperture are creamy white. This species lives on gorgonian corals in shallow waters.

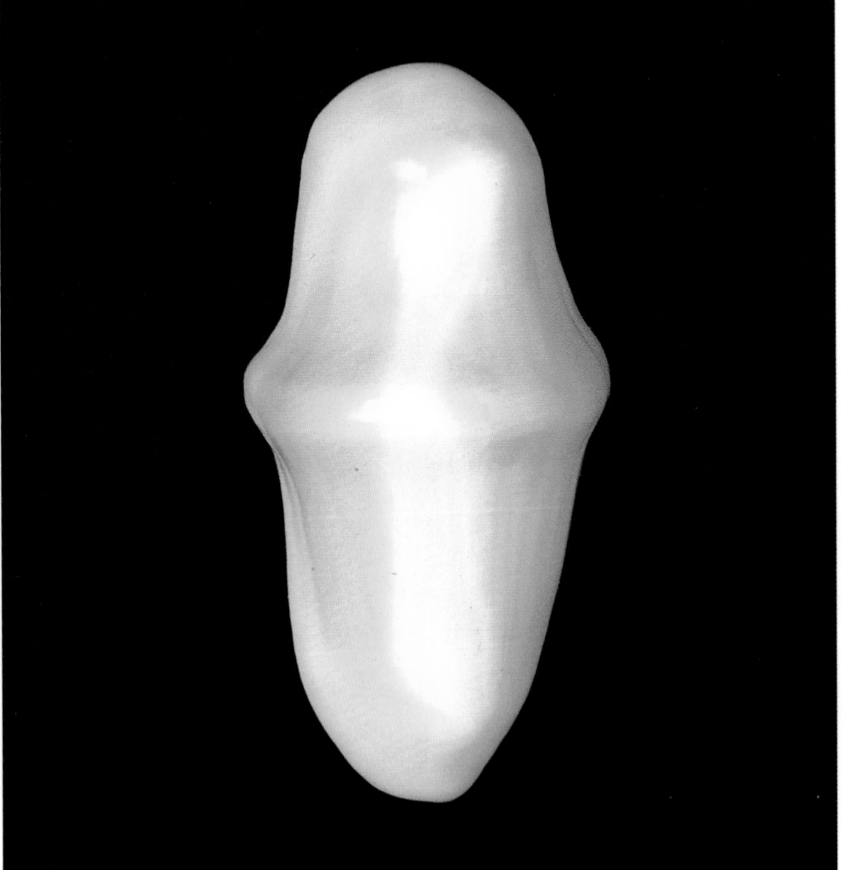

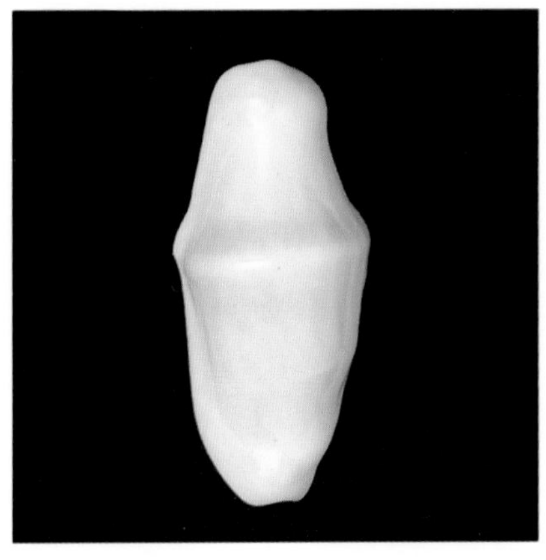

### CYPHOMA SIGNATUM

Fingerprint Cyphoma. *Pilsby and McGinty 1939.* South-eastern USA and Caribbean.

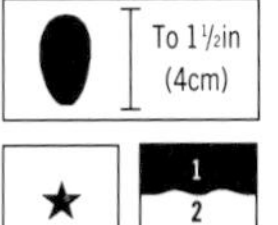

To 1½in (4cm)

Rather similar to *C. gibbosum*, the fingerprint cyphoma tends to be longer and slimmer. The spiral ridge is finer, and there is evidence of another less conspicuous ridge toward the anterior end. The overall colour is a uniform cream. It lives on sea fans, and this particular specimen was fished from Ohio Keys, Florida.

### JENNARIA PUSTULATA

Pustulose False Cowrie. *Lightfoot 1786.* Western Central America.

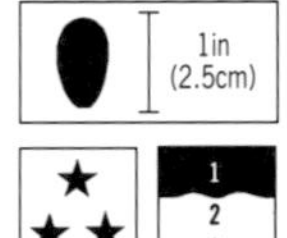

1in (2.5cm)

This species is often thought of as a true cowrie, as there are several *Cypraea* that resemble this shell. However, presumably because of small anatomical differences, it has been placed within the false cowrie family. It is a stunning shell, ovate with a convex base and strong ridged teeth stretching from the aperture to the margins. The dorsum bears raised red ringed spots on a grey background.

### OVULA OVUM

Common Egg Shell. *L. 1758.* Indo-Pacific.

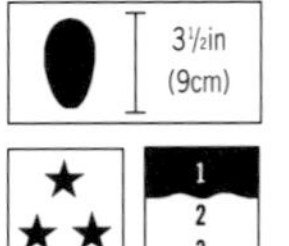

3½in (9cm)

A well-known shell, it is very similar to *O. costellata*, but much larger, inflated and not at all angular. There is no spire, and the lip is coarsely ridged on the underside. The anterior canal is pronounced. The outer shell is a glossy white throughout and the interior is a deep orange brown. A shallow-water reef dweller.

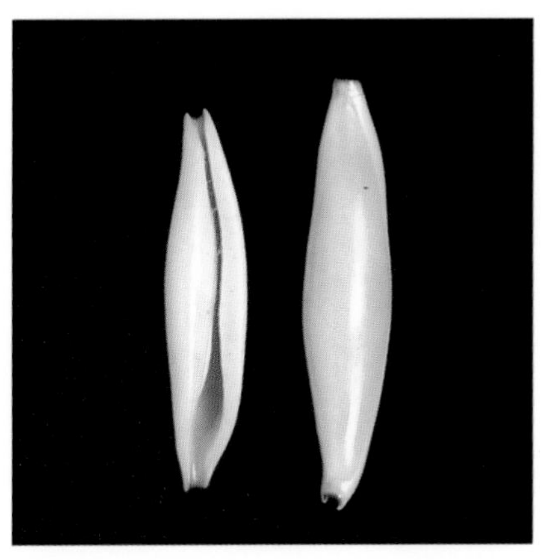

### HIATAVOLVA DEPRESSA

Depressed Volva. *Sowerby 1875.* Western Australia.

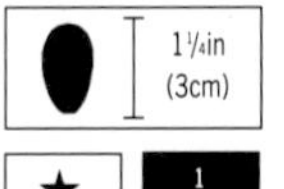

1¼in (3cm)

A delicate long narrow shell, it widens slightly at the centre and has shortened truncated canals. The lip is thick and the aperture is very narrow, widening at the anterior. In colour it is pale pink or yellow, the extremities being tinged with crimson.

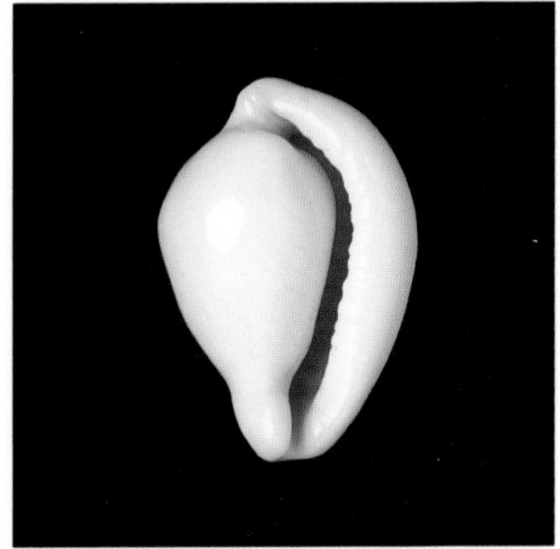

### OVULA COSTELLATA

Pink-mouthed Egg Shell. *Lamarck 1810.* Indo-Pacific.

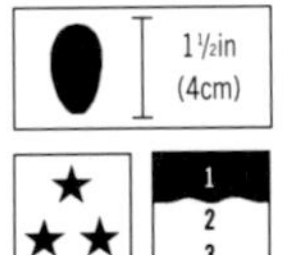

1½in (4cm)

A rather angular shell, it has a central spiral ridge on the dorsum. The labial lip is thickened, and there are fine grooves on the underside. The exterior is pure white, although fine greyish axial lines can be seen on the dorsum, and the interior is a beautiful soft pink. This particular shell was collected on the Great Barrier Reef, Queensland.

### PHENACOVOLVA BREVIROSTRIS

Double-snouted Volva. *Schumacher 1817.* Western Pacific.

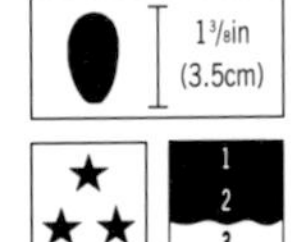

1⅜in (3.5cm)

This is elongate and ovate, with a centrally humped dorsum, and fairly short canals. The lip is thickened and rounded; the columella is smooth. The pale pink shell has a central white spiral band, and its extremities are tinged with orange. This specimen was collected from Manila Bay, Philippines.

**PHENACOVOLVA TOKIOI**
Tokio's Volva. *Cate 1973.*
South-West Pacific.

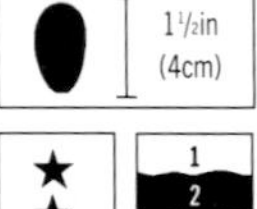

A lovely little shell, it is elongated and narrow, with extended canals, the posterior being rather longer. It is an attractive shade of pale reddish mauve, which deepens in the interior. The extremities are tinged with orange. The lip is narrow but widens toward the anterior end. It inhabits gorgonian corals.

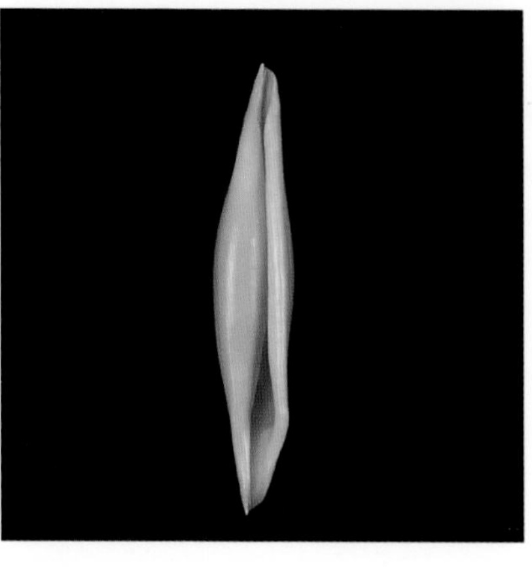

**PHENACOVOLVA SUBREFLEXA**
Stunted Volva. *A. Adams and Reeve 1848.*
Philippines.

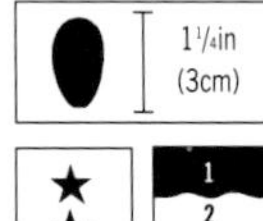

A very slender small shell, it has slightly extended canals and is generally smooth. The lip is thickened and rounded, and the aperture is very narrow, widening at the anterior. It is a pale salmon pink, the underside being somewhat paler.

**PSEUDOSIMNIA CARNEA**
Blood-stained Ovula. *Poiret 1789.*
Med., North-West Africa, West Indies.

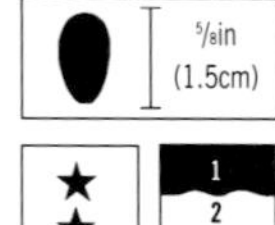

A very widespread species, it is found on both sides of the Atlantic. Colours vary from pale yellow through pale red to a shade that is almost purple. In shape, it is ovate and humped, with minute teeth on the inside of the lip. Both the anterior and posterior canals are slightly extended.

**PHENACOVOLVA LONGIROSTRATA**
Long-snouted Volva. *Sowerby 1828.*
Japan to Philippines.

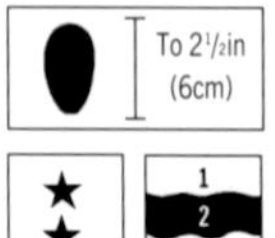

Smooth and slender, the long-snouted volva has long canals and a slightly humped central dorsum. The aperture is narrow but widens at the anterior. The lip is thickened. Shells are off-white to pale pink, the extremities occasionally tinted with russet. The depicted specimen is from the Central Philippines.

**PSEUDOCYPHOMA INTERMEDIUM**
Intermediate Cyphoma. *Sowerby 1828.*
Caribbean to Brazil.

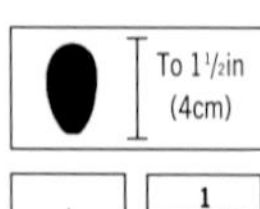

This lightweight shell is ovate, with extended extremities and a moderately humped dorsum. It is very pale pink or cream, the underside being a pale yellow, and there is a faint deep pink tint along the inner edge of the lip. This specimen was dredged in shrimp nets off Vitória, Espírito Santo, Brazil.

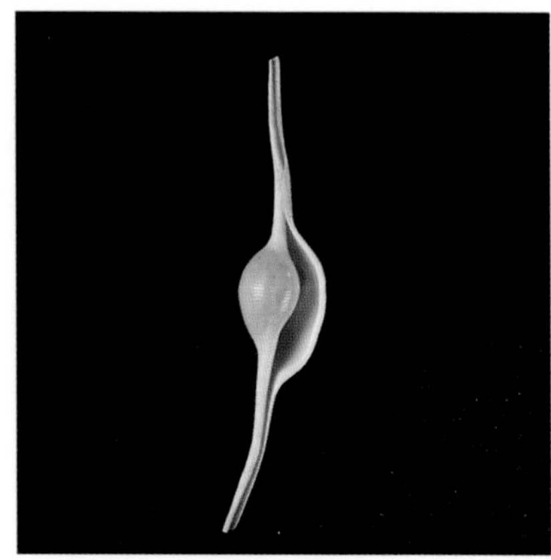

**VOLVA VOLVA**
Shuttle Shell. *L. 1758.*
Indo-Pacific.

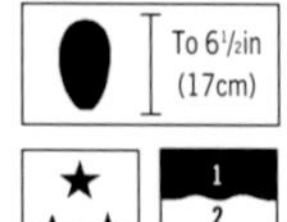

One of the most amazing shells, this has an extraordinary shape: the body whorl is ovate and globose, with fine spiral grooves, the lip being slightly thickened, and the canals are extremely long, narrow and obliquely ridged. Overall, it is a pale cream-to-pink, with very slightly darker extremities. A collectors' favourite, it can be found on or near coral reefs.

SUPER FAMILY
## CYPRAEOIDEA

FAMILY
### TRIVIIDAE
(Allied Cowries)

A small group, they are often termed true cowries, but this can be misleading. Although in many respects the Triviidae resemble *Cypraea*, there are anatomical differences and the former have prominent ridges and are generally less glossy.

SUPER FAMILY
## NATICOIDEA

FAMILY
### NATICIDAE
(Moon or Necklace Shells)

A large worldwide family of smooth, glossy shells with depressed spires and enlarged body whorls, they are all carnivorous, feeding on other molluscs and similar creatures, and living in sand. The group is split into subfamilies, separated by differences in the form of the operculum. There are numerous genera and subgenera, notably *Globularia*, *Polinices*, *Natica*, *Sinum*, *Lunatia* and *Stigmaulax*. Valuable contributions to the study of Naticidae have been made by Mike Dixon (UK) and Marc Streitz (France), both amateur enthusiasts. Professionals Cernorsky, Kilburn and Marincovich have written on the Naticas of certain areas, but a full pictorial guide is still lacking.

**EUSPIRA LEWISI**
Lewis's Moon. *Gould 1847.*
Western USA.

The largest species in the family Naticidae, Lewis's moon is thick and heavy, often scarred or encrusted, and is a chalky beige white, with numerous growth striae. The interior is pale brown as are the outer edges of the lip, columella and calloused parietal wall. There is an open umbilicus. A popular collectors' shell, it lives in sand. The depicted specimen is from Puget Sound, Washington, USA.

**TRIVIA MONACHA**
European or Bean Cowrie. *Da Costa 1778.*
North-East Atlantic and Mediterranean.

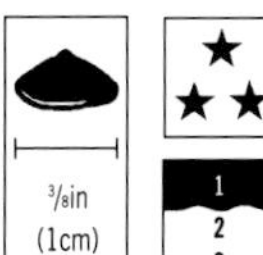


A tiny solid rounded shell, it has a high dorsum and is encircled with tiny ribs. The lip is thickened and rounded. The colour is a pale grey, sometimes pinkish, with three prominent dorsal spots of a grey brown. The base is white. These two specimens were collected on the Portuguese coast.

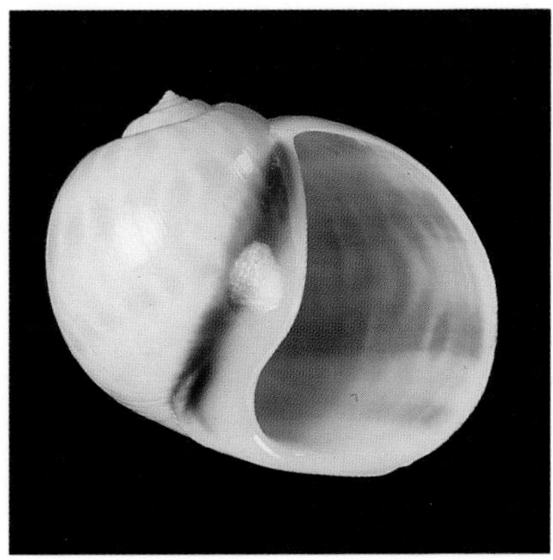

**GLOBULARIA FLUCTUATA**
Wavy Moon. *Sowerby 1825.*
Philippines.

This attractive species has a low spire, large body whorl and a gaping somewhat extended aperture. There is no umbilicus. The columella is white and the parietal area is tinged with dark brown. The exterior pattern consists of white oblique wavy lines over a pale green beige background. There are two broad light brown spiral bands.

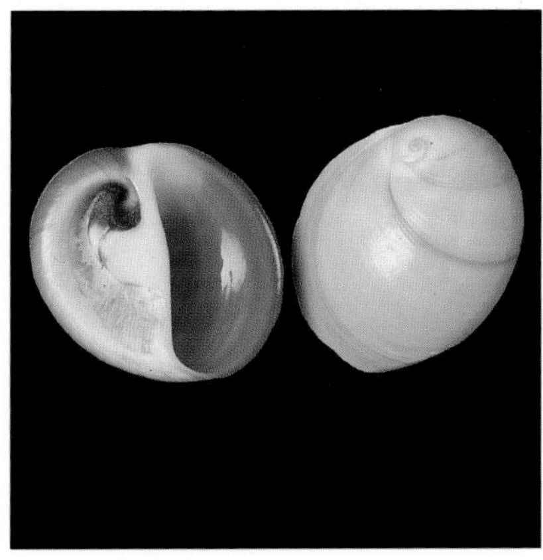

**NEVERITA ALBUMEN**
Egg-white Moon. *L. 1758.*
Indo-Pacific.

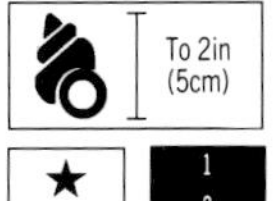


A very flattened glossy smooth shell, it has a small flat spire, and the underside is flat. The umbilicus is large and open, and a flattened calloused funicular pad is attached to the columella. Colours vary from pure white to dark brown. There are fine growth striae. These shells live in sand in either shallow or moderately deep water.

**NEVERITA HELICIODES**
Spiral Moon. *Gray 1825.*
Western Central America.

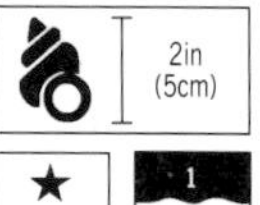

Similar to *N. albumen*, this is larger and not glossy, and numerous strong growth lines are evident. The base is concave and the parietal wall is an oval flat area that covers the umbilicus. The colour is a pale brown or beige grey with a rich shiny brown aperture. This particular shell is from Playas, Ecuador.

**POLINICES GROSSULARIA**
Senegalese Moon. *Marche-Marchad 1957.*
North-West Africa to Angola.

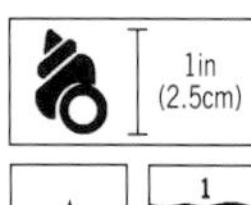

A lightweight fragile species, it has a large rounded body whorl and a distinct umbilicus. The operculum is thin and horny. The shell is a pale beige overlaid with spiral broken bands of brown squares and blotches and with wavy short lines below the suture. This collectors' item comes from moderately deep water and is difficult to obtain.

**POLINICES PANAMAENSIS**
Panama Milk Moon. *Récluz 1844.*
Western Central and South America.

The large body whorl has almost straight sides leading to a small very low spire. Overall, it is a creamy white shell. The operculum is horny and twisted, and there is a large open umbilicus and a calloused parietal wall. This specimen came from Playas, Ecuador.

**NEVERITA PESELEPHANTI**
Elephant's Foot Moon. *Link 1807.*
Indo-Pacific.

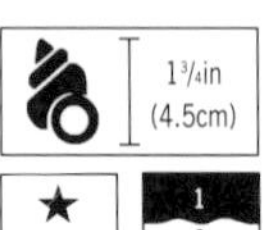

A heavy smooth shell, this is globulate, with a low spire. The columella and parietal areas are white and the umbilicus is partly open. The shell is generally pale to mid-brown, with a broad spiral yellow band below the sutures. The apex is a hazy white. It is found in sand in shallow water.

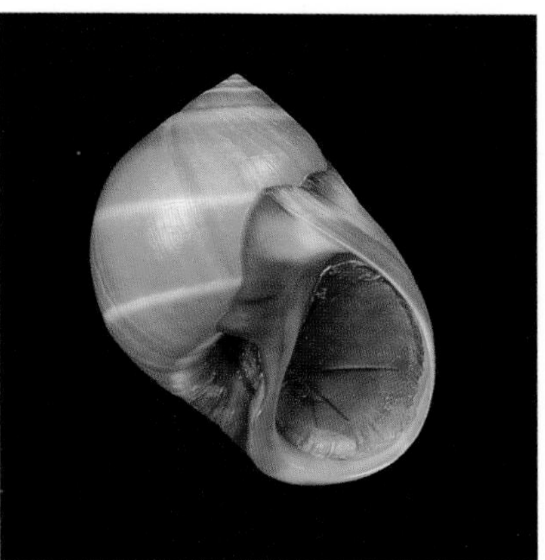

**POLINICES BIFASCIATUS**
Two-banded Moon. *Griffith and Pidgeon 1834.* Western Central America.

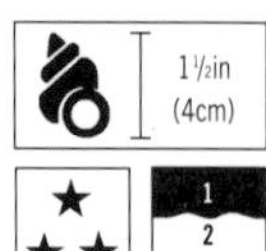

A solid heavy shell, it is rather ovate, with a low-to-moderate spire. There is a large umbilicus, and the parietal wall is calloused. Although the name suggests two, there are in fact three cream spiral bands over a pale brown background. It inhabits intertidal sand or mud. This specimen is from Estero, Sonora, Mexico.

**NATICA STELLATA**
Starry Moon. *Hedley 1913.*
Western Pacific.

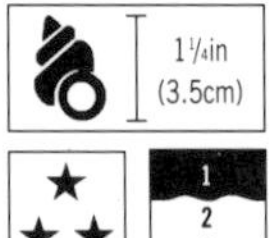

This bright orange glossy shell is very attractive. There are spiral patches of white and yellow. The interior, columella and parietal wall are pure white. The umbilicus is deep, although partly covered by the calloused parietal area. This is another shallow-water sand dweller.

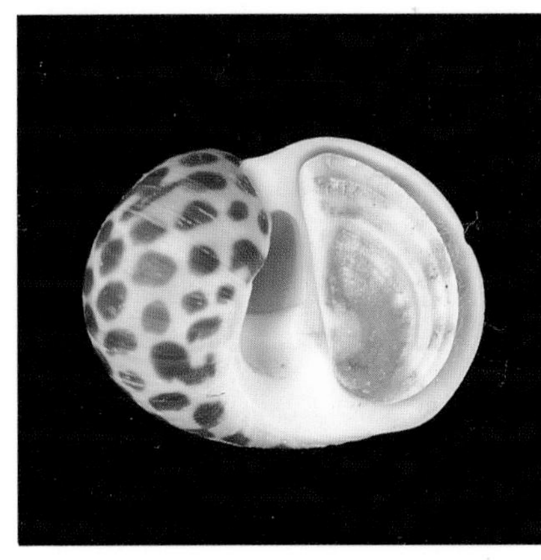

**NATICA ACINONYX**
African Berry Moon. *Marche-Marchad 1957.* West Africa.

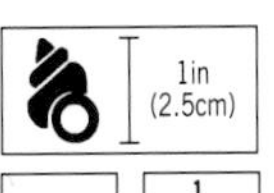

A non-glossy species, the African berry moon is off-white or beige, overlaid with many irregular or rounded dark brown spots. There is a deep, gaping umbilicus. The operculum is a half-moon shape and bears strong incised ridges. A rare shell, it lives in deep water to about 660 feet (200m).

**NATICA VITELLUS**
Calf Moon. *L. 1758.*
Western Pacific and Indian Ocean.

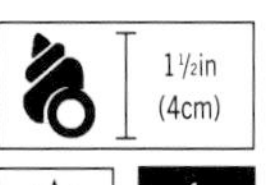

A well-known shell, it has a large bulbous body whorl and a very low spire. The ground colour is off-white, and there are variable spiral bands of cream, pale brown and mid-brown. The aperture is pure white. A shallow-water dweller, this specimen was collected in Quezon, Philippines.

**NATICA RUBROMACULATA**
Red-striped Moon. *E. A. Smith.*
West Africa.

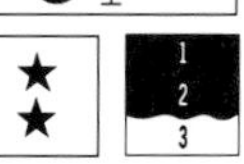

A medium-sized globose shell, it has a moderate spire and is white, with numerous red brown axial stripes and, occasionally, spiral blotches. The aperture, columella and parietal area are all white, and there is a large umbilicus. The depicted specimen comes from Takoradi, Ghana.

**NATICA JANTHOSTOMOIDES**
*Kuroda and Habe 1963.*
Japan.

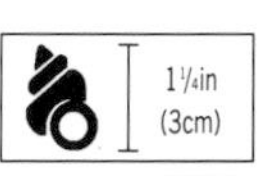

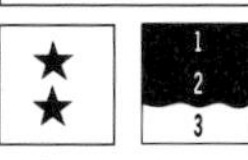

This endemic very rounded moon shell has a silky lustre and fine axial growth lines. The exterior colour is beige, with spiral bands and axial lines of pale brown. The calcareous operculum is off-white and is grooved. The umbilicus is closed. Fished in moderate depths to about 130 feet (40m).

## NATICA ADANSONI

Adanson's Moon. *Blainville 1825.*
Western Africa.

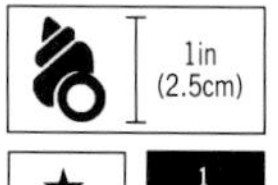



A glossy rounded species with a moderate spire, its background colour of white or cream is overlaid with two broad greyish brown spiral bands and brown axial lines and reticulations – these patterns are quite variable. The operculum is shiny white. There is a narrow umbilicus. This specimen is from Casamance, Senegal, found in shallow water.

## NATICA CANELOENSIS

Canelo Moon. *Hertlein and Strong 1955.*
Western Central America.

A thin globose shell of a pale grey or beige, decorated with two rows of brown dashes or blotches. There is a small neat umbilicus and the operculum is attractively ornamented with spiral grooves. This specimen was trawled at 66 feet (20m) off Perlas Island, Panama.

## NATICA ARACHNOIDEA

Spider Moon. *Gmelin 1791.*
Indo-Pacific.

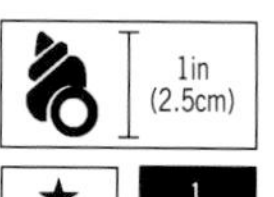



This small sturdy species is highly glossy and smooth, and is attractively but variably patterned – two forms are shown here. The small umbilicus is partly covered by a pure white parietal area. The operculum is a glossy white with very fine spire grooves.

## NATICA TURTONI

Turton's Moon. *E. A. Smith 1890.*
Western Africa.

Another of the scarce West African species, this has similar markings to those of *N. alapapilionis*, but differs slightly in that the spire is somewhat sloping and the shell is almost twice the size. The pattern is quite similar. There is a large umbilicus and the operculum is ornamented with six or seven rounded ridges.

**NATICA GRAYI**
Gray's Moon. *Philippi 1852.*
Western Central America.

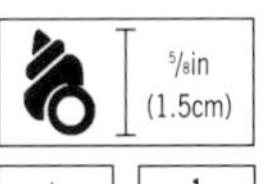


A tiny shell, it is pale grey in colour, with three or four spiral off-white or cream bands marked with brown spots. The aperture is cream, as is the very large funicular pad. The operculum is virtually flat and has a single groove near the outer edge. There is fine radial grooving below the sutures. It inhabits moderately deep water.

**NATICA TIGRINA**
Tiger Moon. *Röding 1798.*
Eastern Asia.

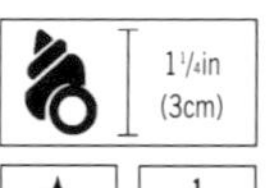


A rounded shell, with a moderate spire, it is generally off-white, with numerous spiral dots, lines and patches of pale grey brown. There is a relatively narrow umbilical opening, and the interior is stained brown. This specimen was fished in the Gulf of Siam.

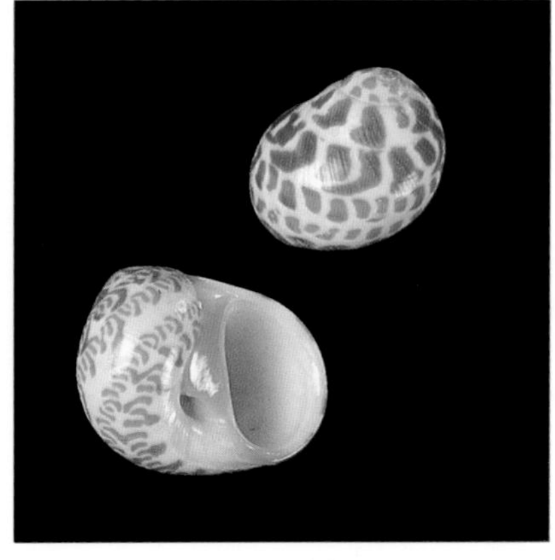

**NATICA VIOLACEA**
Violet Moon. *Sowerby 1825.*
Indo-Pacific.

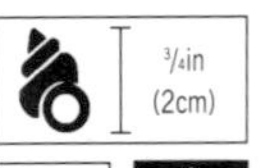

A beautiful combination of pale violet and tan colouring make this a very popular collectors' shell. It is globose, with a rounded spire, and the umbilicus is very small. It inhabits shallow water down to about 66 feet (20m). These specimens were collected by scuba divers at Kwajalein Atoll, Marshall Islands.

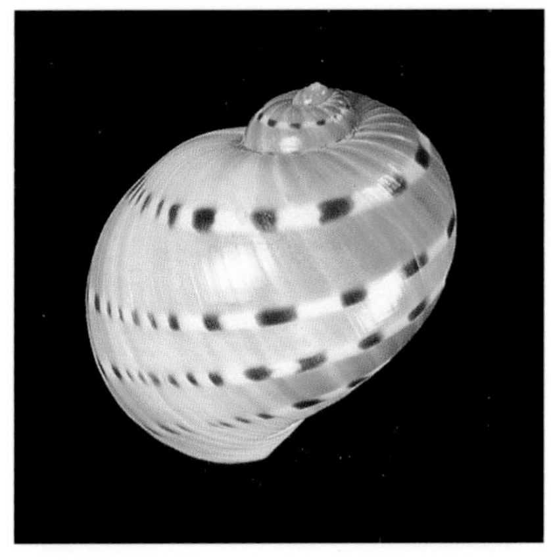

**NATICA ALAPAPILIONIS**
Butterfly Moon. *Röding 1798.*
Indo-Pacific.

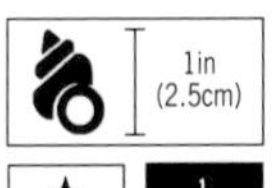


The butterfly moon has a tiny spire and an enlarged globose body whorl. There are radial grooves below the suture, and four very pretty, distinct spiral rows of brown and white bands on a light brown or beige background. The aperture and surrounding area is white. This specimen was fished off southern Thailand.

**NATICA VARIOLARIA**
Fanel Moon. *Récluz 1844.*
Western Africa.

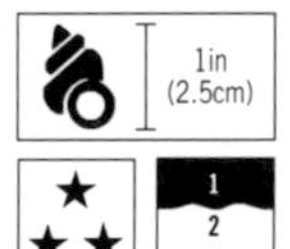


Similar to *N. tigrina*, this species differs in that the spire is very low and the globose body whorl has a high rounded shoulder. It is white or cream, with many dark brown dots. Below the open umbilicus is a narrow funicle which is stained a pale orange brown. The operculum bears strong ridges. These specimens were collected at Guinea Bissau.

**NATICA UNIFASCIATA**
Single-banded Moon. *Lamarck 1822.*
Western Central America.

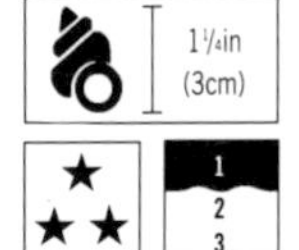


An overall slate-grey is lightened by a creamy yellow spiral band on the whorl shoulders. The columella and parietal wall are white, as is the funicular pad below the umbilicus. The flat calcareous operculum bears no sculpturing. The shells seen here come from Pedro Gonzales Island, Panama.

**NATICA MONODI**
*Marche-Marchad 1957.*
Western Africa.

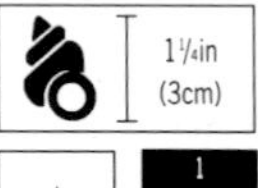

A medium-sized natica, this has a low spire and globose body whorl. It is pale brown or beige with two spiral bands of broken brown markings. There are numerous growth lines. The umbilicus, columella and aperture are white and the lunate operculum is decoratively ribbed. A scarce collectors' item.

**NATICA CAYENNENSIS**
Cayenne Moon. *Récluz 1844.*
West Indies to Brazil.

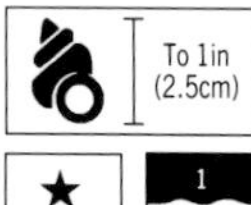

A small smooth shell, with a low spire, it is a dirty beige colour with axial zigzag stripes of pale grey brown. The aperture and umbilical area is white. The calcareous operculum bears a strong central rounded rib. The specimen shown here comes from Guarapari, Brazil.

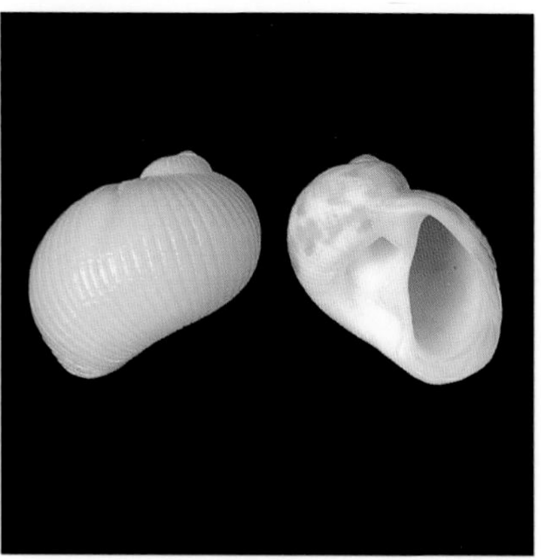

**STIGMAULAX SULCATA**
Grooved Moon. *Born 1778.*
Caribbean.

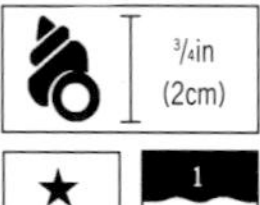

The two specimens shown here display the variation within this species; both come from Antigua, West Indies. They have strong axial grooves and some also have fine spiral ridges, giving a latticed effect. There is a wide umbilicus, and pale orange tinting in the interior.

**NATICA MACULATA**
Hebrew Moon. *Von Salis 1793.*
Mediterranean.

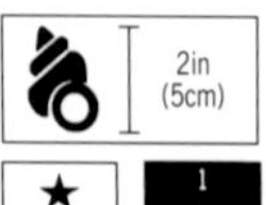

A very variable species, its base colour can be off-white or cream, overlaid with spots, patches or large areas of middle to dark brown, or it can be a plain brown. The umbilicus is open and wide, with a distinct funicle. The lunate operculum is delicately ornamented with raised blade-like ridges. The two variations shown come from Sicily.

**NATICA PULICARIS**
Philippi 1852. Gulf of Oman.

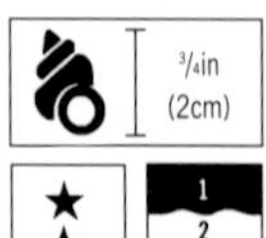

This small but solid shell has a low spire, and almost angular shoulders below the sutures. The umbilicus is small and open and the parietal wall is lightly calloused. There is an intricate pattern of dots, spiral bands and odd patches, all of which are middle or dark brown on off-white. A collectors' item, it is difficult to obtain.

**STIGMAULAX BRODERIPIANA**
Broderip's Moon. *Récluz 1844.*
Western Central America.

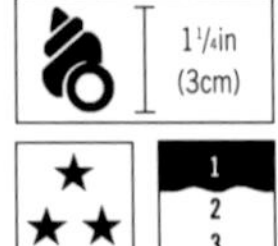

Prettily marked with three spiral bands of dark brown and cream on a tan brown background, this shell also has a thin white band below the suture. Fine radial grooves are in evidence, and there is a wide umbilicus and large funicle. The shiny white operculum has fine radial lirae.

**TANEA LINEATA**
Lined Moon. *Röding 1798.*
Western Pacific.

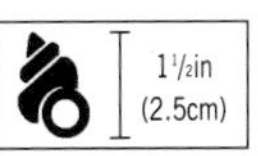


This shell lives in sand or mud in fairly shallow water. It has a low spire and a large body whorl which is patterned with fine axial straight or wavy mid-brown lines. There is an open umbilicus, below which is a strong white funicular pad. The operculum, which is calcareous, bears coarse ridges. These two shells were trawled off south-western Taiwan.

**TANEA UNDULATA**
Wavy Moon. *Röding 1798.*
Japan to the Philippines.

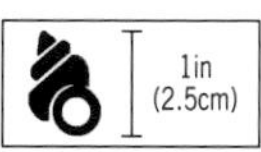


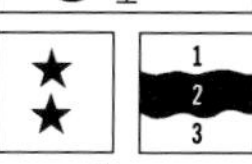


A smallish lightweight glossy shell, the attractively named wavy moon is off-white or cream, with axial wavy or zigzag lines of light tan. The umbilicus is open but is partially covered by a prominent funicular pad. A sand dweller, found in depths to 132 feet (40m).

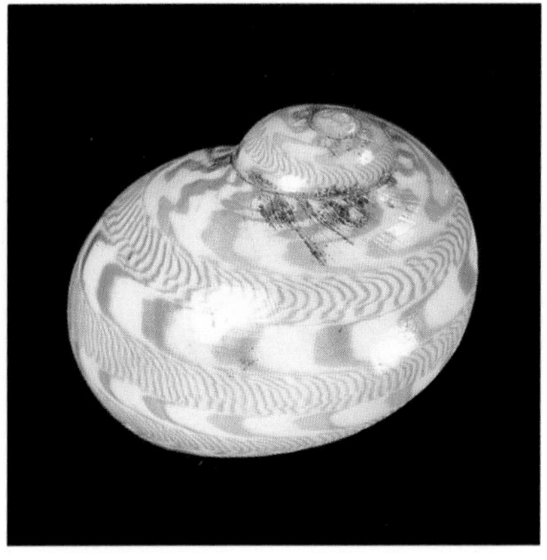

**TANEA EUZONA**
Zoned Moon. *Récluz 1844.*
Indo-Pacific.

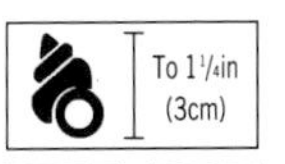


A globose shell with a low spire, its striking markings consist of alternating spiral bands of white with tan brown crescent-shapes and fine close tan brown lines. The aperture, columella, parietal wall and funicle are all white. This particular shell is from the Gulf of Siam in moderately deep water.

**TANEA ZELANDICA**
New Zealand Moon. *Quoy and Gaimard 1832.* New Zealand.

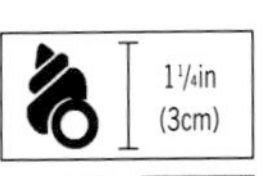


A very rounded shell, with a low spire and enlarged body whorl, it is beige or light brown, with spiral bands of broken pale to mid-brown squares or irregular shapes. The aperture and surrounding area is white. The umbilicus is closed by a large funicle. Endemic, it lives in intertidal and shallow waters.

SUPER FAMILY
## TONOIDEA

FAMILY
## TONNIDAE
(Tun Shells)

The tun shells are so called because of their large rounded or ovate body whorls, the spires being relatively low. Although largish shells, they tend to be rather thin and lightweight. They are carnivorous, feeding on fish, urchins, sea cucumbers and crabs, and they virtually all live in tropical seas in moderate to deep water. They do not possess an operculum. There are three genera: *Tonna*, *Eudolium* and *Malea*.

### *MALEA POMUM*
Pacific Grinning Tun. *L. 1758.*
Indo-Pacific.

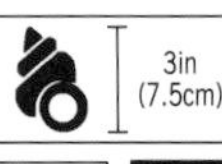


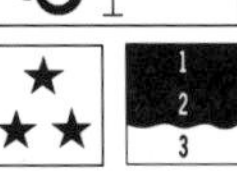


A very solid small tun, it is dominated by coarse low rounded spiral cords. The spire is low; the outer lip is thick and heavily dentate. The colour is a beige pink, with occasional orange or brown patches on the cords. The columella is plicate and the canal very short. The base area is cream and the interior deep orange. It lives in offshore waters.

### *MALEA RINGENS*
Grinning Tun. *Swainson 1822.*
Western Central America.

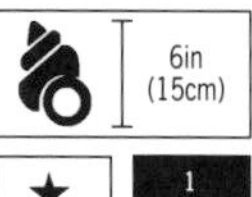


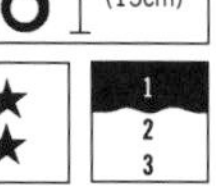


This is by far the thickest and heaviest of the tuns, with very strong spiral rounded cords that encircle the whole shell. The lip is set at right angles to the body whorl and the underside bears strong dentations. There is a deep columella notch. The exterior is a dirty beige, but the interior is orange. The shell lives in sand bars or under rocky ledges.

### *TONNA SULCOSA*
Banded Tun. *Born 1778.*
Indo-Pacific.

A medium-sized species, it has a moderate spire and channelled suture. The body whorl is ovate and bears numerous rather flattened spiral cords. The periphery of the aperture is stepped and the lower edge dentate. The siphonal canal is deep and pronounced. The white shell is encircled with broad brown spiral bands. This specimen is from Central Philippines.

## TONNA DOLIUM

Spotted Tun. *L. 1758.*
Western Pacific and New Zealand.

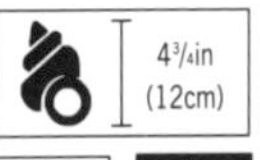

A well-known species, sometimes incorrectly referred to as *T. tessellata*, it is much larger than the latter and lacks lip denticles. The whorls bear low rounded cords, patterned with brown squares or regular blotches. The columella is "twisted". There is a rich brown tinting inside the aperture.

## TONNA OLEARIUM

Giant Pacific Tun. *L. 1758.*
Western Pacific.

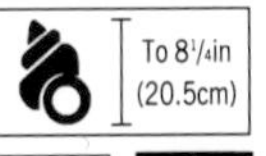


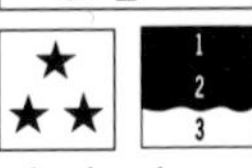


One of the largest species in the family, often confused with and indeed very similar to the Mediterranean *T. galea*, the giant Pacific tun has a very large ovate to rounded body whorl with a moderate spire. There are many strong low rounded spiral cords and axial growth striae are present. The suture is deeply channelled. The shell is beige to brown with a cream aperture. This specimen is from the Philippines. This species is sometimes called *C. cepa* which could be a synonym.

## TONNA CEREVISINA

Beerbarrel Tun. *Hedley 1919.* Queensland to New South Wales, Australia.

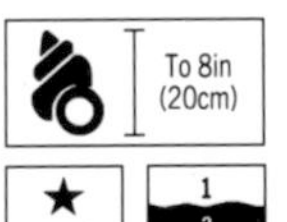


Another very large tun, this bears a close resemblance to *T. variegata*; the sculpturing and size of both are similar and both have variable patterning, so it is difficult to differentiate between them. The beerbarrel tun has coarse, but low rounded cords of yellow alternating with tan. The darker brown dashes and streaks are restricted to the areas around the channelled suture.

## TONNA PERDIX

Partridge Tun. *L. 1758.*
Indo-Pacific.

This species is easily identified by its fairly tall pointed spire and ovate body whorl. There are numerous flat spiral cords. The shell is white, overlaid with pale or tan brown squares and streaks on the cords, and the apex is pale orange. The canal is short. It inhabits offshore sandy areas.

### *TONNA LUTEOSTOMA*
Gold-mouthed Tun. *Küster 1857.*
Western Pacific.

A rounded heavy species, with a low spire and moderately channelled suture, it has prominent rounded spiral cords. The columella is glazed and covers part of the small umbilicus. The outer shell is creamy white, with orange brown streaks and blotches; the interior is an orange brown. A rare find, it is fished in depths to 660 feet (200m). This specimen is from southern Japan.

SUPER FAMILY
## TONOIDEA

FAMILY
## FICIDAE
(Fig Shells)

Fig-like in shape, these are thin and lightweight shells, with no varices or operculae. The spires are more or less flat and a large tapering body whorl and aperture lead to a long siphonal canal. This is a small family, with one main genus – *Ficus*. The shells bear little or no pattern and, apart from their graceful shape, they appear rather drab specimens to many people. Most inhabit sandy areas in tropical seas.

### *FICUS GRACILIS*
Graceful Fig. *Sowerby 1825.*
Japan to Taiwan.

This is the largest member of the family, although it is rather thin and fragile. The enlarged body whorl tapers gracefully to the canal. Fine spiral and axial cords form a "netted" appearance. The columella is smooth and centrally concave. The shell is a beige brown on the outside; the interior is a rich brown, fading to off-white at the margin of the aperture. Found in relatively deep water, this shell was fished off south-western Taiwan.

### *FICUS VARIEGATA*
Variable Fig. *Röding 1798.*
Japan to Taiwan.

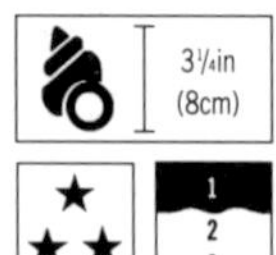


A less fragile species than *F. gracilis*, this is shorter, with an almost flat spire and bulbous body whorl narrowing to a moderate siphonal canal. There are fine spiral cords, and several growth striae are usually evident. The shell colour is a mottled medium-to-dark brown; the aperture is smooth and pale mauve or brown. It is found in sand and mud in shallow water.

**FICUS SUBINTERMEDIA**
Underlined Fig. *Orbigny 1852.*
Indo-Pacific.

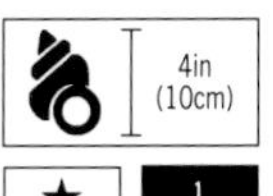


This flat spired shell has an ovate body whorl and a fairly long canal, its raised spiral cords and fine axial lines giving it a file-like texture. Five or so cream spiral bands with dark brown blotches and fine spiral broken lines of mid-brown make this one of the more highly patterned species. Inside the aperture, it is pale mauve.

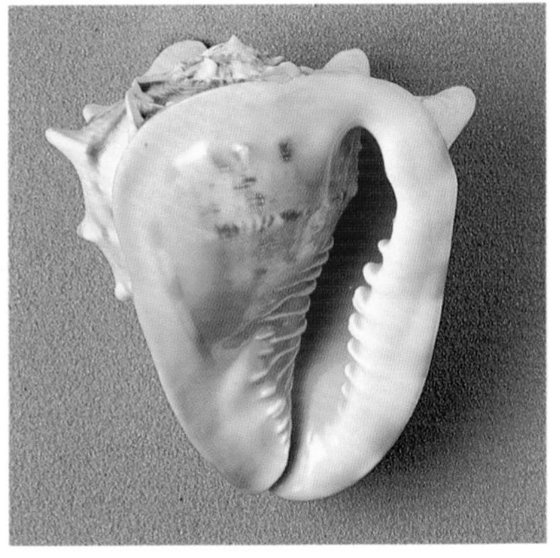

**CASSIS CORNUTA**
Horned Helmet. *L. 1758.*
Indo-Pacific.

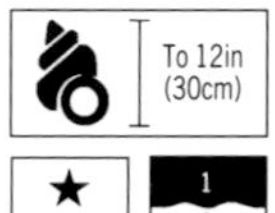


The most obvious feature of this, arguably the largest and heaviest species in the family, is the deep yellowy orange shield-like area on the underside. This comprises a thickened dentate lip, which is joined at the posterior to an enlarged parietal wall and columella. It is a highly glossy area and virtually hides the body whorl when viewed from underneath the shell. There is a low spire and a large angular body whorl, heavily knobbed at the shoulder. A coral reef dweller.

**CASSIS MADAGASCARIENSIS**
Emperor Helmet. *Lamarck 1822.*
Caribbean.

A large species, it has an almost flat spire, its angled body whorl bearing three rows of spiral blunted knobs and fine rounded axial ridges. The large glazed area on the underside is a beautiful peachy orange. The lip bears about ten strong denticles and the columella bears strong white spiral ribs and folds, tinged between with dark brown or black.

SUPER FAMILY
## TONOIDEA

FAMILY
## CASSIDAE
(Helmet or Bonnet Shells)

In total contrast to the tun shells, the helmets are solid and often very heavy, bearing strong ornamentation in the form of nodules and tuberculate varices. It is quite a large family, with several genera, including *Cassis*, *Cypraecassis*, *Galeodea*, *Phalium Casmaria*, *Echinophoria* and *Semicassis*. Some frequently used subgenera and synonymous subgenera such as *Hypocassis* and *Xenopallium* may well be elevated to full generic status as work continues on this family and I have, in a few instances, used these new names. All species prefer warmer seas where they live on sandy substrates, mostly in shallow water. They enjoy feeding on sea urchins. Some of the large species are used for the cameo industry.

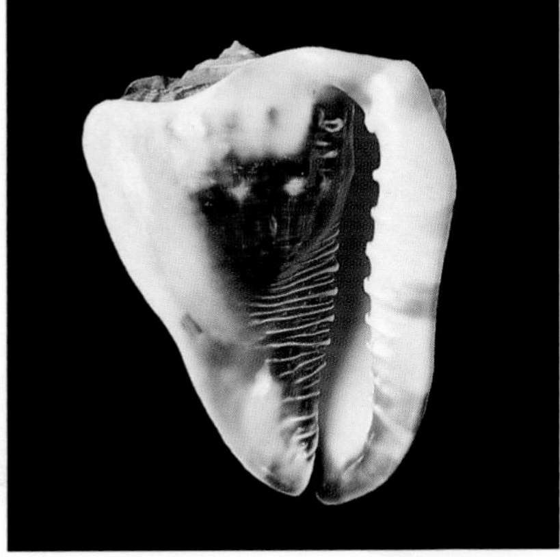

**CASSIS TUBEROSA**
King Helmet. *L. 1758.*
Caribbean to Brazil.

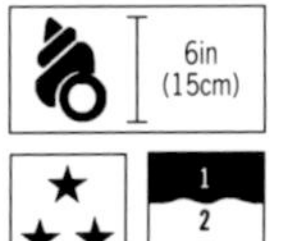


The spirally ridged and heavily knobbed body whorl is also hidden when this species is viewed from the underside, due to the triangular thickened and smooth outer lip, parietal wall and columella area, which again dominate the shell. It is generally beige brown on the dorsum, the large glazed area being cream and dark brown. This is a thick heavy shell.

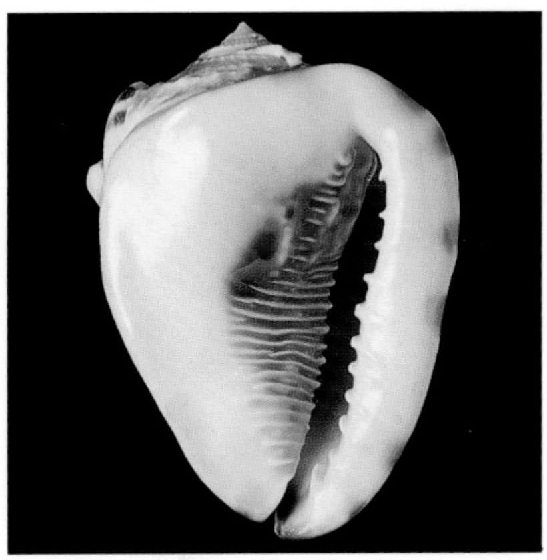

**CASSIS FLAMMEA**
Flame Helmet. *L. 1758.*
Florida and Caribbean.

This is rather similar in shape and weight to *C. tuberosa*, but smaller and more ovate. The spire is low and there are numerous rounded knobs on the body whorl, some pronounced at the shoulders. There is a glossy shield-like area underneath, which is creamy white with a little brown tinging. The siphonal canal is slightly twisted and upturned. This is a shallow-water dweller.

**CASSIS FIMBRIATA**
Fringed Helmet. *Quoy and Gaimard 1833.*
Southern and Western Australia.

A smaller ovate shell, it has a low spire, and its angled body whorl bears about three rows of rounded nodules and numerous fine axial creases. The lip and columella are generally smooth; the siphonal canal is upturned and protruding. Two variations are shown here; the small, more deeply coloured, specimen is from Albany, Western Australia, the larger paler shell is from Port Lincoln, Southern Australia. This shell is sometimes included in the subgenus *Hypocassis*.

**CYPRAECASSIS RUFA**
Bullmouth Helmet. *L. 1758.*
East Africa.

Often referred to as the cameo shell, it is this species, more so than other large cassis, that is used for the manufacture of cameos for the jewellery trade. A solid heavy shell, it is a deep orange red with rounded dorsal nodules; the lip is thick and dentate, and the columella and parietal wall are heavily calloused. It inhabits coral reefs.

**GALEODEA RUGOSA**
Rugose Bonnet. *L. 1758.*
North-East Atlantic and Mediterranean.

A lightweight thin species, it has a high spire and slightly rounded whorls. The shape is ovate, and there are prominent low rounded spiral cords. The thickened and flanged lip bears small denticles, and the columella and parietal area are smooth. The whole of the underside area is white, apart from which the shell is a creamy beige.

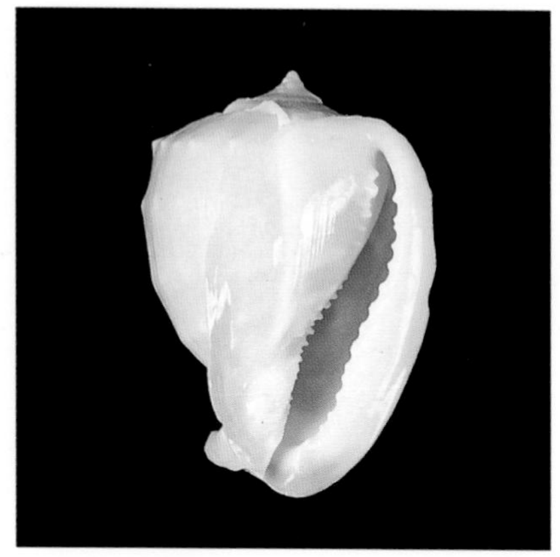

**CASSIS NANA**
Dwarf Helmet. *Tenison Woods 1879.*
Eastern Australia.

One of the smallest cassis, this endemic is somewhat triangular in shape. The spire is low and the body whorls have about four spiral rows of nodules, those at the shoulder being sharp. The outer lip is dentate and the columella has ribs. The exterior of the shell is beige; the underside is pure white. Found in depths between 195 and 990 feet (60 and 300m). This shell is sometimes included in the subgenus *Hypocassis*.

**CYPRAECASSIS TESTICULUS TESTICULUS**
*L. 1758.* Florida to Brazil.

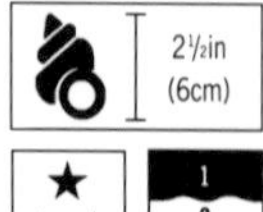


A solid rather narrow ovate shell, its fine spiral grooves and stronger axial ribs create a reticulated effect. The thickened rounded lip is dentate; there are folds on the columella and inner parietal wall. It is an overall beige to orange, with mottled and irregular mid-brown patches on the dorsum, the underside being beige to pale orange. This shell dwells in shallow water.

**ECHINOPHORIA KURODAI**
Kuroda's Bonnet. *Abbott 1968.*
Japan to Australia.

A beautifully sculptured deep-water species, it is lightweight and a lovely cream peach colour. There are several spiral rows of low rounded nodules, slightly more pronounced at the shoulders. The lip is dentate at the periphery and the columella is twisted. A popular and sought-after collectors' item; it has a moderate spire.

**ECHINOPHORIA CORONADOI WYVILLEI** Wyville's Bonnet. *Watson 1886*. Japan to Australia.

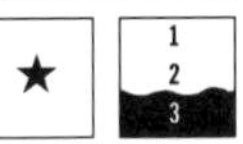


A lightweight globose species, it has a moderately tall spire. There are short rather sharp nodules on the earlier whorls, and very fine spiral threads and axial growth striae. The lip is thin and smooth; the thick columella is twisted and bears several folds. This shell is dredged from deep water, sometimes down to 1,475 feet (450m), and is a choice collectors' item.

**PHALIUM AREOLA** Chequered Bonnet. *L. 1758*. Western Indo-Pacific.

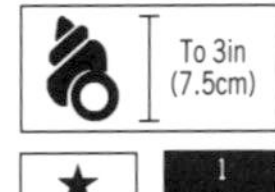


A lovely shell, it is smooth, glossy and patterned with squared markings of rich brown. The ovate shell has a medium-sized spire, and several varices are present. The lip is fairly thin, recurved and dentate, and there are fine columella folds. Prefers sandy mud in intertidal or offshore waters.

**PHALIUM FIMBRIA** Fringed Bonnet. *Gmelin 1791*. Indian Ocean.

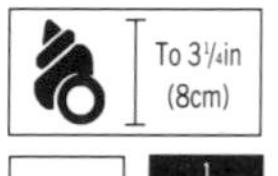


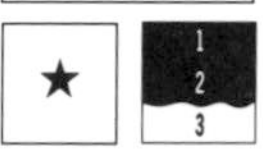


A beautiful and sought-after species, it is an elongated oval shape, with a medium spire. The shoulders have low sharp nodules and there are axial ridges which disappear at the anterior. At least four varices are present. The lip is dentate and the lightly folded columella and the parietal wall are calloused and end in a "lip" at the periphery. The shell is delicately marked with orange beige and dark brown.

**PHALIUM STRIGATUM** Striped Bonnet. *Gmelin 1791*. Japan, Taiwan and Philippines.

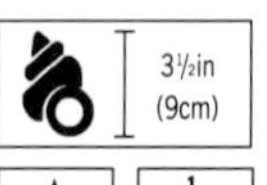


Often incorrectly called *P. flammiferum*, which is a synonym, this is a smooth and glossy ovate shell with a humped dorsum. The spire is of medium size, and there are at least five varices. The lip is thickened, recurved and lightly dentate, and there are columella folds. Conspicuous reddish brown axial bands stand out against the off-white background. It lives offshore, to 330 feet (100m).

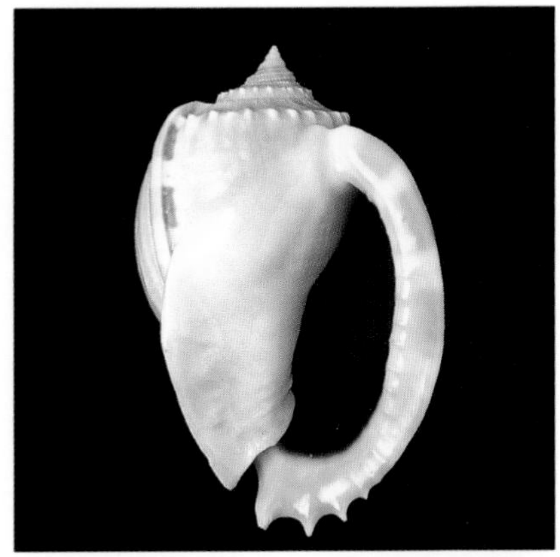

**PHALIUM GLAUCUM** Grey Bonnet. *L. 1758*. Indo-Pacific.

A thick heavy rather rounded bonnet, with a low spire and usually only one varix. The shoulders are flattened below the suture. The much thickened lip is finely dentate, somewhat stepped at the whorl union, and there are about three short sharp processes at the anterior end. The exterior is grey green; the lip and columella are pale orange, and the inside is a deep purple brown.

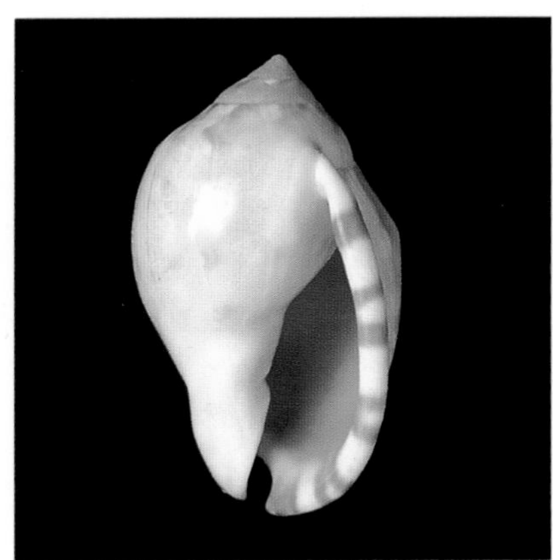

**XENOPHALIUM LABIATUM IREDALEI** Iredale's Bonnet. *Bayer 1935*. South Africa.

A variable subspecies of *P. labiatum labiatum*, this endemic is beige pink with light brown half-moon markings; there are four or five pairs of mauve brown blotches on the lip. It has a medium spire and a rounded-to-ovate body whorl, the shoulder of which sometimes bears low rounded nodules. The columella is smooth and calloused. It inhabits offshore waters.

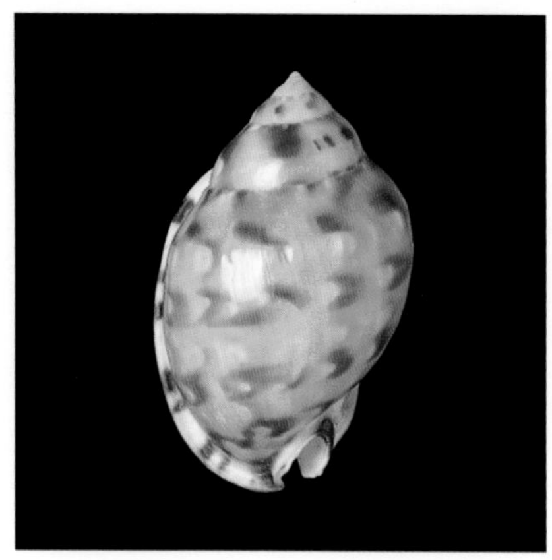

**XENOPHALIUM LABIATUM IHERINGI** Ihering's Bonnet. *Carcelles 1953*. Brazil to Argentina.

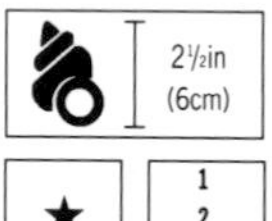

Another subspecies of *P. labiatum labiatum*, it is rarely found, being dredged in deep water – this specimen came from off Rio de Janeiro, Brazil. The shell is similar in size and shape to *P. labiatum iredalei*, but the pattern and colours are more distinctive. Also the inner lip is finely dentate and the columella has folds.

**XENOPHALIUM THOMPSONI** Thompson's Bonnet. *Brazier 1875*. South-eastern Australia.

This fragile endemic shell is trawled in deep water off the coast of south-eastern Australia. It has a high spire and globose body whorl. The shoulders are angled below the suture. There are fine stunted nodules in a row on the shoulders, fine axial striae, and occasional mid-brown blotches on the dorsum and dark brown on the lip. The operculum is fan-shaped, horny and radially ribbed.

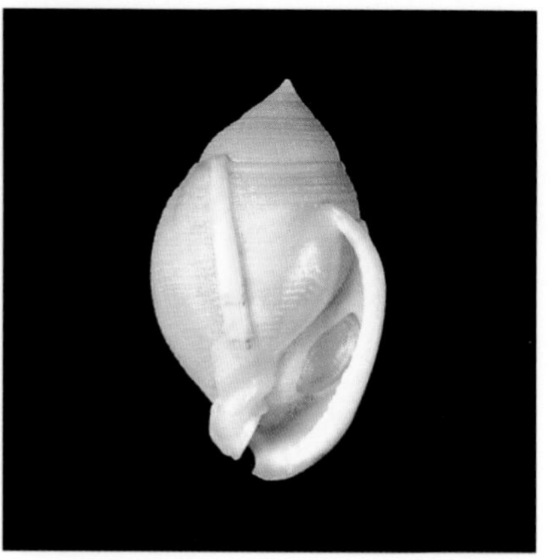

**SEMICASSIS CRATICULATUM** South African Bonnet. *Euthyme 1885*. South and South-East Africa.

An ovate species, with a medium spire, it has rather rounded whorls. There are fine spiral cords and usually one varix is present. The lip is finely grooved and there are strong columella folds. The siphonal canal is short. The colour is a beige throughout, with occasional brown markings on the lip. A deep-water dweller, this specimen was trawled off Zululand.

**XENOPHALIUM PYRUM PYRUM** Pear Bonnet. *Lamarck 1822*. South Africa, Southern Australia and New Zealand.

A fairly solid globose shell, with a low spire, it usually bears weak nodules on the shoulder of the body whorl, although some shells are smooth. The lip is smooth, as is the undulating columella. The background colour is a pale beige grey, decorated with faint pale brown spiral streaks and sometimes with crescent shapes, and there are dark brown blotches on the lip. This specimen was dredged in 99 feet (30m) at Houraki Gulf, northern New Zealand.

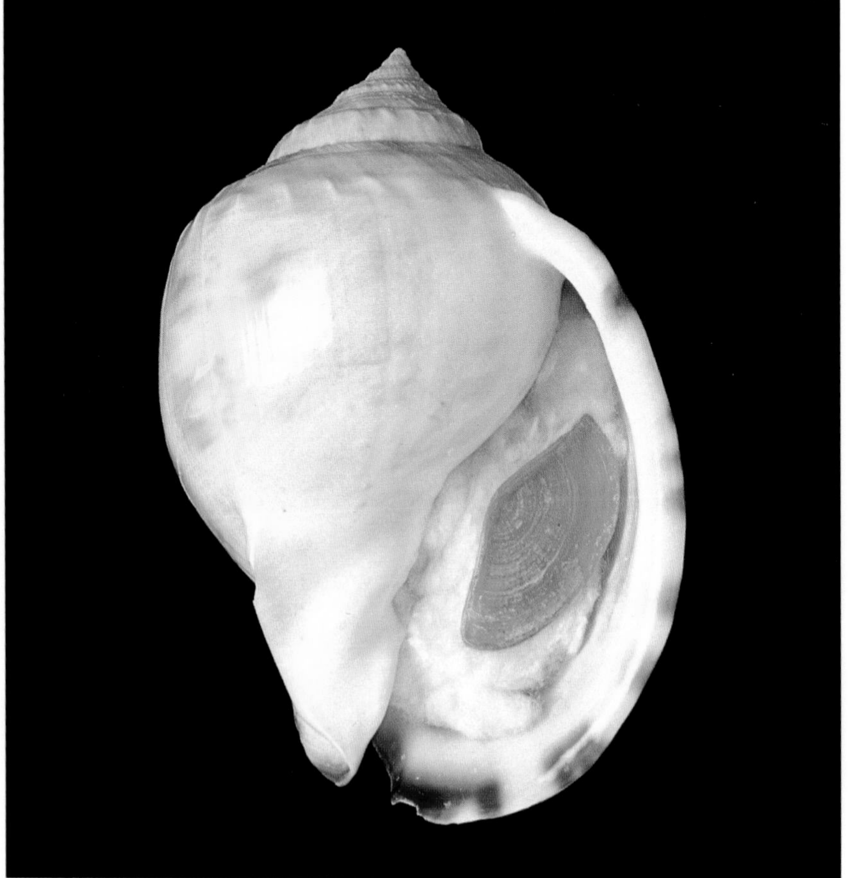

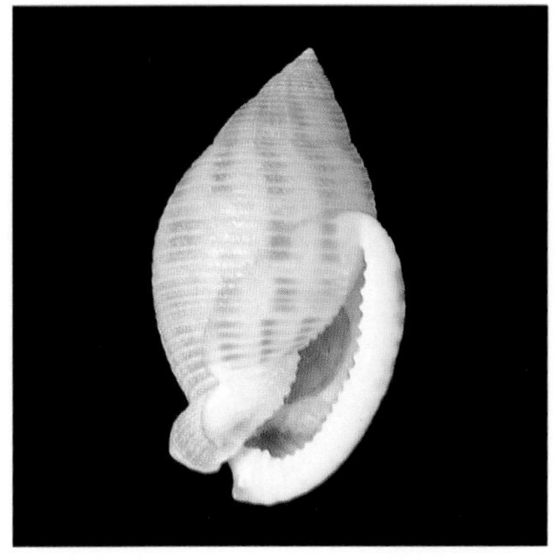

**SEMICASSIS MICROSTOMA**
Narrow-mouthed Bonnet. *Von Martens* 1903. East Africa to Natal.

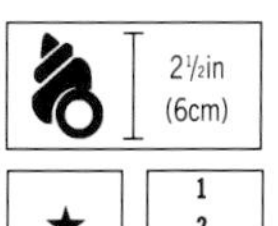


The shell has a high spire, and is ovate. There are strong spiral cords. The lip is recurved, thick and heavily dentate; the columella is calloused and has granular folds. The canal is rather flattened and obliquely laid. The overall colour is beige, and there are broken axial rows of pale brown lines. This shell inhabits deep water.

**SEMICASSIS GRANULATUM CENTIQUADRATUM** Panama Bonnet. *Valenciennes 1822*. Western Central America.

This is very like *S. granulatum granulatum*, but tends to be coarser in texture, with low fairly sharp nodules on the shoulders. There are relatively strong spiral cords above the canal, and the markings are also generally darker. This specimen comes from Ecuador and was fished in offshore waters.

**SEMICASSIS GRANULATUM UNDULATUM** Mediterranean Bonnet. *Gmelin 1791*. Mediterranean.

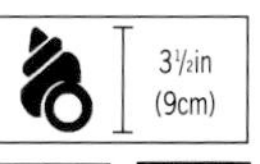


The Mediterranean bonnet has a high spire and is ovate and coarsely ribbed. It is thick and heavy, with rounded whorls. The very thick solid stepped lip bears about 16 prominent denticles. The columella and parietal shield are pustulate and calloused. The beige to pale brown background is decorated with random darker brown bands and a few blotches. The aperture is white, darkening to orange brown within.

**SEMICASSIS GRANULATUM GRANULATUM** Scotch Bonnet. *Born 1778*. South-eastern USA to Brazil.

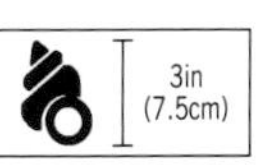


A stocky ovate shell, with a medium spire, the Scotch bonnet appears relatively smooth, but on closer examination there are fine spiral grooves and faint axial growth striae. The lip is thickened, recurved and dentate, and there are numerous pustules on the columella at the anterior and on the shield. It is beige, with brown squared marks on the dorsum, and pure white on the underside.

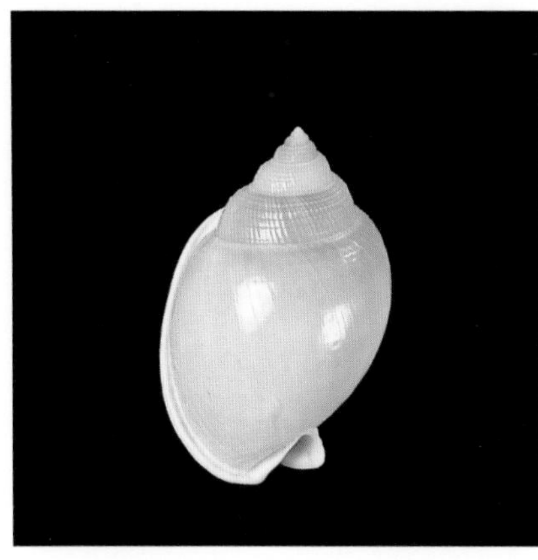

*SEMICASSIS GLABRATUM ANGASI* Angas's Bonnet. *Iredale 1927.* New South Wales to N.W. Australia.

A very lightweight almost transparent bonnet, it has rounded whorls and a medium spire. There are fine cancellations in the early whorls, but the body whorl is smooth and glossy. The rounded lip is dentate and the umbilicus is open behind a folded columella. It is a creamy pink colour.

SUPER FAMILY
## TONOIDEA

FAMILY
### RANELLIDAE
(The Tritons)

An interesting and popular family, the tritons generally inhabit warm tropical seas and are variously shaped, with much ornament. When living, the shells are covered by a thick and often "hairy" or bristly periostracum. The varices usually bear large tubercules. The upper part of the aperture is closed, thus differing from those of the Bursidae family (frog shells), which are open at the posterior. The veliger larvae of some tritons have a free-swimming period of up to three months, and the far-flung localities in which several species occur are possibly a result of this. There has been much alteration and revision of this group. The genera and subgenera worth noting include *Ranella*, *Argobuccinum*, *Gyrineum*, *Biplex*, *Cymatium*, *Ranularia* (which has long curved canals), *Charonia* and *Distorsio*. They are carnivorous, feeding on sea urchins and molluscs.

*ARGOBUCCINUM PUSTULOSUM* Argus Triton. *Lightfoot 1786.* South Africa.

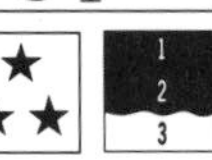


A rather globose flattened shell, this endemic has a medium spire and is decorated with dark brown spiral bands on which are low rounded nodules. The lip is dentate, and there are five or six minute denticles on the lower part of the columella. The aperture area is pure white. Found in offshore waters.

*BIPLEX PERCA* Winged or Maple Leaf Triton. *Perry 1811.* Western Pacific.

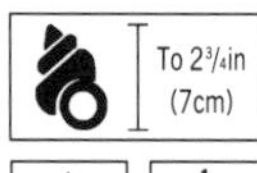


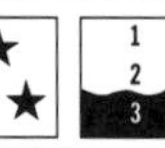


Huge specimens of this deep water shell used to be fished regularly off Taiwan, but this no longer occurs due to changed fishing habits. Shells half the size now come from the Philippines. The winged triton has an amazing shape – very flat with wide leaf-like axially aligned varices – and is a great favourite of mine. It is both spirally and axially ornamented with cords and nodules. The depicted Taiwanese shell measures 3¼in (8cm).

**FUSITRITON MAGELLANICUM**
Magellanic Triton. *Röding 1798.* S. South America, S. Australia and New Zealand.

A graceful pale beige shell, the magellanic triton has a high spire and rounded globose whorls which are coarsely reticulated. There are several low varices. The lip is stepped and smooth inside, and the virtually straight columella is also smooth. The canal is of medium length. This specimen is from deep water off New South Wales.

**GYRINEUM ROSEUM**
Rose Triton. *Reeve 1844.* South-West Pacific.

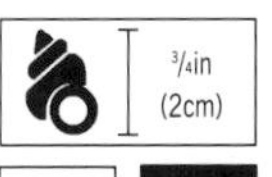

Another shallow-water dweller, its shape is almost the same as that of *G. gyrinum*, but the ribs on the dorsal body whorl appear larger. It is delicately coloured a pale pink orange; the aperture is white, with occasional hints of lavender.

**RANELLA OLEARIUM**
Wandering Triton. *L. 1758.* Caribbean, Med., Africa, Australia and New Zealand.

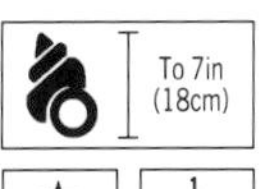

As the common name suggests, this shell is found in many locations. It is thick and heavy, with rounded whorls, a tall spire and large rounded aperture. Despite the world-wide habitats, specimens differ little. The depicted shell was fished in deep water off south-eastern Italy.

**GYRINEUM GYRINUM**
Tadpole Triton. *L. 1758.* Indo-Pacific.

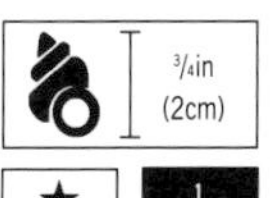

This small but strong little shell is triangular and rather flattened, with a high spire. The whorls bear coarse axial ribs and the varices are axially aligned and are ridged. The inner lip is dentate. The canal is short. Deep brown spiral banding with hints of yellow colour this pretty shell, which inhabits shallow water, living under coral slabs.

**GYRINEUM PUSILLUM**
Purple Gyre Triton. *Broderip 1832.* Indo-Pacific.

This triangular-shaped species has a high spire and short canal. The varices are axially aligned. It is very prettily marked with small white blunt nodules on a tan and grey background; the aperture and inner canal are tinged with purple. These shells live on coral rubble or sand and in muddy areas in shallow water.

**CABESTANA SPENGLERI**
Spengler's Triton. *Perry 1811.* Southern Australia and Tasmania.

A heavy solid triton, it is beige, with mid-brown spiral grooves. The shoulders bear rounded nodules. Shells may have two or three varices, and the lip is expanded and undulating; there are strong lirae within. The columella is smooth, but there is a blunt node on the upper parietal wall. This shell dwells in intertidal rock pools.

## CABESTANA CUTACEA

Mediterranean Bark Triton. *L. 1767.*
North-East Atlantic and Mediterranean.

A very similar shell in shape and colour to *C. spengleri*, it differs in that the whorls are more angular, the colour is pale brown throughout, and the lip is heavily dentate. It dwells in moderately deep water, this specimen coming from southern Italy.

## CABESTANA AFRICANA

South African Triton. *A. Adams 1855.*
South Africa.

A coarse rugged endemic, with robust rounded axial ridges and flat spiral cords, its lip is thickened and there are strong lirae. The columella and parietal area are smooth. Apart from the aperture, which is pure white, the shell is mid-brown throughout. It lives offshore in deep water, and this specimen was collected at Sordwana Bay, North Natal.

## CHARONIA TRITONIS

Trumpet Triton. *L. 1758.*
Indo-Pacific.

The largest species in the triton family, this is a well-known and very beautiful shell, with a tall elegant spire, rounded whorls, and a large flaring lip. The markings are distinctive and the deep orange aperture is particularly attractive. This is one of several shells used as a form of trumpet once the apex has been removed, and is a very popular collectors' shell.

## CYMATIUM RANZANII

Ranzani's Triton. *Bianconi 1851.*
Gulf of Oman, Arabian Sea.

A very coarse, chunky and heavy species, it is triangular in shape, with a high spire. The shoulders are angled below the suture and bear very large rounded nodules. The spiral ribs are low, rounded and coarse. The lip is very large and thickened, almost wing-like when viewed from the underside, and is strongly dentate. The columella and calloused parietal area are smooth. There is a long curved siphonal canal.

**CYMATIUM FEMORALE**
Angular Triton. *L. 1758.*
South-eastern Florida and Caribbean.

A long, rather narrow and misshapen species, the angular triton features strongly sculptured spiral cords, with fine threads between, and has nodulose varices and outer lip. The spire is tall, and the overall colour ranges from dark orange to light tan, with a white aperture. A popular collectors' shell, it likes shallow water, often living on eel grass beds.

**CYMATIUM PARTHENOPEUM**
Neapolitan Triton. *Von Salis 1793.*
Worldwide tropical and warm seas.

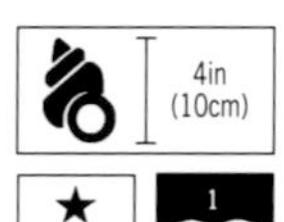


This is a very widespread triton, the specimen shown here coming from South-East Africa. It is solidly built, with heavily corded rounded whorls and a medium spire. The aperture is wide, with a strongly dentate lip, columella and parietal wall. The colour is generally cream and tan, with dark brown markings on the varices, denticles and folds of the columella. It inhabits relatively shallow waters.

**CYMATIUM VESTITUM**
Garment Triton. *Hinds 1844.*
Western Central America.

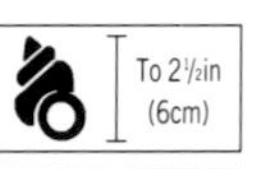


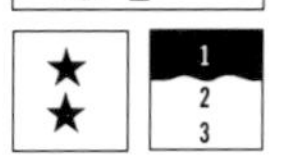

According to some experts, this is the Central American counterpart of the very common Western Pacific species, *C. pileare*. It is shaped in an elongated oval, with a high spire and spirally corded and noduled whorls, and is dark brown with cream or tan spiral bands. It is a shallow-water dweller.

**CYMATIUM PERRYI**
Perry's Triton. *Emerson and Old 1963.*
Southern India and Sri Lanka.

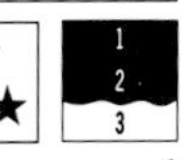

Solid and heavy, with a medium spire, this species is dominated by angular knobbed whorls and rounded ribbed varices. Its colours are striking – pale orange or tan, with cream and dark brown ribs. The dentate inner lip and columella are a reddish orange. The small operculum is ovate and horny. The canal is long and curved.

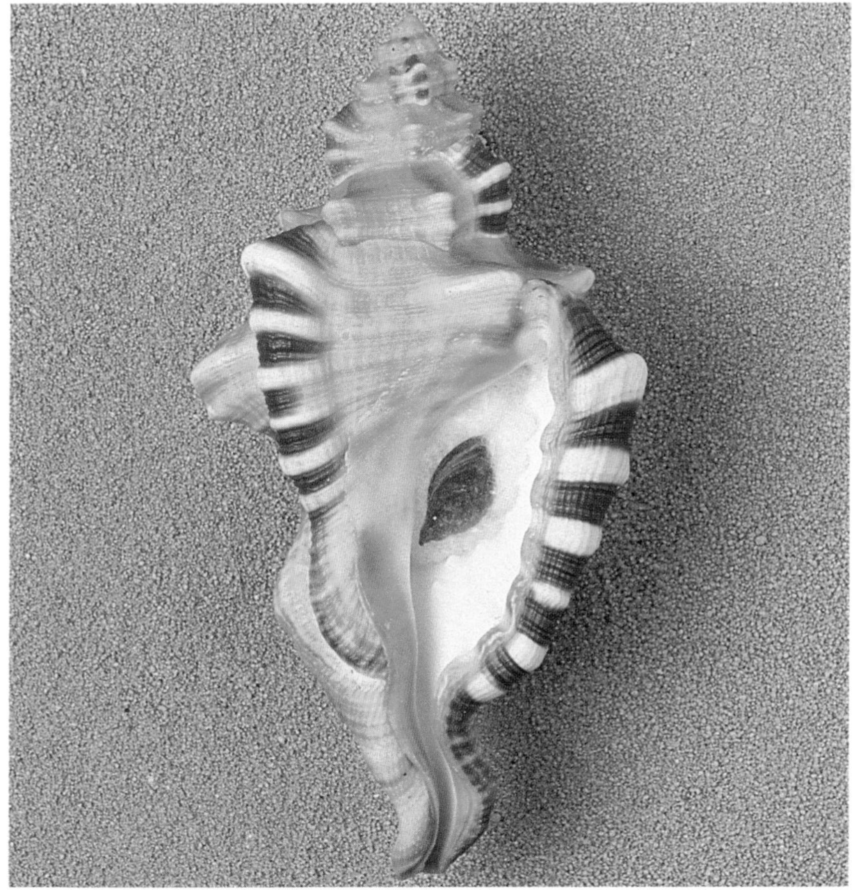

## CYMATIUM AQUITILE
Aquatile Hairy Triton. *Reeve 1844*.
Indo-Pacific.

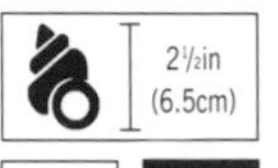


A tall elongate-fusiform species, which is thick and heavy. The orange tan whorls bear low cords and fine spiral grooves, and there are low rounded knobbed ribs. The inner lip carries a double row of strong denticles and the columella and parietal area have many folds. This shell is a lover of shallow water.

## CYMATIUM INTERMEDIUM
Intermediate Hairy Triton. *Pease 1869*.
Central Pacific.

A small stocky shell with strong spirally noduled cords. The columella and parietal wall are plicate, and the inner lip is strongly dentate. The outer lip bears a heavy varix. The overall colour is orange tan, and there are darker brown markings. The aperture is a pale orange. This specimen is from Hawaii.

## CYMATIUM NICOBARICUM
Nicobar Hairy Triton. *Röding 1798*.
Indo-Pacific and West Indies.

This rather distorted angular shell has a tall spire, coarse spiral cords, heavy nodules on the shoulders, and moderate axial ribs. It is a grey beige, with fine black spiral lines between the cords. The columella area is pale orange with cream or white plica; the lip on this specimen is "hollow" and the edge is corrugated.

## CYMATIUM CORRUGATUM CORRUGATUM
Corrugated Triton. *Lamarck 1816*. Med. and West Africa.

A tall elongate-fusiform shell, this has coarse spiral cords with low rounded nodules, especially on earlier whorls. The lip bears very strong sharply ridged denticles, and the parietal wall and columella have fine folds. The canal is of medium length. Two colour forms are shown here – the white shell is from Italy and the beige is from Morocco.

## CYMATIUM TRIGONUM

Trigonal Hairy Triton. *Gmelin 1791.*
West Africa and Southern Caribbean.

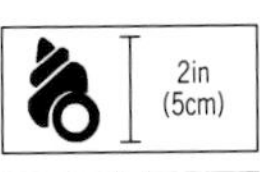


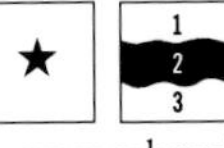


Small and solid, with a relatively low rounded spire, the shell is dominated by spiral cords, irregular nodulose ribs and a thickened long lip which is strongly dentate. The narrow columella and parietal wall bear short rounded nodules. The canal is long. The interior is red or orange; the exterior is a beige cream. The depicted shell is from Senegal, and was found at a depth of 66 feet (20m).

## CYMATIUM TRIPUS

Tripod Triton. *Gmelin 1791.*
Southern India, South-East Asia.

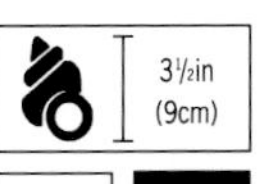


This elongated shell has a medium spire and long siphonal canal. It is decorated with low rounded cords and occasional axial nodules, usually in groups of four. The lip is corrugated, and the columella and parietal wall bear widely spaced folds. The shell is an overall beige colour, the wall being pale pink with darker brown between the folds. This sample was collected in shallow waters off Madras, India.

## CYMATIUM LABIOSUM

Wide-lipped Triton. *Wood 1828.*
Indo-Pacific and West Indies.

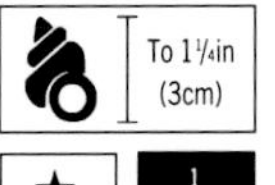


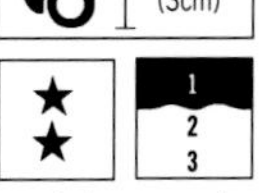


A variable shell – two forms are shown here – it is decoratively sculpted with coarse spiral cords most prominent at the shoulders. There are strong axial ribs, nodulose in places. The canal is of shortish length and slightly umbilicate. It dwells in shallow water, under rocks or on sandy mud.

## CYMATIUM TABULATUM

Shouldered Triton. *Menke 1843.*
Indo-Pacific and New Zealand.

This shell is within the subgenus *Septa*. It is a small solid species, with a medium spire and long curved canal. There are low spiral cords and axial nodules, the whorls appearing angular. It is very prettily coloured with greyish beige and pinkish orange tinges. The mouth area is white. The depicted specimen was collected on an intertidal reef, Dampier, Western Australia.

**CYMATIUM AMICTUM**
Robed Triton. *Reeve 1844.*
Western Central America.

Small, narrow and fusiform, this shell possesses both a tall spire and a long curved canal. It is beige in colour, with a white aperture. There are fine spiral grooves, coarse axial nodules, and both lip and columella are dentate. It dwells in deep water to about 230 feet (70m).

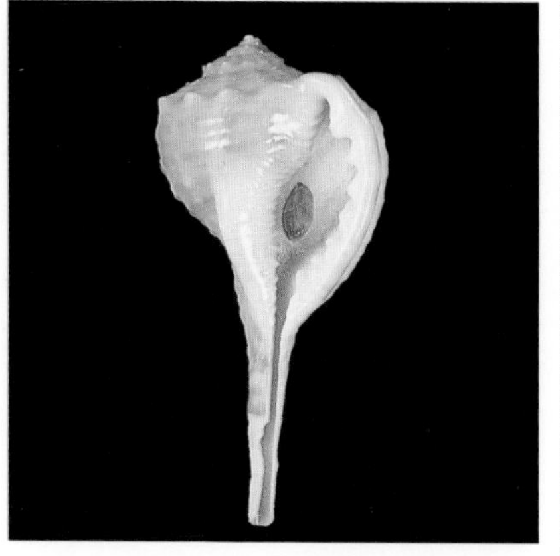

**CYMATIUM RETUSUM**
Blunted Triton. *Lamarck 1822.*
Indian Ocean and South-East Asia.

This strange-looking species has a large globose body whorl, low almost flat spire and a very long siphonal canal. The low flat cords bear small rounded nodules; the lip is very thick, the inside being calloused and dentate. There are numerous folds on the columella and parietal wall. The shell is beige, with a white aperture. This specimen was dredged off Madras, India.

**CYMATIUM TESTUDINARIUM**
Tortoise Triton. A. *Adams and Reeve 1850.* Philippines.

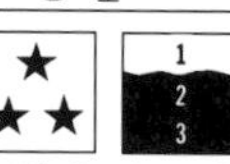

A medium-sized and solid shell, it has nodulose whorls with flat spiral cords. The canal is very long and somewhat recurved. It is generally pale orange; the folded columella and parietal wall are a distinct dark grey brown. This particular specimen is from West Sorsogon.

**CYMATIUM PFEIFFERIANUM**
Pfeiffer's Hairy Triton. *Reeve 1844.*
Indo-Pacific.

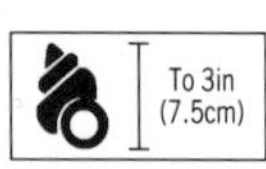

An elongate-fusiform shape, it has a tall spire and long canal. Numerous beaded cords and axial riblets ornament the whorls, giving a cancellated effect. It is variable in colour, and the two forms shown here were collected off Phuket, Thailand, in shallow water.

**CYMATIUM SARCOSTOMA**
Yellow-lipped Triton. *Reeve 1844.*
Western Pacific and Indian Ocean.

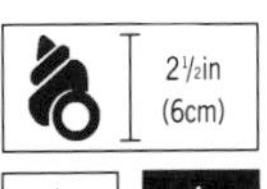

Rather similar in shape to *C. pyrum*, its more common counterpart, this shell has a medium-sized spire and curved siphonal canal. There are low fairly flat spiral cords and short sharp nodulose axial ribs. There is a dip below the corrugated lip edge and internally there are coarse spiral grooves. The columella is plicate and the parietal area bears four or more raised cords. It is a shallow-water species.

**CYMATIUM CAUDATUM**
Bent-neck Triton. *Gmelin 1791.*
Indo-Pacific.

A prettily ornamented shell, this has a large rounded body whorl and its canal is usually long and curved. It has a deeply channelled suture, alternate double and single rows of spiral cords, and nodose axial ridges. The mouth is pure white, the rest of the shell being cream or pale tan. It lives on sand or coral in shallow water.

**CYMATIUM TRILINEATUM**
Three-lined Triton. *Reeve 1844.* Western Pacific, Indian Ocean and Red Sea.

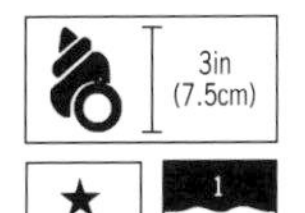

Certainly recorded in the Red Sea and the Philippines, this is a solid and chunky shell with large rounded dorsal knobs and flattened spiral cords. There are strong rounded denticles on the lip and fine plicae on the columella and parietal shield. This cream or orange brown shell has a pinkish aperture.

**CYMATIUM SINENSE**
Chinese Triton. *Reeve 1844.*
Western Pacific and Australia.

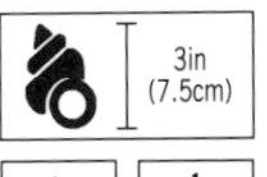

A long narrow shell, the Chinese triton has a tall spire and very long curved canal. It has attractive angular spiral cords, intersected with narrow axial ridges and tiny threads. The columella and parietal area are plicate; the lip is strongly dentate. It is mainly cream or pale yellow, with occasional tan axial streaks following the ridges.

**CYMATIUM EXILE**
*Reeve 1844.*
Philippines.

A small shell, with angular strongly ribbed whorls and a very long curved and twisted siphonal canal, it is an off-white colour with erratic patches of tan or mid-brown. The columella is plicate, and the lip bears short denticles. This specimen is from the Sulu Sea.

**CYMATIUM DUNKERI**
Dunker's Triton. *Lischke 1868.*
Japan.

Although similar to *C. sarcostoma*, this is much larger, with – judging from the limited number that I have examined – more nodose axial ribs. The colour is also different, Dunker's triton being pale beige with blotches of blackish brown on the varices. The aperture is white, but the exterior shell coloration can continue from the parietal area to the interior. This shell lives in depths of about 165 feet (50m) and may be difficult to obtain.

### SASSIA SUBDISTORTA
Distorted Rock Triton. *Lamarck 1822.*
Southern Australia and Tasmania.

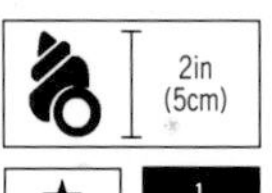

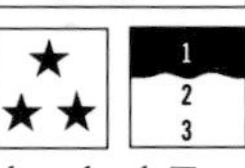


The distorted rock triton has a tall spire, rather angular whorls and a short siphonal canal. There are spirally beaded cords, most prominent at the middle to upper part of the whorl. Two colour forms are shown here. The inner lip is slightly grooved, apart from which the aperture is smooth and white. This is a shallow-water species, living under rocks.

### LINATELLA SUCCINCTA
Lesser Girdled Triton. *L. 1771.*
Indo-Pacific.

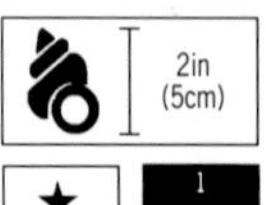


A rounded shell with a medium spire and canal, it is lightweight and ornamented with flat spiral cords which are an attractive dark brown. The background colour is beige. The lip bears numerous flattish denticles, also dark brown. The narrow columella supports rounded ridges at the anterior and two distinct denticles at the posterior. Some experts place *L. succincta* in a separate family, Personidae.

### DISTORSIO RETICULATA
Reticulated Distorsio. *Röding 1798.*
Indo-Pacific.

A lightweight shell, its rounded, distorted whorls are covered with strong cancellate ornamentation. The lip is flattened and supports both fine and coarse denticles. The aperture is complex, with parietal and columella denticles and pustules – more so at the anterior. The whole of this area to the first varix is lightly calloused.

### DISTORSIO SMITHI
Smith's Distorsio. *Von Maltzan 1884.*
West Africa.

A rather angular and distorted species, though less so than *D. reticulata*, Smith's distorsio is generally pale orange or cream with a darker brown glazed and calloused aperture. There are many irregularly-sized denticles and ridges within the opening – a characteristic feature of shells within this genus. This particular specimen is from Takoradi, Ghana.

SUPER FAMILY
TONOIDEA

FAMILY
## BURSIDAE
(Frog Shells)

A small family, very similar and closely related to the cymatiums (tritons), they are small to medium-sized shells, usually sturdy, thick walled and nodulose, with coarse heavy varices. The existence of an anal (exhalant) canal at the upper or posterior end of the aperture differentiates them from the tritons. Most are shallow-water dwellers, found living under rocks or amongst coral in warmer seas. They are an egg-laying family and are carnivores, some feeding on marine worms. There are three main genera – *Bursa*, *Bufonaria* and *Tutufa*; *Crossata* is lesser known, and there are a few subgenera, none of which concerns us here.

### BUFONARIA MARGARITULA
Noble Frog. *Deshayes 1832.*
Indo-Pacific.

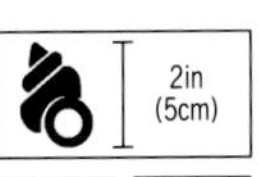


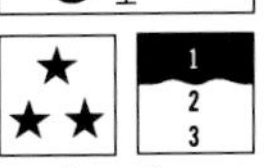


A short stocky shell, it has a medium spire and axially aligned varices. Both canals are prominent; if anything the anal canal is slightly longer. There are fine spirally beaded cords and one row of odd low sharp nodules on each whorl. It is very variable in colour – two forms are shown here. These particular specimens come from Palawan, Philippines.

### BUFONARIA FERNANDESI
Fernande's Frog. *Bell 1977.*
Somalia to Mozambique.

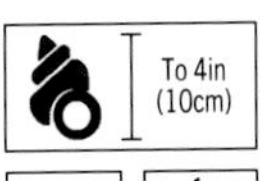


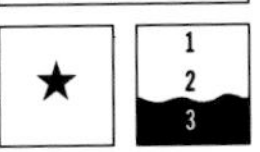


Only recently described, this rarely seen frog shell is occasionally trawled in depths to 577 feet (175m). It is rather long, with a tall spire and angular whorls, these bearing fine spiral threads. The anterior end tapers somewhat to the siphonal canal. The lip is dentate and the columella and parietal wall have strong plicae. Overall a beige brown colour, its aperture is tan with white sculpturing.

### BUFONARIA ELEGANS
Elegant Frog. *Sowerby 1836.*
Indian Ocean.

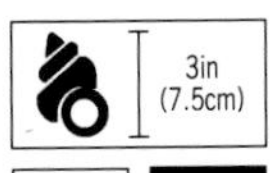


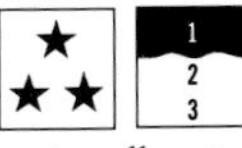


An attractive and rather lightweight shell, it features spiral beading, axially aligned varices and low sharp nodules on the whorls. The varices support larger sharper nodules – virtually spines in many cases. The colour is cream or pale brown, with narrow spiral bands of dark brown; the lip is tinged with orange. A shallow-water dweller.

**BUFONARIA RANA**
Common Frog. *L. 1758.*
Indo-Pacific.

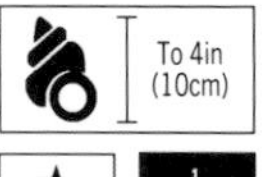

Rather similar at first sight to *B. elegans*, the common frog is larger, heavier and more globose. There are very neat spiral beads, and low sharp nodules on the whorls, these nodules being longer on the varices. The shell is usually a tan colour with a white, sometimes cream-tinged, aperture. This specimen was collected in Manila Bay, Philippines.

**BUFONARIA CRUMENA**
Purse Frog. *Lamarck 1816.*
Indo-Pacific.

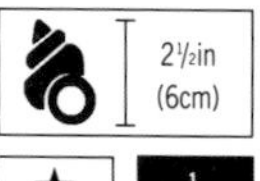

Short, ovate and rather flattened laterally, the shell has axially aligned and weakly noduled varices. The whorls have fine rows of spiral beading and two or three rows of spaced nodules. The dentate lip and anterior portion of the columella are a distinctive orange colour.

**BUFONARIA MARGINARTA**
Margined Frog. *Gmelin 1791.*
West Africa.

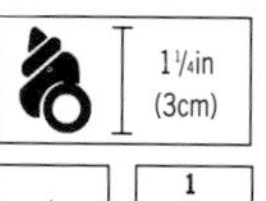

A deep-water sand-dweller, it is somewhat rounded and squat, with a low spire. The shell is reasonably smooth, but there are very fine rows of spiral cording. Three or four very low rounded nodules occur at the shoulders. It is a cream beige except for the aperture, which is white. The lip is finely dentate. The shell shown is from Ghana.

**BUFONARIA SUBGRANOSA**
Granulated Frog. *Sowerby 1836.*
Philippines.

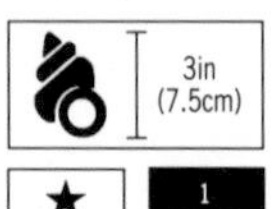

Another species similar to both *B. elegans* and *B. rana* in shape, this shell is dominated by numerous closely packed spiral beads. There are also very low nodules, strongest at the shoulders. The overall colour is an uneven tan-and-white mottling; the aperture is white with a slight lavender hue. Often incorrectly named *B. rana*.

**BUFONARIA CRUMENA**
f. *foliata* Frilled Frog.
*Broderip 1825.* Indian Ocean.

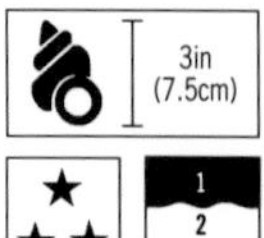

Form *foliata* is an appealing variation of *B. crumena*, the whole of the aperture being a deep orange. There are numerous fine denticles on the lip and plicae on the columella. The coarsely sculptured whorls bear rounded ridges; there are sharp nodules – quite large at the shoulders. In general, this form is not as flattened nor as low-spired as *B. crumena*. The depicted specimen is from Mozambique.

**BUFONARIA ECHINATA**
Spiny Frog. *Link 1807.*
Indian Ocean.

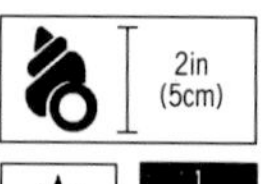

A deviation to the general sculpturing of most Bursidae, this species has axially aligned varices, supporting long narrow projections or spines. There are very fine spiral grooves and odd blunted nodules, sparsely spaced. Overall, it is a dirty grey brown, and it has a creamy white aperture. It is also rather flattened laterally.

### BUFONARIA BUFO
Chestnut Frog. *Bruguière 1792.*
Florida to Brazil.

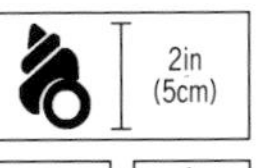

This species enjoys sand, mud or rocky substrate in depths to 330 feet (100m). It has a flattened-ovate shape, with a tall spire. The whorls, which are slightly angled and concave below the suture, bear fine spiral rows of beading. There are one or two blunt nodules on the body whorl. It is pale brown, with greyish spiral bands, and the lip and lower columella are tinted orange.

### BURSA SCROBILATOR
Pitted Frog. *L. 1758.*
North-West Africa and Mediterranean.

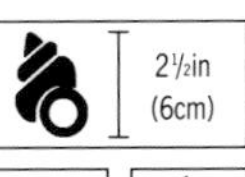

A shell with a tall spire and angular whorls, it is fairly smooth but possesses faint spiral threads. The nodulose lip is dentate on the interior, and there are folds and plicae on the columella. The siphonal and anal canals are of similar length. The shell is tan, with irregular blotches of darker brown. It lives offshore, down to about 132 feet (40m). This specimen was dead-collected in Tenerife.

### BURSA PACAMONI
Pacamon's Frog. *Matthews and Coelho 1971.*
Brazil.

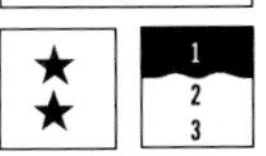

A small species, it is pale beige or cream in colour, with a white aperture. The whorls bear three or four rows of nodulose ridges and the varices are axially aligned. The lip is dentate and crenulated, and the columella has moderate plicae. This particular specimen was collected at 16 feet (5m) on rocks, off Itaparica Island, Bahia, Brazil.

### BUFONARIA NOBILIS
Noble Frog. *Reeve 1844.*
Western Pacific.

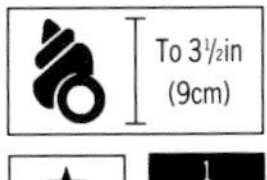

Another laterally "flattened" species, with axially aligned varices, it has a tall spire and a large aperture with an expanded lip. There are numerous spiral rows of beading and low nodules both on the whorls and varices, the latter being rather more sharp and extended. A popular species among enthusiasts of the frog shell family.

**BURSA THOMAE**
St. Thomas Frog. *Orbigny 1842*. South-East USA to Brazil; also Cape Verde Islands.

This is very much like *B. pacamoni* in shape and size, but the nodules are fewer and larger; also the aperture is a delicate lavender colour. Elsewhere, the colour is pale brown to cream. This species lives on or under rocks to about 248 feet (75m).

**BURSA CRUENTATA**
Bloodstained Frog. *Sowerby 1835*. Indo-Pacific.

A coarsely sculptured species, it has heavily nodulose varices and shoulders. There are numerous rows of spiral beading. The lip has denticles and the columella is moderately plicate. Although often encrusted, the colour is generally pale beige or greyish with odd darker streaks, especially on the nodules. The aperture is white and there is black spotting on the parietal wall. This specimen is from the Maldive Islands.

**BURSA LAMARCKI**
Lamarck's Frog. *Deshayes 1853*. South-West Pacific.

A thick and very coarsely sculptured shell, it has obliquely upturned anal canals on the axially aligned varices. It is attractively coloured off-white to cream, with irregular splashes of yellow and dark brown. The aperture is stained brown black and on this area are placed pale orange denticles and plicae. A shallow-water reef dweller.

**BURSA RHODOSTOMA**
Wine-mouthed Frog. *Sowerby 1835*. Indo-Pacific and Red Sea.

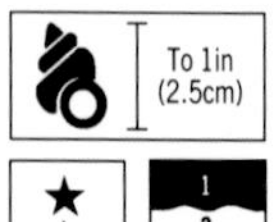

A small but solid shell, it is often encrusted with coarse spirally rounded ridges bearing low nodules. The aperture is an unmistakable lavender colouring; the lip has very small denticles and there are odd pustules on the columella. The depicted shell was collected in 6 feet (2m) on corals at the Gulf of Eilat, Israel.

**BURSA MAMMATA**
Udder Frog. *Röding 1798*. South-West Pacific.

This shell is rather like a large more heavily ornamented form of *B. rhodostoma*, although the interior colour is a deep purple. The anal canal is laid obliquely and is often longer than the siphonal canal. Here is another species that demands painstaking cleaning, as it is usually heavily encrusted with lime deposits. This specimen came from Honiara Reefs, Solomon Islands.

**BURSA BUFONIA**
Warted Frog. *Gmelin 1791*. Indo-Pacific.

The depicted specimen, although much encrusted, has been carefully cleaned to show the apparently pitted nodulose whorls. It is a chunky and heavy shell with conspicuous upturned anal canals and a strongly dentate and very thick lip. This species lives under corals, offshore.

**BURSA TENUISCULPTA**
Finely-sculptured Frog. *Dautz and Fischer 1906.* Canary Islands.

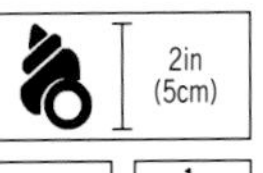
2in (5cm)

This species has a granulose texture to its tall spire and rather angled whorls. There are spirally arranged rows of both fine and strong beads and nodules. The lip is dentate and the columella and parietal area have moderate plicae; at the posterior, these are tinged between with dark brown black. This specimen was collected at 990 feet (300m) off Tenerife Island.

**BURSA AWATII**
Philippine Frog. *Ray 1949.* Philippines.

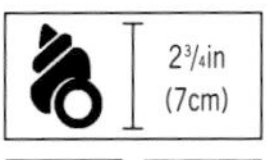
$2^{3}/_{4}$in (7cm)

This endemic species appears to be restricted to the central Philippines, where it inhabits moderately deep water. It is a thin and very lightweight shell, with a tall spire and rounded whorls. These have nodulose spiral ridges and several rows of beading. The depicted specimen was fished off Panglao, Bohol Island.

**TUTUFA BUBO**
Giant Frog Shell. *L. 1758.* Indo-Pacific.

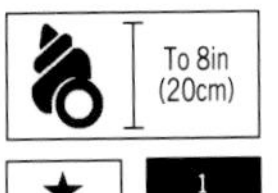
To 8in (20cm)

The largest species in the family, this has a tall spire, angular nodulose whorls and a wide flaring aperture. The lip periphery is scalloped. The siphonal and anal canals are short, and the former is recurved. The shell is mottled with creamy yellow and dark brown, the aperture being an attractive pale yellow or apricot colour, darkening to the interior. A shallow-water dweller.

**BURSA GRANULARIS**
Granulate Frog. *Röding 1798.* Indo-Pacific and Caribbean.

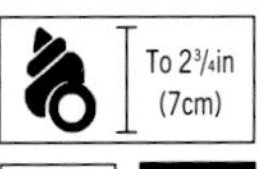
To $2^{3}/_{4}$in (7cm)

A widespread and well-known frog shell, it has a tall spire and rather wide heavily nodulose whorls. All varices are axially aligned. The lip is strongly dentate and the columella has moderate plicae. It has an attractive rich tan and cream coloration, with a white aperture. The dark brown operculum is rather recurved.

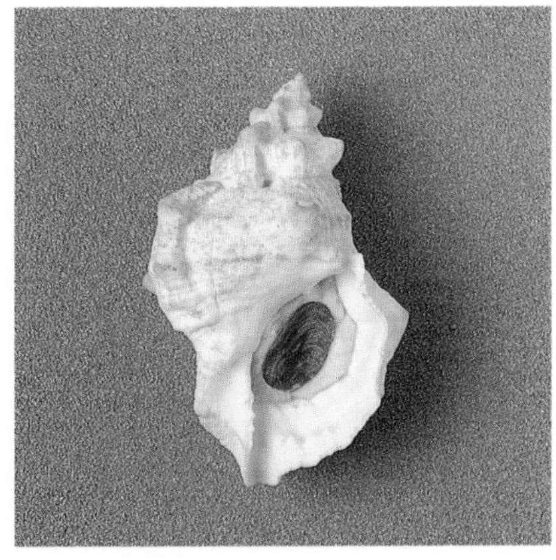

**CROSSATA CALIFORNICA**
Californian Frog. *Hinds 1843.* California to West Mexico.

To 6in (15cm)

This large, rather drab-looking, shell has nodulose shoulders and varices. There are low rounded spiral ridges. Sometimes heavily encrusted, the shell should appear cream-to-beige, with occasional banding and a white aperture. There is a "trough" behind the dentate expanded lip. The columella has four or more small anterior denticles. It lives on offshore rocks.

**TUTUFA BUFO**
Red-ringed Frog. *Röding 1798.* Indo-Pacific.

To 5in (13cm)

The deep red-ringed aperture is the chief characteristic of this species. A sturdy medium-to-large shell, it is coarsely sculptured with spiral cords and ridges and several rows of low rounded nodules. The exterior colour is light brown or beige. An intertidal and offshore dweller.

**TUTUFA OYAMAI**
Oyami's Frog. *Habe 1973.*
Japan to Philippines.

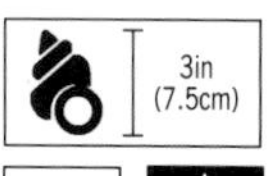
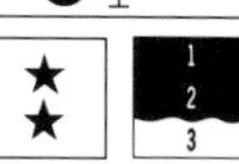

3in (7.5cm)

A medium-sized shell, with a tall spire, its angular whorls display fine spiral beading and two rows of nodules, strongest at the shoulders. The light brown background is decorated with random spiral streaks of darker brown; the aperture is white. The prominent anal canal is set obliquely to the shell axis. The depicted specimen was fished off south-western Taiwan.

SUPER FAMILY
EPITONIOIDEA

FAMILY
## EPITONIIDAE
(Wentletraps)

This wonderful family of exquisitely sculptured and ornamented shells is distributed worldwide, mostly living in shallow water and found among soft corals and sea anemones, on which they feed. They are delicate shells, generally conical, with much axial ribbing or regularly spaced varices. Most have circular apertures and little or no colour. The opercula are corneus, or horny, thin and bear a few whorls. Over the years, there has been much taxonomic division of this moderately large family. According to Vaught, there are numerous genera and subgenera, of which *Epitonium*, *Amaea*, *Cirsotrema* and *Sthenorytis* are of note here. Where the generic placing of some species is doubtful, I have adhered to the largest genus, *Epitonium*. The word wentletrap derives from a German word meaning "spiral staircase".

**AMAEA FERMINIANA**
Ferminiana Wentletrap. *Dall 1908.*
Western Central America.

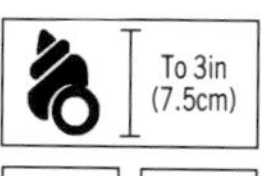
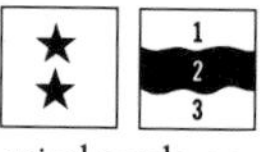

To 3in (7.5cm)

The ferminiana wentletrap has a tall and relatively wide tapering spire with rounded whorls. The sculpturing takes the form of numerous axial growth striations and finer spiral cords, causing a netted effect. The shell is an off-white to grey beige throughout. The operculum is thin, horny and dark brown.

**TUTUFA RUBETA**
Red-mouthed Frog. *L. 1758.*
Indo-Pacific.

To 4in (10cm)

A larger heavy species, its whorls are strongly nodulose, especially at the shoulders. The aperture, which is a deep orange colour, is wide; the lip is expanded, bearing two rows of denticles. The columella and parietal wall are calloused and bear moderate plicae and folds. Elsewhere the colouring is a tan-and-cream mottling.

**AMAEA GUINEENSIS**
Guinea Wentletrap. *Bouchet and Tellier 1978.* West Africa.

2in (5cm)

A short tapering shell, it has a fairly large body whorl and a rounded aperture. The suture is impressed, and each whorl bears a fine network of reticulated ornamentation. Here and there are varices with short upturned blade-like spines below the suture. It is a pale beige grey. It inhabits offshore waters.

**AMAEA MAGNIFICA**
Magnificent Wentletrap. *Sowerby 1844.*
Taiwan to Japan.

To 4in (10cm)

This lovely shell has certainly become much less readily available since Taiwanese fishing habits changed. A choice collectors' shell, it has a tall spire with rounded whorls covered in a reticulated network of cords and striations. It is generally off-white to beige, the apex and interior having yellow tints. A deep-water species.

**CIRSOTREMA ZELEBORI**
Zelebor Wentletrap. *Dunker 1866.*
New Zealand.

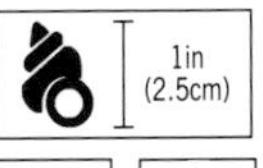


A small solidly built endemic shell, its tall narrow spire is made up of rounded whorls, each bearing numerous ridge-like varices. There are fine spiral cords both on the whorls and the varices. The aperture is rounded. The colour is usually white throughout. The depicted specimen is from Tasman Bay. These wentletraps live in waters down to 99 feet (30m).

**CIRSOTREMA EDGARI**
Edgar's Wentletrap. *De Boury 1912.*
Philippines.

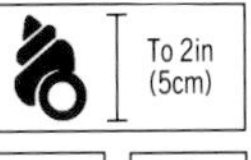

Very similar to *E. rugosum* in shape and structure, it is smaller, has fewer whorls and its axial ribs are more numerous and more fluted. They do not curve up at the posterior – indeed the area below the suture is rather flattened. Fine spiral threads are also evident. A very pretty species, off-white in colour, this endemic is not always readily available to collectors.

**CIRSOTREMA VARICOSA**
Varicose Wentletrap. *Lamarck 1822.*
Philippines.

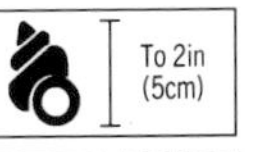

A small solid shell, it has a tall spire and rounded whorls. The axial ribs are almost flat and appear serrated, and there are occasional thick rounded varices. The overall colour is a dirty white or pale grey, and the varices, aperture and apex are white.

**EPITONIUM SCALARE**
Precious Wentletrap. *L. 1758.*
Japan to Northern Australia.

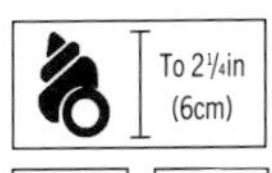

A world-famous shell and at one time a great rarity (see shell-counterfeiting p.27), it is now available in appreciable numbers, the shells coming mainly from Taiwan and the Philippines. It is indeed spectacular, comprising loose rounded whorls separated by strong blade-like varices, which are connected to each other at the open suture. The umbilicus is wide and open. Fished in both shallow and deep water, it is an alabaster white, with occasional cream tones.

### EPITONIUM ACUMINATUM
Pointed Wentletrap. *Sowerby 1844.*
Japan to Northern Australia.

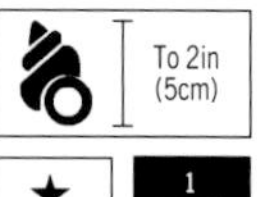


Shells were readily available in the mid 1970s from Taiwan, but they appear to have become more difficult to obtain nowadays. There is a long slender spire of about 16 rounded whorls, all of which have fine axial grooves; the aperture is small. A lightweight and very thin shell, it is a pale greyish brown, with a narrow off-white spiral band.

### EPITONIUM GEORGETTINA
George's Wentletrap. *Kiener 1839.*
Western South America.

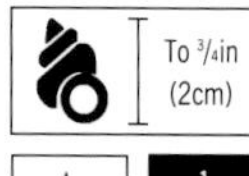


This very small shell is off-white to cream in colour, with about seven rounded whorls and numerous strong varices. The aperture is round and there is no umbilicus. This species inhabits sand or rocky substrate in shallow water. The specimen shown here was collected in Argentina.

### EPITONIUM IMPERIALIS
Imperial Wentletrap. *Sowerby 1844.*
South-West Pacific.

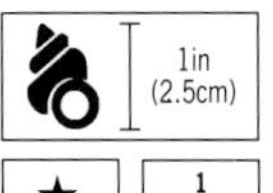


A very thin rather bulbous and squat wentletrap, it has many closely aligned varices. The large aperture is ovate and the umbilicus is small, but open. This species lives in sand in subtidal waters and is a popular collectors' item.

### EPITONIUM AURITA
Eared Wentletrap. *Sowerby 1844.*
Japan.

A small fragile shell, it has a tall tapering spire with rounded whorls on which are very fine white axial ribs and occasional prominent and rounded white varices. The undercolour is a pale to mid-toned grey brown, arranged in spiral bands. The surface is smooth and fairly glossy.

### EPITONIUM CORONATUM
Coronated Wentletrap. *Lamarck 1816.*
South Africa.

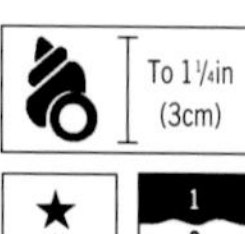


The coronated wentletrap is a smooth glossy shell with a medium spire and rounded whorls. The numerous varices are joined to each other at the suture, the largest and strongest being either near to or at the aperture. The shell is an off-white colour with a small purplish brown narrow band that runs spirally below the suture. This specimen was beach-collected at Jeffrey's Bay.

### EPITONIUM CLATHRUM
Common European Wentletrap. *L. 1758.*
North-East Atlantic and Mediterranean.

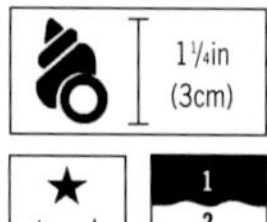


Frequently found on southern British beaches and the Channel Islands, this small narrow but robust shell again has many suture-joined varices that hold together the partly open and rounded whorls. It varies in colour from off-white to a beige with hints of fine brown spiral beading. It lives in intertidal waters.

**EPITONIUM TENELLUM**
*Hutton 1885.*
New Zealand.

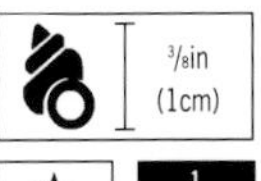


A very small lightweight and fragile species, its rounded whorls bear many closely aligned varices. It is pale brown, rather darker at the apex, and has a wide mid-brown spiral band on the lower part of the body whorl. This specimen is from North Island.

**EPITONIUM PERPLEXA**
Perplexed Wentletrap. *Pease 1868.*
Japan.

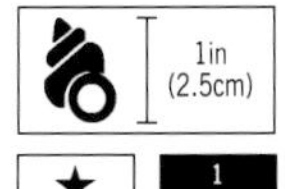


Sometimes placed within the subgenus *Gyroscala*, this is a solidly built species, with a tall tapering spire and rounded whorls. These support strong blade-like varices that are joined at the suture. The aperture is rounded and there is no umbilicus. The colour is pale grey, with white varices and aperture.

**EPITONIUM RUGOSUM**
Rugose Wentletrap. *Kuroda and Ito 1961.*
Central Philippines.

I am reminded of very fine hand-woven lace when I look at this beautiful endemic shell. It has a very tall elegant spire, comprising about 14 whorls. There are many thin closely packed axial ribs; these are blade-like, with serrated edges, and curve upward towards the posterior. There is a rounded smooth aperture and a thin black operculum. A true collectors' item, it is occasionally fished in deep water off Bohol Island.

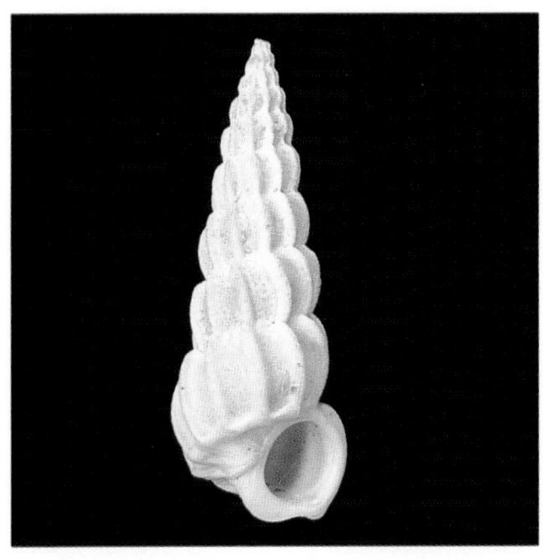

**EPITONIUM AUSTRALIS**
Austral Wentletrap. *Lamarck 1822.*
Southern Australia.

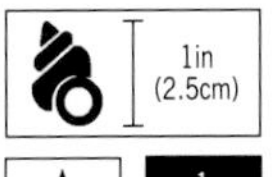


Long and narrow, with almost straight-sided whorls, this wentletrap has numerous blade-like varices joined at the indented suture. The colour is usually off-white and the aperture periphery is a glossy pure white. The depicted shell was collected at Victoria.

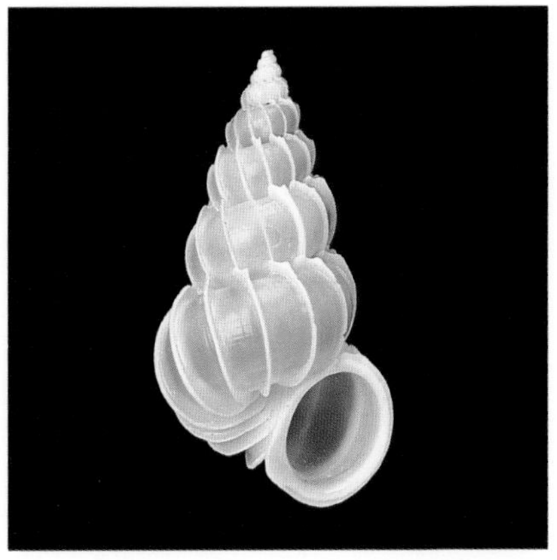

**EPITONIUM PYRAMIDALE**
Pyramid Wentletrap. *Sowerby 1844.*
Philippines.

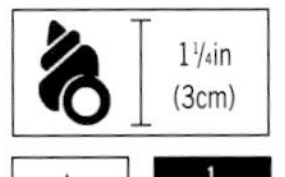


A shell not unlike *E. scalare*, it is, however, much smaller and narrower; it has more joined varices and the whorls are not as separated. The colour is very pale beige with white apex, varices and aperture.

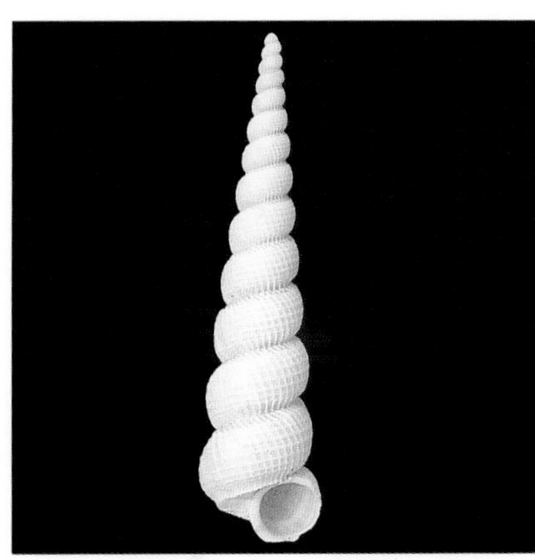

**EPITONIUM FIMBRIOLATUM**
Reticulated Wentletrap. *Melvill 1897.*
Gulf of Oman.

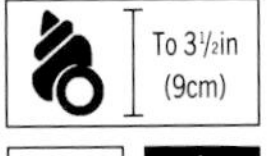


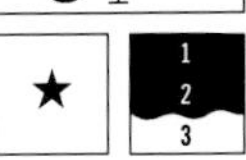


A tall elegant narrow species, this has about 14 rounded whorls covered with a fine network of reticulated ornamentation. The suture is impressed. Shells are seldom available and are usually off-white.

**STHENORYTIS PERNOBILIS**
Noble Wentletrap. *Fischer and Bernardi 1857*. Caribbean.

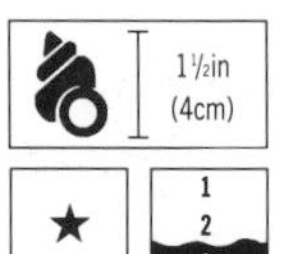


An extremely rare and sought-after species, it is only very occasionally live-taken – usually in fish or lobster traps – and is reputed to dwell as deep as 4,950 feet (1,500m). This specimen was inhabited by a hermit crab, and collected at 594 feet (180m) by David Hunt, offshore, near St. James, Barbados. There appears to be no other species shaped quite like this wentletrap.

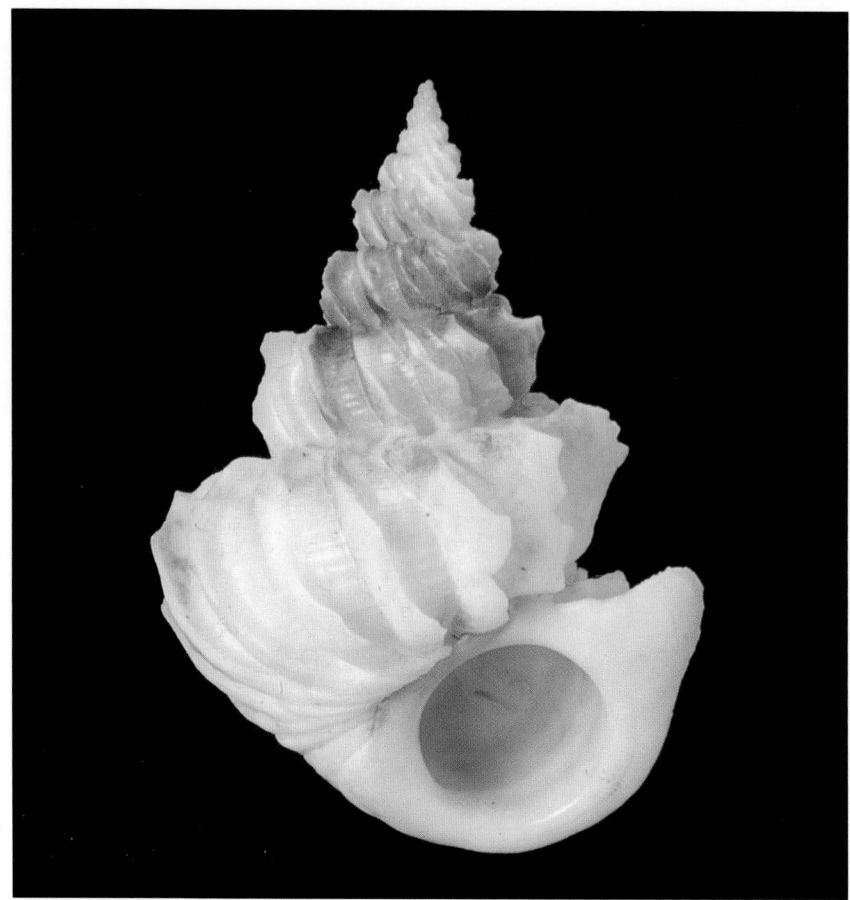

SUPER FAMILY
## EPITONIOIDEA

FAMILY
## JANTHINIDAE
(Purple Sea Snails)

These very delicate snails live pelagic lives – borne along on the surface of warm tropical open seas on a "raft" of mucus-covered bubbles to which they are attached by their foot. They feed on other floating organisms, such as mollusc larvae and small jellyfish. Thousands are often washed ashore after rough storms. The family is very small, numbering possibly ten species in all; there are two genera, the main one being *Janthina*, all of which are purple in colour. Collectors and shell enthusiasts are primarily attracted by the beautiful colour of these shells, but are seldom able to find perfect specimens with intact lips.

**JANTHINA JANTHINA**
Common Janthina. *L. 1758*. Worldwide in tropical seas.

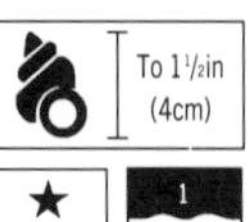


The largest species in the family, the common janthina is variable in shape, some shells having a low rounded spire, while others have a medium-sized spire with almost flat-sided whorls. In either case, the body whorl is large and inflated. The specimens shown here are from northern Queensland and show the two typical shape forms.

**JANTHINA CAPREOLATA**
Capreola Purple Snail. *Montrouzier*. Southern and Western Australia.

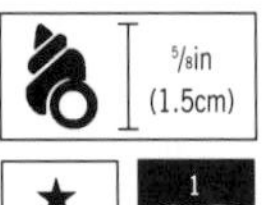


A small very delicate shell, this has a medium spire and large rounded body whorl. The lip is drawn-in at the centre, creating a V-shape on its side, when viewed laterally. There are many fine axial striations. The depicted specimen was collected at Albany, Western Australia.

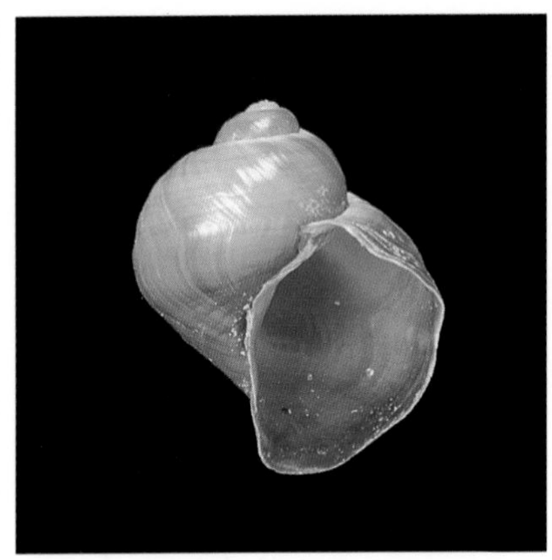

**JANTHINA GLOBOSA**
Globular Janthina. *Swainson 1822.*
Western Pacific and Caribbean.

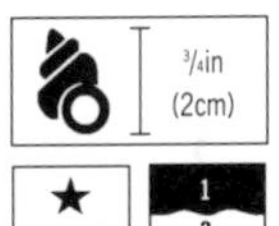

Although rather like *J. capreolata* in shape, the globular janthina has a lower spire, and the whorls are more rounded and bulbous. There is a similar central notch, and numerous very faint growth striations. A narrow white band runs spirally below the suture.

**BOLINUS BRANDARIS**
Purple Dye Murex. *L. 1758.*
Mediterranean.

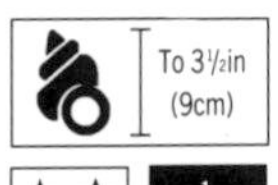

A well-known species, this is one of two murex that were utilized in the manufacture of the Tyrian purple dye that was used from Roman times to the Middle Ages for ecclesiastical and imperial robes. Specimens can be spinose or spineless. This is the type species of the genus *Bolinus*.

**CHICOMUREX SUPERBUS**
Superb Murex. *Sowerby 1889.*
Japan to Philippines.

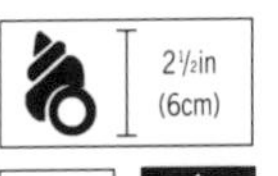

There are three beautifully webbed and ridged varices per whorl and between these are heavy axial nodules. The spiral sculpturing consists of slightly raised beading which is lightly coloured with brown. The varices have odd blotches of pink or beige; otherwise the entire shell is whitish. It is often fished offshore in the central Philippines.

SUPER FAMILY
## MURICOIDEA

FAMILY
## MURICIDAE
(Rock Shells)

The rock shells are a vast family of at least 1,000 widely distributed species enjoying varying habitats, most being found in tropical seas on rocky shores, coral reefs, or stony, muddy or sandy substrates. They are all carnivorous; some are able to drill holes in other molluscs, while others are able to wedge bivalves open with the use of a large projecting tooth on the outer lip. The range of shapes, sizes and sculpturing is bewildering, offering scope for many expert opinions on classification. The shells I have chosen are subdivided into subfamilies as listed by Vaught. The rock shells, being so diverse, endear themselves to collectors and are extremely popular with conchologists. Kay Vaught lists seven subfamilies, 98 genera and at least 50 subgenera! (Sizes quoted are for length of shell without spines.)

**BOLINUS CORNUTUS**
Horned Murex. *L. 1758.*
West Africa.

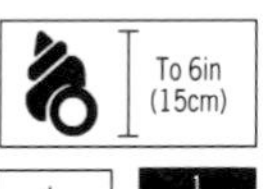

This very dramatic shell can be quite variable, both in size and shape. In most cases, however, it is highly spinose, with heavy hollow recurved spines adorning the body whorl. The long straight canal also has spines, but they are usually much shorter. The calloused inner or columella lip is raised and bent forward. An inhabitant of offshore waters, it is a popular collectors' item.

**CHICOREUS CNISSODUS**
*Euthyme 1889.*
Indo-Pacific.

A most attractive medium-sized shell, it is dominated by numerous frondose spines of varying length, which extend from three varices. There are fine dark brown spiral cords and raised axial nodules. The background colour is off-white or a beige brown. The spire is tall and the canal is long and slightly recurved. The lip is finely dentate.

## CHICOREUS NOBILIS

Noble Murex. *Shikama 1977.*
Japan to Philippines.

A small, very beautiful shell of a deep pink colour, with fine spiral threads of mid-brown. There are three varices per whorl, and each bears medium-length frondose spines decreasing in size towards the posterior; the canal is long, slightly recurved and also spinose. The outer lip is lightly serrated and lirate within. Found in offshore waters.

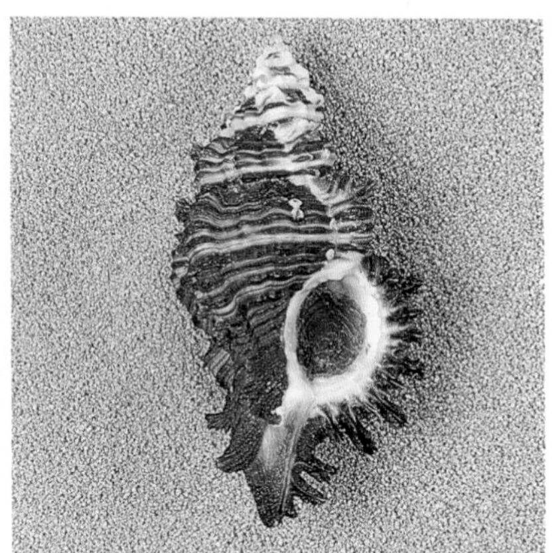

## CHICOREUS MICROPHYLLUS

Curled Murex. *Lamarck 1816.*
Indo-Pacific.

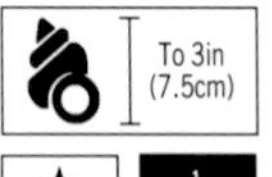

This stocky medium-sized fusiform shell has a high spire, a short canal and a large body whorl. The ornamentation consists of strong spiral cords and rounded axial ribs, and each varix supports very short open fronds, which are more dominant on the last two varices. The cords are a dark brown black and the aperture is tinged with yellow or pale orange. Shells are often heavily encrusted.

## CHICOREUS DENUDATUS

Denuded Murex. *Perry 1811.*
South-eastern Queensland to Tasmania.

A lightweight rather delicate species, it is endemic in its area and has a high spire, a short curved canal and varices bearing short open fronds. There are fine spiral beaded cords and usually one or two axial nodes between the varices. There is a small denticle on the parietal wall. The colour varies between cream, beige and orange.

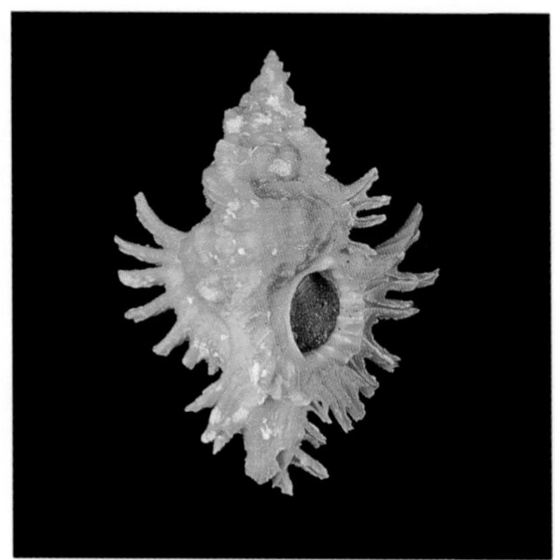

## CHICOREUS CORRUGATUS

*Sowerby 1841.*
Red Sea.

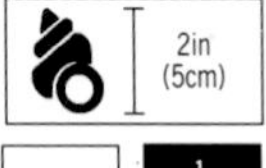

A stout little murex, it is similar in colour to *C. nobilis*, although some shells are reputed to be white or cream. Strong short partly closed spines appear from three varices; the siphonal canal is short. The thin outer lip is expanded, with fine lirae inside. There are two axial nodes between each varix. A choice collectors' item, it is endemic to its Red Sea habitat.

### CHICOREUS BRUNNEUS

Adusta Murex. *Link 1807.*
Indo-Pacific.

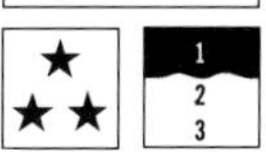


This heavy and highly spinose shell has three varices, each with closely packed fronds of medium length, some of them being recurved. There is a distinctive single large axial node between the varices. Whorl sculpturing consists of coarse and fine spirally-rounded ridges. The white background is decorated with conspicuous dark brown or black fronds and cords. The ventral aspect of the canal is white and the aperture periphery is pink. A shallow-water species.

### CHICOREUS PENCHINATTI

Penchinat's Murex. *Crosse 1861.*
Japan to Philippines.

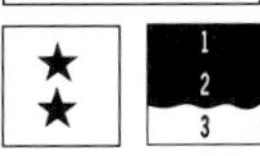


A pretty little shell, this is highly variable in colour – white, cream, pale brown, mid-brown or orange. It is an elongated slender species, with shortly frondose varices and canal. There are fine spiral cords and low axial nodules on the whorls. The lip is minutely dentate. The depicted shell is from the central Philippines.

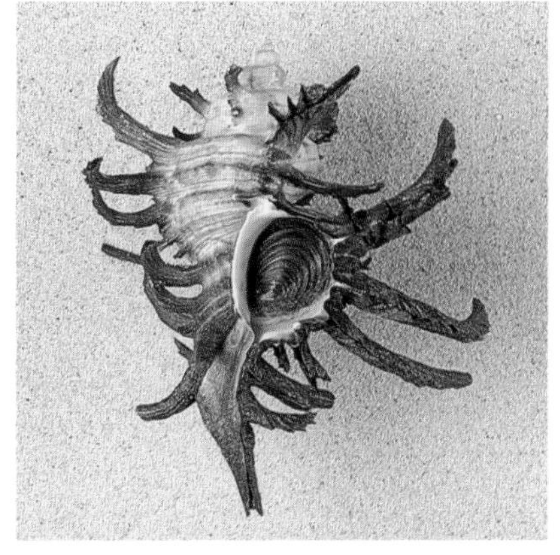

### CHICOREUS CORNUCERVI

Monodon Murex. *Röding 1798.*
Western Australia.

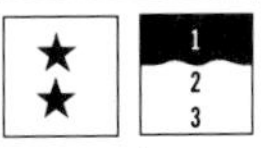


A truly spectacular shell! Fully mature specimens, as depicted, are scarce, but portray the major characteristics: very strong stout long closed fronds, many recurved, some touching those on the earlier varix. The whorls are rounded and spirally corded; the lip bears a large and prominent tooth. Specimens can be white but are more usually very dark brown, with a beige undercolour. A choice collectors' item, it is endemic to its area.

### CHICOREUS PALMAROSAE

Rose-branched Murex. *Lamarck 1822.*
Sri Lanka.

The rose-branched murex is one of my favourite species. It is superbly beautiful and most aptly named – the lovely pink fronds do indeed resemble rose branches in their early growth. Shells are incredibly difficult to clean, being heavily encrusted with marine debris and lime, but the care and time spent cleaning is well rewarded. There are two variations – the shell shown is endemic to Sri Lanka; a less attractive and plainer dark brown form can be found in the Philippines.

## CHICOREUS STEERIAE
*Reeve 1845.*
Central Pacific.

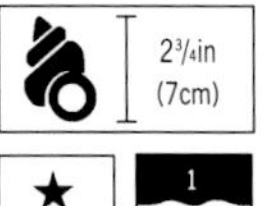


This species is rather like a dark form of C. *saulii*, but it is much wider and more angular, darker in colour and the spire is usually higher. Three varices on the body whorl bear shortish open frondose spines, very strong on the aperture and penultimate varix. It is a pale brown with dark brown spiral cords; the lip and fronds are a pinkish lavender. Generally restricted to Tahiti and the Marquesas Islands.

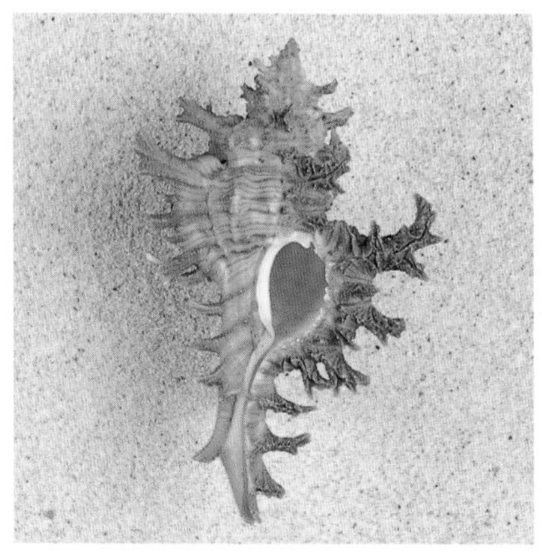

## CHICOREUS SPECTRUM
Spectre Murex. *Reeve 1846.*
Caribbean to Brazil.

The spectre murex is rather similar to C. *palmarosae*, but tends to be more slender; it has three axial nodes instead of two, and the foliated fronds are generally shorter. It is variable in colour; some are off-white with brown fronds, others are all orange, and others are mid-to-dark brown. The specimen depicted is Brazilian.

## CHICOREUS VIRGINEUS
Virgin Murex. *Röding 1798.*
Red Sea.

A robust almost triangular murex, endemic to the Red Sea, it is similar to C. *ramosus*, but is more angular and has far fewer and shorter fronds. The colour is usually white or cream, with occasional brown spiral bands. The columella is pink, and the lip has faint denticles. There is one prominent axial node between the varices.

## CHICOREUS SAHARICUS
Sahara Murex. *Locard 1896.*
West and North-West Africa.

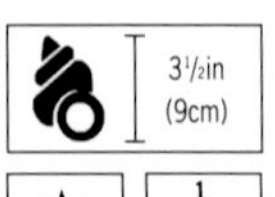


A solid species with high spire, relatively long canal and rounded whorls, each with five varices bearing both short and long open spines, the longest being at the shoulders. Its colour is usually pale cream to light brown throughout, except for the aperture, which is white. The shell depicted was trawled from 297ft (90m) off Cayar, Senegal.

## CHICOREUS RAMOSUS
Ramose Murex. *L. 1758.*
Indo-Pacific.

This is the largest species in the family Muricidae. It is very well known and is abundant in some areas. Mature shells are very heavy and solid. The spire is low and the canal wide, long and recurved. The body whorl is greatly enlarged, and there is a gaping aperture. The short fronds grow from three varices and there is a distinctive strong axial nodule. It is white with occasional brown spiral threads, especially on younger shells, and there is a pink columella.

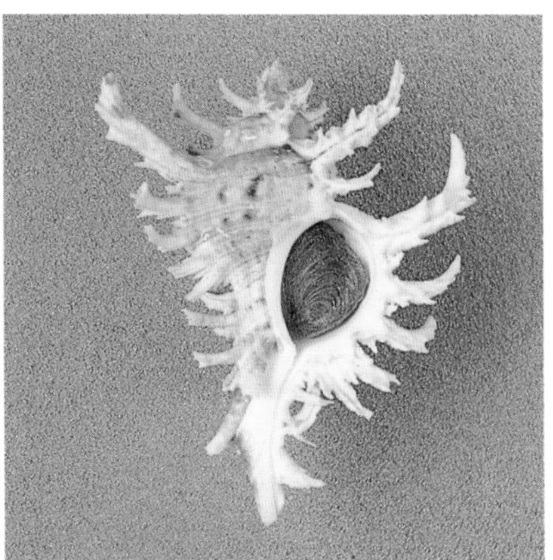

## CHICOREUS ASIANUS
Asian Murex. *Kuroda 1942.*
Japan to Taiwan.

An attractive murex, it has a low spire, rounded and slightly nodose whorls and a long canal. Three varices support both short and long open fronds, the largest of which are most foliated. It is creamy white with very fine spiral threads. There is a pronounced tooth placed at the anterior portion of the lip. An offshore species.

**CHICOREUS INSULARUM**
Insular Murex. *Pilsby 1921.*
Hawaiian Islands.

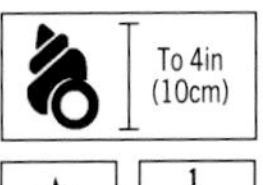

To 4in (10cm)

This heavy coarse murex has strong nodules between three varices. There are low spiral ridges. The fronds are short, open and slightly foliated, but are often worn or eroded, and stunted open spines occur on the earlier varices. The lip bears low coarse denticles. The shell is off-white or cream overall, with red brown cords and a white aperture. This specimen was dredged in 900ft (272m) off Oahu, in the Hawaiian Islands, where it is endemic.

**CHICOREUS ORCHIDIFLORUS**
Orchid Murex. *Shikama 1973.*
Philippines.

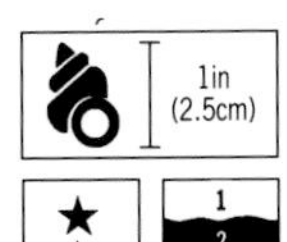

1in (2.5cm)

Although it is reputed to exist in Taiwanese waters, I have known this very delicate and lovely species only to have come from the Camotes Sea. The whorls have thin almost transparent serrated varices. The canal is long, recurved and spinose. The shells are white, orange or pale brown.

**CHICOREUS LONGICORNIS**
Long-spined Murex. *Dunker 1864.*
Eastern Australia.

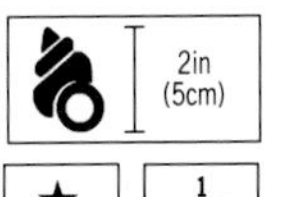

2in (5cm)

A deep-water murex – this particular specimen was trawled in 528ft (160m) off Frazer Island, Queensland – it has a tall spire, and angular spirally corded whorls, with axial nodes; the varices support long closed well-spaced spines. The anterior canal is straight and very long. The lip is minutely dentate; the columella smooth.

**CHICOREUS VENUSTULUS**
Lovely Murex. *Rehder and Wilson 1975.*
Central Philippines.

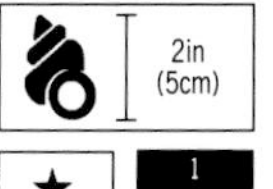

2in (5cm)

The lovely murex can be very variable in colour. It has a medium spire, large body whorl and long rather recurved canal. The whorls have fine beaded cords and varices which bear short sharp spines; these are longer and are lamellated on the lip varix. The two depicted specimens are from Bohol Island and show typical colour forms.

**CHICOREUS PAINII**
Pain's Murex. *Houart 1983.*
Western Pacific.

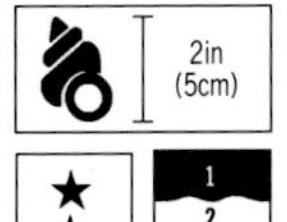

2in (5cm)

A recently described species named after a fellow conchologist of mine, Tom Pain, it is an elongate rather narrow murex with an elevated spire, rounded whorls with low axial ribs, and a long canal which is slightly recurved at the anterior. Three varices per whorl bear short open fronds. It is variably coloured, usually mid-to-dark brown and occasionally beige or orange. The depicted shells were collected in the Solomon Islands.

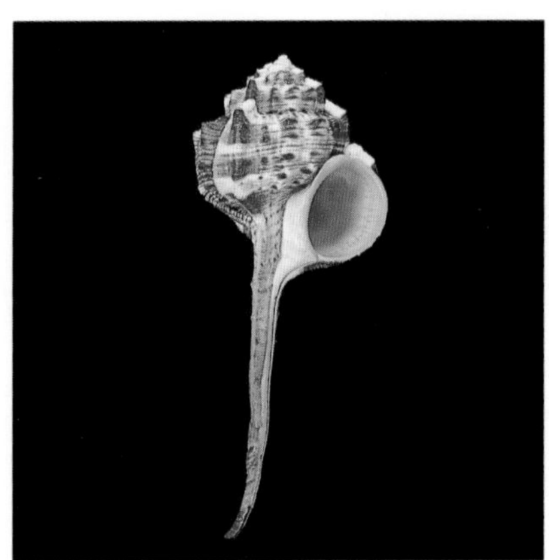

**HAUSTELLUM HAUSTELLUM**
Snipe's Bill Murex. *L. 1758.*
Indo-Pacific.

To 6in (15cm)

A popular murex, this has a distinctive shape: the spire is low; there is a bulbous, enlarged body whorl; and a very long straight siphonal canal, which is often recurved at the anterior. The whorls have fine spiral cords and low rounded nodules, strongest on the shoulders. It is cream in colour, with brown spiral lines and dark brown or black patches on the varices. The smooth rather pronounced large aperture is pink. A shallow-water shell.

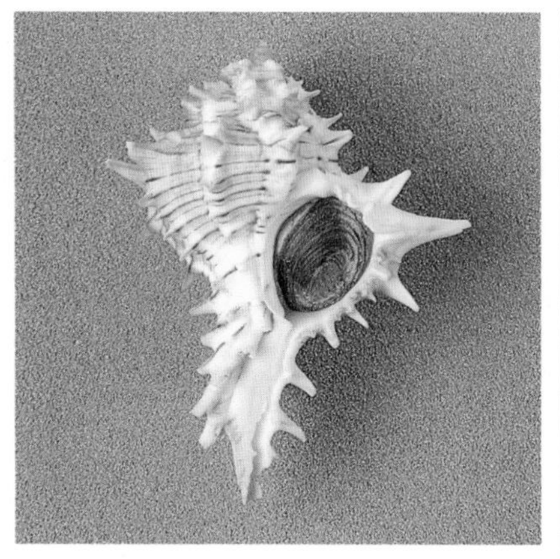

**HEXAPLEX FULVESCENS**
Giant Eastern Murex. *Sowerby 1834.*
South-eastern USA and Florida.

A large solid murex, this has a low spire, large body whorl and long slightly curved canal. There are between six and ten varices, each bearing strong open spines, the largest at the shoulders. The whorls have raised narrow spiral cords. The overall colour is off-white to beige; the cords are a dark reddish brown. It is found in intertidal and offshore waters.

**HEXAPLEX PRINCEPS**
Prince Murex. *Broderip 1833.*
Western Central America.

A handsome shell, it has between five and seven varices which support short open partly foliated spines. There are fine spiral threads. Two superb shells are shown here, portraying the colour variation; they are both from western Panama.

**HEXAPLEX RADIX**
Radish Murex. *Gmelin 1791.*
Panama to Ecuador.

This is similar to *H. nigritus*, but has a lower spire, a more bulbous rounded body whorl and more numerous and closer open spines, which are foliated. The colouring is similar, although more areas of white are usually present on the radish murex. Some experts believe this to be a southerly form of *H. nigritus*. It is often heavily encrusted with lime deposits when collected.

**HEXAPLEX TRUNCULUS**
Trunculus Murex. *L. 1758.*
Mediterranean.

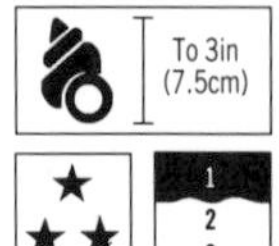


One of the two species used extensively in the manufacturing of Tyrian purple dye in bygone days (the other being *B. brandaris*), it is endemic to the Mediterranean. As the two shells depicted show, the shape can vary, but the colour and markings are fairly constant. Apart from obvious ornamentation, there are numerous extremely fine spirally beaded threads.

**HEXAPLEX NIGRITUS**
Black Murex. *Philippi 1845.*
Gulf of California.

A large and handsome murex, with a low spire, it has an enlarged body whorl with about eight or nine varices and a short wide slightly angled canal. There are many triangular and open spines, the largest being at the shoulders. The shell is white, although the spines, large areas of the shoulders and broad spiral bands, all of which are black, can give it a dark appearance. The aperture is white. It is found in intertidal waters, but perfect sizable collectors' specimens are scarce.

**HEXAPLEX DUPLEX**
Double Murex. *Röding 1798.*
West Africa.

The depicted specimen is from Senegal and is a so-called "giant" form. Although smaller shells are more banded, these large ones show little evidence of this and are usually an overall pale orange or beige, with a vivid pinkish red aperture. There are short open scale-like fronds on the varices and many strong spiral cords and finer threads. A choice collectors' item.

## MUREX TENUIROSTRUM TENUIROSTRUM

*Lamarck 1822*. Indo-Pacific.

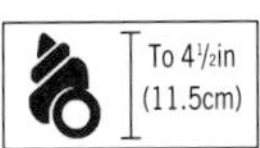

It has a medium-sized spire, rounded body whorl and very long straight closed canal, from which extend closed spines of both short and medium length. There are three varices per whorl, and these bear long and very long, sometimes curved, closed spines. There are spiral cords on the whorls. The shell is pale tan or beige, this specimen coming from south-west Taiwan.

## MUREX TRAPA

Rare Spined Murex. *Röding 1798*. South-West Pacific.

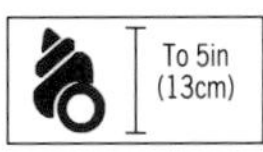


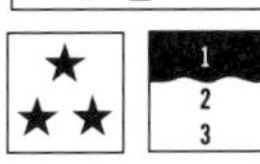


A rather coarse-looking species, it has closed sharp spines of short-to-medium length, coming from the varices. A few short spines occur on the very long straight canal, nearest the aperture. The lip is slightly dentate, with one longer labial "tooth". There are numerous spiral cords and very fine nodules at the shoulders. Shells are generally a pale beige brown, with a greyish tinge on the canal.

## MUREX TROSCHELI

Troschel's Murex. *Lischke 1868*. Western Pacific.

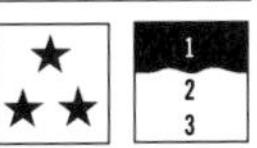


A spectacular species, it bears many long sharp closed spines from the varices and has a long straight siphonal canal. The colour is off-white, with low rounded spiral cords of middle or dark brown. The aperture is white and the lip finely dentate. Perfect specimens are scarce and much sought after.

## MUREX PECTEN

Venus Comb Murex. *Lightfoot 1786*. Indo-Pacific.

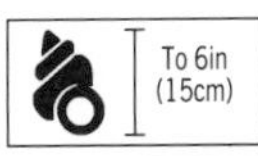

The most spinose – indeed, comb-like – member of the *Murex* genus, this amazing shell is adorned with long, often curved, closed spines, and perfect specimens are collected! The whorls are rounded and bulbous, and bear numerous spiral cords. The inner lip is expanded and raised adjacent to the columella; the outer lip is minutely dentate. Pale beige to mid-brown in overall colour, it has a white aperture. The depicted shell came from the central Philippines.

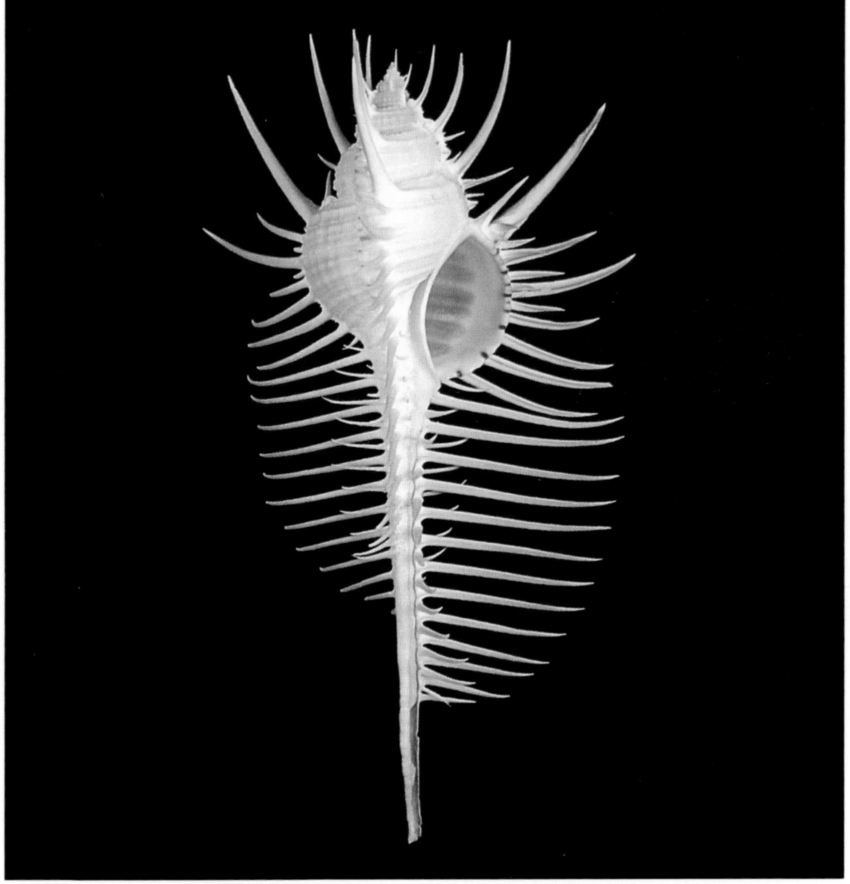

**MUREX ACANTHOSTEPHES**
*Watson 1883.*
Western and Northern Australia.

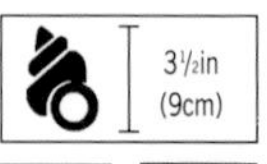


A lightweight rather dainty species, this has a medium spire and rounded whorls. There are low rounded cords and the interspaces are scabrous. Three varices on each whorl support short sharp, occasionally curved, spines. There is a very long straight canal. The lip is finely dentate, with one slightly longer labial tooth. Shells are pale tan or beige, with a white aperture.

**MUREX POPPEI**
Poppe's Murex. *Houart 1979.*
Indian Ocean to South-East Asia.

Described relatively recently, it has a fairly high spire, large rounded body whorl and a very long straight canal. There are both strong and weak spirally rounded cords with very faint scabrous interspaces. Many long narrow sharp spines appear from the varices and the entire length of the canal. The inner lip is calloused, expanded and raised; the outer lip bears denticles, one particularly long and wide. This specimen is from the Andaman Islands.

**PHYLLONOTUS POMUM**
Apple Murex. *Gmelin 1791.*
South-eastern USA to Brazil.

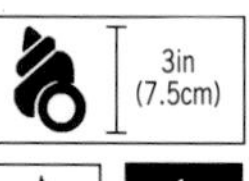


A well-known species, especially in Florida and the Caribbean, where it is fished regularly, it has a high spire, an enlarged body whorl and a strong and slightly curved canal. It is not frondose, but there are coarse spiral ridges and low sharp nodules between the varices. Colours vary, but the most usual colouring is as the depicted specimen. Occasionally pale orange or even pinkish varieties occur. A shallow-water species.

**MUREX ELENENSIS**
Santa Elena Murex. *Dall 1909.*
Western Central America.

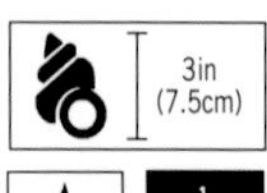


This relatively short stocky murex has a low spire and inflated body whorl. The varices have short sharp spines, both thick and thin, and slightly longer spines continue onto the long anterior canal. Fine spiral threads of brown and yellow are intersected by four or five rows of axially elongated nodules. The lip bears small denticles. This specimen is from Playas, Ecuador.

**NAQUETIA CAPUCINUS**
Mangrove Murex. *Lamarck 1822.*
Indo-Pacific.

A sturdy medium-sized murex, it has a tall spire, slightly angular whorls and a short canal. There are numerous raised spiral cords and three varices per whorl, which are rounded and lamellated. Behind the lip periphery is a trough and a dentate ridge. The shell is normally dark brown or black throughout, and the interior and columella are white or pale grey. It lives among mangrove roots.

**PHYLLONOTUS ERYTHROSTOMUS**
Pink-mouthed Murex. *Swainson 1831.*
California to Mexico.

A dull off-white or beige murex, it is named after its vivid pink aperture. The spire is low and the greatly enlarged body whorl bears four varices on which are blunted triangular open spines. The siphonal canal is wide and recurved. Long-spined variants occur in deeper water; the shell seen here was fished in deep water off the Californian coast.

**PHYLLONOTUS REGIUS**
Regal Murex. *Swainson 1821.*
Western Central America.

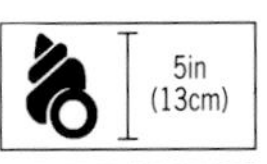

5in (13cm)

A heavy attractive species with both beautiful colouring and ornamentation, it has at least five varices with numerous medium-sized sharp spines which are open and recurved, lying almost parallel to the whorl. Choice specimens are scarce – the shells are often encrusted or eroded, especially at the apex. The aperture is heavily calloused and the lip strongly dentate.

**PHYLLONOTUS BRASSICA**
Cabbage Murex. *Lamarck 1822.*
Western Central America.

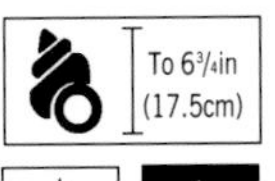

To $6^3/_4$in (17.5cm)

Another heavy shell, this is coarsely sculptured with widely spaced long strong blunted spines, the most prominent being those on the shoulders. It is cream to beige with broad spiral bands of pale brown. The aperture periphery is tinged with pink; the interior is white or pale yellow. The canal is short, open and recurved.

**PTERYNOTUS PELLUCIDUS**
Pellucid Murex. *Reeve 1845.*
Indo-Pacific.

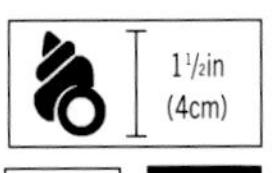

$1^1/_2$in (4cm)

A very delicate off-white species, it inhabits shallowish water down to about 99ft (30m). It is long and slender and is dominated by varical fronds that are ridged and wing-like. The siphonal canal is long and narrow and the small ovate aperture is slightly pronounced ventrally. This particular specimen is from the Solomon Islands.

**PTERYNOTUS MIYOKOAE**
Miyoko Murex. *Kosuge 1979.*
Cebu, Philippines.

To $2^1/_4$in (5.5cm)

A very beautiful species, the Miyoko murex features dominant wing-like varices which are finely ridged and lamellate. There are two axial ridges between each varix and numerous fine spiral threads. A fine collectors' item, endemic to the Philippines, it is occasionally netted off Mactan from deep water, perfect examples being keenly sought-after.

## PTERYNOTUS LOEBBECKEI

Loebbecke's Murex. *Kobelt 1879.*
Southern Japan to Philippines.

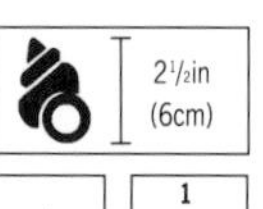

Closely resembling *P. miyokoae*, this tends to be rather heavier, and more stoutly built. The colour is usually a plain pale orange with no spiral bands. A great rarity for many years, this beautiful species remains a choice collectors' item, and perfect colourful shells still command high prices. The depicted shell was collected in deep water from the Camotes Sea.

## PTERYNOTUS ELONGATUS

Clavus Murex. *Lightfoot 1786.*
Indo-Pacific.

A very strangely shaped and therefore popular murex, it has a tall narrow spire with rounded whorls bearing fragmented and eroded blunt flat spines. The body whorl has three distinct varices with flaring and lamellated wings, slightly upturned and folded over themselves at the posterior, which extend onto the long siphonal canal. It inhabits coral reefs in shallow water. Occasionally, pale lavender or pink specimens occur, but most shells are white.

## PTERYNOTUS PINNATUS

Pinnate Murex. *Swainson 1822.*
Japan to Philippines.

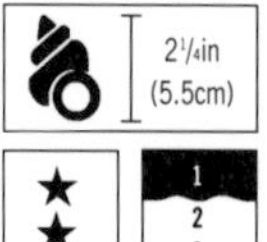

A delicate and pretty all-white murex, this has a tall rather "twisted" spire, a fusiform body whorl, and a long slightly curved canal. Three varices per whorl support thin finely ridged wings. Due to changed fishing habits, the excellent Taiwanese specimens obtainable in the late 1970s are now seldom available. Shells are still collected in the Philippines and Solomon Islands in small numbers.

## PTERYNOTUS PHYLLOPTERUS

Leafy-winged Murex. *Lamarck 1822.*
Lesser Antilles, Caribbean.

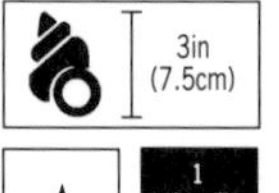

This very beautiful and much prized collectors' murex has dominant undulating wing-like varices, which are virtually continuous from the apex to the canal extremity. There is a double row of fine denticles on the lip; the columella is smooth. Specimens are generally a pale pink or orange. The shell seen here was collected in Martinique from fairly shallow water.

**PTERYNOTUS MARTINETANA**
Fenestrate Murex. *Röding 1798.*
South-West Pacific.

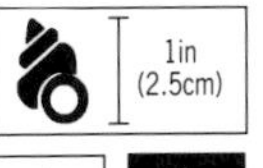

1in (2.5cm)

A frail thin little shell, the fenestrate murex has a medium spire and a long straight canal. The whorls are finely sculptured, with scaly spiral threads, and from the varices extend short and sometimes long open fronds. There are dark brown squared markings between each varix, and the fronds are tinged with pink. This species dwells in coral reefs.

**SIRATUS ALABASTER**
Alabaster Murex. *Reeve 1845.*
Japan to Philippines.

To 6in (15cm)

For many years this very attractive murex, with its long upturned spines and connected web-like varices, was only known from very poor specimens that lacked these distinctive features. Fortunately, in the late 1970s the Camotes Sea, Philippines, yielded up its treasures, and shells of the perfection of the one depicted began to be collected. A highly popular deep-water collectors' item.

**SIRATUS PERELEGANS**
Near Elegant Murex. *Vokes 1965.*
Caribbean.

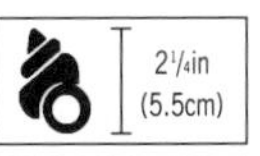

2¼in (5.5cm)

This dainty little murex inhabits moderately deep water, to about 165ft (50m). The fine spiral threads are equally spaced and are a mid-brown colour on an off-white background. The lip is minutely dentate and the columella smooth, apart from a very few tiny denticles at the anterior.

**PURPURELLUS GAMBIENSIS**
Gambia Murex. *Reeve 1845.*
West Africa.

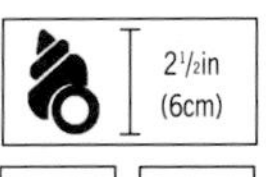

2½in (6cm)

The Gambia murex has an elevated spire, with rather angular whorls, and a broad strong anterior canal. There are raised spiral cords, and the varices are extended into thin ridged processes with a strong recurved spine at the shoulders. A flat hook-like process also occurs at the anterior end, on the canal. Colours vary from white or pale lavender to mid-brown. Often trawled in relatively deep water.

**SIRATUS CONSUELA**
Beautiful Murex. *Verill 1950.*
Eastern Caribbean.

2½in (6cm)

The beautiful murex is aptly named, being tall, slender and delicate, with a medium spire and a long slightly recurved canal. There are very fine spiral threads and low rounded axial ribs. The varices bear short spines which become joined and web-like at the anterior, continuing on the canal. This shell was dead-collected in 99ft (30m) off Piscadera Bay, Curaçao.

**SIRATUS TENUIVARICOSUS**
Thin Bladed Murex. *Dauntzenberg 1927.*
Brazil.

To 4in (10cm)

A stocky heavy medium-sized murex, endemic to Brazil, it has dominant long closed recurved spines. On the lip varix, these spines are linked with short web-like projections. There are low spiral cords and strong axial ribs. The colour is usually off-white or cream throughout. The depicted specimen was collected in deep water on sandy substrate, off northern Brazil.

**FAVARTIA JUDITHAE**
Judith's Murex. *D'Attilio and Bertsch 1980.*
Central Philippines.

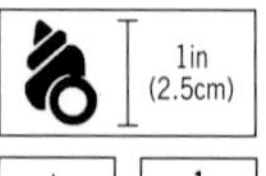


This is one of several very attractive little murex shells to be recently described. This may possibly be endemic to Punta Engano, Cebu. It is highly spinose, the ends of many spines being foliated. The long thin canal is recurved. Often encrusted when collected, it requires careful and patient cleaning.

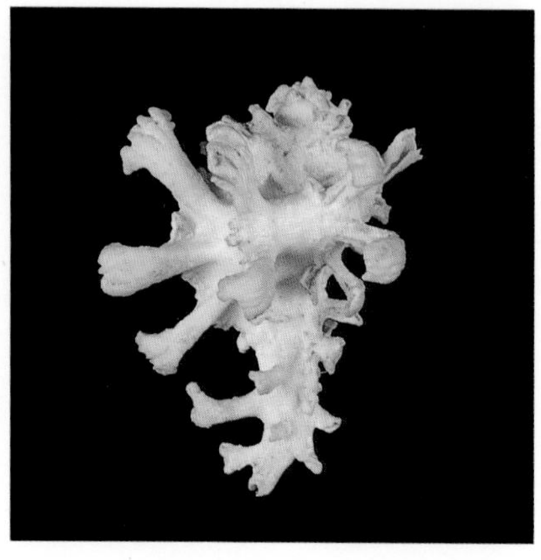

**HOMOLOCANTHA ANATOMICA**
Anatomical Murex. *Perry 1811.*
Indo-Pacific.

Another strange-looking murex, it is not unlike *H. scorpio*, but thicker and heavier. The varical spines are more numerous and stronger; the ends of these are lumpy and can be recurved ventrally. There is low fimbriated webbing between the spines. Shells are usually off-white or cream, with a white aperture. The depicted specimen is from the Red Sea and was collected in shallow water.

**HOMOLOCANTHA MELANAMATHOS**
*Gmelin 1791.*
West Africa.

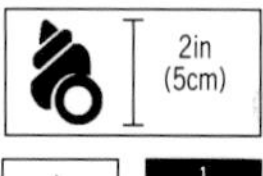


Pyriform in shape, it has about nine varices per whorl, each supporting strong coarsely ridged open, sometimes recurved, spines. The background colour is cream or pale yellow; the varices, spines and canal are dark brown or black. It is a popular and hard-to-obtain collectors' shell. This specimen comes from Luanda, Angola.

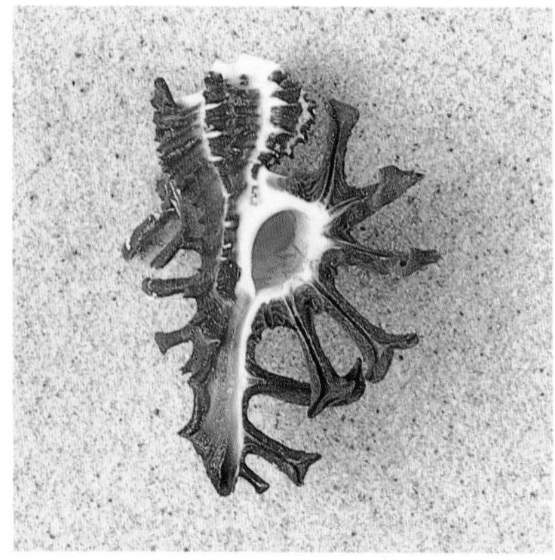

**HOMOLOCANTHA SCORPIO**
Scorpion Murex. *L. 1758.*
South-West Pacific.

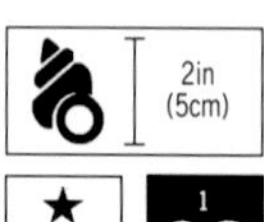


This is the type species of the genus, and is a shell with unusual sculpturing, the spire being low and rather flat, often encrusted or part eroded. The body whorl is enlarged and there is a long straight canal. The suture is impressed, and there is a pit at the suture behind each varix. The varices bear long open spines; those on the lip, which are the largest, are flattened and rather flared. Shells can be white, but are more usually dark brown to black, apex and aperture being white.

**HOMOLOCANTHA OXYACANTHA**
Sharp-spined Murex. *Broderip 1833.*
Western Central America.

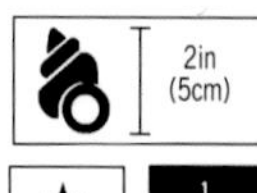


A short stout murex, it has a low spire, large rounded body whorl and strong medium-sized canal. About six varices bear long closely packed and ridged spines; there are also strong spiral ridges. The aperture is lirate, and the columella smooth. Usually beige or light brown in colour, shells are often heavily encrusted.

**MAXWELLIA GEMMA**
Gem Murex. *Sowerby 1879.*
Southern California.

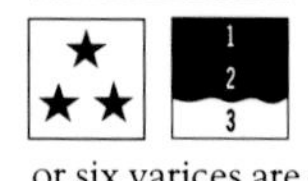


A distinctive little murex, endemic to southern California, it is very solid and has dark brown or black spiral bands on an off-white or cream background. The five or six varices are rounded and smooth, being joined to the ones on earlier whorls by a thin low wing, behind which is a deep pit. The canal is of medium length, recurved and almost closed. This species lives in depths to about 198ft (60m).

## MUREXIELLA BOJADORENSIS

*Locard 1897.*
West Africa.

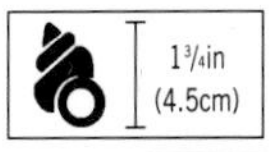


A sought-after collectors' item from offshore waters, this has a low spire, long straight canal, and four or five strong varices. The coarse spines are scaly and those at the shoulders are thickest and longest, the extremities being foliated and recurved. Specimens can be off-white, cream, or mid-to-dark brown.

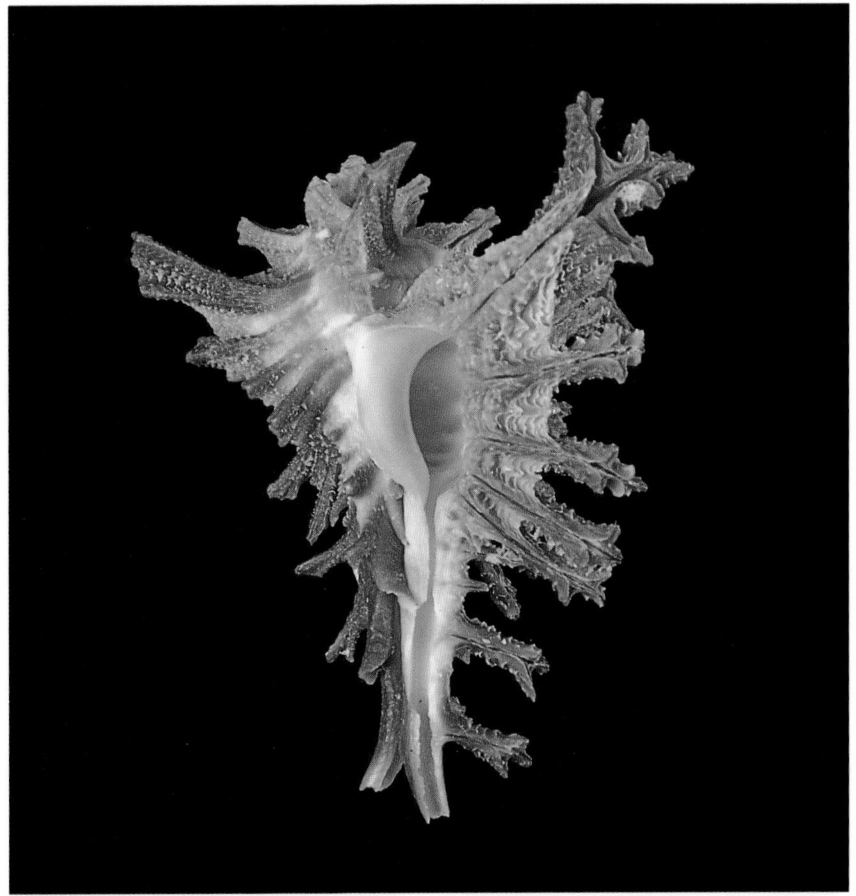

## MUREXIELLA BALTEATUS

Girdled Dwarf Murex. *Sowerby 1841.*
Indo-Pacific.

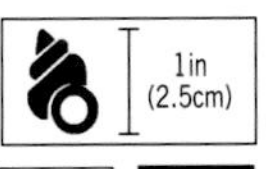


Large delicately coloured specimens of this shell are often fished off Punta Eugaño, central Philippines. The spire is tall, the body whorl ovate and large, the canal short and recurved. The varices bear short sharp open and foliated fronds. Colours can vary, but the depicted shell is of typical coloration.

## MUREXSUL OCTAGONUS

Octagon Murex. *Quoy and Gaimard 1833.*
New Zealand.

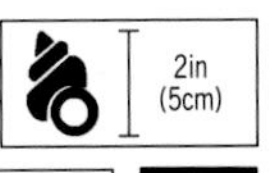


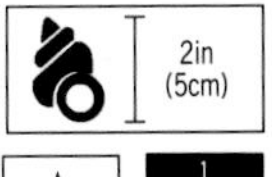

A fusiform shell, with rounded whorls which are angular below the suture, it is endemic to New Zealand. There is prominent dark brown spiral cording, and the eight or so varices bear short open recurved spines. This specimen was collected by a scuba diver at 40ft (12m) on rocks in the Bay of Islands, North Island.

## MURICOPSIS OXYTATUS

Hexagonal Murex. M. *Smith 1938.*
Florida and West Indies.

This slender elongate murex has a tall spire, a short canal and an ovate aperture, the outer lip of which is dentate. There are six varices per whorl, each with short sharp spines and very fine spiral threads between. It is variable in colour, ranging from pure white to pink, and with occasional banded variations.

**CERATOSTOMA BURNETTI**
Burnett's Murex. *Adams and Reeve 1849.*
Japan, Korea and South-East China.

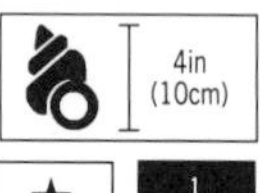

4in (10cm)

A strong ovate species, this has distinctive flaring winged varices. There are low rounded spiral cords which extend onto each varix, causing an undulating effect. The outer lip is denticulate, with one particularly long labial tooth – these also occur on earlier varices. It is a much sought-after collectors' shell, from shallow waters.

**EUPLEURA NITIDA**
Bright Murex. *Broderip 1833.*
Western Central America.

1in (2.5cm)

A small rather flattened shell, with axially aligned prickly winged varices, it has strong spiral ridges and low rounded axial ribs. It is prettily coloured, being white with dark blue-to-black ridges and brown or grey interspaces. The lip has about four small denticles, and there is a straight open canal. It is a shallow-water shell, this specimen coming from Cebaco Island, West Panama.

**OCINEBRELLUS ADUNCUS**
*Sowerby 1834.*
Japan.

1½in (3.5cm)

A rather variable shell, endemic to Japan, some forms are given subspecific names. Five varices per whorl support thin, recurved and grooved wing-like extensions. On the whorls are low rounded cords with scaly interspaces. This squat rather triangular murex is another shallow-water dweller.

**CERATOSTOMA FOURNIERI**
Fournier's Murex. *Crosse 1861.*
Japan, Korea and China.

2in (5cm)

This shallow-water murex has a medium-sized spire, angular whorls and a long recurved canal. Three varices bear leaf-like joined processes, and there is a prominent rounded nodule between the varices. The aperture is white, the shell otherwise varying from off-white to light brown.

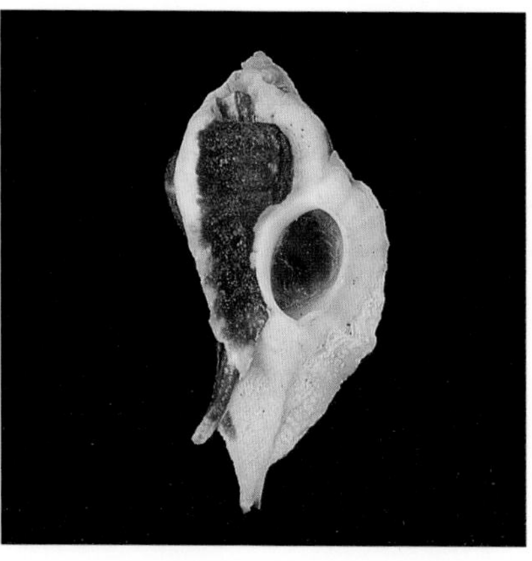

**JATON DECUSSATA**
Decussate Murex. *Gmelin 1791.*
West Africa.

To 2in (5cm)

The species has a low spire, a rather long ovate body whorl and a long closed anterior canal. The poorly developed varices are separated by a prominent humped intervarical node. The anterior portion of the white aperture bears a long sharp denticle. Shells are generally mid-to-dark brown, with off-white apex, varices and canal. They inhabit shallow water.

**OCINEBRA ERINACEUS**
Sting Winkle. *L. 1758.* North-western Europe to North-West Africa.

2in (5cm)

This variably sculptured species has several subspecific names. It is a robust coarse murex with strong spiral ridges and varices that bear prominent, sometimes rounded, or thinner, open spines or nodules. The ventral aspect of the lip varix can be flared, wing-like and lamellated. The species feeds on bivalves in subtidal waters.

## POROPTERON CAPENSIS
Cape Murex. *Sowerby 1841.*
South Africa.

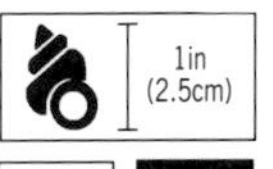

Endemic to South Africa, *P. capensis* is a small lightweight murex, with three varices bearing sharp and upturned spines. Beach-collected specimens are very common, live-taken are less usual. It is found in relatively shallow water and occurs between the Cape and Jeffreys Bay. The species *P. incurvispina* occurs eastwards to East London; the spines of the latter tend to be more curved.

## PTEROPURPURA MACROPTERUS
Frilled-wing Murex. *Deshayes 1839.*
California.

This is a coarsely sculptured murex, with long frilled and wing-like varices. The tall narrow spire and body whorl bear strong rounded nodules – one between each varix – and there are low rounded cords, extending onto the wings. Usually light brown or cream with a smooth white aperture, the species is endemic to California, this particular shell coming from shallow water, San Diego.

## PTEROPURPURA CENTRIFUGA
Centrifuge Murex. *Hinds 1844.*
Western Central America.

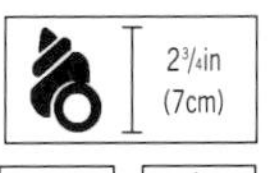

A deep-water species, it can be off-white, beige or tan. There are three extended and frilled varices between which is one low rounded node on the shoulders. The spire and body whorl appear rather angular; the canal is closed, long and generally straight. The shell seen here was collected in 120ft (36m) off Perlas Island, Panama.

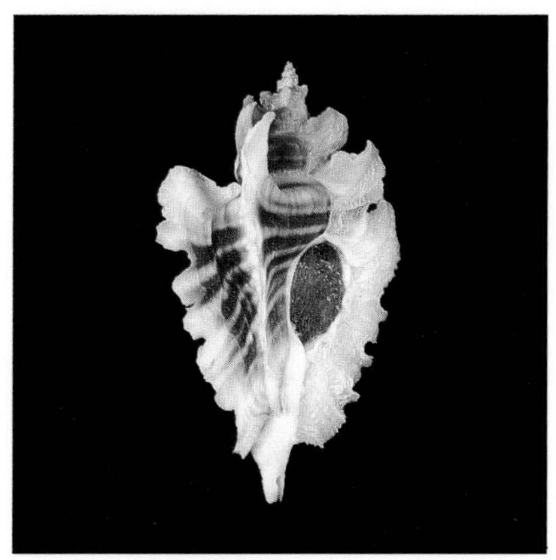

## PTEROPURPURA TRIALATUS
Three-winged Murex. *Sowerby 1834.*
California to Mexico.

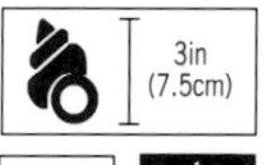

A handsome species, this has a tall spire, rather angular whorls and a long straight closed canal. Normally an intertidal rock dweller, the depicted deeper-water shell displays typically foliated and long winged varices. It is attractively banded with dark brown on cream or white.

## PTEROPURPURA VOKESAE
Voke's False Murex. *Emerson 1964.*
Southern California.

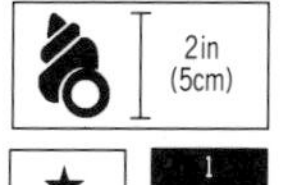

Endemic to southern California, this lightweight species is delicately ornamented, with numerous very fine spiral threads that extend onto the flaring winged and scaly varices. There is one strong intervarical node. The broad siphonal canal is closed, the lip is finely dentate, and the columella is smooth. This specimen was collected in 90ft (27m) off Santa Barbara.

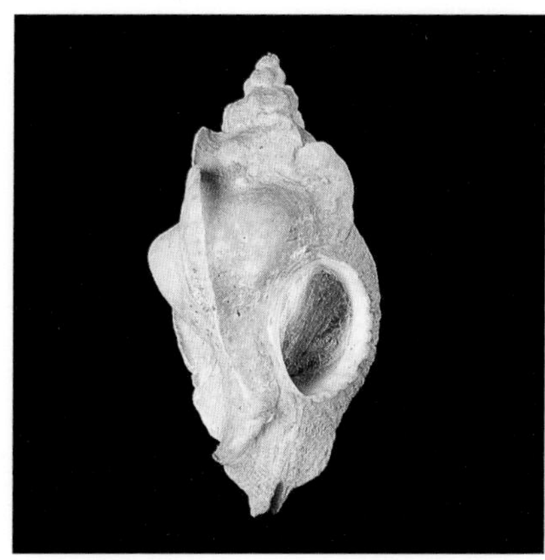

## PTEROPURPURA FESTIVA
Festive Murex. *Hinds 1844.*
California to Mexico.

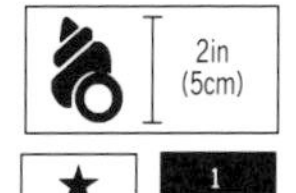

Although the name suggests otherwise, this is rather a drab species and can be encrusted and almost fossil-like. It is dominated by large intervarical nodes; the varices themselves are poorly developed and are rolled backward, partly touching the previous whorl at the posterior. In some, fine spiral threads, which are dark brown or fawn, are evident. A shallow-water dweller.

**TROPHON CARDUELIS**
Thistle Trophon. *Watson 1886.*
South-eastern Australia.

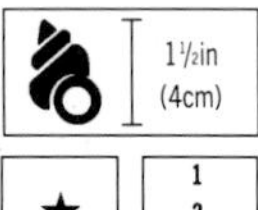


A difficult to obtain deep-water species, this is only rarely obtainable by amateur collectors. I believe that *T. obtusiliratum* may be a synonym. Endemic to south-eastern Australia, it is a tall slender fusiform shell, with sharply angled whorls with numerous fine varices, sometimes bearing rather long upturned open spines. The canal is long, open and straight. Shells are always pure off-white, the depicted shell collected at a depth of 2,100ft (636m) off Sydney.

**ACANTHINA MONODON**
One-toothed Thais. *Pallas 1774.*
Western South America.

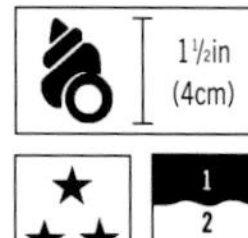


A bulbous and sturdy shell, the one-toothed thais has a very low spire and much enlarged body whorl. The otherwise smooth interior has one short but sharp labial tooth, very near to the siphonal canal. There are a few flat spiral cords and many fine axial growth striae. The variability of colouring is shown in the photograph, these shells coming from Pichidangul, Chile.

**DRUPA MORUM**
Purple Drupe. *Röding 1798.*
Indo-Pacific.

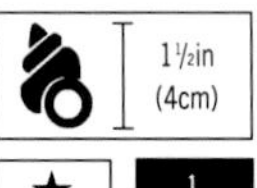


This coral-reef dweller is probably the most well known of the popular genus *Drupa*. The spire is almost flat and the greatly enlarged body whorl bears numerous low rounded nodules. The lip is very strongly dentate, the denticles being laid in groups, with those at the posterior end bifurcated. The columella is strongly folded. A white shell, with black nodules, it has a vivid purple aperture with yellowish margins.

**TROPHON PLICATUS**
Laciniate Trophon. *Lightfoot 1786.*
Brazil and Argentina.

This rather dull species is often called *T. laciniatus*, which is said to be a synonym. It is coarsely sculptured, with many open plate-like varices which are curved forward toward the aperture. The whorls are flat below the sutures, but this is otherwise a rounded, or occasionally elongated, shell. Often heavily encrusted with marine debris or coral, it is a drab grey beige when cleaned, with an aperture of deep reddish brown.

**CONCHOLEPAS CONCHOLEPAS**
Barnacle Rock Shell. *Bruguière 1792.*
Peru and Chile.

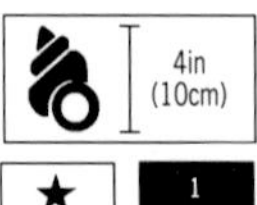


The shell is dominated by a wide flaring aperture which almost hides the body whorl. The spire is depressed and almost non-existent. It is similar to limpets and abalones inasmuch as it attaches itself to rocks by its very strong foot. The axially ridged dorsum is often encrusted with barnacles.

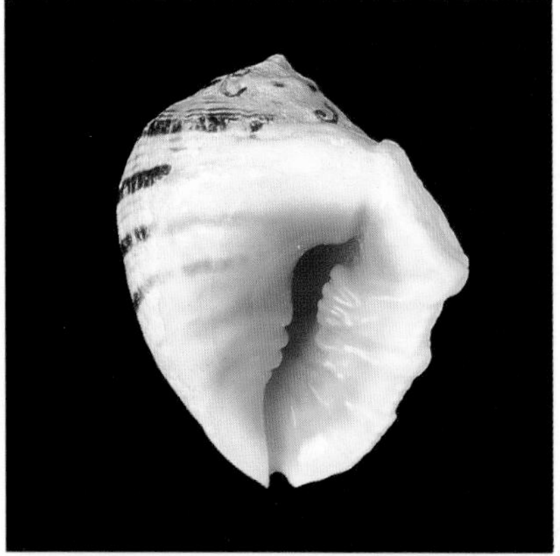

**DRUPA MORUM IODOSTOMA**
Iodine-mouthed Drupe. *Lesson 1840.*
Marquesas Islands.

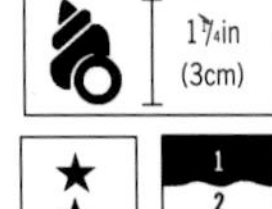


An interesting variant of *D. morum*, this endemic subspecies has a fairly smooth rounded dorsum with dark brown or black spiral bands on a cream or white background. The calloused aperture is similar to that of *D. morum* in structure, but the colour tends to be a deep lavender.

**DRUPA RICINUS**
Prickly Drupe. *L. 1758.*
Indo-Pacific.

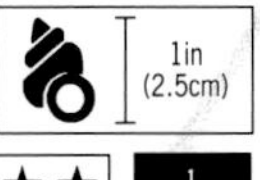

1in (2.5cm)

An attractive drupe, it inhabits intertidal rocks. The enlarged body whorl has well-spaced low blunt nodules, and there are about four long closed spines at the lip margin. The denticles are arranged in a similar fashion to those of *D. morum*; the columella has strong central folds. A white shell, with black nodules, it has a white aperture with a broad broken orange band around the periphery.

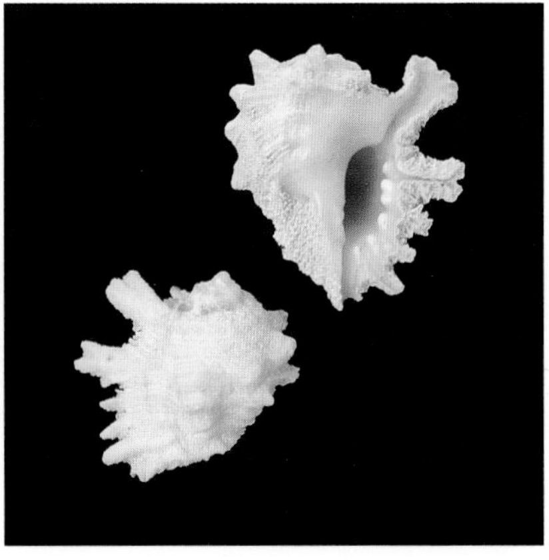

**DRUPA GROSSULARIA**
Finger Drupe. *Röding 1798.*
South-West Pacific.

1in (2.5cm)

The spire is almost flat, and the rather flattened body whorl is greatly enlarged. The exterior has strong scaly rounded cords and odd blunt nodules. The lip bears several opened and flat spines, the largest forming the anal canal; it is also strongly dentate. This shell has a beautiful deep yellow interior and a beige or off-white exterior.

**DRUPA CLATHRATULA**
Clathrate Drupe. *Lamarck 1816.*
South-West Pacific.

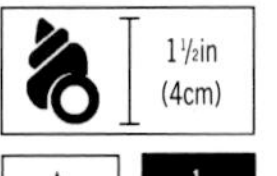

1½in (4cm)

This bulbous drupe has short rounded dorsal spines and – where obvious on lime-free specimens – numerous varices separated by deep axial pits. The aperture has a tan margin, with white strong denticles and plicae, and the shell is pale lavender within. Of the two specimens depicted, one is heavily encrusted and the other was found in lime-free conditions. Both are from Efate, New Hebrides.

**DRUPA RUBUSIDAEUS**
Rose Drupe. *Röding 1798.*
Indo-Pacific.

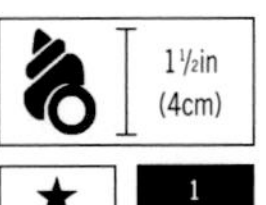

1½in (4cm)

This stocky shell is dominated by short blunt well-spaced dorsal spines and scaly spiral threads. The lip is dentate, and the columella has three plicae; the parietal area is calloused. The exterior colouring is off-white or cream; the aperture is a pretty deep pink, with hints of yellow around the margins. It is a coral reef dweller.

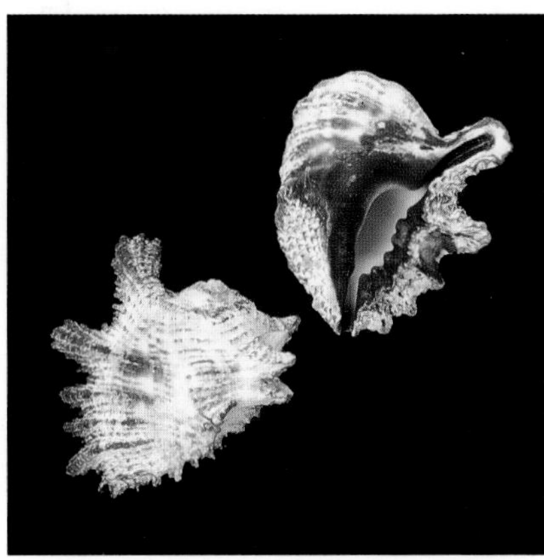

**DRUPA LOBATA**
Lobate Drupe. *Blainville 1832.* Red Sea,
Indian Ocean to Western Australia.

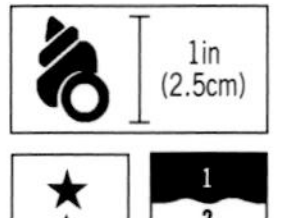

1in (2.5cm)

A species similar to *D. grossularia* in shape and sculpturing, it differs in that the colour of the aperture is a dark chocolate brown, and the interior is a pale yellow. Often heavily encrusted with lime and other deposits, it is a shallow-water shell.

**NASSA FRANCOLINA**
Francolina Jopas. *Bruguière 1789.*
Indian Ocean.

2in (5cm)

A stocky heavy ovate species, it has an enlarged body whorl. There are numerous fine spiral grooves and several prominent growth striae. The lip has extremely small indentations at the edge, and a low blunt nodule at the posterior. There is another blunt nodule on the parietal wall. The shell is a pale cream pink, with large blotched areas of tan; the aperture is white.

### NUCELLA LAMELLOSA

Frilled Dogwinkle. *Gmelin 1791.*
Alaska to California.

2in (5cm)

A solid heavy shell, the frilled dogwinkle has a medium-sized spire and ovate body whorl. The two specimens shown, which come from rocks, at Victoria, British Columbia, show the extremely variable sculpturing within the species. Some forms are banded; others are plain white, beige or pale orange.

### PURPURA PATULA

Wide-mouthed Purpura. *L. 1758.*
Florida and West Indies.

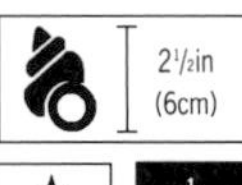

2½in (6cm)

This well-known shell has a low spire, a much enlarged body whorl and a wide gaping aperture. The dorsum is sculptured with rows of low blunt spirally laid nodules and fine cords. There are numerous lirae on the inner lip, and the columella and parietal wall are smooth, wide, curved and almost shelf-like. The exterior is a dull grey brown, the columella is pale orange and the interior wall is white and grey.

### PURPURA PANAMA

Rudolph's Purpura. *Röding 1798.*
East Indies.

To 3in (7.5cm)

A very solid thick-walled shell, it has a medium-sized spire and large ovate body whorl. The whorls are slightly angular and the numerous flat spiral cords are dark brown with cream interspaces. The lip and inner wall are strongly lirate, these being orange on pale peach. The smooth columella and parietal wall are also pale orange.

### NUCELLA LAPILLUS

Atlantic Dog Whelk. *L. 1758.* North-West and North-East Atlantic coasts.

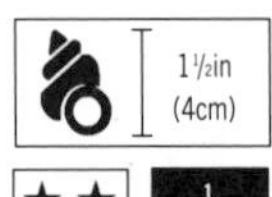

1½in (4cm)

This sturdy little shell lives on rocks and feeds on mussels and other molluscs. It is ovate, with a low narrow spire and enlarged body whorl bearing rounded spiral cords. It is very variable in colour and banding, several forms being shown here, all of them coming from Cornwall, England.

### PURPURA PERSICA
Persian Purpura. *L. 1758.*
South-West Pacific.

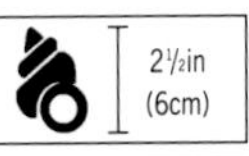


Not dissimilar to *P. patula*, the Persian purpura is heavier, has no nodules and features numerous low spiral cords. The interior of the lip is tinged with dark brown, and this pales almost to white. There are many fine lirae. The columella and parietal wall, which are heavily calloused, are pale orange with dark brown streaks. This species lives on intertidal rocks.

### PURPURA PLANOSPIRA
Eye of Judas Purpura. *Lamarck 1822.*
Western Central America and Galapagos.

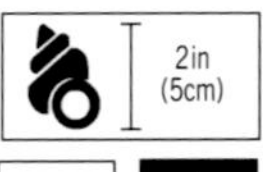


Although considered by some experts to be simply uncommon, I have been aware of only very few specimens available on the market, and the demand obviously exceeds the supply of this very attractive purpura. It has a strange umbilicus set at the posterior, and the ventral aspect is most endearing. The exterior is coarsely ridged and a dull beige brown.

### THAIS HIPPOCASTANUM
Chestnut Rock Shell. *L. 1758.*
South-West Pacific.

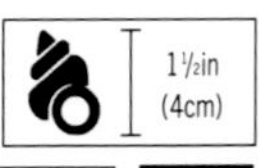


This very strong and heavy shell has a low spire and enlarged ovate body whorl. Axially laid blunt nodules and fine spiral grooves ornament the exterior, while the lip bears four distinct denticles; the columella has one short plica. The colour is dark brown or black, with white irregular patches between the nodules. The apex is often eroded. The species lives on rocky shorelines.

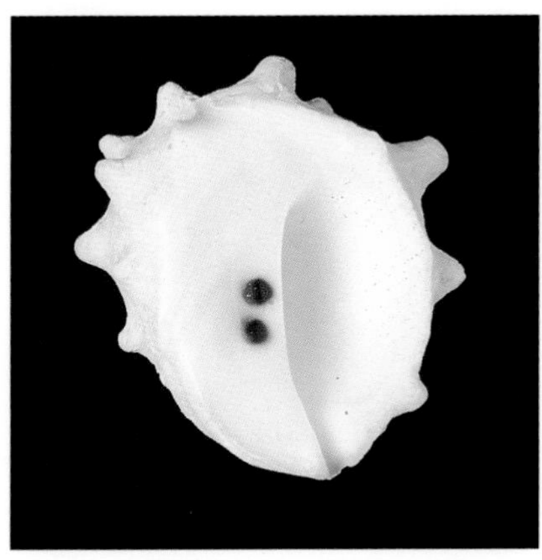

### PURPURA NODOSA
Nodose Purpura. *L. 1758.*
West Africa and Brazil.

The spire is virtually flat; the body whorl is greatly enlarged; and there are well-spaced low blunt nodules. Often, the exterior is heavily lime-encrusted. The extremely smooth and white interior is dominated by two small black spots on the columella. The specimen shown is from Takoradi, Ghana.

### THAIS KIOSQUIFORMIS
Kiosque Rock Shell. *Duclos 1832.*
Western Central America.

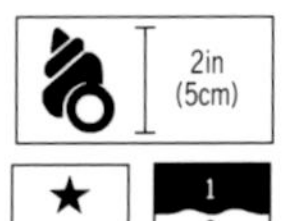


A solidly built thais, it has angular whorls, a tall spire and a short blunt canal. The shoulders bear a double row of rather sharp nodules, and there are numerous spiral cords. At the suture, very thin wavy axially laid ribs stretch to the shoulders. The overall colour is a dark bluish grey with odd thin white bands. The columella is white; the aperture is pale grey.

### THAIS LACERA
Carinate Rock Shell. *Born 1778.*
East Africa and Indian Ocean.

This species is sometimes described with the subgeneric name *Cymia*. It is another solid little shell with prominent nodose whorls and very fine spiral grooving. The suture is somewhat impressed. The lip is finely dentate and the columella and parietal wall calloused; the whole of the aperture is a highly glossy pale orange. The exterior is beige or pale brown.

**THAIS RUGOSA**
Rugose Rock Shell. *Born 1778.*
India and South-East Asia.

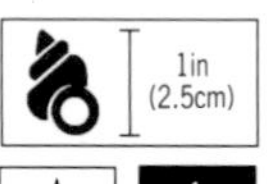


The rugose rock shell is lightweight and has spirally ridged whorls. There are four rows of triangular low spines, the largest at the shoulders. The exterior generally has a very scaly texture. The umbilicus is open and the lip is lirate; the columella is smooth. Shells are a pale orange beige throughout, the spines being tipped with dark brown; the aperture is white. This species lives among rocks or in mud.

**THAIS TUBEROSA**
Tuberose Rock Shell. *Röding 1798.*
South-West Pacific.

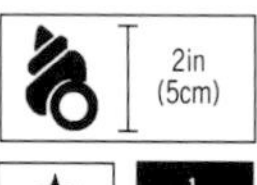


A stocky heavy species, it is dominated by rows of axial blunt nodules. There are also fine spiral grooves. The lip is finely dentate, and the columella is slightly folded. A pale orange or cream shell, it has many dark brown blotches. The aperture is tinged with orange. This specimen was collected at 6½ft (2m) on rocks at Dampier, western Australia.

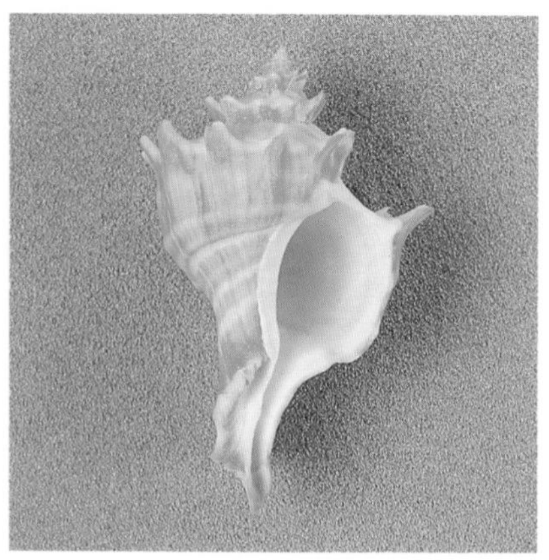

**FORRERIA BELCHERI**
Giant Forreria. *Hinds 1843.*
California to Baja California.

A striking shell, it has angled whorls that are almost pagoda-like in shape. The body whorl is wide, but tapers slightly, and is compressed, with a suture-like indentation which runs spirally around the lower half. The canal is long and slightly recurved. There are low axial ribs with open triangular spines at the shoulders. This specimen was dredged at 165ft (56m) off San Diego.

**THAIS MELONES**
Gourd Rock Shell. *Duclos 1832.* Western Central America and Galapagos Islands.

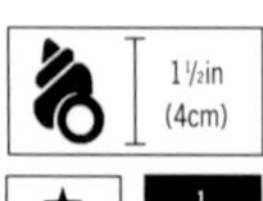


This very rounded virtually smooth and heavy thais has fine spiral grooving. The lip is finely dentate and the columella is smooth. There is a corneus ovate operculum. The shell is a cream colour, overlaid with dark brown or black patches. The inner lip and columella are tinged with pale yellow. A rocky shore dweller.

**VITULARIA MILIARIS**
Spotted Vitularia. *Gmelin 1791.*
South-West Pacific.

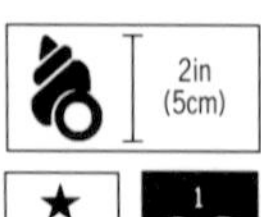


Irregularly shaped and sculptured, this shell has rounded nodulose varices, especially at the shoulders, separated by shallow indentations; the exterior is covered by very small pustules which are obliquely laid, giving the shell a file-like texture. The lip is dentate. Two colour forms are shown here.

**NEORAPANA MURICATA**
Frilled Purpura. *Broderip 1832.*
Western Central America.

A strong and heavy shell, it can be variable in sculpturing. The spire is very low, and the much enlarged body whorl bears four or more strong spiral ridges. These are nodulose, especially at the shoulders. There are numerous scaly axial striations. The glossy aperture is a pale pink or peach colour. Perfect well-cleaned specimens are difficult to obtain.

**RAPANA VENOSA**
Thomas's Rapa Whelk. *Valenciennes 1846.*
Japan, China and Black Sea.

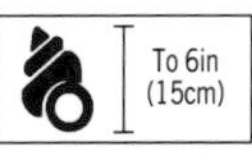


This large heavy shell has a low spire and a large body whorl with a wide flaring aperture. This species was accidentally introduced into the Black Sea when oyster spawn was deposited there, presumably from the Far East. The shell has now become a major pest, feeding on and destroying valuable oyster beds. Large specimens are popular with collectors.

**RAPANA BEZOAR**
Bezoar Rapa Whelk. *L. 1758.*
Japan to Taiwan.

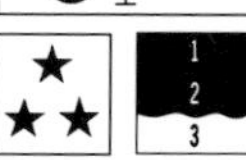


Almost a miniature version of the giant *R. venosa*, it differs in colouring, its aperture being a pale cream or off-white, with numerous strong lirae. The suture is channelled, and there are many low spiral cords. There is a prominent and deep umbilicus. The shell is found in offshore waters.

SUPER FAMILY
MURICOIDEA

FAMILY
## CORALLIOPHILIDAE
(Latiaxis Shells)

Formerly known as Magilidae, latiaxis shells are an exquisite family. Many are adapted to live in and among coral stems, but there are also a number of deep-water species. Although related to the murex, they are parasitic and do not possess a radula; many live in association with sea anemones and their relatives. Much study remains to be done if all the divisions of this group are to be gathered into a logical and worthwhile classification. Recent attempts, such as that of Kosuge and Suzuke, have made a valuable start, but there is still some way to go, especially as new, undescribed deep-water species are still coming to light. Vaught lists 10 genera and seven subgenera. Here, we are primarily concerned with *Latiaxis*, *Coralliophila*, *Babelomurex*, *Hirtomurex*, *Mipus* and *Rapa*.

**BABELOMUREX FEARNLEYI**
Fearnley's Coral Snail. *Emerson and D'Attilio 1965.* Japan, Philippines to Australia.

A coarsely sculptured and fusiform shell, its spiral cords bear short open spines, and the weak axial ribs are strongly spinose at the shoulders. It is off-white, with a pale lavender aperture. The canal is of moderate length and open. The specimen shown is from Cebu, Philippines.

**BABELOMUREX KAWAMURAI**
Kawamura's Coral Snail. *Kira 1954.*
Japan to Philippines, South-East Africa.

This fairly widespread species is quite variable in shape – two local forms are shown here, the smaller is from Port Hedland, western Australia, the larger was found off Natal, South Africa. Both were fished at a depth of over 990ft (300m). The straight-sided whorls have almost flat-topped shoulders with irregular triangular spines that extend laterally. There is fine spiral cording. This shell is always pure white.

**BABELOMUREX FINCHI**
Finch's Latiaxis. *Fulton 1930.*
Japan, Taiwan and Philippines.

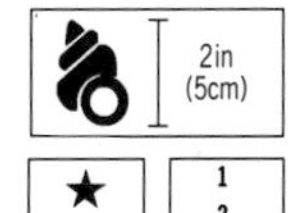


Another white deep-water shell, Finch's latiaxis has a low spire, wide triangular body whorl and broad recurved canal. There are fine spiral cords and upturned triangular flat spines at the shoulders. The umbilicus is open, and there are fine lirae on the inner lip. Both specimens shown here are from south-western Taiwan.

## BABELOMUREX JAPONICUS

Japanese Latiaxis. *Dunker 1882.*
Japan to Philippines.

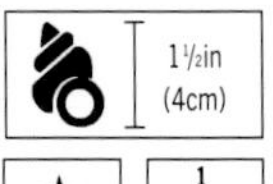


Two specimens are shown of this lovely shell, both fished in deep water off Taiwan. The outstanding features are spinose spiral ridges and small triangular spines, occasionally recurved, at the shoulders. Shells are generally off-white with a pure white aperture.

## BABELOMUREX TAKAHASHII

Takahashi's Latiaxis. *Kosuge 1979.*
Philippines.

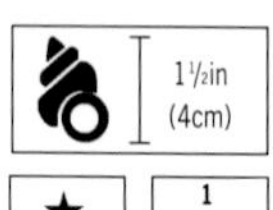


Endemic to the Philippines, this beautiful pink species has highly spinose spiral cords, the spines being longest at the shoulders. The spire is elevated and the whorls angular. The canal is broad, short and recurved. Specimens are occasionally netted in water 330ft (100m) deep, off Bohol Island.

## BABELOMUREX RICINULOIDES

*Schepman 1911.*
Philippines.

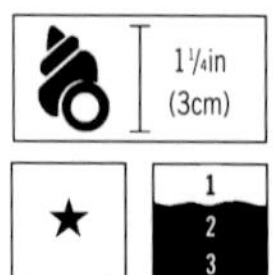


A very attractive latiaxis, it has long, open upturned spines at the shoulders and several rows of rounded spinose ridges on the body whorl. It is finely scabrous in the interspaces. All spines, as well as the ovate aperture, are tinged with a delicate pink. It is often erroneously referred to as *Latiaxis celina muramai*, which is a synonym.

## BABELOMUREX TOSANUS

*Hirase 1908.*
Japan to Philippines.

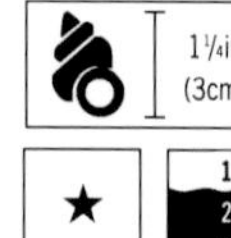


This shell has a tall narrow spire, a rather rounded body whorl and a short recurved canal. The closely packed spiny spiral cords become longer and more triangular at the shoulders. Specimens vary in general shape and length of spines, but are usually off-white.

### *BABELOMUREX HIRASEI*

Hirase's Murex. *Shikama 1964.*
Japan to Philippines.

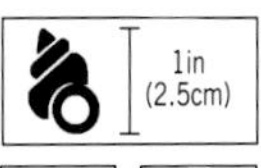


The spire is low, the body whorl straight-sided and depressed at the anterior. There is a sloping shoulder below the suture. Fine spiral scaly threads ornament the whorls, and very large flat slightly upturned triangular spines extend from the shoulders. The umbilicus is prominent and open. A choice collectors' item.

### *BABELOMUREX LISCHKEANUS*

Lischke's Latiaxis. *Dunker 1882.* Japan, Philippines, Australia and New Zealand.

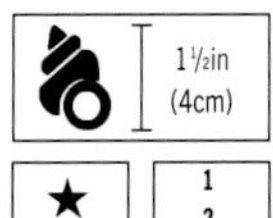


This widespread species can vary from locality to locality. The shell featured here is a particularly beautiful specimen from Taiwan. All variations appear to possess the characteristic highly spinose spiral ridges and large triangular shoulder spines. All are off-white and inhabit deep water.

### *BABELOMUREX SPINOSUS*

Spined Latiaxis. *Hirase 1908.*
Japan to Philippines and Australia.

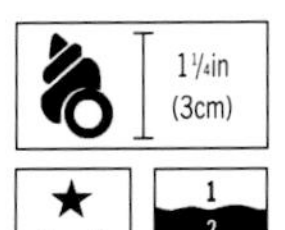


A delicate shell with a tall spire, angular whorls and short narrow recurved canal, it is variably spinose, but the shell in the photograph is a typical example, with long part-open recurved spines extending from the shoulders. Shells are usually off-white, cream or pale brown. This specimen was fished off south-western Taiwan.

### *BABELOMUREX LONGISPINOSUS*

Long-spined Latiaxis. *Suzuki 1972.*
South China Sea and Philippines.

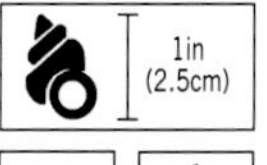


A rather triangular shell, the long-spined latiaxis has a flat spire and almost flat-sided whorls; it has one or two raised spiral ridges and longish irregularly-shaped and sometimes recurved open spines at the shoulders. The umbilicus is open and wide. It is a beige or pinkish shell with a deep rose-red aperture. The depicted specimen is from Bohol Island, Philippines.

### *BABELOMUREX BABELIS*

Babylon Latiaxis. *Requien 1848.*
Mediterranean.

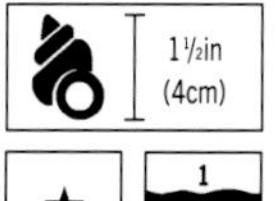


The Babylon latiaxis has a tall conical spire and angular whorls which at the shoulders extend into broad triangular, sometimes recurved, spines. There are rounded axial ribs and scaly spiral cords. The umbilicus is partly closed. The colour is usually off-white, beige or pale yellow. The species is endemic to the Mediterranean, and this specimen was collected in Malta.

### *BABELOMUREX ECHINATUS*

Many-spined Latiaxis. *Azuma 1960.*
Japan, Taiwan and Philippines.

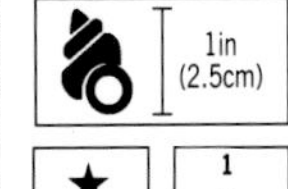


Partly open spines – both long and short – closely pack the whole exterior of this spinose little shell. It has a medium-sized spire, a rounded body whorl and a short slightly recurved canal. The lip is finely dentate, and the columella smooth. Perfectly formed specimens are difficult to find.

**BABELOMUREX AMALIAE**
*Kobelt 1907.*
Mediterranean.

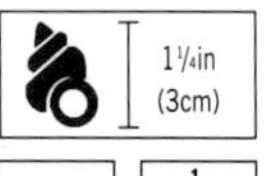


A slender high-spired latiaxis, endemic to the Mediterranean, with strong spiral scaly ridges, its shoulders bear flat spines of varying sizes and generally triangular in shape. The lip has fine lirae and the columella is smooth; the umbilicus is open. The depicted specimen was fished from deep water off southern Italy.

**CORALLIOPHILA VIOLACEA**
Violet Coral Snail. *Kiener 1836.*
Indo-Pacific.

A globose shell, with a low spire, it is usually heavily encrusted and occasionally there are parasitic wormshells on the dorsum. On exposed parts, fine spiral cords are evident. The aperture is a deep violet; there are numerous fine lirae on the inner lip, and the columella is smooth. This specimen is from the central Philippines.

**HIRTOMUREX TEREMACHII**
Teremachi's Latiaxis. *Kuroda 1959.*
Japan to Philippines.

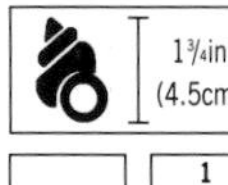


A pure white latiaxis, it is ornamented with very beautiful scabrous spiral cords, separated by fine spiral threads on the body whorl. The largest scabrous projections are at the shoulders. The umbilicus is open and the canal is relatively long. A most popular species, due to its sheer beauty.

**BABELOMUREX INDICUS**
*E.A. Smith 1899.*
Japan to Philippines.

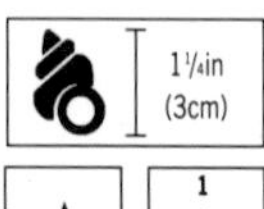


Exquisitely ornamented with fine scabrous spiral ridges and rounded axial ribs, this is a dainty little shell. The spire is of medium height and the body whorl ovate and compressed at the anterior. Both aperture and columella are smooth, and the shell is pure white throughout. The depicted shell, from the central Philippines, was found in deep water.

**CORALLIOPHILA PYRIFORMIS**
Pear-shaped Coral Snail. *Kira 1954.*
Japan to Philippines.

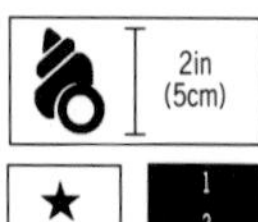


This larger coral snail has rounded whorls and a pyriform body whorl. There are fine scabrous spiral ridges. The aperture is a beautiful pale violet, with fine lirae on the inner lip. The columella is smooth. This is another species that is often highly encrusted when collected.

**HIRTOMUREX WINCKWORTHI**
Winkworth's Latiaxis. *Fulton 1930.*
Japan to Philippines.

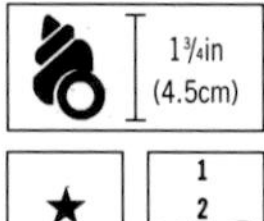


Winkworth's latiaxis is a rather globose thin lightweight shell, with angular whorls and a broad canal and open umbilicus. The sculpturing consists of scabrous and spinose raised spiral cords crossed axially with fine spinose varices. This particular specimen was netted in deep water off Panglao, Bohol, Philippines.

## LATIAXIS MAWAE

Mawe's Latiaxis. *Gray in Griffith and Pidgeon 1834.* Japan, Taiwan & Philippines.

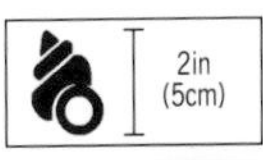

A strangely shaped and very popular latiaxis, its spire is flat or depressed, and the convex sides of the whorls taper at the anterior. The body whorl uncoils, developing outward and downward to a very broad expanded area that includes the gaping umbilicus and open recurved canal. The shoulders can bear triangular, frilly and sometimes recurved spines. Shells are off-white to a dirty beige in colour. Both specimens shown are from Taiwan.

## LATIAXIS PILSBRYI

Pilsbry's Latiaxis. *Hirase 1908.* Japan to Philippines.

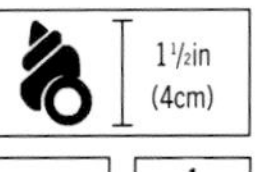


This is similar in shape to *L. mawae*, but the body whorl does not drop and the depressed spire is level with its shoulders, which bear triangular spines. It is also a much lighter and thinner shell. Specimens used frequently to be fished off Taiwan. This source of supply has stopped, perhaps because of altered fishing habits, but shells are still occasionally fished in the central Philippines.

## MIPUS EUGENIAE

Eugene's Latiaxis. *Bernardi 1853.* Japan to Philippines.

A dull off-white to beige species, it has an almost chalky texture. The whorls are distinctly rounded, with an impressed suture; the canal is broad and of moderate length. There are numerous fine spiral cords and occasional axial striae. The umbilicus is open. This specimen was fished in deep water off south-western Taiwan.

## MIPUS GYRATUS

Gyrate Latiaxis. *Hinds 1844.* Japan and South-West Pacific.

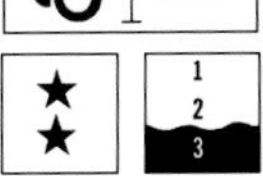

A very angular shell with a high spire and broad slightly recurved canal. The periphery of the shoulders is strongly carinated, as in the specimen shown, but the carina is absent in many shells. Always white, this is an offshore – usually deep-water – species.

SUPER FAMILY

## MURICOIDEA

FAMILY

## BUCCINIDAE

(Whelks)

A large and diverse family of some hundreds of species, whelks live both in cold polar and warm tropical seas. All species are carnivorous, feeding on bivalves and echinoids. The colder-water species tend to be drab, with little colour, whereas the warm-water shells are colourful and patterned. There are many genera and subgenera, among which we are primarily looking at *Buccinum*, *Babylonia*, *Neptunea*, *Phos* and *Cantharus*. This family is not an over-popular group with collectors – many of the cold-water whelks, for example, come from restricted habitats and deep waters in places such as northern Russia and the Bering Sea, thus making many species difficult, if not almost impossible, to obtain; some are rather drab in appearance.

**MIPUS SP.**
North-western Australia.

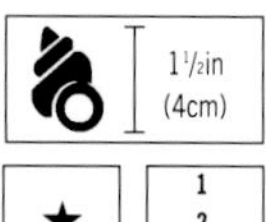


This is possibly an undescribed species, but I felt that it should be included because of the beauty of its shape. The shell in the photograph was trawled at a depth of 1,386ft (420m) off Port Hedland in 1986. The very strong rounded spiral ridges bear extremely close axial striae. I have yet to see another specimen of this particular shell.

**BABYLONIA AREOLATA**
Areola Babylon. *Link 1807.*
South-East Asia.

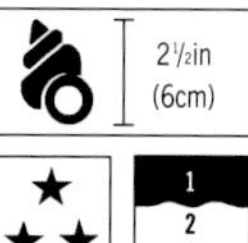


This solid smooth shell has a spire of medium height and rounded whorls, the body whorl being inflated. The suture is channelled, forming a small ledge to the shoulders. The fasciole is strong and surrounds the narrow open umbilicus. The off-white background is dominated by large mid-brown patches, tinged with golden yellow. It lives on sand in shallow water.

**RAPA RAPA**
Bubble Turnip. *L. 1758.*
South-West Pacific.

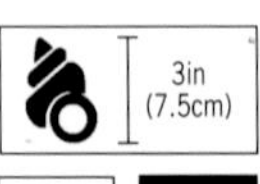


A rather lightweight and fragile, but large, shell, it is very globose, with a flat or depressed spire and a long open, often recurved, canal. There are strong corrugated spiral ridges. Most shells are a pale cream, but some are a dull orange colour; the aperture is always white. The shell lives in soft coral in shallow water.

**ANCISTROLEPIS GRAMMATUS**
Ridged Whelk. *Dall 1907.*
Japan.

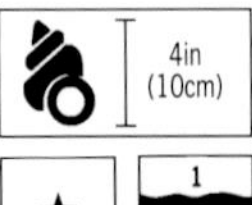


A beautifully sculptured whelk, endemic to Japan, it has a high spire and rounded whorls bearing very distinctive raised strong ridges; the suture is indented. The flaring aperture periphery is crenulated, and there are coarse lirae to the interior. The operculum is thick and horny, and when uncleaned the shell is covered with a thick dark brown periostracum.

**BABYLONIA SPIRATA**
Spiral Babylon. *L. 1758.*
Indian Ocean.

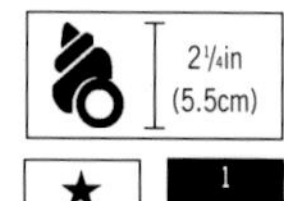


Although it is very similar in shape and build to *B. areolata*, the sides of the whorls are higher and straighter, and the edge of the channel formed by the suture is sharper. The columella and parietal wall are smooth and calloused; the fasciole is wide and the umbilicus is shallow. The depicted shell is from Sri Lanka and shows typical colour and patterns.

**BABYLONIA CANALICULATA**
Channelled Babylon. *Schumacher 1817.*
Arabian Sea.

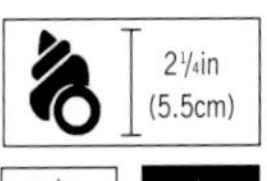

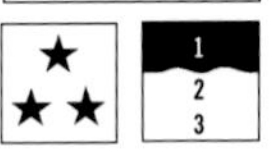

This could be a variant of *B. spirata*, and I am not convinced of its validity as a separate species. However, you will notice a distinct difference at the fasciole and umbilical region, this specimen being totally closed at that area. Also, the columella and parietal wall callous is continuous instead of notched at the umbilical opening, and the spire is lower. This specimen was collected in the Gulf of Oman.

**BABYLONIA JAPONICA**
Japanese Babylon. *Reeve 1842.*
Japan and Taiwan.

Found in shallow offshore water, it is similar in general appearance to *B. zeylanica*, but is rather more elongate and larger. It also has more distinctive and darker markings and it totally lacks violet fasciole staining. There is no sculpturing on the smooth surface, but there are usually several growth striations and scars.

**BABYLONIA LUTOSA**
Lutose Babylon. *Lamarck 1822.*
East Asia.

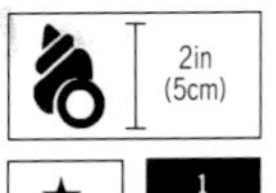

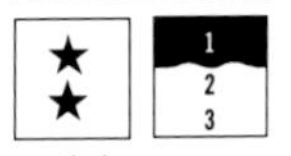

The lutose babylon is rather conical, with a tall narrow spire with slightly rounded whorls; there is a small sloping ledge below the suture. The fasciole is strong and the umbilicus open and deep. A small anal notch is evident, and the siphonal canal is short and deep. Off-white, with hazy beige or pale tan spiral bands and blotches, it is a shallow-water mud-dweller.

**BABYLONIA ZEYLANICA**
Indian Babylon. *Bruguière 1789.*
India and Sri Lanka.

A very smooth babylon, this has a high spire, rounded whorls, slightly impressed suture and a large ovate body whorl. Although its pattern is distinctive, the major characteristic of this species is the violet staining at the fasciole. This specimen is from Trincomalee, Sri Lanka.

**BABYLONIA PERFORATA**
Perforated Babylon. *Sowerby 1833?*
Taiwan.

I have not seen many examples of this species. It may possibly be endemic to Taiwan, but is rarely fished or offered by dealers. The distinctive pattern is of hazy pale brown grey blotches on an off-white background. The shell is rather compressed at the centre and the wide open umbilicus is surrounded by a strongly dentate fasciole ridge.

**BABYLONIA PAPILLARIS**
Spotted Babylon. *Sowerby 1825.*
South Africa.

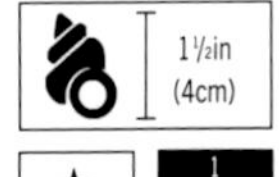

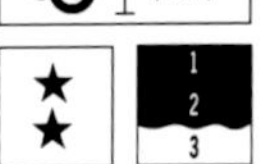

A small narrow elongate shell, with sloping shoulders, it is endemic to South Africa. The suture is slightly channelled. It is a creamy white with orange brown spots and blotches. Some experts name a variation *B. pintado* – this is possibly erroneous. This specimen was collected in Algoa Bay.

## BABYLONIA AMBULACRUM

Walkway Babylon. *Sowerby 1825.*
Western Pacific.

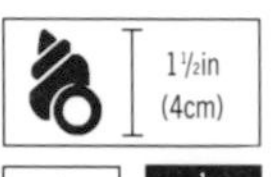


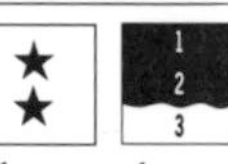


Rather similar to *B. spirata*, the walkway babylon is smaller and more bulbous; the suture channels are narrower; the general colour tends to be an olive brown; and the pattern is closer and resembles a snakeskin. The umbilicus is wide and deep.

## BUCCINULUM CORNEUM

Spindle Euthria Whelk. *L. 1758.*
Mediterranean.

This relatively smooth shell has a high spire and rounded whorls, which are slightly compressed below the suture. The canal is short, open and recurved. There are a few low spiral cords and numerous growth striations axially. It varies in colour from off-white to mid-brown, usually with mottled markings. Endemic to the Mediterranean, it lives in depths to 99ft (30m).

## BUCCINUM STRIATISSIMUM

Striated Whelk. *Sowerby 1899.*
Alaska to Japan.

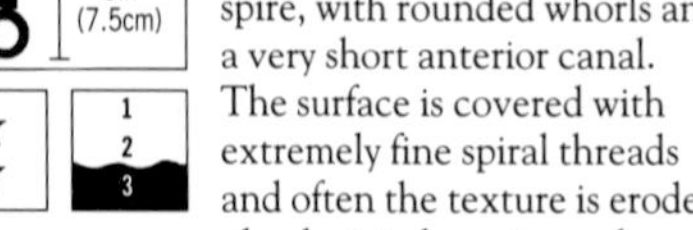

The striated whelk has a tall spire, with rounded whorls and a very short anterior canal. The surface is covered with extremely fine spiral threads and often the texture is eroded or worn away – as the depicted specimen shows. The suture is impressed. The lip is thickened and smooth, the columella and parietal wall smooth and calloused. A dull pale grey in colour, with a cream aperture, this is a deep-water species.

## BUCCINUM UNDATUM

Edible European Whelk. *L. 1758.*
North-West and North-East Atlantic.

Living in varying depths, ranging from shallow to very deep water, it is a scavenger and will feed on virtually anything, including dead and decaying fish. It has been a popular seafood for centuries, and is fished commercially for this purpose. Another drab-looking species, it rarely has any appreciable colour.

**BUCCINUM LEUCOSTOMA**
Yellow-mouthed Whelk. *Lischke 1872.*
Japan.

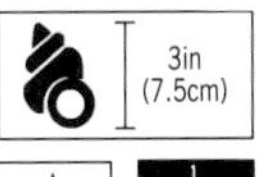


Endemic to Japan, this is an attractive species, both in its graceful shape and in its ornamentation. The enlarged rounded whorls taper to a high spire, and there are two rows of prominent low cords and numerous rows of fine cords on each whorl. There are also axial striations. The aperture is often tinged with pale yellow. A popular seafood source, it is fished commercially.

**JAPELION PERICOCHLION**
Peri Japelion. *Schrenck 1862.*
Japan.

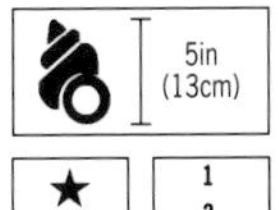


Endemic to Japan, this deep-water species has a very elegant shape, with a high spire and straight-sided whorls that become rounded as they grow larger toward the base. The suture is very deeply channelled. There are numerous axial growth striae. The depicted shell is still covered with its brown periostracum. It is beige beneath; the aperture is a delicate pale orange.

**NEPTUNEA KUROSHIO**
*Oyama 1958.*
Japan.

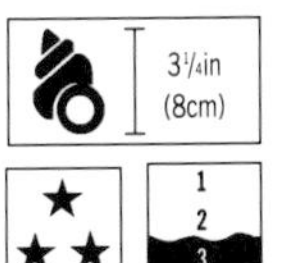


A heavy thickened whelk, it has an enlarged and inflated body whorl. The spire is low and slightly concave; the sculpturing features fine spiral cords, with minute threads in the interspaces. The overall colour is a drab off-white, the aperture being occasionally tinged with cream or yellow. From 240 to 600ft (73 to 182m) deep.

**BURNUPENA PAPYRACEA**
Paper Burnupena. *Bruguière 1789.*
South Africa.

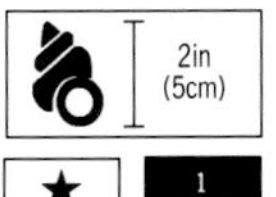


A solid ovate species, endemic to South Africa, it has rounded whorls decorated with fine spiral threads. It is a dull grey brown overall, the white aperture being tinged with pale brown; there are strong lirae within the lip. When alive, the shell is covered by a papery dark brown periostracum. There are several named varieties.

**NEPTUNEA TABULATA**
Tabled Neptune. *Baird 1863.*
Western North America.

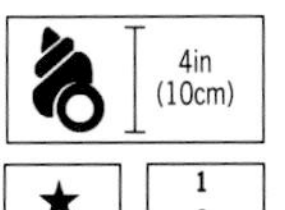


The tabled neptune has a most pleasing shape – a high spire, with fairly straight-sided whorls, the shoulders of which are angled into a ledge, to the suture. There is also a distinct carina around the periphery of the shoulders. The ornamentation is finely reticulated. This shell inhabits deep water to a depth of about 1,320ft (400m), and is a collectors' favourite.

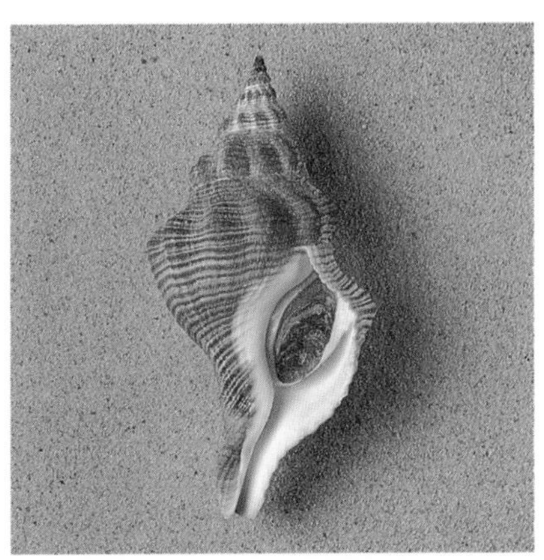

**PENION SULCATUS** f. *adusta*
Northern Siphon Whelk. *Philippi 1845.*
New Zealand.

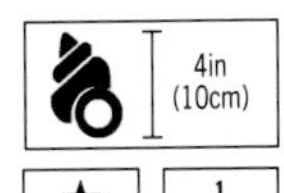


This heavy solid whelk, endemic to New Zealand, is fusiform in shape, with a tall spire, angular whorls, and a long open recurved canal. There are strong nodules at the shoulders, and the exterior is totally covered with coarse spiral cords. The lip is lirate, and the columella is smooth; the overall colour is beige or mid-brown, and it has dark brown cords; the aperture is white. This specimen was trawled in Houraki Gulf, North Island.

**PLICIFUSUS PLICATUS**
Plicate Colus. *A. Adams 1863.*
Japan.

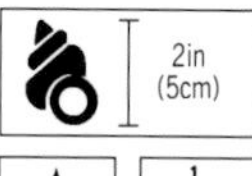

2in (5cm)

A tall and slender shell, the plicate colus has rounded whorls and a short recurved canal. The lip is rather expanded. There are numerous fine spiral threads and strong rounded slightly curved axial ribs. It is a dull pale brown grey, with a creamy aperture. A cold-water whelk, endemic to Japan, it inhabits depths to 330ft (100m).

**LUSSIVOLUTOPSIUS FURUKAWAI**
*Oyama 1951.*
Sea of Okhotsk.

3in (7.5cm)

A deep cold-water whelk, it has well-rounded whorls, and a tall spire with a rounded protoconch. There are numerous fine spiral cords. The interior of the rather expanded lip is smooth, as are the columella and parietal wall. The shell is a dull grey brown with a pale yellow or cream aperture. The exterior surface is usually part-worn or eroded.

**PHOS SENTICOSUS**
Phos Whelk. *L. 1758.*
Indo-Pacific.

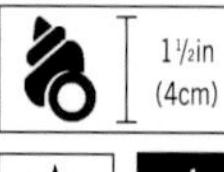

1½in (4cm)

The attractively ornamented little phos whelk has strong rounded axial ribs and sharp narrow spiral cords, these being stronger on the ribs and outer lip margin. The inner lip has fine lirae. The fasciole is strong; the umbilicus is usually closed. Shells vary in colour and decoration, as can be seen from these two specimens.

**SIPHONALIA TROCHULUS**
Hooped Whelk. *Reeve 1843.*
Japan.

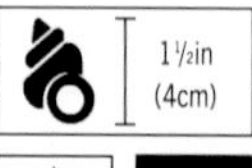

1½in (4cm)

This small rounded species has a low sharp spire and distinctive recurved canal. There are fine spiral threads, and within the thickened lip are strong lirae. The calloused parietal wall bears fine plicae. The shell is a creamy beige or grey throughout.

**NORTHIA PRISTIS**
North's Long Whelk. *Deshayes in Lamarck 1844.* Western Central America.

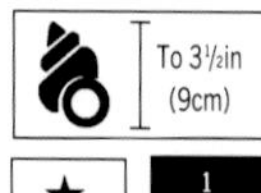

To 3½in (9cm)

A solid shell, it has a smooth texture, with the exception of the earlier whorls, which have axial ribs and spiral threads. Some authorities suggest *N. northiae* to be a separate valid species; the only difference appears to be the presence or lack of short sharp spines on the outer lip, and these differences may be a case of local variation only. The species is found in shallow water.

**PHOS CRASSUS**
*Hinds 1843.*
Western Central America.

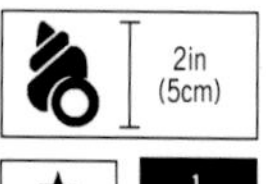

2in (5cm)

Of the several phos whelks in this region, this is the largest and heaviest; it is coarsely ribbed and has low spiral cords. It is variable in colour, although the cream examples tend to be rather uncommon. These two specimens were collected in shallow water at Playas, Ecuador.

## CANTHARUS MELANOSTOMUS

Black-mouthed Goblet Whelk. *Sowerby 1825.* Indian Ocean and Philippines.

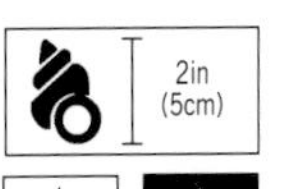


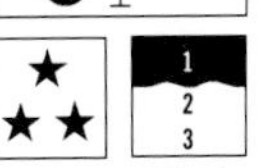


A smallish ovate and coarsely sculptured shell, it has numerous spiral cords and very low broad axial ribs, strongest at the shoulders. It is a rich tan with a distinctive brown or black columella and parietal wall. The lip is dentate and there are moderate lirae within.

## CANTHARUS TRANQUEBARICUS

Tranquebar Goblet Whelk. *Gmelin 1791.* Indian Ocean.

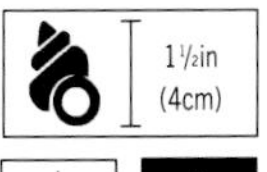


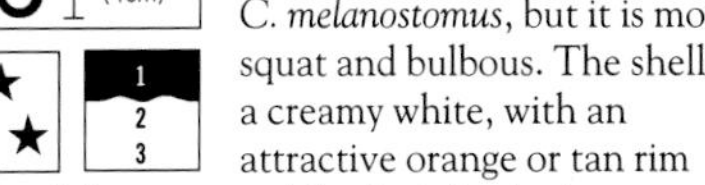


This species is rather similar in sculpturing to *C. melanostomus*, but it is more squat and bulbous. The shell is a creamy white, with an attractive orange or tan rim around the aperture. The lip is finely dentate and lirae are present within. There is a corneus, rather concave, operculum.

## CANTHARUS UNDOSUS

Wavy Goblet Whelk. *L. 1758.* Indo-Pacific.

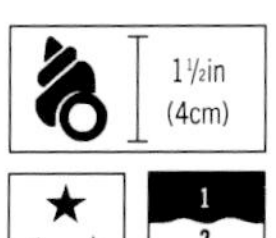


This small, solid and thick whelk has a tall conical straight-sided spire. The body whorl is rounded, and the thickened lip is somewhat expanded at the posterior. There are strong dark brown spiral cords on a beige background. The lip is dentate; there are raised lirae within; and the columella bears several low plicae. It is a shallow-water dweller.

## CANTHARUS LEUCOTAENIATUS

*Kosuge 1985.* Philippines.

Similar in shape and size to *C. melanostomus*, it has spiral threads and low axial nodules, set in threes or fours. A pale beige shell, it is decorated with dark brown threads; the aperture is white and tinged with yellow around the edges. This specimen was collected off Bohol Island.

**ENGINA MENDICARIA**
Striped Engina. *L. 1758.*
Indo-Pacific.

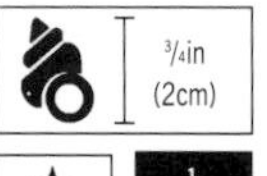


A tiny but solid shell, the striped engina has a spire of medium height and a large tapering body whorl. It is black, with broad yellow spiral bands. The strongly dentate lip and columella are tinged with orange or red. There are small low nodules at the shoulders.

**COLUMBELLA MERCATORIA**
Common Dove Shell. *L. 1758.*
Florida to Brazil, and Caribbean.

Small and solid, this little shell has a spire of medium height and a large body whorl which is compressed at the anterior. There are fine spiral cords; the lip is strongly dentate, and the columella is plicate. The shell is white, with variable patterning and colours. The two specimens shown, which come from Yucatan, Mexico, shown differing colour forms.

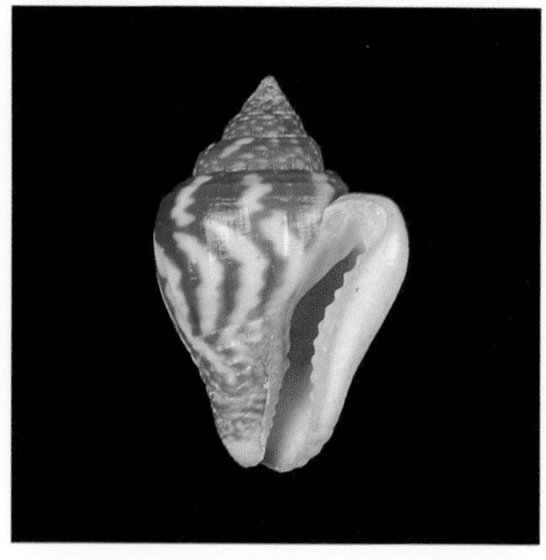

**COLUMBELLA STROMBIFORMIS**
Stromboid Dove Shell. *Lamarck 1822.*
Western Central America.

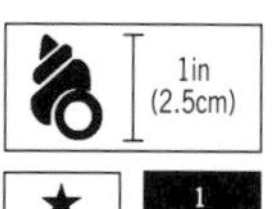


A small solid dove shell, this has a moderate spire and angular whorls. The body whorl is inflated but compressed at the anterior. The lip is much thickened and flaring, and extends to a rounded posterior canal. There are tan or dark brown axial wavy lines, and the dentate lip is tinged with yellow.

SUPER FAMILY
## MURICOIDEA

FAMILY
## COLUMBELLIDAE
(Dove Shells)

A large family of at least 400 species, formerly known as the Pyrenidae; the dove shells are mainly small, relatively smooth and colourful shells, living in warm and tropical seas either on the shore or in deeper water. They are carnivorous scavengers, feeding mainly at night. There are a few specialist collectors of this group, which comprises several genera, notably *Pyrene*, *Anachis*, *Mitrella*, *Strombina* and *Columbella*.

**COLUMBELLA RUSTICA**
Rustic Dove Shell. *L. 1758.*
Mediterranean and North-West Africa.

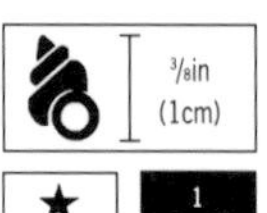


A smooth shell, the attractively named rustic dove has very fine spiral threads on the lower, compressed part of the body whorl. The lip is thickened and strongly dentate, and there are very small plica on the columella. Shells are highly variable in pattern and colour, with areas of spotting, blotches and reticulated markings. The depicted shells, from northern Malta, were collected at low tide.

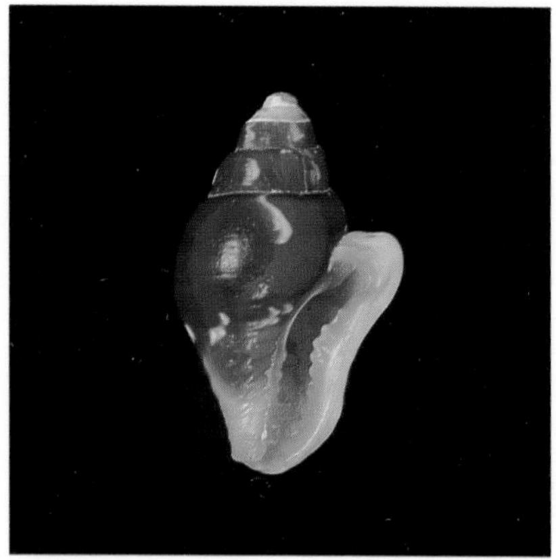

**COLUMBELLA HAEMASTOMA**
Bloodstained Dove Shell. *Sowerby 1832.*
West Central America, Galapagos Islands.

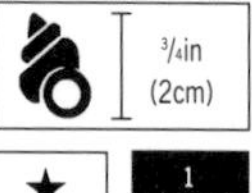


Although rather similar to *C. strombiformis*, it differs in having rounded whorls, and the thickened lip is impressed. This shell is a rich dark brown, with odd white patches and spots; the lip, columella and anterior part of the body whorl are stained pinkish orange.

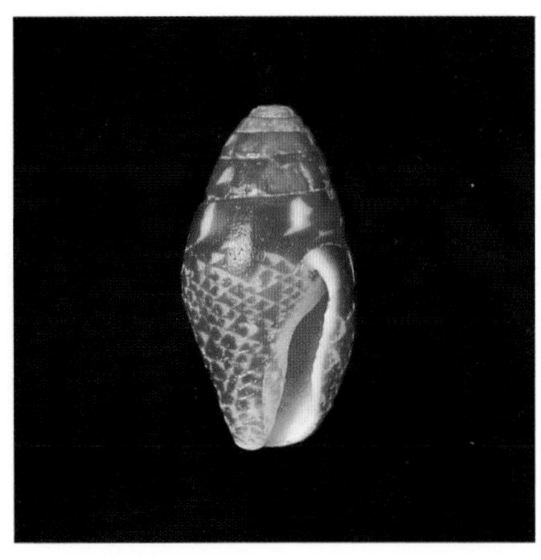

**PYRENE PUNCTATA**
Punctate Dove Shell. *Bruguière 1789.*
Indo-Pacific.

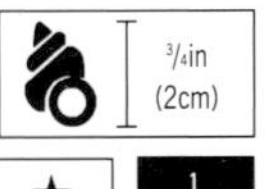


A strong fusiform shell, it has a slightly impressed suture. The lip has fine white denticles and the lower area of the columella is plicate. The pale brown or tan background is blotched or spotted with white, and there are distinct tent-shaped markings on the body whorl. This specimen is from Queensland, Australia.

**PYRENE EPAMELLA**
Philippine Dove Shell. *Duclos 1846.*
South-West Pacific.

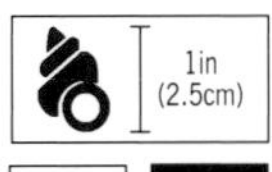


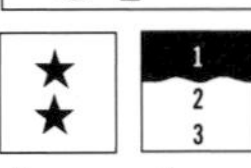


One of the larger dove shells, it is smooth, with a moderately tall spire, and its body whorl is long, tapering at the anterior. It has a wide rounded shoulder; the lip is fairly dentate; the columella is smooth. Shells are off-white, with vivid black axial wavy or zigzag lines. The aperture is tinged pale lemon. A synonym is *P. philippinarum.*

SUPER FAMILY
## MURICOIDEA

FAMILY
## NASSARIIDAE
(Dog Whelks or Nassa Mud Snails)

This large family is chiefly composed of small shells that live in shallow intertidal waters in muddy substrates, though there are some deep-water species. They are carnivorous scavengers, and can detect prey at distances of up to 99ft (30m). In many species, the parietal shield is large and well developed. They live together in large colonies. There are several genera and subgenera, of which *Nassarius, Cyclope, Demoulia* and *Bullia* are well known. This is not a popular collectors' group.

**PYRENE FLAVA**
Yellow Dove Shell. *Bruguière 1789.*
Indo-Pacific.

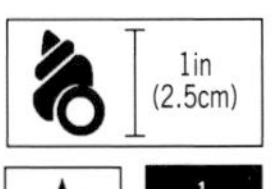


This little dove shell has a slightly impressed suture, a high spire and rather straight-sided whorls, making it slender in appearance. The lip is finely dentate and the aperture is long, narrow and white. The exterior colour is generally tan or orange, with one or two broad brown spiral bands and large white blotches. The shells seen here are from south-eastern India.

**PYRENE OCELLATA**
Lightning Dove Shell. *Link 1807.*
Indo-Pacific.

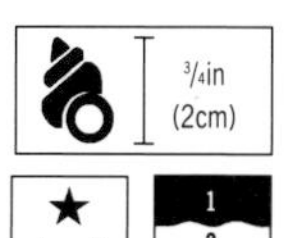


Rather similar in shape and appearance to *P. epamella*, the lightning dove shell is shorter and more rounded at the centre, and its markings are more prominent – a black background with sharply defined white oblique or haphazard streaks. There is a group of four tiny denticles on the inner lip.

**NASSARIUS STOLATUS**
*Gmelin 1791.*
Indian Ocean.

A small, very glossy and smooth species, it has a tall conical spire and an enlarged body whorl. The lip is finely dentate; the columella is plicate; and there is one small raised ridge on the parietal wall. There are low rounded axial ribs, more prominent on the earlier whorls. Shells are variable in colour, but always appear to be spirally banded. This selection is from southern India.

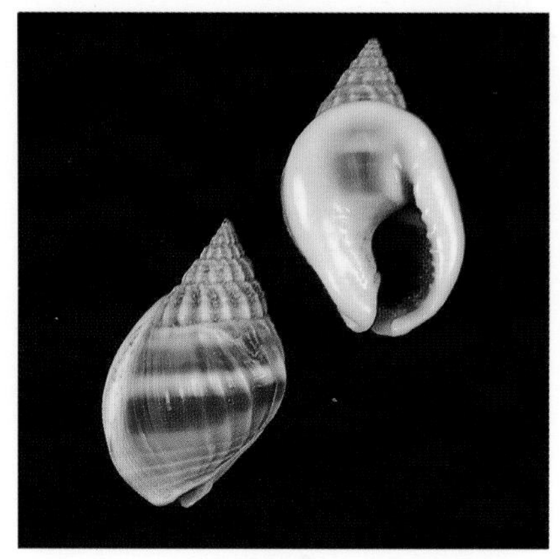

**NASSARIUS PULLUS**
*L. 1758.*
Indo-Pacific.

This little shell has a large smooth and glazed parietal shield and columella; the lip is finely dentate. The dorsum and spire bear fine axial ribs. It is a pale grey colour, with broad brown spiral bands. The glazed area is a rich cream. It lives on mud flats.

**NASSARIUS WOLFFI**
Torben Wolf Nassa. *Knudsen 1956.*
West Africa.

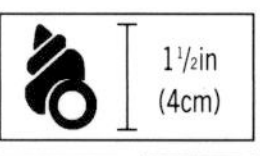

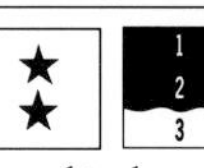

An elegant nassa, it has a tall spire and rounded whorls. The ornamentation is reticulated, with fine spiral cords and axial ribs giving a characteristic netted effect. The siphonal canal is short and recurved. The shell is a delicate cream throughout, with a white aperture. It is an offshore species.

**NASSARIUS CORONATUS**
Crown Nassa. *Bruguière 1789.*
Indian Ocean.

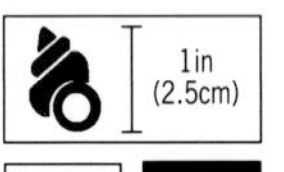

A glossy rounded little shell, the crown nassa is dominated by numerous low rounded nodules; the shoulders are slightly stepped. The lip is dentate, and is lirate within; the columella has several plicae, and the parietal wall is thinly calloused. The aperture area is white, and elsewhere the shell is a rich creamy yellow.

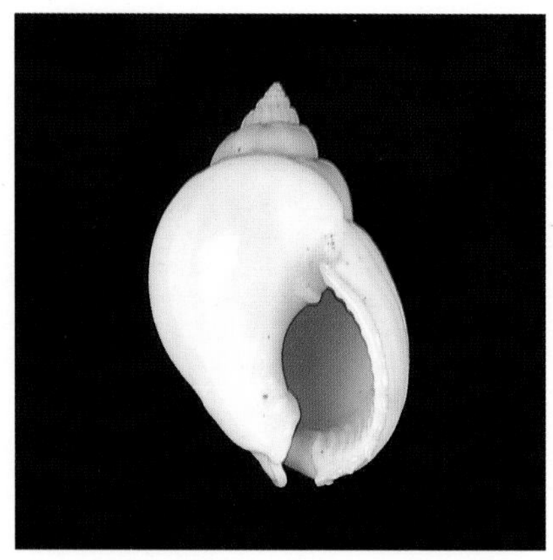

**NASSARIUS CONOIDALIS**
Conoidal Nassa. *Deshayes in Belanger 1832.*
Indian Ocean.

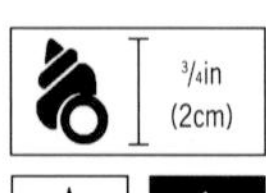

A rounded shell, with impressed sutures and a moderately high spire, it has very low and short axial notches at the shoulders. There is a very large calloused white parietal shield. The lip is dentate, the inner lip being finely lirate. The exterior is a pale beige.

**NASSARIUS LIMA**
Clathrate Nassa. *Dillwyn 1817.*
Mediterranean and North-East Atlantic.

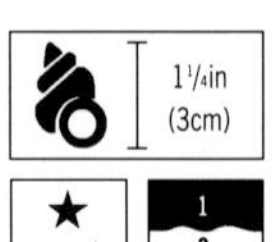

A rather bulbous shell, it features a tall spire and rounded whorls with strong low axial ribs. There is also fine spiral cording. The lip and columella are smooth and white, the exterior colouring being beige or light brown. The depicted specimen is from the northern Adriatic.

**BULLIA TRANQUEBARICA**
Belanger's Bullia. *Röding 1798.*
Indian Ocean.

This very variably coloured shell has a tall slender spire and a narrow body whorl. There are fine beading and axial ribs, especially on the earlier whorls. The aperture is smooth. This selection of colour variations, from Madras, India, was found in shallow water.

SUPER FAMILY
MURICOIDEA

FAMILY
## MELONGENIDAE
(Crown Conch, Swamp Conch)

A relatively small family of shells, ranging in size from medium to very large, they dwell mainly in tropical regions, living in fairly shallow water in brackish or muddy areas, often near mangroves. They are predatory carnivores, feeding primarily on bivalves. This group includes a naturally sinistral (left-handed) species, as well as the largest living gastropod, *Syrinx aruanus*. There are six genera: *Melongena*, *Busycon*, *Pugilina*, *Syrinx*, *Taphon* and *Volema*, and several subgenera. Some are also commonly known as whelks.

### BUSYCON CONTRARIUM
Lightning or Left-handed Whelk. *Conrad 1840.* South-eastern USA.

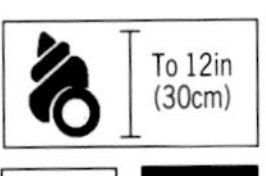


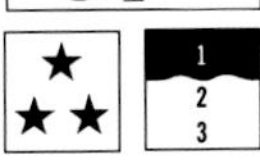

This very large heavy shell is naturally sinistral. It has a low spire and an enlarged, elongated and tapering body whorl, which develops into a broad open canal. Young specimens display the most prominent colour and pattern; very large shells are usually beige or chalky white. It dwells in sand in shallow waters.

### BUSYCON SPIRATUM
Pear Whelk. *Lamarck 1816.* South-eastern USA and North-eastern Mexico.

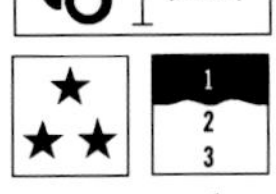

A thin, lightweight and pyriform species, it has a long and open canal. The spire is very low and the suture is channelled. There are fine spiral threads which are stronger at the anterior. The interior is smooth, apart from fine lirae on the inner lip. Two colour variations, both collected in Florida, are shown here.

### BUSYCON CANALICULATUM
Channelled Whelk. *L. 1758.* Cape Cod to Florida, USA.

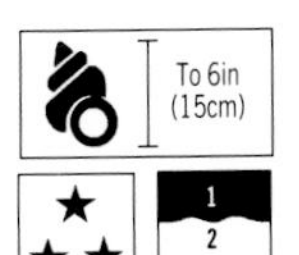


The channelled whelk has a low spire, and straight-sided whorls, angled at the shoulders into a deeply channelled suture. The enlarged body whorl tapers gracefully into a long open siphonal canal. The depicted specimen, which is from Florida, has axial patterning; the colder-water shells are usually a plain pale beige to mid-brown.

## MELONGENA CORONA

Florida Crown Conch. *Gmelin 1791.*
Florida to North-eastern Mexico.

A large attractive shell, the Florida crown conch has distinctive coronated shoulders. There are very fine axial striae and coarse strong growth lines; one strong broken spiral ridge, often spinose, is found on the lower half of the body whorl. The colour is variable: a few are creamy white throughout, but most are banded spirally with brown, grey and pale orange. This species is found in great numbers among mangroves.

## MELONGENA MELONGENA

West Indian Crown Conch. *L. 1758.*
Caribbean.

A large solid species, it lacks the coronated shoulders of *M. corona*, but has rows of blunt nodules laid spirally on the body whorl. The suture are deeply channelled; the spire is low, and the early whorls have axial ribs. The columella and parietal wall are heavily calloused. The spiral bands are usually bluish purple and cream, occasionally dull red. The species dwells in mud in intertidal brackish waters.

## PUGILINA MORIO

Giant Hairy Melongena. *L. 1758.*
Caribbean to Brazil.

A large and solid shell, the giant hairy melongena has a spire of medium height, angular whorls and strongly nodulose shoulders. There are coarse but flat spiral cords. The overall colour is a rich brown-to-black, and this is broken with spiral bands of cream and red brown. When alive, the shell is covered with a coarse hairy periostracum. This specimen was found on rocks in mangroves at 3ft (1m) at East Santo, Brazil.

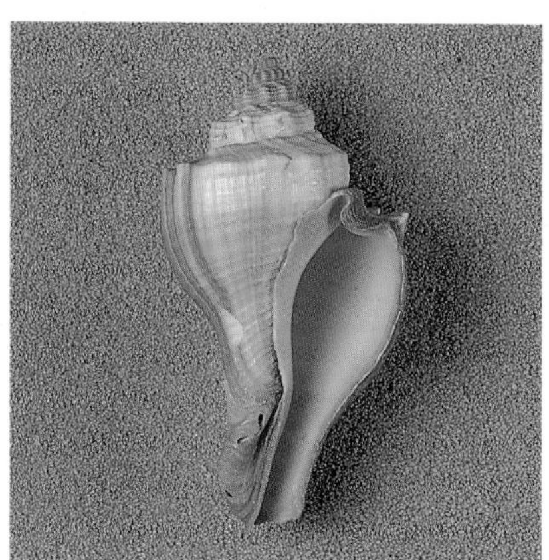

## PUGILINA COCHLIDIUM

Spiral Melongena. *L. 1758.*
Indian Ocean to Philippines.

Another solid heavy shell, this has a lowish spire, angular whorls, which are nodulose at the shoulders, and an enlarged body whorl that tapers into a short broad open canal. The colour is a uniform pale orange or mid-brown throughout; the aperture is a pale orange. The species lives in shallow muddy waters. It is sometimes classified under the genus *Volema*.

**SYRINX ARUANUS**
Australian Trumpet. *L. 1758.*
Northern Australia.

The largest marine gastropod, live specimens are covered with a coarse, flaky periostracum. Young shells have an unusually long protoconch, with many whorls; this erodes away on mature specimens. Although it is a native Australian species, Taiwanese prawn fishers often land these shells and market them, after processing the meat, at lower prices than the Australian dealers. Offshore fishing bans by the authorities do not seem to have stopped them so far.

**FASCIOLARIA TULIPA**
True Tulip Shell. *L. 1758.*
Florida, Caribbean to Brazil.

A large fusiform shell, the true tulip is characterized by its high spire, rounded whorls and strong open canal. It is smooth and glossy, apart from a beaded and ridged suture, and usually has haphazard patches of brown or orange and thin dark spiral bands. The lip margin is finely crenulated, and there are two or more pleats on the columella. An attractive and showy species, it lives on sand in shallow water.

**FASCIOLARIA RUTILA**
*Watson 1882.*
South Africa.

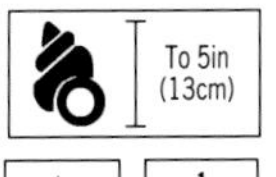


A tall spire, rather globose whorls, a short slightly recurved open canal and very fine spiral threads typify this species, which is endemic to South Africa. It is generally a cream or beige colour with an off-white aperture. The depicted specimen was trawled off Cape Point.

SUPER FAMILY
MURICOIDEA

FAMILY
## FASCIOLARIIDAE
(Tulip and Spindle Shells)

A large and popular group, this is chiefly composed of shells of medium and large size, and encompasses several genera, including *Fasciolaria*, *Pleuroploca*, *Fusinus*, *Latirus* and *Colubraria*. Common names include the horse conch, this being among the largest in the family. Most species live in warm shallow waters and are carnivorous, eating bivalve shells and similar creatures. The family exhibits a wide variety of shapes, ornamentation, colours and patterns, *Fusinus* being particularly distinctive, with very tall spires and long siphonal canals.

**FASCIOLARIA LILIUM HUNTERIA**
Banded Tulip. *Perry 1811.*
South-eastern USA.

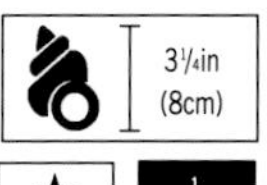


Although much smaller, it is similar in shape to *F. tulipa*. The pattern is less conspicuous, but the spiral bands are much more strongly defined. There are no ridges or beading at the suture. The operculum is ovate and horny. The specimen shown is from Florida and, along with greyish examples, this is the usual colouring.

**PLEUROPLOCA GIGANTEA**
Florida Horse Conch. *Kiener 1840.* South-eastern USA and North-eastern Mexico.

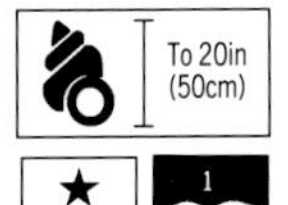


This is the largest of the tulip shells, almost reaching the proportions of *Syrinx aruanus*. The spire is tall, and the whorls, the shoulders of which bear blunt rounded knobs, are angular. The body whorl tapers into a long open siphonal canal. There is broad flat spiral cording and noticeable growth scars may often be seen. Shells are generally beige to light brown, with a pale orange aperture. The species dwells in shallow subtidal waters.

**PLEUROPLOCA TRAPEZIUM**
Fox Head. *L. 1758.*
Indo-Pacific.

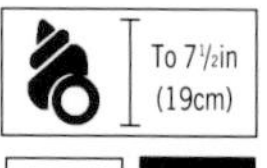


A large, thick and heavy shell, fusiform in shape, its angular whorls bear strong blunt rounded nodules at the shoulders. The lip is dentate, and there are numerous fine raised lirae within. The columella is smooth. Attractively coloured, shells are either an all-over beige or light brown, or have orange tints and almost-black spiral lines. The aperture is a grey pink. The depicted shell is from East Africa.

**PLEUROPLOCA FILAMENTOSA**
Lined Horse Conch. *Röding 1798.*
Indo-Pacific.

This fusiform tulip has a tall spire with rounded whorls and a stout shortish open canal. Broad spiral brown bands pattern the exterior; the lip is dentate, there are very fine orange lirae within and the columella has three pleats. In some, the shoulders can be slightly nodulose.

**FUSINUS CAPARTI**
Capart's Spindle. *Adam and Knudsen 1969.*
West Africa.

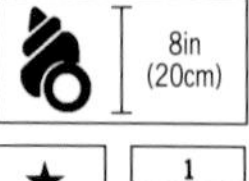
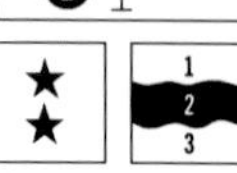

One of the largest in the genus, it is elongated and fusiform, with a very tall spire and long siphonal canal which are virtually of equal length. There is strong spiral cording; the sutures on the rounded whorl is impressed. Raised lirae occur within the lip. Shells are normally white throughout, and are usually dredged on sand at depths between 165 and 265ft (50 and 80m).

**FUSINUS LONGISSIMUS**
Long Spindle. *Gmelin 1791.*
South-West Pacific.

11in
(28cm)

Another of the largest spindle shells, it is all white and is fusiform, elongated and rather broad at the centre. The angular whorls bear a single spiral row of low rounded nodules, and there are numerous spiral cords. The lip is marginally serrated, and there are strong raised lirae within. This specimen comes from the central Philippines.

**_FUSINUS NICOBARICUS_**
Nicobar Spindle. *Röding 1798.*
Indo-Pacific.

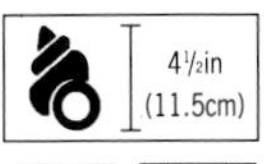


This relatively small but stocky and solid spindle features coarsely sculptured whorls bearing strong rounded spiral ridges and blunt nodules at the shoulders. The white background is decorated with mid-brown axial streaks or "flame" markings. The aperture is white. This particular specimen was fished off south-eastern India in shallow water.

**_FUSINUS DOWIANUS_**
*Olsson 1954.*
Caribbean Sea.

An elongate and medium-sized spindle, its rather broad and rounded whorls support raised spiral cords and axially laid rounded ribs. The lip is dentate and there are strong lirae within. The spiral cords are also evident beneath the very thinly calloused columella. Shells are white in colour, though the earlier whorls are often tinged with beige or cream. The shell seen here was trawled off Honduras.

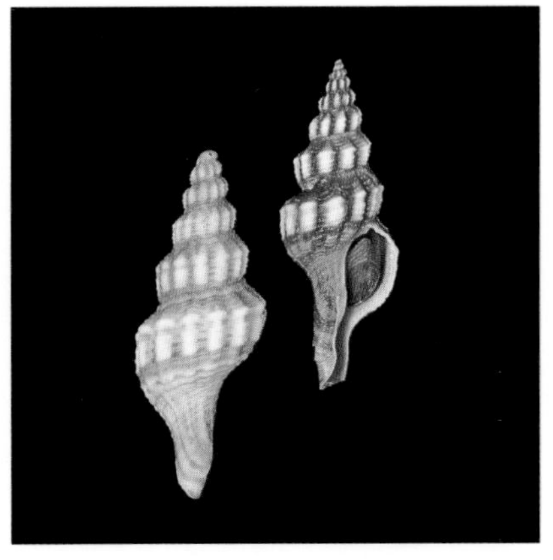

**_FUSINUS SYRACUSANUS_**
Sicilian Spindle. *L. 1758.* Mediterranean, North-West Africa and Canary Islands.

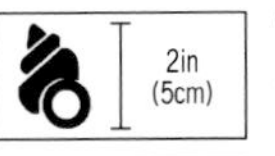


This spindle shell is comparatively small, but it is one of the most brightly coloured of a group composed almost entirely of all-white shells. The angular whorls have rows of axially laid low ribs and there is fine spiral cording. The two depicted specimens display the slight pattern and colour variation. Frequently collected off southern Italy and Sicily.

**_FUSINUS UNDATUS_**
Wavy Spindle. *Gmelin 1791.*
South-West Pacific.

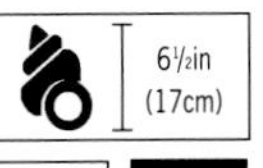


A very thick and heavy shell, the wavy spindle is fusiform, with a very tall spire and broad open siphonal canal. The angular whorls bear spirally undulating rows of blunt nodules at the shoulders. There are fine spiral threads. The lip is dentate and there are lirae within; the columella supports fine plicae. It is off-white to cream in colour throughout.

**_FUSINUS SALISBURYI_**
Salisbury's Spindle. *Fulton 1930.*
Western Pacific and Australia.

A large, fusiform and elongated species, its impressed suture and whorls bear raised spiral cords. There is a row of low nodules at the shoulders. The inner lip is strongly lirate; the columella is smooth. The depicted specimen was trawled in 841ft (255m) off Lady Musgrave Island, Queensland.

**_FUSINUS AUSTRALIS_**
Australian Spindle. *Quoy and Gaimard 1833.* Southern and Western Australia.

The coarsely sculptured little Australian spindle is a shallow-water species. It is an attractive mid-tan colour overall, with a white aperture. The angular whorls bear strong spiral cords and there are fine nodules at the shoulders. This shell is from Cockburn.

**FUSINUS OCELLIFEROUS**
*Lamarck 1816.*
South Africa.

A short, rather broad and solid shell, endemic to South Africa, it can be very variable in shape and form. The depicted specimen portrays the average sculpturing and colouring for this species. Notice the characteristic, almost umbilical, gap beside the columella.

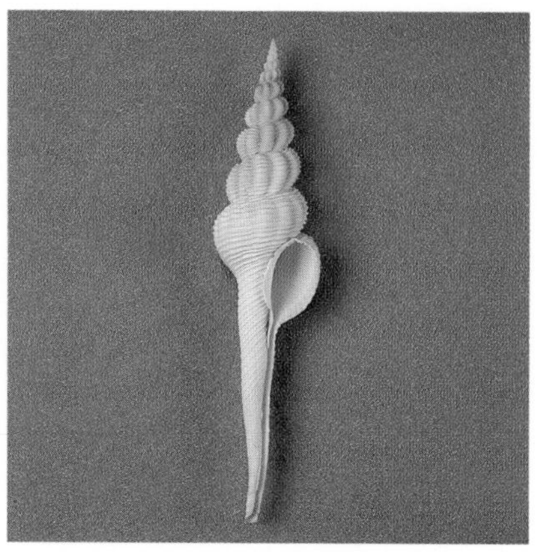

**FUSINUS CRASSIPLICATUS**
Ribbed Spindle. *Kira 1959?*
Japan to Taiwan.

A very attractive elongate and fusiform spindle, it has prominent axially laid rounded strong ribs and coarse spiral cording. The suture is impressed. One of several large spindles that were frequently fished off Taiwan in the 1970s, specimens are rarely offered nowadays and have consequently become sought-after collectors' items.

**GRANULOFUSUS KIRANUS**
*Shuto 1958.*
Western Pacific.

A small and lightweight spindle, this has a tall spire, rounded whorls and a long straight open canal. Raised spiral ridges are joined axially by low ribs. The colour is beige and the ridges are tan. The depicted specimen was collected in the central Philippines.

**LATIRUS POLYGONUS**
Polygon Latirus. *Gmelin 1791.*
Indo-Pacific.

A solidly built shell, with a spire of medium height and a fairly short open canal, it has strong rounded axial ribs and nodules that are usually low but sharp, and most prominent at the shoulders. Attractively coloured with dark brown broken spiral bands on a white or pale orange background, it inhabits intertidal reefs.

## LATIRUS INFUNDIBULUM

Brown-lined Latirus. *Gmelin 1791*.
Florida, West Indies to Brazil.

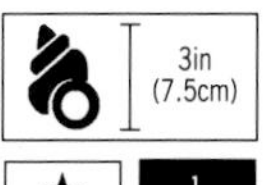
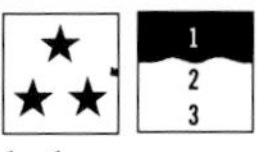

This tall-spired but stocky shell is elongate and rather slender. It has a short, open canal, and the strong rounded axial ribs are crossed by fine raised spiral cords which can be brown or, as in the depicted shell, orange on a beige or cream background. There is a part-open umbilicus. It dwells in offshore waters.

## LATIRUS HEMPHILLI

Hemphill's Latirus. *Hertlein and Strong 1951*. Western Central America.

A stout fusiform latirus, it is rather broad at the centre. The rounded whorls have low axial ribs which are more distinct on the spire than body whorl. The inner lip is strongly lirate, and there are three or four plicae on the columella. The shell is beige to mid-brown, with a white aperture. It is an offshore species; this particular specimen came from Ecuador.

## LATIRUS CARINIFERUS

MacGinty's Latirus. *Lamarck 1816*.
Florida and West Indies.

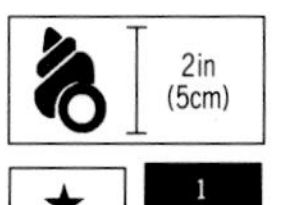

This species dwells in rocky reefs and is fusiform, with a tall spire and a short but broad canal. The narrow umbilicus is open. Strong axial ribs are intersected with several raised spiral ridges. Often encrusted when found, clean shells are attractively coloured with orange, beige and tan with odd dark blotches between the ribs.

## LATIRUS ABNORMIS

Strange Latirus. *Sowerby 1894*.
Natal, South-East Africa.

A difficult to obtain species, it is endemic to South-East Africa, where it lives in deep water at about 265ft (80m). It is fusiform and stocky, with almost straight-sided but nodulose whorls, a rather long body whorl, compressed at the anterior, and a gaping aperture. The small umbilicus is open. The posterior portion of the lip is indented, rather like the characteristic notch of turris shells, for which it can be mistaken.

**LATIRUS FILOSUS**
*Schubert and Wagner 1829.*
West Africa.

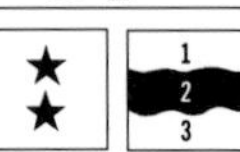


Endemic to West Africa, this graceful species has a tall spire, rounded whorls and a short open canal. There are axial ribs and fine dark brown raised spiral ridges on a white background. Occasionally trawled in offshore waters.

**LATIRUS ARMATUS**
*A. Adams 1854.*
West Africa and Canary Islands.

A short stocky little shell, this is dominated by rows of sharp nodules, which are strongest at the shoulders; there are also raised spiral ridges. For the most part, the shell is a mid-brown colour, but ridges are off-white, and the aperture is white. The inner lip is lirate, and the columella has very fine folds. The shell in the photograph was trawled off Senegal.

**LATIRUS PAETILIANUS**
Paetel's Latirus. *Kobelt 1874.*
South-West Pacific.

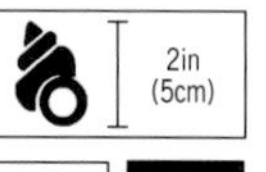


There are strong axial ribs and fine but distinct spiral cords on the whorls of this tall-spired species. The canal is short, open and broad, and the umbilicus is part-open. The inner lip is lirate and the columella smooth. It is an attractive rich brown colour with a dull orange aperture. The depicted specimen is from Dampier, north-western Australia.

**LATIRUS NODATUS**
Knobbed Latirus. *Gmelin 1791.*
Indo-Pacific.

A strong rather thick shell, it has a tall spire and open canal of moderate length. The whorls bear strong low rounded axial ribs of nodules, and several raised spiral cords encircle the exterior of the canal. The shell is a dull beige colour when the thick brown periostracum is removed and the aperture is a beautiful coral pink. It inhabits coral reefs.

**LATIRUS CRATICULATUS**
Red-ribbed Latirus. *L. 1758.*
Indo-Pacific.

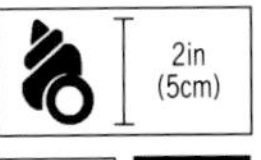

The solid, shiny and attractive red-ribbed latirus has a very tall rather broad spire with almost straight-sided whorls. The canal is short and open. There are coarse spiral cords and very low axial ribs, which are coloured a deep red. The background is cream, the aperture being tinged with yellow. I believe this shell to have been collected in southern Thailand.

**OPEATOSTOMA PSEUDODON**
Thorned Latirus. *Burrow 1815.*
Western Central America.

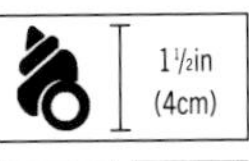

Solid and heavy, the thorned latirus has probably the longest labial tooth in any gastropod. It is assumed that this is used to wedge or force open the plates of barnacles or bivalve shells when feeding. The shell is distinctly marked with almost-black spiral bands on a white background.

**PERISTERNIA INCARNATA**
Fleshy Peristernia. *Kiener 1840.*
Indo-Pacific.

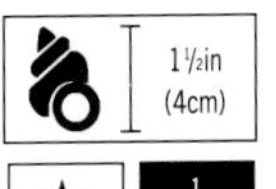

A shallow-water species, living under rocks or coral, the fleshy peristernia is solid, with distinctive smooth rounded axial ribs of a rich orange. The interspaces support fine spiral cords, which are dark brown or black. The aperture is a greyish purple. This shell was reef-collected at 20ft (6m) at Port Hedland, western Australia.

**LEUCOZONIA CERATA**
Waxy Latirus. *Wood 1828.* Western Central America and Galapagos Islands.

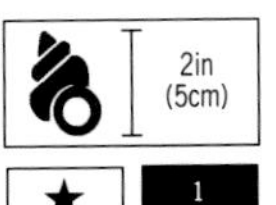

A fusiform shell, it has a tall spire, enlarged body whorl and a short open canal. There are low nodules on the whorls, most prominent at the shoulders, although in some cases these can be absent. Very fine spiral threads are also evident. Three or four folds occur on the columella. A shallow-water dweller, it is found on rocks.

**PERISTERNIA NASSATULA**
Fine-net Peristernia. *Lamarck 1822.*
Indo-Pacific.

A short stocky little shell, and attractively coloured, it is broadly fusiform with strong axial ribs of white. There are fine spiral threads, and at the suture are broad spiral bands of pink or beige. The aperture is a striking mid-purple; this specimen was reef-collected at Honiara, Solomon Islands. The shells are often heavily encrusted.

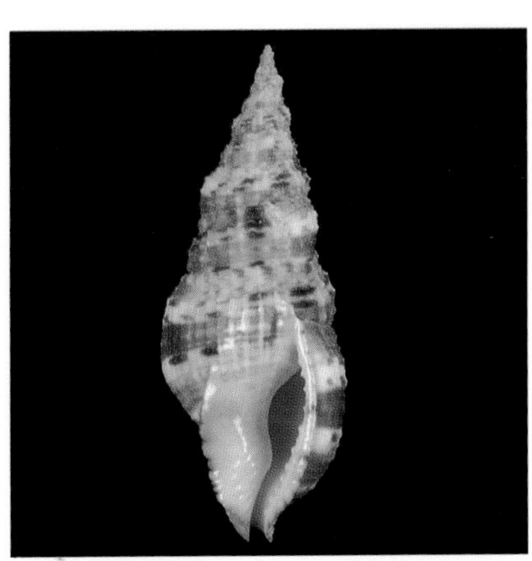

**COLUBRARIA MURICATA**
Maculated False Triton. *Lightfoot 1786.*
Indo-Pacific.

A very thick and solid shell, it has a tall spire, slightly angular whorls and a very short open recurved canal. The ornamentation is reticulated, with very low cords and pustules. There are distinct varices, and the lip is much thickened. The columella and parietal wall is calloused, and the inner lip is dentate.

**COLUBRARIA OBSCURA**
Obscure Dwarf Triton. *Reeve 1844.*
Florida to Brazil.

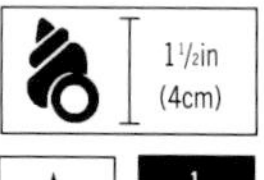


The exterior is finely pustulose, giving the shell a file-like texture. The spire is tall and the body whorl rather inflated. Varices are present and the lip is rounded and thickened. There are lirae within the lip and the columella is finely plicate. A pale beige background is decorated with tan spiral squares and bands. It dwells on shallow reefs.

**VOLUTA MUSICA**
Music Volute. *L. 1758.*
Caribbean.

A popular and well-known volute among collectors, its patterns resemble medieval chant music. This robust stocky shell varies in general shape and colouring, depending on its locality. Of the two shells shown, the paler orange form was collected in Barbados, whereas the darker and more chunky specimen is from the north coast of Trinidad.

**VOLUTOCORBIS ABYSSICOLA**
Deep Sea Volute. *Adams and Reeve 1850.*
South Africa.

A lightweight fusiform shell, it has rather rounded whorls, the body whorl gracefully tapering to a very short canal. Low spiral cords are intersected by low fine axial ribs, giving a reticulated effect. It is beige, with a cream thickened lip and plaited columella. The inner lip has denticles. Endemic to South Africa, it inhabits waters to a depth of about 1,650ft (500m).

SUPER FAMILY
## MURICOIDEA

FAMILY
## VOLUTIDAE
(The Volutes)

A large and very colourful family, the volutes are highly popular with collectors although they lack much elaborate sculpturing. Many are smooth and highly glossy. Most shells are of medium or large size; all are carnivorous, and the most colourful and highly patterned varieties live in tropical seas. Many inhabit deep water and are therefore difficult to obtain, which renders them much sought-after as collectors' items. Most have characteristic columella plaits or plicae and certain genera, such as *Neptuneopsis*, possess operculae. There are numerous genera (Vaught lists 46!), but noteworthy here are *Voluta, Lyria, Cymbium, Cymbiola, Melo, Amoria* and *Scaphella.*

**VOLUTA MUSICA** f. *demarcoi*
De Marco's Music Volute. *Olsson 1965.*
Caribbean.

There are several recently-named forms of the music volute. I have seen numerous colour and pattern variations, and the naming of many of these has added some confusion to an otherwise straightforward group. This particular shell was trawled off Honduras by shrimp boats, and is most attractive.

**LYRIA DELESSERTIANA**
Delessert's Volute. *Petit 1842.*
Madagascar to the Comoros Islands.

This solid little volute has a high spire, and slightly rounded whorls. The shell is dominated by the coarse axial ribs. The columella has numerous strong plicae. It is pale pink with deep orange red haphazard blotches and a white aperture. The form *tulearensis* is also shown, which is generally paler in colour, but with dark spiral bands, and is rather broader.

### *ERICUSA SERICATA*
Silklike Volute. *Thornley 1951.*
Eastern and Southern Australia.

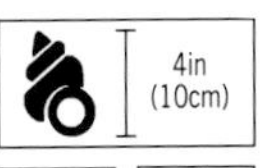


A smooth fairly lightweight species, endemic to its Australian habitat, it has whorls that are virtually straight sided, and a calloused protoconch. The lip is not thickened, and the interior is smooth apart from about four columella plaits. The patterns and colours hardly vary. The depicted shell was trawled in 480ft (145m) in Cape Moreton, Queensland.

### *FULGORARIA RUPESTRIS*
Asian Flame Volute. *Gmelin 1791.*
Japan, Taiwan and China.

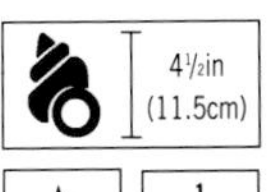


A solid and thick fusiform volute, it has angular whorls, and the protoconch is large and rounded. There are fine spiral grooves and numerous growth striae. The dull beige grey background is overlaid with broad wavy dark brown "flames" and lines. Again, this was frequently fished off Taiwan in the 1970s, but is now less often found.

### *IREDALINA MIRABILIS*
Golden Volute. *Finlay 1926.*
New Zealand.

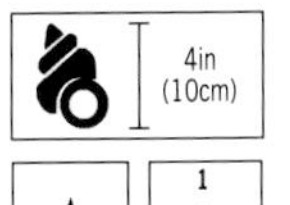


A beautiful deep-water volute, endemic to New Zealand, it inhabits depths to about 2,640ft (800m). There is no external sculpturing; a few inconspicuous growth striae are evident on the body whorl and there are fine columella ridges. The protoconch is compressed and sharp. Shells are always either cream or peach in colour.

### *LIVONIA MAMMILLA*
Mammal Volute. *Sowerby 1844.*
South-eastern Australia.

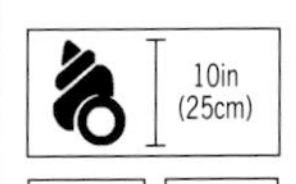


The large ovate mammal volute has a conspicuous rounded and calloused protoconch. The lip is expanded and flaring. It is generally pale orange or cream, with occasional brown tent markings on the exterior and a rich orange aperture. Endemic to south-eastern Australia, it is dredged in deep waters to a depth of about 660ft (200m).

## CYMBIOLA FLAVICANS

Yellow Volute. *Gmelin 1791.*
New Guinea to Northern Australia.

A solid rather bulbous volute, it has a low spire. The body whorl tapers at the anterior, and the lip is flared. There are four strong columella plaits. The shell is a pale cream yellow, with hazy grey axial markings overlaid with small tan dots, and with irregular lines. A shallow-water species.

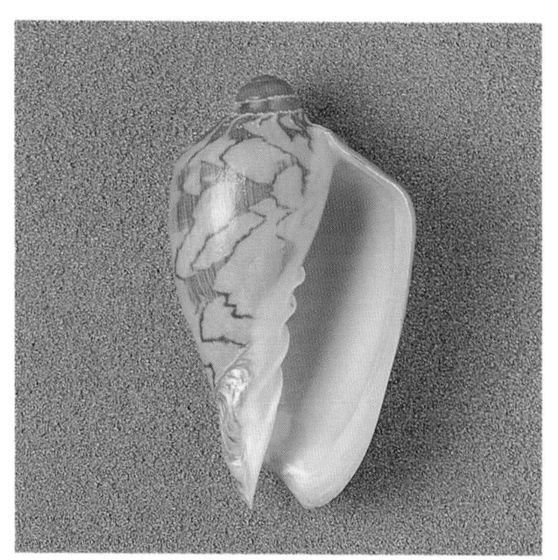

## CYMBIOLA NOBILIS

Noble Volute. *Lightfoot 1786.*
Taiwan to Singapore.

This very solid and heavy shell has a high angular body whorl and a low spire, crowned with a large rounded protoconch. Old shells become coarse and calloused on the interior, and have a much thickened lip. The depicted shell is a young specimen, fished off south-western Taiwan.

## CYMBIOLA MAGNIFICA

Magnificent Volute. *Gebauer 1802.*
Eastern Australia.

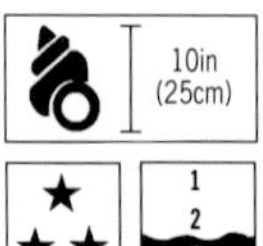

A very large shell, the magnificent volute has a much enlarged ovate body whorl and a short spire with a rounded protoconch. The lip is expanded and flaring. The exterior is generally smooth, but a few low blunt nodules occur at the shoulder. It is attractively decorated with closely arranged tan and dark brown tent markings over a cream background.Endemic to eastern Australia, it is found on sand in moderate depths to about 330ft (100m).

## CYMBIOLA NIVOSA

Snowy Volute. *Lamarck 1804.*
Western Australia.

A most beautiful volute, it is a dark grey brown, with white "snow flake" markings and spiral bands of axially laid dark brown wavy lines. These lines are also closely laid on the whorl shoulders, below the suture. The rounded protoconch supports tiny white axial riblets. The plaited columella is orange, and there is a prominent fasciole. A collectors' favourite.

**CYMBIOLA DESHAYESI**
Deshaye's Volute. *Reeve 1855.*
New Caledonia.

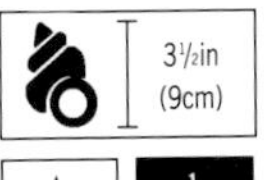

This lovely well-proportioned volute has vivid rich red-orange spirally arranged blotches on a cream background. The large rounded protoconch is off-white. There are low but sharp nodules on the shoulder of the body whorl. On the columella are four very strong plaits. A shallow-water species, it is endemic to New Caledonia.

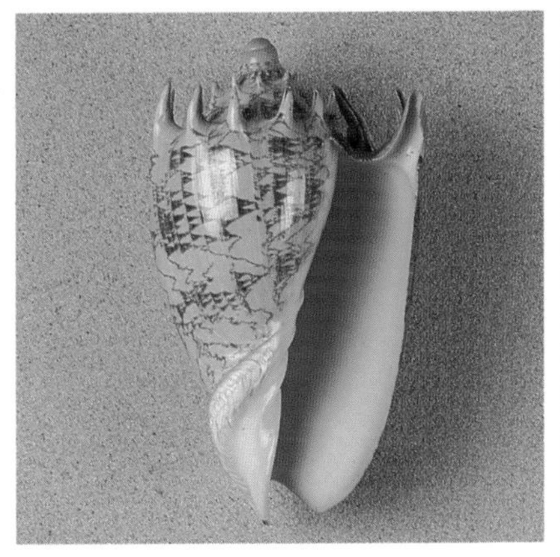

**CYMBIOLA IMPERIALIS**
Imperial Volute. *Lightfoot 1786.*
Sulu Sea.

A large heavy cylindrical-ovate shell, endemic to the Sulu Sea, it has a low spire and a large rounded protoconch. The shoulders support very strong open partly curved spines, giving the shell a coronated effect. There is a very broad calloused fasciole. The form *C. imperialis robinsona* displays identical shape and sculpturing, but has only thin non-coalescing axial zigzag lines. I have doubts on the form's validity, as the specimen shown has markings exactly between both varieties. Where does one draw the line?

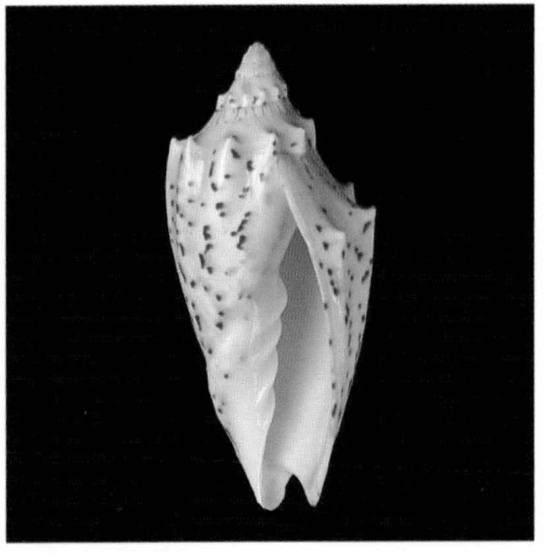

**CYMBIOLACCA PERISTICTA**
Dotted Volute. *McMichael 1963.*
Northern Queensland, Australia.

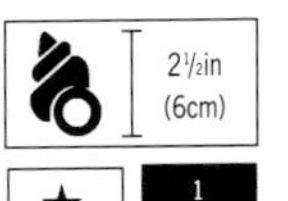

This beautiful shell reminds me of fine porcelain. It is similar in shape to *C. cracenta*, but is much broader and has rather higher shoulders. The pale pink background is overlaid with dots and squiggles of dark brown. Endemic to northern Queensland, it is found on sand in shallow water.

**CYMBIOLA RUTILA**
Blood-red Volute. *Broderip 1826.*
New Guinea to North-eastern Australia.

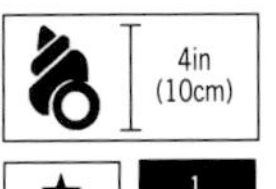

An ovate smooth species, it has a low rounded spire and a rather inflated body whorl. There are about four columella plaits, and the broad fasciole is usually calloused. The cream or off-white background is overlaid with irregular patches and hazy markings of rich red orange. The interior is orange.

**CYMBIOLACCA CRACENTA**
Graceful Volute. *McMichael 1963.*
Queensland, Australia.

A small slender, glossy volute, with small but sharp nodules on the shoulders, it is beautifully marked with broad bands of red brown and haphazard dots of dark brown over a hazy mottling of pale orange and off-white. The heavily pleated columella is pure white. Endemic to Queensland, it inhabits depths to about 165ft (50m).

**CYMBIUM GLANS**
Elephant Snout. *Gmelin 1791.*
West Africa.

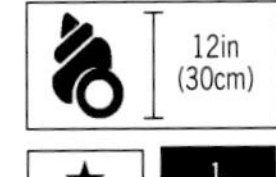

A large elongate ovate shell, endemic to West Africa, it has a distinctive sunken calloused spire surrounded by a sharp outwardly curving shoulder. The lip is flaring and there are strong columella plaits. The whole of the exterior is glazed, and sand grains and other marine debris are often trapped under the glaze. The depicted specimen came from Ghana, and was found in shallow water.

**MELO AETHIOPICA**
Crowned Baler. *L. 1758.*
South-West Pacific.

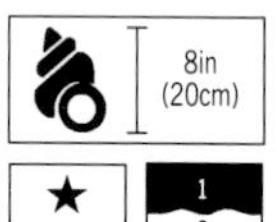

This very large and sometimes heavy globose shell has a flat spire. The shoulders support short sharp open spines, giving the shell a coronated effect. The lip is expanded and gaping. There are many growth striae and scars on the exterior; the columella is strongly pleated and there is a distinct and broad fasciole. Some authorities call this *M. broderippii*, but I have adhered to its more popularly known name.

**HARPULINA LOROISI**
Lorois's Volute. *Valenciennes 1863.*
Southern India and Sri Lanka.

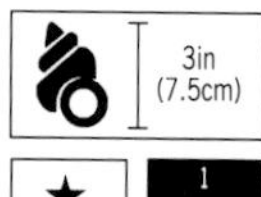

A solid, heavy fusiform volute, endemic to southern India and Sri Lanka, it has a tall spire and rounded whorls. It is strikingly marked with broad axial dark brown wavy bands over a pinkish beige background. The aperture margins are tinged with yellow; the interior is pinkish. An offshore dweller, some authorities class this as a variant of *H. lapponica.*

**HARPULINA ARAUSIACA**
Vexillate Volute. *Lightfoot 1786.*
Southern India and Sri Lanka.

Very similar in shape to *H. loroisi*, and endemic to the same area, it has a slightly lower spire and a prominent rounded protoconch. The shoulders can be slightly nodulose. The background colour is off-white to pale pink, over which are vivid broad spiral bands of rich red orange. Although this is a shallow-water species, shells are scarce and much sought-after by collectors.

**MELO AMPHORA**
Australian Baler. *Lightfoot 1786.*
Australia.

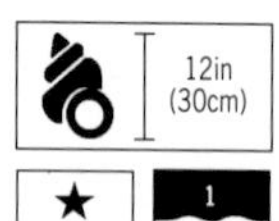

The largest species in the volute family – occasionally as big as 15in (37.5cm) – the shells were originally used by Aborigines and the islanders of the Torres Strait for baling-out their dugouts. This is another species that Taiwanese fishermen have poached from the waters off northern Australia, to such an extent that shells are more readily available in Taiwan than in Australia!

**HARPULINA LAPPONICA**
Brown-lined Volute. *L. 1767.*
Southern India and Sri Lanka.

Also endemic to southern India and Sri Lanka, this is a stout volute with a moderately high spire; the whorls have high rounded shoulders. Dark brown axial wavy lines and odd dots appear over a cream yellow background. The depicted specimen is from Trincomalee, Sri Lanka.

**VOLUTOCONUS GROSSI**
Gross's Volute. *Iredale 1927.*
Eastern and Southern Australia.

A sought-after collectors' item with several pattern and local variations, it is elongated and slender, with a spire of medium height and a curious protoconch. There are numerous axial growth striae. The columella bears three or four strong plaits. The off-white or cream background is overlaid with patches and tent markings of orange. It is a deep-water species.

**AMORIA CANALICULATA**
Channelled Volute. *McCoy 1869.*
Queensland.

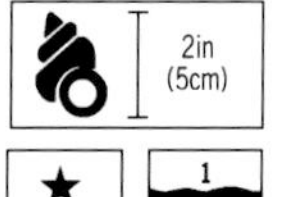

A small but solid, highly glossy volute, endemic to Queensland, it has a deeply channelled suture. The spire is low and the body whorl greatly enlarged. Two colour forms are shown here: the smaller paler specimen is from Lady Musgrave Reef, and the larger from Sandy Cape – both from relatively deep water.

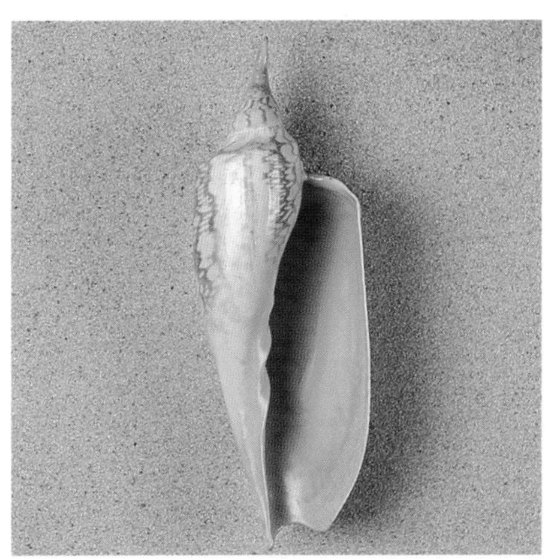

**ZIDONA DUFRESNEI**
Angular Volute. *Donovan 1823.*
Brazil and Argentina.

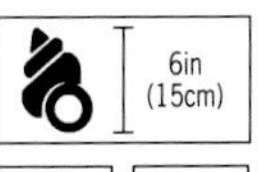

A long slender species, the angular volute has a curious and often heavily calloused curving spire; the whorls are angular, with narrow sloping shoulders. The body whorl curves slightly and the lip is expanded. There are three columella plaits. The exterior has a creamy glaze under which hazy grey axial zigzag lines can be discerned. The aperture area is a pale orange. It inhabits water to about 250ft (76m).

**VOLUTOCONUS BEDNALLI**
Bednall's Volute. *Brazier 1878.*
Northern Territory, Australia.

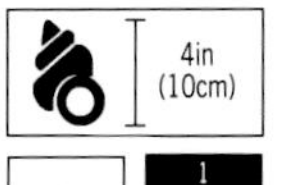

This has always been a firm collectors' favourite, and large specimens command high prices. it is generally fusiform, rather broad at the centre, and its cream base colour is overlaid with unique latticed lines of dark brown. There are fine axial grooves. There is a large yellowish protoconch of about three whorls. It dwells on sand in fairly shallow water, and is endemic to the Northern Territory.

**AMORIA DAMONI**
Damon's Volute. *Gray 1864.*
Australia.

Another highly smooth and glossy species, it includes several named pattern varieties. The commoner form, from western Australia, is the darker of the two depicted specimens; the paler is a variety usually found in Queensland. All forms inhabit shallow water.

**AMORIA TURNERI**
Turner's Volute. *Griffith and Pidgeon 1834.*
Northern Australia.

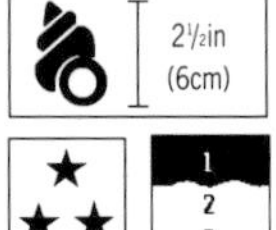


An elongate and fusiform shell, Turner's volute is smooth and glossy. The spire is low and the long body whorl is rather broad at the centre. The shell is pale beige or cream with fairly distinctive axial lines; some darker small patches run spirally at the suture. There are also two broad broken hazy pale brown bands below the glaze. A shallow-water dweller, it is endemic to northern Australia.

**AMORIA GRAYI**
Gray's Volute. *Ludbrook 1953.*
Northern and Western Australia.

Endemic to northern and western Australia, this is virtually the same shape as *A. damoni*, but perhaps rather longer and broader. The colour is an overall creamy beige, with rich brown-stained bands running spirally above the suture. Numerous very fine growth striae are present. The columella is strongly pleated and the fasciole is broad and calloused. The interior is a rich but fairly light mid-brown.

**AMORIA ELLIOTI**
Elliot's Volute. *Sowerby 1864.*
North-western Australia.

This handsome volute, endemic to north-western Australia, is strikingly patterned with distinct wavy axial lines of dark brown. The spire is low and the large body whorl tapers slightly at the anterior. There are strong columella pleats and a broad fasciole. It is a light mid-brown within. A highly smooth and glossy collectors' favourite.

**AMORIA EXOPTANDA**
Desirable Volute. *Reeve 1849.*
Southern Australia.

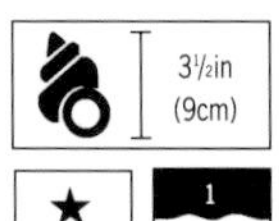


A heavy and solid shell, endemic to southern Australia, it has a large body whorl with a high rounded shoulder; the spire is low. There are three strong columella pleats and a glazed calloused fasciole. The aperture is a beautiful deep orange, and the exterior markings consist of a beige background overlaid with many fine brown tent markings and haphazard squiggles.

**AMORIA UNDULATA**
Wavy Volute. *Lamarck 1804.*
Southern Australia and Tasmania.

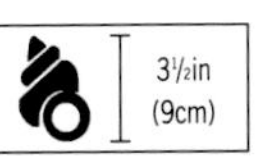


Endemic to its area, this is a solid fusiform shell with a low spire, and an enlarged body whorl that tapers at the anterior. The uniform cream or beige background is overlaid with fine axial zigzag and undulating lines. The aperture margins, including the columella, are tinged with yellow; the interior is orange. There are also random patches of hazy grey brown under the glaze on the dorsum.

**AMORIA KAWAMURAI**
Kawamura's Volute. *Habe 1975.*
Japan and Taiwan.

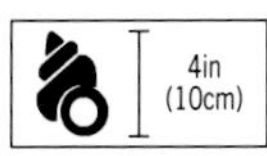


A choice collectors' item, it is smooth and glossy and has very distinctive dark brown wavy axial bands over a greyish beige background. There is a broad spiral orange band above the suture. The cream columella is strongly pleated, and the fasciole is broad.

**AMORIA ZEBRA**
Striped Volute. *Leach 1814.*
Queensland, Australia.

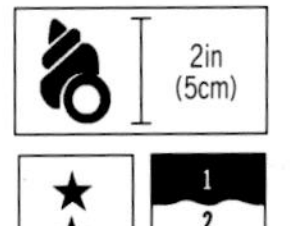


This small solid volute, endemic to Queensland, is found in large colonies on tidal sand banks. It is variable in colour and pattern and some variations have been given subspecific names. Of the three depicted specimens, the golden form is the most uncommon.

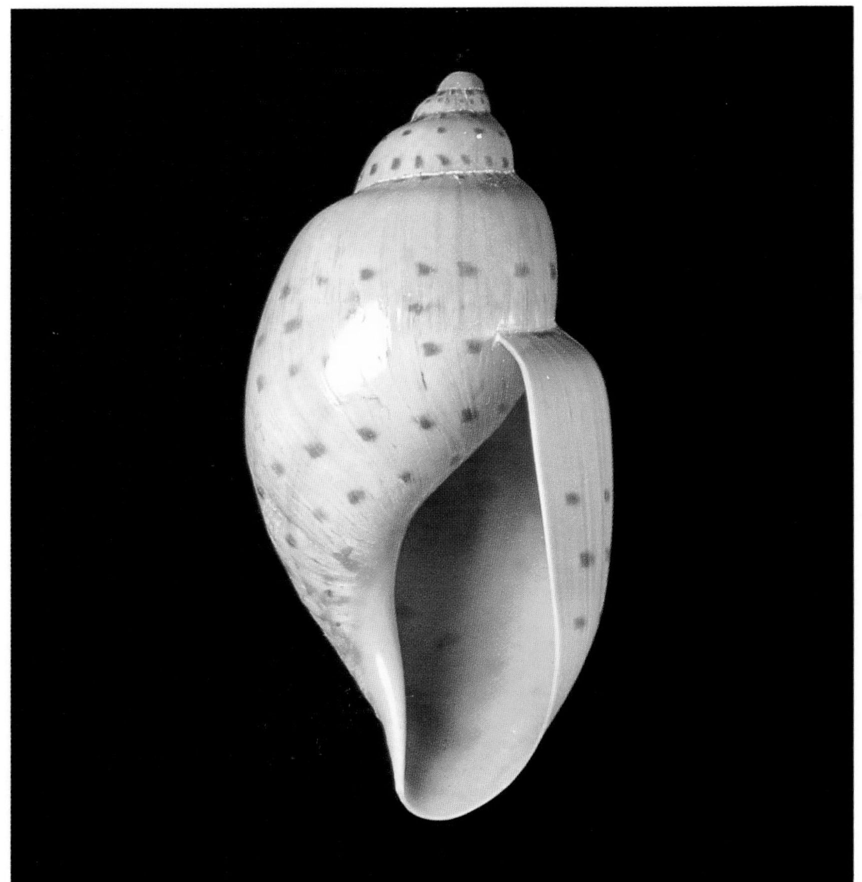

**AMPULLA PRIAMUS**
Spotted Flask. *Gmelin 1791.*
North-East Atlantic.

A lightweight and globose shell, the spotted flask has an enlarged body whorl with high rounded shoulders. Glossy and smooth, it is a dark beige colour with rows of well-spaced small brown squares or spots. It inhabits water at depths of between 65 and 990ft (50 and 300m). A popular collectors' shell.

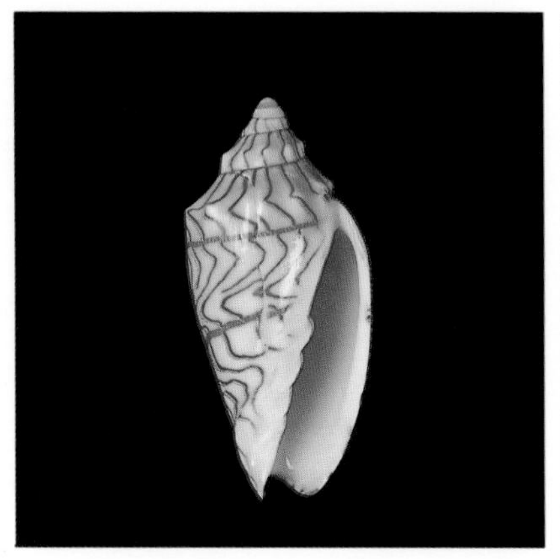

**PARAMORIA GUNTHERI**
Gunther's Volute. *E. A. Smith 1886.*
Southern Australia.

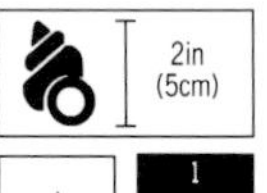


A superb collectors' item, Gunther's volute displays beautiful markings of wavy axial lines and two distinctive spiral bands of rich tan over a pinkish cream background. The aperture margins and columella are cream; the interior a pale peach. The species is endemic to southern Australia, and the depicted shell was collected on a granite reef at 53ft (16m) off Memory Cove, Thorny Passage.

**SCAPHELLA DUBIA**
*Broderip 1827.*
Florida and Northern Gulf of Mexico.

A very slender lightweight fusiform volute, its protoconch is often large and calloused, and there are very fine axial ribs on the earlier whorls. Growth scars can generally be found on the exterior of the shell, which is a pale tan or cream with widely spaced brown squared markings. The columella is stained brown. The depicted shell was trawled at 240ft (73m) off the Mississippi Delta.

**NEPTUNEOPSIS GILCHRISTI**
Gilchrist's Volute. *Sowerby 1898.*
South Africa.

A large, fusiform and rather lightweight volute, inhabiting deep water, it is endemic to South Africa. The rather inflated whorls taper to a calloused protoconch, which is typically set at a slight angle to the rest of the shell. It is overall a beige, light brown or dirty grey colour, and is a popular collectors' shell. This specimen was trawled off Hermanus at 792ft (240m).

**SCAPHELLA JUNONIA**
Juno's Volute. *Lamarck 1804.*
South-eastern USA, Florida.

Endemic to its area, this is another choice collectors' shell, with very striking dark brown squared markings on a cream background. The shell is fusiform, with a moderate spire and long tapering body whorl. Specimens with perfect lips are scarce; they always seem to be filed. The depicted specimen was collected offshore at Apalachicola, Florida.

**FUSIVOLUTA CLARKEI**
Clarke's Volute. *Rehder 1969.*
South-East Africa.

This elongate fusiform species has a tall spire and rounded whorls. The slightly thickened lip is expanded at the posterior; the columella is smooth. There are very fine spiral cords and occasional growth striae. It is pale beige throughout. A deep-water shell, it can be trawled as deep as 1,980ft (600m).

**TEREMACHIA JOHNSONI**
Johnson's Volute. *Bartsch 1942.*
North-western Australia, Taiwan.

This elegant high-spired species has only been available in appreciable numbers over the last ten years or so. I do not believe that the classification is settled as yet, because several variations have been dubiously named. This specimen was trawled off Port Hedland at a depth of 1,320ft (400m). A favourite with volute enthusiasts.

SUPER FAMILY
MURICOIDEA

FAMILY
## HARPIDAE
(Harp Shells)

Harps are a very small family of about 14 species and are highly collectable. They are all heavily sculptured with strong axial ribs, an enlarged body whorl and a wide aperture. The colours and patterns are exquisite, which makes them one of my favourite families! They are carnivorous, feeding mainly on crustaceans, which they tend to cover in a film of sticky saliva and sand before devouring. They are able to cast off part of their foot to avoid capture from an enemy. Most species inhabit sandy substrates in shallow water, but some rarer shells are found as deep as 660ft (200m). The family also includes the genus *Morum*, although some conchologists prefer to place these within the family Cassidae. As things stand, we have three genera to note – *Harpa*, the rare deep-water *Austroharpa* and *Morum*.

### HARPA MAJOR
Major Harp. *Röding 1798.*
Indo-Pacific.

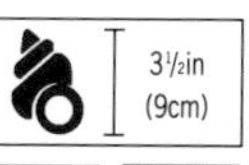


The major harp has a large, ovate and rather inflated body whorl, with a low heavily calloused spire. There are numerous broad flattish axial ribs. The columella has dark brown staining. There is a strongly ridged fasciole. Two views of Taiwanese specimens are shown here – they display characteristic colours and patterns.

### HARPA VENTRICOSA
Ventral Harp. *Lamarck 1816.*
East and South-East Africa.

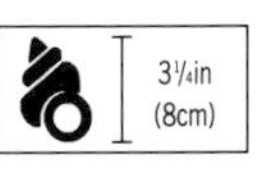


A thick heavy harp, it generally has an ovate body whorl and a moderate spire. The very strong ribs again become spinose at the high shoulders before continuing onto the suture. The exterior patterning consists of broad spiral bands on the ribs and tent markings in the interspaces. These show through on the inner lip wall. Two large dark brown blotches occur on the parietal wall. Both shells seen here are from Mombasa, Kenya.

### HARPA AMOURETTA
Minor Harp. *Röding 1798.*
Indo-Pacific.

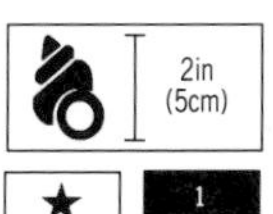


This is an elongate-ovate shell, with a relatively tall spire. The strong axial ribs are spinose at the shoulders, and this continues onto the suture. The basic colour is pale grey or off-white, with spiral bands of grey brown zigzag markings on the interspaces; the ribs have groups of closely set black lines. The exterior ornamentation shows through the inner lip; the columella is a creamy white and calloused. The apex is lavender.

### HARPA COSTATA
Imperial Harp. *L. 1758.*
Mauritius.

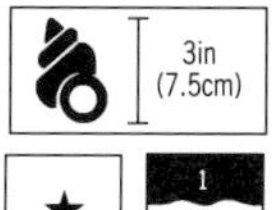


This very handsome harp, endemic to Mauritius, is the rarest of the genus and has very closely laid axial ribs; these become rather spinose at the shoulders, giving the low spire a coronated effect. The apex is pink, apart from which the exterior is creamy yellow, with light brown bands on the ribs. The interior is yellow; the columella and parietal shield are heavily calloused and two dark brown stained patches occur at the posterior. There is a strongly ridged fasciole. It lives in shallow water and is much sought-after.

### HARPA HARPA
True Harp. *L. 1758.*
Indo-Pacific.

The most colourful examples of this species are found in the Sulu Sea. It is a small ovate shell, with a low spire. The ribs can be broad or narrow and have the typical black spiral lines on them; they are sharply spinose at the shoulders. The calloused columella and parietal wall have three hazy brown patches on a cream background.

## HARPA ARTICULARIS
Articulate Harp. *Lamarck 1822.*
Indo-Pacific.

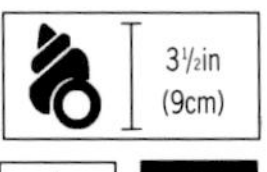


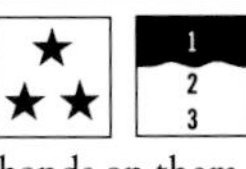


A large fairly lightweight shell, it has a rather inflated body whorl. The strong ribs vary in thickness from shell to shell, but all have conspicuous black or grey purple broad spiral bands on them. There is some callosity above the suture. The columella and parietal wall are glazed dark brown throughout. Both the specimens in the photograph are from the central Philippines.

## HARPA DORIS
Rose Harp. *Röding 1798.*
West Africa.

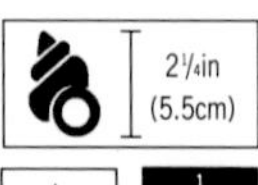


This small lightweight species, endemic to West Africa, has little or no gloss compared to most other species in the genus. The ribs are fine and virtually flat, and are sharply spinose at the shoulders. There are large haphazard patches of dull red; the anterior lip margin is serrated. The depicted specimens are from Gorée, Senegal.

## HARPA CRENATA
Crenate Harp. *Swainson 1822.*
Western Central America.

While similar to *H. doris*, this is larger and has a slightly angular body whorl, and the ribs, although flat, are usually broader. It could be related to *H. doris* (there may well be fossil evidence for this). The coloration is basically a grey brown; the interior is glazed and calloused. The exterior is matt and dull in appearance. This specimen is from west Panama.

## MORUM GRANDE
Giant Morum. *A. Adams 1855.*
Japan to Australia.

An ovate shell, with a moderately high spire, it is the largest species in the genus. The exterior is very coarsely ornamented with rounded and scabrous spiral ridges, and with low axial ribs which are slightly spinose. The much-thickened lip is strongly dentate, and the calloused columella and shield have numerous low plicae. Usually trawled in deep water.

**MORUM CANCELLATUM**
Cancellate Morum. *Sowerby 1824.*
Japan to Taiwan.

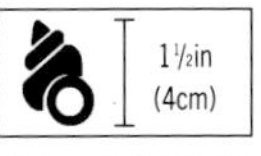
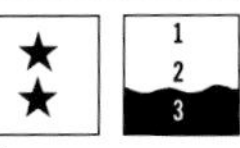

Resembling M. *grande* in shape, the cancellate morum is smaller and less coarsely ornamented. There are low well-spaced spiral cords and axial ridges that are spinose at the intersections. The lip and calloused area are very similar, but the denticles are more closely packed. It is found in deep water to about 495ft (150m).

**MORUM JOELGREENEI**
Joel Green's Morum. *Emerson 1981.*
Central and Southern Philippines.

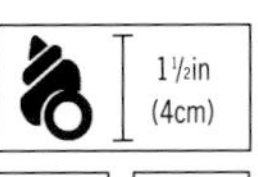
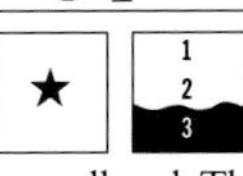

A pretty little shell, endemic to central and southern Philippines, it has coarse sculpturing of low spiral cords and spinose or slightly fluted axial ribs; the low spire is cancellated. There is a sharply defined calloused columella and the parietal shield bears tiny pustules. The shell in the photograph was collected in 660ft (200m) in tangle nets off Davao, Mindanao.

SUPER FAMILY
MURICOIDEA

FAMILY
## VASIDAE
(Vase Shells)

This family contains four subfamilies, *Vasinae, Turbinellinae, Columbariinae* and *Ptychatractinae* (not included here). The *Vasinae* are a small family of solidly built medium to large shells found on tropical coral reefs. There are possibly 25 known species. This group is popular among collectors as many are attractive and some are rare. The genera *Tudicla* and *Afer* have shells with long siphonal canals and are much less coarsely ornamented than those in the genus *Vasum. Turbinellinae* were formerly known as *Xancinae* (chank shells) from the Hindu word *cankh*, meaning a shell. They are a small subfamily of carnivorous snails that eat marine worms and bivalves. *Columbariinae* (pagoda shells) are a subfamily of deep water shells with attractive sculpturing and very long canals.

**MORUM DENNISONI**
Dennison's Morum. *Reeve 1842.*
Caribbean.

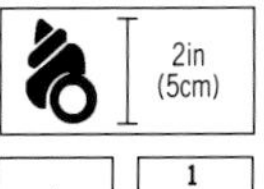

An attractive morum, it is popular with collectors and is occasionally fished or trapped in depths to about 825ft (250m). The main feature of this shell is the orange red calloused columella and the shield, which is covered with small creamy tubercules and plicae. The depicted specimen was dead-collected in deep water by shrimpers off Guyana.

**MORUM MATTHEWSI**
Matthew's Morum. *Emerson 1967.*
Brazil.

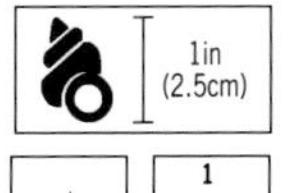

Endemic to Brazil, this is a small ovate shell with a low spire. The broad spiral cords are raised and slightly nodose at the posterior. The thickened lip is strongly dentate, and there are numerous plicae on the columella and shield. It has a beige to mid-brown exterior, an aperture stained with light to dark brown, and is white within.

**AFER CUMINGII**
Cuming's Afer. *Reeve 1844.*
Japan to Taiwan.

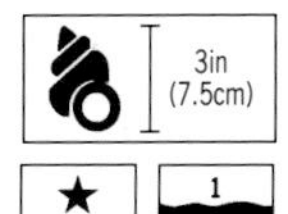

This is a robust shell, with a moderate spire, rounded whorls and a long open canal. There are fine spiral cords and low blunt nodules on the earlier whorls. It is an off-white, with irregular axial and haphazard lines and blotches of tan. It is found in relatively deep water.

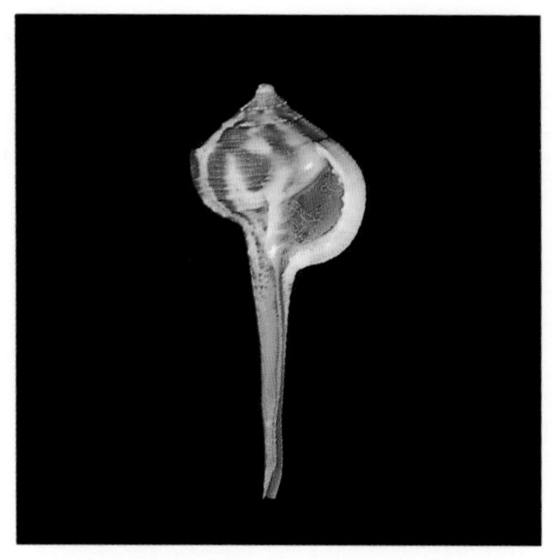

**TUDICLA INERMIS**
Toffee Apple Shell. *Angas 1878.*
Northern and Western Australia.

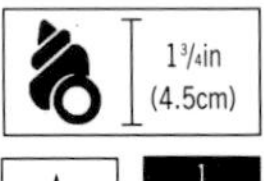

This small species has a large rounded and slightly nodulose body whorl and a very long straight canal. There are fine spiral threads and the inner lip is strongly lirate; the columella has three plicae. The shell is white with broad brown axial "flame" markings; the canal is tinged with pinkish red.

**TUDICLA ARMIGERA KURZI**
Kurz's Tudicla. *Macpherson 1963.*
Northern and Western Australia.

A very attractive vase, it has a high spire, rounded and highly spinose whorls and a long straight open canal. There is a prominent rounded protoconch. The spines are longest at the shoulders and on the canal. A white shell, it is decorated with faint narrow axial lines of pale brown.

**VASUM MURICATUM**
Caribbean Vase. *Born 1778.*
Florida and Caribbean.

This is closely related to *V. caestus*, and indeed looks quite similar, but it is generally smaller, lighter and more delicately sculptured, with fine spiral cords, some spinose on the lower part of the body whorl, and robust sharp nodules at the shoulders. It is creamy white, with a white aperture. The depicted shell is from the Netherlands Antilles.

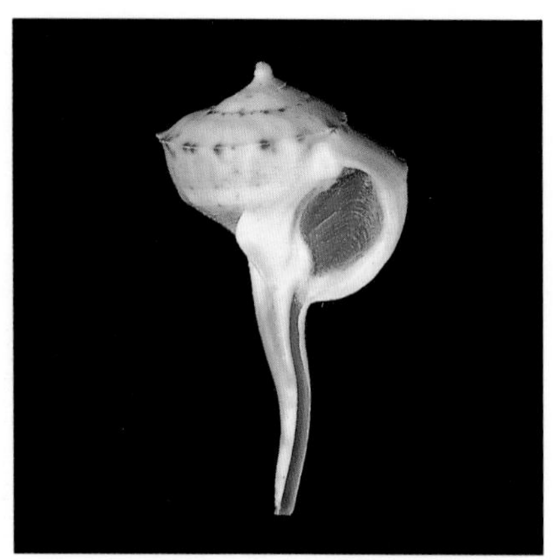

**TUDICLA SPIRILLUS**
Spiral Tudicla. *L. 1767.*
South-eastern India.

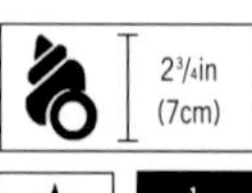

Endemic to south-eastern India, this shell is rather similar to *T. inermis* but larger, and it has a very broad flattened body whorl with a distinctive rounded protoconch. The strong open canal is slightly recurved at the anterior. The inner lip is finely lirate; the columella is smooth. It lives in offshore, shallow water.

**VASUM CAESTUS**
Giant Panamanian Vase. *Broderip 1833.*
Western Central America.

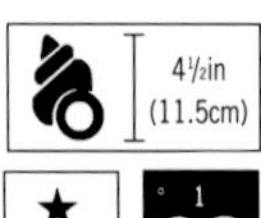

This large and very solid heavy shell has a conical spire of medium height. There are strong blunt nodules at the shoulders and coarse spiral cords on the body whorl. Numerous closely packed axial growth striae occur toward the crenulated lip. There is an open umbilicus. Under a fibrous brown periostracum, the shell is white.

**VASUM CASSIFORME**
Helmet Vase. *Kiener 1841.*
Brazil.

A very attractive and coarsely sculptured collectors' shell, endemic to Brazil, it inhabits shallow water. The body whorl tapers sharply, and the columella and parietal area are usually heavily calloused. Numerous small and large partly closed spines adorn the exterior. This specimen portrays typical coloration.

**VASUM TURBINELLUS**
Pacific Top Vase. *L. 1758.*
Indo-Pacific.

This medium-sized and angular shell has a low spire and an enlarged body whorl which bears coarse nodules or, on some, spines of varying length. It is generally dark brown or black with greyish white patches, often on the spines. The aperture is cream. The depicted shell is from shallow water, Coron, Philippines.

**VASUM TUBIFERUM**
Imperial Vase. *Anton 1839.*
Philippines.

Rather similar to *V. turbinellus*, it is somewhat broader at the centre and generally less angular. The sculpturing consists of both long recurved and short open spines and spiral ridges. The small open columella is encircled by a broad fasciole. Usually dark brown or off-white, this shell is endemic to the Philippines.

**VASUM CAPITELLUM**
Spined Caribbean Vase. *L. 1758.*
Caribbean.

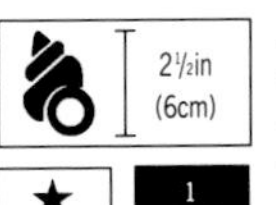

A solid coarsely sculptured vase, it has very strong spiral ridges and axial ribs with blunt low nodules, which are triangularly spinose at the shoulders. The lip margin is crenulated, and there are two columella pleats. The shell is an attractive colour between beige and mid-brown, and has a rich cream aperture.

**VASUM FLINDERSI**
Flinder's Vase. *Verco 1914.*
Southern and Western Australia.

This is better known by its subgeneric name *Altivasum* and is possibly the largest of the vase shells. Shells are frequently trawled dead-collected, but live-taken specimens are scarce. Colours vary from white through to peach and deep orange. The spinose specimen is from western Australia; the smaller shell is from Coffin's Bay, Southern Australia.

**VASUM LATIRIFORME**
Latirus-shaped Vase. *Rehder and Abbott 1951.* South-eastern Mexico.

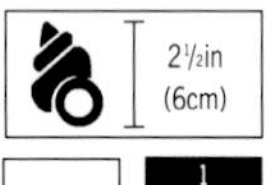


A very difficult-to-obtain vase, endemic to the Bay of Kampeche, it inhabits moderately deep water. It has a curiously formed siphonal canal and spirally ridged and nodose whorls. Most shells are off-white, but a few are pale orange. A much sought-after collectors' shell, it is placed within the subgenus *Siphovasum*.

**TURBINELLA ANGULATA**
West Indian Chank. *Lightfoot 1786.* Caribbean and Eastern Central America.

A very large and heavy shell, the West Indian chank has a high spire, angular and strongly nodose whorls and an open siphonal canal of medium length. There are fine spiral cords below the suture and strong spiral cords on the lower part of the body whorl. Shells are usually creamy white or beige below a coarse periostracum; the aperture margins are tinged with pale orange.

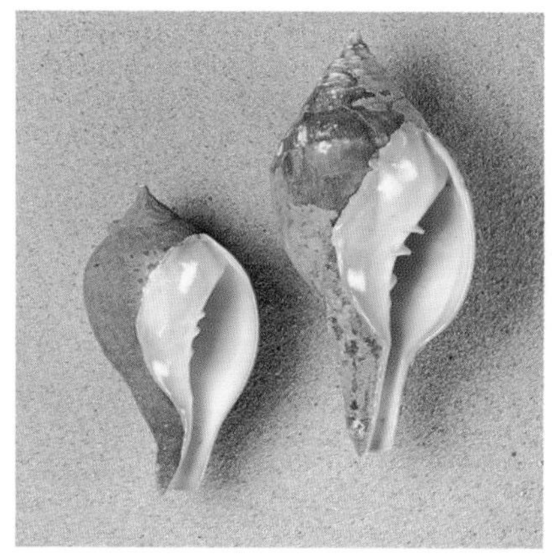

**TURBINELLA PYRUM**
Sacred Chank. *L. 1758.* South-eastern India and Sri Lanka.

This largish very heavy shell, endemic to its area, has an enlarged and bulbous body whorl. Considered sacred to the Hindus, it is used in ceremonial and religious rites and also in various forms of jewellery. Extremely rare sinistral shells are much sought-after and command fantastically high prices from religious Indians. Most collectors, however, are happy with a normal dextral specimen. The smaller of the two shells shown is form *rapa*.

**COLUMBARIUM NATALENSE**
Natal Pagoda Shell. *Tomlin 1928.* Durban, South Africa.

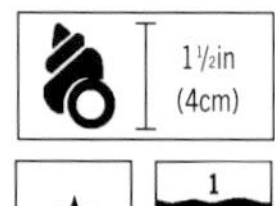


The smallest species of pagoda shell, it has a tall spire, long open canal, strongly corded whorls and spinose shoulders. The suture is impressed. The depicted specimen was dredged in 420ft (127m) off Durban, where the species is endemic.

**COLUMBARIUM ROTUNDATUM**
Rounded Pagoda Shell. *Barnard 1959?*
West coast of South Africa.

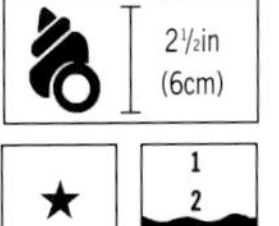

This dead-collected specimen was trawled in 825ft (250m) off Cape Point, the species being endemic to the western coast of South Africa. The spire and canal are almost of equal length and the whorls bear strong low axial ribs. There are also spiral cords. Live specimens possess a thin beige periostracum.

**COLUMBARIUM EASTWOODAE**
Eastwood's Pagoda Shell. *Kilburn 1971.*
South-East Africa.

A medium-sized shell, it has angular whorls, a tall spire and a strong, open and long canal. The central raised spiral ridge bears short triangular flat spires. The suture is impressed. Fine spiral cords are found on the lower half of each whorl and on the canal. It is probably the most common of the pagoda shells in its area.

**COLUMBARIUM PAGODUS**
Common Pagoda Shell. *Lesson 1831.*
Japan to Taiwan.

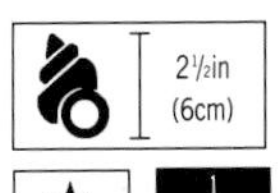

This very attractive and elegant species has an extremely long open siphonal canal. There is a distinctive rounded protoconch. The shoulders bear longish, sharp and upturned spines, and there are several rows of raised spiral and weakly spinose cords. Two slightly differing forms are shown here, both coming from Taiwan.

**COLUMBARIUM RADIALE**
Radial Pagoda Shell. *Watson 1882.*
West coast of South Africa.

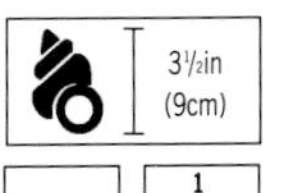

A large chalky white pagoda shell, also endemic to South Africa's western coast, it has a tall spire, rounded and rather globose whorls and a long open canal. The raised spiral cords are slightly spinose around the centre of each whorl. It is very deep-water species, found in depths to about 4,620ft (1,400m).

**COLUMBARIUM SUBCONTRACTUM**
South Africa.

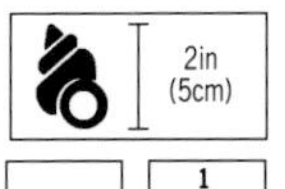

I have no reliable data on this shell, nor can I ascertain the accuracy of this name – it may well be *C. angulare* – but I felt obliged to include it among this group of South African pagoda shells in order to display as many species as possible. I do believe it to be a separate species from other similar South African pagoda shells, however. It was trawled off Natal in deep water.

**COLUMBARIUM PAGODOIDES**
False Pagoda Shell. *Watson 1882.*
South-eastern Australia.

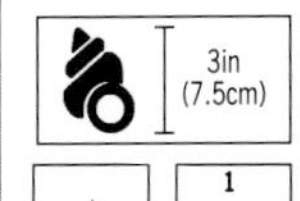

Endemic to south-eastern Australia, this is rather similar in shape to *C. pagodus*, but a little larger and broader; the lower half of the body whorl and the canal bear rows of raised and weakly spinose cords. The depicted shell was trawled off Sydney in 1,800ft (545m).

**COLUMBARIUM HARRISAE**
Harris's Pagoda Shell. *Harasewych 1986.*
Australia.

Possibly the largest and strongest pagoda shell, it is very attractively sculptured with raised spinose spiral cords that are most prominent at the shoulders. The very long canal bears rows of low finely spinose ridges. This specimen was trawled off Musgrave Island.

**COLUMBARIUM SPINICINCTUM**
Spiny Pagoda Shell. *Von Martens 1881.*
Eastern Australia.

A very delicate lightweight shell, endemic to eastern Australia, it is most usually collected off the Queensland coast in waters to 330ft (100m) deep. The angular whorls bear a central row of spiral, triangular and sharp spines; the very long and narrow canal is also weakly spinose. The shell is beige with fine brown axial streaks and lines.

**COLUMBARIUM AAPTA**
*Harasewych 1986.*
Western Australia.

A very elegant species of much interest to pagoda shell enthusiasts. I have seen several of these; all collected off Port Hedland in about 1,485ft (450m) of water. It is often described as *Coluzea aptos*.

**COLUMBARIUM SPIRALIS**
Spiral Pagoda Shell. A. *Adams 1856.*
New Zealand.

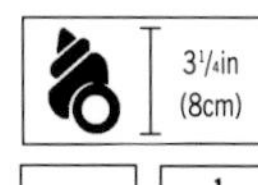

An attractive lightweight pagoda shell, endemic to New Zealand, it has weakly spinose shoulders and spiral ridges. All New Zealand pagoda shells are placed in the subgenus *Coluzea*. This particular specimen was dredged in 180ft (55m) at Houraki Gulf.

**COLUMBARIUM WORMALDI**
Wormald's Pagoda Shell. *Powell 1971.*
New Zealand.

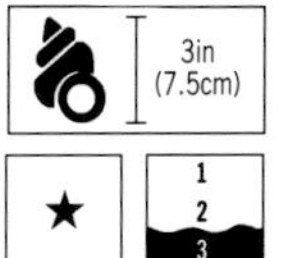

3in (7.5cm)

The whorls of this off-white shell, also endemic to New Zealand, are rounded, with a deeply impressed suture. The spiral cords bear short blunt anterior-sloping spines. The siphonal canal is very long, open and narrow. This specimen was fished at 1,386ft (420m) off Alderman Island.

**OLIVA PORPHYRIA**
Tent Olive. *L. 1758.*
Western Central America.

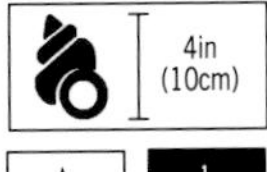

4in (10cm)

This very handsome and attractive shell is the largest in the genus. It has a very low spire with a sharp protoconch; the suture is channelled. The body whorl is very large, elongated and rather bulbous, especially at the centre. The columella is calloused, thickened and strongly plicate, and there is a broad flat fasciole. The colour is a pale violet pinkish tone, overlaid with rich brown tent markings, often closely arranged.

**OLIVA SPICATA**
*Röding 1798.*
Western Central America.

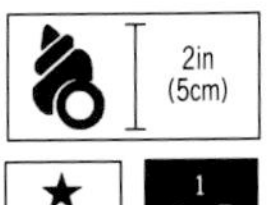

2in (5cm)

A medium-sized olive, it has a pronounced spire and channelled suture. The elongated cylindrical body whorl has somewhat convex sides. The columella plaits extend up to the start of the suture. Its colouring and patterns are not dissimilar to those of *O. sayana*, but there are no central bands. The aperture is white.

SUPER FAMILY

## MURICOIDEA

FAMILY

## OLIVIDAE

(Olive Shells)

Members of this large group of small to medium-sized carnivorous gastropods are generally found in shallow water in warm tropical seas. The main genera are *Oliva*, *Olivancillaria*, *Ancilla*, *Amalda*, *Olivella* and *Agaronia*. Most species have smooth and glossy shells and are often highly coloured or patterned. There has been a recent upsurge of interest in the true olives (genus *Oliva*) due to the publication of various books on the group. I have known many collectors despair of collecting this genus, as the patterns and markings are so very variable. However, the shape of the shell always remains consistent within the species, so for identification, shapes ought to be considered prior to markings. Most species lie hidden under sand during the day; they become active and feed at night.

**OLIVA SAYANA**
Lettered Olive. *Ravenel 1834.*
Florida and Caribbean.

$2\frac{3}{4}$in (7cm)

It has a somewhat extended spire, channelled suture and an elongated cylindrical body whorl. The columella has numerous strong plaits. The greyish yellow background is overlaid with either distinct or hazy grey brown tent marks; dark brown zigzags cross the body whorl in two broad bands. The interior is lavender, the columella white.

**OLIVA POLPASTA**
*Duclos 1835.*
Western Central America.

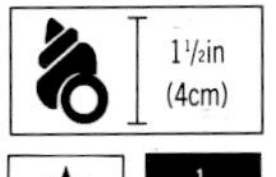

$1\frac{1}{2}$in (4cm)

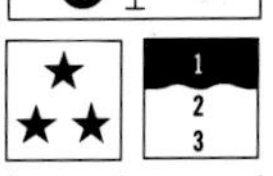

A rather short olive, with an inflated body whorl at the posterior, its low spire has very slightly concave sides. The shell is prettily marked, the pale olive green background being decorated with numerous haphazard broken dark brown zigzag lines; the aperture is white. The depicted specimen is from Pedro Gonzales Island, Panama.

**OLIVA SPICATA** f. *fuscata*
*Marrat 1871.*
Western Central America.

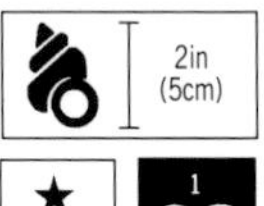

This is a rich brown variant of *O. spicata*, some specimens being almost black. The colour of the shell in the photograph allows the under-markings to be clearly seen. The aperture is pure white. This specimen was collected at low tide, in sand, at Quiros Island, Panama.

**OLIVA FULGURATOR**
Fusiform Olive. *Röding 1798.*
Caribbean Islands.

A thick and heavy shell, it is rather bulbous and broadened at the posterior. The spire is prominent and the suture is slightly channelled. Overall, it is a pale yellow or cream, decorated with axial chestnut brown zigzag markings. The plaited columella and aperture are white. A species only occasionally available to collectors.

**OLIVA SPLENDIDULA**
Splendid Olive. *Sowerby 1825.*
Western Central America.

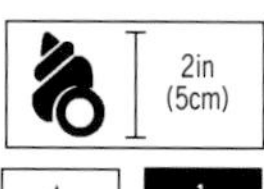

A very attractively marked olive, its patterns and colours seldom vary and the shell is therefore easily identifiable. The two depicted specimens show typical coloration and shape. They were both collected in shallow water at Shells Island, west Panama.

**OLIVA RETICULARIS**
f. *bifasciata* Netted Olive.
*Küster 1878.* Caribbean Islands.

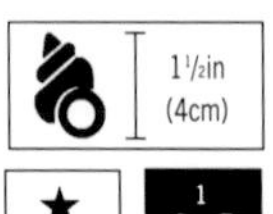

The netted olive is an unusually marked form of a common species, *O. reticularis*. The smallish shell has a moderate spire and slightly convex sides to the body whorl. The pale yellow or cream background bears fine brown tent markings and two spiral bands of rich brown, the central band being narrower. This specimen was collected in Haiti.

**OLIVA JULIETA**
Juliet's Olive. *Duclos 1835.*
Guatamala to Peru.

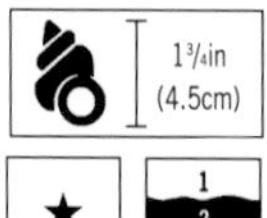

This is the rarest of the western American olives, and is a beautiful species, with conspicuous strong dark brown zigzag markings over a rich cream background. The apex is a pale violet colour. An important feature is the much thickened and expanded lip. The depicted specimen was dredged in sand at 108ft (33m) south of San José, Guatamala.

**OLIVA KALEONTINA**
Woven Olive. *Duclos 1835.*
Western Central America.

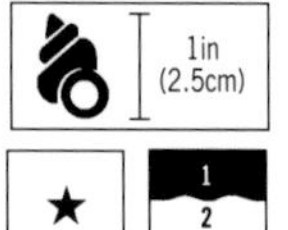

Another rarely obtainable species, it is small, but robust, with a distinctive pale beige to lavender background overlaid with rich brown blotches and thickened arrow marks. The aperture and columella are white. The visual characteristics of this olive also vary very little.

**OLIVA INCRASSATA**
Angled Olive. *Lightfoot 1786.*
Western Central America.

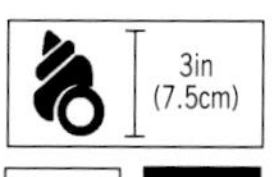

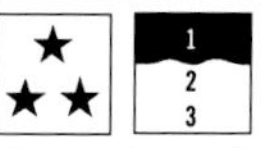


This is the thickest and heaviest olive shell, and is quite easily separated from other species by its solid build and angular appearance. The vivid dark brown markings of the specimen shown are typical.

**OLIVA PERUVIANA**
Peruvian Olive. *Lamarck 1811.*
Peru and Chile.

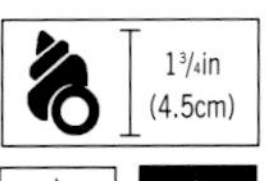


This stocky medium-sized olive is broad and ovate, and the body whorl sometimes has convex sides or, as shown, an angled shoulder and swollen posterior. It is invariably very pale creamy lavender with axially laid thickened lines or blotches of pale brown. The columella, calloused parietal wall and aperture are white.

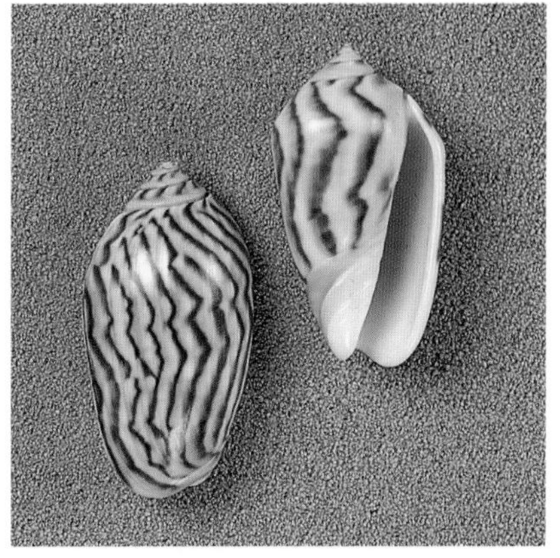

**OLIVA PERUVIANA**
f. *fulgurata* Striped Peruvian Olive.
*Martens 1869.* Peru and Chile.

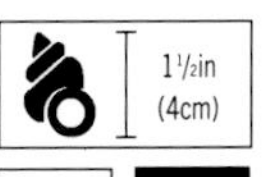


One of several colour and pattern forms of *O. peruviana*, it has very distinctive broad axial rich brown streaks over an off-white background. As can be seen, the shapes vary, as in all forms of this particular species, which is a most popular collectors' olive.

**OLIVA INCRASSATA**
f. *burchorum* Burch's Angled Olive.
*Zeigler 1969.* Chile.

A lovely colour form of *O. incrassata*, this is considered by some experts to be endemic to the Gulf of California, but the two shown are from Chile. The mottled shell is possibly a transitional form between *O. burchorum* and *O. incrassata*. This pale orange shell rarely reaches the size of its more common counterpart.

**OLIVA RETICULARIS**
*f. olorinella* Pearl Olive.
*Duclos 1835.* Bahamas.

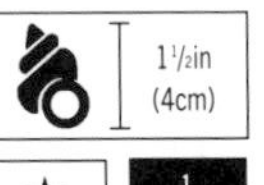

An albino form of its common counterpart, *O. reticularis*, it is usually only found in the Bahamas. It is devoid of markings. The spire is of moderate height, with straight-sided whorls, slightly channelled suture and a body whorl with convex sides. The columella is strongly pleated.

**OLIVA BULBOSA**
Inflated Olive. *Röding 1798.*
Red Sea; Indian Ocean to Indonesia.

A very well-known shell, it is variably marked, but its shape, however, is constant – much thickened and bulbous centrally, the spire is partially sunken below a raised suture; there is a thickened calloused ridge at the posterior tip of the aperture on the body whorl. Several pattern variations are shown here; the albino shell being form *immaculata*. All are from East Africa.

**OLIVA MINIACEA**
Gold-mouthed Olive. *Röding 1798.*
Indo-Pacific.

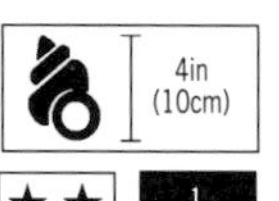

A most well-known and widespread species, it is characterized by its size and distinctive deep orange aperture. The colours and patterns vary, but most specimens have a pale orange or beige background with strong dark to mid-brown broken bands, patches and arrow marks, irregularly laid.

**OLIVA FLAMMULATA**
Flamed Olive. *Lamarck 1811.*
West Africa.

A smallish cylindrical species, the flamed olive has a low rather concave spire. It is prettily marked with broken dark brown zigzag or tent marks over a cream yellow background, on top of which are large areas of hazy pale greyish blue. The depicted specimen is from shallow water, Mussulo Bay, Luanda, Angola.

**OLIVA CAERULEA**
Purple-mouthed Olive. *Röding 1798.*
Indo-Pacific.

A medium-sized shell, it has a low spire and a cylindrical body whorl with rather convex sides. The cream shell is overlaid with both hazy and distinct grey blue and almost black lines and blotches. The aperture is a beautiful deep purple colour. The smaller of the two depicted shells is possibly form *lugubris*, from the Solomon Islands.

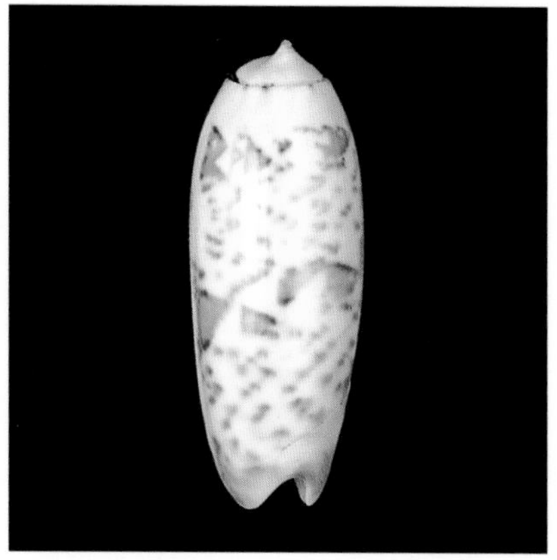

**OLIVA LIGNARIA**
Ornate Olive. *Marrat 1868.*
Indian Ocean and Western Pacific.

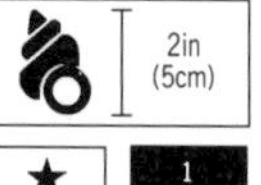

The ornate olive is an elongate and slender species with a characteristic callous-filled low spire; the suture is channelled. Shells are usually off-white or cream, overlaid with grey or bluish tent and arrow markings of varying sizes. The aperture and finely plaited columella are white.

**OLIVA LIGNARIA** f. *cryptospira*
Orange Ornate Olive.
*Ford 1891.* Southern Philippines.

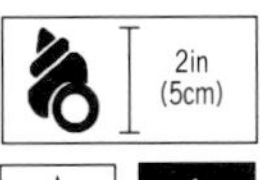


This lovely colour form of *O. lignaria* is common in its restricted range, the Sulu Archipelago. The variety displays all the major shape characteristics of its more common cousin. The deep gold-coloured glaze is often thin enough to allow faint pale grey spiral zigzag or tent marks to show through.

**OLIVA TRICOLOR**
Three-coloured Olive. *Lamarck 1811.*
Indo-Pacific.

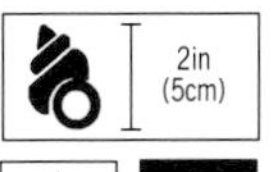


It is indeed marked with at least three attractive colours – mottling and reticulations of olive green, bluish beige undertones, and pale orange or salmon fasciole and columella. The shell is cylindrically oblong, with a short calloused spire. A characteristic feature are the near-black oblique tessellations, or lines, on the spire.

**OLIVA TIGRINA**
Tiger Olive. *Lamarck 1811.*
Indo-Pacific.

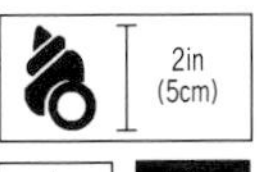


The broad and heavy tiger olive has a low spire and a calloused low ridge at the posterior end of the aperture. The colour is a creamy yellow, overlaid with indistinct hazy greyish blue dots and tent markings. The depicted specimen is one of many beautiful examples now coming from Mozambique.

**OLIVA LIGNARIA** f. *fordi*
*Johnson 1910.*
Southern Philippines.

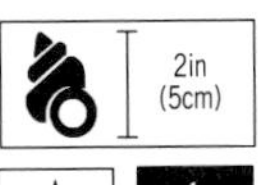


The dark brown form, and the albino form *albescens*, which is shown alongside it, are again restricted in habitat to the Sulu Archipelago. All four variations of *O. lignaria* are very popular with olive enthusiasts.

**OLIVA RETICULATA**
Blood Olive. *Röding 1798.*
Indo-Pacific.

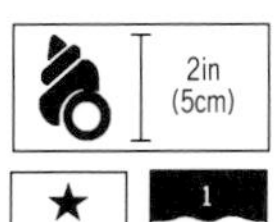


A solid, elongate and medium-sized shell, it is slightly convex. There is a distinctive calloused ridge at the posterior end of the aperture on the body whorl – rather similar to several other species in the genus. It bears rich dark green brown markings over a pale green or yellow background; the columella and fasciole are a deep red orange.

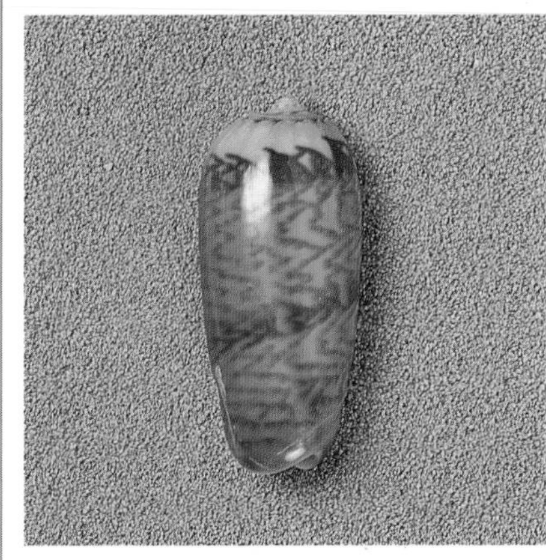

**OLIVA HIRASEI**
Hirase's Olive. *Kira 1959.*
Japan to Philippines.

An elongated cylindrical olive, with a high rounded shoulder, its spire is very low and somewhat calloused. It is attractively marked with two or three spiral bands of closely aligned tent marks, with numerous hazy zigzag lines between them, over a dull orange or cream background. The darkly coloured and patterned shell seen here is from south-western Taiwan.

**OLIVA TIGRINA** f. *glandiformis*
Black Tiger Olive.
*Marrat 1871*. Indian Ocean.

Virtually identical to its more common counterpart *O. tigrina*, this colour form is distinctly different, in that there is no evidence of dots or tent marks, the shell being completely or mostly a dark greyish black; sometimes there are broken spiral bands of cream or off-white. The aperture is white as is the columella apart from its base, which is tinged with salmon. Both shells here are from Mozambique.

**OLIVA ANNULATA** f. *carnicolor*
Blood-coloured Olive.
*Dautzenberg 1927*. South-West Pacific.

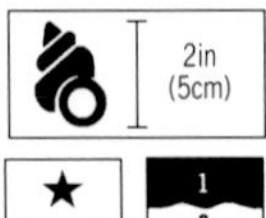

One form of several within the *O. annulata* complex, it is a beautiful apricot to pinkish orange colour, and in most cases it has a broad body whorl which is often centrally and spirally ridged, a characteristic of some forms. The columella is strongly plaited; the interior is white. This specimen is from the Sulu Sea.

**OLIVA ANNULATA** f. *intricata*
*Dautzenberg 1927*.
South-West Pacific.

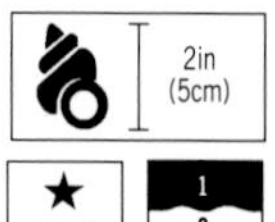

The background of this beautiful form is cream, overlaid with haphazard hazy and distinct tent markings of pale brown and greyish black; the raised spire, with its channelled suture, is partly calloused and is a deep salmon colour. The interior is deep orange; the columella off-white, but darker at the anterior, and the broad fasciole bears striking blue black oblique lines.

**OLIVA RUFULA**
Reddish Olive. *Duclos 1835*. South-West Pacific, particularly Philippines.

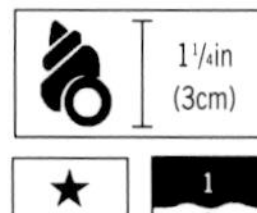

A short cylindrical olive, it has a low spire and channelled suture. It is invariably marked with broad chestnut brown spiral or oblique bands over a fawn background. There is a small calloused ridge at the posterior end of the aperture. The finely pleated columella is white, but tinged with pale orange at the anterior.

**OLIVA CARNEOLA** f. *bizonalis*
*Dautzenberg 1927.*
South-West Pacific.

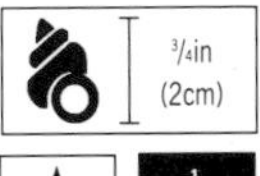

This is an extremely variable group of tiny olives, giving rise to numerous named forms and varieties. The very pretty two-banded form occurs in several colours, as shown. Occasionally the bands are raised into spiral ridges, as seen in the smaller yellow shell.

**OLIVA BULBIFORMIS**
Rounded Olive. *Duclos 1835.*
Indo-Pacific.

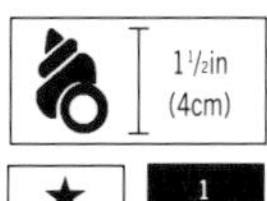

As the name implies, this is short, rather swollen and bulbous; it is variable in colour, and the three shells show some of the numerous variations. They all, however, display very fine tent markings throughout. The interior is usually a greyish white, and the inner edge of the lip is tinged with the exterior colour. These specimens are from the Philippines.

**OLIVA OLIVA**
Common Olive. *L. 1758.*
Indo-Pacific.

This is the true type species of the genus. I think this olive has confused more collectors, due to its great variation of pattern and colour, than any other species in the genus; the shape and the dark grey interior is, fortunately, always constant. Much interbreeding takes place, and the result is numerous named forms and varieties. For simplicity's sake, I have selected a few of the many variants, most originating from New Guinea.

**OLIVA SIDELIA**
Pretty Olive. *Duclos 1835.*
Indo-Pacific.

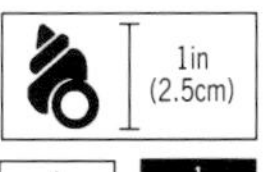

A small cylindrical and elongated species, the pretty olive is again very variable in colour and pattern and there are several named forms. I believe there is much hybridization within the complex, and have therefore included all the forms shown under the one species. All the shells seen here were dredged off Cuddalore, India.

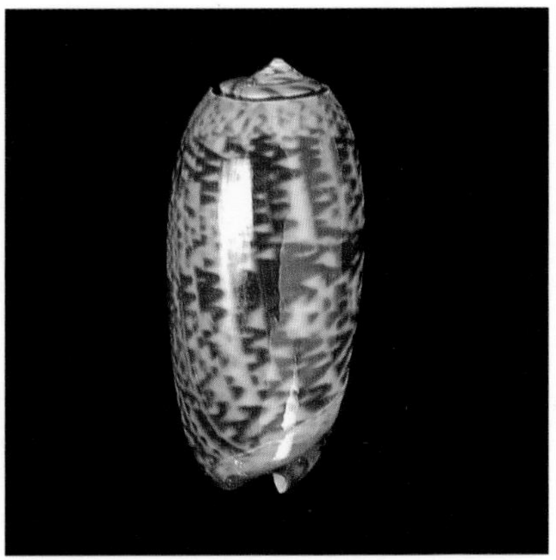

**OLIVA FUNEBRALIS**
*Lamarck 1811.*
South-West Pacific.

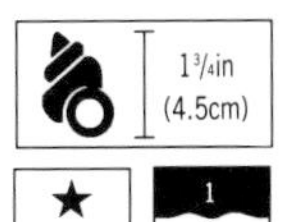

A handsome medium-sized olive, it has a low partly calloused spire and channelled suture; the body whorl has rather convex sides. The pale olive green background is overlaid with black tent or arrow markings that are thickened and axially arranged. The coarsely plaited columella and aperture are white.

**OLIVA OLIVA** f. *oriola*
Little Black Olive. *Lamarck 1811.*
South-West Pacific.

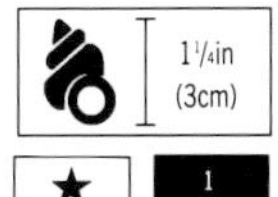

This is one form, the classification of which I happen to agree with. I have seen literally hundreds of specimens and they have always been identical – apart from the length of the shell. They are very commonly fished in the central Philippines.

**OLIVA MINIACEA** f. *marrati*
*Johnson 1871.*
South-West Pacific.

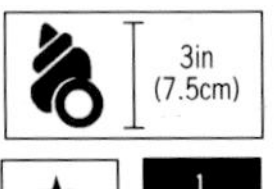

3in (7.5cm)

This very handsome dark brown, almost black shell, with its deep orange interior, is a colour form of the more common O. *miniacea*, described elsewhere. Choice shells that are large and unscarred are difficult to find; the depicted specimen is from the Sulu Sea.

**OLIVA VIDUA**
Black Olive. *Röding 1798.*
Indo-Pacific.

2¼in (5.5cm)

This olive comes in many named colour forms, but the shape varies little. It is a large shell, elongated, slightly ovate, and somewhat swollen at the posterior. The spire is usually flat, and there is a distinctive calloused ridge at the posterior end of the aperture on the columella side. Shells are dark brown or black, with a white aperture.

**OLIVA VIDUA** f. *cincta*
*Dautzenberg 1927.*
Indo-Pacific.

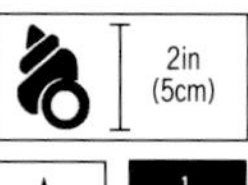

2in (5cm)

This attractive variant of O. *vidua* is a pale to mid-toned olive green, overlaid with prominent black blotches and bands that are obliquely and spirally laid. The aperture is white, as is the columella, although the anterior tip is a salmon colour. This specimen is from Kuta, Bali.

**OLIVA TEXTILINA**
Textile Olive. *Lamarck 1811.*
South-West Pacific.

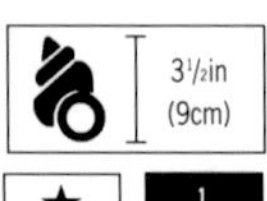

3½in (9cm)

A large, thick and somewhat broad species, this is slightly variable in pattern, although all display numerous hazy or distinct tent marks or zigzag lines, some in closely packed spiral bands. There is a strong callosity on the columella side of the posterior end of the aperture. Spires can be sunken or raised, as seen in the two depicted specimens.

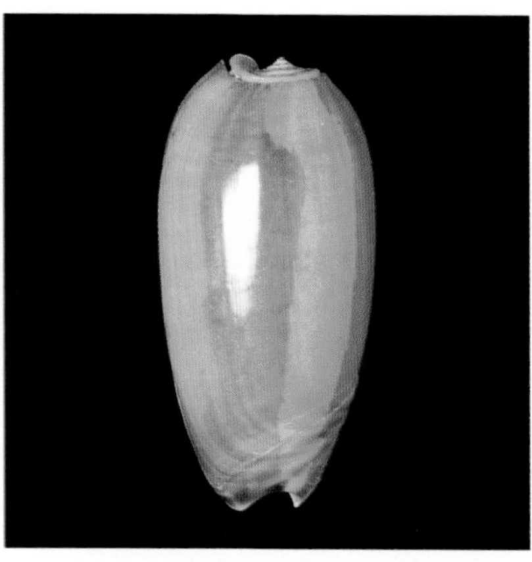

**OLIVA VIDUA** f. *aurata*
*Röding 1798.*
Indo-Pacific.

2in (5cm)

A rich orange brown colour variation of O. *vidua*, it portrays the major shape characteristics of the species. The colour form shown falls between paler, more yellowish green and mid-brown species. The depicted shell was collected in Bali.

**OLIVA TREMULINA** f. *concinna*
*Marrat 1871.*
South-West Pacific.

2in (5cm)

The O. *tremulina* complex is another controversially arranged group, with several named variations. The dark brown form shown seems to be the accepted colour for the form, and the lighter golden shell could be described as the form *chrysoides* by some. Again, I believe there is much hybridization within the species. Both shells are from the New Hebrides.

**OLIVA TREMULINA** *f. oldi*
Old's Olive. *Zeigler 1969.*
South-West Pacific.

This colour and possibly locality variant seems to vary little. The shell is a pale creamy orange, overlaid with attractive grey tent and zigzag markings; often, there are broad spiral bands. The columella is a pale salmon colour. The larger of the two shells is from the Solomon Islands, while the smaller is from Vila, New Hebrides.

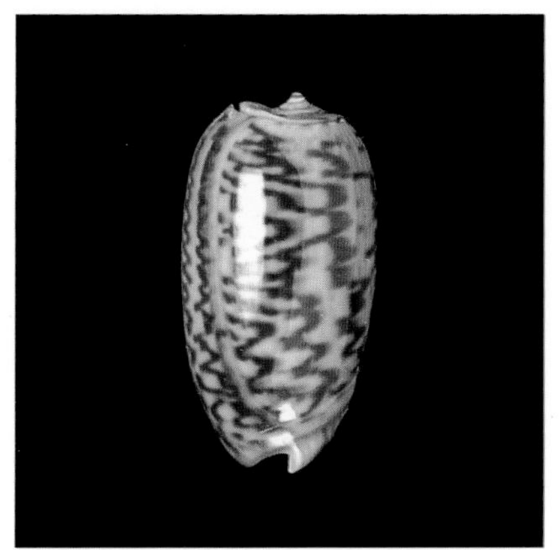

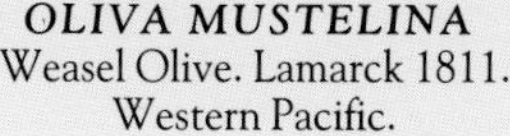

**OLIVA MUSTELINA**
Weasel Olive. Lamarck 1811.
Western Pacific.

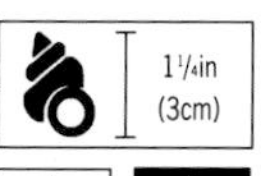

A smallish cylindrical elongate species, it has a depressed spire and a channelled suture. There is a low but thickened and calloused ridge at the posterior end of the aperture on the columella side. The shell is a pretty violet colour within, and the pale grey green exterior bears strong black axial zigzag lines. This specimen is from Rabaul, New Britain.

**OLIVA MULTIPLICATA**
*Reeve 1850.*
Japan and Taiwan.

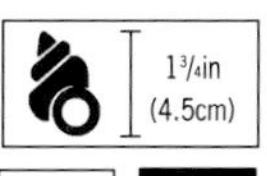

Many specimens – like those depicted here – used to come from Taiwan, but in common with many other shells from that region their supply has dwindled, due to changed fishing methods. The shell is slender and tall, with almost straight sides and a high spire. This is one of the few olives with numerous very fine columella plaits. The colour and pattern variations that exist are similar to those specimens shown.

**OLIVA AUSTRALIS**
Australian Olive. *Duclos 1835.*
Australia and New Guinea.

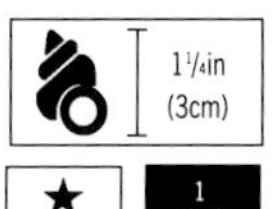

This is one of very few olives which hardly vary, either in shape or pattern and colour. It is a slender fusiform shell with a high spire. A creamy white, it is overlaid with fine oblique and irregular lines and squiggles. The depicted specimen is from southern Australia.

## OLIVA TESSELLATA

Tessellated Olive. *Lamarck 1811.*
Western Pacific.

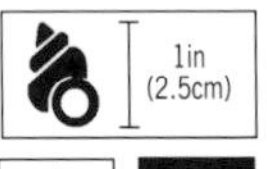


A stocky little olive, it is ovate, with a low calloused covered spire. The pattern and colour are more or less constant – a rich creamy yellow overall, with haphazard small spots or blotches of bluish purple. The aperture and columella plaits are a vivid and rich purple. The lip margin and canal extremity are white.

## OLIVA BAILEYI

Bailey's Olive. *Petuch 1979.*
Solomon Islands.

A recently described and attractive species, endemic to the Solomon Islands, it is elongate and cylindrical with an almost flat spire and channelled suture. The shell is a creamy yellow, overlaid with quite strong oblique light brown lines, not unlike those of *O. rufofulgurata*, but more coarsely marked. The depicted shell was dredged in 540ft (164m), which is deep for an olive, off Yandina, Russell Islands.

## OLIVA BULOWI

Bulow's Olive. *Sowerby 1889.*
New Britain Islands.

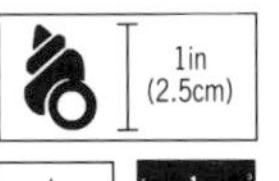


A pretty, small but solid olive, it is rather similar in shape and size to *O. parkinsoni*, but lacks the distinctive angled and ridged shoulder, although it is rather inflated at that point. The shell is attractively patterned with oblique and broad, both hazy and clear, purple maroon lines, over a cream or orange background. The aperture and columella are white. The species is endemic to the New Britain Islands.

## OLIVA RUFOFULGURATA

*Schepman 1911.*
Western Pacific.

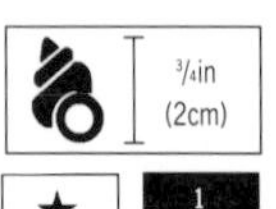


A tiny cylindrical little shell, it is slightly inflated at the posterior. The spire is low; the suture is channelled; and the columella is finely plaited. The shell is prettily and delicately marked with very fine axial zigzag and oblique lines of pale orange brown on a creamy yellow background.

## OLIVA PARKINSONI

Parkinson's Olive. *Prior 1975.*
New Guinea.

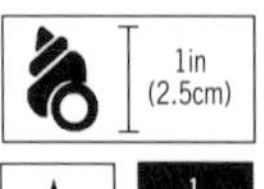


Endemic to New Guinea, this is a very distinctive little olive with a tall spire and somewhat "stepped" whorls; the body whorl is angled and ridged at the shoulder. Pattern and colour vary little, and are adequately displayed by the two specimens shown. This is a popular collectors' shell.

## OLIVA RUBROLABIATA

Red-lipped Olive. *H. Fischer 1902.*
New Hebrides.

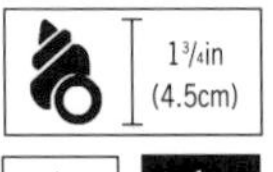

One of the most striking and attractive olives, it is endemic to the New Hebrides and is most sought-after by collectors. The thickened lip and plaited columella are vividly coloured with a rich red orange; elsewhere there are spiral lines and bands of charcoal grey over a pale grey or creamy yellow background. There is also a prominent calloused ridge at the posterior end of the aperture.

**OLIVANCILLARIA GIBBOSA**
Gibbose Olive. *Born 1778.*
Southern India and Sri Lanka.

A solid heavy shell, endemic to southern India and Sri Lanka, it has an enlarged and inflated body whorl. The moderately tall spire is calloused and this extends around the suture to a thickened parietal wall and finally down to a plaited columella. The lip margin is thin. Shells are usually greyish, with a broad band of streaked brown and yellow above the fasciole. A pale orange form occurs occasionally.

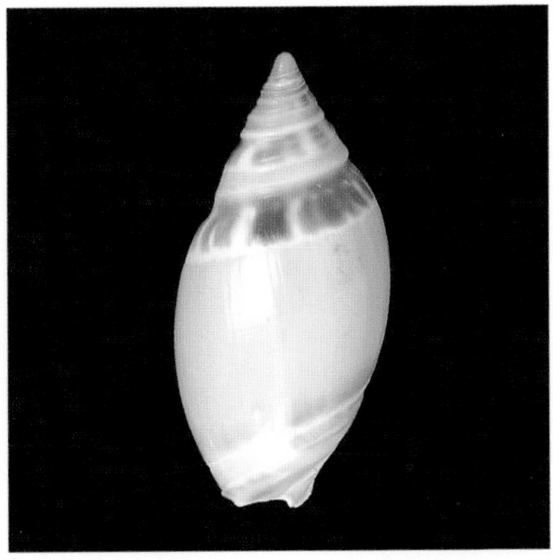

**AMALDA MARGINATA**
Margin Ancilla. *Lamarck 1811.*
Southern Australia.

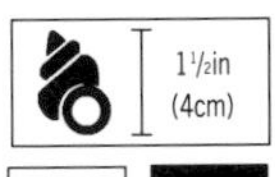


A small lightweight rather inflated shell, it has a tall spire, and there is a fine raised spiral ridge above the suture. The columella is plaited and slightly twisted. The overall colour is a creamy beige, and there are dark brown broken spiral bands at the shoulders. A shallow-water dweller, in sand, it is endemic to southern Australia.

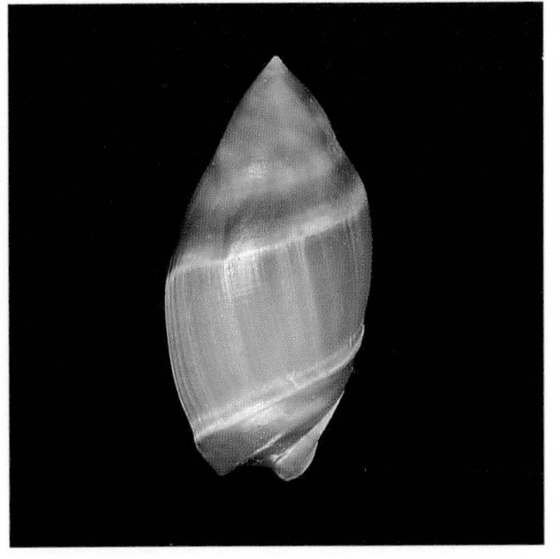

**AMALDA AUSTRALIS**
Southern Ancilla. *Sowerby 1830.*
New Zealand.

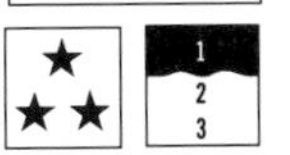


This attractive dark-coloured ancilla is short and rather bulbous. The high spire is heavily calloused. The columella is plaited, the fasciole broad and ridged. The interior is a deep grey brown, while the exterior is bluish grey, with a brown spire and fasciole. The columella is white. The species is endemic to New Zealand.

**OLIVANCILLARIA URCEUS**
Bear Ancilla. *Röding 1798.*
Brazil and Argentina.

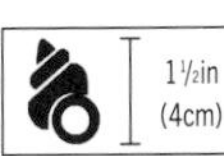


A heavily triangular shell, it has a flat heavily calloused spire and straight-sided body whorl. The parietal wall is much thickened and calloused, and this extends down to the columella. The pale grey shells bear numerous axial growth striae. There is a broad brownish fasciole. The depicted shell is from Guaraja, Brazil.

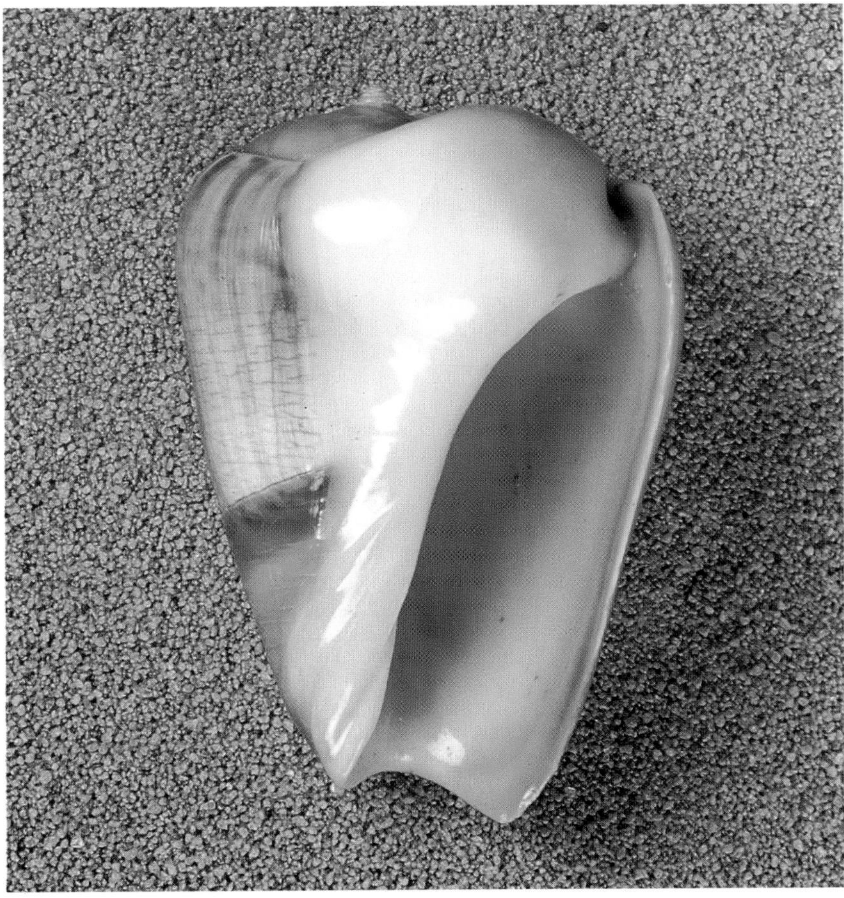

### AMALDA OBTUSA

Blunt Ancilla. *Swainson 1825.*
South Africa.

This bulbous heavy species has a low and rounded calloused spire. The plaited and twisted columella is white and extends upward to a large calloused white parietal area. The exterior of the shell is beige, with broad brown bands and a thin white band at the centre. There is a wide off-white groove above the fasciole. A deep-water species, rarely live-taken, it is endemic to South Africa.

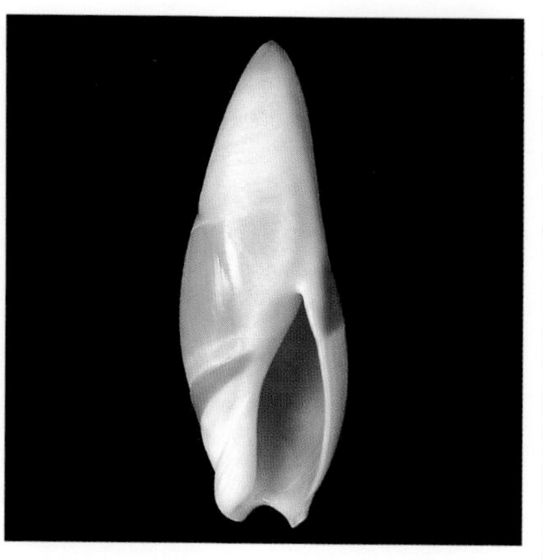

### AMALDA HINOMOTOENSIS

*Yokoyama 1922.*
Japan and Taiwan.

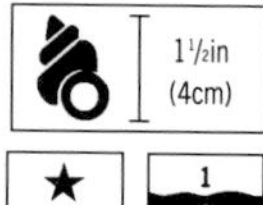


A small slender species, it has a tall and heavily calloused spire – more so ventrally, where the callosity joins the upper parietal wall. The slightly inflated body whorl is fawn in colour and has two broad brown bands – one at the shoulder and the other on the fasciole. This shell is occasionally fished in moderately deep water.

### ANCILLA CINGULATA

Honey-banded Ancilla. *Sowerby 1830.*
Eastern and South-eastern Australia.

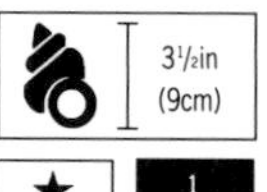


Also popularly known by its synonym, *A. valesiana*, this is a very lightweight and thin shell with rounded glossy whorls and a tall spire. The shoulders are slightly angled below the suture. The early whorls are a rich honey or amber colour, as is the fasciole. The apex and body whorl shoulder are white, and the rest of the shell is a pinkish cream. There are extremely fine axial striae and spiral threads. This shell is endemic to eastern and south-eastern Australia.

### AMALDA MONTROUZIERI

Montrouzier's Ancilla. *Souverbie 1860.*
New Caledonia and Fiji.

An off-white to pale cream ancilla, it has a slender fusiform shell. The spire and body whorl shoulder are calloused. An open groove runs above the fasciole, and the columella has two or three plaits. A rare species, it is seldom available to collectors.

### ANCILLA LIENARDI

Lienardo's Ancilla. *Bernardi 1858.*
Brazil.

This most beautiful shell of rich orange coloration is smooth and highly glossy. It is ovate and rather inflated with rounded calloused whorls. There is a white depressed groove running above the fasciole and a large gaping umbilicus. The interior is pure white. Very popular with collectors, it is endemic to Brazil.

### ANCILLA ALBOCALLOSA

*Lischke 1873.*
Japan.

A thicker more solid shell than *A. cingulata*, it has a typically calloused tall spire and an inflated body whorl. It is greyish beige, with a rich brown shoulder and lower spire; the strongly ridged fasciole is brown and there is a broad white groove above this. The species is endemic to Japan, and the specimen shown here was found 300ft (91m) deep off Suruga Bay, Shizuoka.

**ANCILLA GLABRATA**
Golden Ancilla. *L. 1758.*
Caribbean.

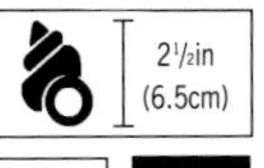

This large and heavy species is very close to *A. lienardi* in shape, but the colours are less vivid, being a pale cream to a pale orange or apricot. The spire is thickened and calloused. There is a large open umbilicus and a much-twisted columella and fasciole.

**ANCILLA MAURITIANA**
Mauritian Ancilla. *Sowerby 1830.*
Western Indian Ocean.

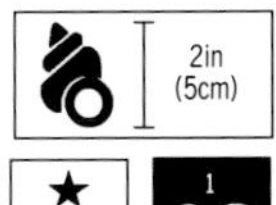

A lightweight and globose species, it has a very low rounded and calloused spire and a much enlarged body whorl. The exterior colours vary from white through to dark brown. The aperture is white. The columella is slightly twisted and there is a broad fasciole.

**ANCILLISTA MUSCAE**
Orange-tipped Ancilla. *Pilsbry 1926.*
Northern Australia.

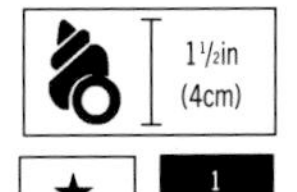

A very thin and lightweight species, it is broad at the anterior and gradually tapers to a tall spire with a rounded and deep orange protoconch. Apart from this, the shell is pure white. There are minute axial striae and a strong broad fasciole. This species inhabits intertidal sand flats.

**ANCILLA *Sp.***
Western Australia.

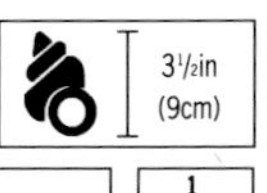

This shell has recently been trawled off Port Hedland at a depth of 660ft (200m) and so far I have been unable to trace a reliable classification. A superb example of the genus, it is fusiform with a tall spire with virtually straight sides, and an enlarged and centrally broadened body whorl. Of the few specimens I have seen, the depicted shell portrays the general appearance and colour of them all.

**ANCILLA CASTANEA**
Chestnut Ancilla. *Sowerby 1830.*
North-West Indian Ocean and Red Sea.

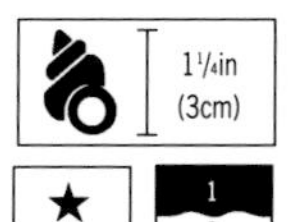

A robust and solid little shell, the chestnut ancilla is ovate with a low and heavily calloused spire. The aperture is wide and gaping. The colour is either pale, mid-toned or very dark brown throughout, and there is a fine yellow groove above the fasciole. The shell in the photograph was collected in shallow water in the Gulf of Oman.

**OLIVELLA VOLUTELLA**
Volute-shaped Olivella. *Lamarck 1811.*
Western Central America.

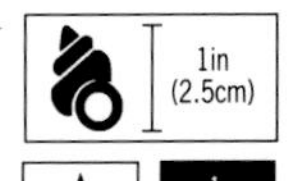

This short slender little shell has a moderately tall spire. The suture is channelled, and there is a groove above the fasciole. The columella has fine plicae. Colours vary from albino and cream, through to dark purplish brown. These two specimens are from Pedro Gonzales Island, Panama.

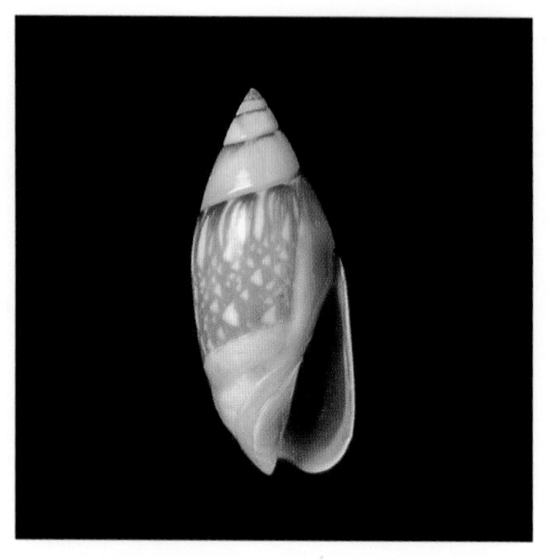

**OLIVELLA DAMA**
Dama Dwarf Olive. *Wood 1828.*
Western Central America.

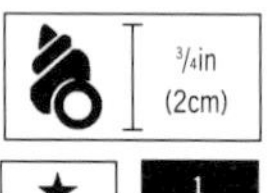

This is the type specimen of the genus. It is short and robust, with a moderate spire. The suture is slightly impressed. The shell is creamy white, overlaid with fine pale brown axial lines and reticulations on the body whorl. The interior, columella and parietal wall are tinged with violet. The fasciole is broad and yellowish cream. The depicted shell is from San Felipe, Mexico.

**AGARONIA TRAVASSOSI**
Travasso's Ancilla. *Morretes 1938.*
Brazil.

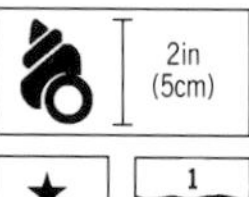

A fusiform shell, endemic to Brazil, it has a tall rather sharp spire and a body whorl which is inflated at the centre. The suture is channelled. The two shells in the photograph portray the major pattern and colour characteristics. They are both from deep water off Rio de Janeiro.

**AGARONIA PROPATULA**
Open-mouthed Ancilla. *Conrad 1849.*
Western Central America.

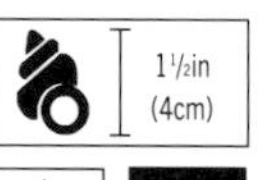

A slim fusiform ancilla, it is a particularly appealing greyish blue. The columella is finely pleated and there is a broad fasciole of dark grey. The apex and early whorls are creamy white. The shell seen here was collected in 20ft (6m) off Costa Rica.

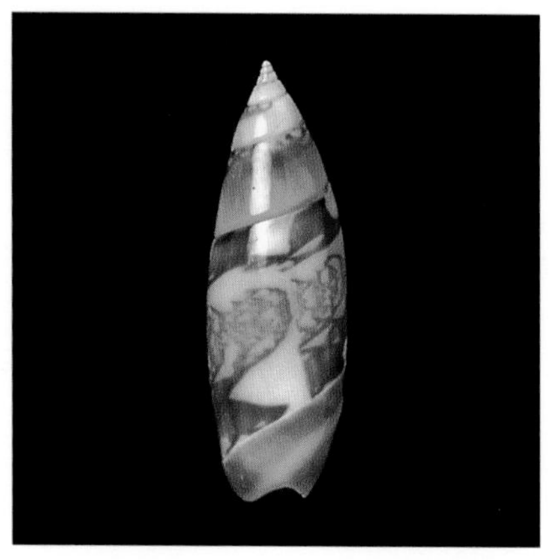

**OLIVELLA GRACILIS**
Graceful Dwarf Olive. *Broderip and Sowerby 1825.* Western Central America.

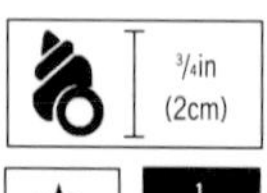

A very slender highly glossy little shell, with most attractive patterns, it usually displays two broad spiral brown bands of zigzag markings with fine reticulations between them. The undercolour is creamy white. This particular specimen is from shallow water, Nayarit, Mexico.

**AGARONIA ACUMINATA**
Pointed Ancilla. *Lamarck 1811.*
West Africa.

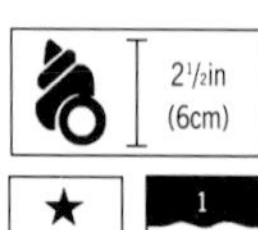

A smooth fairly glossy species, the pointed ancilla is fusiform in shape, with a low spire and channelled suture. The colours vary from an overall pale cream through to strongly marked specimens, as in the smallest of the three depicted specimens. These were all collected in Angola in shallow water.

**AGARONIA LUTARIA**
*Röding 1798.*
Indonesia.

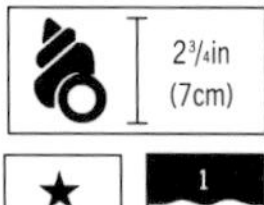

A tall and elegantly fusiform agaronia, it comes from a restricted range, possibly only Java and surrounding islands. The spire is tall, and the body whorl is inflated at the centre. The suture is channelled and a calloused area above this runs around the whorls to the tip of the aperture. The cream shell is overlaid with both distinct and hazy reticulation. There is a very broad tan and cream fasciole.

**AGARONIA CONTORTUPLICATA**
Twisted Olive. *Reeve 1850.*
Uruguay to Brazil.

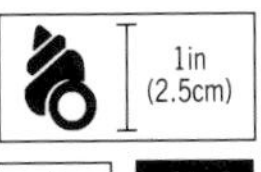

A small ovate shell, it has a lowish spire, channelled suture and a twisted and impressed columella – from which comes its name. There is a broad cream band above the fasciole, apart from which the shell is a pale to mid-grey colour. The interior is a rich brown.

SUPER FAMILY
MURICOIDEA

FAMILY
## MARGINELLIDAE
(Margin Shells)

This very large family contains at least 600 species, mostly small or very small highly colourful smooth and glossy shells. The majority of species are shallow-water sand dwellers, found in warm tropical waters, especially in West Africa, where many occur. The lip edge is thickened – hence the name "margin" shell. Classification is complex and confusing, but in a simplified form, the following genera are to be considered: *Marginella, Bullata, Glabella, Persicula, Prunum* and *Cryptospira*, and, within another subfamily, based on the details of the radula, is *Afrivoluta*.

**BULLATA MATTHEWSI**
Matthew's Marginella. *Van Mol and Tursch 1967.* Brazil.

A medium-to-large species, it is virtually identical in shape to *B. bullata*. The sunken spire is calloused and the thickened rounded lip is minutely dentate. The rather twisted columella has at least four strong plaits. The shell is an overall pale tan colour, with darker mid-brown spiral bands and lines. The depicted specimen was collected ex-pisce of Fortaleza.

**SYLVANOCOCHLIS ANCILLA**
*Hanley 1859.*
South Africa.

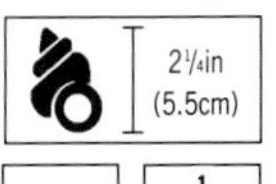

A robust solid shell, endemic to South Africa, it is inflated at the centre. It is an overall dirty beige to light brown colour, with numerous very fine growth striae. There is a deep open groove above the fasciole. The columella and parietal wall are white and calloused. The shell depicted was trawled in 396ft (120m) on Agulhas Bank.

**AUSTROGINELLA MUSCARIA**
Fly Marginella. *Lamarck 1822.*
Southern Australia and Tasmania.

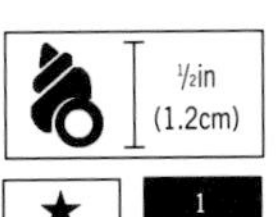

A tiny off-white or cream margin, the fly marginella resembles a small strombus. The spire is tall; the body whorl is rather flattened; and the parietal area, columella and lip are calloused and thickened. The two specimens shown are from Pambula, New South Wales, found in shallow water.

**BULLATA BULLATA**
Bubble Marginella. *Born 1778.*
Brazil.

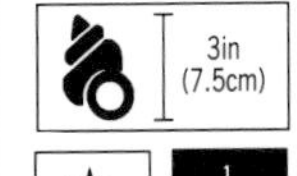

Apart from *Afrivoluta pringlei*, this is the largest margin in the family. It is a solid, smooth and highly glossy shell, with a calloused and sunken spire and a very large body whorl which is inflated at the posterior. Its colour and insignificant markings vary little. The shell depicted was collected in sand at 66ft (20m) off Itaparica Island.

### CLOSIA LILACINA
Lilac Marginella. *Sowerby 1846.*
Brazil.

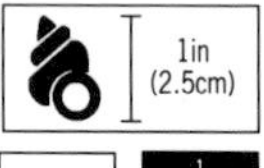


This is rather like a miniature *B. bullata*, but it is more squat. The spire is sunken and the body whorl inflated. The lip is much thickened, and finely dentate, and is a rich pink colour. The rest of the shell is a pale pinkish grey with three broad darker bands. An offshore dweller.

### CRYPTOSPIRA STRIGATA
Striped Marginella. *Dillwyn 1817.*
South-East Asia.

The large showy striped marginella has a depressed callous-filled spire and a very large ovate body whorl which is inflated at the posterior. The two depicted specimens are the normal axially striped form and a variant, which totally lacks markings and is known as *C. s. unicolor*; both are from southern Thailand, in shallow water.

### CRYPTOSPIRA ANGUSTATA
Narrow Marginella. *Sowerby 1846.*
Southern India and Sri Lanka.

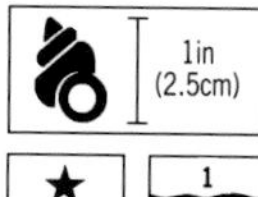


This elongated margin is somewhat inflated at the centre. The spire is totally hidden by callouses and this callosity extends along the outer margin of a thickened smooth lip. It is an overall grey fawn, with several broad and fine spiral bands of grey. Its range extends from offshore to deep water.

### CRYPTOSPIRA VENTRICOSA
Broad Marginella. *Fischer 1807.*
South-East Asia.

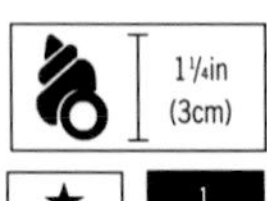


This species inhabits shallow water in mud. It has a very low, almost flat, spire, and an enlarged ovate body whorl which is broadened at the posterior. There are about five columella plaits; the thickened lip is more or less smooth. It is pale to mid-grey throughout, with an off-white interior.

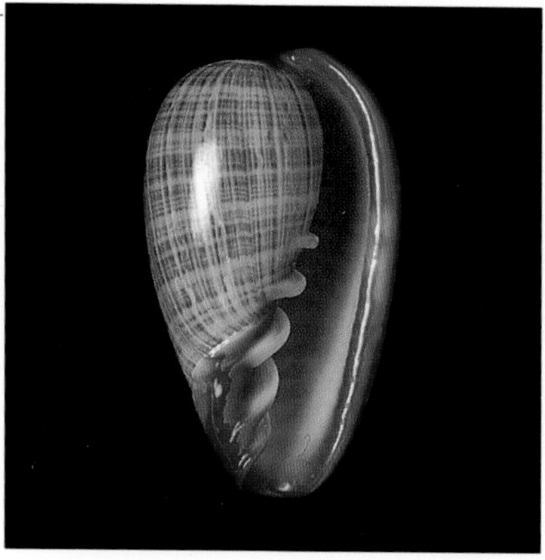

### CRYPTOSPIRA ELEGANS
Elegant Marginella. *Gmelin 1791.*
South-East Asia.

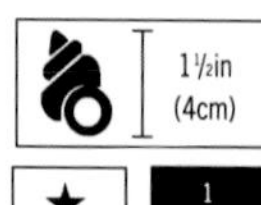


Virtually identical in shape and size to *Cryptospira strigata*, the elegant marginella differs in that the patterning is of broad and mid-grey spiral bands on a pale grey background, intersected by numerous axial pale grey lines. Also the lip and lower columella and fasciole area are of a deep reddish brown. It is found in shallow water in sand.

### GLABELLA ADANSONI
Adanson's Marginella. *Kiener 1834.*
West Africa.

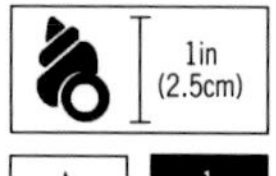


A small species, it has low axial ribs on the shoulders and a thickened rather recurved lip. There are strong columella pleats and very fine denticles on the inner lip. It is attractively marked with thin black axial wavy lines over a greyish green background.

**GLABELLA HARPAEFORMIS**
Harplike Marginella. *Sowerby 1846.*
West Africa.

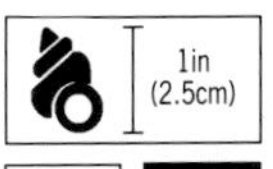

Though it is very similar in shape to G. *adansoni*, the ribs of this species tend to be a little longer, and the colouring is entirely different, being a creamy grey overlaid with tiny black spirally-laid dots. The inner lip is dentate and there are four columella pleats.

**HYALINA PERGRANDIS**
Pink Marginella. *Clover 1974.*
Gulf of Oman.

This is another elongate and cylindrical species which is rather bulbous at the centre. It has a very low spire with a pink protoconch; the thickened white lip has pink patches, and the greyish pink dorsum is overlaid with irregular white blotches. It inhabits intertidal sandy areas, and is endemic to the Gulf of Oman.

**MARGINELLA CLERYII**
Clery's Marginella. *Petit 1836.*
West Africa.

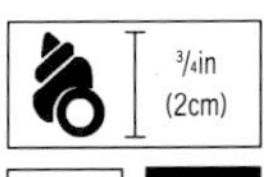

This is a beautifully marked shell, with vivid black axial wavy lines over a pale greyish-green background; some broad hazy spiral bands may be present. It is fusiform, with a high spire. There are about four strong columella plaits, and the thickened lip is smooth

**GLABELLA PSEUDOFABA**
Queen Marginella. *Sowerby 1846.*
West Africa.

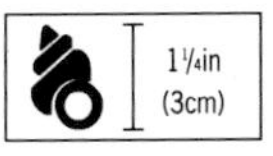

A beautiful collectors' item, the queen marginella is similar in shape to both G. *adansoni* and G. *harpaeformis*, but is much larger and broader. The shoulders are sharply ribbed and the lip much thickened and dentate. The shell is off-white with hazy blue grey wavy bands, on top of which are numerous vivid small black squares.

**HYALINA RUBELLA**
f. *navicella*. *Reeve 1864.*
Cape Verde Islands.

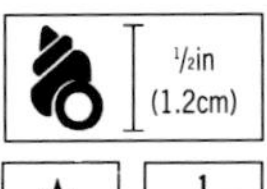

A very small smooth shell, endemic to the Cape Verde Islands, it is elongate and cylindrical. The spire is almost flat and rounded. The lip is thickened and smooth, and there are fine columella plaits. The colour varies from cream or beige to pink, with several broad spiral bands of darker colouring.

**MARGINELLA NEBULOSA**
Clouded Marginella. *Röding 1798.*
South Africa.

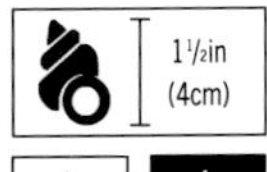

A lovely marginella, it is off-white or cream, overlaid with broad axial bands or haphazard patches of bluish grey. There are four strong columella plaits, the thickened lip has dark grey spots on the outer edge. The aperture area is white. The depicted shell is from western Cape Province.

**MARGINELLA FLOCCATA**
Woolly Marginella. *Sowerby 1889*.
South Africa.

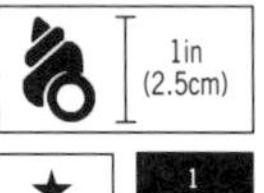

The woolly marginella has a lowish spire, with a rounded protoconch and a high shouldered body whorl which tapers at the anterior. The colour is off-white with hazy pale grey axial lines, over which are spiral rows of broken thin grey-brown lines. The plaited columella and smooth lip are white.

**MARGINELLA AURANTIA**
Golden Marginella. *Lamarck 1822*.
West Africa.

The name is rather misleading, as the basic colour is usually a dull reddish pink. The shell is similar in shape to *M. rosea*, but tends to be slimmer, with a taller spire and a rounded protoconch. The depicted specimen was collected in shallow water off Senegal.

**MARGINELLA GLABELLA**
Shiny Marginella. *L. 1758*. North-West Africa and Cape Verde Islands.

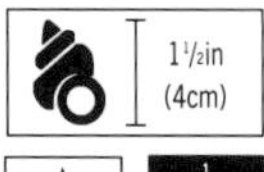

A solid, medium-sized species, it has a moderately tall spire, and the body whorl is rather inflated at the centre. The thickened lip is finely dentate and there are four columella plaits. Colours and patterns vary, but the depicted specimen shows a typical colour form. Its range extends from shallow to fairly deep water.

**MARGINELLA ROSEA**
Rosy Marginella. *Lamarck 1822*.
South Africa.

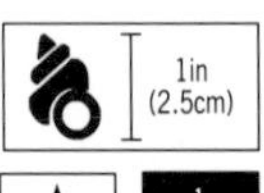

A very variably coloured species, it has a low spire and high shouldered body whorl. The inner lip is dentate. The three specimens shown portray some of the colour variations that exist. Live-taken specimens have become more readily available with increased scuba-diving activity in the region.

**MARGINELLA MUSICA**
Music Marginella. *Hinds 1844*.
South Africa.

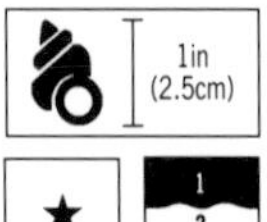

This rather thick and robust little shell has strong columella plaits and a thickened, rounded lip. It is most strikingly marked, with distinct black spiral bands on a greyish-green background. Live-taken shells are very scarce.

**MARGINELLA IRRORATA**
Glistening Marginella. *Menke 1828*.
West Africa.

This small, solid fusiform little shell has a tall spire with rounded whorls. The body whorl broadens at the centre. The shell is a creamy white, with a fine network of pale pink-grey markings with some larger, darker blotches on the shoulder. It is rather similar to *M. glabella* in shape, but much smaller.

**MARGINELLA SEBASTIANI**
Sebastian's Marginella. *Marché-Marchard and Rosso* 1979. West Africa.

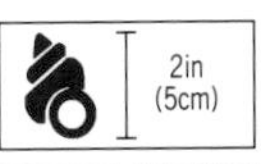


At one time this rather large and attractive margin was always erroneously known as M. *goodalli*. It has a large globose body whorl and a low rather calloused spire with a rounded protoconch. Beautifully coloured, its pinkish orange background is overlaid with numerous haphazard and large creamy-beige spots. It is possibly endemic to Senegal, in offshore waters.

**MARGINELLA PIPERATA**
Peppered Marginella. *Hinds* 1844. South Africa.

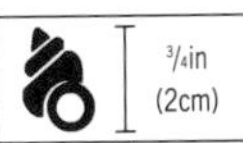


A very attractive little shell, it is often found beached, – live-taken specimens are scarce. This unusual form, known as M. *piperata albocincta*, has distinctive broad white spiral bands, between which are very fine dark grey reticulations. The thickened lip has strong dark grey lines.

**PERSICULA PERSICULA**
Spotted Marginella. *L.* 1758. West Africa.

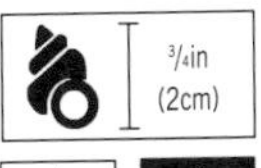


An ovate and rather bulbous margin, it has a flat or depressed, usually calloused, spire. The strong columella plaits extend up to the parietal area. It is beige or fawn, overlaid with large pinkish-brown spots.

**MARGINELLA DESJARDINI**
Desjardin's Marginella. *Marché-Marchard* 1957. West Africa.

Another beautifully marked and coloured margin, it is fusiform, with a long gently tapering body whorl. The spire is low and calloused. The depicted specimen, which shows typical colours and pattern is from Gorée Bay, Senegal, from moderately deep water. Shells are usually found at depths to 330 feet (100m).

**PERSICULA CINGULATA**
Girdled Margin. *Dillwyn 1817.*
West Africa.

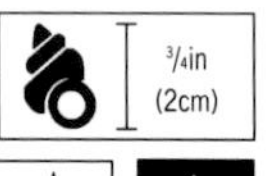

An ovate and inflated shell, this is very similar in shape and form to *Persicula persicula*. It is a creamy white, with conspicuous strong spiral brown lines. The specimen shown here was collected in shallow water in Senegal.

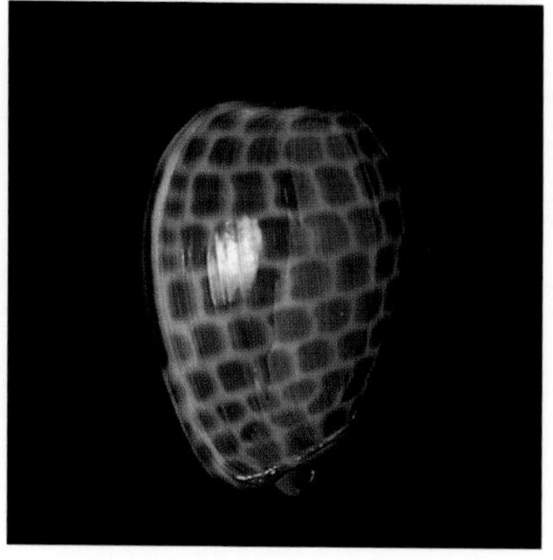

**PERSICULA ACCOLA**
Twinned Marginella. *Roth and Coan 1968.*
Panama.

A very handsome little shell, it displays unique dark grey squared-type markings on a pale creamy green background. The flat spire is callous covered, as are the columella and parietal wall. The lip margin is tinged with rich dark brown. A collectors' favourite, it is endemic to Panama.

**PRUNUM PRUNUM**
Plum Marginella. *Gmelin 1791.*
Caribbean to Brazil.

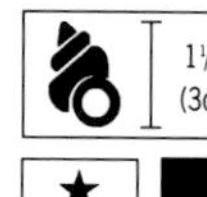

The plum marginella is an elongate ovate margin with a low calloused spire. The lip is thickened and smooth, and there are four strong narrow plaits on the columella. The lip margin is usually tinged with yellow and the overall colour varies from pale tan to mid-grey. (The specimen shown is rather pale in colour.)

**PERSICULA CORNEA**
Pale Marginella. *Lamarck 1822.*
Senegal, West Africa.

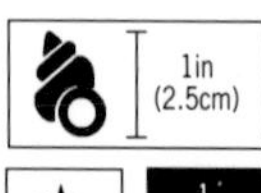

A rather elongate ovate margin, endemic to West Africa, it has a flat or sunken spire. There are fine lirae within the lip and the plaited columella and parietal wall are thinly calloused. These specimens of varying colours were collected in 49ft (15m) at Goree, Senegal.

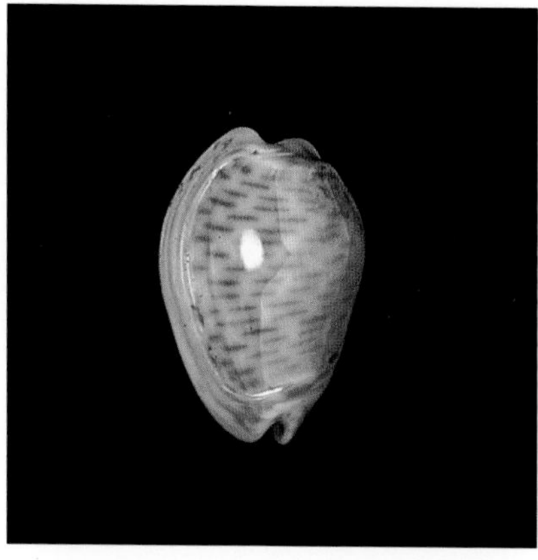

**PERSICULA INTERRUPTOLINEATA**
Broken-line Marginella. *Mühlfeld 1816.*
Caribbean.

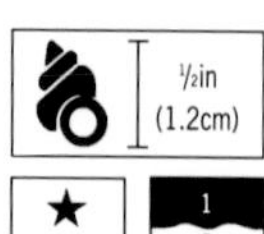

A tiny species with a virtually non-existent spire and an inflated body whorl, its lip is much thickened; there is a calloused glaze over the columella and parietal wall. It is a pale greenish beige overall, with very fine broken dark grey spiral lines.

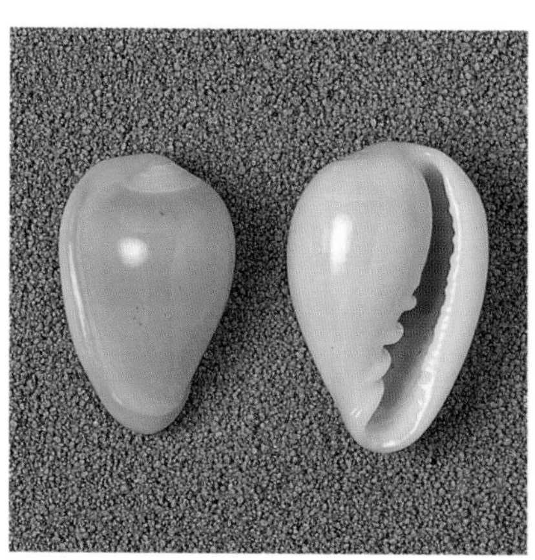

**PRUNUM LABIATA**
Royal Marginella. *Kiener 1841.*
Central America and Caribbean.

A solid thick medium-sized margin, this shell is rather inflated at the posterior. It is a beautiful rich cream colour, with a yellow-tinged and very thick lip on which are fine denticles. The spire is flat and heavily calloused. It is a sand dweller, living in intertidal waters.

**PRUNUM CINCTA**
Encircled Marginella. *Kiener 1834.*
West Africa.

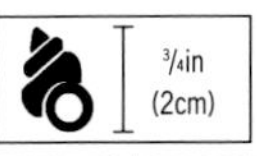


This attractively coloured species has the peculiarity of a deep orange callosity encircling the entire shell periphery. The underside and aperture are pure white. This shell lives in depths to about 132ft (40m).

SUPER FAMILY
MURICOIDEA

FAMILY
## MITRIDAE
(Mitre Shells)

Mitre shells are a very large group of several hundred carnivorous species inhabiting warm, shallow seas, although a few live in deep water. Most are colourful and attractive, and they are popular with collectors. They are generally slender, fusiform shells with tall spires, and they possess a prominent siphonal notch. There are several notable genera: *Mitra, Pterygia, Imbricaria, Scabricola, Subcancilla* and *Cancilla.* They have a worldwide distribution.

**MITRA PAPALIS**
Papal Mitre. *L. 1758.*
Indo-Pacific.

This mitre is large and heavy, with a very tall spire and almost straight-sided whorls. The shoulders are coronated at the suture; the lip bears sharp serrations; there are about five strong columella plaits. White overall, it displays very distinctive large crimson or maroon spots and blotches. The aperture and interior are cream. It inhabits coral rubble to about 99ft (30m).

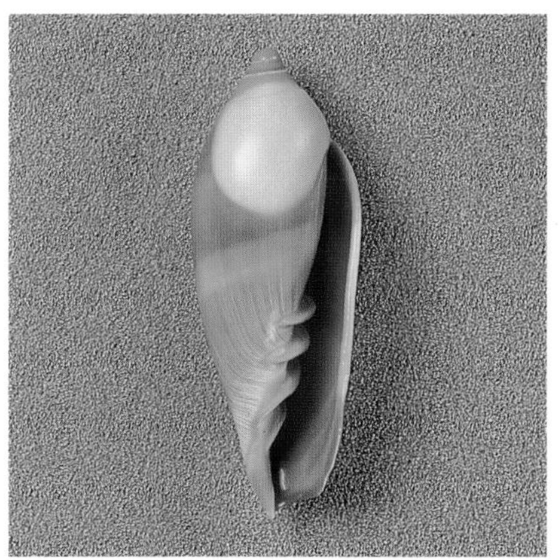

**AFRIVOLUTA PRINGLEI**
Pringle's Marginella. *Tomlin 1947.*
South Africa.

For many years, this, the largest known marginella, was considered to be a volute, but studies have shown this to be untrue. It is unique in form, with a distinct and very large calloused blotch from the spire to the posterior end of the aperture. A deep-water species, and very popular with collectors, it is endemic to South Africa.

**MITRA MITRA**
Episcopal Mitre. *L. 1758.*
Indo-Pacific.

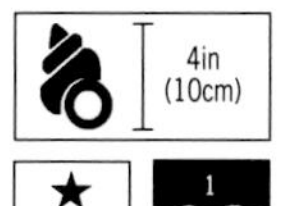


A very attractive and well-known shell, the episcopal mitre is patterned with vivid rich red squares and blotches on a white background. It is elongate-ovate in shape, with a tall spire with slightly convex-sided whorls. The lip is dentate and the columella bears strong plaits. The aperture colouring is creamy yellow. It is a shallow-water sand dweller.

**MITRA BOVEI**
Bové's Mitre. *Kiener 1838.*
Red Sea and Persian Gulf.

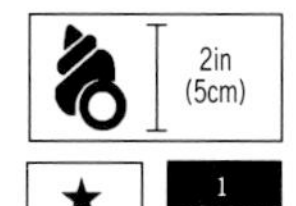


A fusiform shell, it has a tall spire and straight-sided whorls; the body whorl is enlarged at the centre. There are low rounded nodules below the suture. The depicted specimen, which was collected at 3.3ft (1m) in sand, under coral at Nabek, Gulf of Aqaba, shows typical colour and pattern for the species.

**MITRA INCOMPTA**
Tessellate Mitre. *Lightfoot 1786.*
Indo-Pacific.

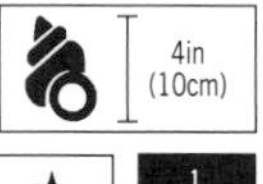

An elongate and narrow mitre, this has a tall spire and more or less straight-sided whorls. There are fine low axial ribs and pitted spiral grooves, creating a reticulated effect. The lip is crenulated and the columella has strong plaits. It is a cream shell, with distinct dark to mid-brown axial "flame" markings. A shallow-water reef dweller.

**MITRA CARDINALIS**
Cardinal Mitre. *Gmelin 1791.*
Indo-Pacific.

A shallow-water sand dweller, the cardinal mitre is distinctively patterned with spirally laid reddish brown squares or blotches on a creamy white background. It is a solid shell, with a medium height spire and convex whorls. The body whorl is rather inflated at the centre. There is a finely crenulated lip.

**MITRA BELCHERI**
Belcher's Mitre. *Hinds 1844.*
Western Central America.

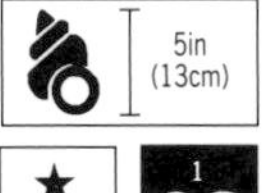

A large and heavy species of handsome proportions, Belcher's mitre is a pale cream or beige shell, covered with a black periostracum when alive. There are coarse flat spiral cords and wide incised interspaces. The suture is channelled. The lip margin is scalloped, and there are usually three strong low plaits on the columella.

**MITRA FRAGA**
Strawberry Mitre. *Quoy and Gaimard 1833.*
Indo-Pacific.

An attractive shell, with strong spiral cords, its suture is slightly impressed and the whorls have rather convex sides. The colour is variable, ranging from pale orange to deep red; some examples have pale spots on the cords. The lip is finely crenulated and there are lirae on the interior. There are four or five columella plaits.

**MITRA FUSIFORMIS** f. *zonata*
Zoned Mitre. *Marryat 1818.*
Mediterranean and North-West Africa.

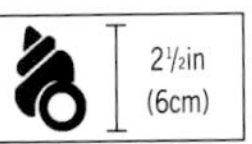

A most popular and sought-after collectors' shell, it is most usually retained with the periostracum intact – as seen here. It is a long and slender fusiform species, with a tall spire and a slightly channelled suture. The lip margin is thin and smooth. It inhabits depths from subtidal water to about 430ft (130m).

**MITRA PUNCTICULATA**
Punctured Mitre. *Lamarck 1811.*
Indo-Pacific.

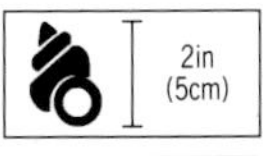

A richly coloured mitre, it is red and orange with off-white spots or blotches. The widely spaced spiral grooves are punctate; the whorl shoulders are coronated at the suture. This attractive shell inhabits intertidal coral reefs.

**MITRA RETUSA**
Blunt Mitre. *Lamarck 1811.*
Indo-Pacific.

This small solid species is ovate, with a low spire and an enlarged body whorl. The thickened lip margin is crenulate, and there are a few strong columella folds. Fine spiral grooves are present on the lower portion of the body whorl. Attractively patterned, it has rich dark brown or black axial streaks or stripes on a white and orange background.

**MITRA PYRAMIS**
*Wood 1828.*
Indo-Pacific.

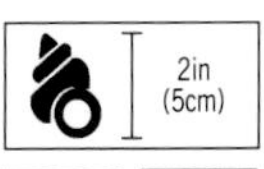

A beautiful shell, it is fusiform in shape and has an entirely cancellated texture, with low axial ribs and spiral grooves. The background is a reddish orange, embellished with white ribbing. The aperture is smooth and a pale creamy orange. The depicted specimen is from Bogo, Philippines.

**MITRA VEXILLUM**
*Reeve 1844.*
Indo-Pacific.

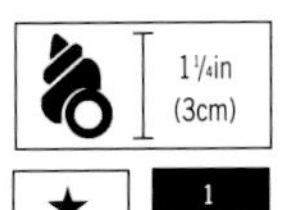

A medium-sized shell, this has a tall spire and slightly convex-sided whorls. Some specimens bear low spiral cords, but the depicted shell is smooth throughout. The pale orange background is overlaid with broad dark or mid-brown spiral bands. The species inhabits coral reefs, and this particular specimen is from Mahé, Seychelles.

**MITRA CHALYBEIA**
Steel Mitre. *Reeve 1844.*
Western Australia.

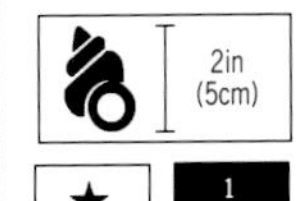

This species inhabits crevices or caves in tidal or subtidal rocky reefs and the depicted specimen, which portrays typical colour and pattern, was collected by a scuba diver off Carnac Island, Fremantle.

**PTERYGIA DACTYLUS**
Finger Mitre. *L. 1767.*
Indo-Pacific.

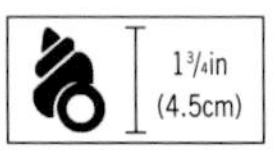


A medium-sized rather heavy and ovate shell, it has a low spire and inflated body whorl. The spiral grooves are fine and well spaced and there are numerous indistinct growth striae, although some specimens are completely smooth. The colour is off-white, with irregular hazy patches of pale grey or brown; and there are very fine spiral continuous or broken brown bands.

**PTERYGIA SINENSIS**
Chinese Mitre. *Reeve 1844.*
Japan to the Philippines.

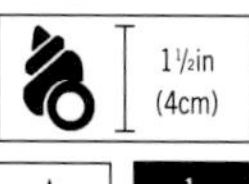


Rather similar in shape to *P. fenestrata*, this is narrower and more elongated. The shell is covered with fine reticulations and axial and spiral cords. The long lip margin is crenulate, and there are about nine columella folds. The colour is usually a dull greyish beige. It is found offshore in relatively shallow waters.

**IMBRICARIA OLIVAEFORMIS**
Olive-shaped Mitre. *Swainson 1821.*
Indo-Pacific.

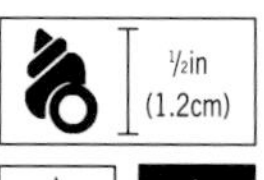


This tiny mitre is smooth in texture, with a spire of moderate size and a sharp protoconch. The colour varies between white and yellow; the apex and base of the columella are tinged with purple. It is an intertidal sand dweller.

**PTERYGIA FENESTRATA**
*Lamarck 1811.*
Indo-Pacific.

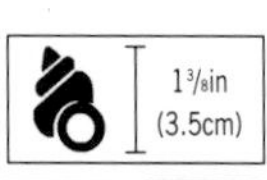


A small solid mitre, it is elongated and ovate, with a low spire. The aperture is long and narrow. There are several small sharp columella folds. The shell is coarsely sculptured, its low axial ribs intersected with spiral grooves creating a nodulose texture. Shells are variable in colour, and two forms are shown here, both originating from the Honiara Reefs, Solomon Islands.

## NEOCANCILLA CLATHRUS
*Gmelin 1791.*
Indo-Pacific.

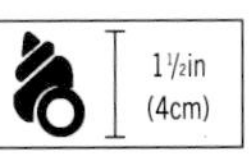

1½in (4cm)

I often confuse this medium-sized shell with *Scabricola variegata*. Certainly, the shape is similar, but both pattern and texture differ. This species has numerous very fine spiral and beaded cords intersected with occasional axial striae. The cream or beige background is overlaid with broad brown bands and irregular white blotches. The aperture is tinged with pink. The shell shown is from Rameshwaram, southern India.

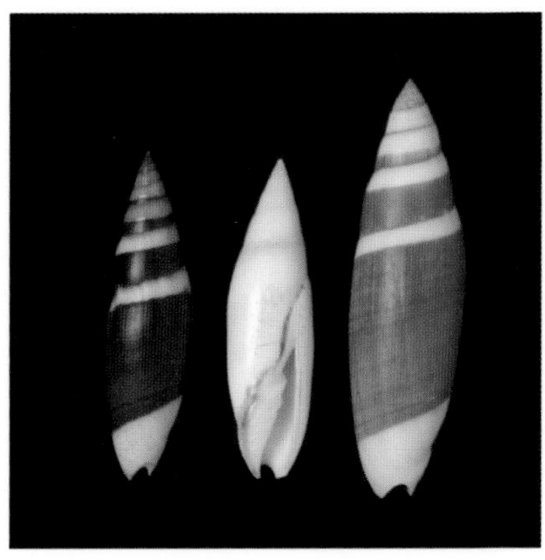

## SCABRICOLA CASTA
Chaste Mitre. *Gmelin 1791.*
Indo-Pacific.

2in (5cm)

This tall-spired elongated and smooth mitre is one of several shells which have a decorative periostracum. Although it would appear that the shell itself is coloured with a broad brown band, this can be removed by cleaning, leaving a totally white shell! Both examples are shown here. The species is a sand dweller.

## SUBCANCILLA INTERLIRATA
Ridged Mitre. *Reeve 1844.*
Western Pacific.

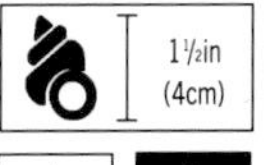

1½in (4cm)

A slender elongated species, it has a tall spire and rather convex-sided whorls. There are numerous raised and sharp spiral cords. The colour is variable, but is often off-white to beige, overlaid with fine axially aligned streaks of orange or brown. The depicted specimen is from the Solomon Islands.

## SCABRICOLA NEWCOMBII
Newcomb's Mitre. *Pease 1869.*
Hawaii and Midway Islands.

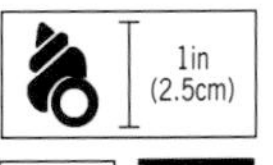

1in (2.5cm)

A small elongate-ovate species, it can vary in shape, colour and texture. The two depicted shells were collected at Pokai Bay, Oahu, Hawaii; the smaller shell is entirely smooth, whereas the larger has very fine reticulations on the spire and upper half of the body whorl. Shells can be found subtidally in sand in Hawaii and the Midway Islands, to which the species is endemic.

## SCABRICOLA VARIEGATA
Snake Mitre. *Gmelin 1791.*
Western and Central Pacific.

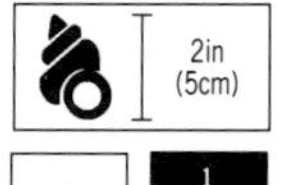

2in (5cm)

A beautifully patterned species, the snake mitre is likened to snakeskin, hence the common name. It is a robust shell, with flat broad spiral cords between which are punctated interspaces. The lip margin is crenulated, and there are several columella folds. This particular specimen is from shallow water in the central Philippines.

## SUBCANCILLA HINDSII
Hind's Mitre. *Reeve 1844.*
Western Central America.

1½in (4cm)

An elongated mitre, its very tall slender spire occupies about half of the entire length of the shell. The overall colour is white, the sharp raised spiral cords being dark to mid-brown. The white aperture is stained brown or orange within. The lip margin bears short indented lirations and there are two or three columella folds.

**ZIBA FULGETRUM**
*Reeve 1844.*
Western Pacific.

This small slender mitre is basically smooth in texture but very variable in colour and pattern. The specimens shown here portray two colour and pattern variations; they were collected in Guam Island. On close examination, the smooth shell is occasionally interrupted with very fine spiral grooves.

**COSTELLARIA SEMICOSTATUM**
*Anton 1838.*
Western Pacific.

Some authorities place this species under the subgenus *Pusia*. It is a beautiful little mitre – usually orange or red, with distinct white spirally laid spots or blotches. There are low rounded axial ribs. This shell generally inhabits reefs in relatively shallow water. The two shells in the photograph were fished off Punta Engaño, Philippines.

**COSTELLARIA RUBROCOSTATUM**
Red-striped Mitre. *Habe and Kosuge 1966.*
Western Pacific.

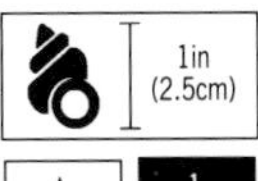


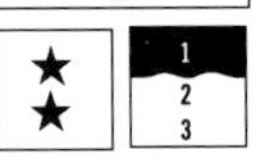


A slender and elongated shell, it has a tall spire and slightly convex-sided whorls. This lovely mitre bears distinctive crimson axial ribs on a white background. Fine spiral grooves intersect the ribs, creating a beaded effect. The aperture rim and lower columella are stained black, as is the apex. A most popular collectors' species.

SUPER FAMILY

## MURICOIDEA

FAMILY

## COSTELLARIIDAE

(Mitre Shells)

These very close relatives to the Mitridae family have been separated from them in recent years due to anatomical differences, principally concerned with the radula. Most have distinctive surface sculpturing and the aperture is lirate, whereas members of the Mitridae are generally smooth. Most species are relatively small to medium in size and inhabit sandy substrates in shallow waters. Again, this is a family that generates much interest among collectors. The principal genus is *Vexillum* and there are two subgenera of note, *Costellaria* and *Pusia*. They are still commonly referred to as mitre shells.

**COSTELLARIA ZELOTYPUM**
*Reeve 1845.*
Western Pacific.

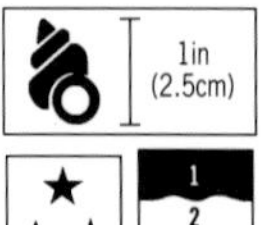


A small but solid shell, it displays coarse sculpturing of fine sharp spiral cords and rounded axial ribs which are sharply nodulose at the shoulders, creating somewhat angular whorls. The colour is off-white or cream; the anterior end of the aperture and columella are stained with lavender. This particular specimen was collected in sandy rubble on Honaria Reefs, Solomon Islands.

**PUSIA CANCELLARIODES**
Cancellated Mitre. *Anton 1839.*
Indo-Pacific.

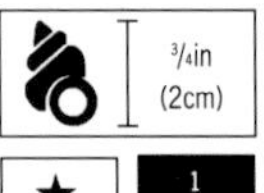


A small, solid and bulbous little shell, it is ornamented with obliquely laid axial ribs, crossed by incised spiral grooves, the combination forming a nodulose texture. The columella bears several strong folds. The overall colour is off-white, and the aperture is a creamy yellow. This specimen is from Tahiti and was collected on a rocky reef.

**PUSIA PATRIARCHALIS**
Patriarchal Mitre. *Gmelin 1791.*
Indo-Pacific.

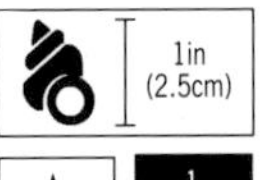

A very beautiful little shell, the patriarchal mitre is rather squat, with a stepped spire and sharply nodulose shoulders. There are numerous fine spiral grooves. As can be seen from the three depicted shells, the colouring varies; these are all from shallow water at Vairao, Tahiti. A sought-after collectors' shell.

**VEXILLUM VULPECULA**
Little Fox Mitre. *L. 1758.*
Indo-Pacific.

This is a well-known and popular species, primarily due to its variability in colouring and pattern variation. Of the three depicted specimens, all of which are from the central Philippines, the yellow form would appear to be the least common and the boldly banded form the most common. The species inhabits sand in shallow water.

**VEXILLUM DENNISONI**
Dennison's Mitre. *Reeve 1844.*
Philippines.

This elegant and attractive shell has a tall spire and numerous low axial rounded ribs; there are also fine spiral grooves. The off-white to pinkish background is overlaid with broad bands of orange and a narrow grey band at the shoulders. The lirate aperture is deep orange. The species inhabits shallow water to moderate depths, and I believe it to be endemic to the Philippines.

**PUSIA LAUTUM**
Elegant Mitre. *Reeve 1845.*
Western Pacific.

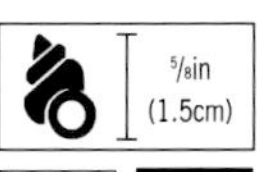

Small and stocky, with a rounded body whorl, it features low rounded axial ribs and strong columella folds. The shell is a deep red or crimson colour, with spirally laid white dots or blotches. The aperture is a pale yellow or cream. The depicted shell is from New Hebrides.

**VEXILLUM VULPECULA JUKESII**
Jukes's Mitre. *L. 1758.*
Northern and Western Australia.

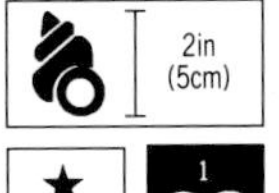

This is a sub species of *V. vulpecula*, and appears to have a restricted range. Of the specimens I have examined, the low axial ribs are stronger and the colour banding – usually of orange, white and black – darker than that of *V. vulpecula*. This particular shell was collected off Darwin.

**VEXILLUM RUGOSUM**
Rugose Mitre. *Gmelin 1791.*
Indo-Pacific.

A coarsely sculptured mitre, it inhabits sand or sandy mud in shallow water. There are low spiral cords and rounded axial ribs, which are nodulose at the shoulders. It is rather variable in colour and pattern, but the two depicted specimens, which are both from the central Philippines, show typical forms.

**VEXILLUM LYRATUM**
Lyrate Mitre. *Lamarck 1811.*
Indo-Pacific.

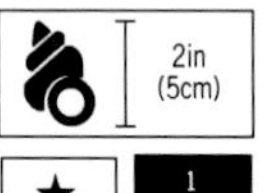

Very tall and slender, this attractive species is pale grey or bluish in colour, with well-spaced narrow spiral bands of brown or dark grey. There are numerous fine spiral grooves and the shell is dominated by low narrow axial ribs. The aperture is narrow; the inner lip is lirate and there are about three columella folds.

**CANCELLARIA RETICULATA**
Common Nutmeg. *L. 1767.*
South-eastern USA, Caribbean to Brazil.

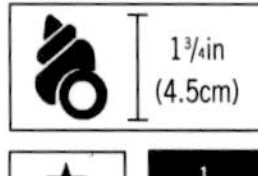

One of the best known of this family, it is relatively large and solid, and has a lowish stepped spire and an enlarged rounded body whorl. There are numerous low spiral cords and axial striae, creating a typical netted effect. The aperture is strongly lirate, and there are two or three strong columella plaits or folds.

**CANCELLARIA PULCHRA**
Beautiful Nutmeg. *Sowerby 1832.*
Western Central America.

This solid and very rounded species has a low spire. The axial ribs are nodose and sharp, especially at the shoulders, and there are strong spiral cords. It is off-white with bands and lines of pale to dark brown. The umbilicus is partly open, and there is a small but noticeable fasciole. The shell inhabits offshore waters to about 170ft (52m). The specimen shown is from Cebaco Island, Panama.

SUPER FAMILY
CANCELLARIOIDEA

FAMILY
## CANCELLARIIDAE
(Nutmeg Shells)

This family is chiefly composed of small shells living in warm seas, generally in moderate to deep water. Many are found off the western coasts of tropical America. Most are sculptured with axial ribs and spiral grooves or cords, creating a reticulated network. Few are highly coloured, and the attraction, albeit one felt by only a select few collectors, is the variable shape and the texture of the shells. Little is evidently known of the animal's feeding habits, but judging from the structure of the radula, they possibly feed on shell-less micro-organisms on the sea bed. There are numerous genera, but I would consider *Cancellaria* and *Trigonostoma* to be the principal and best known.

**CANCELLARIA CANCELLATA**
Cancellate Nutmeg. *L. 1767.*
North-West Africa and Mediterranean.

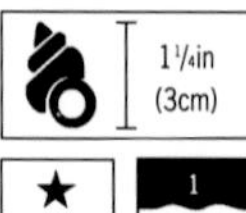

A lovely species, the cancellate nutmeg is dominated by broad dark brown bands on a cream or off-white background. Strong sharp spiral cords are crossed by narrow axial and sharply nodose ribs. The whorl sides are convex and the suture slightly impressed; there are strong columella folds; and the aperture is lirate. A shallow-water dweller.

**CANCELLARIA CASSIDIFORMIS**
Helmet Nutmeg. *Sowerby 1832.*
Western Central America.

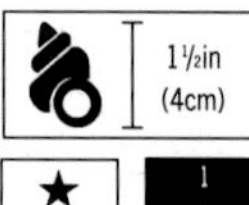

A large nutmeg, it is thick and heavy, its large body whorl being compressed at the anterior end. The spire is low, and has rather concave sides. The very low axial ribs are developed into small blunt nodules at the shoulders. It is a pale tan colour, with an off-white coarsely-lirate aperture. There are strong folds and a few tubercules on the columella. An intertidal species, it is found to about 120ft (36m).

## CANCELLARIA NODULIFERA

Knobbed Nutmeg. *Sowerby 1825.*
Japan.

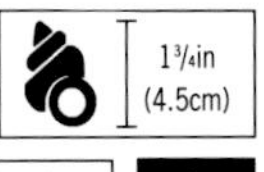


Endemic to Japan, this nutmeg has a very rugged exterior, with strong thin spiral cords which cross low nodulose axial ribs and striations. There is a distinct and open umbilicus and a strong fasciole. The columella bears tubercules and two or three folds at the anterior end. The lip margin is crenulated. The pale tan or beige shell has an off-white to pinkish aperture.

## CANCELLARIA LYRATA

Lyrate Nutmeg. *Brocchi 1814.*
West Africa.

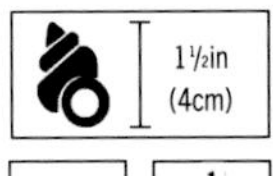


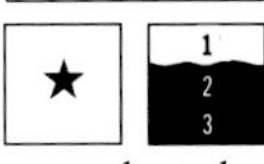


A largish species, its tall and narrow spire appears somewhat twisted. The whorls are angular and the sharp raised axial ribs are crossed at the centre of each whorl with a raised spiral cord; there are also numerous fine cords on the lower halves of the whorls. The depicted specimen, which shows typical coloration, was dredged in 990ft (300m) off Senegal.

## CANCELLARIA OBLONGA

*Sowerby 1825.*
Indo-Pacific.

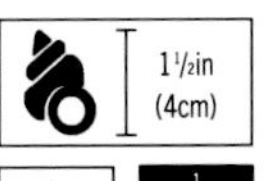


A medium-sized nutmeg, this has a tall spire and rounded whorls. The large aperture is lirate, and there are small folds and plicae on the columella. A very fine network of ribs and cords can be seen, and the shell colour is beige or cream with two or three broad pale brown spiral bands. This shell was collected off south-eastern India, in moderately deep water.

## CANCELLARIA SPENGLERIANA

Spengler's Nutmeg. *Deshayes 1830.*
Japan.

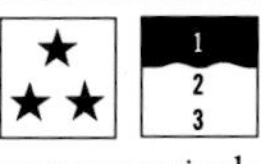


Another nutmeg restricted in range to Japanese waters, it is a very handsome shell, both in proportion and sculpturing. As can be seen from the depicted shell, the typical nutmeg reticulated texture is evident. The axial ribbing develops into fairly sharp nodules at the shoulders. It inhabits shallow water in Japan, to which it is endemic.

**CANCELLARIA PISCATORIA**
Fisherman's Nutmeg. *Gmelin 1791.*
West Africa.

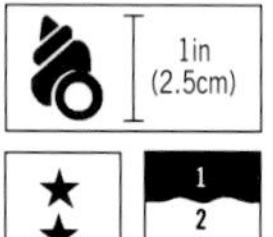


The fisherman's nutmeg is a small fairly lightweight shell, with a low stepped spire. Its enlarged body whorl has a gaping aperture, and there are low well-spaced spiral cords and axial striae. The shoulders bear very small but sharp nodules. The exterior colour is a pale bluish grey, with occasional brown patches; the aperture margin and columella are white, and the interior is a deep greyish brown.

**CANCELLARIA CRAWFORDIANA**
Crawford's Nutmeg. *Dall 1891.*
California.

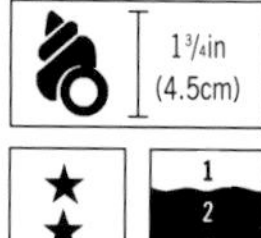


Endemic to California, this medium-sized shell is not unlike *C. cooperi* in general shape, but the former has rounded whorls and a latticed texture of intersecting cords and ribs. It is generally white to pale beige. The two depicted specimens were collected in 600ft (182m) off Goleta.

**CANCELLARIA ASPERELLA**
*Lamarck 1822.*
Western Pacific.

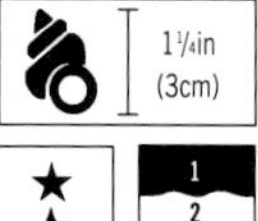


While rather similar in shape to *C. laticosta*, this is smaller and the cancellations are very much finer. It is an overall mid-tan colour; the aperture is creamy grey, and there are distinct lirae. The depicted specimen is from Thevenard Island, western Australia.

**CANCELLARIA COOPERI**
Cooper's Nutmeg. *Gabb 1865.*
California to West Mexico.

One of the larger nutmegs, this is reputed to grow to 3in (7.5cm) on occasions. It inhabits moderate to very deep water and is a sought-after collectors' item. Fusiform in shape, it has a tall spire and angular whorls. There are low rounded axial ribs. The dirty beige background is decorated with distinctive thin mid-brown spiral bands. The columella is white; the aperture is creamy yellow.

**CANCELLARIA LATICOSTA**
*Löbbecke 1886.*
Japan.

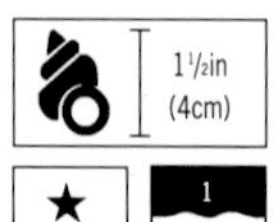


A largish ovate nutmeg, this has a high spire, rounded whorls and coarsely-sculptured ornamentation of sharp axial ribs and spiral cords. It is pleasantly coloured with mid-brown and pale brown or cream bands. The beige aperture is lirate; the lip margin is crenulated. It is a shallow-water dweller.

**CANCELLARIA MERCADOI**
Mercado's Nutmeg. *Old 1968.*
Philippines.

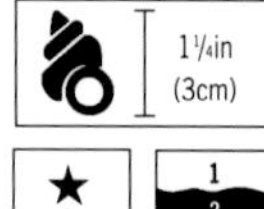


This very attractive species, endemic to the Philippines, has only been available in appreciable numbers during the last 10-15 years and its habitat appears to be restricted to moderately deep water in Tayabas Bay. It has been named after Mario Mercado, a shell dealer of Zimbales. The broad, raised and angular ribs and convex whorls are typical of this shell, the specimen seen here portraying the normal colouring of tan and yellow.

**PISANELLA VIVA**
*Habe and Okutani 1981.*
Philippines.

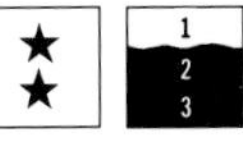

Although this species in some way resembles *C. lyrata*, it does not conform to the usual nutmeg "shapes" and appears closer to some *Colubraria* species. Radula examination, however, persuades experts to place it within the Cancellarias. It is a tall fusiform shell, rather slender, with low ribs and fine spiral cords. The thickened lip is dentate and there are small folds and tubercules on the columella. The depicted shell was fished in 480ft (145m) off Punta Engaño.

**TRIGONOSTOMA ELEGANTULUM**
Little Elegant Nutmeg. *M. Smith 1947.*
Western Central America.

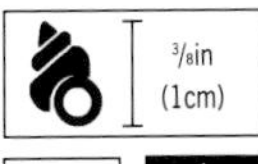


This is similar to *T. pellucida*, but it is generally much smaller, has a larger open umbilicus and the axial ribbing is coarser. The colour varies, ranging from off-white overall, to beige or greyish brown. The aperture margins are white and shells are occasionally deep red brown within. This particular shell is from Gubernadora Island, Panama.

**TRIGONOSTOMA WITHROWI**
Withrow's Nutmeg. *Petit 1975.*
West Africa.

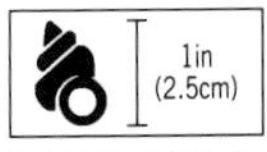


A small but solid, rather angular shell, with stepped whorls which are flat between the suture and the shoulders, its exterior is ornamented with coarse well-spaced axial ribs and fine spiral cords. The lip is thickened and lirate within. The umbilicus is large and open. The depicted shells were collected in 99ft (30m) off Cap de Naze, Senegal.

**TRIGONOSTOMA PELLUCIDA**
Triangular Nutmeg. *Perry 1811.*
South-West Pacific.

A beautifully shaped little shell, the triangular nutmeg has a tall spire, strongly stepped whorls, which are flat between the suture, and sharply keeled and coronated shoulders. The sides of the whorls slant inward toward the anterior end. The umbilicus is wide and open and the aperture is unusually triangular. A choice collectors' shell.

**TRIGONOSTOMA CONTABULATA**
*Sowerby 1833.*
Western Pacific.

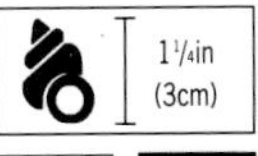


This light brown or beige nutmeg is similar in shape to *C. crawfordiana*, but is more squat and has stepped whorls and a channelled suture. The obliquely laid ribs are crossed with fine spiral ridges. The aperture is off-white, and the columella bears two or three low folds.

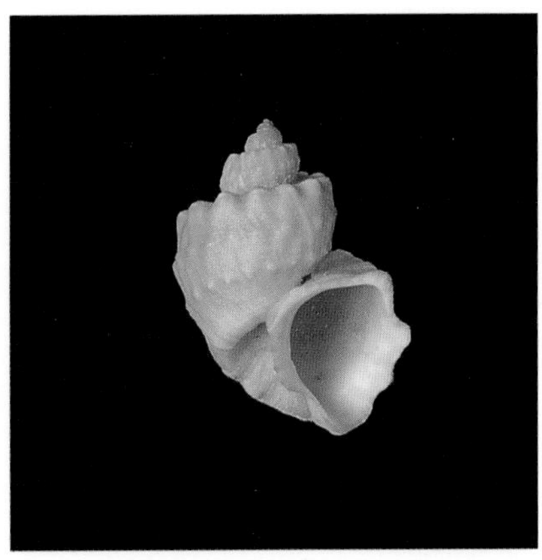

**TRIGONOSTOMA TENERUM**
Philippi's Nutmeg. *Philippi 1848.*
Southern Florida and Gulf of Mexico.

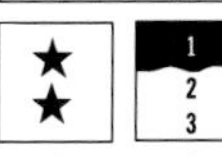

Philippi's nutmeg is similar in shape to *T. withrowi*, but is compressed ventrally and the coarse ribs are absent. The angled shoulders are nodulose, and there are two further nodose cords at the centre of each whorl. There is an open umbilicus. Shells are generally cream or pale brown in colour. The specimen shown is from Yucatan, eastern Mexico.

**TRIGONOSTOMA SCALARIFORMIS**
*Lamarck 1822.*
Indo-Pacific.

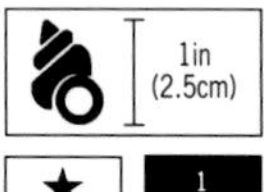


This attractive nutmeg has a moderately tall spire, convex-sided whorls and a channelled suture. There are strong rounded axial ribs. The overall colour is off-white, with broad bands of tan brown; the aperture area is white. The depicted specimen was fished off south-western Taiwan.

**TRIGONOSTOMA SEMIDISJUNCTA**
*Sowerby 1848.*
South Africa.

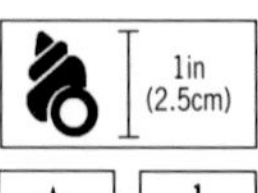


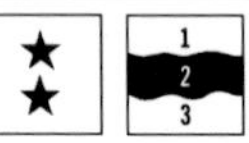

A small squat shell, it has very rounded globose whorls, a moderate spire and a deeply channelled sutures. There are raised spiral cords and occasional axial striae. The colour is off-white or beige, with pale brown or tan axial streaks. The aperture is ovate and the umbilicus large and open.

SUPER FAMILY
## CONOIDEA

FAMILY
## CONIDAE
(Cone Shells)

Cone shells are arguably the most popular of all families among collectors, although I would tend to place them second to the cowries (Cypraeidae). They are a very large group of shells, small to very large in size, totalling well over 300 named species; the largest species, *Conus pulcher* Lightfoot 1786, exceeds 8in (20cm), the world size record at the time of writing being 10in (25cm). Cones generally inhabit warm seas, and are most prolific in the tropical Indo-Pacific; the Philippines boasts at least 185 valid species. They are a carnivorous family, preying on fish, other molluscs and worms (most cones fall into the worm-eating group). They are a highly successful predaceous family, and all species possess a specialized radula system through which a poisonous barb is injected into the prey. It is thought that the species with the largest apertures (usually fish-eating) are the most dangerous. Indeed several human fatalities have been reported over the years due to careless handling of live specimens. All cones are covered with a periostracum when alive, and it is interesting to note that this is generally thick, so that it is virtually impossible to see any colour or pattern beneath. The true beauty of the cone shell can only be revealed after collecting and cleaning. Kay Vaught lists one major genus, *Conus*, and numerous subgenera. Much controversy exists among scientists and collectors regarding the systematics of this major group. I believe that there is much inter-breeding and hybridization within species, but there will always be those who enjoy creating new species, groups and variations, which inevitably adds to the already confusing array of names. Where possible, I have included variations and so-called subspecies in one photograph, to enable the reader to appreciate possible identification problems.

**CONUS GEOGRAPHUS**
Geography Cone. *L. 1758.*
Indo-Pacific.

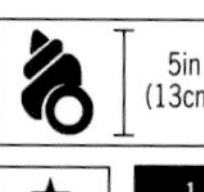


A large but lightweight cone, this curiously named species has a distinctly large aperture. It has claimed at least one human fatality – the guilty specimen is housed in the British Museum (Natural History). The two Philippines specimens depicted here portray typical coloration and markings.

**CONUS THALASSIARCHUS**
Bough Cone. *Sowerby 1834.*
Philippines.

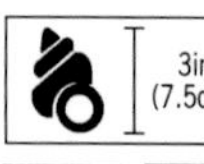


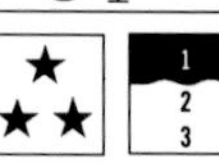

A tall graceful shell, with a very low concave spire and straight-sided tapering body whorl, its aperture is rather wider at the anterior end. Three local variations are shown here; the slightly larger of them is the most usual colour and pattern, while the other two have had varietal names attributed to them.

**CONUS RATTUS**
Rat Cone. *Hwass 1792.*
Indo-Pacific.

1½in (4cm)

A very common and well-known species, the rat cone inhabits shallow water. The spire is low and the large body whorl has rather convex sides. The texture is smooth with a high gloss. The colour is off-white, overlaid with large areas of olive green or brown. The aperture is tinged with violet grey.

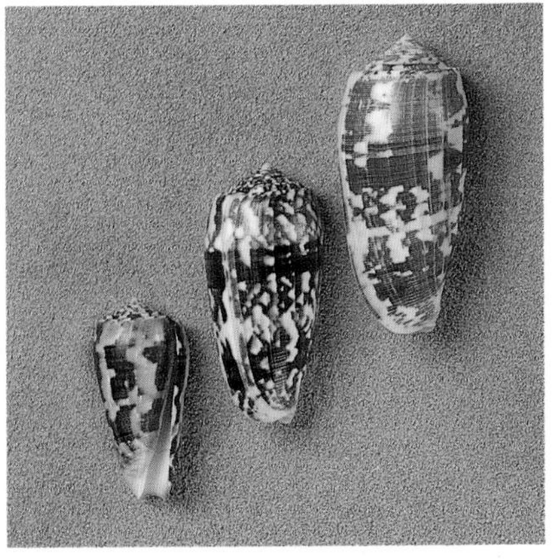

**CONUS STRIATUS**
Striated Cone. *L. 1758.*
Indo-Pacific.

4in (10cm)

This medium-sized cone has a low spire with concave whorls. The very large body whorl has convex sides toward the posterior and gradually tapers to a broad anterior canal. Three colour forms are shown here; the largest shell is from the Philippines, the virtually black specimen is from southern India, and the smallest shell has a purple tinge and is from Réunion Island. All specimens have a moderate gloss and very fine and numerous spiral grooves.

**CONUS MILES**
Soldier Cone. *L. 1758.*
Indo-Pacific.

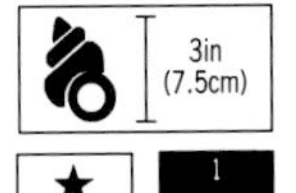

3in (7.5cm)

A well-known species, with striking marks, it is moderately large and heavy, and has a low spire, straight-sided whorls and very slightly convex body whorl. Shells are off-white, with two broad dark brown spiral bands and orange or tan axial streaks and patches. They are glossy, and have several low spiral cords at the anterior end of the body whorl.

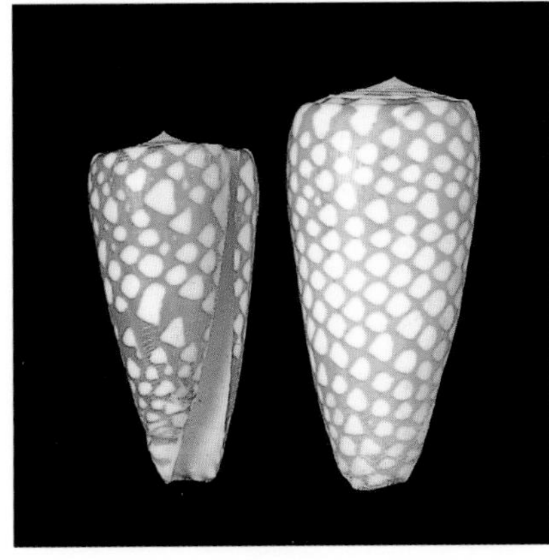

**CONUS NOBILIS NOBILIS**
Noble Cone. *L. 1758.*
Western Pacific.

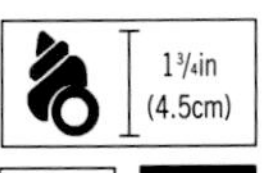

1¾in (4.5cm)

The noble cone, a lovely shell, is mustard yellow or pale tan, overlaid with distinctive white tent markings. The spire is very low or almost flat, with concave whorls. The body whorl has slightly convex sides tapering at the anterior. A smooth shell, with a moderate gloss, it is popular with collectors.

**CONUS TESSULATUS**
Tessellated Cone. *Born 1778.*
Indo-Pacific.

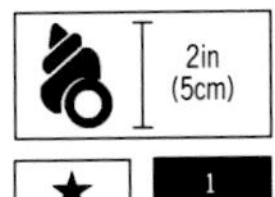

2in (5cm)

An attractive species, it is white, with vivid red tessellations or large spiral dashes; the columella tip is tinged with lavender. The spire is very low and the body whorl has a slightly rounded shoulder and straight tapering sides. The smallest of the three shells seen here is from Cocos Island, Panama, and is rare from this locality.

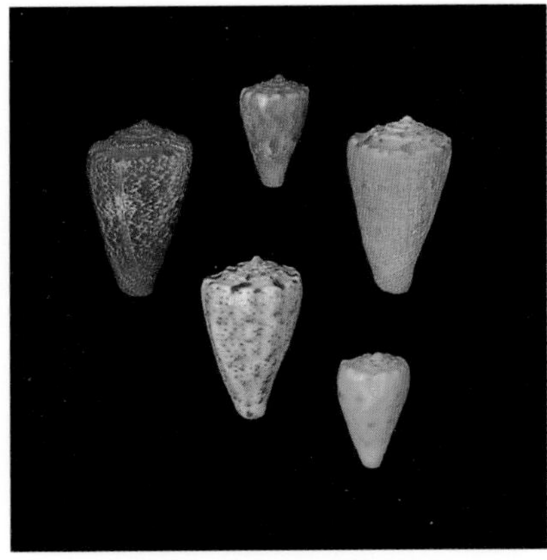

**CONUS RUTILUS**
Burnished Cone. *Menke 1843.*
Southern Australia and Tasmania.

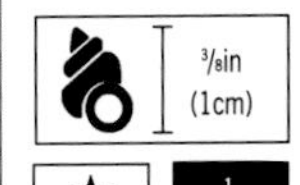

⅜in (1cm)

This is the smallest-known *Conus*, and is very variable in colour. The shells depicted show a typical range. Some are plain, others have minute bands and mottling of darker colour. Many specimens are beached, as few are live-taken. Close examination shows the flat or very low spire to be lightly coronated.

**CONUS AUSTRALIS**
Austral Cone. *Holten 1802.*
Japan to Philippines.

This tall shell has a spire of moderate size, and slightly concave whorls. The body whorl is convex, being widest below the shoulder and tapering to the canal. The depicted shells were fished off south-western Taiwan and show the extremes of pattern and coloration. It would appear to be most common off Taiwan but, as mentioned elsewhere, little material is currently available from this locality.

**CONUS CAPITANEUS**
Captain Cone. *L. 1758.*
Indo-Pacific.

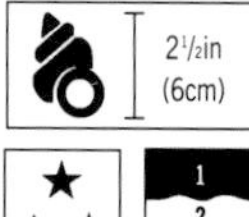


This handsome species can vary in coloration, though the pattern seems to remain fairly constant. The spire is low and the body whorl has virtually straight sides, tapering to the canal. The background is white, with broad bands of pale brown, olive green or grey, with black axial streaks and fine spirally laid spots and blotches. All shells seen here were collected in the central Philippines.

**CONUS AULICUS**
Princely Cone. *L. 1758.*
Indo-Pacific.

A truly handsome and aptly named cone, it is most strikingly marked, with vivid white tent markings on a rich reddish brown background. The spire is low with straight-sided whorls; the body whorl is very large, elongated and rather inflated at the centre. There are numerous fine spiral striae. The aperture is widest at the anterior end and is rich creamy yellow in colour. A most popular collectors' item, it is a shallow-water reef dweller.

**CONUS SPONSALIS**
Marriage Cone. *Hwass 1792.*
Indo-Pacific.

A small solid species, it has a low spire, and an inflated convex body whorl. It is often encrusted, and gem specimens are scarce. Two forms are shown here, the smaller shell having a coronated spire and pustulose body whorl. Shells are invariably cream, with centrally placed reddish brown patches; the anterior tip is black or purple.

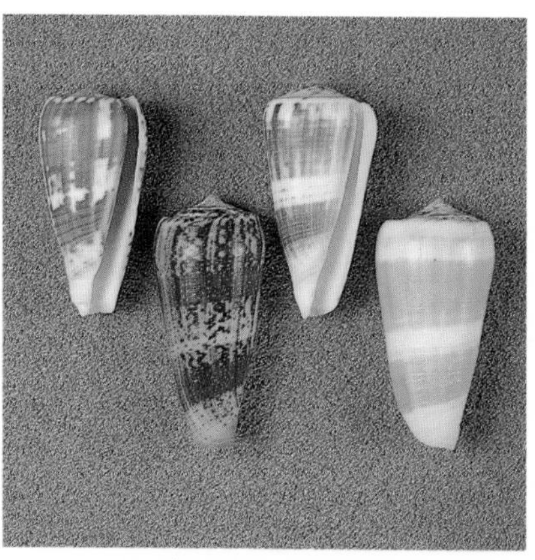

**CONUS MAGUS**
Magical Cone. *L. 1758.*
Indo-Pacific.

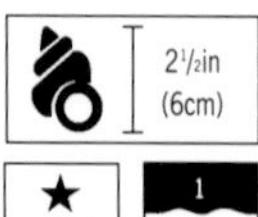


This must be one of the most variably patterned or coloured cones known. The Philippines alone can yield at least a dozen forms, and there are many more further afield, including those from the Solomon Islands and New Hebrides. As can be seen here, the shape remains more or less constant. Novices are often confused when only one or two specimens are available; you need to see many shells in order to acquaint yourself with the variations!

**CONUS GLORIAMARIS**
Glory of the Seas Cone. *Chemnitz 1777.*
Central Philippines.

Alongside *Cypraea aurantium*, this shell is the most sought-after of all species and commanded very high prices until very recently. It was extremely rare during the 18th and 19th centuries and has only become available in great numbers during the last 15-20 years. It is not spectacular by any means, but over the years it has taken a legendary place in the history of shell collecting and still commands interest and conversation. It is highly glossy.

**CONUS MILNEEDWARDSI**
Glory of India Cone. *Jousseaume 1894.*
Indian Ocean and China Sea.

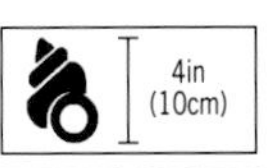


Another much sought-after collectors' cone, of elegant proportions and attractive patterning, it is a slender and fairly large shell, its stepped spire occupying one-third of the total length. The body whorl is straight-sided, tapering toward the canal. The depicted specimen shows typical colour and markings. Many specimens have noticeable growth scars.

**CONUS BENGALENSIS**
Bengal Cone. *Okutani 1968.*
Bay of Bengal and off Burma and Thailand.

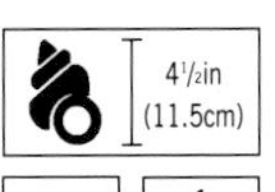


A beautiful tall and slender shell, it has a long gently tapering body whorl and low stepped spire. Not unlike *C. gloriamaris* in general appearance, it is narrower and has a much larger and distinctive pattern of rich brown tent markings on a white background. It has a high gloss.

**CONUS CARACTERISTICUS**
*Fischer 1807.*
Indian Ocean and Western Pacific.

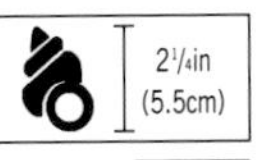


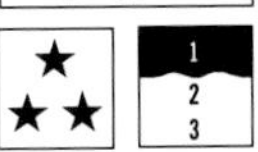


A very heavy and solid shell, with a very low spire, its body whorl is inflated and has slightly convex sides, tapering to the canal. The shell has a low gloss and numerous growth striae are evident. Off-white to cream in overall colouring, it is overlaid with tan streaks, blotches and spots arranged in spiral bands. These two specimens were collected in shallow water, Quezon, Philippines.

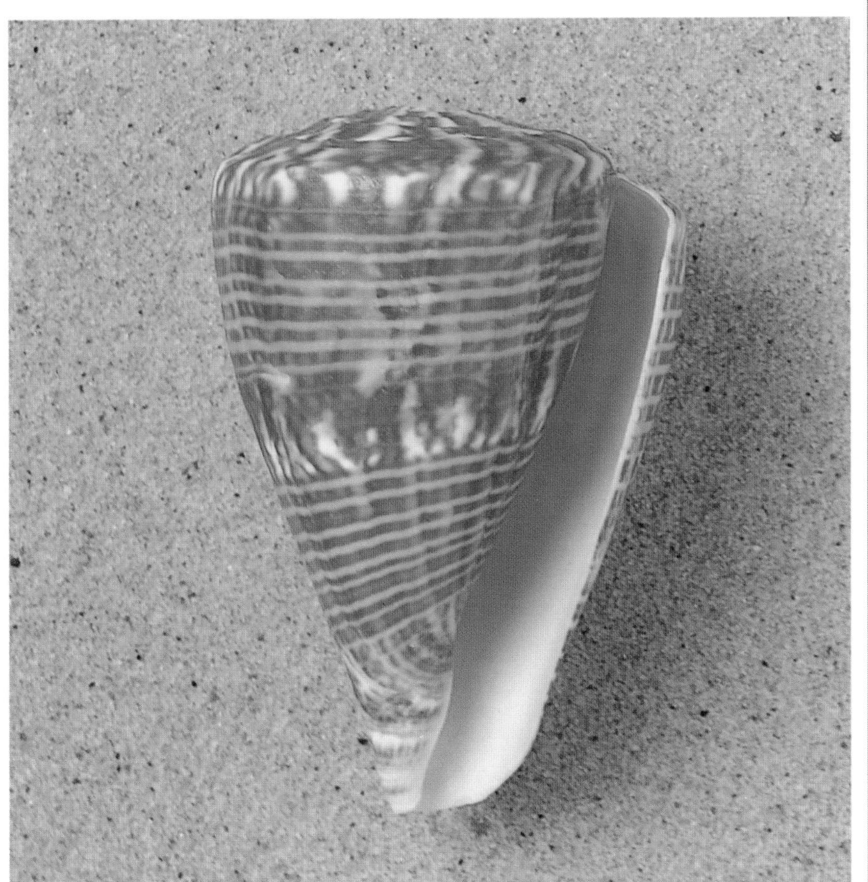

**CONUS TRIGONUS**
Trigonal Cone. *Reeve 1848.*
Northern and Western Australia.

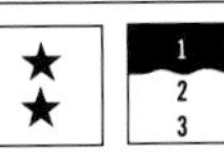


As the name implies, it is very triangular in shape, with a flat spire, wide shoulder, and body whorl sides which taper sharply to the canal. The gloss is low. The depicted specimen shows the darker of several colour and pattern forms found within this species; it was collected in shallow water off Broome.

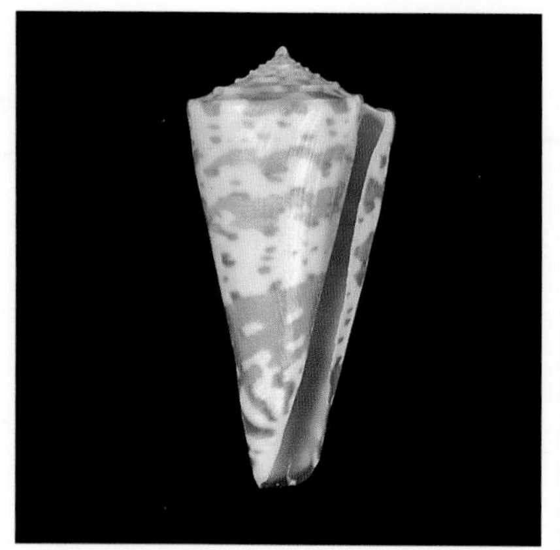

**CONUS SCULLETTI**
Scullett's Cone. *Marsh 1962.* Southern Queensland and New South Wales.

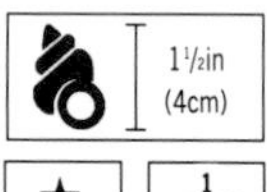

This is a lightweight, small and slender cone. Most specimens have a low slightly stepped spire with a distinct protoconch. The body whorl sides can be straight or concave. The gloss is moderate and the shell colour is off-white with large pale tan spots and blotches. The shell in the photograph was taken in 480ft (145m) off Cape Moreton, Queensland.

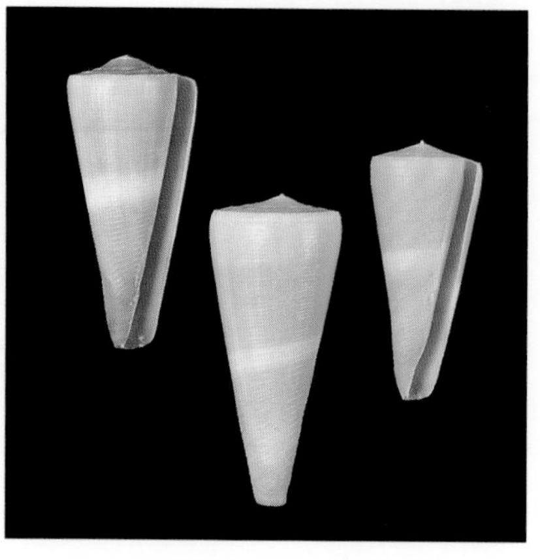

**CONUS KINTOKI**
*Coomans and Moolanbeek 1982.* Central Philippines.

This elegant slender cone has until relatively recently been confused with other similar species. There is little or no pattern, but the shell has numerous fine spiral cords; the colour varies from pale pink, through lavender to orange. A lovely species, it is endemic to the Mactan Islands area of the central Philippines.

**CONUS ARGILLACEUS**
Clay Cone. *Perry 1811.* North-West Indian Ocean.

A species which is seldom available to collectors, the clay cone is medium sized and has a low spire with slightly concave sides and a straight-sided body whorl. It is attractively marked with large tan or mid-brown patches overlaid with darker spiral dashes and lines on a white background. The depicted specimen was reef-collected off Yemen.

**CONUS TEXTILE**
Textile Cone. *L. 1758.* Indo-Pacific.

A most common yet beautiful species, it is popular with collectors. The textile cone has many forms and variations, giving rise to numerous names – some valid, others to be accepted or agreed upon. The smaller, "blue" form shown alongside the typically marked and coloured specimen is known as *C. euetrios*, and has recently appeared on the market, coming from Mozambique.

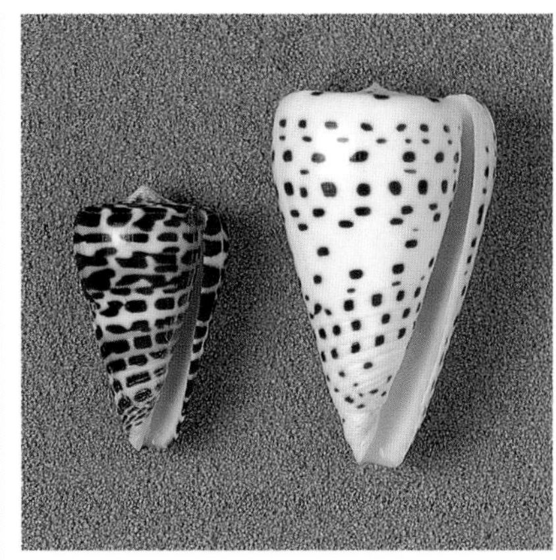

**CONUS EBURNEUS**
Ivory Cone. *Hwass 1792.*
Indo-Pacific.

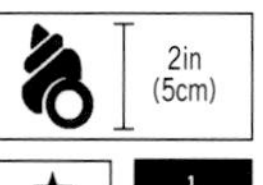

A solid triangular-shaped species, it has a moderate to high gloss; the shell is smooth apart from a few spiral grooves at the anterior end of the body whorl. There are several pattern forms; the larger of the two specimens is the normal form, the smaller darker shell is the attractive variety, *C. eburneus polyglotta*. Both inhabit shallow reef areas.

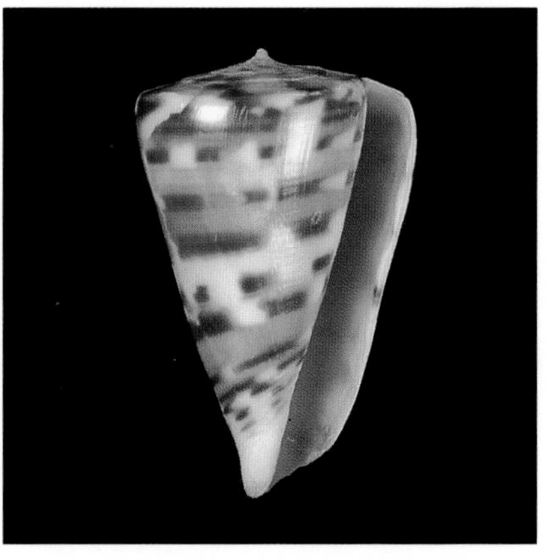

**CONUS ADVERTEX**
Reference Cone. *Garrard 1961.* Southern Queensland and New South Wales.

An uncommon species, it is similar in shape to *C. trigonus* but is perhaps rather less triangular, with more gently sloping body whorl sides. The spire is flat, with a distinct protoconch. Shells are off-white to pinkish, with broad continuous spiral bands of pale orange or tan, and broken narrow bands of dark brown. The depicted shell is from Cape Moreton.

**CONUS CYLINDRACEUS**
Cylindrical Cone. *Broderip and Sowerby 1830.* Indo-Pacific.

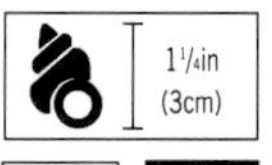

The cylindrical cone is small, glossy and slender, elongated and bullet-shaped. It has a tall spire and convex sides, and is strikingly marked with spirally laid patches and streaks of white on a rich tan or mid-brown background. The aperture is white. The shell seen here was collected at Pango, New Hebrides.

**CONUS CHALDEUS**
Wood Cone. *Röding 1798.*
Indo-Pacific.

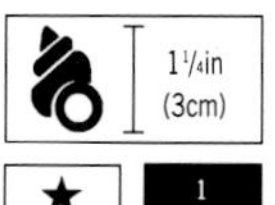

A small stocky shell, the wood cone has a smooth or moderately rough texture and a low gloss. The colour is white, overlaid with black axial streaks and stripes, some shells being almost totally black. The shoulders bear very small nodules and there are fine spiral cords. The species is a sand dweller, found in shallow water.

**CONUS ZEYLANICUS**
Obese Cone. *Gmelin 1791.*
Indian Ocean.

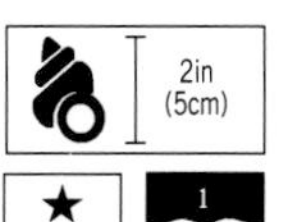

A most attractive species, the obese cone is very heavy and rather bulbous in shape. It has a pale pink or lavender background, overlaid with white spots and patches or streaks of purplish brown or black. The aperture is tinged with pink. Occasional growth striations are evident. The two depicted specimens were fished off south-eastern India in shallow water.

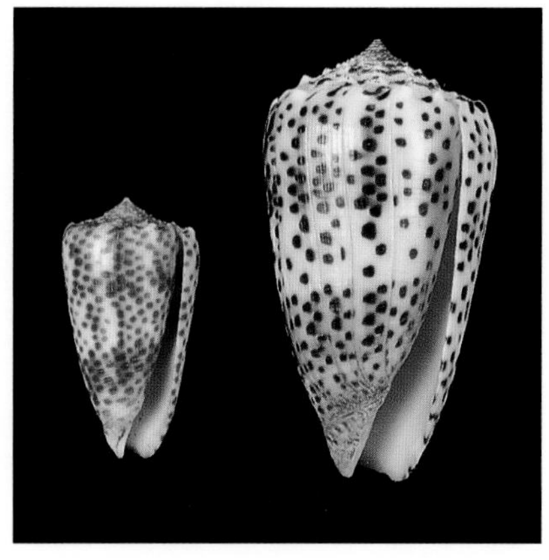

**CONUS PULICARIUS**
Flea-bite Cone. *Hwass 1792.*
Indo-Pacific.

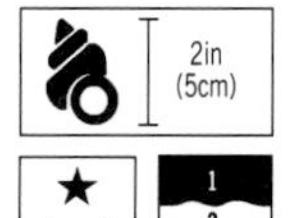

A solid cone, this has a low coronated spire and concave sides. The body whorl is rather elongated, with slightly convex sides. The larger of the two depicted shells shows the typical pattern for the species; the smaller specimen is a variation known as *C. vautieri* and appears to be endemic to the Marquesas Islands. The species is an intertidal sand dweller.

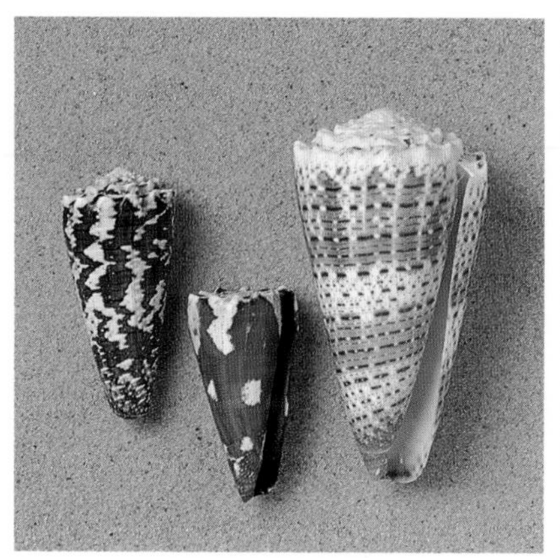

## CONUS IMPERIALIS

Imperial Cone. *L. 1758.*
Indo-Pacific.

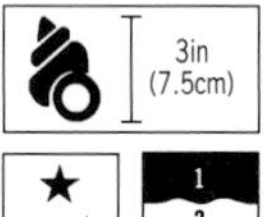

A handsome intertidal reef dweller, it has a long straight-sided body whorl, tapering to the canal, and a distinctive low or flat coronated spire. It is off-white in colour and there are two very broad spiral bands of pale orange, overlaid with many greyish blue bands, dots and dashes. The lower third of the shell is spirally pustulose. The two smaller and darker shells shown are the East African form, *C. imperialis fuscata*.

## CONUS GENERALIS GENERALIS

General Cone. *L. 1767.*
Western Pacific.

A very handsome and attractively marked species, this is very variable both in pattern and colour. The spire also can be flat or raised, with concave sides. Of the three specimens shown, two are true *C. generalis* whereas the mid-brown form with the broad central white band is *C. generalis maldivus*, which occurs from East Africa to the Bay of Bengal. I believe there to be some intergrading where habitat ranges overlap.

## CONUS ATERALBUS

*Kiener 1849.*
Cape Verde Islands.

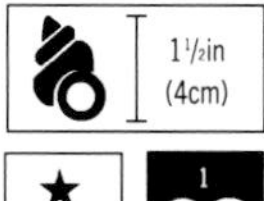

An attractive shell, it is virtually black overlaid with irregular, but often centrally placed, white spots and blotches. The very low, almost flat spire is often eroded, as this part is exposed in its habitat in sand. The body whorl sides are slightly convex, tapering gently to the canal. The interior is white or tinged with greyish blue. This species is one of many endemic Cape Verde cones to have come onto the market in recent years.

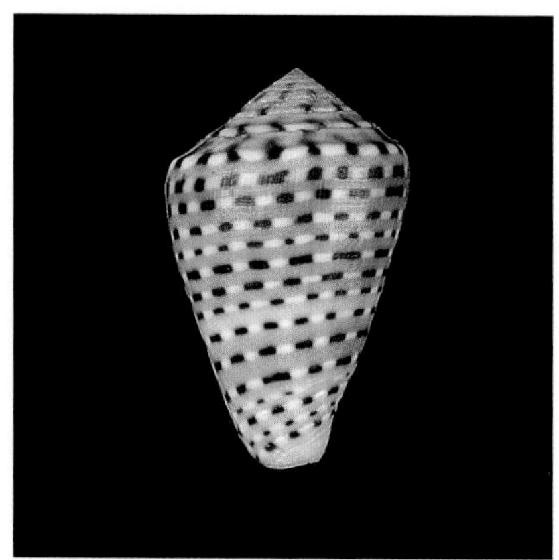

## CONUS TAENIATUS

Ringed Cone. *Hwass 1792.*
Red Sea and North-West Indian Ocean.

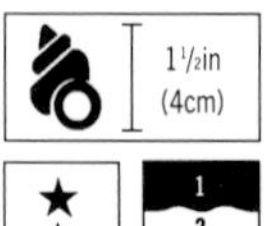

This beautifully marked little cone has a pale bluish grey background overlaid with distinct spiral bands of alternate black and white dashes. The aperture is greyish, with brown tints. The depicted specimen was collected in the Gulf of Oman.

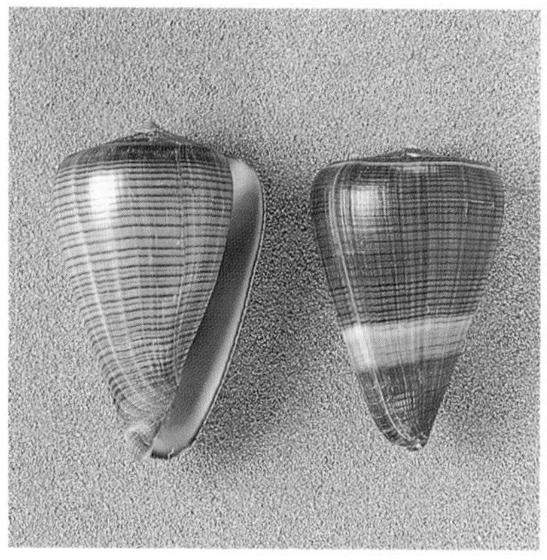

## CONUS FIGULINUS

Fig Cone. *L. 1758.*
Indo-Pacific.

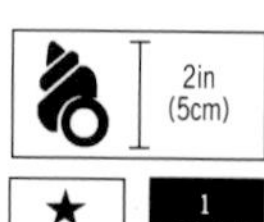

A rich brown triangular-shaped species with rounded shoulder and very low spire with concave sides. The numerous close spiral black lines are raised on the lower third of the body whorl. The aperture is greyish white. This species is a shallow-water dweller.

## CONUS MOZAMBICUS

*Hwass 1792.*
South Africa.

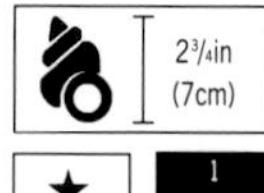

This is an extremely variable cone, with forms ranging in colour from pale yellow and lavender to deep brown or purple. The two variations that are shown here originate from False Bay. The shape, however, is constant: a moderate spire, with rather convex whorls and an enlarged and elongated body whorl, widest below the shoulder.

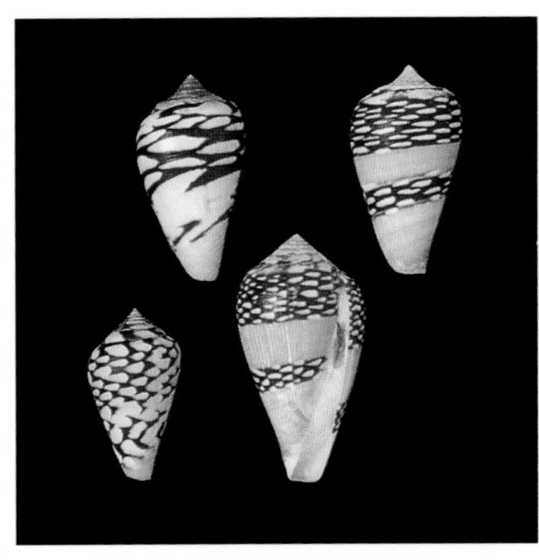

**CONUS MERCATOR**
Trader Cone. *L. 1758.*
West Africa and Cape Verde Islands.

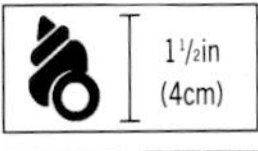


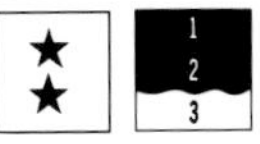


This small cone has a low spire with straight or concave sides; the body whorl has rather convex sides and is generally inflated at the rounded shoulder. The beautiful markings can vary greatly, as can be seen in the specimens shown; many subspecific names have been attributed to the various forms. The spires of some shells are eroded. The species is very popular with collectors.

**CONUS BARTSCHI**
Bartsch's Cone. *Hanna and Strong 1949.*
Western Central America.

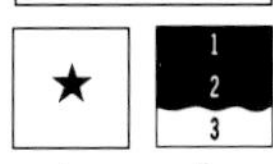


A small species with a low coronated spire – often encrusted – and straight-sided smartly tapering body whorl, it is a smooth shell with a little gloss; growth scars and axial striae are often evident in mature specimens. Shells are off-white, with tan or mid-brown spiral dashes and large blotched areas. The depicted cone was dived for in 80ft (24m) off San Carlos, Sonora, Mexico.

**CONUS PATRICIUS**
Pear Cone. *Hinds 1843.*
Western Central America.

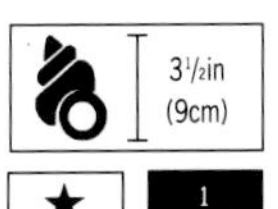


1
2
3

A beautiful cone, it has a flat spire and slightly raised apex. The body whorl is pyriform and tapering; it is compressed at the anterior end and has a rounded shoulder. In colour, it is a mixture of lavender and creamy yellow, with a white aperture. Younger, smaller specimens portray the best attributes of this graceful shell. The depicted shell was collected at low tide, in mud at night, at Pedro Gonzales, Panama.

**CONUS BULBUS**
Onion Cone. *Reeve 1843.*
South-West Africa.

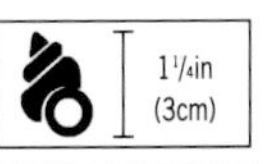


1
2
3

A pyriform shell, it has a very low spire and a much rounded shoulder. It has striking mid-brown axial streaks on an off-white or cream background; there is a low gloss. The spire is often eroded, as with several other West African cones, and there are occasional growth scars. It inhabits intertidal and shallow water. The depicted specimen was collected from Angola.

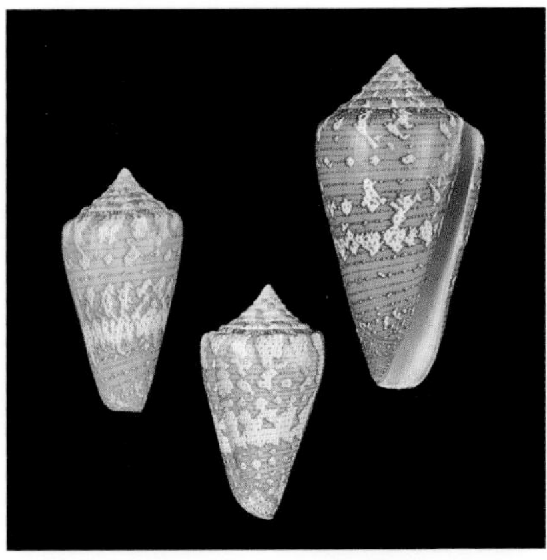

**CONUS CEDONULLI**
Matchless Cone. *L. 1767.*
West Indies.

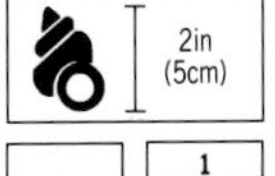


1
2
3

This rare and much sought-after cone is very occasionally brought up in lobster nets in deep water off St. Vincent. It has a low spire with convex whorls; the body whorl is straight-sided, tapering toward the anterior end. Shells are almost always patterned with spiral lines, with both small and large irregular blotches, especially at the centre; the background colour varies, as can be seen with the three depicted specimens.

**CONUS XIMENES**
Interrupted Cone. *Gray 1839.*
Western Central America.

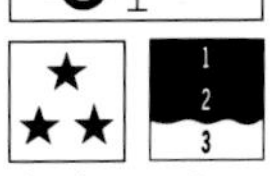


An attractive species, it has a moderate spire with concave whorls and a body whorl with straight sides; the shoulder is rounded. Two colour forms are shown here – the larger shell displaying the more typical coloration is from California; the smaller darker specimen is from Panama.

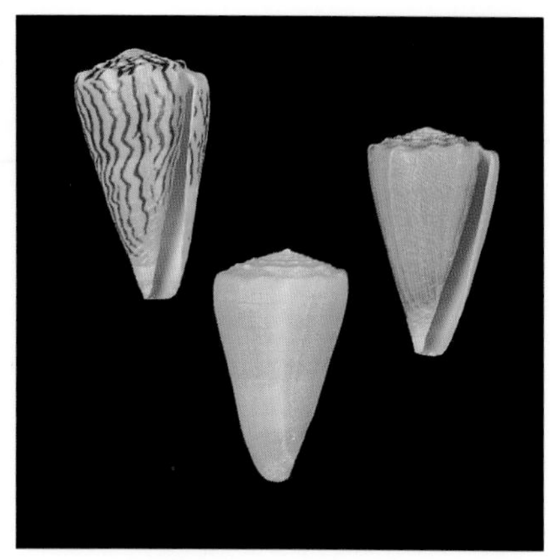

## CONUS PRINCEPS

Prince Cone. *L. 1758.*
Western Central America.

A very handsome species, the prince cone has distinctive dark brown or black axial streaks and zigzag markings on a rich orange background. The two named variations also shown here are *C. princeps lineolatus*, which has very fine axial lines, and *C. princeps apogrammatus*, which exhibits no markings at all. These shells are most popular with cone collectors.

## CONUS LUCIDUS

Spiderweb Cone. *Wood 1828.* Western Central America and Galapagos Islands.

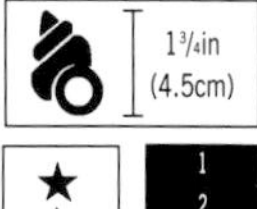

This attractive cone is uniquely marked with a fine web-like network of thin rich brown lines and dashes. It has a medium gloss, and there are a few raised cords at the anterior end of the body whorl. Large perfect specimens are much sought-after by collectors, but many shells have growth scars and healed breaks.

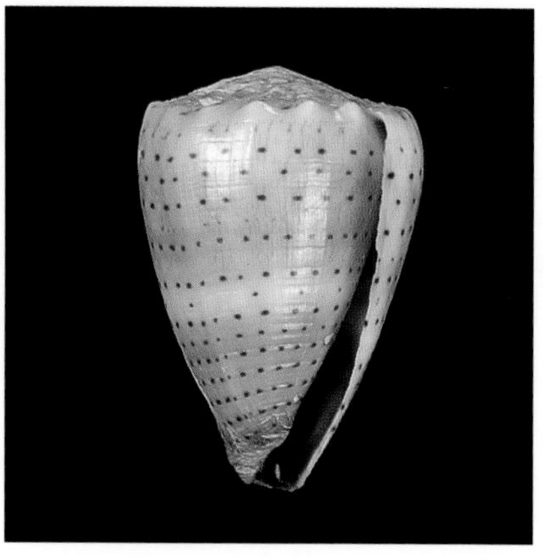

## CONUS ABBREVIATUS

*Reeve 1843.*
Hawaiian Islands.

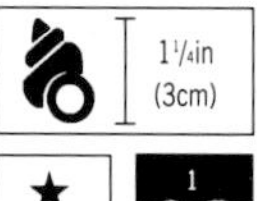

Endemic to the Hawaiian Islands, this is a short stocky little cone with a low, indeed almost flat, coronated spire and slightly convex body whorl sides. It is attractively patterned with broad pale lavender or light grey bands, over which are laid tiny spiral rich brown dots. The aperture is tinged with dark brown. This shell is from Ala Moana Reef, Oahu.

## CONUS PURPURASCENS

Purple Cone. *Sowerby 1833.*
Western Central America.

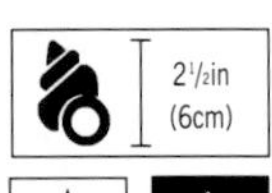

A colourful medium-sized species, this has a low spire, with straight or concave sides; the body whorl can have either straight or slightly convex sides. The pink or pale lavender background is overlaid with dark blotches and dashes of grey, dark blue or brown; the shell has a low gloss. Both specimens here are from Palo Seco, Panama.

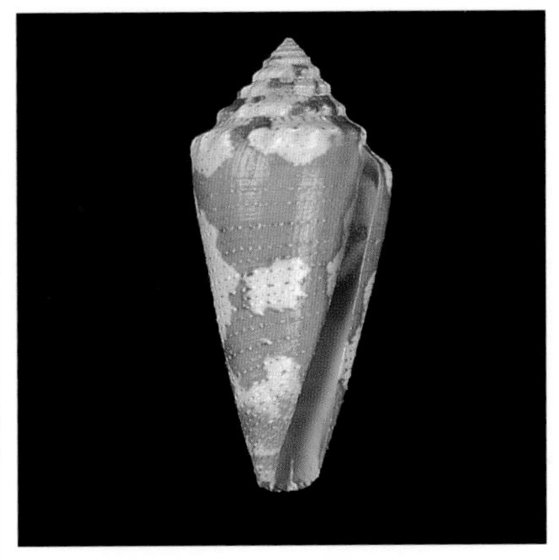

**CONUS AURANTIUS**
Golden Cone. *Hwass 1792.*
Southern Caribbean.

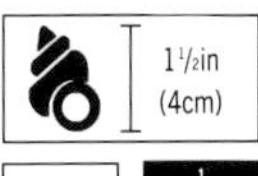
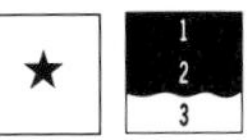

A much sought-after and beautiful collectors' item, it is rarely available in pristine condition. Although the name suggests a golden colour, many specimens are dark or mid-brown. The shell is rather long and narrow, with a straight-sided body whorl and a moderate, stepped and slightly nodulose spire. There are spiral rows of fine tubercules on a smooth glossy surface. This specimen is from Curaçao.

**CONUS GRADATUS**
*Wood 1828.*
Western Central America.

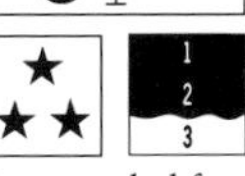

This medium-sized and sharply angled species is, according to some authorities, *C. regularis*, but here again there is confusion, due to several closely related and intergraded forms. It is variable in pattern, the colour being fairly constant, as can be seen in the two specimens here; the shape, you will note, will also vary. Both shells come from Sonora, Mexico.

**TIARITURRIS SPECTABILIS**
*Berry 1958.*
Western Central America.

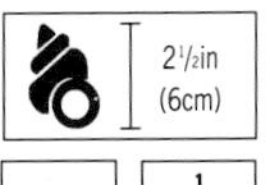
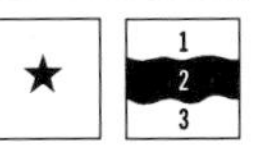

Similar in shape and size to *K. tuberculifera*, this differs in having less pronounced nodulose whorls, and there are small axial ribs on the earliest whorls. The colour and pattern is off-white, with dark brown zigzag lines and larger patches of brown below the suture. The depicted shell was dredged in 300ft (91m) off Medidora Island, Panama.

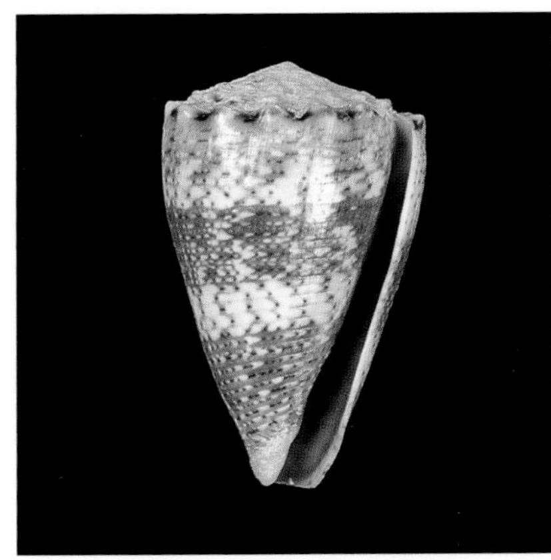

**CONUS ENCAUSTUS**
Burnt Cone. *Kiener 1845.*
Marquesas Islands.

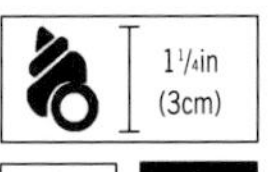
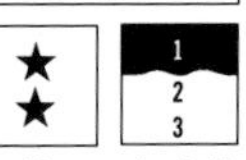

This little cone is one of several species of a similar shape and pattern, such as *C. abbreviatus*, *C. miliaris* and *C. fulgetrum*. This particular species, as depicted, is sufficiently different in colouring and pattern from the others to preserve its individual identity. Shells are restricted to shallow water in the Marquesas Islands. Unfortunately, as with many species, several specimens of each named shell need to be seen alongside each other if one is to appreciate the differences.

SUPER FAMILY
## CONOIDEA

FAMILY
## TURRIDAE
(Turrid Shells)

This is by far the largest group of molluscs, numbering over 1,000 described species, placed into numerous genera and subgenera. (Vaught lists over 200 genera alone!) Apart from taxonomic problems, I find the turrids extremely fascinating, due to the complexities and variations in their shape and structure. Indeed, one of my favourite species, *Thatcheria mirabilis*, is within this group. The identification clue to any turrid is the slit-like anal notch or sinus on the edge of the upper lip. All species are carnivorous and have a venomous gland which is used in association with the radula. They inhabit all seas of the world, in both shallow and very deep water. Of the species discussed here, most are within currently accepted genera – I have endeavoured to omit spurious and problematic species.

**DRILLIA ENNA**
*Dall 1918.*
South-West Pacific.

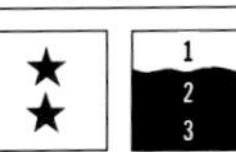

A heavy medium-sized turrid, it has a tall spire and axially nodulose whorls; the canal is very short and broad. There are fine spiral cords and the notch is U-shaped. Shells are variable in colour, as can be seen from these two specimens, both of which were collected in deep water in the Mactan Trench, central Philippines. Some authorities place this within the genus *Clavus*.

**DRILLIA ROSACEA**
Rose Turrid. *Reeve 1845.*
West Africa.

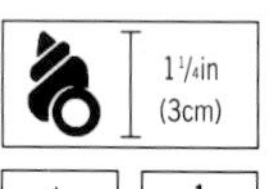

A beautiful small species, this has a tall spire, an impressed suture, and a small body whorl with a short but broad open canal. There are strong low axial ribs; the U-shaped notch is placed at the top of the aperture. The overall colour is a delicate pale pink, with darker pink tints on the inner lip and columella base.

**GEMMULA CONGENA CONGENA**
E. A. *Smith 1894.*
Philippines.

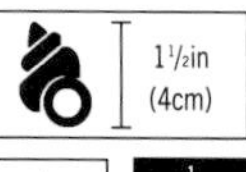

This small, slender and dainty turrid is fusiform in shape, with a tall stepped spire. The body whorl tapers to a long narrow open canal. The numerous fine spiral cords are beaded at the shoulders. The pale lavender background colour is offset by a broad tan spiral band running below the suture.

**GEMMULA KIENERI**
Kiener's Turrid. *Doumet 1840.*
Western Pacific and Australia.

A beautiful species, it has a tall spire and a centrally inflated body whorl which abruptly tapers to a canal of moderate length. The ornamentation takes the form of strong raised spiral cording, beaded at the shoulders, between which are numerous fine threads. The strong cords are brown, tending to reddish brown between the beading; there are also fine spiral dashes of brown on the lower part of the body whorl. The depicted shell is from Cape Moreton, Queensland.

**FUSITURRIS UNDATIRUGA**
Wrinkled Turrid. *Bivona 1832.*
Mediterranean.

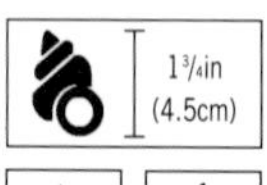

The wrinkled turrid is a popular and well-known species, and attractive both in shape and colouring. The tall spire has virtually straight-sided whorls, angled at the suture, and the body whorl is compressed and tapers to an open canal of moderate length. There are numerous axial or oblique low ribs and fine spiral grooves. A pale orange shell, it is decorated with brown spiral bands that run around the lower part of each whorl.

**GEMMULA GRAEFFEI**
Graeffe's Turrid. *Weinkauff 1875.*
Western Pacific.

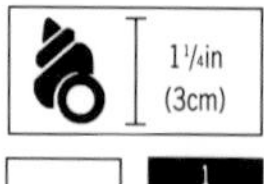

Another delicate little shell, this is fusiform, with a tall beige spire and a long narrow open canal which is a most beautiful lilac colour. There are close strong spiral cords, beaded at the centre, and a small but distinct notch. The Philippines species *G. concinna* is very similar and could well be a synonym. The depicted specimen was collected in Dingo Bay, Queensland.

**POLYSTIRA ALBIDA**
Giant White Turrid. *Perry 1811.*
South-eastern USA and West Indies.

A large heavy fusiform turrid, it has a tall spire, convex whorls and a stout broad siphonal canal. There are distinctive strong and narrow spiral cords. The aperture is smooth and white, but elsewhere the shell is cream or beige. Growth scars and healed breaks are often evident.

**PTYCHOSYRINX CHILENSIS**
Chilean Turrid. *Berry 1968.*
Chile.

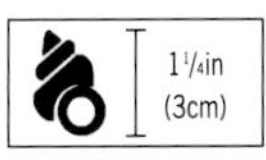

An extremely rare species, it is seldom available on the collectors' market. It has a tall spire, with rounded whorls which bear blunt low nodules at the centre. There are two strong and several fine spiral cords on the lower half of the body whorl. The suture is impressed. The depicted shell was trawled in 990ft (300m) off Coquimbo, Chile.

**XENOTURRIS CINGULIFERA**
Necklace Turrid. *Lamarck 1822.*
Japan and Western Pacific.

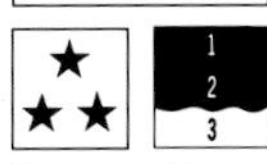

A medium-sized species, it is solid, with a tall spire which dominates the shell and has about 12 slightly convex-sided whorls. The smallish body whorl is compressed at the lower end into a large open canal. There are numerous spiral small beaded cords and one large raised cord on each whorl; the notch is prominent. The shell is off-white to beige, with brown dots and small patches.

**COCHLESPIRA ELEGANS**
Elegant Star Turrid. *Dall 1881.*
Florida to Cuba.

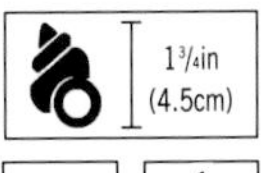

A most difficult species to obtain, due to its deep-water habitat, this is scarcely to be seen in amateur collections. It is a very attractive turrid, with a tall spire and sharply keeled and crenulated whorls, flat at the suture; there are numerous very fine spiral cords. The specimen shown here was dead-collected in deep water off western Florida. Most shells are off-white or cream.

**TURRIS UNDOSA**
*Lamarck 1816.*
Philippines.

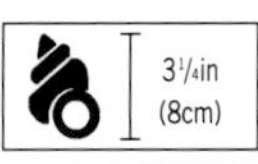

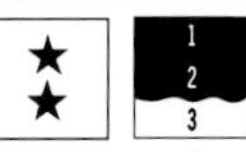

A fusiform shell, it has a very tall sharply tapering spire and a relatively short body whorl with a moderate open canal. There are both fine and strong rounded spiral cords. The aperture, columella and canal are pale purple; elsewhere, the shell is off-white, with mid-brown streaks and patches. An attractive and popular species.

**COCHLESPIRA PULCHELLA SEMIPLOTA**
Dull Star Turrid. *Powell 1969.*
Philippines.

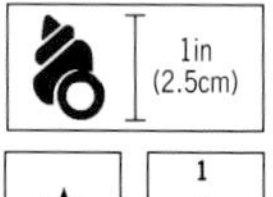

1in (2.5cm)

A small lightweight delicate and most beautiful turrid, it inhabits deep water in the Camotes and Sulu Seas. It is pagoda-like in shape, with sharply spinose keeled whorls and a very long and narrow canal. There are very fine spiral threads. It is beige to light brown in colour.

**COMITAS KADERLYI**
Kaderly's Turrid. *Lischke 1872.*
Japan to Australia.

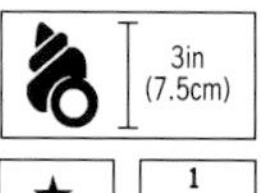

3in (7.5cm)

The depicted specimens were both trawled off Port Hedland, Western Australia in 1,155ft (350m) of water, and were supplied to me with the above name. The more slender shell, with the more pronounced axial ribs, looks not unlike *C. kamakurana* of Philippine origin. It is quite possible that one or both shells are intergrades, which exist between these species.

**FUSITURRICULA MAESAE**
Maese's Turrid. *Rios 1985.*
Brazil.

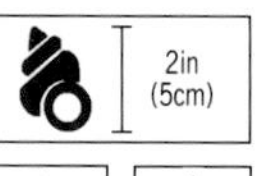

2in (5cm)

Very similar in shape, general appearance and colour to *Turricula*, this species is more slender and smaller, with finer nodules on the shoulders. The depicted specimen was dredged by shrimp fishermen in nets at 231ft (70m) off Rio de Janeiro.

**COCHLESPIRA CEDONULLI**
*Reeve 1843.*
Western Central America.

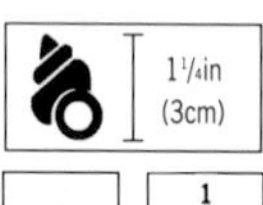

$1^1/_4$in (3cm)

Another delicate and beautiful shell, this is very much like *C. pulchella semiplota*, except that it has longer sharper spines on the keel and is smooth and glossy, with no threads. The depicted shell was dredged off Medidora Island, Panama, in 300ft (91m) of water.

**FUSITURRICULA JAQUENSIS**
Surinam Turrid. *Sowerby 1850.*
Colombia to Brazil.

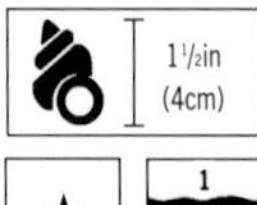

$1^1/_2$in (4cm)

This slender narrow shell has a tall spire and broadly shouldered whorls that are flat below the suture. The body whorl is compressed at the centre and tapers to a long wide open canal. There are numerous fine spiral cords and very low nodules on the earlier whorl shoulders. The shell is cream with light brown spotting and dots.

**KNEFASTIA TUBERCULIFERA**
Knobbed Turrid. *Broderip and Sowerby 1829.* Western Central America.

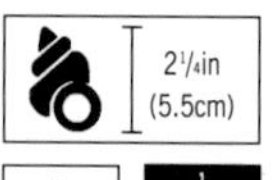

$2^1/_4$in (5.5cm)

The knobbed turrid has a tall spire, and whorls with heavily nodulose shoulders; the compressed body whorl tapers to a moderate open canal. The shell is attractively coloured off-white with rich brown broad spiral bands; the columella area is tinted pale orange or tan.

**NIHONIA MIRABILIS**
Remarkable Turrid. *Sowerby 1914.*
Japan.

A slender fusiform shell, endemic to Japan, it has a tall elegant spire, rounded whorls and a long straight and open canal. There are strong spiral cords. In colour, it is cream to light brown with tan axially laid streaks; the aperture is white. This specimen was trawled in 600ft (182m) off southern Japan.

**TURRICULA TORNATA**
Turned Turrid. *Dillwyn 1817.*
India to Thailand.

An elegant shell, the turned turrid has a tall spire, rounded whorls and a long and open canal. There is a flat spiral cord above the suture, and this is patterned with tan blotches. Elsewhere there are fine crossed or zigzag tan lines on a cream background. There are also fine spiral cords on the lower half of the body whorl. This specimen is from Phuket, Thailand.

**CLAVATULA MURICATA**
Muricate Turrid. *Lamarck 1822.*
West Africa.

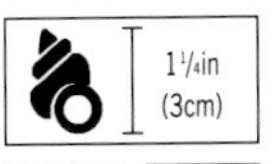


This small squat turrid has a tall spire, an enlarged body whorl and a short wide open canal. There is a row of short but sharp nodules below the suture and numerous low beaded cords on the lower half of the body whorl. Most shells are off-white or cream throughout.

**TURRICULA JAVANA**
Java Turrid. *L. 1767.*
Indo-Pacific.

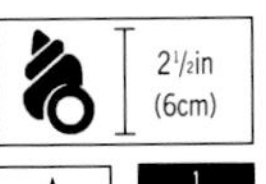


A fairly large but lightweight shell, with a tall spire, it has angled whorls and a long open siphonal canal. There are numerous very fine spiral cords and a series of low rounded blunt nodules on the shoulders. Its colour varies, as can be seen from the two depicted shells; the darker specimen is from Phuket, Thailand, the larger from Taiwan.

**CRASSISPIRA SEMIINFLATA**
*Grant 1931.*
California, USA.

This elongated slender shell has a black periostracum if left uncleaned. The spire is tall with convex-sided whorls, and there are numerous low axial and rounded ribs which are coloured a rich brown; the background is generally cream or beige. Three examples, including one with its periostracum, are seen here.

**CLAVATULA TAXUS**
Yew Turrid. *Chemnitz 1923.*
South Africa.

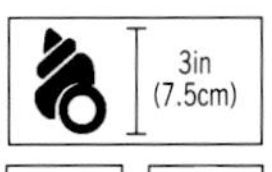


Endemic to South Africa, this is a large, fairly heavy and coarse-looking turrid, with a very tall spire and small body whorl that tapers to a short but broad open canal. The suture is distinctive in that it overlaps the whorl above it and is irregular in outline. Shells generally have several growth breaks and scars, and are almost always off-white or cream. A deep-water species, it is rarely offered by dealers or fishermen.

**BATHYTOMA LUHDORFI**
Lühdorf's Turrid. *Lischke 1872.*
Japan to Philippines.

Descriptions of this species in certain other sources suggest an off-white or creamy beige shell with some reddish brown spiral cords. The depicted two shells show no evidence of the brown markings, but their shape and ornamentation would appear to identify them as belonging to this species. The smaller of the two was fished off south-western Taiwan; the larger comes from the Camotes Sea.

**THATCHERIA MIRABILIS**
Miraculous Thatcher Shell. *Angas 1877.*
Japan to North-western Australia.

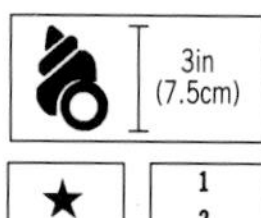


This is a wonderful pagoda-like lightweight shell of elegant proportions. A deep-water species, it is still regularly fished off Taiwan, but in recent years large and usually paler specimens have been trawled off Port Hedland, western Australia in about 825ft (250m) of water. It is a firm favourite of mine – and this is probably true of most collectors!

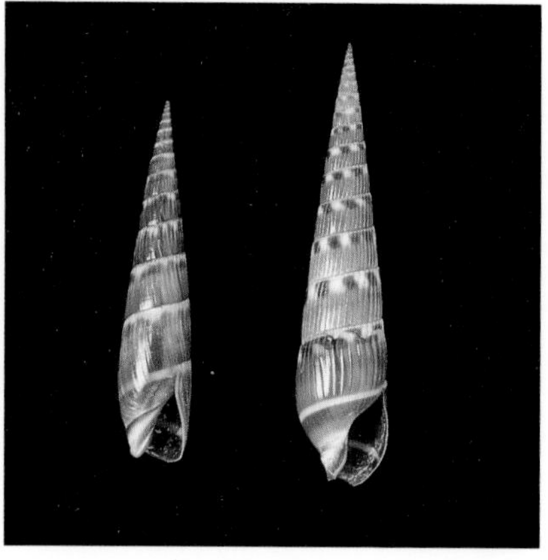

**HASTULA STYLATA**
Wide-mouthed Auger. *Hinds 1844.*
Indo-Pacific.

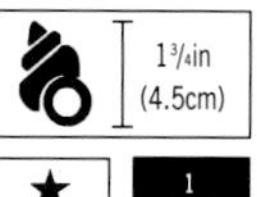


This small and glossy species has very fine axial grooves. Most specimens are a greyish brown, with pale cream spiral bands below the suture which can be spotted with black on some shells. The smaller of the two shells in the photograph portrays the characteristic gaping aperture and comes from Arue, Tahiti. The larger specimen originates from the Philippines.

**PLEUROTOMELLA AGUAYOI**
*Carcelles 1953.*
Brazil.

A squat lightweight little shell, it has a high spire, an inflated body whorl and a very short but broad canal. There are fine spiral grooves and numerous fine axial striations; the shoulders are rather angled and bear very small sharp nodules. The overall colour is beige, decorated with broad pale brown spiral bands. This specimen was collected by shrimp fishermen off Rio de Janeiro.

SUPER FAMILY
## CONOIDEA

FAMILY
## TEREBRIDAE
(Auger Shells)

This is a large family of very long and slender shells, ranging from small to large in size, and with numerous whorls. They are carnivorous and for the most part inhabit warm seas. The group arouses only modest interest among collectors, although many species are decorative and colourful. They all possess a thin horny operculum, and live in sand. Unlike many other highly glossy shells, the augers are not covered with a periostracum when living. There are eight main genera according to Vaught; we are primarily interested in *Terebra* and *Hastula*. There are also numerous subgenera.

**TEREBRA MACULATA**
Marlinspike Auger. *L. 1758.*
Indo-Pacific.

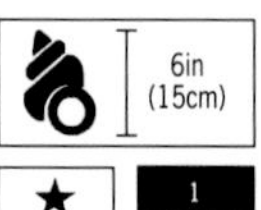


A very substantial heavy shell, this is the largest species in the family – the current world size record stands at over 10½in (27cm). The spire is very tall, with about 15 slightly convex-sided whorls, and the body whorl is narrow and rounded, with an ovate aperture. The suture is impressed. It is an attractively patterned shell, with spiral rows of greyish blue and brown squared patches and streaks on a cream and fawn background.

**TEREBRA GUTTATA**
Spotted Auger. *Röding 1798.*
Indo-Pacific.

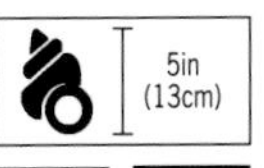

The handsome spotted auger has a tall acute spire, with more or less straight-sided whorls; these are slightly inflated below the suture. The colour is an unusual pinkish beige, with prominent large white spots on the upper part of each whorl. Large specimens, exceeding 6in (15cm), occur from time to time in the Sulu Sea.

**TEREBRA DIMIDIATA**
Dimidiate Auger. *L. 1758.*
Indo-Pacific.

A smooth and glossy shell, it displays a beautiful pattern of pinkish orange squared markings and bands on off-white. There are about 15 very slightly convex-sided whorls. One spiral groove occurs below the suture. Large perfect specimens exceeding 4¼in (11cm) are scarce.

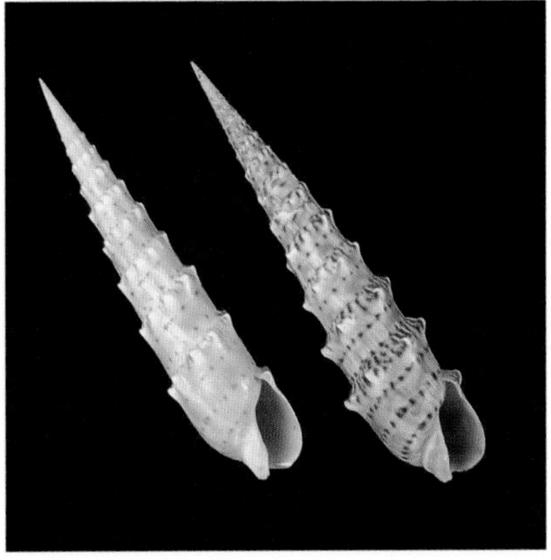

**TEREBRA CRENULATA**
Crenulated Auger. *L. 1758.*
Indo-Pacific.

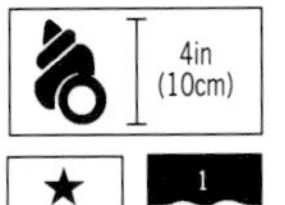

A medium-sized and stocky shell, it has rather variable sculpturing and pattern. Some forms have virtually smooth straight-sided whorls; others, as depicted, are strongly nodulose below the suture. The two shells also display some colour and pattern variations. The darker shell is from the Solomon Islands; the paler from Tahiti.

**TEREBRA SUBULATA**
Subulate Auger. *L. 1767.*
Indo-Pacific.

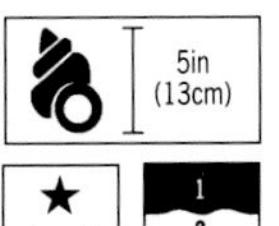

A tall and slender shell, its spire comprises at least 20 slightly convex-sided whorls. The suture is impressed. The body whorl, as in all augers, narrows to a short open canal. The creamy beige background is overlaid with two distinct spiral rows of dark brown squared blotches.

**TEREBRA AREOLATA**
Flyspotted Auger. *Link 1807.*
Indo-Pacific.

This species is often confused with *T. subulata*, and vice-versa. It differs, however, in that it is generally more inflated toward the anterior end, and there are three distinct spiral bands of brown markings. There are slight columella folds.

**TEREBRA CHLORATA**
Short Auger. *Lamarck 1822.*
Indo-Pacific.

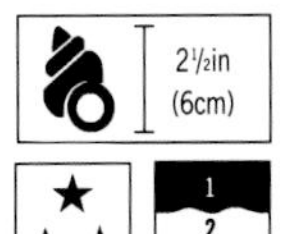

A shortish rather stumpy shell, it lacks the tall elegance of some species. The whorls are straight-sided and there is one spiral groove below the suture. The cream background is overlaid with pale bluish grey spiral blotches and pale tan axial wavy lines. The columella has a strong fold.

**TEREBRA STRIGATA**
Zebra Auger. *Sowerby 1825.* Western Central America and Galapagos Islands.

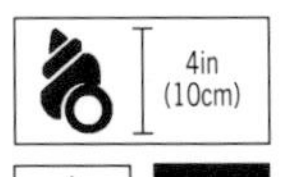


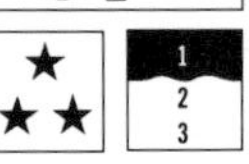


A stocky auger, it has an inflated body whorl and an acute tall spire. There is one fine spiral groove below the suture and numerous low axial ribs on the earlier whorls. It is a most strikingly marked shell, with vivid dark brown axial streaks and "flame" markings on a dull cream background. Shells often have healed breaks and growth scars. This specimen is from Gubernadora Island, Panama.

**TEREBRA TAURINA**
Flame Auger. *Lightfoot 1786.* South-eastern USA to Brazil.

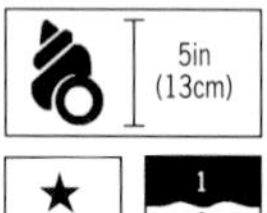


Long and slender, with about 20 convex-sided whorls, the flame auger is of dull texture and there are many closely set growth striations. The colour is cream, with numerous hazy dark brown patches and "flame" markings.

**TEREBRA ORNATA**
Ornate Auger. *Gray 1834.* Western Central America and Galapagos Islands.

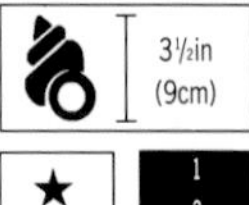


A medium-sized sturdily built species, it has straight-sided whorls. The suture is impressed, and there is one spiral groove midway between it, on each whorl. The shell is matt in appearance, and the cream background is decorated with spiral rows of neat hazy brown spots. A sought-after collectors' shell.

**TEREBRA ROBUSTA**
Robust Auger. *Hinds 1844.* Western Central America and Galapagos Islands.

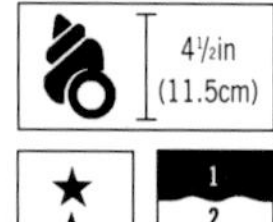


Often confused with *T. taurina*, the robust auger can be distinguished by its more prominent and less hazy axial "flame" marks or streaks. It also lacks the fine growth striations, and has fine nodulose ribs on the earlier whorls. It is a shallow-water sand dweller. The depicted shell is from western Panama.

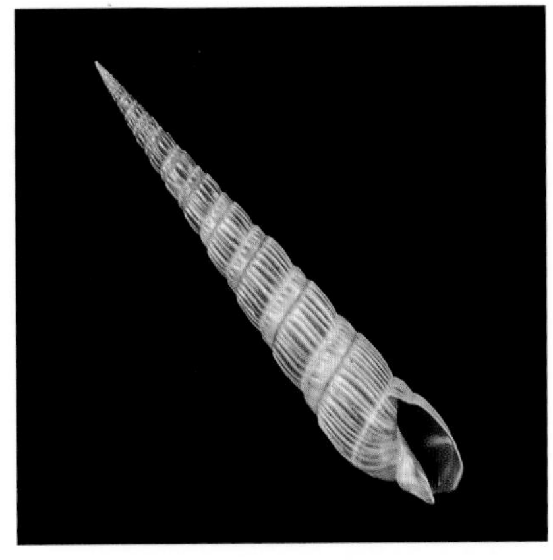

**TEREBRA DUSSUMIERI**
Dussumier's Auger. *Kiener 1839.*
Japan to Taiwan.

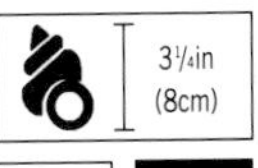


A medium-sized and glossy shell, it has distinctive low axial ribbing and broad spirally beaded bands below the suture. The colour is a greyish beige. These shells were in adequate supply before Taiwan altered its fishing habits, but nowadays the species is difficult to obtain in reasonable numbers.

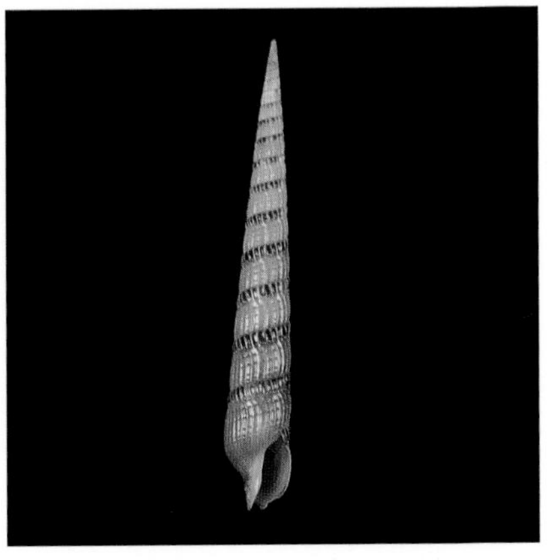

**TEREBRA PERTUSA**
Perforated Auger. *Born 1778.*
Eastern Indian Ocean to Hawaii.

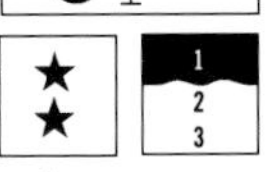

This is a small slender auger with a high gloss. The 15 or so straight-sided whorls have very fine ribs and are crossed with spirally laid rows of neat indentations. An attractive pale orange overall, it has brown bands at the suture. Shells frequently display healed breaks and scars.

**TEREBRA DISLOCATA**
Common American Auger. *Say 1822.*
South-eastern USA to Brazil.

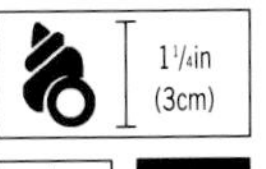


This small dainty shell is pale grey in colour and has straight-sided whorls, each bearing fine axial ribs. There is a broad beaded band above the suture. The aperture is brown. The surface is moderately glossy. The depicted specimen was collected in 3ft (1m) of sand at Texas Beach, Florida.

**TEREBRA SENEGALENSIS**
Faval Auger. *Lamarck 1822.*
West Africa.

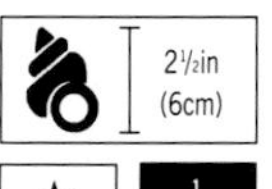


A smallish smooth shell, it has a moderate gloss and is very similar in shape to *T. chlorata*, though it is rather narrower than the latter. The beige background is overlaid with hazy and indistinct patches and squares of grey brown. The earlier whorls have fine axial ribs. The shell in the photograph was collected in sand off Mussulo Bay, Angola.

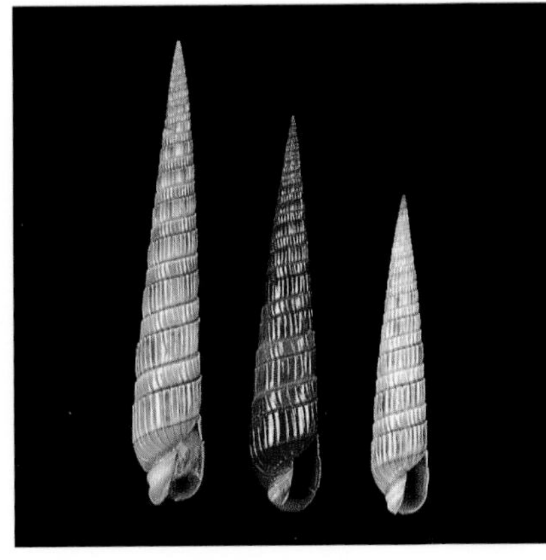

**TEREBRA DUPLICATA**
Duplicate Auger. *L. 1758.*
West Pacific/Indian Ocean.

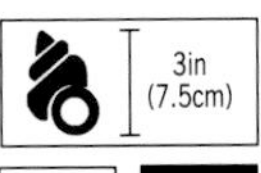


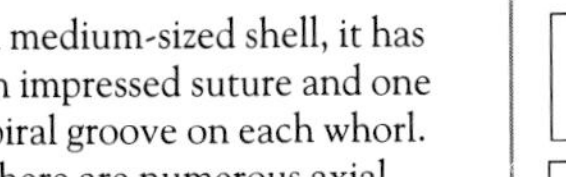

A medium-sized shell, it has an impressed suture and one spiral groove on each whorl. There are numerous axial grooves. The shell is highly glossy and occurs in a range of plain colours, a selection of which can be seen in the three depicted specimens. The species is placed by some authorities within the subgenus *Duplicaria*.

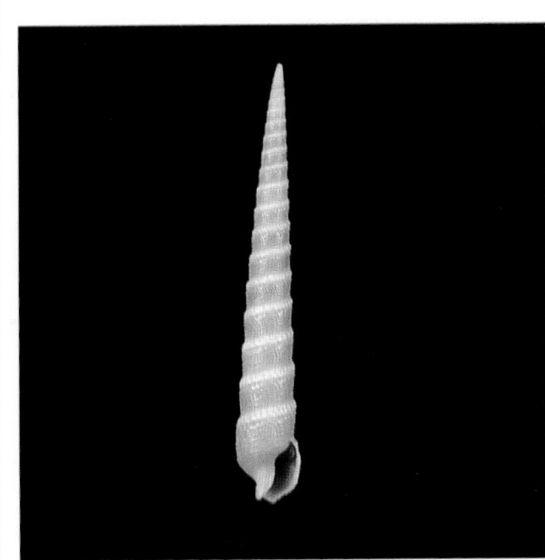

**TEREBRA LAEVIGATA**
*Gray 1834.*
Western Pacific.

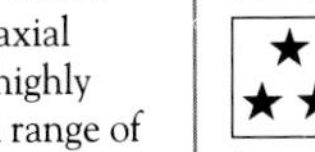


A very slender auger with about 18 straight-sided whorls, it has many very fine spirally beaded threads and a double row of stronger ones below the suture. The greyish beige or creamy yellow colour is sometimes offset by one paler spiral band per whorl. This particular specimen came from the Solomon Islands.

**TEREBRA NEBULOSA**
Red Cloud Auger. *Sowerby 1825.*
Tropical Indo-Pacific.

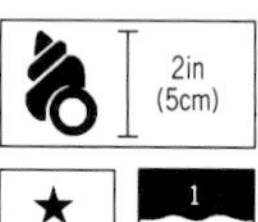


An attractively coloured shell, it is off-white with reddish orange axial patches or streaks. There are numerous low rounded ribs and one ribbed spiral band on each whorl below the suture. This specimen was collected on Honiara Reef, Solomon Islands.

**TEREBRA CORRUGATA**
Corrugated Auger. *Lamarck 1822.*
West Africa.

An attractive medium-sized shell, it has a low gloss. Below the suture occurs a row of very low nodules which on the smaller earlier whorls appear as small indentations. It is an off-white to cream shell, with small reddish brown dots and axial streaks. It inhabits shallow to moderately deep water.

**TEREBRA VARIEGATA**
Variegate Auger. *Gray 1834.*
Western Central America.

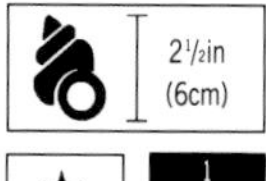


A medium-sized shell, its rounded whorls number about 15 in mature shells. Below the suture are broad bands bearing small rounded nodules; between these are fine spiral cords. It is prettily patterned with brown spots and axial streaks on a grey background.

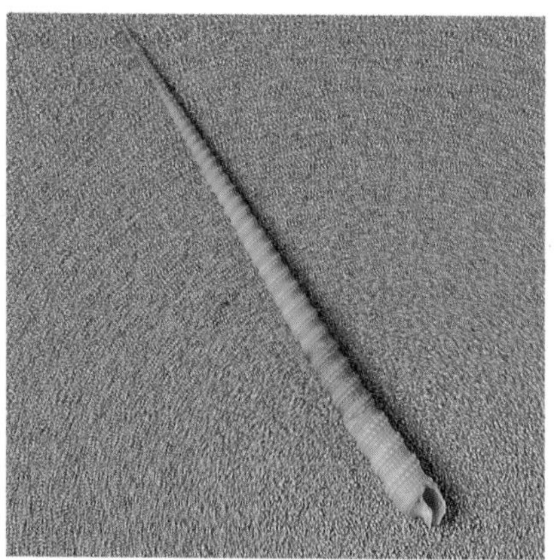

**TEREBRA TRISERATA**
Triseriate Auger. *Gray 1834.*
Japan, Taiwan and South-West Pacific.

This is an amazingly long and very narrow species – there can be at least 35 whorls in mature specimens. Between a double row of strong spiral beading is a minute reticulation of ribs and grooves. The colour is a dull orange or pale brown. Choice specimens are now seldom available from Taiwan, where they were once fished in good numbers.

**TEREBRA CRACILENTA**
*Li 1930.*
Western Central America to Ecuador.

A smallish robust auger, its straight-sided whorls are slightly angular above the suture. The texture is totally beaded, the strongest row running spirally below the suture. A creamy beige colour, it inhabits offshore waters in depths of about 100ft (30m).

**TEREBRA NASSOIDES**
*Hinds 1844?*
Gulf of Oman.

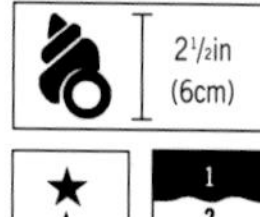


This species is very similar in shape to *H. stylata*, but is almost twice the size. It is completely smooth and is much paler than *H. stylata* in colour, being off-white, with beige or pale orange axial streaks and a neat spiral row of reddish brown dots below the suture. The shell has a high gloss. It is possibly endemic to the Gulf of Oman.

SUPER FAMILY
ARCHITECTONICOIDEA

FAMILY
## ARCHITECTONICIDAE
(Sundial Shells)

This is a small family of flat, disc-shaped shells, with low spires and a sharply keeled periphery; they have a large and open umbilicus. They possess a horny operculum and inhabit varying depths of water, generally in tropical seas. There are several genera, of which *Architectonica*, *Heliacus*, *Philippia* and *Discotectonica* are of interest to us. Differences between the larger species are not easy to detect by pattern and markings alone; more study is required before the collector can satisfactorily differentiate between them – no one handbook or guide facilitates quick identification of this rather confusing group.

### ARCHITECTONICA NOBILIS
American Sundial. *Röding 1798.* Caribbean and West Central America and West Africa.

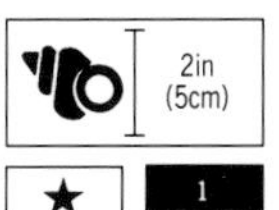


The medium-sized and heavy American sundial has a low spire and a slightly convex base. The shell is generally pale in colour, with occasional brown spots and blotches. There are several large raised and flat cords on the whorls, and a very thick nodular ridge surrounds the moderate umbilicus. The smaller of the two specimens is from Senegal; the larger is from south-western Florida.

### ARCHITECTONICA PERDIX
Partridge Sundial. *Hinds 1844.* West Pacific/Indian Ocean.

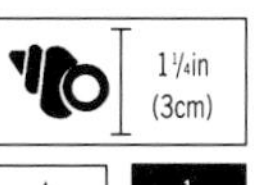


This little shell has beaded spiral cords and, on close examination, very fine axial striae. The open and deep umbilicus is encircled by the typical strongly ribbed or beaded ridges. The off-white to pale cream background is offset with neat rows of spirally laid pale brown blotches. The depicted shell is from Keppel Bay, Queensland.

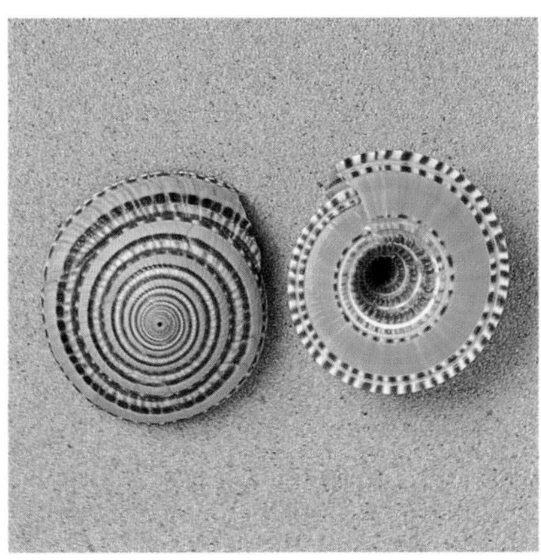

### ARCHITECTONICA PERSPECTIVA
Clear Sundial. *L. 1758.* Indo-Pacific.

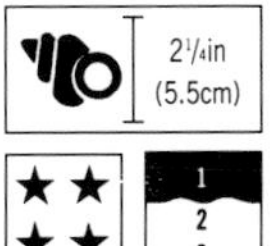


A large solid shell, it has a low spire and a flat base. On each whorl is one deep spiral groove below the suture and one strong raised cord above. There are two raised cords above the periphery keel of the body whorl. There are numerous fine axial grooves on the earlier whorls. Two beaded ridges and one groove border the wide and deep umbilicus. The species is a shallow-water sand dweller.

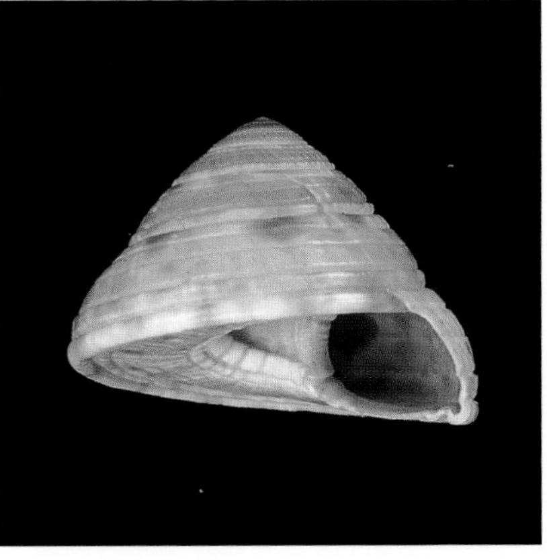

### ARCHITECTONICA LAEVIGATA
Smooth Sundial. *Lamarck 1816.* Indian Ocean.

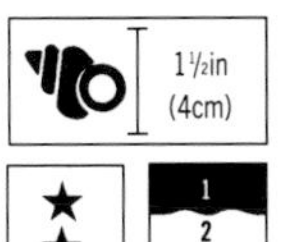


A small shell, the smooth sundial has a moderate to tall spire, with whorls bearing about four spiral grooves. Its texture is, as one might assume, smooth compared to other species, and is fairly glossy. The base is somewhat concave. This shell is a pale beige to lavender, with haphazard blotches of orange brown.

### *DISCOTECTONICA ACUTISSIMA*
Sharp-edged Sundial. *Sowerby 1914.* Japan to Northern Australia.

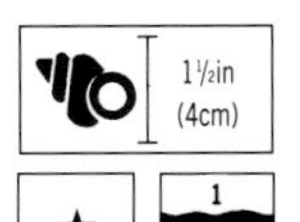


An almost flat species, with a very sharp keel, it has a rather convex base. The whorls bear extremely fine spiral threads. The deep and open umbilicus is bordered by several rows of beaded cords. The overall colour is beige; the base is paler, being cream or off-white. The two shells shown are from deep water in the central Philippines.

**HELIACUS STRAMINEUS**
Straw Sundial. *Gmelin 1791.*
Indo-Pacific.

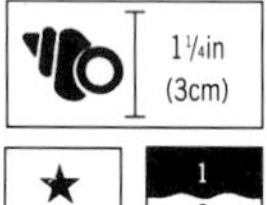


A sundial with a moderately tall spire, its whorls bear numerous spiral cords which are crossed by very fine axial striae. The body whorl has no keel and is wide and rounded. The aperture is circular and large, and the umbilicus is open and deep – the base of the apex can be seen within it. This specimen was collected off south-western Taiwan, in shallow water.

**PHILIPPIA RADIATA**
Radial Sundial. *Röding 1798.*
West Pacific/Indian Ocean.

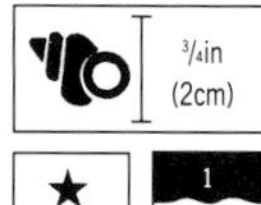


Another small species, this has a tall humped spire. The shell is smooth in texture and has a moderate gloss. There are two fine raised cords on the lower part of each whorl. There is a small open umbilicus; the base is rather convex. An overall cream colour, the shell has a tan or pale orange spiral band and axial streaks.

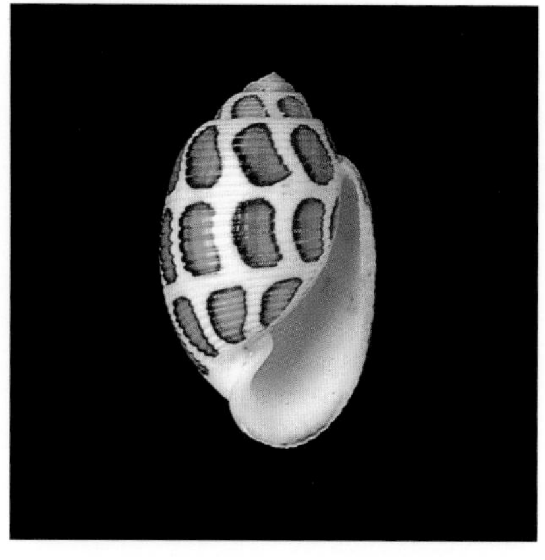

FAMILY
## ACTEONIDAE

**ACTEON ELOISAE**
Eloise's Acteon. *Abbott 1973.*
Oman.

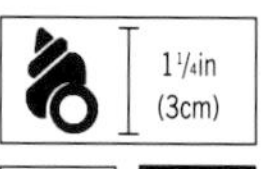


This beautifully marked and most desirable species has a fairly strong ovate shell, with a low spire. The suture is channelled, and there are many low spiral cords. It is pure white, with vivid reddish-tan blotches, encircled with black. The species is endemic to Oman.

**HELIACUS VARIEGATUS**
Variegated Sundial. *Gmelin 1791.*
West Pacific/Indian Ocean.

One of the smallest of the family, this little shell has a flat or slightly raised spire, with whorls bearing strong striated or beaded cords. The open umbilicus is surrounded by a beaded ridge. Usually cream or off-white, it features dark brown irregular spots or axial streaks and patches.

SUPER FAMILY
## PHILINOIDEA

The subclass Opisthobranchia comprises a group of molluscs that are mostly shell-less and without an operculum. This group includes the sea hares (Aplysiidae) and sea slugs, Nudibranchs, and generally do not concern us here. There are, however, within this section species that do possess shells and are of interest to the conchologist and amateur collector, namely the bubble shells. The families that are of interest are Acteonidae, with several genera, including *Acteon* and *Pupa*; Hydantinidae, with the genus *Hydatina* and subgenus *Aplustrum*; Bullidae, with the genus *Bulla*; and finally Hamineidae, with the genus *Atys*. They are all small-to-medium, lightweight, rounded or ovate shells, with a wide distribution. For the following species, the family heading is given but not discussed, after which the genus and species are described as normal.

**ACTEON VIRGATUS**
Striped Acteon. *Reeve 1842.*
South-West Pacific.

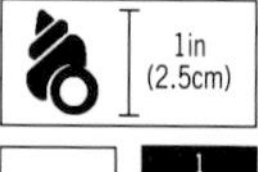


A stocky little shell, it is ovate in shape and has a low spire. The body whorl is much enlarged. It is patterned with wavy axial brown lines on a creamy white background. There are extremely fine spiral grooves at the lower end of the body whorl. The depicted shell is from Efate, New Hebrides.

FAMILY
# HYDATINIDAE

### *APLUSTRUM AMPLUSTRE*
Royal Paper Bubble. *L. 1758.*
Indo-Pacific.

An attractive bubble, it has an ovate shape and a flat spire; the suture is channelled. The shell is patterned with two broad pink and four thin black spiral bands on a white background. This particular specimen displays good colour; many are unfortunately very dull in appearance.

### *HYDATINA PHYSIS*
Paper Bubble Shell. *L. 1758.*
Indo-Pacific.

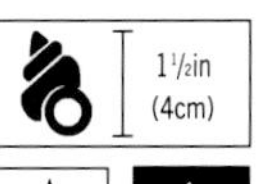

An extremely thin lightweight ovate or rounded shell, it has a depressed spire and an enlarged and bulbous body whorl. It is most prettily decorated with olive green to dark brown slightly wavy spiral lines, set against a cream background.

### *HYDATINA ZONATA*
Zoned Paper Bubble. *Lightfoot 1786.*
Indo-Pacific.

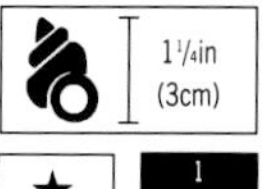

This very lightweight paper-thin species has a depressed spire and a large bulbous body whorl. The aperture is large and gaping. The off-white shell is patterned with broad brown spiral bands – two at the centre – between which are many fine axial pale brown lines. It inhabits shallow to moderately deep water.

### *HYDATINA ALBOCINCTA*
White-banded Bubble. *Van der Hoeven 1839.* Taiwan and Japan.

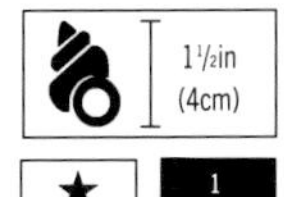

Very thin and lightweight and very similar in shape to *H. zonata*, the white-banded bubble has a larger and more gaping aperture. The spire is depressed. The shell is vividly marked with four broad brown spiral bands on a dull creamy background.

FAMILY
## BULLIDAE

### BULLA STRIATA
Common Atlantic Bubble. *Bruguière 1792.*
Florida to Brazil and Mediterranean.

This fairly sturdy bubble shell is usually ovate, with a depressed spire. The body whorl is compressed at the posterior end. Shells are most variable in pattern and colour, but all have white, brown and grey hazy blotches; the aperture is white. These two pretty specimens were collected off Yucatan, Mexico.

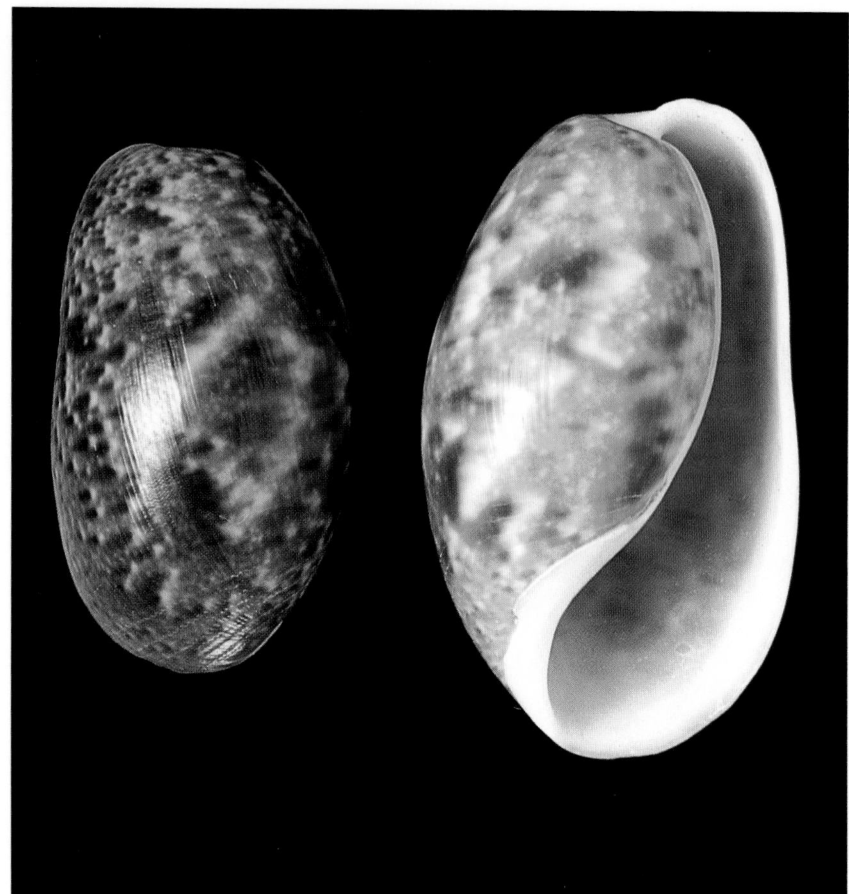

### BULLA MABILLEI
Mabille's Bubble. *Locard 1896.*
Canary Islands.

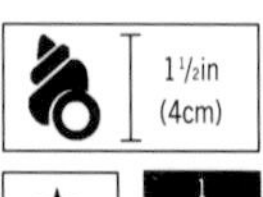


An attractive shell, it is very similar in shape to *B. striata*, but is generally larger. The pretty markings consist of purple and greyish white spots and blotches on a lilac background. The aperture and columella are white. This particular shell was collected in 165ft (50m) off Agaete, north-western Gran Canaria.

FAMILY
## HAMINEIDAE

### ATYS NAUCUM
White Pacific Atys. *L. 1758.*
Indo-Pacific.

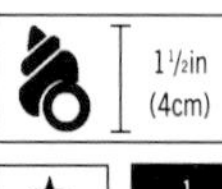


This lightweight shell is white and almost translucent, with very fine spiral threads. It is rather globose, and the posterior lip margin extends up and over the virtually absent depressed spire. There is a small columella fold. The depicted shell is from the central Philippines.

### ATYS CYLINDRICUS
*Helbling 1779.*
Indo-Pacific.

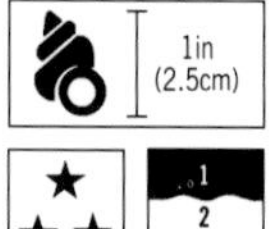


An ovate and cylindrical shell, it has a depressed spire and is white throughout, with no ornamentation apart from fine axial growth striations. The lip is solid, and the posterior margin extends up above the apex. The species is an intertidal sand dweller.

# CLASS: BIVALVIA

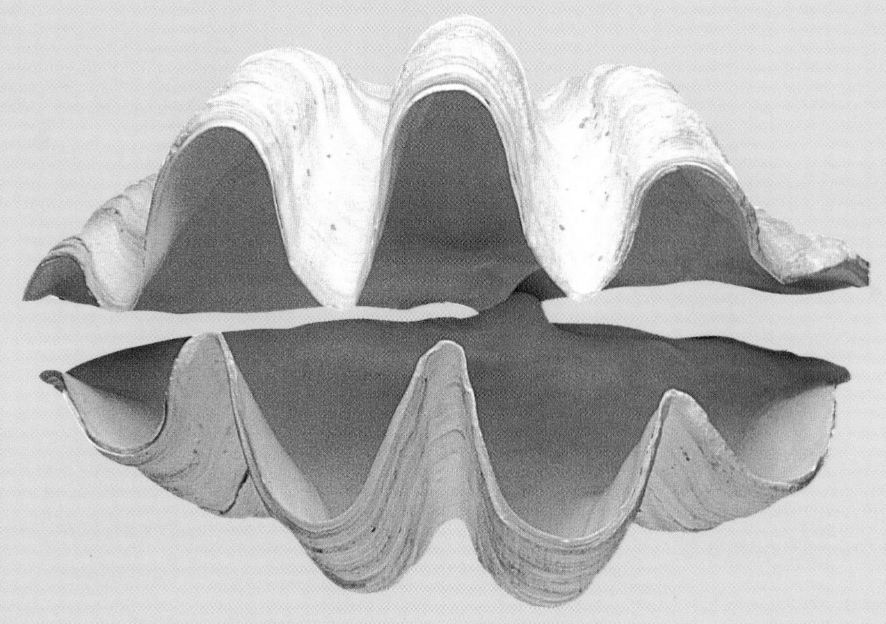

SUPER FAMILY
## ARCOIDEA

FAMILY
### ARCIDAE
(Ark Shells)

A medium-sized family, it contains about 200 species, most of which live in warm seas. They are heavy, solid shells, with a long straight hinge bearing a row of many fine interlocking teeth (toxodont). They usually live attached to rocks and in cliff cracks and crevices by a byssus of hair, which serves as an anchor. Most species inhabit shallow water, but a few live in very deep habitats. This is not a particularly popular group with collectors. There are several genera, of which *Arca*, *Anadara*, *Trisidos* and *Barbatia* are the best known.

**ANADARA MACULOSA**
Maculose Ark. *Reeve 1844.*
South-West Pacific.

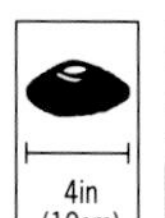


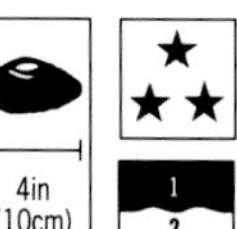


A large and solid shell, it has equal and inflated valves. The umbones are large, and the escutcheon is chalky white, with black zebra-like stripes. There are strong radial ribs and concentric growth lines toward the lip margins. When the thick brown periostracum is removed, a pure white shell is revealed.

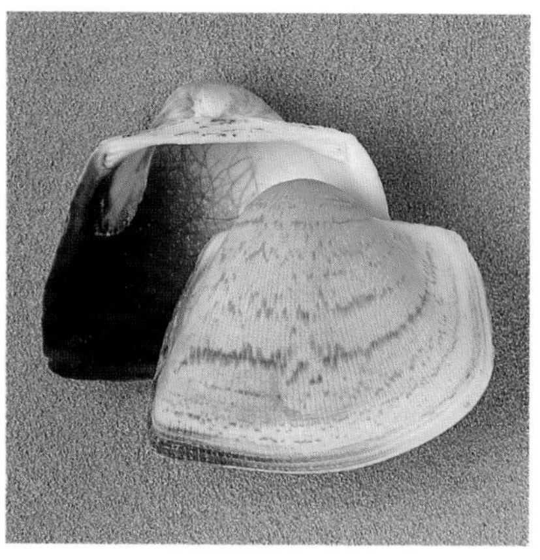

**CUCULLAEA LABIATA**
Hooded Ark. *Lightfoot 1786.*
South-West Pacific.

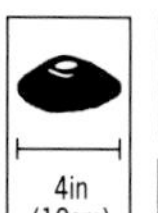

A large medium-weight shell, it has inflated equal valves and low umbones. The shell is reticulated, with many fine radial grooves and crossed by concentric striations. This species can be termed a living fossil, as it has survived the passage of time over thousands of years without change in form or structure. The depicted shell shows typical colour and pattern although some have all-white interiors. It is from the central Philippines.

**TRISIDOS SEMITORTA**
Half-propeller Ark. *Lamarck 1819.*
Japan to the Philippines.

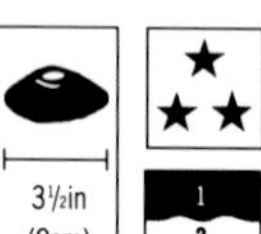


This solid heavy chalky white species has inflated long valves which are twisted at the posterior end. There are numerous fine radial ridges and several concentric growth lines. Some shells, such as the one in the photograph, have a yellow interior. The hinge teeth are toxodont.

SUPER FAMILY
## ARCOIDEA

FAMILY
### CUCULAEIDAE
(Ark Shells)

This very small family contains one genus, *Cucullaea*, which consists of primitive bivalves, very closely related to the true ark shells (Arcidae). The Cuculaeidae are inflated, and one valve usually overlaps the other at the lip margin. The teeth are long and are either oblique or parallel to the hinge line.

SUPER FAMILY
## LIMOPSOIDEA

FAMILY
### GLYCIMERIDIDAE
(Bittersweet Clams)

These are rounded thick and heavy shells, with toxodont teeth which are similar to those of the ark shells. There are well over 100 species, of which most inhabit shallow water in the Indo-Pacific region. The shells are porcellaneous and have a thick periostracum. There are several genera, of which *Glycymeris* is the best known. Many species are edible.

**GLYCYMERIS GIGANTEA**
Giant Bittersweet. *Reeve 1843.*
Gulf of California.

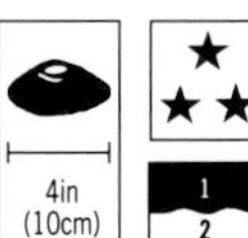
4in (10cm)

This attractive shell has rounded, thick and very heavy symmetrical valves with low umbones and a long narrow and deep escutcheon. There is a very obvious row of coarse toxodont teeth, and the white interior has some purple or brown staining. The off-white exterior is overlaid with rich brown streaks and zigzag markings.

**GLYCYMERIS PECTUNCULUS**
Comb Bittersweet. *L. 1758.* Tropical Indo-Pacific and North-West Indian Ocean.

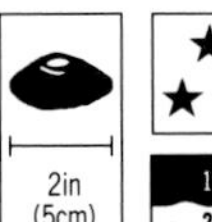
2in (5cm)

This bittersweet has rather compressed, rounded and solid symmetrical valves, dominated by strong radial ribs. It is cream to brown, with dark brown wavy concentric bands and blotches. The teeth are obviously toxodont, and the off-white interior is stained with brown. This specimen was collected in 3ft (1m) in sand at Obhor Creek, Jeddah, Red Sea.

SUPER FAMILY
## MYTILOIDEA

FAMILY
## MYTILIDAE
(Mussel Shells)

The species belonging to this large family occur in a world wide range of locations, usually in shallow intertidal waters. The shells are relatively thin, elongated and oval, with a very weak hinge structure, and a few have fine teeth. Most species live in colonies, attached to rocks by means of a byssus, but some genera burrow in rocks or coral. Many mussel species are edible. The important genera are: *Mytilus*, *Perna*, *Modiolus* and *Lithophaga*. The shells are covered with a periostracum and the interiors are often nacreous.

**AULACOMYA ATER**
Black-ribbed Mussel. *Molina 1782.*
Eastern and Western South America.

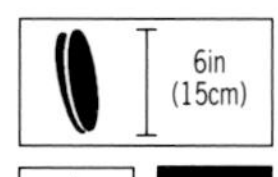
6in (15cm)

A large species, with wavy low radial ribs, it is ovate in shape, with sharply tapering almost pointed umbones; the valves are equal. There is a long fine ligament hinge and one rather large primitive tooth, with a corresponding notch in the opposite valve. The shell in the photograph is a small immature specimen, portraying more colour than larger shells; it is from Chiloe, Chile.

**_MYTILUS EDULIS_**
Common Blue Mussel. *L. 1758.*
Worldwide (not polar seas).

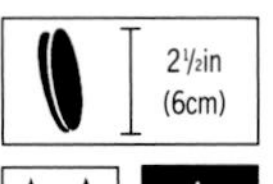

A well-known and most popular sea food, this species is found on rocky shorelines in great numbers, and is often farmed in "mussel beds". Beneath the brown periostracum is a purplish blue shell with a silver blue nacreous interior. The valves are attached by a long thin ligament. The umbones are rounded and sharply pointed.

**_PERNA VIRIDIS_**
Green Mussel. *L. 1758.*
Indian Ocean and South-West Pacific.

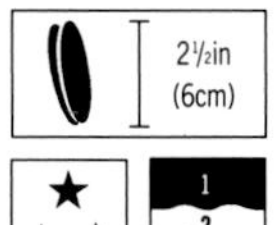

Another attractive species, this has a green periostracum. It is elongated, narrow and rather curved, with tapering umbones. There are many concentric growth lines on the exterior. The interior is an iridescent pale blue/green. This specimen was collected in southern Thailand.

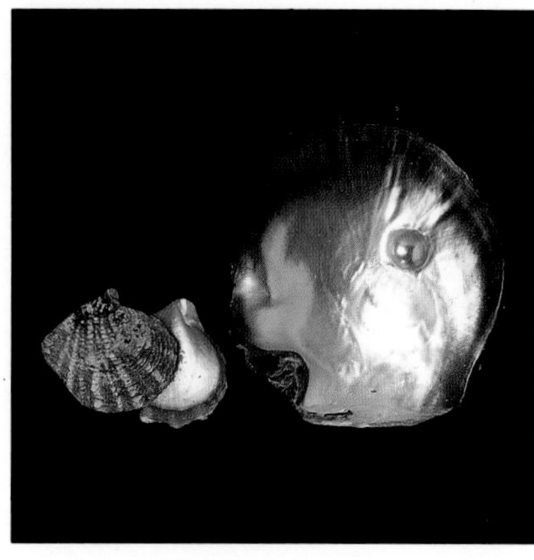

**_PINCTADA MARGARITIFERA_**
Black-lipped Pearl Oyster. *L. 1758.*
Indo-Pacific.

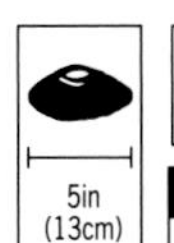

A large oyster, this has equal compressed valves with a rich silver grey nacreous interior edged with greyish black. The exterior is formed from concentric layers of flaky green and grey lamellae. Some whitish radial bands are also evident. The large specimen bears a blister pearl which has been cultured or induced artificially.

**PERNA CANALICULUS**
Channel Mussel. *Gmelin 1791.*
New Zealand.

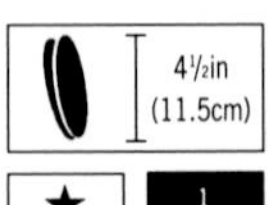

This large, ovate and elongated shell has a very attractive rich green periostracum, under which are several rows of black radial lines. The umbones are rounded but pointed, and there is a rudimentary tooth structure and a long ligament. The depicted shell, from the Houraki Gulf region, is one of many that are farmed and subsequently exported to Britain for the retail food trade.

SUPER FAMILY
## PTERIOIDEA

FAMILY
### PTERIIDAE
(Wing and Pearl Oysters)

The wing and pearl oysters are a large family of bivalves living, for the most part, in tropical seas. They have a highly nacreous interior, and many are capable of producing pearls, the genus *Pinctada* producing pearls of gem quality. The shells grow a byssus, by which *Pinctada* species attach themselves to coral rubble and *Pteria* species to gorgonian stems. The main characteristic of the genus *Pteria* is a long wing-like extension of the hinge line; all species have a byssal notch (through which the byssus extends for anchorage) on the anterior margin of the lower valve.

**PINCTADA MARTENSII**
Marten's Pearl Oyster. *Dunker 1872.*
Western Pacific.

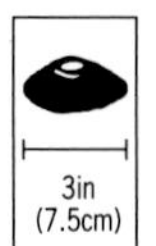
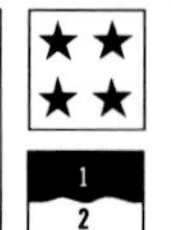

This is the mother shell of the famous Japanese cultured pearl, and is farmed in great numbers solely for this purpose. The shell is of medium size, and is rather inflated and fragile. The exterior is rough and covered with layers of greyish purple lamellae, which extend over the margins. The byssal notch lies below a small winged projection of the hinge line.

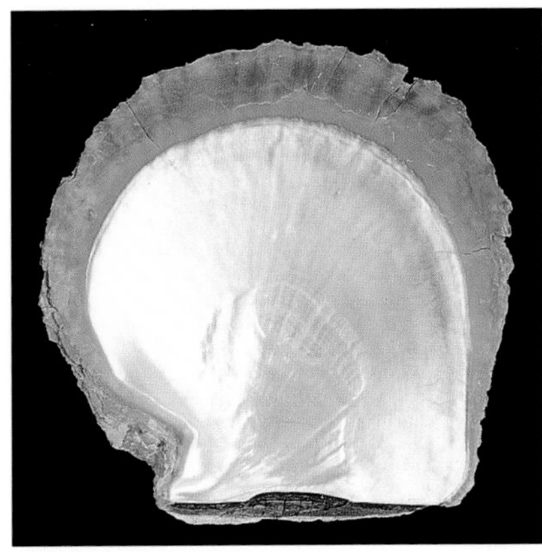

**PINCTADA MAXIMA**
Gold-lip Pearl Oyster. *Jameson 1901.*
Western Pacific.

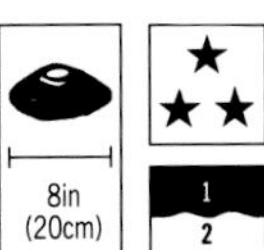


This, the largest of the pearl oysters, boasts the highest quality mother-of-pearl, and the shell is widely used in the mother-of-pearl industry. The silver yellow nacre is edged with a greenish gold tint, hence its common name. The depicted single valve clearly shows the interior, with its large muscle scar and the coarse and overlapping flaky lamellae from the exterior; the byssal notch indentation and the long hinge, to which some black ligament is still attached, can be clearly seen.

SUPER FAMILY
PTERIOIDEA

FAMILY
## MALLEIDAE
(Hammer Oysters)

A small curious family of bivalves, the hammer oysters have semi-nacreous interiors and a general hammer-like appearance, due to greatly extended hinge lines. The body of the shell is elongated, irregular and narrow, and consists of rough coarse overlapping lamellae. There is a small pit or indentation in the centre of the top edge of the hinge, to accommodate the ligament. Most species inhabit intertidal reefs in tropical waters. There is one well-known genus – *Malleus*.

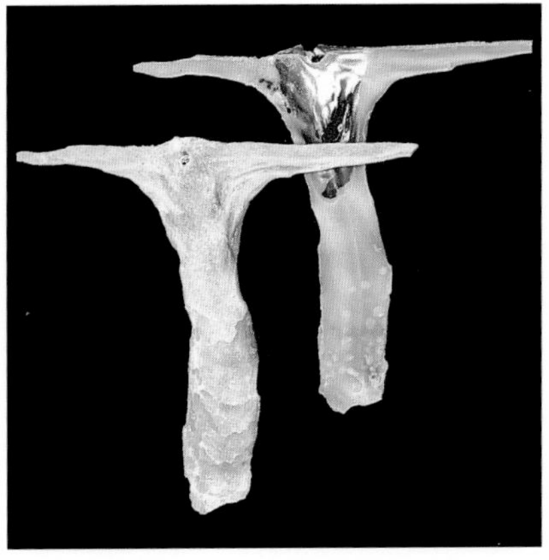

**MALLEUS ALBUS**
White Hammer Oyster. *Lamarck 1819.*
Indo-Pacific.

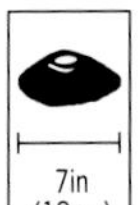


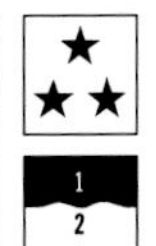


The white hammer oyster has extended hinge lines of almost equal length, looking like narrow ears, and a long narrow undulating body. It is creamy beige in colour (seldom white) and has an attractive blue grey nacreous interior with one dominant muscle scar. This species is frequently available in the Philippines and is popular with bivalve collectors.

**PTERIA PENGUIN**
Penguin Wing Oyster. *Röding 1798.*
Indo-Pacific.

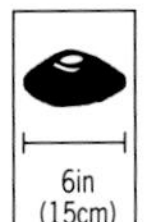

An ovate and fairly fragile shell, it has unequal valves, the upper, or right, valve being more inflated. The depicted specimen clearly shows the characteristic extension of the hinge line. As is the case with most oysters, parts of the shell expand and crack when they are in a dry warm atmosphere. This shell is from the central Philippines.

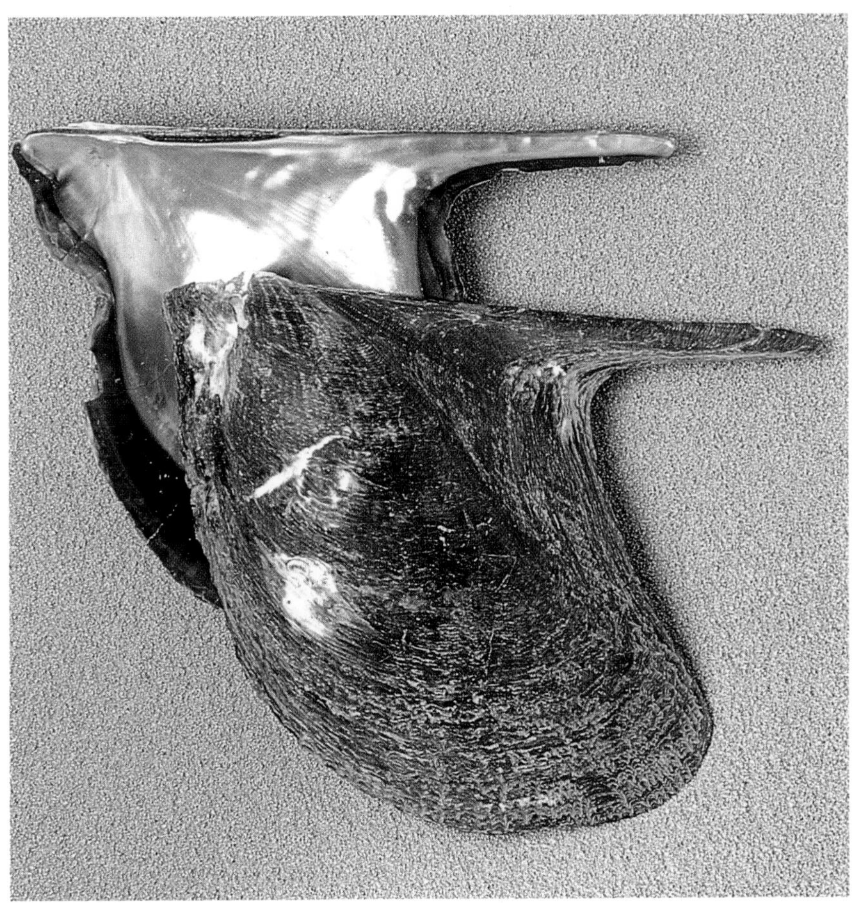

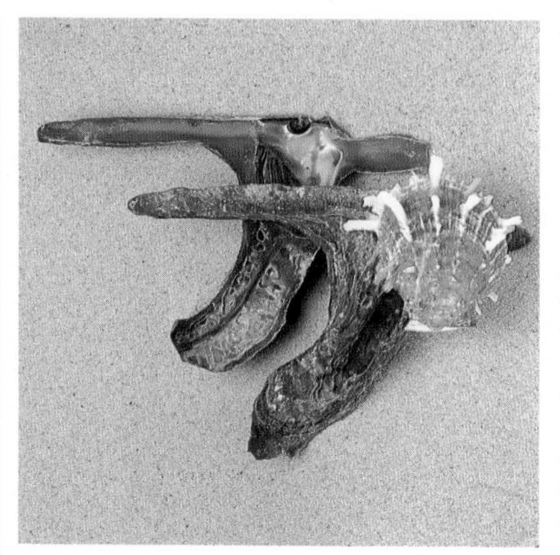

**MALLEUS MALLEUS**
Common Hammer Oyster. *L. 1758.*
Indo-Pacific.

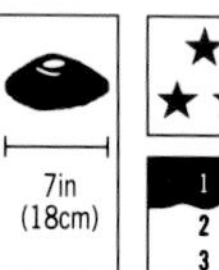

7in (18cm)

Although quite similar in shape to M. *albus*, this is much more rugged in appearance, less regular in shape and its extensions are rarely of equal length. The exterior and interior are a dull greyish black with a bluish nacreous area. This particular specimen, which originates from the central Philippines, has a specimen of *Spondylus* attached to its dorsum.

**PINNA RUDIS**
Rude Pen Shell. *L. 1758.* Mediterranean and North and West Africa.

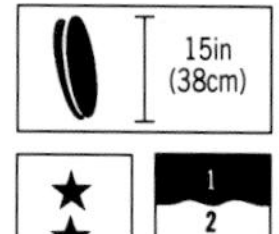

15in (38cm)

This large but thin and fairly fragile shell has sharply tapering valve sides leading to the pointed umbones. The exterior has low radial ridges from which extend upturned open flutes, or hollow spines nearer the margins. The thin shell is translucent and orange brown. The interior surface is smooth but uneven and is a nacreous silver colour at the narrow end. This immature shell was collected in Goree Bay, Senegal.

**ACESTA RATHBUNI**
Philippine Giant Lima. *Bartsch 1913.*
Central Philippines.

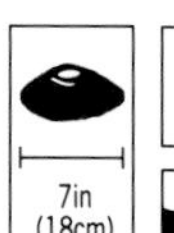

7in (18cm)

Endemic to the central Philippines, this large, ovate, lightweight and almost translucent shell is rather inflated. The short umbones are set at the anterior end of the straight and narrow hinge line – the ligament is internal. The pale lemon yellow shell is smooth and glossy; the interior has a slightly nacreous finish. The species has been popularized only within the last 10 to 15 years, being fished off Bohol Island in deep water.

SUPER FAMILY
PINNOIDEA

FAMILY
## PINNIDAE
(Pen Shells)

The Pinnidae are a small family of large, thin, fan-shaped shells with equal valves. They inhabit calm warm seas and live vertically, with their narrow end embedded in sand or mud and anchored by the byssus to rocks and similar stable objects. The thin silk-like threads of the byssus of some species were in former times woven into very fine material – the famous "cloth of gold". Some museums still exhibit gloves and stockings that have been woven with this very fine substance. Of the two main genera, *Pinna* and *Atrina*, *Pinna* have a weak groove at the centre of each valve, whereas *Atrina* species do not.

SUPER FAMILY
LIMOIDEA

FAMILY
## LIMIDAE
(File Clams)

The file clams are a relatively large family of bivalves the exteriors of which bear many small spines, creating a file-like texture. There are both small and large species, some living in shallow, others in deep water. They are free-swimming and highly mobile shells, moving with the help of long tentacles. For camouflage or protection some build a nest of pebbles and shell fragments on the substrate, by the byssus, which is exuded by the foot. There are several genera, the most well known being *Lima*. *Acesta* is also included here.

**LIMA LIMA VULGARIS**
Rough File Clam. *Link 1807.*
Western Pacific.

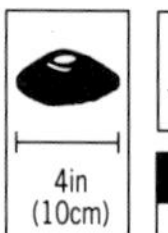

4in (10cm)

This is a much larger variation of the *Lima lima* which is found in the Caribbean. The rough file clam is fan-shaped, with equal valves, and has a narrow hinged area and short pointed umbones. The strong rounded radial ribs bear sharp open upturned spines; the interior is smooth and has radial grooves. The shell is pure white.

**LIMA TENERA**
*Sowerby 1851.*
South-eastern USA.

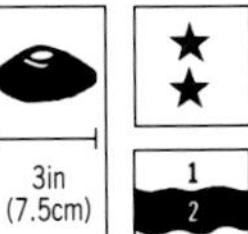

A medium-sized file clam, this is a thin almost translucent shell. There are very fine spinose radial ribs; the "ears" and hinge area are thickened and strong. The interior is smooth and highly glossy. The depicted shell was fished at 108ft (33m) off Pompano Beach, Florida.

**OSTREA EDULIS**
Common European Oyster. *L. 1758.*
Western Europe and Mediterranean.

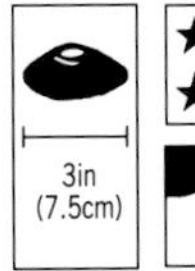

This is the edible oyster of the gourmet and is farmed widely on a commercial basis in Britain and elsewhere. It is roughly circular, the upper valve being inflated, the lower virtually flat. The interior is greyish white and smooth; the exterior is covered with rugged layers of radial ribs and scales and is beige or grey in colour. This specimen is from Langstone Bridge, Hampshire, England.

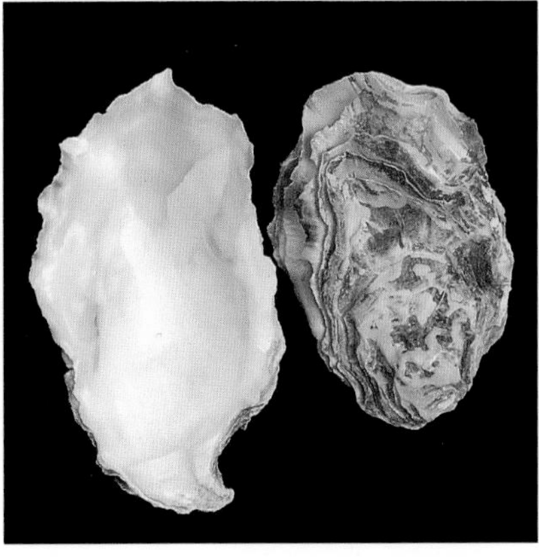

**CRASSOSTREA ANGULATA**
Portuguese Oyster. *Lamarck 1822?*
Western Europe and Mediterranean.

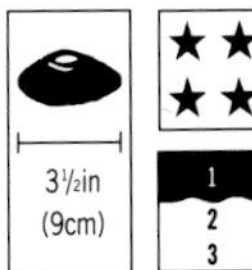

This irregularly shaped and rugged species was introduced into Britain from Portugal on a commercial basis; this particular specimen has been farmed in a marine-water loch in the North-West of Scotland. It is very variable in shape – some shells are rounded, others ovate. The interior is smooth and white, and the muscle scar can be white or purple.

SUPER FAMILY
## OSTREOIDEA

FAMILY
## OSTREIDAE
(True Oysters)

True oysters are a major food source and occur worldwide. They are generally dull in appearance, but vary greatly in shape and form. The interior is not nacreous but porcellaneous – often white or greyish. The exteriors are usually very rough and lamellate. The family is of little interest to most collectors, although *Lopha cristagalli* is most popular. Of the numerous genera, *Ostrea*, *Crassostrea* and *Lopha* are worthy of note.

**OSTREA IMBRICATA**
*Lamarck 1819.*
Japan.

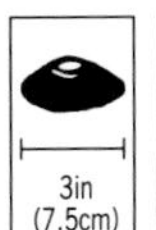

This roughly ovate or circular shell has a very coarse undulating scaly and scabrous texture, and is greyish purple in colour. The interior is fairly smooth and is creamy white. There is a short ligament. The species inhabits shallow water.

**LOPHA CRISTAGALLI**
Cock's Comb Oyster. *L. 1758.*
Indo-Pacific.

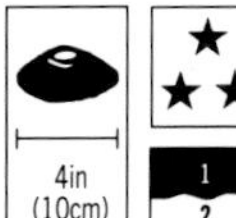

This is a most unusual greyish purple oyster. From the misshapen umbones radiate sharply angular ribs which form deep V-shaped folds on both upper and lower valves. Small irregular spines occur along the edges of the ribs near the umbonal area. The shells grow in clusters and often attach themselves by these spines to coral and pebbles.

SUPER FAMILY
## PECTINOIDEA

FAMILY
## PECTINIDAE
(Scallop Shells)

Because of the diversity of pattern and colour, and also because they are easy to store, the scallops are very popular with collectors. It is a large group of several hundred species, occurring worldwide. Many are found in tropical waters, and very few in polar seas, but species occur in both deep and shallow habitats. Many species are capable of swimming by flapping their valves; usually to escape their major predators, starfish. There is a byssal notch in the anterior, on the right-hand valve. Their characteristic fan-shape remains fairly constant, but variation occurs in the surface sculpturing and the size or shape of the hinge-like "ears" either side of the umbones. The genera, are often referred to as "pecten" by amateur collectors. Wherever possible, I have used the genera as listed by Vaught.

### *AEQUIPECTEN TUMBEZENSIS*
*Orbigny 1846.*
Western Central America.

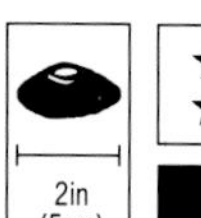


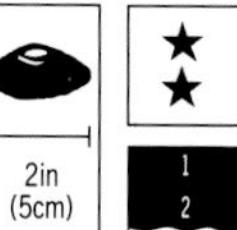


A rounded shell, it has equal valves and inequal ears. There are large well-formed radial ribs and very fine concentric growth striae. The lower valve is white, and the upper is also white, but with greyish brown or tan ribs and ears. The depicted shell was fished by shrimp boats in 180ft (55m) off the Bay of Panama.

### *ARGOPECTEN FLABELLUM*
African Fan Scallop. *Gmelin 1791.*
West Africa.

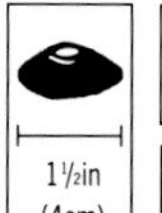

A beautifully coloured and rounded shell, it has equal inflated valves and low rounded radial ribs. The interior is usually white, and bears prominent muscle scars. The depicted specimen shows the typical vivid red form, but shells can occur in pale orange, beige and lavender, often with white patches that are more distinct on the upper valve.

### *AEQUIPECTEN LINEOLARIS*
Wavy-lined Scallop. *Lamarck 1819.*
Florida and Caribbean.

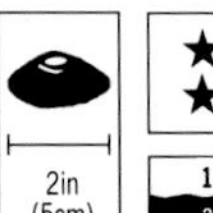


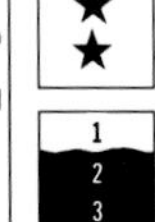


A medium-sized thin shell, it has inequal valves, the lower tending to be rather more inflated than the upper. The ears are equal. There are low and almost flat radial ribs, and the pink or pale brown shells are patterned with numerous very fine concentric wavy lines. The lower valve can be either plain or patterned. The shells in the photograph are from the Gulf of Venezuela.

**ARGOPECTEN CIRCULARIS**
Circular Scallop. *Sowerby 1835.*
Western Central America.

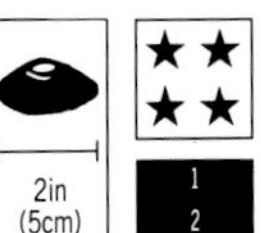


As the name suggests, this is a rounded shell, with inflated equal valves and ears. There are about 18 strong rounded ribs. The shells in the photograph show some of the vast array of colour and pattern variations – all of which are most beautiful. A major seafood source, it lives in subtidal to moderately deep waters.

**ARGOPECTEN PURPURATUS**
Purple Scallop. *Lamarck 1819.*
Western South America.

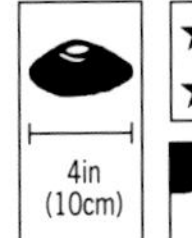


Another commercially fished edible species, this is a large shell, its valves being equal, and rounded and less inflated than those of other *Argopecten* species. The strong and fat radial ribs are a deep purple on a white background, the colours being more vivid on the upper valve. The interior pallial line is tinged with purple. A sand-dwelling species, it is found in shallow water.

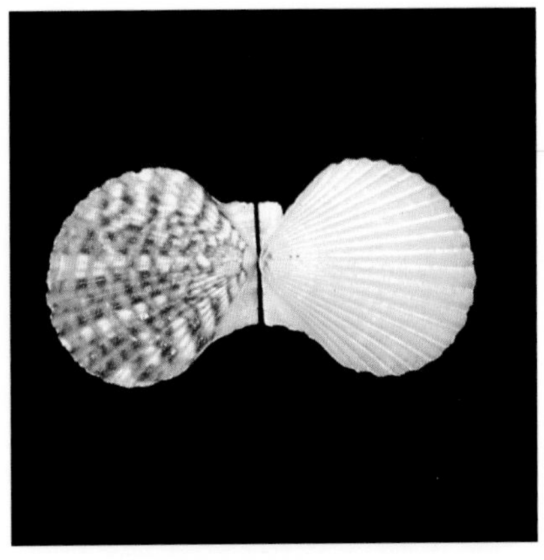

**ARGOPECTEN JUDDI**
Judd's Scallop. *Dall, Bartsch and Rehder 1938.* Hawaii.

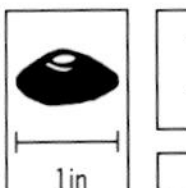

A small dainty species, endemic to Hawaii, it has rounded inequal valves. The upper valve, which has numerous fine ribs, is flattish; the lower, with its rather larger ribs, is slightly more inflated. The off-white background is overlaid – on the upper valve – with reddish brown and pink mottled markings. The lower valve is white.

**ARGOPECTEN GIBBUS**
Calico Scallop. *L. 1758.*
South-eastern USA to Brazil.

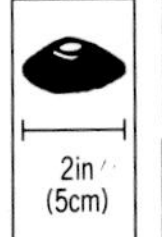


This looks almost like a Caribbean version of the *Argopecten circularis*, the shape being very similar. The shell, however, is lighter in weight, and the ears are lower and smaller. Again, it is to be found in a large range of colour and pattern variations, although the interior is always white. The depicted specimens were fished off south-western Florida.

**ARGOPECTEN AEQUISULCATUS**
*Carpenter 1864.*
Western Central America.

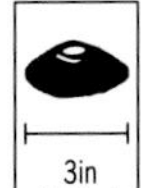
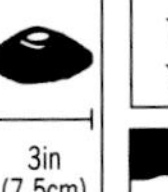

A medium-sized and rather lightweight scallop, it has equal and inflated valves. It can be either fan-like in shape, or rounded, with equal ears. There are numerous strong rounded ribs. Colours vary, but the depicted specimen shows a typical form. The lower valve is usually less darkly patterned. This shell was collected at low tide in sand at Estero San José, Baja Cal Sur, Mexico.

**ARGOPECTEN SOLIDULUS**
Solid Scallop. *Reeve 1853.*
West Africa.

1¼in (3cm)

This small species has rounded equal valves, with umbones set off-centre. The ears are inequal. There are about 18 low but strong radial ribs. The colour displayed in the depicted specimen is typical for the species, which inhabits both shallow and moderately deep water.

**CHLAMYS ASPERRIMA**
Prickly Scallop. *Lamarck 1819.*
Southern Australia and Tasmania.

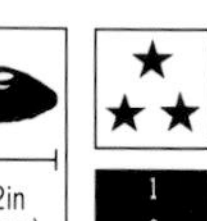

This small delicate shell has fan-shaped valves that are more or less equal in size; the ears are unequal. There are numerous fine angular radial ribs on which grow small scabrous spines. The range of colours is great, as reflected in the specimens shown.

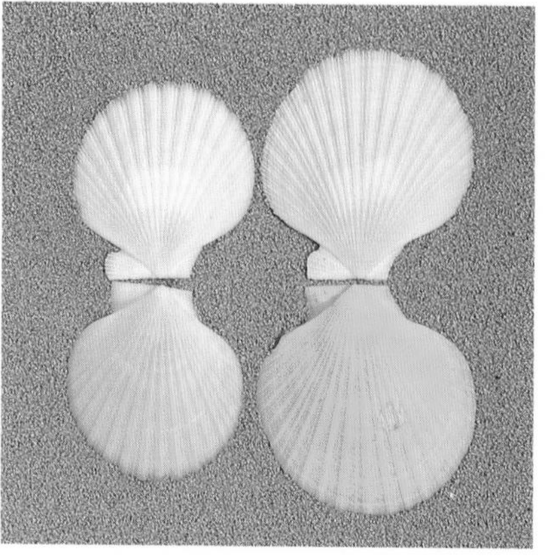

**CHLAMYS DELICATULA**
Delicate Scallop. *Hutton 1873.*
New Zealand.

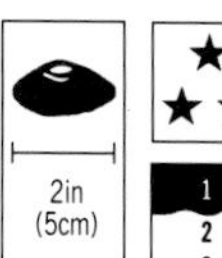


A fine, delicate and very thin species, endemic to New Zealand, it is rounded, with equal compressed valves and inequal ears. There are numerous both strong and coarse radial ribs. The interior is white, and although variable in exterior colour shells are most commonly beige to lemon yellow. The lower valve is usually white.

**CHLAMYS LISCHKEI**
Patagonian Scallop. *Dunker 1850.*
Eastern and Western South America.

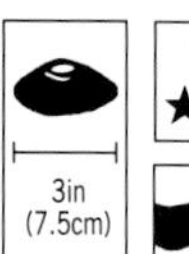

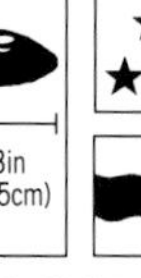


A very thin and delicate scallop, this has rounded equal flattish valves, which sharply taper at the umbones. The ears are inequal. Set against a cream background are numerous pale brown ribs, which are very fine. The lower valve is white. The depicted shell was fished at 264ft (80m) south of Lobos Island, Uruguay.

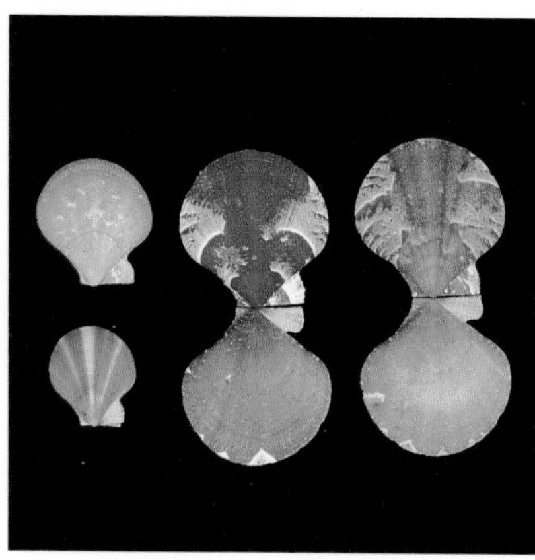

**CHLAMYS TIGERINA**
Tiger Scallop. *Müller 1776.*
Iceland, Norway to Spain.

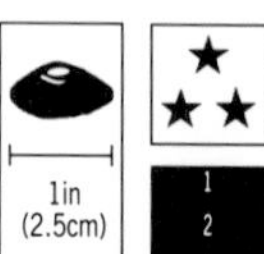


This small rounded shell tapers sharply at the umbones, and has inequal ears and equal valves. It has a smooth surface with a dull finish. The shells in the photograph show some of the colour variations and were dredged in 480ft (145m) off southern Iceland. Although common, they are generally rejected by North Sea fishermen and thrown back into the sea, as a result of which they are difficult to obtain.

**CHLAMYS SQUAMOSA**
Squamose Scallop. *Gmelin 1791.*
South-West Pacific.

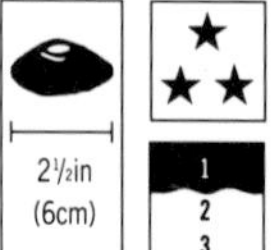


This attractive trio were collected under intertidal rocks off Broome, western Australia. The valves are equal and rather flat; the ears are inequal, the anterior being the largest. The well-spaced low ribs are covered with small but sharp fluted scales. The external colour is usually reflected on the interior margins and below the umbones, apart from which the interior is white.

**CHLAMYS TOWNSENDI**
Townsend's Scallop. *Sowerby 1895.*
North-West Indian Ocean.

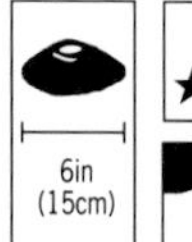


One of the largest species of scallop, this has very thick and heavy inflated valves, which are more or less equal. There are strong rounded radial ribs and concentric growth striae. The lower, right-hand valve, contains a distinct byssal notch. Shells are usually a dull reddish or greyish brown, with irregular white mottling. The shell seen here is from the Gulf of Oman.

### CHLAMYS DIEFFENBACHI

Dieffenbach's Scallop. *Reeve 1853.*
New Zealand.

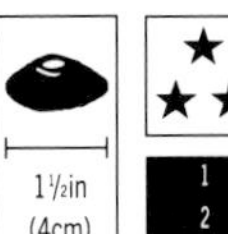

1½in (4cm)

Endemic to New Zealand, this small and rather coarsely sculptured shell has sharp finely scabrous radial ribs. It is fan-shaped, with equal valves and inequal ears, the anterior ones being twice as large as the posterior. The attractive colour range shown here were fished in 66ft (20m) of water off Bird Island, in the Stewart Islands.

### CHLAMYS SENTIS

*Reeve 1853.*
South-eastern USA to Brazil.

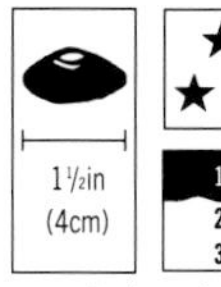

1½in (4cm)

This is a small fairly fragile species, with numerous finely scabrous sharp radial ribs. It is very variable in colour, as the depicted specimens show. The red specimen with a mottled umbonal area and larger fluted scales is the variation C. *mildredae*, which some believe to be a hybrid between C. *sentis* and C. *ornata*.

### ANNACHLAMYS MACASSERENSIS

Macassar Scallop. *Chenu 1845.*
South-West Pacific.

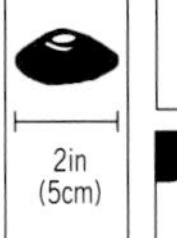

2in (5cm)

A small scallop, it has equal ears and inequal valves, the lower being slightly inflated, while the upper is flatter. The shell is prettily marked, with low ribs coloured with mottled and striped areas of orange, pink, red and purple. The white interior is occasionally tinged with yellow at the margins. It has a faintly rough texture, due to minute concentric ridges.

### CHLAMYS TINCTA

Tinted Scallop. *Reeve 1853.*
South Africa.

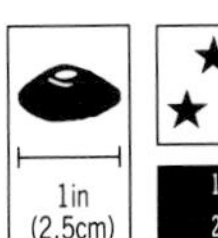

1in (2.5cm)

The small fan-shaped tinted scallop has equal valves. The anterior ear is very much larger than the posterior. There are finely scabrous small and neat radial ribs. Many colour forms exist, as can be seen here. These particular shells were collected by a scuba diver in 83ft (25m) in False Bay among kelp beds.

### CHLAMYS DIANAE

Diana's Scallop. *Crandall 1979.*
Southern Japan.

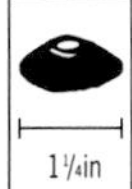

1¼in (3cm)

Named relatively recently, Diana's scallop was described by Philip Crandall, a dealer situated in Okinawa. I have placed it within the genus *Chlamys*, but is often put within the genus *Bractechlamys*. It is a most variably coloured and attractive species, as can be seen here. These specimens are all from 160ft (48m) off Zampa, Okinawa, and the species might be endemic to this area.

### DECATOPECTEN PLICA

Plicate Scallop. *L. 1758.*
Japan and Western Pacific.

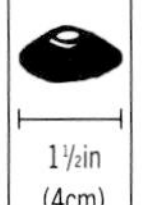

1½in (4cm)

A small but solid scallop, it is fan-shaped and tapers toward the umbones. The ears are equal and large. There are five very large and low rounded radial ribs and numerous minute ones. Colours and patterns vary; the two depicted shells show typical variations.

**EXCELLICHLAMYS HISTRIONICA**
*Gmelin 1791.*
Western Tropical Pacific.

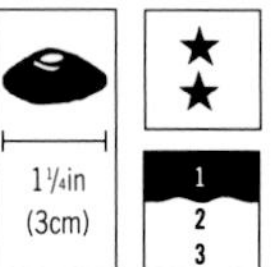


A small, delicate and lightweight shell, it has inequal valves and ears; the lower valve is slightly inflated, and the upper is flat. There are about 12 rounded ribs. The pretty markings consist of dark brown, pink and white irregular small blotches on an off-white or cream background.

**LYROPECTEN NODOSA**
Lion's Paw. *L. 1758.*
South-eastern USA to Brazil.

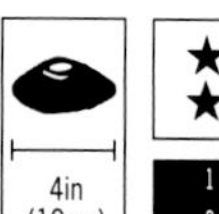


This remarkable species has fan-shaped equal valves with abut eight very large fine rounded radial ribs, often bearing large rounded nodular protuberances; the ears are unequal, the anterior being larger. Variable in colour, shells are generally reddish brown, but rare specimens are orange or yellow. A choice collectors' shell.

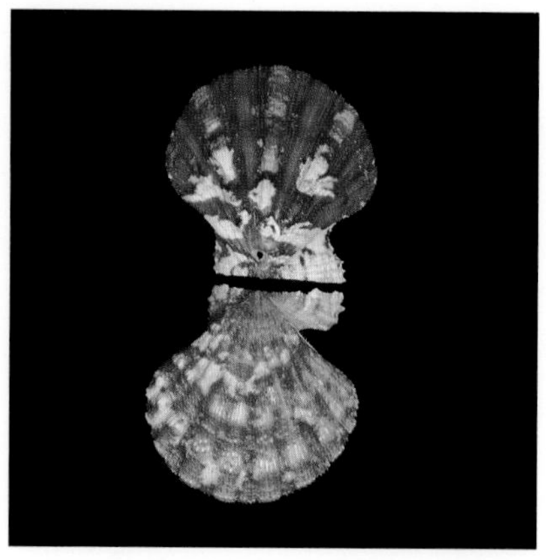

**LYROPECTEN CORALLINOIDES**
Coral Scallop. *Orbigny 1834.*
Canary and Cape Verde Islands.

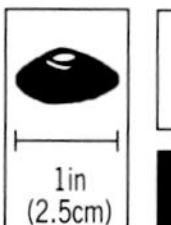

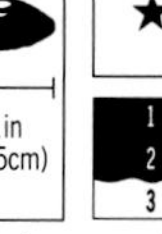


This small, highly colourful and rounded scallop has equal valves and inequal ears, the largest ear being at the anterior. The large low rounded ribs are slightly nodulose on the upper valve. The colours are a mixture of red, pink, orange and white, arranged in blotchy formations. The interior is usually tinged with pink on white.

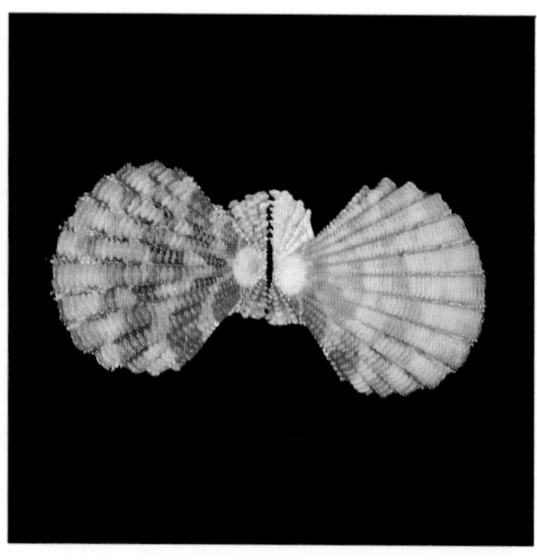

**GLORYPALLIUM SPECIOSUM**
*Reeve 1853.*
Japan to Philippines.

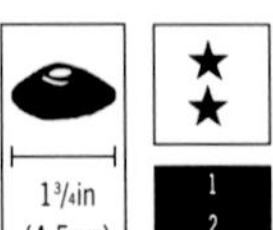


A very beautiful species, shells are deep pink and red, with equal and rounded valves and inequal ears. There are about 12 wide fluted radial ribs, that are rounded and closely aligned. The lower valve usually differs slightly in colour. The interior is white. The depicted specimen was collected in 160ft (48m) off Bolo Point, Okinawa.

**LYROPECTEN SUBNODOSA**
Pacific Lion's Paw. *Sowerby 1835.*
Western Central America.

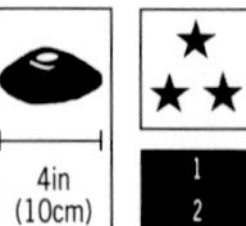


This Pacific equivalent to the Caribbean lion's paw is not dissimilar to the latter, but it is generally larger and heavier, and there are no rounded nodules on the strong radial ribs. Valves are equal and inflated; ears are unequal. Again, shells are variable in colour, but are usually dull reddish brown, and only rarely orange. The depicted specimen was collected off western Panama.

**MESOPEPLUM TASMANICUM**
Tasman Scallop. *Adams and Angas 1863.*
Tasmania and South Australia.

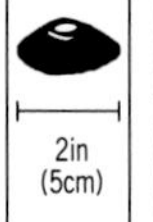


This species, which is sometimes placed within a synonymous subgenus *Notochlamys*, has rounded equal valves and inequal ears. There are five strong radial ribs and numerous fine ones. The colour is usually pink-to-reddish purple, with fine white haphazard lines. The lower valve is white, with pink staining. This specimen came from Port Lincoln.

## MIRAPECTEN MIRIFICUS

Miraculous Scallop. *Reeve 1853.*
Japan, Philippines to Hawaii.

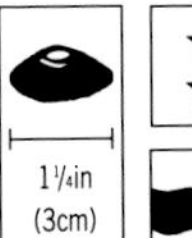


A delicate, very thin and lightweight little shell, the miraculous scallop varies in colour from yellow, to orange and deep red. It is fan-shaped, and has inequal valves and ears. There are eight strong ribs, from which grow fluted scales (these also occur above the hinge area on the ears). The two specimens shown are from Bolo Point, Okinawa.

## PECTEN SULCICOSTATUS

*Sowerby 1842.*
South Africa.

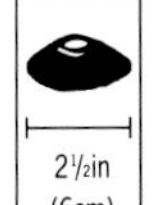

This is the largest of the few South African scallops. It is fan-shaped, and has large equal ears and inequal valves. The upper inflated valve has broad radial ribs and very fine radial grooves; the lower is concave and has narrower ribs. Most shells are creamy white or beige with some pink or brown coloration, particularly on the lower valve.

## PECTEN CHAZALIEI

Chazalie's Scallop. *Dantzenburg 1909.*
Florida to Brazil.

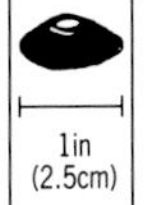


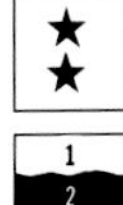

A fragile and thin little shell, it is very delicately marked with concentric bands and zigzag lines of beige, brown, cream and pink. The lower valve is flat; the upper is inflated. The ears are more or less equal. The depicted shell was dredged at 420ft (127m) off Guajira Peninsula, Colombia, in muddy sand.

## PECTEN NOVAEZELANDIAE

New Zealand Scallop. *Reeve 1853.*
New Zealand.

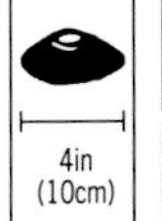


A large solid shell, it has inequal valves, the lower being flat, and the upper very inflated. The shell is fan-shaped, with rounded umbones and more or less equal ears. There are about 18 strong rounded radial ribs. Colours and patterns vary greatly, ranging from white through beige, to tan, dark brown and maroon, many shells being blotched with white. The interior is always white.

## PECTEN RAVENELI

Ravenel's Scallop. *Dall 1898.*
South-eastern USA and West Indies.

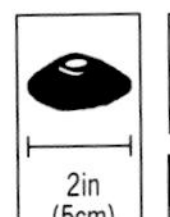


A medium-sized scallop, it has rounded inequal valves, the lower being rather concave, and the upper inflated. The prominent ears are equal. There are many low radial ribs. The interior is white, and the exterior is variably coloured and patterned. The two shells in the photograph portray typical variation and were collected off Content Keys, Florida.

## DECATOPECTEN RADULA

Radula Scallop. *L. 1758.*
Indo-Pacific.

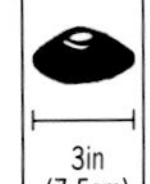

A large robust shell, the radula scallop has inequal valves, the upper being flat, and the lower slightly inflated. The ears are equal. There are about nine strong and rounded radial ribs, and numerous fine ones. The beige background is overlaid with tan streaks and blotches. Some authorities place this within the synonymous subgenus (according to Vaught) of *Comptopallium*. The species is a reef dweller.

**PLACOPECTEN MAGELLANICUS**
Atlantic Deep-sea Scallop. *Gmelin 1791*.
Eastern Canada to North Carolina.

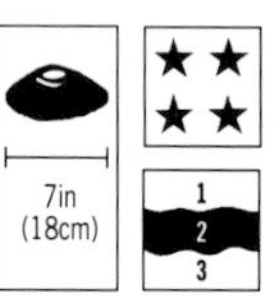


Another of the larger members of the scallop family, it is commercially fished in offshore waters. It has equal, well rounded valves with neat equal ears. There are very fine radial threads and occasional concentric growth striae. Shells vary in colour from white and yellow to mid-brown; some are radially rayed. The white interior has a large distinctive muscle scar.

**AMUSIUM PLEURONECTES**
Asian Moon Scallop. *L. 1758*.
South-West Pacific, Japan and India.

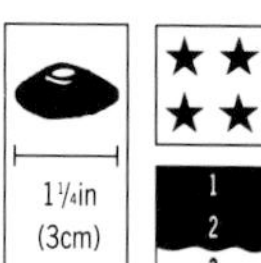


A very rounded, flat, smooth and glossy species, its lower valve is slightly more convex than the upper. The smallish ears are equal. There are numerous fine mid-brown concentric lines on a pale brown background; the ears are reddish brown. The lower valve is pure white.

**AMUSIUM BALLOTI**
Ballot's Saucer Scallop. *Bernardi 1861*.
New Caledonia and Northern Australia.

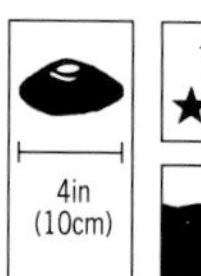


This is possibly the largest species in the genus *Amusium*, its rival for the title being *A. japonicum*. All species within the genus are more or less consistent in shape and form. This rather heavy shell has numerous reddish brown concentric lines and odd blotches on a pale brown background. The equal ears are a deep reddish brown. The species is commercially fished off the Queensland coast.

**PATINOPECTEN CAURINUS**
Giant Pacific Scallop. *Gould 1850*.
Alaska to California.

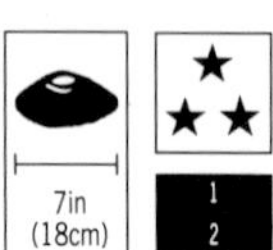


Probably the largest scallop, this has rounded, equal and slightly convex valves. The anterior ear is rather larger than the posterior. There are low, but strong and rounded, radial ribs, and fine concentric growth striae toward the lip margins. The colour is beige or pale brown with a deep tinting of reddish pink below the umbone of the top (left-hand) valve; the lower valve is a plain cream or beige, and the shell is white inside. The species is fished commercially.

**AMUSIUM LAURENTI**
Laurent's Moon Scallop. *Gmelin 1791*.
Florida and Caribbean.

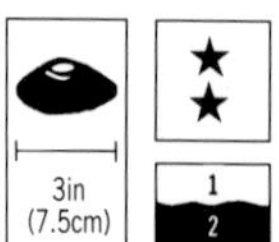


This is similar in shape and valve proportions to *A. pleuronectes*. The lower valve is creamy white, with pale yellow tints at the margins. The upper valve is a dull reddish brown, with broad darker brown radial bands; there are odd creamy beige streaks and zigzags near the umbones. The equal ears are tinged with pale purple.

**PROPEAMUSIUM SIBOGAI**
Siboga Glass Scallop. *Dautzenburg and Bavay 1912*. Japan.

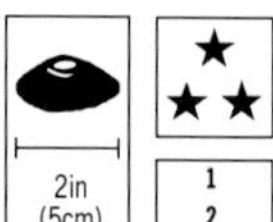


A very thin, fragile and almost translucent shell, the siboga glass scallop is pale yellow with seven broad orange radial bands. The upper valve is large and slightly inflated, totally overlapping the much smaller and flatter lower valve. The tiny ears are equal. The shells seen here were fished in deep water off Wakayama.

SUPER FAMILY
## PECTINOIDEA

FAMILY
## SPONDYLIDAE
(Thorny Oysters)

A small group of highly spinose bivalves, the thorny oysters are closely related to the scallops and live permanently attached to coral and rocks. Sometimes known as chrysanthemum shells, they possess a unique "ball and socket" hinge structure which rather resembles the human elbow joint. This family is very variable in shape, size and colour, making identification difficult for the amateur. I have deliberately chosen less obscure species for inclusion here. Most species, however, are very popular with collectors, and long-spined choice specimens are much sought-after. In their habitat, these shells are covered with sponge, algae and encrustations, making collecting and cleaning difficult. Vaught lists one main genus, *Spondylus*, and two subgenera.

### SPONDYLUS AMERICANUS
American Thorny Oyster. *Hermann 1781.*
South-eastern USA to Brazil.

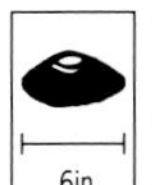

A large very variably coloured species, it has long – sometimes very long – curved spines. Colours vary from pure white through pink or pale yellow to orange and, rarely, red. The equal valves are inflated; the ears are small. There is a distinctive large white triangular escutcheon between the umbones. Large, perfect and colourful specimens command high prices. The unique hinge structure can be seen within the white specimen.

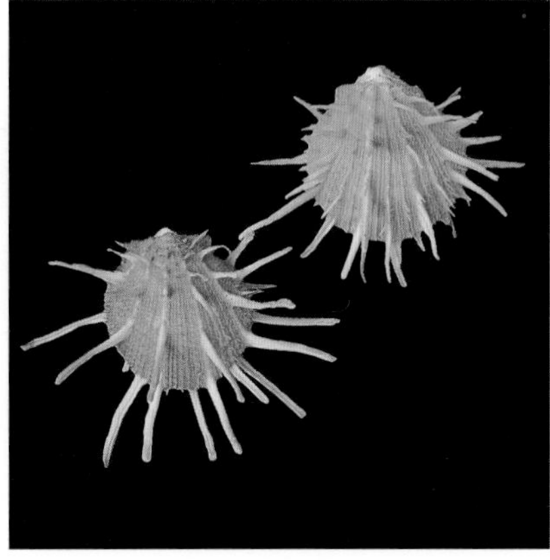

### SPONDYLUS REGIUS
Royal Thorny Oyster. *L. 1758.*
Western Pacific.

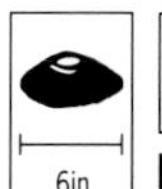

This is rather similar in shape and size to some forms of *S. americanus*. Specimens with valves that are small to medium in size usually have longer spines than those with very large and greatly inflated valves. Between the widely spaced ribs bearing long spines are numerous scabrous or finely spined radial ridges. Most shells are a dull pinkish brown; orange shells are uncommon.

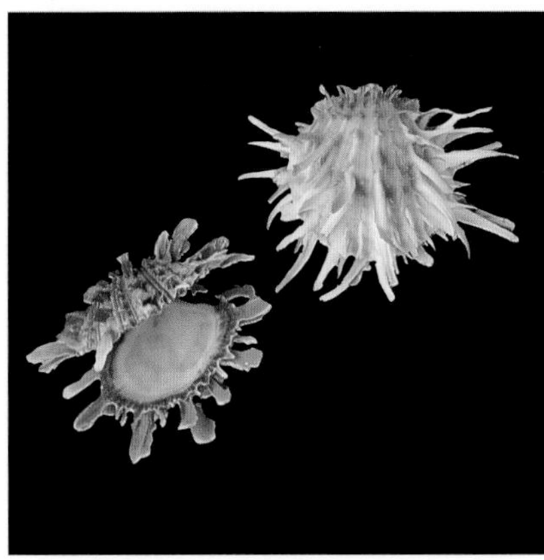

### SPONDYLUS PRINCEPS
Pacific Thorny Oyster. *Broderip 1833.*
Gulf of California to Panama.

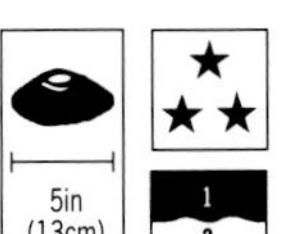


Both valves are inflated and equal; the ears are indistinct. The surfaces of both upper and lower valves bear numerous short and long flattened or spatulate spines. The shell is difficult to clean, which makes perfect specimens a rarity. Most shells are white with orange tingeing, but a few are red throughout.

### SPONDYLUS VARIANS
Water Thorny Oyster. *Sowerby 1829.*
Philippines.

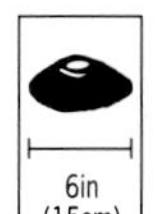

This is the largest of all *Spondylus*, although the spines rarely exceed 1in (2.5cm) in length. The very thick and heavy valves are pure white, the upper valve often being almost flat. The umbonal area is vividly coloured in crimson, yellow or orange. There is a very large triangular escutcheon which is split, revealing part of the interior ligament. Sometimes, sea water is trapped in hollows in the interior surfaces and is covered with a thin flaky calcareous membrane. The current world size record exceeds 12in (30cm).

### SPONDYLUS PICTORUM
*Schreiber 1793.*
Red Sea.

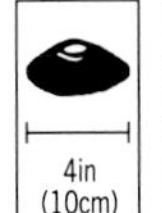

A highly spinose shell, with rounded valves, it usually lives attached to coral in moderate depths. The ears are barely evident and there is a prominent escutcheon. Although this particular specimen is white, with pinkish umbonal tinting, I am sure that other colour variations occur. It was collected by a scuba diver off Eilat.

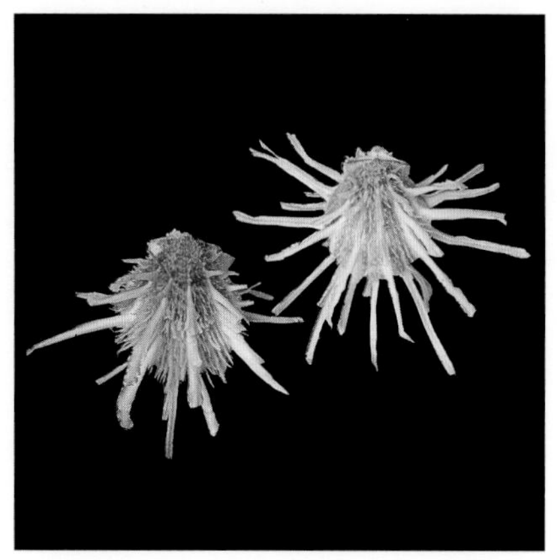

**SPONDYLUS WRIGHTEANUS**
Wright's Thorny Oyster. *Crosse 1872.*
Western Australia.

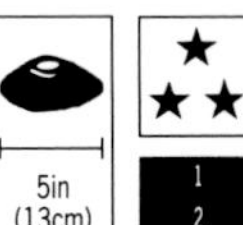


A beautiful species, it has small rounded inequal valves, the lower being rather flat and the upper inflated. The largest flat spines at least double the overall size of the shell. There are also many closely packed short sharp spines. The colour varies from off-white to pink or lavender; the longest spines usually remain white. The species is endemic to Western Australia.

**SPONDYLUS GAEDEROPUS**
European Thorny Oyster. *L. 1758.*
Mediterranean and North-West Africa.

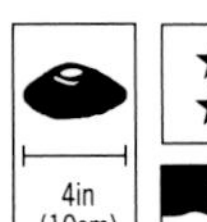


A variable shell, it has more or less equal valves, but these are often misshapen. The spines can be either fairly long or short, and haphazardly placed or not present at all. The upper valve is usually coloured purple or brownish crimson; the lower valve is often white and has marine debris attached to it. The darker of the two specimens shown has parasitic worm shells and barnacles attached to the upper valve.

**SPONDYLUS SQUAMOSUS**
Scaly Thorny Oyster. *Schreibers 1793.*
Philippines.

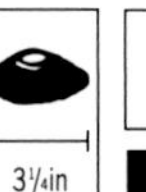


This fairly small species has rounded inequal valves, the upper being rather flatter than the lower. There are numerous radial ribs, both small and large, and the spines are flat and leaf-like and largest toward the margins. The colour is a mottled purplish brown; the spines and interior are white.

**SPONDYLUS TENELLUS**
Scarlet Thorny Oyster. *Reeve 1856.*
Southern and South-western Australia.

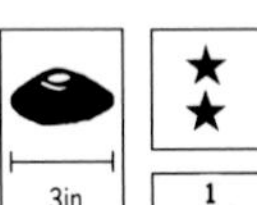


A relatively small shell, the scarlet thorny oyster has fan-shaped equal valves bearing numerous short stocky spines. The ears are inequal. Specimens are collected by scuba divers, but are often difficult to locate, due to camouflage by marine growths; they are also occasionally trawled. Most commonly pink in colour, the shell is white within.

**SPONDYLUS ANACANTHUS**
Nude Thorny Oyster. *Mawe 1823.*
Japan to the Philippines.

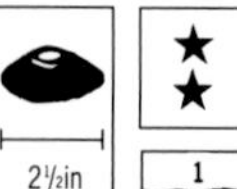


An ovate species, it tapers sharply to the umbones. The upper valve is rather flatter than the deeply set lower valve. Although the name suggests otherwise, some variations are very spinose. Small spines can be seen on the pink shell, which comes from the Camotes Sea; the orange-rayed virtually spineless specimen is from deep water off Taiwan.

**SPONDYLUS SINENSIS**
*Schreibers 1793.*
Philippines.

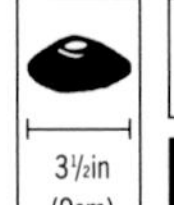

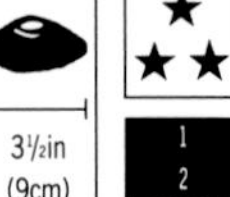


A medium-sized shell, it has rounded valves. The lower valve is deep and inflated, the upper is less so. There are well-spaced low radial ribs, and short and medium length flat spines, which are infrequently placed. Between the umbones is a prominent white triangular escutcheon. The two depicted specimens from the Sulu Sea show typical colour variation. The interior is always white.

**SPONDYLUS BUTLERI**
Butler's Thorny Oyster. *Reeve 1856.*
Western Pacific.

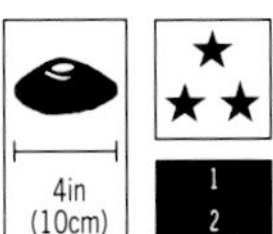

An attractive shell, this has more or less equal valves, although the shape varies. There is a large rather curved escutcheon; the valves are equal. The entire upper valve is covered with fairly short but closely packed spines. The lower valve is usually less spinose, and often has overlapping irregular scale-like projections. The colours vary greatly, as can be seen with these shells from Thailand.

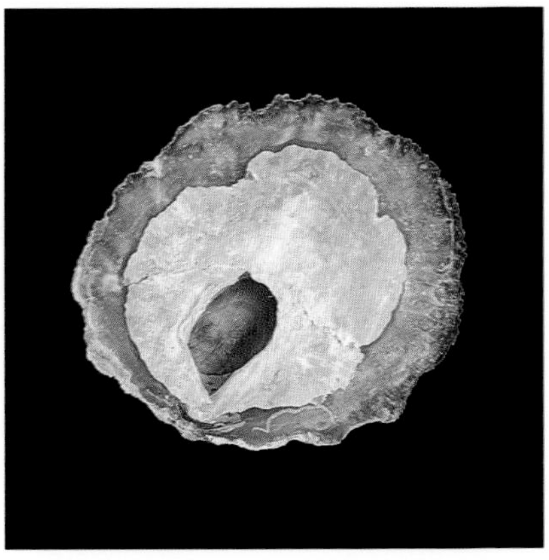

**ANOMIA EPHIPPIUM**
European Jingle Shell. *L. 1758.* Norway to the Mediterranean and Black Sea.

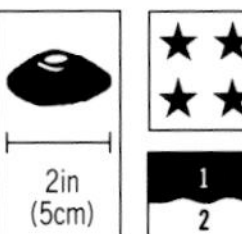

The exterior of the larger upper valve of this rounded species is a pale greyish brown; the interior is iridescent silver green or orange. There is a large muscle scar. The small fragile lower valve is white, and has an irregular and crinkly surface; it has the characteristic hole.

**PLACUNA EPHIPPIUM**
Saddle Oyster. *Retzius 1788.*
South-West Pacific and South-East Asia.

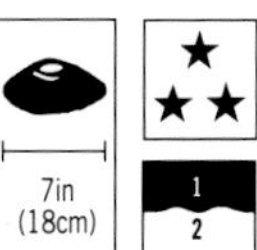

This large solid shell is roughly ovate in shape. The two valves, which are of equal size and shape, are curved outward and downward, giving the shell its characteristic saddle shape. The exterior surface is rough and scaly. The interior is a nacreous silvery grey or brown, with a central muscle scar and two obliquely placed strong interlocking teeth.

SUPER FAMILY
ANOMIOIDEA

FAMILY
## ANOMIIDAE
(Jingle Shells)

This is a small and unusual group of shells which are irregular in shape. In most species the lower valve is smaller, translucent and has a hole through which protrudes the foot and byssus. Jingle shells live in colonies, attached to other shells, rocks, wood and other man-made objects. There are no hinge teeth. They inhabit worldwide localities, mostly in shallow waters. There are six genera, of which *Anomia* is possibly the best known.

SUPER FAMILY
ANOMIOIDEA

FAMILY
## PLACUNIDAE
(Saddle and Window Pane Oysters)

This is a very small group of bivalves, with thin often translucent valves. Some are very flat, and the adult animals live unattached; others are saddle-shaped. These shells inhabit shallow warm water and are often attached to substrate by a byssus. The species *Placuna placenta* (discussed below) has been widely used for many years for small window panes, and is now commercially farmed for the shellcraft industry in the Philippines. There are two genera, of which *Placuna* is widely known.

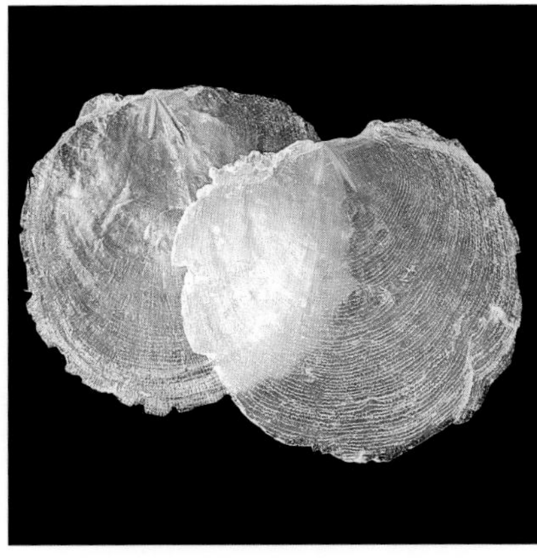

**PLACUNA PLACENTA**
Windowpane Oyster. *L. 1758.*
Philippines and South-East Asia.

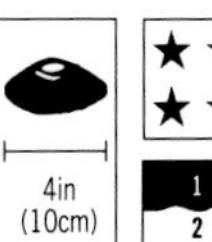

An almost transparent pearly cream-coloured shell, it has flat valves with irregular margins. There are numerous fine concentric growth striae and the interior is smooth and glossy. The muscle scar is centrally placed, and there are two diagonal interlocking teeth. Farmed by the million for shellcraft, it is exported worldwide from the Philippines.

SUPER FAMILY
TRIGONIOIDEA

FAMILY
## TRIGONIIDAE

Many fossil forms of this ancient group are known, but there is only one recent genus: *Neotrigonia*. There are possibly no more than two species in existence, and these are restricted in range to south-eastern Australia. They are dredged offshore in relatively deep water to 165ft (50m) and are used in the jewellery industry for the shell's nacreous interior.

**NEOTRIGONIA BEDNALLI**
Bednall's Brooch Clam. *Verco 1907*.
South-eastern Australia.

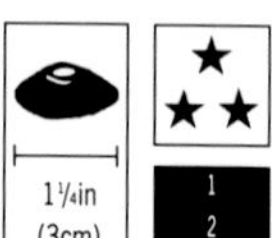

1¼in (3cm)

This small solid shell is roughly ovate; it is rounded at the anterior end and blunt at the posterior. Strong radial ribs bear low concentric scales. The interior is highly nacreous and can be lavender or pale orange. The complex hinge structure is V-shaped and ridged.

SUPER FAMILY
LUCINOIDEA

FAMILY
## LUCINIDAE
(Lucina Clams)

A large family, it consists chiefly of white bivalves with thick and solid shells which are circular-to-ovate in shape. They inhabit both shallow and deep water and occur in a worldwide range of locations. The siphon is not usually long, so the animals make a tube to the surface with their foot. There are many genera and a few subgenera. The most well known of these are *Codakia*, *Anodontia* and *Divaricella*. These are not popular with collectors.

**CODAKIA TIGERINA**
Pacific Tiger Lucina. *L. 1758*.
Indo-Pacific.

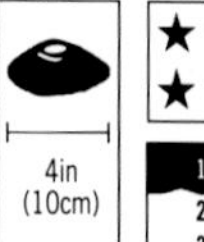

4in (10cm)

An attractive rounded shell, the Pacific tiger lucina has a distinctive reticulated texture of small radial ribs and concentric striations. The teeth are small for the size of shell, but the hinge area and ligament are large. The exterior is chalky white, while the interior is a beautiful pale yellow tinged with pinkish red around the entire valve periphery.

SUPER FAMILY
LUCINOIDEA

FAMILY
## FIMBRIIDAE
(Basket Lucines)

A small family, it contains for the most part ovate shells which burrow into sand or mud and are generally found in warm tropical seas. The sculpturing invariably consists of overlapping concentric and radial ribs or cords forming a reticulated surface. Several species are very attractive and are therefore reasonably popular with collectors. There is only one genus, *Fimbria*.

**FIMBRIA FIMBRIATA**
Frilly Basket Lucine. *L. 1758*.
Indo-Pacific.

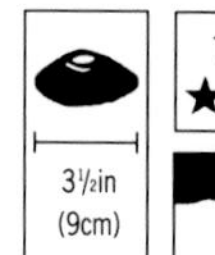

3½in (9cm)

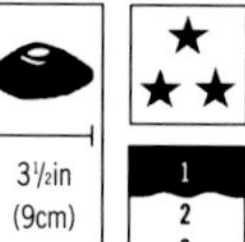

An ovate, solid and heavy shell, it has low flat concentric ridges and tiny radial grooves, giving a netted effect. The ornamentation becomes coarser and more bead-like at the posterior end. The exterior is white; the interior is smooth and is off-white, with a cream-tinted margin. The interlocking teeth are strong, and there is a long hinge line and ligament; the lunule is pinkish.

**FIMBRIA SOVERBII**
Sowerby's Basket Lucine. *Reeve 1841.*
South-West Pacific.

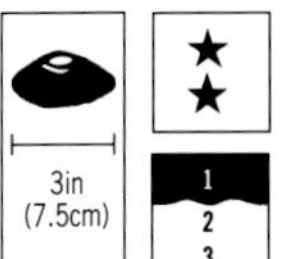


A most beautiful and sought-after collectors' shell, it is elongated and ovate, with slightly inflated valves. The concentric ridges are sharp and raised, and are lamellose at the anterior. The exterior is white, with delicate but distinct radially laid pink rays; the interior is smooth, white and tinted with pale yellow at the centre.

SUPER FAMILY
## CARDITOIDEA

FAMILY
## CARDITIDAE
(Cardita Clams)

The carditas are a moderately large family of thick-walled and strongly ribbed shells, most of which are found in shallow waters around the world, except for Arctic seas; some deep-water species, however, do exist. There is a yellow-to-brown periostracum, which is sometimes hairy. The umbones are set off-centre, often well to the anterior end. Many produce and use a byssus. This group is not particularly popular or well known among collectors. Nineteen genera are listed, of which *Cardita* is the most widely known.

**CARDITA CRASSICOSTA**
Leafy Cardita. *Lamarck 1819.*
Philippines to Australia.

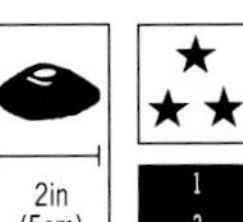


An ovate and elongated bivalve, the leafy cardita has a short ligamental area. The four or so very large, low and rounded radial ribs and six or seven small ribs which are set at the anterior, below the umbones, all bear strong fluted scales. There is a large colour range, as can be seen here in these specimens fished in the Sulu Sea.

**CARDITA LATICOSTATA**
Wide-ribbed Cardita. *Sowerby 1833.*
Western Central America.

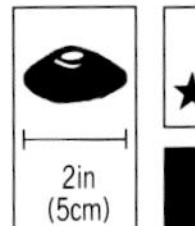


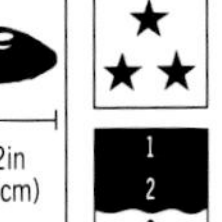


This very thick and solid shell is oval to triangular in shape. There are about 15 strong ribs, bearing small concentrically laid scales on mature specimens. There is a strong hinge structure, with two large cardinal teeth. Shells are usually off-white, with concentric bands of either beige or various tones of brown. The interior is white.

**CARDITA INCRASSATA**
*Sowerby 1843.*
Western Australia.

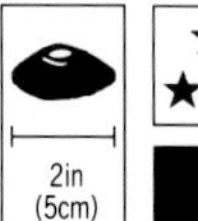
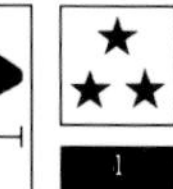

2in (5cm)

An oval-shaped and much-thickened cardita, it has large, strong, well-rounded and closely set radial ribs, numbering perhaps 16 or 17 in all. The depicted specimen was collected in 80ft (24m) of water, in weed at Cockburn Sound, Fremantle.

**ARCINELLA ARCINELLA**
True Spiny Jewel Box. *L. 1767.*
West Indies to Brazil.

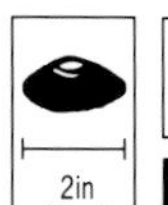
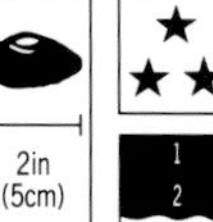

2in (5cm)

The triangular, sometimes almost crescent-shaped, true spiny jewel box has numerous radial ribs bearing both short and long coarse spines. Shells are usually white; the interior is occasionally stained with lemon, pink or purple. There is a heart-shaped lunule. This shell is very solid and heavy.

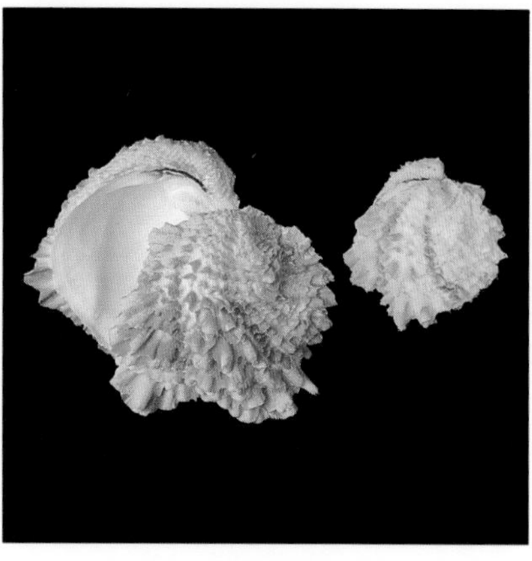

**CHAMA BRASSICA**
Cabbage Jewel Box. *Reeve 1846.*
Philippines.

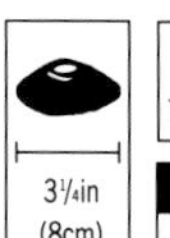

3¼in (8cm)

An attractive thick and heavy shell, it is covered with concentrically laid scaly lamellae. The colours vary – these two specimens, which originate from the Sulu Sea, show two forms. The interior is, however, always white. Occasionally, anchorage debris can be found in the lower valve, which is often less scaly.

SUPER FAMILY
CHAMOIDEA

FAMILY
## CHAMIDAE
(Jewel Boxes)

A colourful and very variable group of bivalves, both in shape and colour, the jewel boxes to some extent resemble the thorny oysters. They live attached to rocks or coral and inhabit shallow water, mostly in tropical areas. They grow numerous scaly plates, frills or spines, and all possess a rudimentary hinge structure. Although many species are difficult to identify, due to their great variability, several are most popular with collectors. Vaught lists three genera and four subgenera.

**ARCINELLA BRASILIANA**
Spiny Jewel Box. *Nicol 1953.*
Brazil.

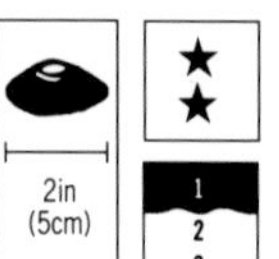

2in (5cm)

An attractive collectors' shell, it has radial ribs bearing numerous fine and strong spines of varying length. The interspaces have a pitted texture. The large single tooth has fine interlocking ridges. Usually pinkish beige in colour, it has a white interior. The species lives on rocks and other hard substrates, and is endemic to Brazil.

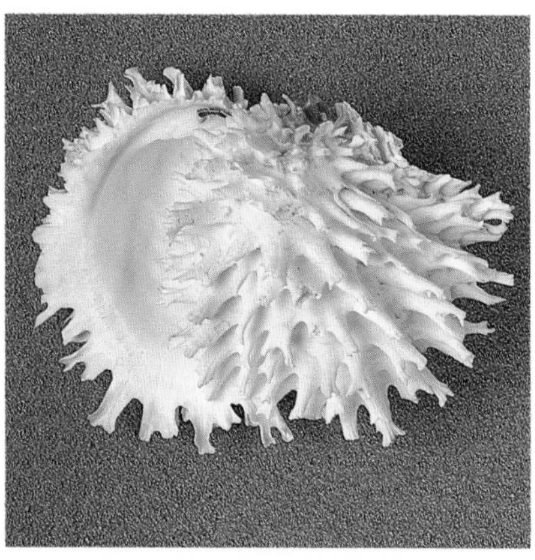

**CHAMA LAZARUS**
Lazarus Jewel Box. *L. 1758.*
Indo-Pacific.

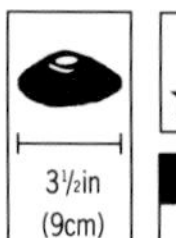
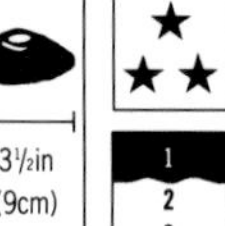

3½in (9cm)

Usually oval or generally rounded in shape, the lazarus jewel box has valves that bear very large and strong scaly lamellae, many of which extend into forked and spatulate spines. Shells are almost always white, with pastel umbonal colouring; but they can occasionally be a pale lemon colour. They are often collected in twos or threes, with attached marine debris, coral, and the like.

**CHAMA** *Sp.*
Indian Ocean.

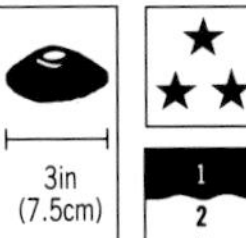


I have included this attractive and colourful jewel box, although I cannot satisfactorily identify it. Many were collected by conchologists who served with the British forces in Gan, in the Maldive Islands in the early 1970s, and I have seen many specimens, generally with little variation in colour or shape. It is probably erroneously named *Chama broderippi* – could it be *C. rubea* or *C. reflexa?*

***ACANTHOCARDIA TUBERCULATA***
Tuberculate Cockle. *L. 1758.* Southern England to Mediterranean; Canary Islands.

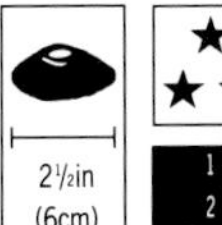


A solid species, the tuberculate cockle has equal and inflated valves and very large rounded umbones, which in some shells touch and erode each other. There are prominent rounded radial ribs. The colour can be attractive – cream or beige, occasionally with tan to dark brown concentric bands, and with a pale orange to brown tint on the interior.

**CARDIUM COSTATUM**
Great Ribbed Cockle. *L. 1758.*
West Africa.

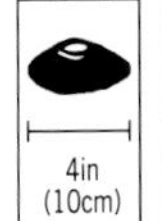


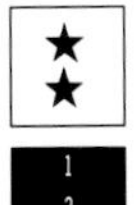


A large, showy and lightweight shell, it has equal and inflated valves. There are well-spaced hollow high-keeled radial ribs. The long hinge line or plate bears strong sharp cardinal and lateral teeth. The valves gape at the posterior end. White or off-white overall, it has pale tan or orange interspaces near the rounded umbones. A choice collectors' item.

SUPER FAMILY
## CARDIOIDEA

FAMILY
## CARDIIDAE
(Cockle Shells)

This is a large and very well-known family, composed chiefly of edible bivalves, which live in worldwide locations in both shallow and deep water. Ranging in size from medium to very large, most species display radial sculpturing and can be either smooth, scaly or spinose. They are rounded or oval in shape, inflated and have large rounded umbones. There are numerous genera and subgenera. The genus *Corculum* is most unusual in that the shells are flattened, with keeled margins and overlapping umbones, and are distinctly heart-shaped. Due to their diversity of shape, form and to some extent coloration, the members of this family are most appealing to collectors.

**ACANTHOCARDIA ECHINATA**
European Prickly Cockle. *L. 1758.*
Western Europe to North-West Africa; Med.

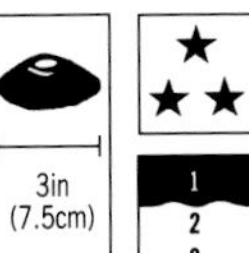


Rounded to oval in outline, this has inflated and equal valves. The well-spaced and low ribs bear strong broad spines which are sharp toward the posterior and rather more rounded and nodulose at the anterior. The right valve has two anterior lateral teeth and one posterior tooth; the cardinal teeth in the left valve are of similar size.

**PLAGIOCARDIUM PSEUDOLIMA**
Giant Heart Cockle. *Lamarck 1819.*
East Africa.

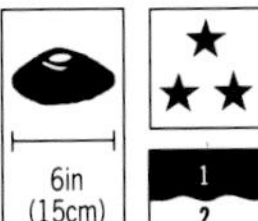


This is one of the largest of the cockles, with rounded-to-ovate very inflated and heavy valves. The numerous low radial ribs bear small thick scaly spines; these are often eroded, but are most in evidence at the anterior end of the shell. The depicted specimen, which comes from Mombasa, shows typical colour, but albino shells occasionally occur.

**PLAGIOCARDIUM SETOSUM**
Hairy Cockle. *Redfield 1846.* South-West Pacific and Northern Australia.

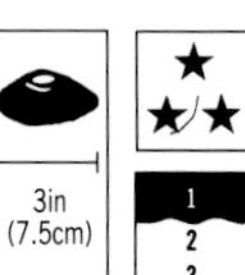


A cockle of handsome proportions, it is oval, with inflated equal valves and large umbones – a typical cockle shape. Numerous low ribs bear irregularly placed very small blunt nodules; the colour is beige or pale tan, with slightly darker concentric bands. The lip margins are serrated and interlocking. The interior is white.

**TRACHYCARDIUM CONSORS**
Partner Cockle. *Sowerby 1833.* Gulf of California to Ecuador.

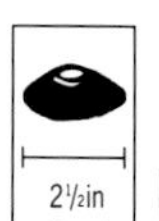


This handsome shell has equal valves and large inflated umbones. The low radial ribs bear imbricated scales (rather like overlapping roof tiles). The colour is pale beige, with irregular and large patches of tan or mid-brown. The interior is flushed with pale pink. The lip margins are strongly crenulated.

**CORCULUM CARDISSA**
True Heart Cockle. *L. 1758.* Indo-Pacific.

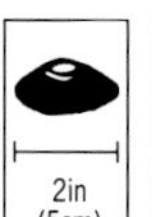

This cockle has a virtually unique form. When viewed from the anterior, it is much flattened and heart-shaped, with overlapping umbones, from which extends a sharp keel, bearing small fluted projections around the periphery. There are numerous low slightly spinose ribs. From the posterior, the small exterior ligament can be seen, and the valve surface here is smoother and bears only fine grooves. Shells are usually off-white, but pale lemon or pink forms often occur.

**TRACHYCARDIUM REEVEANUM**
Reeve's Cockle. *Dunker 1852.* Australia.

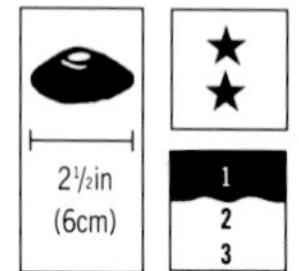


A beautiful species, Reeve's cockle is oval in shape, with equal valves bearing strongly ridged radial ribs which are slightly spinose at the posterior side and nodulose at the anterior side of each valve. The shell is attractively coloured in mottled creamy beige; the lip margins are stained with deep orange and are crenulated. The interior is white. This specimen was dredged in 10ft (3m) off Gladstone, Queensland.

**TRACHYCARDIUM BELCHERI**
Belcher's Cockle. *Broderip and Sowerby 1829.* West Mexico to Panama.

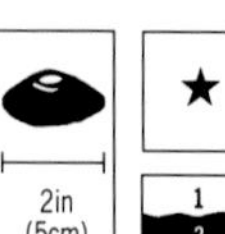


Belcher's cockle is dominated by unusually ridged and saw-like radial ribs, which are well spaced. The colour is attractive – creamy yellow within and an exterior with blends of beige, pale orange and pinkish red. Most shells inhabit moderately deep waters.

**CTENOCARDIA VICTOR**
Victor's Prickly Cockle. *Angas 1872.* Western Pacific.

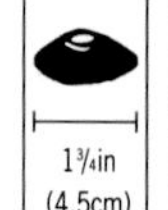


A popular and most attractive cockle, its narrow radial ribs bear numerous mostly short recurved spines. These are longest on the ridged area of the valve and very short at the posterior end. This is a very pale pinkish orange shell, with irregular deep orange red blotches. The interior is a pastel pinkish orange. This specimen is from Okinawa Island.

**FRAGUM HEMICARDIUM**
Pacific Half-heart Cockle. *L. 1758*. South-West Pacific and Northern Australia.

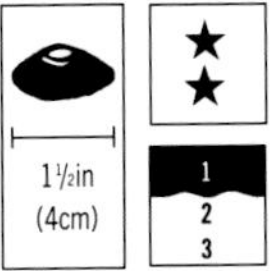


This attractive and unusual cockle has strong equal valves and sharply incurved umbones, from which the keel or ridge extends to the lower posterior margin. There are rather flat broad ribs with grooved and pitted interspaces. Usually white overall, shells occasionally have pastel pink or yellow markings, and are distinctly heart-shaped when viewed from the posterior or anterior.

**CERASTODERMA EDULE**
Common European Cockle. *L. 1758*. North-East Atlantic.

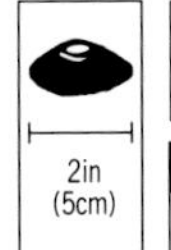


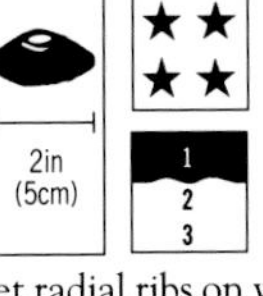

A well-known seafood, this species is farmed on a large scale. A medium-sized shell, it is oval in shape and has solid thickened valves. There are numerous low and closely set radial ribs on which are very small concentrically laid scaly spines. The exterior is usually off-white to beige; the interior is white, with a little brownish grey staining on the posterior muscle scar.

SUPER FAMILY
TRIDACNOIDEA

FAMILY
## TRIDACNIDAE
(Giant Clams)

The giant clams are a small but well-known family of large and very large shells, the largest of which, *Tridacna gigas*, can exceed 4ft (1.2m) in length. They are a valuable seafood source; due to indiscriminate over fishing, collecting of all species is now monitored; they are farmed in some areas. All species inhabit shallow tropical waters and live embedded in coral or rocky substrate hinge-down, so that the gaping aperture can encourage sunlight to foster algal growth within the large mantle, on which the animal feeds. There are two genera, *Tridacna* and *Hippopus*.

**LYROCARDIUM LYRATUM**
Maroon Cockle. *Sowerby 1841*. Japan to Northern Australia.

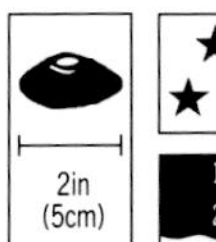


A medium-sized rounded cockle, it has large umbones and inflated equal valves. This is a cream shell, but collectors invariably retain the maroon-coloured and very attractive periostracum. Sculpturing is divided equally; there are fine radial ribs at the anterior, and obliquely laid ridges that are sharp but almost flat on the posterior portion of each valve. The lip margins are finely serrated.

**LAEVICARDIUM ELATUM**
Giant Pacific Egg Cockle. *Sowerby 1833*. Western Central America.

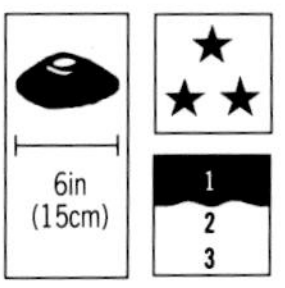


Another of the very large species in the family, it is an ovate-to-triangular shell, with very large rounded umbones. It is fairly smooth and glossy, with fine very low ribs which are most evident at the margins. Shells are usually pale yellow in colour, with a creamy white interior. They are most commonly found on the shallow mud flats in the Gulf of California.

**HIPPOPUS HIPPOPUS**
Bear's Paw Clam. *L. 1758*. South-West Pacific.

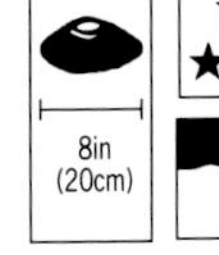


A medium-to-large clam, the bear's paw is distinctly triangular in shape, with very deep and inflated valves. These are strongly sculptured, with about seven large and, in the interspaces, numerous small minutely scaly ribs. The hinge line is long – half the length of the shell – and the lunule area is very wide and compressed. There is virtually no byssal gape. Shells are off-white, with much mottling of crimson, orange and yellow. The interior is white.

### *HIPPOPUS PORCELLANUS*

China Clam. *Rosewater 1982.*
Central and Southern Philippines.

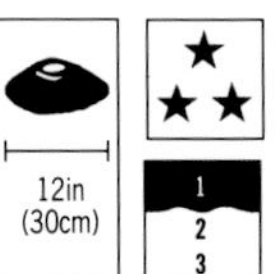


A large species, the China clam is similar in shape to *H. hippopus*, but it is more ovate and has slightly less inflated valves. The low rounded radial ribs are more or less smooth; there are many concentric growth striations. Small or young shells have a little yellow or orange coloration at the umbones; apart from this the shell is off-white. The interior is pure white and porcellaneous. This species dwells on coral reefs.

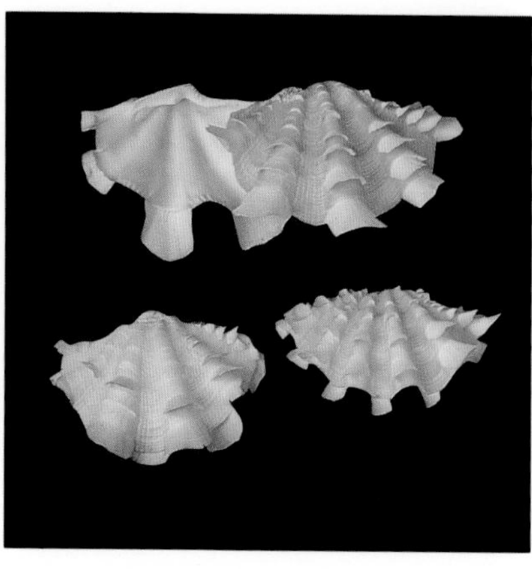

### *TRIDACNA SQUAMOSA*

Fluted Clam. *Lamarck 1819.*
Indo-Pacific (not Hawaii).

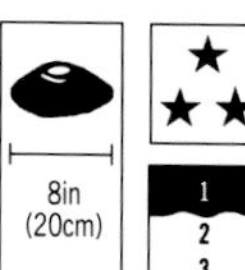


A large ovate and attractive species, it has equal inflated valves on which are about five strong radial ribs, bearing large sharp upturned and hollow scales or flutes. The hinge line occupies half the length of the shell; there is a large byssal gape behind the umbones. Many pastel colours occur, including cream, pink, lemon and pale orange.

### *TRIDACNA MAXIMA*

Elongate Clam. *Röding 1798.*
Indo-Pacific.

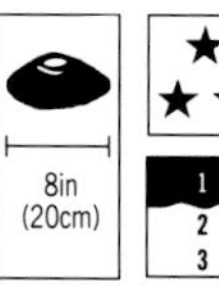


This thick and heavy, elongate slender species has very low but broad radial ribs, on which are numerous large and undulating concentric scaly ridges. The hinge line is about one-third of the shell's length; the byssal gape is large. The exterior is usually off-white to cream; the interior is white. It is a shallow-water reef dweller.

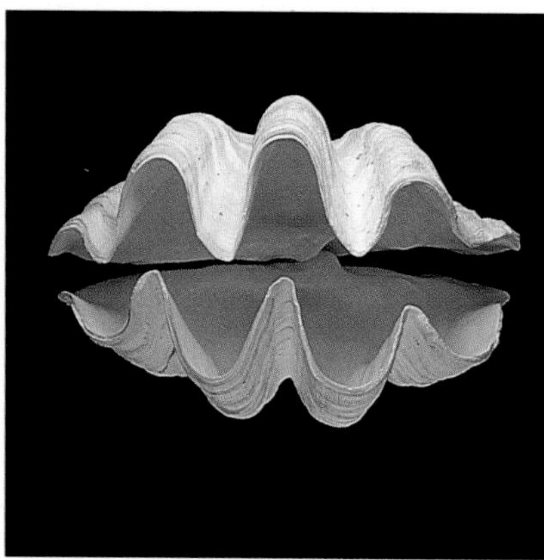

### *TRIDACNA GIGAS*

Giant Clam. *L. 1758.*
South-West Pacific.

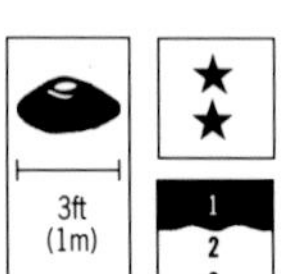


This is the largest and heaviest known mollusc – the two valves can weigh as much as 500 lbs (230kg). The elongated-oval shell, with its equal valves, has about five very large undulating and rounded ribs, with numerous concentric growth striae. Mature shells are encrusted with lime deposits and much marine debris. Most shells are not particularly attractive. The interior is porcellaneous and white.

### *TRIDACNA CROCEA*

Crocus Giant Clam. *Lamarck 1819.*
South-West Pacific.

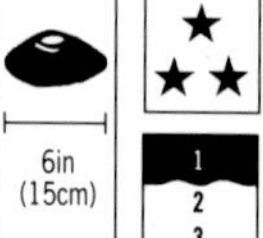


A rather elongated and heavy medium-sized clam, it has equal valves and broad low radial ribs that bear growth lines that are concentrically arranged and scaly. There is a relatively short hinge line and a very large byssal gape. Shells appear in a range of pastel colours, including pale yellow, or orange and yellow, or cream. The interior is pure white. This species dwells on coral reefs.

SUPER FAMILY

## MACTROIDEA

FAMILY

## MACTRIDAE

(Mactra Clams)

Mactra clams, also known as trough or surf clams, have a worldwide distribution, mainly in shallow water, and perhaps number 100 or so species. There is no byssus, and shells can either be smooth or have concentric ornamentation. There are about 24 genera, of which *Mactra* and *Spisula* are the principal ones. These shells are not popular with collectors, but many are edible.

**MACTRA CORALLINA**
Rayed Mactra. *L. 1758.*
British Isles to Mediterranean.

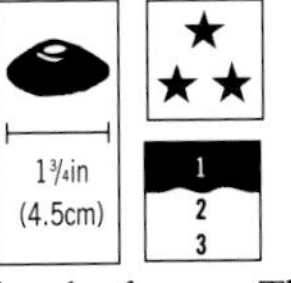

A smooth and lightweight shell, this is somewhat triangular in shape, with rounded margins. It is a pale reddish brown with both narrow and broad radial bands of cream. The interior is a pale lavender. The ligament is internal. It is a shallow-water species; this specimen was collected at Camber Sands, Sussex, England.

**SOLEN MARGINATUS**
European Razor Clam. *Montagu 1803.* West Europe, Mediterranean and West Africa.

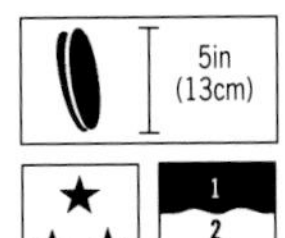

A long straight-sided shell, the European razor clam has equal valves and truncated ends. Each valve possesses one cardinal tooth, but lateral teeth are absent. The shell is beige to dirty yellow, with a mid-brown periostracum. A characteristic groove runs parallel to and just behind the anterior margin. There are concentric growth lines. These shells are from Camber Sands, Sussex, England.

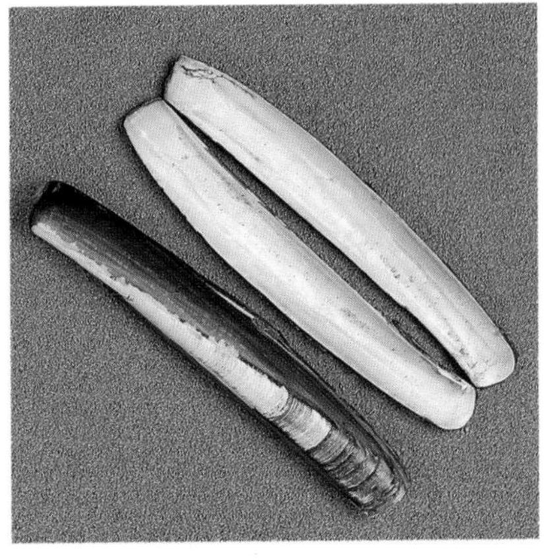

**ENSIS ARCUATUS**
*Jeffreys 1865.*
Norway to Spain, Great Britain.

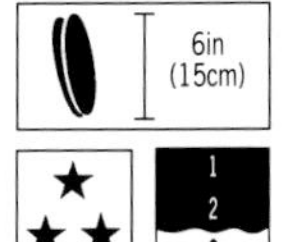

This is very similar in shape and appearance to *E. ensis*, but it is much larger, more strongly constructed and is either very slightly curved or almost straight. In addition, the ends of the valves are more truncated and less curved. The species burrows into sand or shell gravel from the intertidal zone down to about 119ft (36m).

S U P E R  F A M I L Y
## SOLENOIDEA

F A M I L Y
## SOLENIDAE and CULTELLIDAE
(Razor Shells and Jackknife Clams)

These two families consists for the most part of long, narrow and thin-walled bivalves that burrow in sand or mud. Many are edible, and the species are distributed worldwide, from Arctic to tropical waters. Of the principal genera, *Solen* (Solenidae) and *Ensis* (Cultellidae) have truncated ends; *Siliqua* (Cultellidae) differ in that they have ovate and elongated shells, with round ends.

**ENSIS ENSIS**
Narrow Jackknife Clam. *L. 1758.*
Norway to Mediterranean.

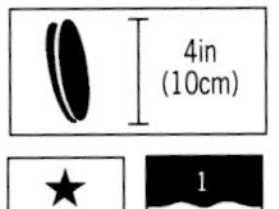

A fragile and lightweight shell, this is long, narrow and curved slightly, with equal valves. The periostracum is a pale olive green and is visible on the shell in the photograph. Fine concentric growth lines are evident on the pinkish grey shells. The right valve has one small cardinal and lateral tooth; the left valve has two cardinal and two lateral teeth. The ligament is external.

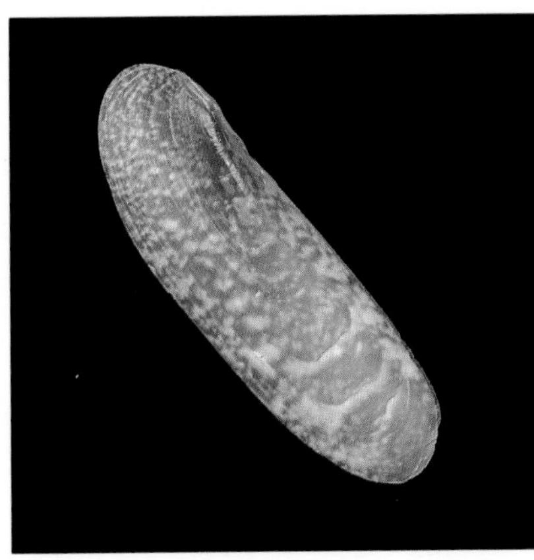

**PHAXAS CULTELLUS**
*L. 1758.*
Japan to Philippines.

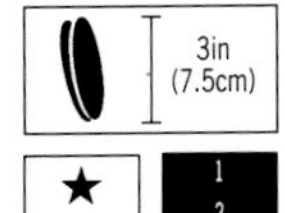

Similar in size and weight to *S. radiata*, this is less broad, however, and is slightly curved, with valves that gape at the anterior end. The shell is smooth, with a moderate gloss, and is marbled with pale grey or brown on a pale lavender background. The shell in the photograph is from Taiwanese waters.

**SILIQUA RADIATA**
Sunset Siliqua. *L. 1758.*
Indian Ocean.

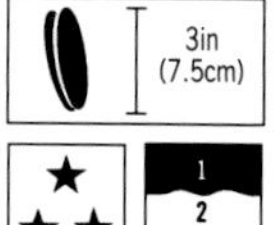


A very thin and fragile shell, it is often thought of as a species of tellin. The long, narrow and ovate valves have rounded ends. There is a very small exterior ligament. This shell is a beautiful pale purple, with four broad white radial rays. It is smooth and glossy.

**TELLINA ALFREDENSIS**
Alfred Bay Tellin. *Bartsch 1915.*
South Africa.

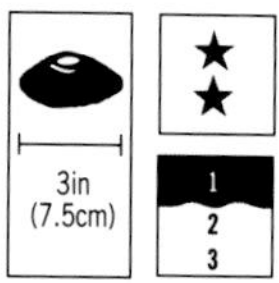


A large relatively thick-walled tellin, it has virtually equal triangular valves with rounded margins. The exterior is smooth, with a low gloss; there are numerous very fine concentric growth lines. The interior is flushed with a rich pink colour, and the periphery of the valve is white. A popular collectors' shell.

**TELLINA RADIATA**
Sunrise Tellin. *L. 1758.*
South-eastern USA and Caribbean.

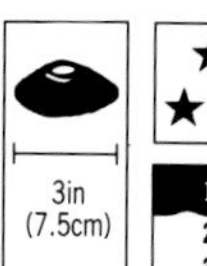


This very smooth and highly glossy shell is elongated and oval. It is usually cream, with broad radial bands or rays of pink. All-cream specimens are sometimes known as *T. unimaculata*. The interior of both forms is tinged with rich yellow. The species lives in coral sand.

SUPER FAMILY
TELLINOIDEA

FAMILY
## TELLINIDAE
(Tellins)

Tellins are a family of at least 200 species of bivalves. Very small to medium in size, they are usually thin and ovate, and occur in most parts of the world in shallow water, where they burrow in sand or mud. Most are smooth and glossy, although some species have concentric lines or ridges. The umbones are very small; there are two small cardinal teeth in each valve, and the hinge plate is narrow. The best known of numerous genera and subgenera are *Tellina*, *Strigilla*, *Macoma* and *Semele*.

**TELLINA ALBINELLA**
Little White Tellin. *Lamarck 1818.*
Southern Australia.

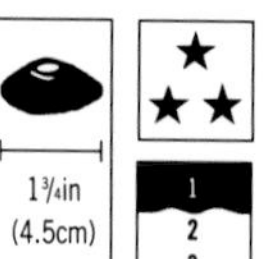


Although occasionally white, the species appears to be more commonly pink or pale orange, with fine white concentric lines. This ovate and rather elongated thin shell is compressed at the posterior end.

**TELLINA PULCHERRIMA**
Beautiful Tellin. *Sowerby 1825.*
Western Pacific.

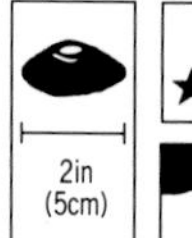


A smallish tellin, it is oval in shape, and compressed at the posterior. There are numerous fine concentric growth striae and very fine scaly spines at both ends of each valve – these do not occur at the centre. The exterior is a rich pink colour, with cream radial rays. The interior is pale pink. The specimen shown is from south-western Taiwan.

**TELLINA FOLIACEA**
Foliated Tellin. *L. 1758.* North-East Indian Ocean and South-West Pacific.

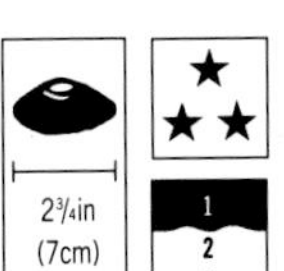

2¾in (7cm)

The large ovate foliated tellin is thin and lightweight. The valves are flat and more or less equal, with a low ridge or keel running from the umbones to the lower posterior margin. The upper posterior margin, alongside the exterior ligament, bears small flattened scaly spines. Shells are deep yellow or orange in colour, the two shown here coming from Oman.

**TELLINA ROSTRATA**
Rostrate Tellin. *L. 1758.* South-West Pacific.

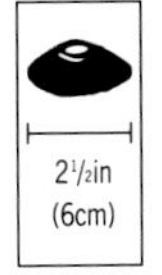

2½in (6cm)

A very thin lightweight tellin, this is elongate and its posterior margin is rostrated. The surface is smooth and glossy, with extremely fine concentric striations. It is a most beautiful coral pink colour, deepening toward the umbones.

**DONAX SERRA**
Giant South Africa Wedge Shell. *Röding 1798.* South Africa.

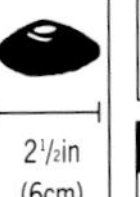

2½in (6cm)

A large thick species, it has equal ovate valves which are sloping and truncated at the posterior. The surface is smooth and glossy apart from the posterior portion, which has small wavy concentric ridges. The lips are finely dentate just within the shell. It is pale purple in colour, greyish at the umbones outside and purple and white inside.

**TELLINA VIRGATA**
*L. 1758.* Indo-Pacific.

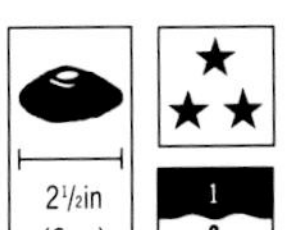

2½in (6cm)

A medium-sized ovate shell, it has a fine concentrically grooved surface and a matt finish. It is a pale pastel pink, with cream radial rays. There is a deep groove running from the umbone to the lower posterior margin of the left valve. The shell is white, with yellow staining within.

SUPER FAMILY
TELLINOIDEA

FAMILY
## DONACIDAE
(Donax or Wedge Clams)

These small triangular or wedge-shaped shells are a group of perhaps 50 species. They inhabit warm temperate or tropical waters, where they burrow in sand near the surface in the intertidal zone. Many are edible, some species being used in quantity in a soup preparation. Of four listed genera, *Donax* is the principal.

**DONAX SCORTUM**
Leather Donax. *L. 1758.* Indian Ocean and East Indies.

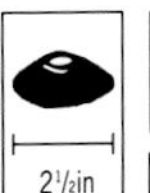

2½in (6cm)

The leather donax is large and triangular, with inflated and concentrically ridged valves; the posterior area slopes, and is flattened from the umbones to the lower posterior margins. The shell is off-white to grey, with a large white lunule. The interior is white, tinged with purple. The specimen shown is from Cuddalore, southern India.

SUPER FAMILY
ARTICOIDEA

FAMILY
## ARCTICIDAE
(Arctica Clams)

This small family was well represented in prehistoric times, and there are numerous fossil forms, but there is only one recent genus – *Arctica*. The shells are similar to Venus clams, but have two or three cardinal as well as well developed lateral teeth.

SUPER FAMILY
GLOSSOIDEA

FAMILY
## GLOSSIDAE
(Heart Clams)

This family is a very ancient group, with numerous fossil forms, but few surviving species. The rounded inflated valves have coiled umbones, which give the shells a swollen, heart-like shape. The few known species occur both in cool and tropical seas. Due to their unusual and appealing shape, all species are popular collectors' items. There are two main genera, *Glossus* and *Meiocardia*.

**MEIOCARDIA VULGARIS**
Vulgar Heart Clam. *Reeve 1845.*
Philippines.

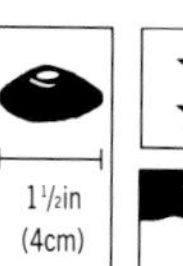


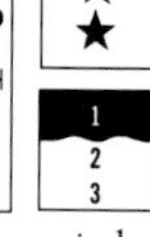


There seems to be some confusion between this and *M. moltkiana*, which it closely resembles. The characteristic features – acutely rolled umbones and a keeled ridge – are present in both species. The vulgar heart clam, however, has stronger and broader concentric ridges and a sharper keel; there are occasional small brown blotches on the exterior.

**ARCTICA ISLANDICA**
Ocean Quahog. *L. 1767.*
North Atlantic and North Sea.

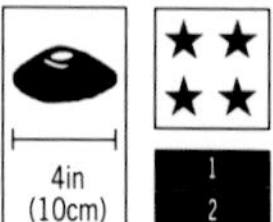


A very solid and heavy shell, it has equal and inflated valves which are sometimes ovate or circular in outline. There are numerous fine concentric lines and, as can be seen here, the beige or off-white shell is covered with a thick dark brown or black periostracum. The interior is a dull white, with distinct muscle scars and pallial line. The species is an important food source.

**GLOSSUS HUMANUS**
Oxheart Clam. *L. 1758.*
Iceland, Norway to the Mediterranean.

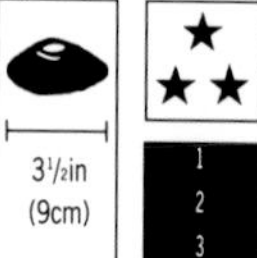


A large lightweight shell, the oxheart clam has equal and inflated valves and high rounded umbones which are rolled toward the anterior. There are numerous concentric growth lines. There are three cardinal teeth and one lateral per valve. The shell is cream or beige, with tan radial markings; the interior is off-white. The species lives on sand or mud at depths from 26 to 1,000ft (8-300m).

**MEIOCARDIA MOLTKIANA**
Moltke's Heart Clam. *Spengler 1783.*
Western Pacific.

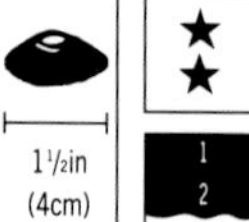


A beautifully shaped shell, it has finer concentric ridges than *M. vulgaris*, and the keel edges are less acute. The colour is a pale creamy white, with occasional very pale yellow tinting. The interior is pure white. A choice collectors' item.

SUPER FAMILY
## VENEROIDEA

FAMILY
## VENERIDAE
(Venus Clams)

A very large and varied family, the largest group of bivalves, containing over 400 species. Venus clams have solid-walled shells, and there is much texture and sculptural variation, making the family fascinating to the enthusiast and collector. They occur in many locations, in both cold and warm waters, inhabiting soft substrates. Most prefer shallow water, but some species live deep. Many are edible. Of numerous genera and subgenera, the notable ones are *Venus*, *Periglypta*, *Chione*, *Bassina*, *Mercenaria*, *Pitar*, *Callista*, *Tapes*, *Paphia*, *Dosinia* and *Lioconcha*.

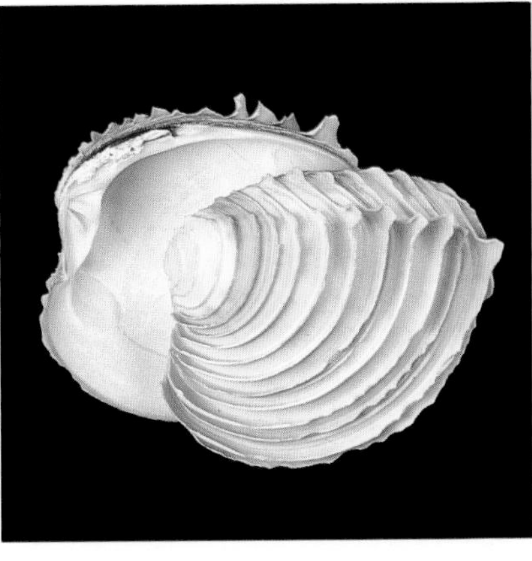

**CIRCOMPHALUS FOLIACEOLAMELLOSUS** Scaly-ridged Venus. *Schröter 1788.* West Africa.

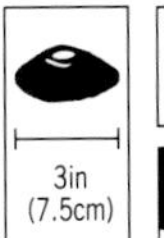

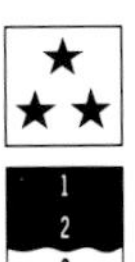


A large and rather heavy shell, with prominent concentric scaly ridges or lamellae, it is similar to *B. disjecta*, but with more ridges and with less inflated but equal valves. The colour is beige or cream with pink tints in the umbonal area. There are strong cardinal teeth and distinctive muscle scars and pallial line.

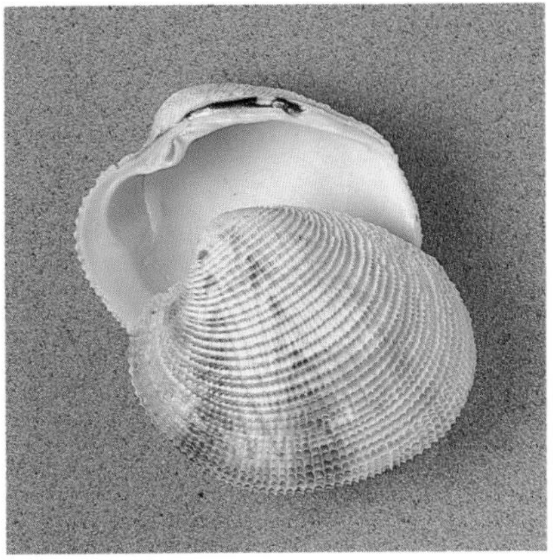

**PERIGLYPTA CHEMNITZI** Chemnitz's Venus. *Hanley 1844.* South-West Pacific.

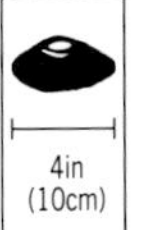

A large and heavy species, it has inflated equal valves, bearing closely set low and crenulated thin ridges; there are very fine radial grooves. The shell is off-white to cream, with pale brown rays or zigzag lines, the interior being white. There are three strong cardinal teeth in each valve.

**ANTIGONA LAMELLARIS** Lamellate Venus. *Schumacher 1817.* West Indies.

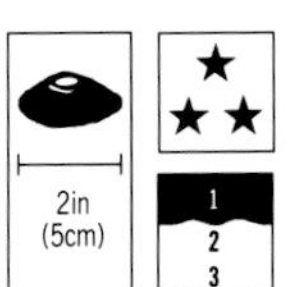


Although within the *Venus* genus, this shell is better known under its subgeneric name *Antigona*. It is an attractive species, triangular in shape, with rounded and serrated margins. There are radial grooves and the low thin flat concentric ridges are crenulated. The specimen shown depicts typical coloration, both interior and exterior.

**PERIGLYPTA MAGNIFICA** Chocolate Venus Clam. *Sowerby 1875.* Philippines.

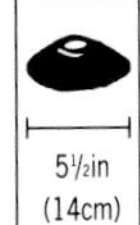

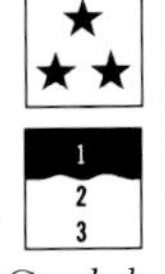


The chocolate Venus clam is probably the largest and heaviest species in the family, and I cannot understand why no shell-guide has included it since it was first described in Reeve's *Conchologia Iconica* back in the middle of the 19th century. It is indeed a handsome shell, with strong concentric growth lines which are crossed by very flat narrow radial ribs, giving a reticulated effect. It is pinkish beige, with dark purplish grey margins. There are very strong cardinal teeth and distinct muscle scars and pallial line. The valves are rounded and equal.

**PERIGLYPTA PUERPERA** Youthful Venus. *L. 1771.* Indo-Pacific.

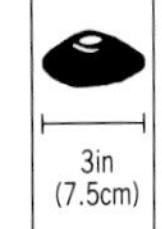

An attractive shell, the youthful Venus has thick heavy equal valves, which are covered with reticulations of fine concentric ridges and radial lines. The off-white shell has broad brown radial rays, darkest on the posterior portion. The interior is also off-white, with deep purple staining within and around the pallial sinus area.

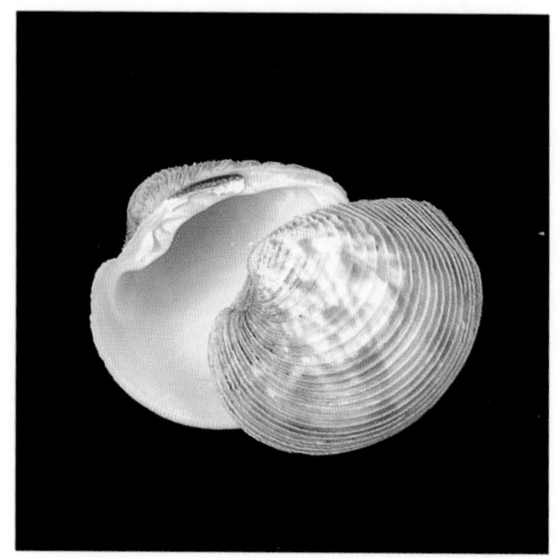

## VENTRICOLARIA RIGIDA

*Dillwyn 1817.*
Southern Florida, West Indies and Brazil.

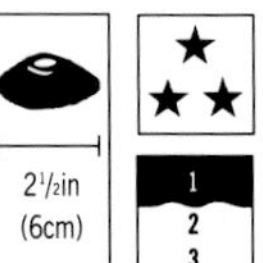


This Venus clam is rounded, with inflated equal valves. There are numerous concentric low scaly ridges and a rounded lunule. The exterior is beige or cream, with tan blotches of V-shaped markings; the interior is white. This is a shallow-water dweller.

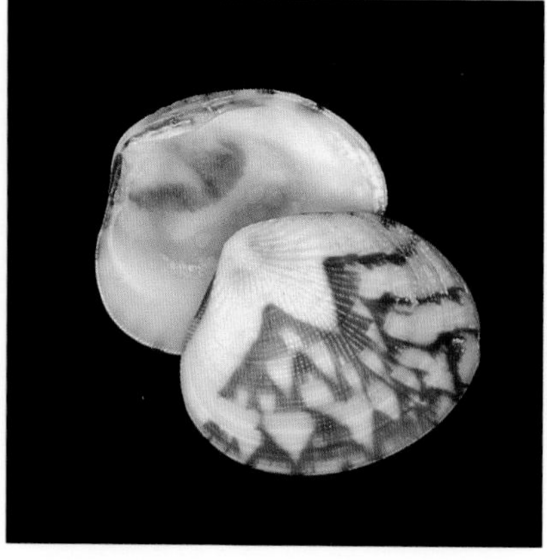

## GAFRARIUM AEQUIVOCUM

Forked Venus. *Holten 1803.*
Indo-Pacific.

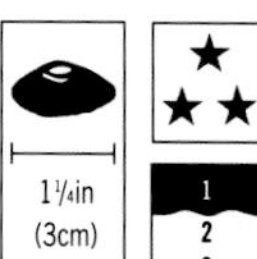


An ovate shell, with equal valves, its umbones are placed off-centre, toward the anterior. Fine radial cords diverge out from the centre. The off-white exterior displays tan or dark brown tent markings or zigzag lines, the interior is white, with brown staining at the centre.

## BASSINA DISJECTA

Wedding Cake Venus. *Perry 1811.*
South Australia and Tasmania.

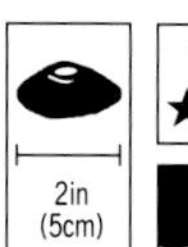


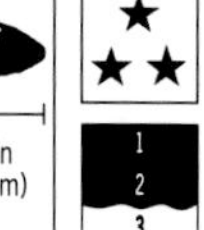


This wonderful shell looks indeed like carefully iced layers of a wedding cake! It is a pinkish cream colour and has equal and inflated valves, with the umbones directed to the anterior. The sculpturing is of strong and distinctive concentric and continuous frilly lamellae. A popular collectors' shell.

## VENUS VERRUCOSA

Warty Venus. *L. 1758.*
North-East Atlantic and Mediterranean.

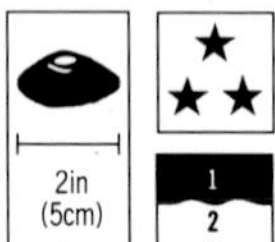


A solid and heavy medium-sized Venus, it has equal and rather inflated valves. The strong concentric ridges are slightly and irregularly nodulose, especially toward the anterior and posterior margins. The shell in the photograph portrays typical colour and is from shallow water off Cadiz, Spain. This is an edible species.

## ANOMALOCARDIA SUBRUGOSA

Partially-rough Venus. *Wood 1828.*
Western Central America.

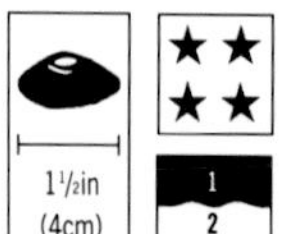


The partially-rough Venus has very thick solid equal valves with strong rounded concentric ridges. There are two cardinal teeth in each valve. The dirty beige background is overlaid with about four broad dark grey or brown rays. The species lives on intertidal mud flats and is an important food source. The larger specimen here is from Ecuador.

## BASSINA CALOPHYLLA

Wooden Venus. *Philippi 1836.*
Philippines to Northern Australia.

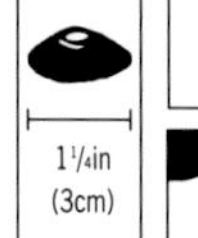


Although rather similar to *B. disjecta*, the wooden Venus is rather more triangular in shape, has less prominent concentric lamellae or ridges, and is smaller. I have also encountered this species under the genus *Clausinella* and the subgenus *Callanaitis*.

**CHIONE GNIDIA**
Gnidia Venus. *Broderip and Sowerby 1829.*
Western Central America.

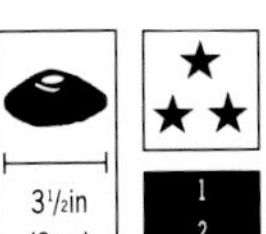

3½in (9cm)

Rather triangular in shape, it has rounded margins. The equal valves bear numerous radial grooves and the concentric flat ridges are crenulated, especially on younger specimens, as seen in this photograph. The overall colour is pinkish beige.

**CHIONE LATILIRATA**
Imperial Venus. *Conrad 1841.*
South-eastern USA to Brazil.

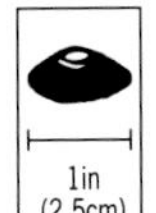

1in (2.5cm)

This small but very solid and chunky Venus shell has large raised and recurved concentric ridges. Off white, with pale brown rays, it is triangular in shape and not dissimilar to *C. paphia*.

***MERETRIX LUSORIA***
Pokerchip Venus. *Röding 1798.*
India to Eastern Asia.

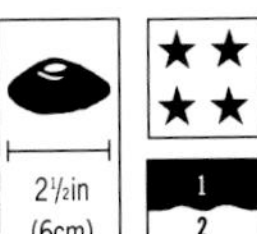

2½in (6cm)

A thick heavy shell, the pokerchip Venus has smooth equal valves and a high gloss. Some are devoid of pattern; others have brown rays or zigzag lines. The specimen in the photograph has pale grey rays on a creamy grey background. The interior is cream, with purple staining at the posterior margin and between the teeth.

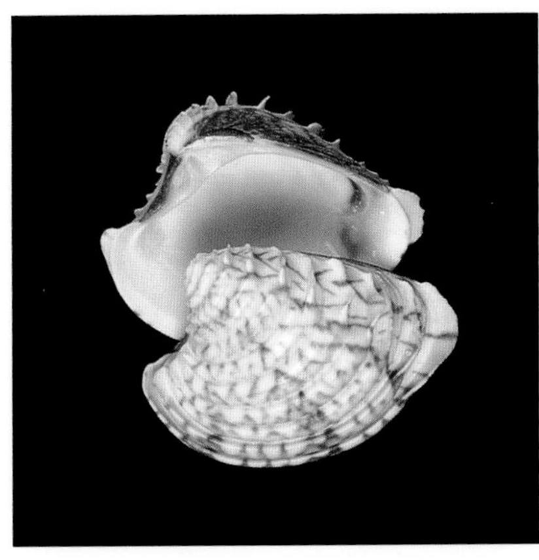

**CHIONE PAPHIA**
King Venus. *L. 1767.*
West Indies to Brazil.

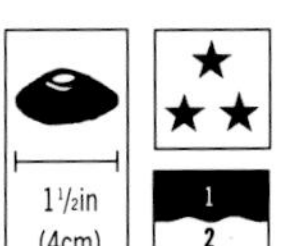

1½in (4cm)

A very handsome robust little shell, it has inflated equal valves, with broad flat concentric ridges which are scaly at the posterior end. The anterior margins are slightly upturned; the lunule is distinctive and heart-shaped. There are brown rayed bands or tent markings on an off-white background.

**CLAUSINELLA GRAVESCENS**
Heavy Venus. *Meake 1843.* South-western Pacific and Northern Australia.

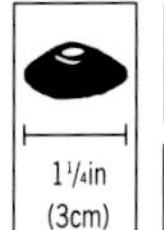

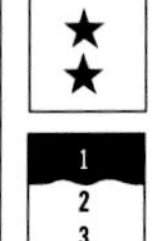

1¼in (3cm)

This little Venus is similar to *B. calophylla*, but is less inflated, and the concentric flat ridges are less raised. The off-white background displays faint pale tan rays. The interior is tinged with rose red or purple. This particular specimen is from subtidal sand, Shark Bay, Western Australia.

***TIVELLA COMPRESSA***
Compressed Tivella. *Sowerby 1851.*
South Africa.

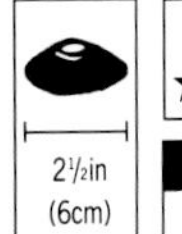

2½in (6cm)

This solid and triangular shell tapers to rounded and centrally placed umbones. The beige colouring is overlaid with greyish brown radial rays, and the effect is most attractive. There are numerous fine concentric lines. The interior is between off-white and creamy grey in colour.

### *AMIANTIS PURPURATUS*
*Lamarck 1818.*
Brazil and Argentina.

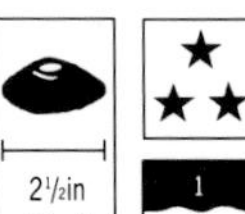


An ovate shell, it has rounded margins and equal, rather inflated, valves. There are concentric growth lines and the surface has a moderate gloss. The exterior colour is a greyish lavender or mid-brown; the interior is pure white. There is a large pallial sinus. This particular shell was collected in sand at Rio Grande do Sul, Brazil.

### *LIOCONCHA FASTIGIATA*
*Sowerby 1851.*
Japan, Western Pacific and Australia.

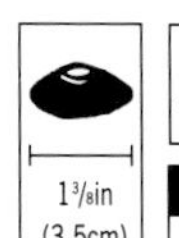


The umbones of this small, almost triangular Venus are slightly rolled to the anterior. There are numerous very fine concentric grooves. The shell is attractively marked with small dark brown tent markings on a cream background. The white interior is stained yellow.

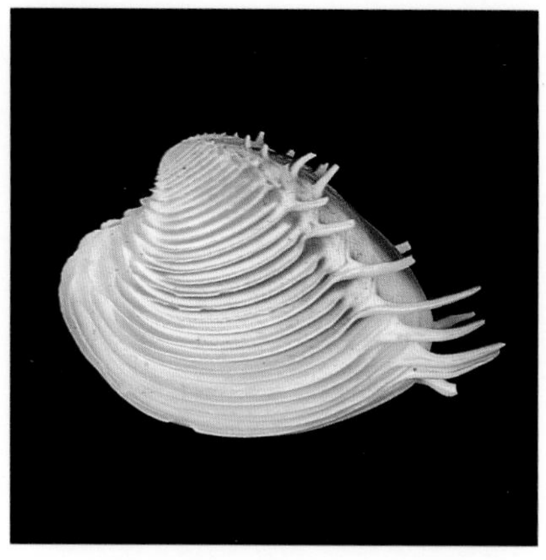

### *PITAR DIONE*
Royal Comb Venus. *L. 1758.*
Caribbean.

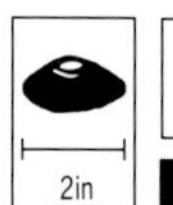


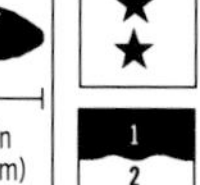


A much desirable and sought-after species in the 17th and 18th centuries, it is still a popular bivalve. The equal valves have strong concentric flat ridges. Curved and strong spines extend from the ridge which runs from the umbones to the lower posterior margin. The shell is off-white, with pale lavender tints.

### *CALLISTA ERYCINA*
Reddish Callista Venus. *L. 1758.* South-West Pacific, Japan and Indian Ocean.

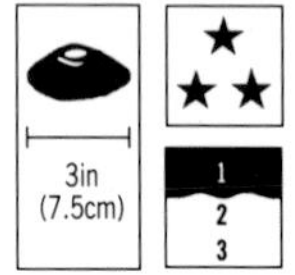


A beautiful shell, it has equal valves and large rounded umbones. the glossy surface is sculptured with strong and raised concentric ridges. The cream surface is patterned with broken brown and tan rays, and the periphery of the valves is tinged with rich orange. This specimen is from south-eastern India.

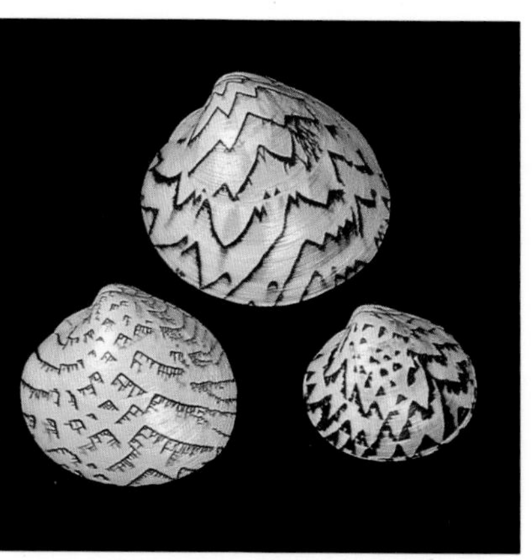

### *LIOCONCHA CASTRENSIS*
Chocolate-flamed Venus. *L. 1758.*
Indo-Pacific.

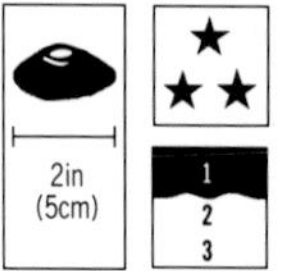


This is a most attractive Venus clam and certainly one of my favourites! The rounded-to-oval shell has equal and somewhat inflated valves with fine concentric ridges. It is cream in colour, with hazy greyish blue patches, overlaid with vivid dark brown zigzag lines or tent markings. All the shells here are from the central Philippines.

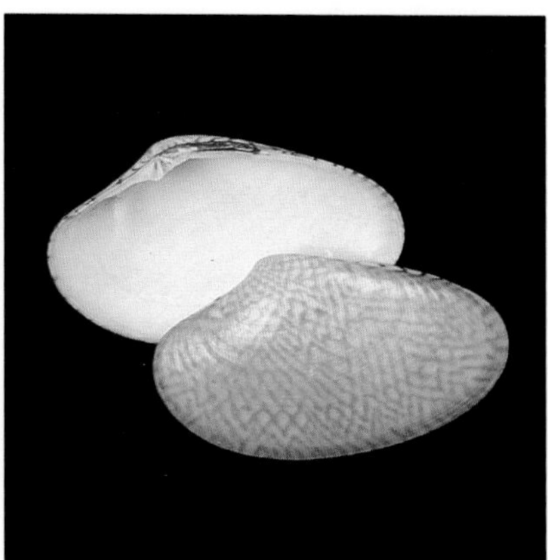

### *PAPHIA UNDULATA*
Undulating Venus. *Born 1778.*
Indo-Pacific.

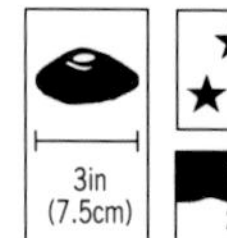


A triangular elongated species, it has more or less flat and equal valves. The surface is smooth and glossy, but there are a few very fine concentric lines. The beige shell has purplish grey zigzag or tent markings; the interior is white.

**PAPHIA AMABILIS**
Lovely Venus. *Philippi 1847.*
Western Pacific.

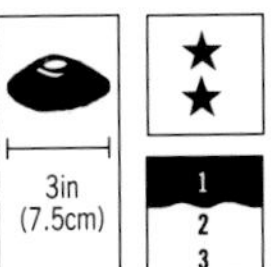


An elongated and ovate thick-walled species, the lovely Venus has bulbous valves which bear strong, low and rounded concentric ridges. Shells are beige or pale tan, with occasional dark brown irregularly placed spots. The interior is white, and there is some pale yellow staining within the pallial line area.

***DOSINIA VARIEGATA***
*Gray 1838.*
Indo-Pacific.

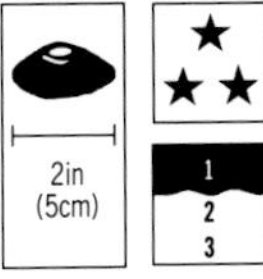


This Venus has rounded flattened equal valves that are sculptured with low closely laid concentric flat ridges. The colouring is variable, as can be seen in these two specimens. The variegated form shown here is from Shark Bay, Western Australia.

**CYRTOPLEURA COSTATA**
Angel Wing. *L. 1758.*
South-eastern USA to Brazil.

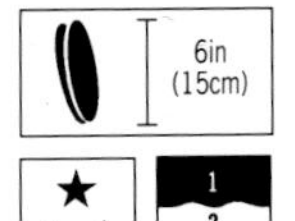


Unlike the rather drab *P. dactylus*, this species is very beautiful, with elongated and inflated white valves. The sculpturing consists of raised and scaly radial ridges and fine concentric lines. Although the specimen shown exceeds 7½in (19cm), the specimens that I see nowadays are rarely larger than 5in (13cm). The current size record is 8in (20cm).

***TAPES LITERATUS***
Lettered Venus. *L. 1758.*
Indo-Pacific.

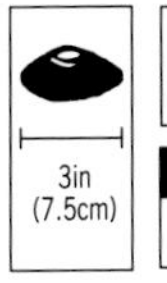


A shallow-water Venus, this has rather flat equal valves, with the small umbones placed well to the anterior portion of the shell. There are many concentric grooves; the pattern and colour varies, two forms being shown here. The smaller of the two shells comes from the Solomon Islands.

SUPER FAMILY
PHOLADOIDEA

FAMILY
## PHOLADIDAE
(Piddocks or Angel Wings)

This is a family of bivalves that have thin but strong elongated shells which gape at both ends and have ribbed surfaces. Apart from the two main valves, there are various accessory plates. Members of this worldwide group are to be found in Arctic, temperate and tropical seas. They are able to burrow or bore into various substrates, such as coral, rock, soft limestone and mud, as well as man-made materials like wooden harbour piles. Of the several genera, *Pholas*, *Barnea* and *Cyrtopleura* are the best known.

***PHOLAS DACTYLUS***
European Piddock. *L. 1758.*
North-East Atlantic and Mediterranean.

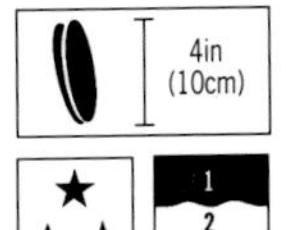


The animal of this species has remarkable phosphorescent properties, in that its outline glows in the dark with a green blue light. It is capable of boring into sand, peat, shale, chalk or red sandstone. The shell is not particularly attractive, but the surface ornamentation is somewhat pleasing to the eye.

# *CLASS: POLYPLACOPHORA*

ORDER
## NEOLORICATA

This is a large class of molluscs, known as chitons or coat-of-mail shells. The group contains about 1,000 species of more or less ovate shells, consisting of eight overlapping plates which can, in a limited fashion, move between each other (hence "coat of mail"). These plates are set into a tough muscular material known as the girdle. The chitons are vegetarian and usually inhabit rocky shallow water. They eat after dusk – usually small algae and, on rare occasions, small invertebrates. The arrangement of this Class is complex. There is one order, Neoloricata; then three suborders and nine super families. Of the many genera, we are here interested only in four; other well-known ones are *Stenoplax*, *Mopalia* and *Tonicella*.

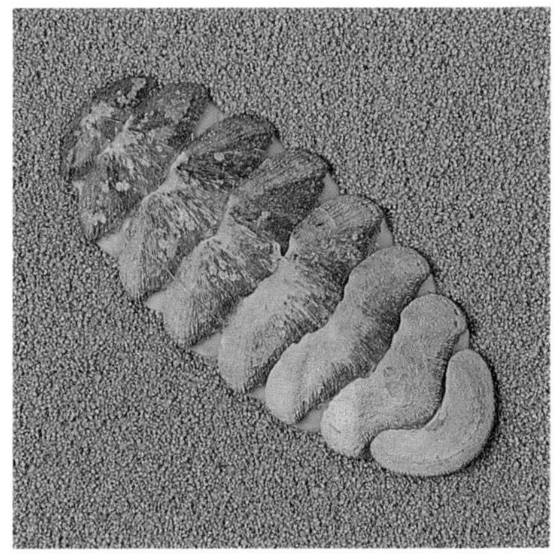

### *DINOPLAX GIGAS*
Giant South African Chiton. *Gmelin 1792.*
South Africa.

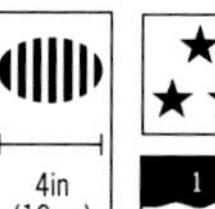


The largest of the South African chitons, it has thick and solid plates. The specimen shown here has had the girdle removed and, because of its relative immaturity, the fine surface sculpturing can be seen. On large shells, the exterior is usually encrusted. The underside of the plates is off-white. Shells are often found washed up on beaches.

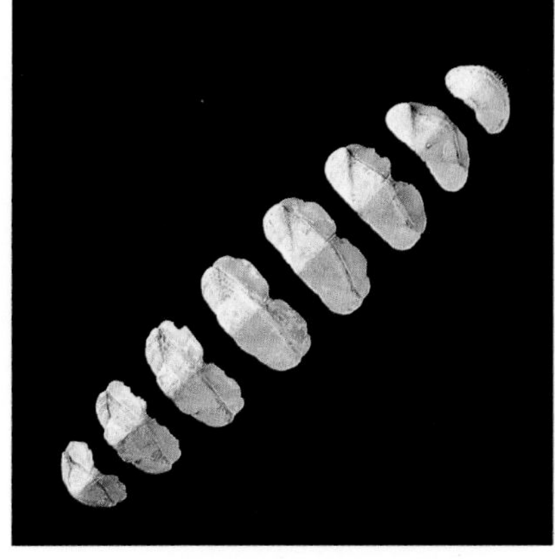

### *DINOPLAX GIGAS*
Giant South African Chiton. *Gmelin 1792.*
South Africa.

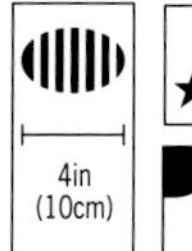


This specimen has had the tough leathery girdle removed to show the eight separate plates that make up chiton shells. The last small plate has a minutely serrated margin which resembles a miniature half-set of dentures! These end plates, which are often found on beaches, are frequently known as "false teeth" locally.

### *ISCHNOCHITON SUBVIRIDIS*
Green Chiton. *Iredale 1916.*
Southern Australia.

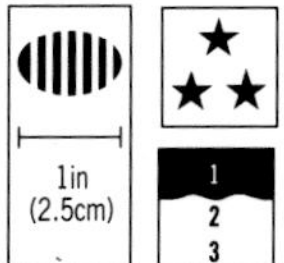


An elongated and rather narrow species, it has very finely grooved plates on the exterior or dorsum, the colour being a greenish grey, with beige markings on the central ridge. The plates on the underside are a blue grey colour. These two specimens are from Kangaroo Island, southern Australia.

### *LEPIDOCHITONA CINEREUS*
*L. 1767.* Scandinavia, Western Europe and Western Mediterranean.

This is a small lightweight and fairly fragile chiton, the dorsum of which is usually beige to greyish brown, but is often encrusted. The underside of the plates is a pale blue green. This specimen was found clinging to the underside of chalk boulders below the high tide level at Eastbourne, Sussex, England.

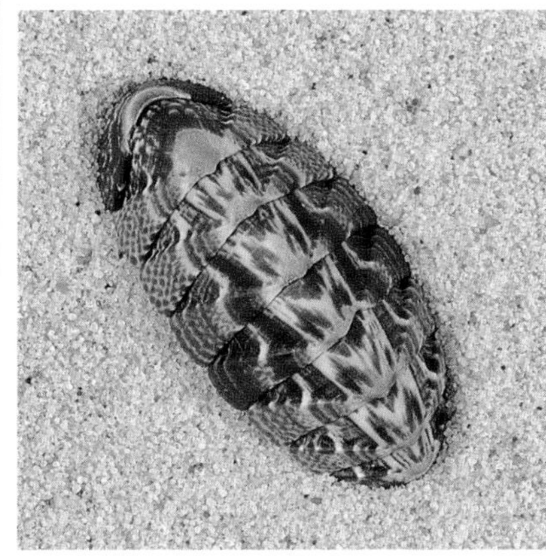

### *CHITON TULIPA*
Tulip Chiton. *Quoy and Gaimard 1834.*
South Africa.

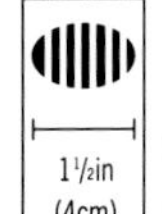


A prettily marked and coloured species, it is narrow and elongated with a high central ridge. The pattern and colours can be very variable, although the underside of the plates is generally a bright bluish green.

# *CLASS: CEPHALOPODA*

FAMILY
## NAUTILIDAE
(Chambered Nautilus Shells)

This is a small family of perhaps four or five species. I still believe that the arrangement of these shells is in need of revision, due to confusion in specific names and local variants. There is a subclass and an order – Nautiloidea and Nautilida respectively. They have external shells, the animal occupying the last and largest chamber. The shell itself is large and coiled and closely resembles the Ammonite, its fossil ancestor, of which there were once many. (This remarkable group is discussed in more detail in the biology and fossil section of this book.) There is one genus, *Nautilus*.

FAMILY
## SPIRULIDAE
(Spirulas)

Closely related to the *Nautilus*, this family of one species consists of a thin, fragile, closely coiled shell with internal chambers. The animal, a small deep-sea squid, entirely covers its shell when alive. It is within the subclass Coleoidea and order Sepiida. Many hundreds of these shells are regularly discovered washed up on beaches in numerous worldwide warm sea areas. There is one genus, *Spirula*.

### *SPIRULA SPIRULA*
Common Spirula. *L. 1758.*
Worldwide in warm seas.

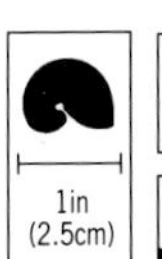

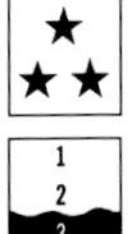


The species lives in depths of about 3,300ft (1,000m) and is usually only beach-collected. Through the thin walls of the coiled off-white shell the partitions inside can be clearly seen. The thin divisional walls are nacreous, and one can be seen at the open end.

### *NAUTILUS POMPILIUS*
Common Chambered Nautilus. *L. 1758.*
Western Pacific.

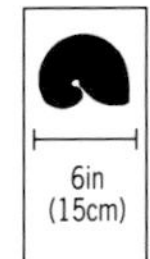

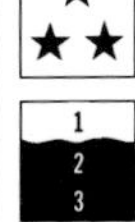


This well-known species has a large and coiled shell, with an indented (involute) spire and large and gaping aperture (the male tends to have a larger aperture). The shell is off-white, with distinctive tan, "flame"-like radial bands. There is a black calloused area facing the aperture on the compressed part of the coiled shell. Unlike other species, this has no umbilicus. The half-section clearly shows the internal chambers which are used ingeniously as a buoyancy aid.

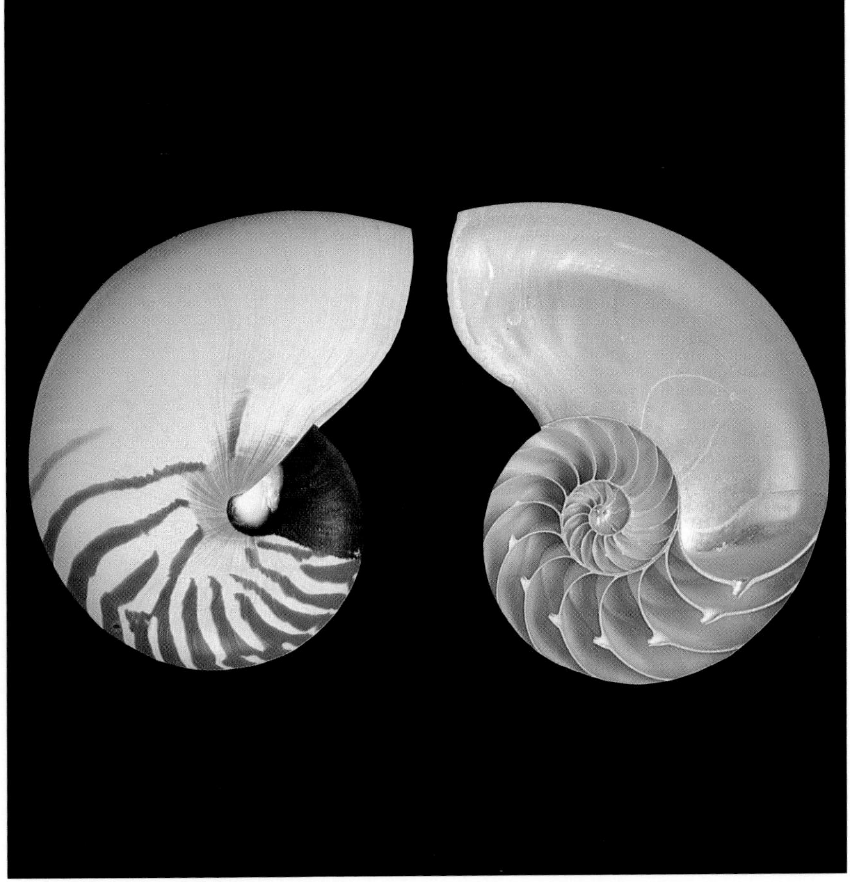

SUPER FAMILY
## ARGONAUTOIDEA

FAMILY
## ARGONAUTIDAE
(Paper Nautilus)

Argonauts are octopus-like animals which do not have true shells, producing instead a shell-like egg case which in shape is most beautiful. The "arms" of the female secrete the material to form the shell as a receptacle in which to cradle the tiny eggs. There are less than a dozen known species, all of which inhabit warm open seas. Many such egg cases are found washed ashore after storms, but they are often incomplete. These shells are very popular collectors' items.

### ARGONAUTA NODOSA
Knobbed Paper Nautilus. *Lightfoot 1786.* Indo-Pacific.

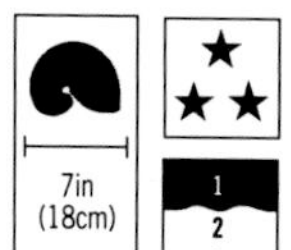


While similar in shape to *A. argo*, this has a wider keeled area, its sides are more inflated, and the sculpturing is nodulose and not ridged. The shell is rather more thickened and heavy, but still fragile. Like other species of paper nautilus, they can occur in one locality in great numbers and then vanish for years – obviously seasons and ocean currents are to be taken into consideration when accounting for this phenomenon.

### ARGONAUTA HIANS
Brown Paper Nautilus. *Lightfoot 1786.* Warm Pacific and Atlantic and Indian Oceans.

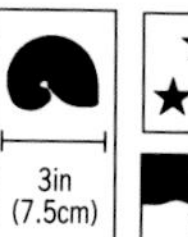

A much smaller, more inflated shell than *A. argo*, this has fewer and proportionately larger keel nodules. In some, two prominent and sharp projections form outwardly either side of the aperture margin adjacent to the spire. This can be seen in the darker form which is from the Gulf of Oman; the large pale shell is from the Philippines.

### ARGONAUTA ARGO
Common Paper Nautilus. *L. 1758.* Worldwide in warm seas.

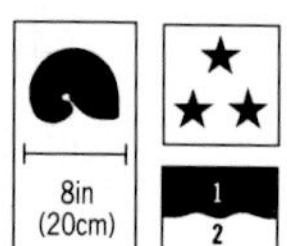


This beautiful delicate structure is very thin and lightweight. There are numerous low wavy radial ridges extending from the narrowly coiled spire to the margin, where a double row of short sharp nodules extends in a keel-like fashion around the shell. The shell is off-white to cream in colour, the early part of the keel and spines being tinted with greyish black.

# *CLASS: SCAPHOPODA*

FAMILY

# DENTALIIDAE

(Tusk Shells)

There are at least 1,000 known species of tusk shells, many of which are very small. They occur in worldwide locations, inhabiting either shallow or, more likely, deep water, where they burrow in sand or mud with their posterior end exposed. Their range extends from temperate to tropical seas. The species vary little and are generally curved, long, tapering at the posterior and hollow. In some shells the posterior portion has a notch or slit, or a small terminal "pipe". They are a carnivorous group, feeding on protozoans, foraminifera and other micro-organisms. The family has only luke-warm popularity among collectors.

## DENTALIUM APRINUM

Boar's Tusk. *L. 1766.*
Indo-Pacific.

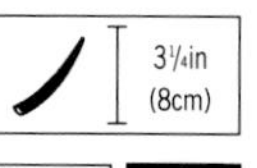


This small and very narrow tusk shell is curved and tapers almost to a point. There are at least 10 raised longitudinal low ridges. It is an attractive pale green colour. Frequently collected in the central and southern Philippines.

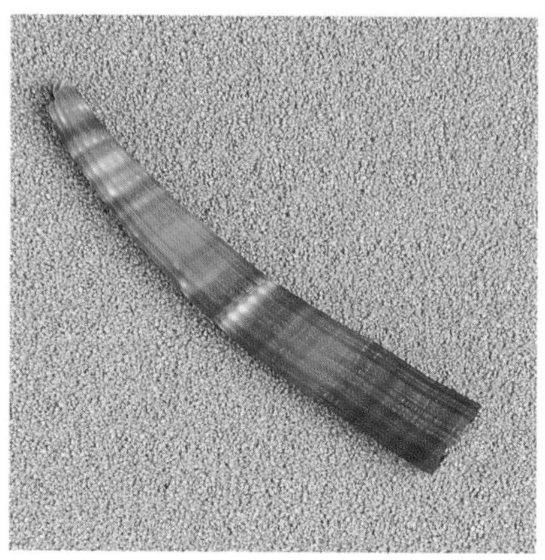

## DENTALIUM FORMOSUM

Formosan Tusk. *Adams and Reeve 1850.*
Japan to the Philippines.

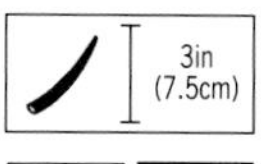


A relatively short and stocky species, it has numerous low longitudinal ribs. At the narrowed posterior, there is a short open terminal pipe. The shell is most attractive in colour, graduating from maroon to a dull brick red with odd spiral bands of cream or white. The species inhabits fairly shallow water, but is only infrequently offered, usually from Japanese waters.

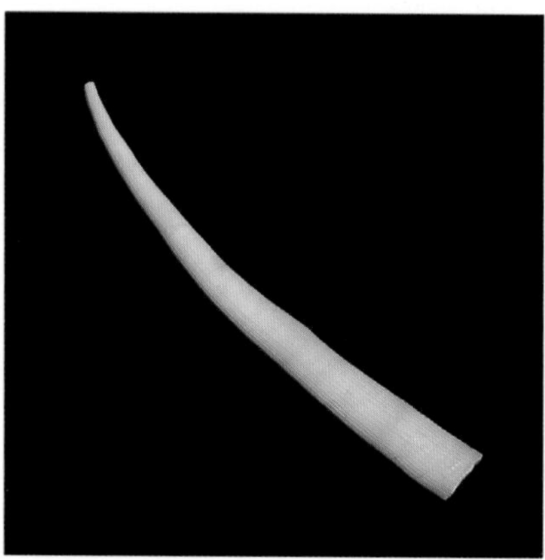

## DENTALIUM VERNEDI

Vernede's Tusk. *Sowerby 1860.*
Japan to the Philippines.

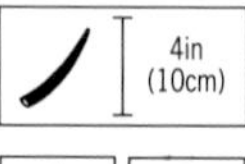


A long slender yellowish beige shell, it is slightly curved and tapers narrowly to the posterior tip, where there is a neat notch. There are numerous very closely set longitudinal grooves and a few indistinct spiral growth bands. The interior is white. This particular shell is from south-western Taiwan.

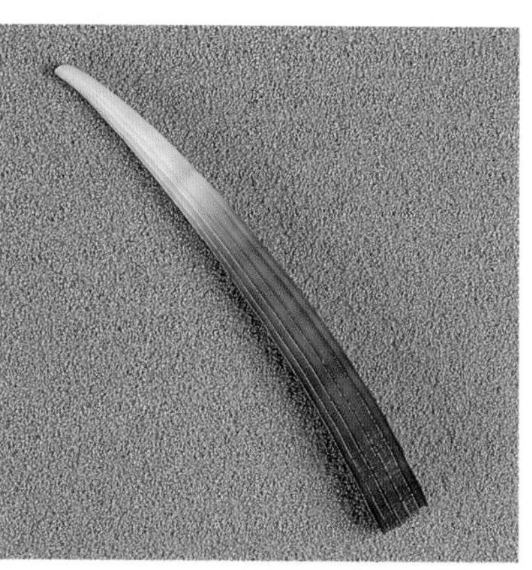

## DENTALIUM ELEPHANTINUM

Elephant Tusk. *L. 1758.*
Japan to Philippines.

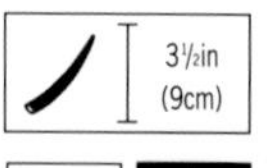


The popularity of this attractive species is due mainly to its good size and lovely dark green colour, which pales to white at the posterior end. It is solidly built and heavy, with a slight curvature. About 10 strong rounded ribs run the length of the shell. This particular specimen is from the Sulu Sea.

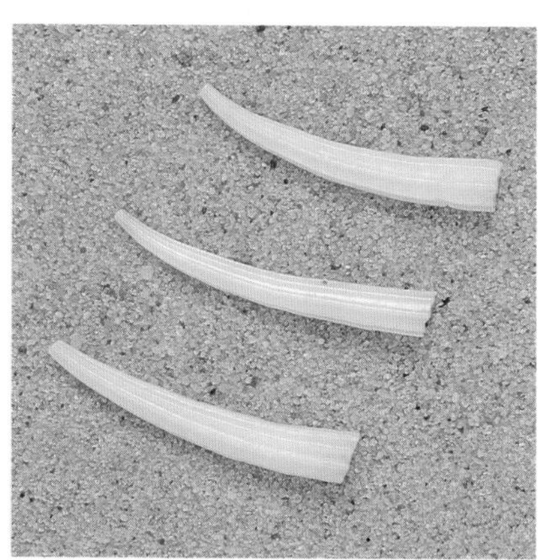

## DENTALIUM OCTANGULATUM

Octagonal Tusk. *Donovan 1804.*
Indo-Pacific.

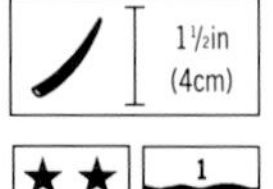


This small species is white, highly glossy and has eight quite prominent longitudinal ribs. The size appears to vary according to its locality; the shells in the photograph are small specimens – 1in (2.5cm) – and were collected off south-eastern India.

# Glossary

**axial:** following or parallel to the shell axis, usually applied to gastropods.
**axis:** an imaginary line around which the whorls revolve, drawn from the anterior to the apex of gastropods.
**beads:** very small, usually rounded knobs, these are often spirally laid, resembling a string of beads.
**body whorl:** the largest section of a gastropod, this encloses the soft parts.
**byssal/byssus:** some bivalves have a byssal area, through which the byssus (fine, thread-like filaments) extend for anchorage.
**calcareous:** a chalky, usually white appearance, due primarily to the presence of calcium carbonate.
**callous:** a thickened, often smooth area, usually found around the aperture or on the parietal wall.
**cancellation:** a sculptured area of lines crossing others at right angles, in a lattice-like effect; also referred to as reticulation.
**carina:** a sharp ridge or keel.
**columella:** the spirally-twisting pillar surrounding the axis of a gastropod.
**concentric:** following the direction of growth lines, usually in bivalves.
**cord:** rope-like ornamentation, usually spiral.
**coronated:** having nodules on the shoulder or spire; crown-like.
**corrugated:** structured with ridges or folds.
**crenulation:** notches or small indentations on ridges or margins.
**dead-collected:** a shell devoid of its animal; often found on beaches, such shells are sometimes referred to as "beached".
**denticle:** a small tooth-like projection; shells with denticles around the margins or inside the lip are "dentate" or "denticulate".
**dorsum:** the back of a shell, opposite the aperture.
**endemic:** confined to a restricted area or geographical region.
**fasciole:** a groove or raised spiral band, formed by successive growth stages and found at the base of certain gastropods.
**fimbriate:** edged or bordered by thin, wavy sculpturing of an ornamental nature.
**frondose:** leaf-like.
**funicular:** a pad-like calloused area found on or above the umbilical portion of some moon snails.
**fusiform:** spindle-shaped.
**globose:** rounded or almost spherical.
**impressed:** indented – a term usually applied to the suture.
**keel:** a raised, often sharp ridge or carina.
**lamellate:** covered with thin scales or plates.
**lirae:** fine ridges, often found on the inner surface of the outer lip.
**maculated:** irregularly blotched or spotted.
**nacreous:** resembling mother-of-pearl.
**nodule:** a sharp or rounded knob or node; where several are present, the shell is described as nodulose.
**ocellated:** having eye-like spots.
**operculum:** grown on the foot of many species of gastropod, this is an oval or rounded structure which seals the aperture when the animal withdraws into its shell.
**ovate:** oval.
**pallial line:** a curved scar line seen on the interior walls of bivalve shells at the point where the edges of the mantle were attached.
**parietal area/wall:** occasionally referred to as the inner lip, this is the area in gastropods that lies opposite the outer lip and above the columella.
**periostracum:** the fibrous and skin-like outer covering of many shells.
**plicate:** plaited or folded portions of the columella; bearing plicae.
**porcellaneous:** a porcelain or china-like texture.
**process:** a spine or projection.
**protoconch:** the tip or apex of a gastropod, formed in its larval stage.
**pustulose:** a surface covered with pustules or tiny pimple-like swellings.
**pyriform:** pear-shaped.
**radial:** ray-like ornamentation or sculpturing, diverging from the umbones of bivalves.
**reticulation:** a pattern of oblique intersecting ridges or striae; also known as cancellation.
**rib:** a raised or elevated structure, usually laid parallel to the axis.
**scabrous:** a rough, scaly surface.
**stria/striae:** fine raised or grooved line(s) on the surface of a shell, sometimes an indication of growth stages.
**suture:** the junction of two whorls, it is often depressed or indented.
**threads:** very fine sculptural lines, usually in a spiral pattern.
**trigonal:** triangular.
**tubercule:** a projection, usually rounded, that is larger than a pustule but smaller than a nodule.
**trochoidal:** shaped like a spinning top; rounded at the bottom and tapering to the top, as in top shells.
**truncated:** finished off abruptly; a term often applied to bivalves with a square-ended appearance and to gastropods with abruptly-terminated spires.
**umbilicus:** the lower open axis around which the whorls of a gastropod are coiled.
**umbo:** sometimes referred to as the beak, this is the part of a bivalve that is the first to be formed; the plural is umbones.
**varix:** a growth resting stage that often appears as a raised and thickened ridge; murex shells bear several varices.
**veliger:** a mollusc in its young, free-swimming larval stage.
**ventral:** in gastropods, the surface on the same side as the aperture; in bivalves, the portion opposite the hinge, where the valves are widest.
**whorl:** a complete coil of a gastropod shell.

# Index to Common Names

Note: All shells described in main section are accompanied by illustrations. Page numbers in *italics* indicate illustrations in introductory chapters.

# *Index to Latin Names*

Note: All shells described in main section are accompanied by illustrations. Page numbers in *italics* indicate illustrations in introductory chapters. Where relevant, subfamilies follow the genus name – the subfamily name is within brackets and ends -inae.

# Bibliography

Conchologists of today are privileged to have at their disposal not only a wide range of high quality modern literature with first class photographs, but also superb antique, often leather-bound, volumes containing beautiful hand-painted or engraved plates. Of many notable titles, I would make particular mention of Martin's *Universal Conchologist* (1784–7), Reeve's *Conchologia Iconica* (1843–78) and the Sowerby family's *Thesaurus Conchyliorum* (1842–87). Books such as these, however, are rarely offered for sale and thus remain virtually out of reach of the amateur collector, although they may be viewed in specialist libraries, such as that of the Linnaean Society, London.

The following list of titles comprises books used as reference for this work and those that I consider will be of particular interest to the reader.

*A Classification of the Living Mollusca.* Vaught (American Malacologists Inc. 1989). A useful reference of the latest framework of systematics.
*A Collectors guide to seashells of the World.* Eisenberg (McGraw Hill 1981). A comprehensive general guide.
*Catalogue of dealer's prices for marine shells.* Rice (Of Sea & Shore Pubs.). A useful collection check-list and price guide. Periodical.
*Compendium of Seashells.* Abbott & Dance (Charles Letts, London 1991). The most comprehensive world-guide to have been published.
*Cone Shells.* Walls (T.F.H. Publications). Popular text book on this large family.
*Cowries of the World.* Burgess (Seacomber Pubs. 1985). The major text book on this most popular family.
*Olive Shells of the World.* Zeigler & Porreca (Rochester Polychrome Press 1969). The first and possibly most popular work on Olive shells.
*Red Sea Shells.* Sharabati (KPI Ltd. 1984). Excellent photographs of shells of restricted habitat.
*Seashells of the World.* Oliver (Hamlyn Pubs. 1975). An excellent pocket-guide.
*Seashells of the World.* Lindner (Blandford Press 1977). A good introductory guide, now out of print.
*Seashells of Tropical West America.* Keen (Stanford University Press 1958). A well-known and popular work on this area.
*Seashells of the West Indies.* Humfrey (Collins 1975). Well-written book on an interesting area. Now out of print.
*Shells of the Philippines.* Springsteen & Leobrera (Carfel Shell Museum 1986). The first book on this area to have been published.
*The Murex Book.* Fair (Ruth Fair 1976). A very good reference book on this large family, sadly now out of print.
*The Living Volutes.* Weaver & DuPont (Delaware Museum 1970). The major work on this large and popular family.
*What Shell is that?* Coleman. A well-illustrated guide to marine species of Australia and the South Pacific.

# Contacts

**BRITISH MUSEUMS**
**(IN WHICH EMINENT OR NOTABLE COLLECTIONS ARE HOUSED)**
*Natural History Museum,* Cromwell Road, London SW7
*National Museum of Wales,* Cathays Park, Cardiff
*The Manchester Museum,* The University, Manchester
*Royal Scottish Museum,* Chambers Street, Edinburgh
*The Ulster Museum,* Botanic Gardens, Belfast, N. Ireland
*Northants N.H.S. & Field Club,* The Humfrey Rooms, Castilian Terrace, Northampton

**CLUBS & SOCIETIES**
*The Conchological Society of Great Britain & Ireland.* (Regular meetings held at the Natural History Museum, London.)
*The British Shell Collector's Club.* Hon Sec Mr. K. Brown, 12 Grainger Road, Isleworth, Middx. (Meetings bi-annually, held in London.)

**CURRENT JOURNALS & PERIODICALS**
*Journal of Conchology.* Published by the Conchology Society.
*Pallidula.* The magazine of the British Shell Collector's Club.
*Hawaiian Shell News.* Published by the Hawaiian Malacological Society, PO Box 10391, Honolulu, Hawaii 96816.
La Conchiglia (The Shell). Published by Kety Nicolay, via C. Federici 1, 00147 Rome, Italy.

**CONSERVATION SOCIETIES**
*Marine Conservation Society.* 9 Gloucester Road, Ross-on-Wye, Herefordshire.

# Acknowledgments

Conchology is a complex subject, and hardly a shell book is published without the inevitable errors. It was in the hope that any such errors be kept to a minimum that I enlisted the help and advice of the following fellow-enthusiasts and conchologists. My grateful thanks extend to:-

Mr. Alex Arthur (Ranellidae); Mr. Kevin Brown (General); Mr. Mike Dixon (Naticidae); Mr. Tom Pain (Muricidae, Astraeinae, Bursidae and Buccinidae); Dr. Endre Sandor (Olividae and Coralliophilidae); Mr. Alan Seccombe (Cassidae); Mr. Andy Wakefield (Marginellidae); and Mr. Derek Worth (British Marine).

I am also indebted to Mr. Colin Harper who kindly loaned the 'fake' Epitonium scalare.

Lastly, and by no means least, I wish to express my gratitude for her support, to my wife, Brenda, who helped in proof-checking, and exercised patience and long-suffering over the months of my working at home amidst mounds of paper, transparencies and shells.

The publishers would like to thank the following for providing photographs and for permission to reproduce copyright material. p.7 Heather Angel; p.9 al Uffizi, Florence, ar Sotheby's, c Shell Oil, br Moira Clinch; p.11 bl and br Quarto; p.13 al Heather Angel; p.18 bl Heather Angel; p.20 a & b Heather Angel; p.21 al Heather Angel; p.23 Heather Angel; p.24 al Wildlife Matters; John Feltwell/Courtesy of Fabré's Museum, Orange; p.26 Quarto